Statistical Methods for Communication Science

Statistical Methods for Communication Science

ANDREW F. HAYES
The Ohio State University

LEA LAWRENCE ERLBAUM ASSOCIATES, PUBLISHERS
2005 Mahwah, New Jersey   London

Senior Acquisitions Editor: Linda Bathgate
Assistant Editor: Karin Wittig Bates
Cover Design: Kathryn Houghtaling Lacey
Textbook Production Manager: Paul Smolenski
Text and Cover Printer: Hamilton Printing Company

This book was typeset by the author using the LaTeX language and delivered to the publisher as camera-ready copy.

A web page supporting this book can be found at
http://www.comm.ohio-state.edu/ahayes/smcs/

Lawrence Erlbaum Associates, Inc., Publishers
10 Industrial Avenue
Mahwah, New Jersey 07430

Library of Congress Cataloging-in-Publication Data
Hayes, Andrew F.

   Statistical methods for communication science/Andrew F. Hayes

   p. cm.

   Includes bibliographic references and index

   ISBN 0-8058-5487-8 (hard cover: alk. paper)

   1. Communication—Statistical Methods. 2. Communication—Research

   I. Hayes, Andrew F. II. Title

   P93.7.H39 2005

   302.2′02 dc–22   2005040570

Books published by Lawrence Erlbaum Associates are printed on acid-free paper, and their bindings are chosen for strength and durability.

Printed in the United States of America
10 9 8 7 6 5 4 3 2 1

To **Carole**

CONTENTS

Preface

Why do we need yet another book on statistical methodology when there are so many books already available? When I started writing this book, I entertained this question myself and, obviously, decided that another book was needed. My primary motivation for writing this book is that, prior to its publication, no statistical methods book on the market was tailored to the field of communication. Typically we send students to other departments to get statistical training—psychology, sociology, or statistics, for instance. This is a shame because there is plenty of evidence that suggests that people learn better when information is personalized. Of course, when planning and teaching my courses I could have simply adopted a book written for another field or for the general social sciences and then use communication examples during lectures. I tried this for a couple of years and found that it didn't work well. I couldn't find a single book that students liked or that didn't focus excessively on concepts that I felt weren't particularly relevant to the way that communication scientists conduct their business. Without a statistical methods book written for the field of communication, I found it difficult to engage students in the material and maximize their success in acquiring what may be some of the more difficult material that burgeoning communication scientists need to understand—and understand thoroughly.

So that is why I wrote this book. In the spirit of these reasons, I have tried to couch most of my examples in this book in terms of communication research and questions in the hope that this will cognitively involve students (and faculty, and practitioners) in the field more and make them see the relevance, indeed the tremendous importance of statistics to the field of communication and to success as a communication scientist. I wrote this book thinking in particular of the reader who has some background in research methodology and perhaps even some prior exposure to introductory statistics. However, even without this background, anyone should be able to read and understand the material in these pages. Although this book is suitable as a text, my hope is that the writing and examples are clear enough that any motivated reader can come away having learned something useful without the formal guidance provided in a classroom context.

I have always believed that although a good understanding of the mathematical basis of statistics is helpful to mastery of statistical methodology, it is by no means necessary. Perhaps several years or so ago I wouldn't have said this because hand computation predominated statistics education. But the age of high-speed, low-cost computers is here. The result of this widely available technology is an increasing use of complex statistical procedures because they are available to all at, literally, the touch of a button. Of course, the danger of the convenience and user-friendly nature of statistical software is the temptation to use a statistical procedure with which you may not be familiar merely because the computational obstacles no longer exist. There is no substitute for conceptual understanding because it is necessary to make sense of what a computer tells you. This book is motivated by a desire to bring that conceptual understanding to everyone interested and motivated, regardless of their mathematical sophistication.

There is a CD that comes with this book as well as a web page supporting the book that I believe you will find useful. The URL is

http://www.comm.ohio-state.edu/ahayes/smcs/

Using the data files on the CD and the web page (available in multiple formats), you should be able to replicate most of the analyses reported in this book. The web page contains some files mentioned in this book that are not on the CD as well as additional documents that you will find useful that were developed after this book went to print.

To the Student

One of the student's greatest barriers to mastering statistics is fear of mathematics. Many students just lock up with anxiety when they are asked to do any computation, and this anxiety typically interferes with the ultimate goal of conceptual understanding. I hope you will not let this happen to you. Statistics has a bad reputation that is perpetuated by the way most statistical methods books are written. In this book, I depart company with many of my book-writing colleagues by minimizing the computational aspects of statistical methods while maximizing their conceptual presentation. You will find as you read through this book that it is possible to understand conceptually how the statistical procedures discussed in this book are used without completely understanding their mathematical basis. Many mathematicians I know can barely add and subtract without the help of a calculator. Their brilliance resides in their ability to solve problems using their knowledge of mathematics concepts and theory. Because computers are used for statistical computations, in my opinion, your time is best used by developing an understanding of the concepts presented here.

This is not to say that mathematics is irrelevant to complete mastery of statistics. Mathematics is the language of statistics. If you do want to study statistics formally, you eventually will have to come to terms with some complex mathematical operations and the mathematical basis of statistical theory. My assumption is that if you are reading this book, your primary goal is to understand how to use statistics intelligently rather than understand the mathematics behind the statistics. An additional assumption I make is that if you are interested in the mathematics, you will seek that information on your own. There are many good books similar to this one but with a greater focus on mathematics that will undoubtedly serve you well as a supplement to this book.

To the Instructor

As a science educator, you may have a great interest in if not a total passion (such as I do) for the nitty-gritty of statistics. On the other hand, most likely your students don't share this passion. Many of them will be taking your course because they have to. And many of your students probably have developed a fear of statistics, perhaps because of bad experiences they've had in the past. And most certainly, mathematics is something that the typical communication student would prefer to avoid. To be sure, one or two students in an average size class will really enjoy the elegance and subtle details of mathematics and statistical theory. But those students are in the minority, and so it makes no sense to design a course with only them in mind. But one thing all students in your class have in common is a need to use statistics. Thus, a class and text needs to teach students how to use statistics to accomplish their research objectives. A student's interests are better served, in my opinion, by teaching them how to use statistical methods intelligently rather than trying to turn them into miniature statisticians. (Those who have such an interest or ability will undoubtedly seek out more information on their own). My approach in this book is one where the concepts are presented in such a way that students, regardless of their background or motivations, will acquire the skills needed to use statistics.

I believe that professional methodologists such as myself spend a whole lot of time thinking, writing, and arguing about things that for the user of statistics rarely matter that much. I believe that when teaching statistical methodology, one should focus on the things that matter much or most of the time rather than spending time on things that matter rarely. What does matter to the student is to understand how to use their statistical knowledge. So you will find that many of the lively and interesting controversies and debates in the statistical methodology literature are given little to no treatment in this book (although I do occasionally make reference to that literature) because those controversies and debates just won't matter to how most students end up using statistics.

I had the student and not the professional methodologist in mind when I wrote this book. The end result is that rather than trying to satisfy everyone by talking a little bit about everything, I emphasize certain things that I think are more important while under emphasizing or completely ignoring others, knowing that the instructor who feels that important things are missing or who prefers to spend more time than I on certain topics can supplement the book with additional readings. Many good sources of supplementary reading are available. I have found the *Quantitative Applications in the Social Sciences* series published by Sage Publications most helpful both as an educator and as a professional methodologist. These small volumes are ideal supplements because they provide further detail while still being both readable and friendly on the wallet.

The advent of high-speed desktop computers has revolutionized the way that statisticians think about statistics and inference. Many of the procedures communication scientists use are old and, frankly, a bit outdated. To be sure, they work relatively well, but they are a bit klunky and conceptually or philosophically ill-suited to how communication research is actually done. For example, although some communication researchers do conduct research using random samples, most researchers do not. Yet almost all statistical methods communication researchers use are based on what I call the "population model" of inference. According to this model, the goal of statistics is to give the researcher a means of inferring some unknown characteristic of a population by randomly sampling from that population, as if we are all closet public opinion pollsters. But we aren't. Furthermore, many of the methods used by communication scientists make questionable assumptions. Modern and computationally intensive methods of data analysis, such as randomization tests and bootstrapping, are largely unknown to communication scientists but conceptually better suited to the way we conduct research. To be sure, classical methods are important to understand, and I still emphasize them in this book. But the time is right to introduce some of these modern developments into the introductory classroom. You will find discussions of some of these new conceptualizations of statistical inference and what "chance" means scattered at appropriate places throughout the book. If you choose not to cover these materials in your course, no harm done. But I strongly encourage you to consider exposing your students to some of these exciting even if seemingly (but not actually) unorthodox ways of thinking about statistical inference.

Acknowledgments

Many people have contributed to this book either directly or indirectly. Rather than list them all, let me simply say thank you, knowing that you know who you are. But a few people whose contributions were most profound should be acknowledged. First, I want to acknowledge the patience of several years of graduate students in the M.A. and Ph.D. programs in communication at The Ohio State University. They suffered through various drafts of these chapters and somehow managed to make sense of their contents in spite of the typos, poor grammar, and verbal belches. Next, Richard Darlington needs acknowledgment because he profoundly influenced the way I think about data analysis. I entered Ph.D. study at Cornell University thinking I was pretty smart when it came to statistical methods. After exposure to Dick's thinking and writing, I eventually realized how little I actually did know. I'm sure he and others familiar with his work will see his influence on me in these pages. Robert Witte also influenced me during my undergraduate study at San Jose State University in ways that are hard to overstate. Rather than scaring me away from statistics, he made the topic interesting and lively. Linda Bathgate and the production staff at Lawrence Erlbaum Associates contributed in an important way by giving me the freedom and a sufficiently large page budget to produce the kind of book I wanted to produce. I've learned that a book is never complete—you simply run out of time. But had I been forced to cut corners, this book would have turned out differently than I had originally envisioned it. I also thank my wife Carole and several anonymous reviewers who read and reread earlier drafts. They contributed tremendously to the production of this book, and each suggested modification improved the final product. Carole, my son Conor, and my daughter Julia have also contributed through their support, encouragement, and patience over the years it took to complete this book. Finally, the hard work of everyone who has been involved in the production of the LaTeX system must be acknowledged for their selflessness in providing their code free of charge for the world to use.

Andrew F. Hayes
Columbus, Ohio
April 2005

ONE

Statistics and Communication Science

1.1 Welcome

Let me be the first to welcome you to the exciting world of statistics and data analysis. Statistics is a way of organizing, describing, and making inferences from data, and statistical methods are used throughout the physical, natural, and social sciences, including the field of communication. Statistics is a way of thinking, a language, and a means of making an argument based on data available (Abelson, 1995). Most importantly, statistics is fundamental to the scientific process. It may seem a strange way of thinking at first, but with enough perseverance and practice, thinking statistically will eventually become second nature to you. Once you have developed the ability to understand and apply statistical principles and concepts to your scientific investigations, you will find that your everyday thinking has changed as well. You will find yourself more analytical, more rational, and you may even possess a new and healthy skepticism when it comes to interpreting information and evaluating claims people make. Furthermore, you will be able to participate in the exciting world of knowledge generation that is the field of communication. So again, welcome.

The field of communication has not always been recognized as a leader in the use of statistical methods, but any observer of the communication literature would recognize statistics as fundamental to the discipline by spending only 10 minutes or so looking through the major journals in the field. The majority of the articles published in such places as *Communication Research, Human Communication Research,* the *Journal of Communication,* the *Journal of Broadcasting and Electronic Media,* and *Media Psychology* read much like the research articles found in other social sciences, with detailed method and results sections where the research design and data analysis procedures the researcher used to collect and analyze the data are described. Several communication programs, such as mine at The Ohio State University, are appropriately located in the same administrative colleges as other disciplines that use statistical methods reside, such as psychology, sociology, and political science. And it is common, more so now than in the past, for graduate programs in communication to require students to take a few and often several data analysis courses.

There are at least two mutually interdependent components of the scientific process. The first component is research design—the various approaches you might take to collecting the data to answer your question of interest. You may have taken a research methods course at some point in your education. If so, the course probably focused primarily on how to collect data and the various categories of research designs, such as surveys, experiments, content analysis, archival research, observational studies, interviewing, and so forth. The second component is the process of data analysis—how to evaluate the data with respect to the original question that motivated the research in the first place. As you work through this book, you will come to appreciate the interdependence of design and analysis. In the field of statistics there is a saying: "garbage in, garbage out." This means that even the best data analyst can't take data from a poorly designed study and produce something useful or meaningful. What you put in is what you get out. It is important before embarking on any study to carefully think through what questions you want your study to help you answer. Before collecting the data, you have to constantly keep sight of why you are doing the study and how to best conduct the study to attain those objectives. The questions you are attempting to answer will determine how your study is designed. During the design phase, you need to think about how others might criticize your study and how you can preempt such criticisms with a better design. If your study isn't designed well, no amount of data analysis can turn badly collected data into something meaningful and interpretable with respect to your original question.

Good design is extremely important to the research process. However, the focus of this book is squarely on the data analysis aspect of science. This is a book about statistics, and as such, it focuses on statistical methods for describing and making inferences from data. Along the way, there will be the occasional discussion of design issues, as design and analysis are intertwined. Chapter 3, for instance, discusses sampling strategies—ways of recruiting "units" for your study, whether those units are people, newspaper columns, advertisements, or whatever. This is a design issue, but it is also a statistical one in the sense that our method of recruiting research units affects the kinds of inferences we can make with statistics. Although I cannot help but talk about research design, I focus primarily on data analysis in this book.

If you approach statistics as an exercise in mathematics rather than as an integrated part of the scientific process, you probably will ever understand just why a background in statistics is not only helpful but essential to success as a communication scientist. But before diving head first into the topic of statistics, it is worthwhile to first do a brief overview of just what science is, how communication scientists use the scientific method, and to make explicit the assumptions that communication scientists make when going about their business.

1.2   Why Do Science?

There are as many definitions of science as there are scientists. When I use the term *science* I am referring to something very explicit, but at the same time a bit nebulous. When you think of science, your mind probably conjures up images of people wandering around laboratories in white coats, looking through microscopes, mixing chemicals, filling test tubes, or peering through a telescope at the stars. This is how the media portrays science. Indeed, if you were to read the science section of any newspaper, most likely it would be filled with stories of biology, medicine, chemistry, geology, and astronomy. But to the scientist, science is more a way of thinking about and answering questions rather than a specific discipline, like chemistry or physics or biology. Science is more a *process* than a thing. Someone who is engaging in science is using a particular set of methods, based on a common philosophy about knowledge and discovery, to answer questions of interest to him or her or the scientific community.

But not all disciplines are scientific ones, even if the discipline does focus on the discovery of knowledge and the answering of questions. For instance, philosophy and history are two fields of study not traditionally known as relying on the scientific method even though understanding and discovery are a part of these fields. Other disciplines do share this common method called science (or the "scientific method"). Stereotypically, we think of only the hard or natural sciences as scientific—chemistry, biology, physics, and astronomy, for instance. But there are also the *social sciences*—sociology, psychology, economics, and communication, for example—all of which use the scientific method as a means of discovery and exploration.

I've already described science as a process rather than a thing. I've also described it as a way of thinking and as a collection of methods for answering questions. These are all true. Others define science differently. Looking through the books I have conveniently available in my office, science has been defined as "a process of disciplined inquiry" (Liebert & Liebert, 1995, p. 3) or as "the development of knowledge through a combination of rationalism and empiricism" (Stewart, 2001, p. 4) where rationalism is the use of logic and empiricism is the use of observation and the senses. Both definitions suggest that science is a method of discovery guided by rules. But what are we trying to discover? What is the purpose of doing science?

Science as Problem Solving. One purpose of science is to try to solve some problem of relevance to the world. That world need not be the entire world, in the sense of the planet Earth. That "world" may be a very confined one—a business, for example, or it may be larger, such as a city, state, or country. Communication scientists often do scientific research as a means to solving some problem of relevance to our daily lives and the world in which we live. For example, AIDS can be thought of as a problem of global proportions, and it is clearly a problem with behavioral origins. A large proportion of infections occur through unprotected sex. If we want to reduce or eliminate human suffering resulting from the proliferation of AIDS, what needs to be done? Scientific research can be helpful here by helping us to discover the sources of the behavior (e.g., lack of knowledge, feelings of invulnerability) and evaluate methods to change that behavior (e.g., making condoms conveniently available, educating people on the causes of the disease, informing them how to protect themselves, and so forth). Scientific research that focuses on some kind of real world problem is sometimes called *applied research.*

Science as Information Acquisition. We often engage in scientific discovery for the purpose of information acquisition. Information is important in all aspects of life, including the quest to understand and explain communication processes and to influence behavior. Information is also very useful or even necessary before deciding on a course of action. Suppose, for example, that you are running for a political office and are developing a campaign strategy. What kind of information would be helpful in designing your campaign? You could just campaign on the issues that you find important, but this strategy probably won't get you elected. You need to know what issues are important to your potential constituents. Science could help you figure out what your platform should be so potential voters will pay attention to your message. Or imagine you work for a public relations firm trying to help a fast food chain capture greater market share. Why do some people prefer the competition, and what can you do to get people through the doors of your client's chain and enjoy the experience, thus enhancing the likelihood they will return? You might want to know if people have had bad experiences at your client's chain, whether the prices are perceived to be lower at the competition, or whether the physical environment of your client's chain is unappealing or unwelcoming. The scientific method could help you answer these questions, thus arming you with information about what your client needs to change.

Science as the Development and Testing of Theory. Most disciplines have a large body of theories that researchers in the discipline study. Just like there are many definitions of science, there are many definitions of theory. A *theory* can be thought of as an explanation of a process or phenomenon. There are many scientific theories, some of which you have undoubtedly heard about and equate with "science," such as Einstein's theory of relativity or Darwin's theory of natural selection. Communication has many theories too, such as *communication accommodation theory* (e.g., Giles, Mulac, Bradac, & Johnson, 1987), *spiral of silence theory* (Noelle-Neumann, 1993), and the *elaboration likelihood model of persuasion* (Petty & Cacioppo, 1986). Entire books are devoted to nothing but a description and discussion of communication theories (e.g., Littlejohn, 2001; McFleur & Ball-Rokeach, 1989; Severin & Tankard, 2001), illustrating that communication scientists are busy trying to understand and explain the communication process. These theories may be based on lots of prior research, or they may be based on the theorist's intuition, personal experiences, or the application of rules of logic. Regardless, theories are only attempts at explaining. They may not adequately explain the phenomenon or process. We use science to test the validity of those theories, to see if predictions the theory makes actually work out when they are put to the test. And we do science to determine how theories should be modified to better describe and explain the process under investigation. Research motivated by the testing and development of theory is sometimes called *basic research.* However, this does not mean that basic research is never guided by applied concerns, nor does it mean that applied research is never theoretical. People who conduct basic research often are very focused on eventual application but may feel that their understanding of the process is not sufficiently developed for them to apply the theory in a particular context of interest.

Consider the *elaboration likelihood model of persuasion,* which predicts that "peripheral cues" to persuasion such as a messenger being a well-liked celebrity should have a greater effect on people who are uninvolved in or don't care much about the topic compared with those who are more involved. If a researcher found that the same message when delivered by a celebrity was more persuasive than when it was presented by someone who was not a celebrity, but only for people who didn't care about the topic, then this gives support to the theory—it has passed at least one test. If the data are not consistent with the theory's prediction, and assuming the study was well designed, this is a strike against the theory. If the theory fails repeatedly when put to the test, this suggests that theory is invalid. A theory can't be an adequate explanation of the process if predictions it makes about what a researcher should find in a study designed to test it are rarely or never right. Indeed, it has been said that falsification through disconfirming evidence is the only way that theories can be tested, because a confirmation of a theory's prediction is only suggestive of the accuracy of the theory. There could be (and perhaps is) some other theory that would make the same prediction. However, if data aren't consistent with a theory, this is strong evidence against the validity of the theory.

Chaffee and Berger (1987) discuss in considerable detail the important role that theory development and testing plays in the life of the communication scientist. In the end, we can all create theories, and we routinely develop our own intuitive theories as we manage our day-to-day social affairs, but that doesn't mean that these theories are good. Researchers in a discipline are in charge of evaluating the many theories that attempt to explain some process or phenomenon of interest to the discipline, and they do this using the scientific method. If you are a graduate student, at least some of your time as a student will likely be spent learning about, testing, and evaluating theories through the methods of science.

Science as the Satiation of Curiosity. We also do science simply because we are curious. Curious people are naturally drawn to science because science provides people with a systematic method for answering their own questions. If you are someone who likes to wonder or invent your own explanations or theories for something, then you will enjoy science. Few things are more exciting than answering your own questions through the scientific method. But such pleasures usually are short lived because curious people have many curiosities and there is always some new curiosity to be satiated, some new question to answer.

I've presented these uses of science as if they are nonoverlapping and unrelated, but a researcher may use science for any of these reasons in combination. For example, a researcher may have a natural curiosity in persuasion and is perhaps interested in applying his or her study of persuasion to the development of information campaigns focused on improving childhood health. But just where are the health problems? Are children getting sufficient vitamins at critical stages of development? Are vaccines available and being used? What deters a parent from vaccinating his or her child? Answers to these questions are important before an information campaign can be developed. There are many theories of persuasion, and the researcher may not know which would be most helpful or maximally effective in a particular situation. So the researcher may conduct various tests of the different theories by focusing on issues relating to childhood health. If a theory doesn't make accurate predictions in this context, it probably shouldn't be used when developing an information campaign in that context.

1.3   Assumptions and Philosophies of Scientific Investigation

There are many disciplines that use the scientific method as a means of answering questions, and each discipline tailors the scientific method to suit the special issues and problems conducting research in that discipline. However, users of the scientific method, including communication scientists, make a number of common assumptions when they apply it to their field of study.

The World is Orderly. Scientists are in search of the logic and orderliness of the world. That is, we assume that there are rules or laws governing human behavior and thought. If there were no laws of human behavior, studying human behavior scientifically would be pointless because every situation would lead people to respond, think, or act differently. There would be nothing about the "human condition" to explain, discover, or understand. And there would be no way of systematically attempting to influence or change human behavior because each person's thinking and behavior would be guided not by some common processes or principles but instead by their own whims and idiosyncrasies. Social scientists, such as communication scholars, believe that there are laws of human behavior to be discovered even if they don't always apply to everyone in every situation. These laws are propensities to think, feel, or act in certain ways.

For example, it is well accepted that similarity breeds attraction (Byrne, 1971). We tend to like and be attracted to people that are similar to us. This relationship can be thought of as a behavioral law because it is such a consistent finding in the literature on human attraction. To be sure, laws may have boundary conditions, meaning that they may apply only to certain people in certain situations. We know that in some circumstances dissimilarity breeds attraction, but such circumstances are rare. The important point is that if we didn't believe that there are such laws to be discovered, then there would be no point in doing research in communication. Communication scientists generally believe that such laws exist and can be discovered and described with the methods of science.

Empiricism. Researchers who use the scientific method believe that research should be based on observation that is objective and replicable. Science largely rejects subjective data that are not visible or replicable, such as anecdotes, rumors, or other data that can't be publicly observed and verified. This does not mean that what we study must be directly observable. Communication scientists study things that you can't actually see. Communication anxiety, for instance, is a widely studied construct that you can't actually see directly. But you can indirectly study it by examining observable characteristics of communication anxiety such as how a person responds to a question about his or her worries about speaking in public, or how that person acts when communicating. Furthermore, the methods we use must be replicable. Someone else should be able to conduct the study exactly as we have. To replicate a study, it is important that we clearly describe how the study was conducted and the data analyzed so that others can attempt to replicate not only our methods but hopefully our findings too.

Related to the assumption of empiricism is the importance of *measurement* or *measurability.* To be able to study something, we have to be able to measure it, usually in some quantitative form (although there is some debate about whether it must be quantified). If something can't be measured or, at minimum, categorized, then we can't study it with the scientific method. However, nearly anything of interest can be measured, and so nearly everything can be studied through the scientific method.

This empiricist philosophy when combined with the assumption that the world is orderly is sometimes known as *positivism.* Positivism is akin to the belief that "the truth is out there," and that anyone can discover that truth if they approach it objectively, using a systematic set of replicable methods that can be communicated to other researchers. Nevertheless, not everyone believes that there is a single truth to be known. Some researchers believe that truth is subjective and in the eye of the perceiver (rather than some reality to be observed objectively). According to this philosophy, the conclusions one reaches after observation depend on who is doing the observing. Two people observing the same phenomenon may have very different interpretations of that "reality," and to really understand what makes a person think and act as he or she does, we must understand that person's social environment and how he or she interprets the world. As such, reality is subjective and cannot be known in the same way that a positivist believes is possible. Researchers that reject empiricism or positivism tend to use a different set of methods than do strict positivists and approach knowledge and discovery very differently. But a strong positivist would argue that any approach to knowledge acquisition that doesn't allow the object of study to be perceived objectively and the "truth" to be discovered is pseudoscientific at best. As you can imagine, for researchers in one camp or the other this can be a very emotional issue.

Parsimony. Also known as *Occam's Razor*, the rule of parsimony states that scientists should not evoke explanations for a phenomenon that are more complicated than need be to adequately describe it. In other words, simpler is better. When two competing explanations are used to describe the same thing and can do so equally effectively, the one that is simpler and that makes fewer assumptions is the one that should be preferred. That does not mean that the simpler explanation is always the correct one. It merely means that when two explanations that differ in complexity are equally consistent with the data, the simpler one is to be preferred until new data are available to contradict the simpler explanation and that favor the more complicated one.

Progression in Small Steps. A researcher who believes in the importance of the scientific method is also a modest one. No single research study is ever the definitive one. The development of knowledge through the scientific method is a slow process that progresses in small steps. If you were working on a puzzle, each piece that you fit into its proper place gets you closer to the picture. The result of a single study is like a single piece of the puzzle. However, unlike is true when working on a puzzle, each study often raises new questions, making the puzzle even bigger. Imagine what it would be like if each piece you correctly fit into a puzzle increased the size and complexity of the picture. But that is a little what science is like!

The Nonexistence of Proof. If you ever hear someone say "a study was done that proved" such and such, you know that person isn't familiar with the doctrines of science because no scientist would ever use that word to describe the state of any knowledge we have (at least not in the company of other scientists). No single study is itself especially revealing. More important is what the collection of studies on a similar topic says because a single study is open to multiple interpretations and always has some limitations. Our knowledge is cumulative and evolving. What we know today may not be true tomorrow because new data are always coming in, and there are always alternative explanations for something that can't be categorically ruled out. And just because we can't think of an alternative explanation doesn't mean some other explanation doesn't exist. A theory that is widely accepted today may not be accepted tomorrow. So nothing is ever proven. The things we believe to be true we believe only because the data seem to compel us to accept them as true, but we shouldn't get too comfortable with that truth because it may change as more data become available. So we talk about theories or explanations being *supported* by the data or that the data *suggest* the correctness of such and such explanation. Our beliefs are always tentative ones that we hold until the day that some data lead us to reject those beliefs in favor of something else. That day may never come in our own life time, but that doesn't mean the day will never come.

The fact that proof doesn't exist in science is important to keep in mind when analyzing data and interpreting the results of an analysis. It is all too easy to assume that the statistics tell the story objectively and, because statistics cannot lie (although users of statistics can), the proof of one's claim is to be found in the numbers. Such an assumption places far more importance on statistics than is justified. Any study result, the statistics included, has only limited meaning in the context of a single investigation. There usually are many different ways of quantifying the results of a study, some of which may be better than others. Someone who analyzed your data differently might come away with a very different interpretation or conclusion. Statistics is an area that, like any area of science, is controversial. Professional statisticians disagree on such seemingly uncontroversial matters such as how to best quantify "average" and "variability," and yet we use these concepts routinely in communication science. There are many different ways of analyzing data, and your interpretation of the results of your research must be done in light of this fact. Indeed, throughout this book you will see there are many different statistical tests that have been proposed to answer the same statistical question, and it isn't always clear which test is best in a particular circumstance. What is important in the scheme of science is consistency. Do many studies, conducted using different methods and using different approaches to data analysis all converge on a similar result or interpretation? To the extent that the answer to this question is yes, we can be more confident in our interpretation of the corpus of studies on a topic. But we can never say with 100% confidence that anything has been proven.

Falsifiability. An explanation for some phenomenon must be falsifiable, which means, therefore, that it must be testable and it must be possible for evidence inconsistent with the explanation to exist. Not all theories or claims are falsifiable. One example in communication is McCluhan's phrase "the medium is the message." McCluhan appreciated that the phrase is ambiguous and could have multiple interpretations across people and over time (Sparks, 2002). As such, it is very difficult to falsify and so it is very difficult to study whether there is any "truth" to this phrase using the scientific method. Similarly, could we ever falsify the well accepted claim that "We cannot not communicate"? As alluring and obvious this "fact" might seem, I'm not sure how a study to discredit such a claim could even be undertaken. If it cannot be discredited, if no data inconsistent with the claim could ever be produced, then it is not falsifiable and not in the realm of things amenable to scientific investigation.

1.4   Building Your Statistical Vocabulary

Statistics is an important part of the scientific process because it is through statistics that we extract information from our application of the scientific method to a research problem. As we will discuss later, we use statistics both to describe what we found when conducting a study and to make inferences from the data. Unfortunately, statistics is a topic that often scares the burgeoning scientist. When someone takes his or her first statistics course, sometimes anxiety about mathematics interferes with the ultimate goal of conceptual understanding. This is based on the belief that statistics is about numbers and math. But it is not. Statistics is more like a language; it is a means of communicating ideas and evidence. To understand how to use statistics in science, you need to grasp the concepts as well as the vocabulary used to discuss those concepts. Computers are used to do much of the computational work, so one's initial exposure to statistics is best focused on understanding how statistical procedures are used and getting a handle on the vocabulary. Formulas are always available in printed form, here and elsewhere, and you will rarely need to do computations by hand. But computers are limited in their role as number crunchers. You, the user of statistics, need to understand the concepts and the vocabulary to truly master statistics and interpret what a computer is telling you. In this section, I begin to define some of the more widely used and important terms that are used in this book and throughout the scientific community.

We typically conduct research to answer some kind of question. As you read the communication literature, you will frequently come across the term *research question*, often denoted symbolically as *RQ*. A research question is simply a question that a researcher poses in an investigation. These questions are often vague and abstract, like theories are, but they are much more limited in scope and rarely if ever attempt to explain a process in the same way that a theory does. Someone studying persuasion might ask the following research questions:

RQ_1: To what extent does the depth of one's thinking while being exposed to a message influence whether attitude change is short or long-lasting?

RQ_2: Does distraction during presentation affect the persuasiveness of a health-related message?

In contrast to a research question, which is usually a vague statement, a *hypothesis* (sometimes denoted in the literature with the letter H) is a prediction about what the researcher expects to find in a study. Two hypotheses corresponding to the research questions posed above might be

H_1: The more time a person spends thinking about a message, the longer any attitude change resulting from that message will persist.

H_2: The more tasks the person is given when being exposed to a persuasive message, the less attitude change the message will produce.

Notice that these are much more specific than the research questions because they explicitly state what is being predicted. Hypotheses can take various forms. A *one-tailed* or *directional* hypothesis makes a prediction about the direction of the result expected. The following hypotheses are one-sided or directional:

H_1: Males will spend more time reading the sports section than females.

H_2: People who read the print form of the news will learn more current events than those who read the online version of the same paper.

Observe that these hypotheses make a prediction about how the groups should differ. The hypotheses predict not only the groups will differ, but that one group will do more of something (such as learn more or read more). The corresponding hypotheses presented in *two-tailed* or *nondirectional* form don't specify the precise direction of the result expected. For example:

H_1: Males will differ from females in how much time they read the sports section

H_2: There will be a difference between readers of print and online newspapers with respect to how much they know about current events.

Hypothesis testing is an important part of the scientific process because theories often lead to predictions about what an investigator should find if the theory is a good representation of the process. In this book I devote considerable space to how to test a hypothesis using statistics.

When you conduct a research study, at some point you will be collecting *data*. Data refers to some kind of representation, quantitative or otherwise, of a variable or variables in a research study. For instance, if we asked 10 students their grade point average, their answers (such as 3.4, 2.4, 3.93, etc.) constitute our data. If we administered the *Personal Report of Communication Apprehension* (see Rubin, Palmgreen, & Sypher, 2004) to a classroom of tenth graders, their scores on this measure in addition to perhaps information about their age and sex would be our data. If we wanted to know how much violent television a person watches during the typical week, we might ask the person which shows they regularly watch and then count up the number of shows watched that could be classified as violent. Our data would be the number of violent shows each person reported watching. Data need not be quantitative. For example, the sex of the 10 students is qualitative rather than quantitative information. The term can also be used to refer to a collection of statistics or more generically to refer to any kind of evidence. Someone might ask if you have any data to support your claim. You might ask yourself what your data tell you about the process you are studying. A *data set* is simply a collection of data. After data collection, the researcher will typically enter the data into a computer prior to analysis, and this file constitutes the data set.

The term *case* is often used to refer to each unit that provides data to the researcher. The unit may be a person, or it may be a single advertisement in a collection of advertisements being analyzed, or it may be one of several letters to the editor of major newspapers that are being content analyzed. Each of the students in the example above is a case in the data. If you had 100 letters to the editor or a collection of advertisements that you were content analyzing as part of a study, each letter or advertisement would be a case in the data set.

Each case in the data set is typically measured on one or more *variables*. A variable is anything that the units providing data in your study vary or differ from each other on. Take a group of newspapers, for example. On any given Sunday, the front section of the *New York Times* has a certain number of pages. *The Washington Post* may have a different number of pages in the front section that day, and the *Los Angeles Times* may have still a different number. The number of pages varies across newspapers, and thus it can be thought of as a variable. Other variables might be the number of square inches of total space devoted to advertising or how many stories about crime are printed on a given day. The *New York Times* may have had 12 stories last Sunday, whereas the *Washington Post* had only 10. So the number of stories about crime that different newspapers print in a day could be considered a variable.

People are also the unit of study quite frequently in communication research. People vary from each other in a lot of ways, such as sex, religion, or years of formal education. People may have different reactions to an advertisement—some may like the advertisement, others may dislike it, and others may not have even noticed. People may differ with respect to how much they think others support their own opinion on some social topic, such as affirmative action or the death penalty. Some may think they are in a minority and others may think they are in a majority. So perceived support for one's opinion is a variable. Other things can vary between individuals, such as how long a person reads the newspaper each day. Some people may regularly spend two hours with the paper. Others may not read the paper at all. "Variable" is an extremely important term, and we will use it a lot. We will often talk about the relationship between variables in this book. Theories make predictions about how variables should be related to each other. We test hypotheses and theories by looking at whether the relationship we find in a study between two or more variables is in the direction a theory or hypothesis predicts it should be.

In research, we often distinguish between two types of variables. The definitions you see people use vary, so I'll do my best to capture the flavor of all of them. When we conduct research or theorize, we often think of one variable as coming before another in time or sequence or that one variable is some how causally prior to another. That variable, the one that affects something else, that is presumed to be the cause of, is used to predict something, or that in some way "explains" variation in something else is referred to as the *independent variable*. It is also called the *explanatory* or *predictor variable* or sometimes the *exogenous variable*. In contrast, the *dependent variable* is on the other side of this chain. The dependent variable is thought to be the result of some process or affected by something else in the model or theory. Usually, the outcome of some process we are interested in studying is the dependent variable. The dependent variable is also sometimes called the *criterion, outcome,* or *endogeneous* variable.

This sounds like a confusing set of definitions, so I'll make it more concrete with some examples. Arguably, the more you are exposed to news through various media outlets, the more informed you will become. In this case, exposure to the news is the independent variable and knowledge is the dependent variable. We presume, as phrased above, that exposure to news causes an increase in knowledge. And it has been said that managers who give workers the freedom to determine how they do their job tend to be liked more by their employers. If we were studying this process, we would think of how much freedom the manager gives the employees as the independent variable, and the employees' liking of the manager as the dependent variable. But sometimes it doesn't matter which variable is the dependent variable and which is the independent variable. For example, you may be interested in determining whether people who fear public presentations tend to be anxious in the course of their daily lives. You may have no particular interest in claiming that being anxious causes fear of public presentations or that fear of giving public speeches leads to general anxiety, nor may you be trying to make the case that there is some causal relationship between them. Therefore, it doesn't matter which is conceptualized as the independent variable and which is defined as the dependent variable.

In a single research study, a variable can serve as both an independent and a dependent variable. For example, the *knowledge gap* refers to the tendency for people with low socioeconomic status to be less informed about things going on in the community or world than those higher in socioeconomic status (Tichenor, Donohue, & Olien, 1970). It could be argued that relatively poor people tend not to get exposed to the media, and because the media is a major source of information, poorer people tend not to get as much information about the community or current events in the world as people with more money. In this process, media exposure is both an independent and a dependent variable. It is a dependent variable in the relationship between socioeconomic status and media exposure (being poor leads to less exposure), and an independent variable in the relationship between exposure and knowledge (knowledge results from exposure to media). This example also illustrates what we will call a *mediating variable* in Chapter 15. Low socioeconomic status causes people to be less exposed to media, and as a result of that low exposure, people low in socioeconomic status tend to know less. Therefore, media exposure is a mediating variable in the relationship between socioeconomic status and knowledge.

Another kind of variable is the *moderating* or *moderator variable*, discussed in more detail in Chapter 16. A moderating variable is one that determines or is related to the size, strength, or direction of the relationship between two variables. For example, suppose men who play sports more often than most other men also spend more time than those other men reading the sports section of the newspaper on the weekend. But suppose there is no relationship between how often women play sports and how much time they spend reading the sports section. So the relationship between sports activity and sports reading is different in men compared to women. As such, we say that gender *moderates* the relationship between sports activity and how frequently a person reads the sports section, and so gender is a moderator variable. If variable Z moderates the relationship between X and Y, we also say that X and Z *interact* in explaining variation in Y.

Of course, there are many other important terms that you need to be comfortable with eventually, and they will be introduced at the appropriate times throughout this book.

1.5   The Role of Statistics in Scientific Investigation

As discussed at the beginning of this chapter, science consists of at least two interdependent stages—research design and data analysis. Research design involves such issues as how to measure the variables of interest, how to approach the data collection procedure, who to include as participants in the study, how to find them, and other matters pertaining to procedure. Data analysis involves how to describe the results of the study and how those results relate to or reflect upon the research question or hypothesis being tested. Relatedly, statistics focuses on the kinds of inferences that can be made about the people or process being studied given the data available. The branch of statistics known as *descriptive statistics* focuses on graphical and numerical summaries of data. We use descriptive statistics to summarize a set of measurements taken from a sample from a population as well as when we have measurements taken from every member of the population. *Inferential statistics*, on the other hand, focuses on the kinds of inferences that can be made from the data collected from a sample to either some broader population from which the sample was derived or to the *process* under investigation. Both categories of statistics are important.

When we collect data, we often assume that the units providing data to the researcher are only a small subset of all the possible units that could have provided data but simply did not. For example, you may be interested in studying gender differences in the importance that people place on the television in the course of their daily lives. So you administer the *Television Affinity Scale* (see Rubin et al., 2004) to 10 men and 10 women. These 20 men and women who provide data to you constitute your *sample.* In contrast, you may have some specific *population* of interest from which your sample was derived. If you are interested in sex differences in general, your population may be defined as all males and females. Your population, however, may be more specific, depending on your research interests and objectives. Perhaps you are interested not in men and women in general but *adult* males and females. Thus, your population is defined as all men and women over 18. Or you may be focusing only on college men and women, so your population is all men and women enrolled in college. If your unit of analysis is not people but something else, such as newspaper advertisements, your sample may be a small subset of the newspaper advertisements that appeared in major newspapers that week, and your population is newspaper advertisements published in major newspapers. Ideally, you should specify your population in advance before collecting your sample from that population, although this is not often done. It goes without saying that your sample should be derived from your population of interest. If you were interested in college men and women, you would want to make sure that the data that you analyze come only from men and women enrolled in college.

After you have administered the *Television Affinity Scale* to your sample of men and women, you will probably want to examine the data in some way and describe what you found. A possible data set as it would be set up in *SPSS*, a data analysis program widely used by communication scientists, can be found in Figure 1.1. This figure illustrates the way that a data set is typically entered in a computer program and shows how some of the concepts described in the previous section relate to the data set. Each case gets a row in the data matrix, and the variables measured are

Cases (rows)

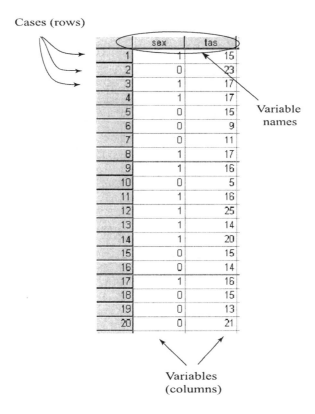

Figure 1.1 An example data set as it might appear as an SPSS data file.

represented in each column. So if the variable "sex" codes whether the participant in the study is a male (1) or female (0), then case 12 is a male that scored 25 on the *Television Affinity Scale* (named "tas" in the data file). This is a relatively small data set. In reality, the data set from a typical research study would be much larger than this example, with many rows (cases) and many columns (variables).

Making sense of the data in this format is difficult. Researchers usually condense or transform their data into a format that is more digestible and easier to interpret using various numerical and graphical approaches to describing data. To forecast where we are headed, you might compute a measure of central tendency such as the *arithmetic mean*, as well as a measure of variation such as the *standard deviation*. Such numerical summaries of the data would tell you that the 10 men scored higher on the *Television Affinity Scale* than 10 women *on average* but that the women differ from each other more than the men. Such descriptions are an important part of the scientific process for they are a simple way of representing a study's results.

One thing is for certain, and that is when you conduct a study, you will get some result. For instance, if you are comparing two groups of people in their response to some question, most certainly there will be some difference between the groups in your data. The question that needs to be answered is how much faith can be placed in the result you found as a good description of what is true in the population under investigation, or what it reflects about the process producing the pattern of results observed. Had you used 10 different women and 10 different men in the study, it is entirely possible that there would be no difference between men and women on average in their responses to the *Television Affinity Scale*. Or perhaps in a different set of 10 men and women, the women would actually be *higher* on average than the men. Researchers must acknowledge that any result found may just be the luck of the draw—the fact that the data were collected on these 20 men and women rather than some other group of 20 that could have provided data but that did not. *Chance* can be used to explain any study result, and we will talk about several models of chance throughout this book. Inferential statistical procedures are often used to gauge the role of "chance" in producing a study result and give the researcher a means of testing whether any result could be reasonably attributed to this thing we call "chance."

Suppose a theory predicts that men would feel television is more important in their lives than would women. The data in Figure 1.1 support this prediction. But as I just described, if a different group of 10 men and women participated in the study, this could have produced a different result. Before making some grand claim that men and women in the population of interest differ, or whether the theory is supported by the data, it is necessary to contend with the possibility that chance is the best and sole explanation for our obtained result. Chance is generally regarded as the simplest explanation for a study result, and in accordance with the rule of parsimony, scientists assume chance is the mechanism until we have evidence to the contrary. Inferential statistical procedures are used to assess whether such evidence exists. Again, to forecast where we are headed, you may use an inferential statistical procedure to estimate that if you assume that men and women in the population of interest don't actually differ on average in their television affinity, then chances of getting a difference favoring men as large or larger than you found is only about 1 in 50. When a research finding is determined to be unlikely to occur "just by chance," then chance is discounted as a good explanation for the result and this leads us to infer that the result reflects a real difference between men and women in the population from which the sample was derived.

Before closing this first chapter, I want to make one point regarding inferential statistics. The model I just described, where one uses the results from a small group of units in the study to some larger population is only one way of thinking about statistical inference, the so called *population model* or *random sampling model* of inference. This model of inference is used to make *population inferences*, which are statements about some broader population using information obtained from a subset of that population. Other models of inference are very appealing and arguably more appropriate for many of the research problems that communication scientists confront, such as the *random assignment model*. Alternative models of inference are not widely known or discussed in the communication literature, and I feel obligated to bring them to your attention when appropriate. Having said this, the population model of inference is so pervasive that it is important that you understand it thoroughly. So I will emphasize this model in much of my discussion of statistical inference in the chapters that follow.

1.6   Summary

Communication is a scientific discipline. Communication researchers use the scientific method to test theory, to help solve real world problems, to acquire information, and to satiate their own curiosities about the world. Researchers who subscribe to the canons of science acknowledge the importance of being objective and systematic in their approach by using only observable data to answer research questions and test hypotheses that are falsifiable. They recognize that science is a cumulative process and that the results of a single study are only one small part of a bigger puzzle being put together. They live their professional lives knowing that nothing can be proven and that "facts" exist only to the extent that there is no compelling evidence to the contrary. Researchers recognize that evidence disconfirming what they believe to be true could surface at any time. Communication scientists are active users of both descriptive and inferential statistics. They use statistics to reduce and summarize a complex data set into simpler and more interpretable forms and to assess the extent to which chance is the more parsimonious explanation for a study result. They also use statistics as a means of acknowledging the uncertainty attached to any findings resulting from collecting data from only a sample of a larger population.

My hope is that after working through this book you will appreciate that statistics is not simply a form of mathematics, where you plug numbers into one end of an equation and get another number out the other end. Statistics is a field of inquiry, not just a branch of mathematics. As in any field of inquiry, when a bunch of smart people work independently to solve a problem without a correct answer, they are bound to disagree while at the same time believing that their own solution is the best or most correct. In that way, statistics is just like the field of communication in that it is filled with controversies, differences of opinion, strong personalities, and people who are trying to find the "truth" in a world where truth is often elusive.

CHAPTER

TWO

Fundamentals of Measurement

Statistical procedures are used in communication science to both describe study results and to make inferences from a study result to some population or process that the investigator is studying. The use of statistics ultimately involves some kind of mathematical operation on numbers and then a translation of those numbers into something interpretable in the context of the study design and its purpose. The numbers in the data set being analyzed are almost always the result of some kind of measurement of the units on one or more constructs. A *construct* is simply a concept—typically discussed with some kind of verbal label—that we use to describe a psychological, cognitive, biological, or behavioral process or attribute of the object being studied. Media exposure, shyness, attitudes toward censorship, interest in politics, aggression, news learning, gender, nonverbal sensitivity, and family communication patterns are among the many constructs that communication scientists study. It is through the measurement process that we are able to do such things as quantify the association between constructs, compare groups in their behavior, thoughts, or feelings, or otherwise test hypotheses that our intuitions, curiosities, or theories suggest. Because measurement is important to statistics and the scientific process, it is important to understand some of the fundamental concepts in measurement, the topic of this chapter.

2.1 Measurement Concepts

In Chapter 1, I described the philosophy of empiricism—that scientists use observable data and that to be studied empirically the constructs must be measurable. But just what is measurement, and how is measurement done? There are many definitions of measurement, such as "a scheme for the assignment of numbers or symbols to specify different characteristics of a variable" (Williams & Monge, 2001, p. 11) or "careful, deliberative observations for the purpose of describing objects and events in terms of the attributes composing a variable" (Baxter & Babbie, 2004, p. 107). I think of measurement as *the process of meaningful quantification*. When we measure something, we are assigning numbers to the units on some construct, as Williams and Monge's definition states. But it is not enough, in my judgment, merely to assign numbers to objects to qualify as measurement because those numbers may not be meaningful. To be considered meaningful quantification, those numbers must actually correspond to some kind of quantitative attribute of the object being measured. This important property of measurement will be described shortly. But first, what methods of measurement do communication scientists typically use? How do we obtain the measurements that we subject to data analysis?

2.1.1   Methods of Measurement

Do portrayals of violence on television or other media forms facilitate or promote aggressive, violent behavior in society? Although for experts in the field this question is largely resolved (e.g., Anderson, Berkowitz, Donnerstein et al., 2003; Anderson & Bushman, 2002), the popular media still discuss this debate, and communication researchers continue to conduct research on the specific processes linking exposure to violent media and aggression (see e.g., Slater, Henry, Swaim, & Anderson, 2003). Suppose you wanted to determine whether exposure to violent media is related to a person's tendency to act aggressively or violently. Where would you get the data you would need to answer this question?

One possibility is to develop a questionnaire that asks people to list all the television shows they watch regularly. From their responses, you could count up the number of shows the person watches that could be construed as violent. This could be your measurement of each person's exposure to violent TV. Those data could then be compared to ratings that the participants in the study receive from family members, friends, or acquaintances about how violent or aggressive they tend to be. This hypothetical study illustrates one simple method of measurement: the *survey*. Self-report methods such as surveys are a common source of data that communication scientists use. Indeed, they are perhaps the most common method of measurement in communication research. Surveys are conducted over the telephone, in person, by mail, or over the Internet, and can be administered in either written, oral, or electronic format. Surveys have obvious problems and disadvantages, including such worries as whether people can accurately report the information that you are requesting and the possibility that respondents will not be truthful. Nevertheless, they remain an important source of data to communication researchers and will continue to be used widely.

Another possibility would be to recruit a group of children to a laboratory. You show some of them a series of violent TV shows over a week long period, whereas you show others a series of nonviolent shows. After this exposure period, the children in the study could be placed into a situation that provides an opportunity to respond in an aggressive manner such as in a playroom with a group of other children. The interaction could be videotaped and each child's aggression in that situation quantified in some manner later (such as the number of times a child pushes or hits another child). This is an example of an *experiment*. In this study, exposure to violent television is *manipulated*, whereas aggression is measured through *observation*. Communication scientists often conduct experiments through the manipulation of one or variables because experiments are one of the best ways of assessing cause-effect relationships. Observation, although a bit more complicated and not as widely used by communication scientists, has some obvious advantages over other methods of measurement such as self-report surveys. Observational measurement does not require the study participants to reflect on or recall their own behavior, and if behavior is what you are ultimately interested in measuring, it is hard to argue that the data you obtained do not reflect on a person's actual behavior, unlike self-reports collected through survey methods.

Still another possibility is to examine if the publication of news stories about violence is related to later crime statistics, such as the number of homicides in the community. To conduct such a study, you might select a number of cities throughout the country and examine how many column inches the major newspaper for each city published during a month-long period that contained references to some violent act (such as homicides, assaults). This information could then be compared to crime statistics in those cities a month later compiled by various government agencies after adjusting in some fashion for the amount of crime in the previous month. This study illustrates measurement through *content analysis* and *archival data sources*, both methods of measurement that enjoy frequent use by communication scientists. Content analysis involves the quantification and analysis of information contained in a stream of communication, be it in print, visual, or auditory form. Archival data are data a researcher uses that someone else collected, perhaps some time ago but for a different purpose. Archival data can also be publicly available information that a researcher compiles from public records. Archival data are the primary source of measurement used in many empirical articles published in the communication literature. The *National Election Study*, for example, is a continuously updated, expanding, and publicly-available data set maintained by the University of Michigan and used by many political scientists and political communication scholars interested in political processes and the role of communication in political activity. Data files from the National Election Study are available free on the Internet (http://www.umich.edu/~nes/), as are the data from many other surveys (for example, from polls regularly conducted by the Pew Center for People and the Press, available at http://www.people-press.org, or the Inter-University Consortium for Political and Social Research, at http://www.icpsr.umich.edu/).

Although this is not an exhaustive list of methods of measurement, and the specific studies described above are in many ways ill-designed to answer the research question unequivocally, the methods described above do capture perhaps ·75% or more of the methods that communication researchers use to collect data. This is book is about data analysis more than research design, so I refer you to specialized books on the topic of design and data collection for more details on the methods of measurement communication researchers use (e.g., Baxter & Babbie, 2004; Shadish, Cook, & Campbell, 2002; Frey, Kreps, & Botan, 1999; Fowler, 2001; Krippendorff, 2003; Neuendorf, 2001).

2.1.2 Operationalization

Before you can measure using one or more of the procedures described above, you first need to decide how to operationalize the constructs you intend to measure. *Operationalization* is a term used in two different ways in science—as a noun and as a verb. As a noun, an operationalization is the specific manner in which a construct is measured in a research study. But used as a verb, operationalization is the process of translating a construct into a measureable form. Let's consider this concept of operationalization by continuing with the earlier example of examining the relationship between exposure to violent media and aggression.

Although it may seem on the surface that exposure to violent media is a simple enough construct, the fact is that how to best measure it is far from simple, and it is certainly controversial. A number of possible operationalizations of exposure to violent media exist. Using survey methods you could ask people to rate their exposure to violent television with a simple question asking them to rate on a 1 (not at all) to

10 (very frequently) scale how much television they watch that they would consider violent. Or you might impose a definition of violent television on them by asking them to indicate which television shows in a list of violent shows you provide to them they watched in the last month. Or you might choose a method of data collection that doesn't require people to self-report. For example, if you had the technical know-how or access to such technology, you might provide participants in your study with a device to attach to their TV that records the shows that are on the channel the TV is tuned to when it is on. Over a course of a month, this would provide a relatively objective measure of at least what programs were being projected into the person's living room (although it may not adequately capture what a specific person in the household is actually watching). Or you might control how much violent TV the participants in your study are exposed to by controlling, temporarily, which shows your participants are allowed to watch. This might be easy to do if your participants were children, as the parents could regulate the shows the children are allowed to watch under your instruction. Rather than controlling the content children are exposed to, it might be easier to ask the child's parents to indicate which shows the child watches and then quantifying how much violent content those shows contain in order to quantify each child's exposure to violent television images. Each child's "exposure score" might be the average violence content of the shows that his or her parents say that the child watches regularly.

It is through the process of operationalization that social science is possible. Many of the constructs that communication scientists study, such as communication apprehension, nonverbal sensitivity, media exposure, political knowledge, and the like are abstract, nebulous, and somewhat difficult to define. To study these things, we need to be able to measure them concretely and specifically. A good source of information for how to operationalize various communication-related constructs is Rubin, Palmgreen, and Sypher's (2004) *Communication Research Measures*. Although it focuses almost exclusively on self-report survey-based measures, I believe that every communication researcher should have a copy of this useful resource in their personal library. Other good resources on operationalization include *Measures of Personality and Social Psychological Attitudes* (Robinson, Shaver, & Wrightsman, 1990), *Measures of Political Attitudes* (Robinson, Shaver, & Wrightsman, 1998), the *Handbook of Marketing Scales* (Bearden, 1998), and the *Sourcebook of Nonverbal Measures* (Manusov, 2005). A more thorough overview of the process of operationalization than I have provided here can be found in Baxter and Babbie (2004).

Choosing an operationalization. As the example above illustrates, the same construct can be measured in different ways, and none of the operationalizations of exposure to TV violence described above are perfect. So how do you choose how you should operationalize your constructs of interest in your specific study? There are a lot of things to consider.

First, you should use an operationalization that is going to be convincing to potential critics and anyone who might read your research. Faulty operationalization is a reason many papers are rejected when they are submitted for publication in the communication field. The research community will not hear much about your research if you don't measure well, using a sound operationalization of the constructs you intend to be measuring. For this reason, operationalizations that others have used in published research, particularly in research journals that have a peer-review system, are a relatively safe choice because those studies have gone through a screening process focused on the quality of the design of the study prior to publication. And it is easier to defend yourself by citing precedent rather than just saying "I made it up!" Having said this, there are some obvious dangers to blindly following the lead of others. For example, you may end up making the same mistakes that others have made. So keep up with the scientific literature in your area of interest because that literature often informs you not only how to operationalize and measure what interests you, but the literature is also peppered with criticisms of operationalizations others have used and that perhaps you should avoid.

Second, if possible use more than one operationalization. Imagine you found that people who watch lots of violent television tend to be perceived by their friends and neighbors as aggressive. This finding could be used as evidence supporting your claim that exposure to violent media is related to a person's tendency to be aggressive or violent. But wouldn't it be even more convincing if you could also report that those same people were more likely to have been arrested for some kind of violence-related crime, were more likely to endorse statements such as "sometimes a punch in the mouth is the only way to resolve our differences," and were evaluated by a clinical psychologist as prone to sociopathic behavior? When you get the same finding when measuring something different ways, you can say you have *converging evidence* for your claim. A finding based on a single operationalization of the construct may be interesting and even important, but the results can be highly vulnerable to criticism. A set of consistent findings obtained with several different operationalizations of the construct is more difficult to criticize and considerably easier to defend.

Third, you should use operationalizations that are consistent with the resources you have available. Some operationalizations produce data quite easily and nearly anyone can use them. For example, finding people to respond to a set of questions about their attitudes, beliefs, or behaviors (unless you are studying young children or people who have some kind of disability that makes communication difficult) is fairly easy. Other operationalizations may be difficult or next to impossible for you to use. If you were studying anxiety reactions to fear-arousing advertisements, you may not have access to sophisticated equipment to measure physiological markers of anxiety such as heart rate or skin conductance. Or if you wanted to use something such as crime statistics, the community you are studying simply may not have the data you need, or it may be too costly to obtain.

2.1.3   Levels of Measurement

Stevens (1958) popularized a scheme for conceptualizing *levels of measurement* on a continuum from low to high. According to this scheme, the highest level of measurement is the *ratio level*. Measurement at the ratio level has the following properties:

1. A measurement of "zero" implies a complete absence of what is being measured.

2. A one-unit increase on the measurement scale corresponds to the same increase in what is being measured regardless of where you start on the scale.

Exposure to violent TV programs, defined as the number of violent TV shows you reported watching last week, is an example of ratio-level measurement. The difference between 4 shows and 3 shows is the same as the difference between 2 shows and 1 show. And zero implies an absence of what is being measured. Zero truly means zero—no TV shows were watched. Other examples include minutes spent reading the newspaper today and how many children you have.

The existence of an absolute zero point that corresponds to an absence of what is being measured means that ratios of measurements can be interpreted to mean that two research units who differ by a certain ratio on the measurement scale can be said to differ from each other by the same ratio on the construct being measured. For instance, someone who reports that he watches 6 hours of television a week can be said to watch television twice as frequently as someone who reports watching television only 3 hours a week.

Measurement at the *interval* level is said to be of a "lower" level of measurement than the ratio level. Interval-level measurement also has the property that equal differences on the scale correspond to equal differences in what is actually measured. However, with interval-level measurement, the value of zero does not imply the absence of what is being measured. Temperature on the Fahrenheit or Celsius scale is often used as a generic example. The difference between 20 degrees and 30 degrees corresponds physically to the same actual difference in temperature as the difference between 10 and 20 degrees. But zero does not imply an absence of temperature. So you cannot say that 80 degrees is twice as hot as 40 degrees. As I soon discuss, true interval-level measurement is fairly rare in communication research.

The next lowest level of measurement, the *ordinal* level, does not have the property that interval and ratio level measurement share—equal differences in the scale corresponding to equal differences in the construct being measured. Ordinal measurement quantifies only with respect to a *relative* but not *absolute* amount of what is being measured. For example, a customer might provide an evaluation of an Internet service provider's service as excellent, good, not so good, poor, or very poor. We can assign numbers to these ratings in a meaningful way: 5 = excellent, 4 = good, 3 = not so good, 2 = poor, 1 = very poor. The numbers themselves are arbitrary, but at least they seem to scale the quality of the service along an ordinal continuum where the lowest value on the scale (a value of "1") indicates the worst evaluation, and the highest value ("5") indicates the best evaluation. Furthermore, increasing steps on the arbitrary numerical scale seem, on the surface at least, to indicate increasing quality of the service. An alternative may be a simple rating scale where you ask someone to judge something on a 1 (worst) to 10 (best) scale. Another common ordinal-level measurement procedure is the Likert-type scale, where you ask a person to indicate the extent to which he or she agrees with a statement.

Unlike ratio and interval level measurement, ordinal level measurement doesn't provide precise information about *how much* two measurements differ from each other on the construct being measured. Even though the difference between 1 (very poor) and 2 (poor) is the same as the difference between 2 (poor) and 3 (not so good) in the numerical representation, we don't know that the difference in quality is the same in the minds of those interpreting the scale. The same one point difference between 1 and 2 and between 2 and 3 may not correspond to the same difference in what is actually being measured.

Ordinal measurement is very common in communication research, whereas interval-level measurement is rather rare. But many researchers treat ordinal-level measurement as interval level. Indeed, the practice of conceptualizing ordinal-level data as if were measured at the interval level is so common that rating scales such as those described above are sometimes used as examples of interval measurement in some textbooks (e.g., Frey, Kreps, & Botan, 1999). With interval-level data, you can legitimately apply arithmetic operations to the measurements, like adding and subtracting, knowing that the result means the same thing regardless of where you start with respect to the amount of what is being measured. So it is sensible to say that someone who reads the newspaper twice a week reads it one day more than someone who reads it only once a week and that this difference of one day is the same as the difference between 2 people who read the paper 4 and 3 days a week. But it is difficult at least in principle to justify doing arithmetic operations on ordinal data. Suppose, for example, we ask 4 people to respond to the statement "There is too much violence on television" with one of 5 options: strongly disagree, disagree, neither agree nor disagree, agree, or strongly agree. It would be common to assign numbers to these responses, such as 1 through 5, as a way of quantifying level of agreement. Imagine Jerry responds agree (4), Carroll responds strongly agree (5), Chip replies neither (3), and Matt says disagree (2). We cannot say that the difference in agreement between Jerry and Carroll is the same as the difference between Matt and Chip. Nor can we say that Jerry agrees with the statement twice as much as Matt. The numbers we assign to their responses belie the fact that they are arbitrary and carry only relative information, not absolute information, about what is being measured (level of agreement).

Because many statistics used in research require such mathematical operations, many people treat ordinal measures as if they were interval data and don't worry about it. This is very controversial from a measurement perspective, but it also very common. For example, grade point average (GPA) is based on arithmetic operations on a set of ordinal level measurements (where A = 4, B = 3, C = 2, D = 1, F = 0). But GPA is rarely questioned as a legitimate measure of academic performance. Communication researchers routinely compare people based on ordinal evaluations they provide of something, and they often arithmetically combine a set of ordinal measurements. The statistical methods literature is replete with research on the legitimacy of treating ordinal-level data as if it were interval. The research suggests probably no serious harm is done in doing so under many of the conditions that communication researchers confront (e.g., Baker, Hardyck, & Petrinovich, 1966). Some have called ordinal measures treated like interval as "quasi-interval," a term that I think deserves recognition, reflecting the fact that many of the measurement procedures communication researchers use produce data that, though ordinal, can be treated like interval without doing too much damage.

In Steven's (1958) measurement scheme, the lowest level of measurement is known as the *nominal* level. A variable measured at the nominal level does nothing other than categorize into groups. A person either does or does not speak their opinion when asked in class. The leadership style of a CEO may be classified as either authoritarian, laissez-faire, or democratic. A person's primary source of news might be either the newspaper, the television, the radio, or the Internet. So nominal "measurements" are those that place people in categories. Although widely discussed as such, I do not consider this measurement because measurement requires meaningful quantification according to my definition. Nominal measures do not meet my definition of measurement because they do not reflect the assignment of a number that indicates the *amount* or quantity of something. Consider a construct such as religious affiliation. Recalling William and Monge's (2001) definition of measurement, we can come up with a scheme that assigns numbers (a symbol) to objects (people) depending on whether they are Protestant (religion = 1), Catholic (religion = 2), Jewish (religion = 3), Muslim (religion = 4), Nondenominational (religion = 5) or "Other" (religion = 6). But the numbers themselves have no quantitative interpretation, and thus this is not meaningful measurement. A Jewish person isn't somehow more religious or more affiliated with a religion than a Protestant. Categorization is not really measurement by my definition. It is simply categorization.

2.1.4   Measurement Precision

Another way of conceptualizing measurement is in terms of its fineness versus its courseness. A fine measure has very many possible values. A course measure, in contrast, has few possible measurements. The finest possible measurement is called *continuous*. A continuously measured variable has an infinite (or at least a very large) number of possible values. The number of seconds it takes you to answer a question correctly is continuous, in that there is no limit to the number of possible values a measurement could take because time can be measured at an infinitely fine level (e.g., one hundredths of a second), and often there is no upper bound imposed on measures of time. The number of children a woman has, however, is not continuous. Human biology imposes a limit on how many children a woman can conceive, and it is not possible for a person to have 1.2 children, 2.6 children, or any number of children that is not an integer.

By contrast, a *discrete* measure has a limited number of possible values. Examples of discrete measurement include the number of days a week you read the newspaper at least once (only 8 values possible), your rating of the quality of care your doctor provides (1 = very poor, 2 = poor, 3 = adequate, 4 = good, 5 = very good), how many of your grandparents are still alive (only 5 values possible—0 to 4), and how many children a person has.

Whether a measurement procedure produces continuous or discrete measurements is not always obvious, and it depends in part on how you use the measuring instrument. Consider you allowed a person up to 60 seconds to view a web page, and you recorded the number of seconds the person chose to view it in one-second intervals. Technically, this is discrete measurement. Had you recorded it in milliseconds, while technically there is a limit to the number of possible values, the measurement is so fine (there are 60,000 possible measurements) that it would be sensible to think of this as essentially continuous. Differences of less than one millisecond would have no importance to any communication-related research using this fine of a measure, although in other fields such a difference might be meaningful. You can always record time even more precisely than the millisecond, so theoretically, time could be construed as continuous when measured at a fine level. However, it is clear that the number of children a person has could never be thought of as continuous. It is clearly discrete.

It is also sensible to conceptualize measurement precision not only in terms of possible values but plausible values. Though it might be possible for a person to have 60,000 children, and thus 59,999 is possible, as is 59,998, and so on, you could think of such a measure as continuous (using the same logic as above). But it is implausible that you'd ever get a measurement greater than perhaps 10 or so in everyday use of such a measure. It is therefore sensible to think of this as discrete measurement. Although the number of possible values is perhaps quite large, the number of plausible values is relatively small.

Analyzing data using the highest level of measurement precision available to you is generally best. It is far too common for a researcher to reduce measurement precision by making a continuous or nearly continuous set of measurements discrete. For example, participants in telephone surveys are often asked their year of birth to derive a measure of their age in years by subtracting the reported birth year from the year of data collection. In that case, age is a ratio-level variable that can be treated as practically continuous in analyses involving age. But to their misfortune, researchers often first turn age into an ordinal variable by classifying people into age groups (e.g., under 18, 19 to 35, 36 to 50, 50 or older) prior to analysis. Another common example is the *median* or *mean split*, where an investigator creates "high" and "low" groups by classifying respondents' measurements on some dimension as either above or below an arbitrary cutoff. For instance, a study participant might be classified as either high or low in self-esteem based on whether or not his or her score on the Rosenberg self-esteem index exceeds the sample median or mean. This practice has little value and should be avoided unless there are justifiable reasons for treating people lumped into ordinal or discrete groups as if they are the same on the variable being measured. For a discussions of the many reasons for avoiding this practice, see Cohen (1983), MacCallum, Zhang, Preacher, & Rucker (2002), Irwin & McClelland (2003), Maxwell & Delaney (1993), and Streiner (2002).

2.1.5 Qualitative Data versus Quantitative Measurement

A final distinction pertinent to measurement is the distinction between qualitative and quantitative data. Qualitative data describe or code the object being measured in qualitative rather than quantitative form. You will recognize the nominal level of measurement as qualitative. For the same reasons I gave when discussing the nominal level of "measurement," qualitative measurement cannot be considered true measurement by my definition. Quantitative measurements, in contrast, represent the object of measurement in quantitative terms on the dimension being measured. Ordinal-, interval-, and ratio-level measurement all qualify as quantitative measurement, although an argument could be made that ordinal-level measurement possesses both qualitative and quantitative features depending on what is being measured.

2.2 Measurement Quality

Science requires measurement, but good science requires good measurement. Anybody can measure something, but it takes effort to measure well. The quality of one's measurement of a construct can vary along a continuum from poor to perfect (although if you ever succeed in measuring something perfectly you deserve an award, as perfect measurement is next to impossible). No single numerical index of measurement quality exists. However, measurement quality can be judged on two important dimensions: *reliability* and *validity*.

2.2.1 Reliability of Measurement

Reliability assesses how much numerical error there is in the measurements. The quantification of reliability of measurement is too advanced a topic at this stage of the book because a complete understanding requires some familiarity with material not yet introduced. The theory of reliability and ways of quantifying reliability are discussed in Chapter 6 after some of the relevant prerequisite statistical concepts are introduced. But at this stage we can discuss some of the basic ideas.

A method of measuring some construct, such as a self-report questionnaire, produces an *observed measurement* of that construct. This observed measurement is the empirical quantification of the unit on the construct being measured. But this observed measurement is unlikely to be equal to that unit's *true score* on what is being measured. The true score is the actual amount of the construct possessed by that unit. The observed and true scores are not necessarily the same thing. The observed measurement is linked to the true score by the equation

$$\text{Observed Measurement} = \text{True Score} + \text{Measurement Error}$$

So the observed measurement contains both the true score of the unit on that construct as well as some error in measurement. The smaller the error, the higher reliability. Various reliability indices that exist are means of quantifying how large these errors in measurement tend to be.

Reliability is often conceptualized as the repeatability of a measurement or set of measurements. If you measured your height with a ruler, recorded your height in inches on a piece of paper, and then measured your height again, you'd be surprised if your measurement changed. Your surprise would stem from that fact that your intuition tells you that a ruler is a reliable measure of height. By the same reasoning, you expect your weight not to vary much from measurement to measurement. To be sure, at different times of the day your weight may fluctuate (depending how much you had eaten recently, what you are wearing, etc), but you'd be surprised if it varied by more than a few pounds from measurement to measurement. This is because most measures of weight, such as a bathroom scale, are very reliable measures of weight. These same ideas can be applied to measures of communication-related constructs, such as media exposure, communication apprehension, and the like. If a measuring instrument produces measurements that contain little error, you would expect that if you repeatedly measured something on the same unit in your study and the unit has not actually changed on what you are measuring, the resulting measurement should be the same or at least very similar time after time. As will be discussed in Chapter 6, rarely would you expect two measurements of the same unit over time to be exactly the same even if the unit has not changed on the construct being measured, but if the measurement instrument is a good one (that is, if the measurements contain relatively little error) then those repeated measurements should be very similar.

But as will be discussed later, repeatability is an *outcome* of high reliability, not the definition of reliability. To be sure, if a set of units is measured on some construct X with relatively little measurement error, then repeated measurement of those same units should be similar over time. But reliability refers to the amount of measurement error that pervades a set of measurements or the measurement process, not just the repeatability of those measurements over time.

2.2.2   Validity of Measurement

Validity of measurement speaks to whether the obtained measurements can be thought of as sensible and high quality quantifications of what the researcher *intends* to be measuring. Whereas reliability quantifies how much *numerical error* exists in the measurement, validity assesses *conceptual error*. A bathroom scale is a reliable measure, but it is not a valid measure of height. Even though a scale will provide consistent measurements, it would be silly to use someone's weight as a measure of his or her height. Indeed, tall people tend to be heavier, but a person's weight is not a sensible or valid measure of his or her height.

Although this example illustrates the point, determining whether or not a method of measurement is valid is typically not at all clear cut. There is no way to prove that a measuring instrument or set of measurements are valid. Validity is assessed through logical argumentation and research. Unfortunately, many researchers just

---

Box 2.1: The *Television Affinity Scale*

For each statement, please indicate the extent to which you strongly disagree, disagree, agree and disagree, agree, or strongly agree as it applies to you. Circle a number from 1 to 5, where 1 = strongly disagree, 2 = disagree, 3 = both agree and disagree, 4 = agree, 5 = strongly agree.

(1) Watching television is one of the more   1 2 3 4 5
     important things I do each day.

(2) If the television set wasn't working I would   1 2 3 4 5
     really miss it.

(3) Watching television is very important in   1 2 3 4 5
     my life

(4) I could easily do without television for   1 2 3 4 5
     several days

(5) I would feel lost without television to watch   1 2 3 4 5

TO COMPUTE YOUR TELEVISION AFFINITY, FIRST SUBTRACT YOUR RESPONSE TO THE FOURTH QUESTION FROM 6. THEN ADD TO THE RESULT THE SUM OF YOUR RESPONSES TO QUESTIONS 1, 2, 3, and 5. YOUR SCORE SHOULD BE BETWEEN 5 and 25.

---

assume that a measurement procedure they are using is producing valid measurements of the construct they want to measure without providing any kind of argument or research to support that claim. A good measurement instrument should meet many different criteria of validity if it is to be accepted as valid. Not all measures will meet all criteria, and not all criteria are relevant for all measures.

Face Validity. We talk about a measuring instrument's *face validity* as a kind of intuitive feeling that the measure seems or feels right. When you look at a measuring instrument and compare it conceptually to the construct you intend to measure and find yourself thinking "yeah, it seems about right," then you are saying the measure has face validity. Consider for instance the *Television Affinity Scale* (see Box 2.1), which reportedly measures the importance one attaches to television in the course of day to day life (see Rubin et al., 2004). This is known as a *summated rating scale*, and it yields a single score for each person who responds to the questions. This single score is constructed by adding up the person's responses to each of the questions, as described in Box 2.1, such that a higher score reflects a greater sense of the importance of television to the person. For example, someone who responded agree or strongly agree to questions 1, 2, 3, and 5 and disagree or strongly disagree to question 4 would have a relatively high score on the measure—in the 20 to 25 range. The opposite pattern of responses would yield a low score—in the 5 to 10 range. If you look at this measure and you agree that it seems like a reasonable and sensible measure of this construct, then you are agreeing that the measure has face validity. This is a very subjective judgment, and if all you can say is that a measure has face validity, you haven't really said that much. Surprisingly, however, some of the published research in the communication literature includes measures that at best satisfy only the face validity criterion. Researchers often construct measures ad hoc, based on their needs for the particular study, and never give any kind of evidence, logical or otherwise, that the measurement procedure they are using is actually measuring what they claim. This is a problem not in just the field of communication; it permeates the social sciences and reflects the fact that demonstrating that a measurement procedure meets the more rigorous criteria of validity described below is a lot more difficult.

Content Validity. A closely related kind of validity is *content validity*. A measurement instrument is said to be content valid if the items in the measure adequately represent the universe of relevant behaviors or indicators of that construct. Consider a test of your mastery of the material presented in this book up to this point. If this test had 90% of its questions on levels of measurement and nothing on the philosophies and assumptions of science (in the previous chapter), you could reasonably criticize such a test on the grounds that it is not a content valid measure of your mastery of the material because it does not adequately cover all the material or even a decent representation of it. Similarly, people often criticize many measures of "intelligence" as low in validity because they fail to measure abilities that could be argued are intelligence, such as creativity or the ability to interact appropriately with people in various situations. Or if you were measuring "aggressive tendencies" by asking a person if he or she has ever punched someone in the face, that clearly would not be a content valid measure of "aggressive tendencies." Aggression can take many physical forms, as well as many nonphysical forms. Consider the *Television Affinity Scale* again. To assess its content validity, you need to ask whether something important may have been left out. Think about this for a minute. Might there be an item or two missing that would improve this measure?

I leave this question unanswered to illustrate that both content validity and face validity are somewhat difficult to assess objectively. You could say that a measurement instrument you are using has content and face validity, but someone else may disagree. All you can do is argue about it, duke it out verbally, and no one can really be "proven" right or wrong. So what can you do? Probably the best way to assess face and content validity is to show the instrument you are using to a group of experts on the topic of interest and see if they feel like the measure is missing something important. Does an expert or a group of experts feel like you are adequately capturing all the relevant domains, dimensions, behaviors, and so forth, that are relevant to the construct?

Criterion-related Validity. If the *Television Affinity Scale* is a valid measure of the importance that one places on television from day to day, then you'd expect that people who score low on the *Television Affinity Scale* would also watch relatively little television compared to those who score relatively high on the index. If that was the case, it would be reasonable to say that the *Television Affinity Scale* has *criterion-related validity*. Criterion-related validity is assessed by seeing if scores on the measurement instrument are related to other things that you'd expect them to be related to if the measure is measuring what you claim it is measuring.

There are a few special forms of criterion-related validity, but in practice the distinction between them is not important, and the terms I describe next are often used interchangeably. *Concurrent validity* refers to the extent to which a measurement instrument produces measurements that are similar to the measurements that a different measure of the same construct yields. For example, if you were developing a measure of shyness, you would hope that people who score relatively high in shyness on your measure also score as relatively shy on other measures of shyness. *Predictive validity*, also a form of criterion-related validity, assesses the extent to which scores on a measure accurately predict something that they should be able to predict. For example, you could argue that your measure of shyness is valid if it accurately predicts performance on a job in which shyness should inhibit good performance, such as a door-to-door sales.

With the concept of criterion-related validity now introduced, it is worth making the distinction between validating a measurement instrument and validating its *use*. We use measurement instruments to accomplish certain research objectives, such as examining the relationship between exposure to violent TV and aggression. If the measure allows us to accomplish those research objectives because our measures are measuring the constructs we want, then they are valid for that use. But there are other ways that a measure can be valid, even if we don't accept the validity of the measure as a measure of something in particular. You may not believe that such college admission tests as the SAT or ACT are valid measures of scholastic aptitude because they focus so much on verbal and mathematical skills. But they are valid predictors of college grade point average, and so it is perfectly legitimate from the perspective of making good decisions to use SAT or ACT scores of applicants for admission as a criterion in college admission decisions.

Here is another admittedly absurd example that makes the same point. The U.S. government employs thousands of people in the Transportation Security Administration (TSA) as airport security screeners. How does the TSA know if an applicant for a position as a security screener is going to be good? Suppose for argument's sake that research found that good screeners, when given the choice, prefer bananas to oranges whereas bad screeners prefer oranges over bananas (I doubt this is true, but let's pretend it is true). Fruit preference clearly is not a valid measure of the skills required to be a good screener using the simple definition of validity I gave earlier. But it is a valid predictor of performance in this example. As such, on the surface at least, it doesn't seem unreasonable to use an applicant's response to such a question to determine who should be and should not be hired if it is a valid predictor of performance as a screener.

Construct Validity. The final form of validity is *construct validity*. In my judgment, construct validity is really what most people are interested in when they ask whether a method of measurement can be said to be validly measuring the desired construct. We can say a measure has construct validity if it meets most of the criteria I've been describing. Does it "feel" right. Do others agree that the measure is representing the relevant dimensions or indicators of the construct the instrument reportedly measures? And is the pattern of associations between scores on the instrument and measures of other constructs consistent with the claim that the instrument is measuring the desired construct?

This latter criterion is probably the most difficult to grasp, so let me use an example from my own research on a construct I developed and named *Willingness to Self-Censor* (Hayes, Glynn, & Shanahan, in press a). Willingness to Self-Censor refers to a person's general, cross-situational willingness to censor their opinion expression around others thought to disagree with that opinion. I developed the *Willingness to Self-Censor Scale*, an 8-item self-report instrument to tap this individual difference in people (see Box 6.1). To establish that the *Willingness to Self-Censor Scale* is a construct-valid measure of this individual difference, I embarked on a series of studies to examine its correlates with other individual differences you would expect people who are relatively high versus relatively low on this construct to differ on. For instance, expressing an opinion that others don't agree with can result in an argument or some kind of interpersonal conflict. Therefore, you would expect people who are relatively more willing to censor their own opinion expression would be relatively averse to argumentation, a construct measured with the *Argumentativeness Scale* (Infante & Rancer, 1992). Indeed, I found that people who scored relatively high on the *Willingness to Self-Censor Scale* (compared to those relatively low) did indeed score relatively low on the *Argumentativeness Scale*. Additionally, I argued that the expression of a dissenting opinion is a risky act that you would expect people to do only if they were relatively confident in their own goodness, because our opinions are reflections in part of the things we value and find important and define who we are as people. To test this prediction, I administered the *Willingness to Self-Censor Scale* to a group of people and also had them respond to a series of questions that are known to measure self-esteem. I found that, as expected, people who scored relatively low on the *Willingness to Self-Censor Scale* were relatively higher in self-esteem. Furthermore, in an experimental context, I showed that people who scored high on the *Willingness to Self-Censor Scale* were more sensitive to the distribution of others' opinions when deciding whether or not to voice their opinion publicly than were people who scored relatively low on the scale (Hayes, Glynn, & Shanahan, in press b). These findings, combined with several others described in the validation paper and elsewhere, all can be used as evidence that the *Willingness to Self-Censor Scale* is a construct valid measure of this individual difference. It is measuring this construct rather than something else.

Validation of a measurement instrument is a complex and long process. If you are being innovative and creating a new instrument or method of measurement, it is very reasonable for a reader of your research to expect you to provide some evidence or argument that your measurement method is producing measurements of what you claim it is producing. If you are using a measurement instrument that others have used before and that others accept as valid when used in the way you used it in your research, then most are willing to give you the benefit of the doubt that your method of measurement is valid for that purpose. For an advanced discussion of measurement validation, see Cronbach and Meehl (1955).

Before closing this chapter, it is important to make the distinction between a set of observed measurements and the measuring instrument or procedure. A measurement instrument or procedure is what yields the observed measurements. A self-report measure such as the *Interpersonal Attraction Scale* (Rubin et al., 2004) is a measuring instrument, and if it is a valid measure of interpersonal attraction, it will produce observed measurements for a person's attraction to another (on three dimensions—social, physical, and task). We often talk about measurement instruments as being reliable or valid and that is a sensible thing to do. Some measures of communication constructs are certainly more reliable and valid than others. But it is not necessarily true that a reliable and valid measure will yield reliable and valid measurements in all circumstances. For example, a measure of self-esteem may have been developed and validated based on the responses of people 18 years old and older living in the United States. And it may produce reliable and valid measurements when administered to adult residents of, for example, the state of Ohio. Whether it produces reliable and valid measurements in adolescents, or residents of Sydney, Australia, or Barcelona, Spain is open to question. You can assume that the measure would be reliable and valid if used on adolescents or Australians or Spaniards, but that doesn't mean it is. Therefore, it is important whenever possible to report at least the reliability of your measurements when describing your research. A reader will want to know if your method of measurement yielded reliable measurements. Whether the instrument is reliable for other investigators who have used it in their research is only indirectly relevant. Of course, the chances of the observed measurements being reliable are much higher if you use a measurement instrument that has lots of evidence supporting its reliability in many circumstances or many populations. In contrast, there is almost no way of knowing whether a measurement instrument is valid in all circumstances or situations in which it is likely to be used. You can only assume it is valid, make the argument that it is valid, or provide data suggesting that it is valid.

2.3 Summary

Communication researchers typically quantify the constructs they are interested in measuring. The process of operationalization results in a means of measuring the constructs of interest to the researcher. The outcome of the measurement process is a set of observed measurements of the research units on the constructs being measured. These measurements, and the methods of measurement being used, can vary in precision and in quality. Communication researchers should strive to measure their constructs with as little error as possible (reliability) and ensure that they are measuring what they intend to be measuring (validity). Although reliability can be quantified (see Chapter 6), establishing the validity of measurement is considerably more complex and as much a logical and argumentative process as a statistical one, ideally buttressed by data when possible.

THREE

Sampling

Before any data analysis can begin, you have to have some data to analyze. Where do your data come from, and how do you go about obtaining the data you need to test your hypotheses and answer your research questions? Data can take many forms, it can come from many different sources, and there are various approaches to finding the data you want. As discussed in Chapters 1 and 2, data are the outcome of the measurement or categorization process. But before you can measure, you have to have someone or something to measure. In other words, you need to have recruited participants for your study or otherwise obtained the research units to be measured on the variables relevant to your study. In this chapter, I give a broad overview of the various approaches to recruiting or otherwise obtaining the research units that provide data to the researcher.

3.1 Population Inference

When we conduct research, we are often interested in some kind of inference. In statistics, the most common conceptualization of inference is *population inference*—the practice of making a statistical statement about a collection of objects from a subset of that collection. For example, if 60% of 200 people you ask approve how the president is doing his or her job, you might make the claim that around 60% of *all* people (rather than just those 200 you asked) approve. In so doing, your claim that 60% of all people approve is a population inference. To make such an inference, you must be very careful in how you go about recruiting or finding research units to be measured (e.g., people who respond to a question or participate in the research in some fashion) because most statistical methods make some kind of assumption about how the units were obtained in order to apply those methods to making population inferences.

When conducting research, we usually collect data only from a *sample*—a small subset of the population. The *population* is the universe of objects you are trying to make some kind of inference about, whereas the sample consists of a collection of members of the population (see Figure 3.1). The sample will almost always be smaller in size than the population and typically *much* smaller. We often (but not always) are interested in the population that a sample represents and not the individuals in

Population

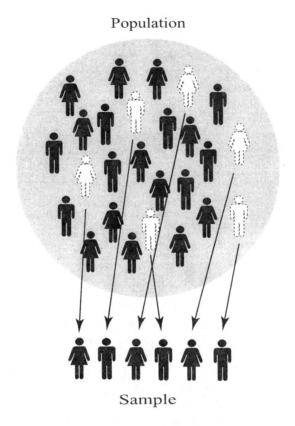

Sample

Figure 3.1 Population versus sample.

the sample itself. Public opinion polls are a good example of this. When a pollster calls 1,000 people on the telephone and asks their opinion on some issue, the pollster is interested in understanding the population of people from which the sample was derived. So the focus of the inference is on the entire population, not just the 1,000 people telephoned. Of course, it would be far too burdensome (and typically impossible) to obtain data from the entire population. But if you were somehow able to obtain data from every member of the population, then you would have what is technically called a *census*. Fortunately, when population inference is the goal of the research, it isn't necessary to obtain a census of the population because the sample can provide a window through which the population can be viewed if proper sampling procedures are followed.

Similarly, a media researcher may be interested in how news broadcasts (the population) portray minorities, but the researcher will probably examine this by studying only a small subset of news broadcasts, such as all 10 o'clock news broadcasts from four local networks in Los Angeles, Dallas, Chicago, and New York for a week (the sample). The researcher will have data about how this small subset portrays minorities, and if proper sample procedures are followed, he or she can use this small subset to make statements about the broader population of interest. Just how population inference is accomplished constitutes the theory of estimation, aspects of which are discussed in Chapter 7 and elsewhere in this book.

When we make a population inference, we are making a numerical statement about a population by generalizing a statistical description of the data in the sample to the population from which the sample was derived. But there is another kind of inference that is equally or even more important than population inference—*process inference.* Any research finding is constrained in some respects by who provided the data and how the units were recruited to participate in the study. When a researcher's primary interest is a process inference, there is less focus on specific numerical descriptions of the population (such as 60% of the U.S. population approves of the president, or people watch 2.5 hours of TV per week on average). Furthermore, who provided the data and how the participants were obtained typically take a back seat to other concerns when interpreting study results. Instead, the focus is on whether the theory or hypothesis is being adequately tested given the design of the study and whether the study helps to illuminate the process that is producing the effect observed. Process inference is usually the primary interest of communication researchers. This important distinction between a process and a population inference will be made clearer toward the end of this chapter and elsewhere throughout this book. For now, we will focus on sampling methods as a means of making good population inferences.

3.1.1   The *Literary Digest* Poll: Population Inference Gone Awry

Most of the statistical methods that communication researchers use are based on the *population model* of inference. The concept of population inference is probably best illustrated by first discussing one of the most well known population inference failures, the infamous *Literary Digest* poll of 1936. The *Literary Digest* was a magazine published in the early half of the 20th century, and the publishers had been conducting a poll to predict U.S. Presidential election results since 1916. Until 1936, it had correctly predicted the winner of the presidential election every single time. But in 1936, it got it wrong by predicting that Republican Alf Landon would beat Democrat Franklin Delano Roosevelt, with Landon garnering roughly 57% of the votes. This prediction was a population inference, reflecting their estimate (57%) of the percent of the U.S. voting population that would vote for Landon, as well as a qualitative inference that Landon would win the election. But history tells us Roosevelt won the Presidency, not Landon, and by a huge margin (62% vs. 37%).

To understand how the *Literary Digest* got it wrong, it is necessary to understand the methodology of the poll in some detail. To conduct this poll, they mailed ballots to roughly 10 million people. The respondents were asked to indicate on the ballot who they were going to vote for in the upcoming election and then return the ballot by mail. The 10 million people were obtained largely from automobile registration lists and telephone books. Roughly 23% of those that received the ballot did return it; a sample size of over 2 million, which is a very large sample by any standard. But sample size is not everything because from responses returned, the *Literary Digest* incorrectly forecasted that Landon would win the election.

Just what went wrong has been a source of debate for some time, and although we will never know for certain just what happened, Squire (1988) published a rather convincing paper in *Public Opinion Quarterly* that attributed the failure to both data collection methods and nonresponse bias. His data came from an opinion poll conducted in 1937, just after the election. This poll contained questions about how the respondent voted in the 1936 election as well as whether he or she owned a car or telephone, received the *Literary Digest* ballot, and if so, whether he or she filled it out and returned it to the *Digest.*

One explanation that had been offered for the failure of the *Literary Digest* poll is that the list of 10 million people who were sent the ballot did not adequately represent the people of the United States. Of concern was the possibility that the use of automobile registrations and phone lists produced a collection of respondents who were more well-to-do than the U.S. population as a whole and therefore more likely to vote Republican. Remember that this was 1936, when the richer segment of the population would have been much more likely to own a car or telephone and therefore receive a ballot. However, Squire's data suggests that this explanation doesn't completely explain the failure of the *Literary Digest* poll. To be sure, those with neither a car nor a telephone were much more likely to vote for the Democrat (Roosevelt) than the Republican (Landon) by about a 4 to 1 margin (79% vs. 19%). But even among those who owned both a car and a telephone, Roosevelt received more votes than Landon (55% to 45%).

Squire also examined whether people who received the ballot were more likely to vote for Landon than those who did not receive it. Indeed, those that reported that they did not receive the *Literary Digest* poll were much more likely to vote for Roosevelt (71%) than Landon (27%). However, even those that reported that they did receive the poll were more likely to vote for Roosevelt (55% vs. 45%, respectively). Combined, these findings suggest that there were differences between those who did and did not receive the poll with respect to how they voted, and people of different income levels probably did vote differently. But in none of the subgroups of this sample discussed thus far was there a preference for Landon over Roosevelt.

A better explanation for the source of the failure of the poll to correctly forecast the election is *nonresponse* bias. Squire tabulated how the respondents in the 1937 poll voted as a function of whether or not they received and *returned* the ballot. The results were striking. Of those who received but did not return the ballot, 69% reported they voted for Roosevelt. Of those who both received *and* returned the ballot, the majority voted for Landon (51% vs. 48% for Roosevelt). So the failure of the *Literary Digest* poll can be attributed, at least in part, to the fact that those who participated in the poll by returning the ballot did not represent the views of the American public as a whole. Probably less important, although its influence cannot be ruled out, was the tendency for wealthier people to be more likely to receive a ballot, who were more likely to vote for Landon than the less wealthy. In the end, the results from their poll were not generalizable away from their data (the 2+ million respondents to the ballot) to the larger group the publishers of the *Digest* were interested in understanding—the U.S. voting population as a whole. The population inference was wrong.

It is tempting to attribute the failure of the *Literary Digest* poll to early 20th-century methodological ignorance. Certainly, such a huge mistake could never happen again by expert, modern-day researchers. To be sure, there were lessons learned from the *Literary Digest* failure that changed the way that pollsters collect and interpret data. But there is evidence that the same processes that lead the *Literary Digest* to overestimate support for Landon in 1936 lead Edison Media Research and Mitofsky International, the companies that managed the November 3, 2004 exit polls in the U.S. Presidential election between Senator John Kerry and President George W. Bush, to overestimate how many people were voting for Kerry on election day. Exit polls are conducted just after voters cast their ballots, the results of which are given to the media so a winner can be forecasted after the polling stations close but before votes are counted. Historically, exit polls have been very accurate, but in this case Bush ended up winning many of states the exit poll data said should have been won by Kerry. The discrepancies between exit poll data and voter returns resulted in many conspiracy theories of election day fraud and vote rigging. But when the exit poll data were closely analyzed, it turned out that in many voting precincts, exit poll staff were more successful at recruiting Kerry supporters to participate in the exit poll than they were at recruiting Bush supporters (Edison Media Research & Mitofsky International, 2005). As a result, Kerry supporters were more likely to have their opinions registered in exit poll data, and the result was an inaccurate inference from sample to population. So even expert researchers well-versed in sampling theory and methodology are not immune to errors in inference.

3.1.2   Population Inference Through Representativeness

If the goal of the research is to generalize from the data to some population of interest (which was the goal for the *Literary Digest* publishers), we want to do our best to make sure that the sample is *representative* of the population. A sample is representative if it is *similar to the population in all important aspects relevant to the research.* To clarify, suppose you are interested in the political attitudes of the people of the city you live in. So you conduct a study by getting 500 residents of the city to fill out a questionnaire in which you ask various questions about political orientation, voting habits, and so forth. To the extent that the 500 people in your study are similar to the population as a whole on aspects relevant to your research, you can say that your sample is representative, and you can probably generalize your results from your sample to the population.

But on what important aspects relevant to the research would you want to see high correspondence between the sample and the population? For starters, you'd probably want to make sure that the sample contains men and women in about the same proportion as the population. We know that political attitudes of men and women are different, and if you want to generalize from sample to population, you'd want to make sure that your sample didn't substantially overrepresent males or females, lest your findings may be slanted in the direction of the overrepresented group. Similarly, income is also related to many political attitudes. If it was known that 20% of the city is lower class, 50% middle class, and 30% upper class (how these categories are defined is not important for our purposes), it would be important to make sure that your sample is similar in this respect. It would probably be all right, however, if your sample did not represent the population with respect to something irrelevant to the research, like pet ownership. Whether or not someone owns a pet is probably unrelated to their political attitudes, so you probably wouldn't care too much if 90% of your sample respondents had a pet even though only, say, 30% of the residents of the city own a pet. Of course, a difference on a seemingly irrelevant characteristic such as pet ownership might reflect other differences between the sample and the population that affect representativeness (e.g., perhaps pet owners are more likely to own a house and thus are more likely to have a higher income).

Although it is important that the sample be representative of the population when the goal is to make a population inference, we never really know whether or not it is representative. Why? Because you won't usually know in advance (a) all the aspects of the population that are relevant to the research and (b) just how the population differs from the sample on those characteristics. There are some things, however, that you can check after sampling, such as demographic similarity. For instance, the U.S.

Census Bureau keeps lots of statistics pertaining to the demographic make up of cities all over the United States. You could see if your sample is similar to the population by comparing the demographic characteristics of the sample to the statistics compiled by the Census Bureau. Or you could attempt to make a logical argument that even though your sample may not be representative of the population, you are safe in making a population inference from your data. Of course, you can argue all you want, and that doesn't mean you arguments are valid and the resulting inference will be correct. Therefore, it is best that you not end up in a situation having to defend your population inferences on logical grounds. Instead, maximize representativeness through the use of a good sampling strategy.

3.2   Sampling Methods

If your goal is population inference, you should focus your energy on obtaining research units that make it likely that your sample represents the population by the careful selection of sampling method. Although there is no way to guarantee a representative sample, there are things that you can do to enhance the likelihood that it will be representative. But first it is worth overviewing methods of sampling that tend to produce poor population inferences.

3.2.1   Nonprobability Sampling

A *nonprobability sampling method* is any method of recruiting or obtaining units for analysis in which inclusion in the sample is not determined by a random process. Just what is meant by a "random process" will be clearer in section 3.2.2 when I discuss probability sampling. For now, I describe two common methods of nonprobability sampling.

Convenience Sampling. If the investigator selects who (if the unit is people) or what (if the unit is something else, such as newspaper advertisements) provides data merely because those units are conveniently available to the researcher, then that investigator is conducting a *convenience sample.* Perhaps the people live in the same neighborhood as the investigator, or they are students in the researcher's college class, or they happen to shop at a local shopping mall. Or suppose a media researcher examines newspapers that he or she happens to subscribe to or that are available at the local newsstand or library. Although the use of convenience samples is very common in social science research, including communication research (see, e.g., Potter, Cooper, & Dupagne, 1993; Rossiter, 1976; or Sears, 1986), it is very difficult to make accurate population inferences from a sample of convenience. This is not to say that other forms of inference are not possible, and often (or even typically) population inference is not the goal of the researcher. But when it is, population inference rests on very shaky ground when a sample is based on convenience of the research units.

Why? The major problem is that there is no way of knowing that units conveniently available to the researcher are representative of the population to which the population inference is being made. For example, if I were interested in numerically estimating gender differences in communication apprehension by walking around the campus of The Ohio State University and asking men and women to fill out McCroskey's *Personal Report of Communication Apprehension* (see Rubin et al., 2004), all kinds of processes could render any difference (or lack of difference) I find ungeneralizable to people in general, college students in general, or even college students at The Ohio State

University. For instance, I might hesitate to approach someone if he or she appears angry, unhappy, or unsociable. Or I may have some other conscious or unconscious bias that leads me to approach only certain types of people, such as tall people or physically attractive people. To the extent that attributes of a person that lead me not to approach that person are related to what I am measuring (or things related to what I am measuring), my sample will be not be representative of any population, except perhaps the trivial population of people that I find approachable. I think it is easy to see how such people might differ in important ways related to communication apprehension. They may be especially outgoing, gregarious, and not at all anxious about communication. As a result, I may find no sex differences only because I only approached the more sociable and outgoing people I ran across wandering around campus. By the same reasoning, newspapers that a researcher happens to subscribe to or that are locally available may not represent newspapers in general. The community in which the researcher lives may be especially conservative or liberal, with newspapers in the area reflecting the political or social environment of the region. It would be difficult to make any kind of population inference (such as the proportion of editorials in major newspapers that are critical of the president's foreign policy) from what such a restricted sample of newspapers yields, unless the population of interest was the regional newspapers or newspapers with similar characteristics to those locally and conveniently available.

Another problem with samples of convenience is that it isn't clear just what the population being sampled is. Consider again my convenience sample of men and women I approach around campus. Just what is the population from which I sampled? Is it all people? Probably not. Is it young adults? Probably not. Students? People who live or work around The Ohio State University? I don't know, and there is no way I could determine what the population I sampled is. So even if the sample was representative, it isn't clear just what population it represents.

Volunteer Sampling. Another nonprobability sampling method that enjoys wide use is *volunteer sampling*. In a volunteer sample, the researcher recruits people to participate in the research, and those who volunteer to participate are included in the sample. In some sense, almost all samples of people are volunteer samples because you can't force a person to participate in a research study. What makes volunteer sampling distinguishable is the method of recruitment. Volunteer sampling procedures include advertising a study in the newspaper, posting a sign-up sheet in a classroom or around campus, or emailing potential participants. Volunteer samples suffer from the same problems as convenience samples, in that it is very difficult to know how representative your sample is of your population of interest, and when you obtain your sample, it usually isn't clear just what population your sample does represent. There is considerable evidence that (a) people interested in the topic of the research are more likely to volunteer to participate in that research, (b) when given the choice of several studies to participate in, volunteers who choose different studies sometimes differ in potentially important ways such as personality, (c) that students who volunteer to participate in research early in the academic term differ from those who volunteer later, (d) and that people who require more coaxing to participate in research may differ from those who more willingly participate (see, e.g., Abeles, Iscoe, & Brown, 1954–1955; Jackson, Procidano, & Cohen, 1989; Rosenthal & Rosnow, 1975; Wang & Jentsch, 1998). So there is no question that volunteers often differ from nonvolunteers in ways that might be relevant to the research. They are not likely to be representative of the population of interest, and population inference is often unwarranted and unjustifiable.

As I will soon discuss, convenience samples or other samples derived from a nonrandom sampling plan can be an efficient way of collecting data, depending on the kinds of inferences one wants to make. But if the goal is population inference, convenience samples should be avoided whenever better alternatives are possible.

3.2.2 Probability Sampling

Probability sampling methods are better suited to research where population inference is the goal. Probability sampling procedures are those where the determination of who or what provides data to the researcher is determined by a random process. In a probability sample, the only influence the investigator has in determining who is included in a sample is in the determination of the population to be sampled. Once the population is identified, the researcher (or his or her assistants or associates) has no say in who ends up in the sample. Random selection of the sample greatly increases the likelihood that the sample will be representative of the population in all aspects relevant to the research.

Simple Random Sampling. The simplest form of random sampling is *simple random sampling*. To conduct a simple random sample, all members of the population are identified and enumerated in the form of a list or database of some kind. Members of the population are then included in the sample through a random selection procedure, such as having a computer randomly select from the list, or even putting the names or identifiers of each member of the population on a slip of paper, putting the slips into a container and drawing out the desired number of members to be included in the sample. The key to conducting a simple random sample is to make sure that each member of the population has an equal chance of being included in the sample. If you are successful at doing so, this means that all possible samples of size n are equally likely samples. For example, if my population contained $N = 25$ members and I wanted a sample of size $n = 5$ from that population, there are 53,130 possible samples of size $n = 5$ (where that number comes from will be discussed in Chapter 7). A simple random sampling procedure guarantees that all 53,130 of these possible samples of size 5 are equally likely samples.

A simple random sample is in some ways the statistical ideal. However, in practice, it is difficult or impossible to collect a truly simple random sample because for most populations of interest to a researcher, there is no list or from which the sample can be derived in a simple random fashion.

Systematic Random Sampling. Another probability sampling method is *sequential random sampling*. In systematic or sequential random sampling, the researcher selects a random start point in the list of the population and then includes every k^{th} member of the population from that point, selecting k so that the desired sample size is obtained once the end of the list is reached. For example, if the population is of size $N = 100$ and a sample of size $n = 20$ is desired, a starting point in the list between 1 and 5 is randomly selected and then every fifth person in the list from that point is included in the sample.

Interestingly, this kind of sampling strategy is possible even if the population list is not available. Suppose a researcher wanted to sample people who visit a particular mall (the population of interest). The researcher could stand at the entrance to the mall over a series of days or weeks and interview or otherwise collect the relevant data from every 20th person that enters the mall. If the researcher followed this procedure, then we know that he or she will not be influencing who is ultimately approached to provide data.

Stratified Random Sampling. Another kind of random sampling is *stratified random sampling*. A stratified random sampling procedure might be used if the researcher wants to make sure that the sample represents the population on one or more especially important dimensions, such as the distribution of males versus females. In a stratified random sample, the researcher first identifies two or more *strata*, defined by values on the stratification variable. A *stratum* (the singular of strata) is defined as a subset of the population the members of which share a common feature. For example, a researcher might want to stratify based on sex. Therefore, sex is the stratification variable, and the two strata are the males in the population and the females in the population. A stratified random sample is obtained by taking a simple random sample from each stratum, ensuring that the proportion of the total sample obtained from each stratum reflects the distribution of the population on the stratification variable.

For example, in a study I conducted on high school English teachers in California (Barnes & Hayes, 1995), we used a stratified random sampling procedure to select teachers to be interviewed. It was important in this study to make sure teachers at large, medium, and small schools (defined by enrollment) were represented according to their frequency in the population of schools. From a list of schools the state provided, it was possible to determine the proportion of schools that were large, medium, and small defined by enrollment. Knowing that 40% of schools were large, 40% were medium, and 20% were small using our definition of size, 40% of our sample was obtained by simple random sampling from the list of teachers at large schools, 40% was obtained by simple random sampling from the list of teachers at medium sized schools, and the remaining 20% were obtained from a simple random sample of teachers at small schools. As a result, the distribution of school size in the sample exactly mirrored the population distribution of school size.

If a simple random sample is difficult to obtain because of the difficulty of obtaining a list of the entire population from which the sample can be derived, a stratified random sample is often even more difficult because in addition to having a list from which to sample, you must have some kind of information that identifies which stratum in the population each member belongs. If that information is available, all well and good, but often it is not, making stratification impossible.

Cluster Sampling. Another random sampling method is *cluster sampling*. Cluster sampling is similar to stratified sampling in that the members of the population must first be identified and classified based on some characteristic. Whereas the groups sharing the stratification characteristic are called strata in stratified sampling, in cluster sampling those groups are called *clusters*. In cluster sampling, the population of clusters is randomly sampled. For each randomly selected cluster, *all* members of that cluster are included in the sample. This differs from stratified sampling, in that stratified sampling is based on a random sampling of members of each strata.

To illustrate the distinction, let's imagine you wanted to sample all members of the faculty at a particular university. To conduct a cluster sample, you might randomly select departments from the population of departments and then include in your sample all members of the departments that were randomly selected from the population of departments. By contrast, a stratified sample would randomly sample members from *each and every department* in such a way that the proportion of people in the *sample* from each department corresponds to the proportion of the entire faculty that resides in each of the departments.

Cluster sampling can also be useful for sampling a large geographical area. A map of a region can be divided into smaller regions (clusters), and then the population of clusters is randomly sampled by randomly selecting clusters and including every person living in those randomly selected clusters in the sample. Similarly, neighborhoods can be sampled by dividing up the neighborhood into city blocks and then randomly sampling city blocks and including each resident of those blocks that were selected in the sample.

Notice that cluster sampling does not necessarily require a list of all members of the population prior to sampling. For example, it might be tough to get an accurate list of employees at all North American McDonald's restaurant franchises. Indeed, the corporation might be quite reluctant to provide that information even if it had it available. But it would probably happily provide a list of all of its franchises in North America. You could randomly sample from the list of franchises and then approach the manager of each restaurant that was selected randomly and ask if he or she would be willing to let the employees of that restaurant participate in the research.

Random Digit Dialing. With the exception of cluster sampling, the sampling methods described above presume that it is possible to first enumerate the entire population prior to selecting a sample. There is another way of randomly sampling a population that enjoys widespread use in public opinion research and some other areas of communication research as well. The method of *random digit dialing* capitalizes on the fact that although there are few readily available lists of the population of a city, state, or country, most people can be identified with a phone number. When a researcher conducts a random sample using random digit dialing (often abbreviated *RDD*), people are contacted by dialing a random phone number. Whoever answers the phone and meets the desired selection criteria (e.g., someone over 18) is then included in the sample. By focusing the random dialing on a particular area code (the first three digits) or telephone exchange (the next three digits), it is possible to randomly sample small regions, such as states, cities, or even neighborhoods.

The use of the telephone to recruit participants has a number of clear disadvantages however. Not all telephone numbers are residential numbers. Many are businesses, fax machines, or disconnected. So it takes a lot of dialing to obtain the desired sample size because many phone numbers are not linked to a person. Furthermore, not everyone owns a phone, and we know that phone ownership is related to things that may bias the sample in important ways so that certain types of people (e.g., unemployed, homeless, or poor) are less likely to end up in a sample using RDD sampling. Relatedly, people who only use a cell phone will not be included in public opinion polls because of restrictions placed on pollsters and telemarketers on the calling of cell phone numbers for research and marketing purposes and the fact that there is no database of active cell phone numbers.[1] Also, some people have more than one phone number, meaning such people have a greater chance of being included in the sample. To the extent that having multiple phone lines or a cell phone only is related to things relevant to your research, you could end up with a sample that is biased in favor of such people or types of people.

For these and other reasons, it is relatively rare these days for researchers to use pure random digit dialing as a sampling method. More likely, a research firm will sample from a list of working telephone numbers compiled from one of many different databases. Because not all working telephone numbers are likely to be included in such

---

[1]This may change in the future, as more and more people abandon traditional "landline" phones in favor of cellular phones.

databases, the last few digits of the phone number might be randomly switched in an attempt to capture at least some unlisted numbers.

Sampling methodology is a very large and technical topic, and it is impossible to do it justice in just a few pages. Many books on the topic are available, and you could spend years developing knowledge and expertise in the area. Stuart (1984) provides a good and relatively nontechnical introduction to some of the more complicated issues in sampling. But the basic introduction I presented here should give you a feeling for the options available and used by communication researchers to recruit research units.

3.3   Is Nonprobability Sampling Really So Bad?

The probability sampling methods described above are the best approach to producing a sample that maximizes the ability to make sound population inferences. The random selection of participants, (if well conducted and the sample is not adulterated by response biases of some sort) allows the researcher to be reasonably confident that a sample represents the population from which sample was derived, and this representativeness affords the researcher the ability to make inferences about the population from information obtained from a sample of members of that population.

Given this, it might seem discouraging to acknowledge the fact that true probability sampling is rarely ever done in communication research. More typically, the samples that communication researchers collect are not selected randomly from any population. Indeed, the population from which a sample is derived is rarely explicitly defined either before or after data collection. Given this, how is it possible to make inferences from sample to population? The simple answer is that, technically, it isn't possible to make population inferences. However, in thinking about this problem, it is clear that the question is better framed not as whether or not it is *possible* but instead whether or not the researcher *wants* to make a population inference. If the researcher does not want to make a specific statistical statement about a population (such as females are 2.3 units more shy than males on average), then the question of whether the sample is random or not becomes moot. If the intent of the researcher is not to make a population inference but instead make a *process inference*, then the origin of the sample should loom less large in our evaluation of that research (Mook, 1983).

Just what do I mean by process inference? This concept is best understood by remembering that we often do research to test theory or a hypothesis (whether or not derived from a theory). Theories make predictions about what researchers should find in a research study motivated by the theory. Theory-driven research focuses less on estimating the size of an effect (such as the average difference between men or women on some measure in the population of interest) than it does on determining whether a prediction the theory makes about what should happen in a research study actually does happen (c.f., Frick, 1998; Mook, 1983). The data are collected, and the researcher analyzes the data to see if the data are consistent with the prediction that the theory makes. If so, then this provides some support to the theory. Remember that theories are explanations of a process. So if the theory is supported by the data, it is sensible to say that, at least in the circumstances in which the theory was tested, the process is probably at work and that in similar circumstances or situations, it is probably at work as well.

I need to be more concrete than this, so here is an example of what I mean. The *elaboration likelihood model of persuasion* (Petty & Cacioppo, 1986) postulates that people will deeply process the contents of a message aimed at persuading only if they are motivated and able to do so. How would you be able to determine if people who are motivated to process a message are actually thinking about the contents of the message more deeply than people less motivated? In other words, how would you be able to test this theoretical proposition? One approach taken by persuasion researchers has been to assess whether people's attitudes are affected by a manipulation of the strength of the arguments in the message. If people are paying attention to the message and thinking about the contents of the message at a deep level, then they should be more persuaded by strong arguments than by weak arguments. But if they are not paying attention and processing the message because they aren't motivated or able to do so, then strong arguments should be no more persuasive than weak ones. To test this, you might recruit some people who happen to be conveniently available to participate in a study. Perhaps the participants are college students or people who happened to respond to an advertisement you placed in the local paper in search of participants. First you determine whether the contents of the message will be of interest to them or relevant to each participant's life. For those people for whom the answer is yes, consider those people motivated to process the message. Those who don't care about the topic or who find it irrelevant to their lives you can consider unmotivated to process the message. Then randomly assign these participants to receive a persuasive message containing either mostly strong arguments or mostly weak arguments, and then assess their agreement with the message after they are exposed to it. The *elaboration likelihood model* predicts that the argument strength manipulation should have a bigger effect on the people motivated to process the message. For those who don't care about the topic or find it irrelevant to their lives, they would be less likely to notice whether the arguments are strong or weak because they aren't processing the message deeply when it is presented. So there should be relatively little difference between the strong and weak argument form of the message in terms of their agreement with it. In contrast, those who are motivated to attend to the message and process it more deeply should be more persuaded by strong arguments than by weak ones, as anyone paying attention to and processing the message deeply should be.

Suppose that you conducted this study using a group of university sophomores who were conveniently available to you, and you found exactly what the *elaboration likelihood model* predicts you should have found. From my discussion of sampling methods, it would seem that this tells you next to nothing given how the sample was obtained. Without knowing which population was sampled, who knows if the results are generalizable to any interesting population, such as "people in general" or even college students (a population of trivial interest in general unless you are particularly interested in studying college students specifically). But this criticism of the study is invalid on the grounds that process inference rather than population inference was the goal. The focus of the study was to test a theoretical proposition, which predicted that people motivated to process a message would attend to the contents and think about it more deeply. The fact that those highly motivated were more persuaded by strong arguments than weak ones compared to those less motivated suggests that the process the theory is attempting to explain about persuasion and the processing of messages is accurate. It matters not at all that the participants were not randomly selected from some larger population of interest because the intent of the study was process inference, not population inference.

And if the data are not consistent with the theoretical prediction? This suggests that either the theory is inaccurate, the researcher didn't adequately test the theory, or the theory has boundary conditions (i.e., it may not apply in all circumstances, or to all people, or it is sensitive to the choice of operationalization the investigator uses). As such, it is sensible to then say that the process at work producing the data is different than the process the theory proposes, it doesn't work this way in the circumstances or situation in which the researcher explicitly examined it, or it doesn't apply to the participants that actually participated in the study. As Mook (1983) aptly stated, it is the process at work that we are often interested in making inferences about, not the specific size of the effect in some population that we may (or may not) have sampled from. Importantly, process inference does not require us to randomly sample. The question as to whether the result generalizes beyond the conditions of the study or the people who participated is based not on the random sampling process but on *replication* of the research in different circumstances, using different methodologies, and different units of analysis. You can always criticize a study on the grounds that the people in the study perhaps had some quality that makes them different from everyone else (e.g., they are students, they are young, they are uneducated, and so forth). If that criticism is valid, if the findings are an artifact of the sample used, then future researchers will discover this when they fail to replicate your finding. Generalizability of a research result is an empirical question as much or more so than a statistical one.

But what about research that is not motivated by theory testing? The same argument applies, although the form of the argument is slightly different. A researcher may conduct a study motivated by curiosity using research units that are conveniently available. After collecting data, the researcher will have some finding, and a good researcher will probably at least attempt to speculate on why he or she found what was found. What is the process that produces the result found? And a good researcher will recognize that the generalizability of the finding away from the constraints of the design (both who provided data and how the data were collected) is dangerous. But those speculations or explanations, by advancing them in a research paper, become fuel for future research. Researchers have to take a "leap of faith" in their peers in the scientific community and trust that science is a self-correcting process (Aronson, 1977). If other people find our research interesting, it will motivate further research. It will serve as the source of some future researcher's predictions about what he or she should or might find in a study. If an explanation for a finding turns out to be wrong, future researchers will discover this. If that explanation is correct, the findings will be replicated when the explanation is put to the test in a new study. So the generalizability of our findings and the correctness of our explanations for a phenomenon are determined by replication not by random sampling (c.f., Amir & Sharon, 1991; Frick, 1998; Hendrick, 1991).

Random sampling also never results in a sample that is verifiably and unequivocally representative, so perhaps it shouldn't be put on a pedestal as the ideal method of recruiting research participants. Consider random digit dialing methods used frequently in public opinion polls. Not everyone is going to own a phone, and not everyone who owns a phone is going to be willing to answer your questions when you call them. There is no way of knowing the extent to which those variables (phone ownership and willingness to cooperate) are related to what you are measuring. How do you know for that certain that your sample doesn't under or over represent certain groups of people in important ways? The answer is that you can't be certain. To be sure, you could at least compare, for example, the demographic makeup of those who actually answered the phone and cooperated with you to see if the distribution of demographic variables in the sample matches population statistics derived from some place such as the U.S. Census Bureau.

Finally, it is important to keep in mind that all samples, including random ones, will yield results that do not necessarily generalize over time. When a public opinion pollster measures, for example, approval of the president's job performance, the result (say, 65%) is generalizable only to the population from which the sample was derived at that time. Next week, approval of the president's performance may be different. Populations change physically (people die and people are born continuously), and the social environment that influences that population on things you might be interested in measuring is in constant flux. Even process inferences may apply only to the time in which the study was conducted. As society changes, the social forces at work that communication theories often attempt to explain change as well, so a theory that is good now (i.e., one that is consistent with the data and makes accurate predictions) may not be an adequate description of the same process in the future. Of course, some theories are based on processes that are not likely to change substantially. We wouldn't expect major changes over time in the way people process information or interact face-to-face, for example, so communication theories that attempt to explain such processes probably are safe from substantial threats to validity resulting from population or social change.

3.4 Summary

Researchers are typically interested in some kind of inference. If population inference is the goal, random sampling methods are the most appropriate methods of recruiting research units. However, even nonrandom sampling plans can be useful to researchers more interested in process inferences. As this chapter illustrated, inference is best phrased as a question or set of questions. What form of inference do you want to make, population, process, or both? And does your sampling method and research design allow you to make the desired inference?

CHAPTER FOUR

Data Description and Visualization

When you conduct research, at the end of the data collection phase you will have a data set of some kind. This data set contains the measurements of each research unit on each variable measured and can be used in a number of ways in your research. You may use this data set to statistically test hypotheses that a theory makes about what you should find in your research. Or you may examine the data without any specific theory in mind, just to see what the data tell you about what you are studying. Ultimately, this process requires at some level the description of your data. The data set is largely a disorganized batch of numbers with no obvious meaning or interpretation. In this chapter, I describe various statistical and graphical approaches to summarizing measurements on a variable and discuss how to quantify the direction and strength of the relationship between two quantitative variables.

4.1 Graphical and Tabular Descriptions of Data

About twice a year, I teach a lecture course on communication research methods. On the first day of class, I distribute a questionnaire and request each student to respond to each of the questions prior to returning to class on the next day. The resulting data file, collected over a three year period, is described in Appendix E1 on the CD and is available on the book web page at http://www.comm.ohio-state.edu/ahayes/smcs/ as well as on the CD that comes with this book. One of the questions on the questionnaire asks the students: "On an average day, how many hours do you spend watching TV?" The responses of all 610 students in the data file to this question can be found in Box 4.1.

4.1.1 Frequency Tables

How many respondents reported that they watched one hour of TV on a typical day? Two hours? Five or more hours? Looking at the data in Box 4.1, you could answer these questions but it wouldn't be easy. You'd have to scan through the data, tallying up each response that satisfies some criterion you are searching for on a sheet of paper or trying to keep track in your head. After scanning all 610 responses, you would have the answer. It would be quite a bit easier to answer these questions if you could

---

Box 4.1: Responses to a Question About TV Viewing

"On an average day, how many hours do you spend watching TV?"

3,1,1.5,1,0.25,6,2,2,2.5,3,5,1.5,1,3,5,3,1,2.5,5,2.5,2,2,4,2,4,2,3,2,2,4,
2,0.5,5,4,2,6,2,4,4,1.5,4,1,3,3,5,4.5,1,2,0.5,1,3,2.5,4.5,4,2.5,0,3.5,2,
4.5,6,0,2,4.5,2,3,2,1,2,4,0.5,1,2.5,0.5,2,1.5,2,3,2.5,2,3,2.5,2,3,1.5,4,
0.5,1,1.5,2,1,1,2,2,1,2.5,1.5,2,1,2,2,0.5,1.5,4,4,3,2.5,2,2,2,4,4,2,3,2,
2,3,2,4,3,4,1,1.5,3,2,2,1,3,5,4,2,2,1,9,4.5,3,1.5,2,0.5,5,1.5,0.5,1,3,2,
1,1.5,2,0.5,4.5,2,1,1,1,2,2,2,1,3,2,2,0,1,3,5,3,1.5,2,3,4,2,2.5,2,3,2,2,
2.5,3,0.5,1.5,1.5,1,1,4,2,2.5,3,4,2,1,0.5,1.5,3,2,1,2,3,6,5,4.5,2,2,2,
2,5,4,2,4,1,2,0.75,2,5,2,0.5,2,1.5,2,2,2,5,2,2,4,2,1,4,4,2,3,3,2,3,1.5,3,
2,4,4,1.5,4,2,1.5,1,1,4,4,2,3,1.5,1,1,2.5,2,2,1.5,2,2,3.5,2,5,4,2,2,1,5,
0,1,1,3,2,3,4,1,6,3,2,3,6,3,2,2,3,10,.,2,3,2,2,4,1,2,5,1,3,1,1.5,2,2,2,1,
3,4,3,3,2,1,1,2,3,2,2,1,0,0.5,1,0,2.5,1,3,4,3,2,2,1,2,1,4,5,2,2,2.5,3,3,1,
1,1.5,2,2,2,4,2,1,6,1,1,1.5,1.5,1,2.5,2,1,0.5,2,3,1,5,1,2,3,1,3,2,3,2,2,4,
1.5,4,2,2,1,1,4,3,1,2,3,3,2,4,2,1,3,3,3,1,2,3,2,0.5,2,2,2,5,3,2.5,3,2,1,3,
3,2,2.5,2,3,3,3,1,0.5,2,2,2,1.5,2,2,1,7,3,3,4,2,1,1,1,3,2,2,4,3,2,3,4,1.5,
5,2,0.5,1,2,1,2,0,1,7,2,2,4,3,0,2,2,2,2,2.5,2,4,4,2,2,1,3,5,2,1,2,3,0.5,2,
3,1,4,3,4,3,3,3,1,3,1.5,1,5,2,2,4,6,3,2,1,4,1,2,2,2,1,2,2,2.5,2,1,1,2,0,
4,2,2,3,1.5,2,2,2,0.5,3,2,2,4,2,1,2,4,1.5,3,2.5,4,2,2,3,5,2.5,3,2,2,2,4,3,
0.15,2,3,2,5,3,3,1,3,6,1,1,2,0.5,0.5,0.25,2,1,1,3,4,2,2,2,1,2,0.5,1.5,2.5,
2,4,3,5,3,1,3,2,2,1,3,1,2,1,5,3,1,2,2,1,3,3,1,2,2.5,1,4,1.5,3,3.5,5,1,3,1,
4,2,2,0.5,1,4,2,4,4,2,2,2,3

$n = 610$ students enrolled in a research methods course.

---

construct some kind of a table that organized the data in an easily digestible format. A *frequency table* is a table that, at the very minimum, displays how many times in a data set each measurement or "score" for a variable occurs in the data. A good frequency table will display more than this, although with just this information additional bits of information can be derived. A frequency table is sometimes called a *frequency distribution*. The term *distribution* is a bit difficult to define, but it is widely used in statistics, and I will use it frequently. The term is typically used to refer to any collection of measurements on a variable, much like the term *data set* except data set and distribution don't have quite the same meaning. We often talk about characteristics of a distribution, such as its center, or its shape, or its variability. So the 610 responses to the TV use question can be thought of as the distribution of responses to this question—a distribution that can be described using a variety of statistics discussed in this chapter.

Although it is possible to make a frequency table by hand, computers can do the work more efficiently once the data are entered into a good statistical program. A frequency table for the data in Box 4.1 can be found in Table 4.1. Organized with a frequency table, it is much easier to answer my earlier questions. Each row in the table corresponds to a value on the variable in the data set, and the columns contain information about how frequently that value occurs in the data. A close examination of Table 4.1 reveals that 101 of the 610 students reported that they watched one hour of TV on a typical day, 196 claimed to watch 2 hours of TV, and $26 + 9 + 2 + 1 + 1 = 39$ reported that they watched 5 or more hours per day. Apparently one student didn't answer the question or otherwise provided an answer that couldn't be interpreted and is therefore listed as "missing." This case is represented in the data with a "." (look

Table 4.1
A Frequency Table of the TV Viewing Data

Measurement	Frequency	Cumulative Frequency
0.00	9	9
0.15	1	10
0.25	2	12
0.50	23	35
0.75	1	36
1.00	101	137
1.50	34	171
2.00	196	367
2.50	25	392
3.00	105	497
3.50	3	500
4.00	63	563
4.50	7	570
5.00	26	596
6.00	9	605
7.00	2	607
9.00	1	608
10.00	1	609
Missing	1	
Total	610	

in the tenth row of the data in Box 4.1). Notice that the respondents tended to round their answers to the nearest hour, but not everyone did. Thirty students reported watching one and a half hours, and one reported around 10 minutes on a typical day (which is about 0.15 hours).

Knowing the frequency of each measurement in the data and the total number of cases in the data file (listed in the row labeled "Total"), we can easily compute the *relative percent*. The relative percent or frequency is just the frequency rescaled to be between 0 and 100. It is computed by dividing the frequency by the total number of cases in the data and multiplying the result by 100. So $(101/610) \times 100 = 16.557\%$ of respondents reported watching only one hour of TV per day, and $(196/610) \times 100 = 32.131\%$ of respondents reported watching two hours of TV. If you don't do the multiplication by 100, you get a number referred to as a *proportion, relative proportion,* or *relative frequency*. So what proportion (or relative proportion) of the students reported watching three hours of TV per day? Easy: $105 / 610 = 0.172$. Observe that a proportion is just %/100. As such, a relative proportion will always be between zero and one, whereas a relative percent will always be between zero and 100.

Relative proportions, percents, and frequencies are important because they allow you to compare two groups that may differ in size. For example, suppose that 100 females and 55 males in a history of communication course were asked how many hours of TV they watched last weekend. Suppose 20 females and 11 males reported they watched no TV. You might be tempted to say that women in this class were more likely to report watching no TV because 20 females reported zero hours compared to only 11 males. But notice that $(20/100) = 0.20$ or 20% and $(11/55) = 0.200$ or 20%. So by expressing these frequencies as relative proportions or percents, it is clear men and women reported zero hours with equal relative frequency, and the difference in the size of the frequencies reflects nothing more than the fact that there are more females than males in the class.

Another useful statistic that can be derived from a frequency table is the *cumulative frequency*. Some statistical programs will provide cumulative frequencies in a frequency table for you, but they can be calculated relatively easily from just the frequency information. The cumulative frequency tells you how many cases in the data set have a measurement equal to a specific value *or smaller* on the variable being tabled. Table 4.1 displays the cumulative frequencies for the TV viewing data. As can be seen, 137 students reported watching one hour of TV or less on a typical day, and 497 students reported watching three hours or less.

4.1.2 The Histogram

A *histogram* is a handy way of visually representing the distribution of quantitative measurements. A histogram visually depicts frequency information by representing frequency with bars of different heights. A histogram is constructed by first by selecting a number of *intervals* to be used in constructing the histogram. Each interval defines a minimum and maximum measurement value that will be represented in that interval. The number of cases in those intervals is then plotted visually as a bar, with the height of the bar in the histogram reflecting the frequency or relative frequency of cases in that interval. Typically, missing data are excluded from a histogram.

Figure 4.1 contains a histogram of the data in Box 4.1, generating using SPSS. SPSS is a statistical program widely used in communication, and most examples of statistical program output in this book will be from SPSS. The statistical analysis program that you use is up to you, but all respectable programs can generate a histogram. But different programs will format the output from its statistical routines differently, and nothing can substitute for familiarity with your program of choice. Familiarity with a program will come with practice, a good user's manual, and perhaps the guidance of a local expert on the program you use.

Different statistics and graphics programs differ in how they label the lower axis in a histogram and how the cases are assigned to a bar in the figure. In Figure 4.1, the numbers on the lower axis represent the endpoints of the interval represented with each bar. For example, the height of the bar between the numbers zero and one depicts the number of observations in the data set with a value between zero and one, including zero but *not* including one. From the histogram, that number is somewhere between 35 and 40 or so (observe from the frequency distribution in Table 4.1 the exact number is 36). Other programs might include one but not zero in that interval, and still other graphics programs will display the midpoint of the interval rather than the endpoints.

Different computer programs will also differ in how they construct the intervals. Most good statistical programs will allow you to determine how many intervals the histogram will contain by instructing it how wide to make each interval. The wider each interval is, the fewer the number of bars the histogram will contain. The appearance of the histogram will depend substantially on how many intervals are used in its construction.

Histograms can be used to display frequency information for quantitative data. If the data are qualitative (such as gender, ethnic grouping, etc.), a histogram is typically referred to as a *bar chart*.

4.1.3   Describing the Shape of a Distribution

A histogram can reveal the *shape* of a distribution. There are four characteristics frequently used to describe the shape of a distribution of measurements.

Symmetry. A distribution of measurements can be symmetrical or asymmetrical. Imagine a histogram of a set of measurements with a line drawn vertically down the center of the distribution. If the part of the histogram on the left side of the line is more or less a mirror image of the right side of the histogram, then the distribution is said to be *symmetrical*. If the distribution is *asymmetrical*, then the two sides will not be mirror images of each other. Many symmetrical distributions are used widely in statistical theory, but the distribution of measurements in your own research will rarely ever be perfectly symmetrical.

Skew. A distribution is said to be *positively skewed* (also called *right skewed* or *skewed to the right*) if the scores tend to cluster on the lower end of the measurement scale (i.e., the smaller numbers). The distribution of people's income is an example of a positively skewed distribution. The incomes of most people tend to be on the lower end of the scale of possible incomes, but some people make a lot of money, with very high incomes rather rare. The TV viewing data in Box 4.1, visually represented in Figure 4.1, is another example of a positively skewed distribution. Notice from the

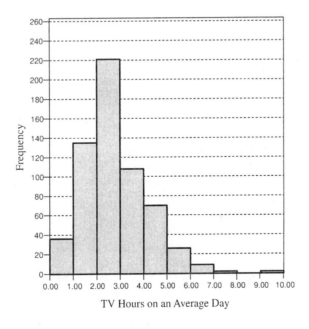

Figure 4.1 A histogram of the TV viewing data.

histogram that most of the students in this sample watch relatively little television, and increasingly fewer watch lots of TV.

By contrast, a *negatively skewed* distribution is just the opposite. In a negatively skewed (also called *left skewed* or *skewed to the left*) distribution, larger measurements tend to be more frequent, with relatively fewer measurements on the smaller end of the scale. Age at retirement is an example. Most people retire relatively late in their lives (in their mid to late 60s or early 70s), some people retire in their 50s, and relatively few retire in the 40s or earlier. The distribution of the number of meals a person ate last week is probably also negatively skewed. Most people would report eating 15 or more meals, some might report between 10 and 15, and relatively few would report less than 10. A mathematical definition of skewness is provided in section 4.4 after I introduce measures of central tendency and variability.

Modality. Distributions are sometimes described by their modality. A distribution is *unimodal* if there is one obvious "peak" in the distribution of scores. A distribution is said to be *bimodal* if there are two distinct peaks. If there are more than two distinct peaks, the distribution is called *multimodal.* Imagine that you were developing a measure of shyness and to validate the measure you gave it to two groups of people: door-to-door salespeople and librarians. A distribution of the scores of a combined sample of librarians and door-to-door salespeople on the shyness scale might be bimodal, with an obvious peak or clumping around a low score (reflecting the relatively low shyness of door-to-door salespeople) and another obvious peak or clumping around a high score (reflecting the likely introverted nature of people who become librarians). Bradley (1977) discusses some other scenarios where a distribution can be expected to be bimodal or multimodal.

Figure 4.2 displays some generic examples of how distributions of different shapes might appear visually in a histogram. A distribution shape in Figure 4.2 we have not yet discussed—the *normal distribution*—plays an important role in statistics. I devote a part of Chapter 5 to the normal distribution, so I don't discuss it here. Suffice it to say that although many people claim that the normal distribution is a wonderful fact of nature, the reality is that almost nothing that social scientists measure can be described as normally distributed (see, e.g., Micceri, 1989). To be sure, some distributions are similar to the normal distribution, but a truly normal distribution is relatively rare except in theory.

Kurtosis. A distribution can also be described by its degree of *kurtosis.* There is some disagreement among statisticians about what kurtosis is. In most statistical methods books, kurtosis is discussed as a measure of the extent to which the measurements cluster more toward the center of the distribution or more toward the extremes. The larger the kurtosis, the more "peaked" the distribution. A distribution with high kurtosis is sometimes called *leptokurtic.* In contrast, a *platykurtic* distribution has smaller kurtosis and relatively more of the measurements in the extremes or "tails" of distribution relative to a leptokurtic distribution. Such a distribution will look "flatter." However, as Darlington (1970) and Moors (1986) discuss, kurtosis as it is typically quantified is better conceptualized as a measure of the extent of bimodality of a distribution, in that bimodal distributions will tend to have smaller kurtosis than unimodal distributions. A mathematical definition of kurtosis is provided in section 4.4 after I introduce measures of central tendency and variability.

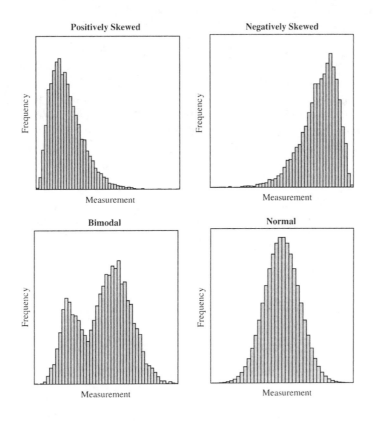

Figure 4.2 Examples of distributions of different shapes.

4.2 Measures of Central Tendency

Graphical and tabular depictions of data are quite useful and widely used in research. These methods provide you with a quick summary of what measurements exist in the data and in what frequency. Even more widely used are various statistical indices that describe the "center" of a distribution of measurements. These measures, known as measures of *central tendency*, attempt to reduce the data down to a single descriptive statistic that quantifies something akin to the "typical" or "average" measurement, although various measures of central tendency differ in how they define "typical" or "average."

4.2.1 The Mode

The simplest measure of central tendency is the *mode*. The mode of a distribution is the most frequently occurring measurement in the data. As can be seen from the frequency table in Table 4.1, the most frequent response to the TV viewing question is two, so two is the mode of the distribution, or the modal measurement or response. But notice that it is not necessarily accurate to say that the *majority* of responses are at the mode. Even though two is the mode, the majority of the measurements are not two. Although it is possible that the mode will be the majority measurement, more often it is not.

Earlier, I mentioned that one way of characterizing the shape of the distribution is with respect to its modality. A unimodal distribution has a single mode, and a bimodal distribution has two modes. But how can there be more than one most frequently occurring measurement? By describing a distribution as bimodal, we are simply acknowledging that the distribution has more than one obvious hump, peak, or clustering of scores around a particular value. There is some subjectivity to this judgment. A distribution may show two peaks or humps that are very close to each other. Two people may look at the same distribution but differ in whether to call such a distribution unimodal or bimodal.

4.2.2 The Median

The *median* of a distribution enjoys wider use than the mode as a measure of central tendency. The median quantifies the ordinal "middle" of the distribution, and is most easily understood by considering a simple example. Consider the following measurements of some variable from a sample of 11 people:

$$4, 5, 12, 4, 2, 10, 1, 1, 3, 4, 6$$

Now sort these data from low to high:

$$1, 1, 2, 3, 4, 4, 4, 5, 6, 10, 12$$

The middle score in this sorted distribution of 11 scores is the sixth measurement in this list, which is 4. So the median of this distribution of scores is four. But this computational procedure works only if the number of measurements in the distribution is odd. When the number of measurements is even, there is no single middle score. For example, consider this set of 10 measurements:

$$1, 5, 4, 2, 6, 5, 7, 3, 4, 10$$

The sorted data look like this:

$$1, 2, 3, 4, 4, 5, 5, 6, 7, 10$$

Because there is no single middle score here, consider the 2 scores that straddle the middle. If there are 10 measurements, then the 2 measurements that straddle the middle position would be the fifth and sixth measurements, which are 4 and 5. The median is then defined as the midpoint between these 2 scores, computed as their sum divided by 2. So the median in this distribution is $(4 + 5)/2 = 4.5$.

The median is sometimes defined as the value of the measurement in the distribution at which 50% of the cases are below and 50% are above. For this reason, the median is also known as the 50th percentile. However, this definition will not always correspond to the realities of your data, so it should be used only as a rule of thumb. If many cases in the data are equal to the median on the variable measured, then it won't be true that 50% of the cases have a measurement less than the median. The first example above illustrates this. Even though 4 is the median in this distribution of 11 scores, it is not true that 50% of the scores are less than four.

Although a good statistical program will tell you the median of a set of scores if you ask for it, it can be extracted from a frequency distribution of the data relatively easily. An examination of the frequency table in Table 4.1 reveals that the median must be two. With $n = 609$ cases (cases missing on the variable are not included in the computation of the median), the median score would be the 305th score in the sorted distribution. You can convince yourself by looking at the frequency table that the 305th score in the sorted distribution is two. This also illustrates how the median may not perfectly cut the distribution in half if there are lots of measurements at the median.

4.2.3 The Arithmetic Mean

Although the median is more popular than the mode as a measure of central tendency, by far the most commonly used measure of center is the *arithmetic mean*. There are many different kinds of means, but the term *mean* is generally used interchangeably with the term *arithmetic mean* or *average* so whenever I use the term *mean* or *average*, I will be referring to the arithmetic mean.

The arithmetic mean is simply the sum of the measurements for the variable divided by the number of cases contributing to the sum. So if there are n cases in the data set, each with a measurement on a variable X, the arithmetic mean is defined as

$$\boxed{\text{Mean} = \frac{\sum X}{n}}$$

(4.1)

where $\sum X$ means to add up the n values of X in the data set. The letter n is typically used to refer to the *sample size*, meaning the total number of cases in the data file. But acknowledging that not everyone will provide data for every variable, I will use the letter n throughout this book to refer to the "effective sample size" or "valid sample size," meaning the number of cases in the sample that provide data on the variable or variables being analyzed. Therefore, n is not a property of the data file itself but instead can vary from analysis to analysis, depending on how many cases provide data to the statistic being computed or the analysis being conducted.

Applying equation 4.1 to the data in Box 4.1, the mean number of hours students in this research method class reported watching TV per day is

$$\frac{\sum X}{n} = \frac{3 + 1 + 1 + 5 + \cdots + 2 + 2 + 2 + 3}{609} = 2.373$$

Why is the mean the most commonly used measure of central tendency? One reason is that the most widely used statistical methods known to communication scientists focus on means, probably because they are the most widely-taught methods in undergraduate and graduate programs. Communication scientists are not special in this regard. Most social scientists focus on the mean when describing the central tendency of their data, and inferences often focus on means. But perhaps more important is that fact that statistical theory is well described and widely communicated for statistics based on sums and therefore means. In short, the mean is a simpler statistic for scientists to work with than other measures of central tendency.

The mean has a number of interesting and useful interpretations. First, it is the arithmetic "balancing point" of a distribution. Define a case's *error* as the difference between that case's measurement on X and the mean of X. If you add up all the negative errors in a distribution, then remove the negative sign from that sum, you will find that the result is exactly equal to the sum of all the positive errors. Because the negative errors, ignoring sign, sum to the same value as the sum of the positive errors, it must be true that the sum of the errors is zero. Therefore the mean of all the errors is zero. So the average difference (i.e., error) between the measurements and the mean is zero. Given this fact, the mean can be thought of as the number that most closely approximates the original measurements.

A second interpretation of the mean is that it is the best guess you can provide about any measurement in the distribution. Suppose we knew the mean of a distribution, but we didn't know the original measurements in the distribution. If you had to guess each of the original measurements, no guessing strategy would outperform merely guessing the mean every time if you measure the accuracy of the guess as the difference between the guess and the actual measurement for the case whose value is being guessed. If you guess the mean every time, on average, your guessing error would be zero.

Equation 4.1 yields the *unweighted* arithmetic mean. It is called unweighted because each case in the data set contributes equally to the value of the mean. Public opinion pollsters and researchers in some other fields often instead describe the center of a distribution of measurements with the *weighted mean*. The weighted mean is defined as

$$\text{Weighted Mean} = \frac{\sum w_i X_i}{\sum w_i}$$

$$(4.2)$$

where w_i is case i's weight and X_i is case i's value on the X variable, and both summations are over all n cases in the data. Notice that if all n weights are set to one, equations 4.2 and 4.1 are the same because $\sum w_i = n$. Using a weighted mean, different cases in the data file contribute more or less to the computation of a mean, depending on its weight.

Although the unweighted mean is far more widely used than the weighted mean, in some circumstances it is desirable to weight the cases in a data set differently. For example, people who have more than one telephone number are more likely to be included in public opinion polls or other forms of research based on a random digit dialing sampling method. It is routine to ask people at the end of a telephone survey how many telephone lines they have and then use this information to generate weights for each case based on their answer when calculating various descriptive measures of the data such as the mean. Responses to questions from people with more than one phone line are weighted less than those with only one line. Many other measures of central tendency discussed in the statistics literature are based on equation 4.2, with those measures differing from each other by how the weights are generated. But throughout this book, whenever I use the term *mean*, keep in mind that I will be referring to the unweighted mean (equation 4.1).

4.2.4   Choosing a Measure of Central Tendency

With three sensible measures of central tendency, which measure should you use? Ideally, the choice should be dictated by what is most sensible given your data, but in reality, the mean is almost always used in communication research. Because inferential statistics (discussed later in the book) are so widely used and because so many of the well-known statistical methods are based on means, if you used something other than the mean as your measure of central tendency, you'd have to have a lot of extra knowledge on the application of inferential statistics than most scientists have. And if you used a different measure of central tendency other that what most researchers are familiar with, they would be less able to understand how you analyzed your data.

Having said this, it would be wrong for me to say that you should always use the mean and not worry about it. The reality is that the mean does suffer from one major limitation: its susceptibility to extreme or unusually large or small measurements, what scientists sometimes call *outliers*. The median and mode do not suffer from this limitation. You can verify this for yourself by constructing a small list of numbers, computing the mean, and then adding another number to the list that is very large or very small relative to the other numbers in the list and recomputing the mean.

It is often recommended that the median should be used for distributions that are highly skewed, and the mean for distributions that are roughly symmetrical. The rationale is that skewed distributions often have outliers that pull the mean in their direction, making the mean somewhat less representative of the distribution of scores as a whole. I think this recommendation is a bit misguided. It is relatively uncommon to find communication researchers reporting the median of a distribution even with measurements that are likely to be highly skewed. Many variables that communication researchers measure are likely to be skewed, and if we followed the guideline of reporting medians in such circumstances, communication researchers would have to develop a greater understanding of more complicated inferential methodologies. There is nothing wrong with increasing the size of our statistical toolboxes, but the reality is that it isn't likely that the communication discipline is going to embrace major changes in practice without compelling reasons for doing so. The susceptibility of the mean to extremes is not a compelling reason. This is because although it is true that the mean is highly influenced by extreme measurements, it is relatively unusual for a single measurement or two to drastically influence the mean in such a way that you end up completely misled about your research findings using the mean rather than the median. No doubt it can happen, so you should be on guard for the possibility, but one or two cases in a data set don't usually drastically affect an analysis unless the sample size is small.

However, you should be sensitive to the fact that the mean is susceptible to the influence of extreme measurements and report a more sensible measure of central tendency when it really does matter. Whether or not it matters will depend on how drastically different the mean is from the median and whether you will be substantially misrepresenting your research findings by reporting the mean rather than the median. In some situations reporting the median may be a better approach. Suppose, for example, you have developed a new method of training high school graduates how to prepare for job interviews. Before you developed your method, suppose those who took your interview preparation course obtained jobs with a mean salary of $38,000 and a median salary of $34,000. After taking your course, your students were obtaining jobs with a mean salary of $46,000 and a median salary of $34,000. What is the real story here? Sure, the mean salary has increased, but perhaps that is because one or two of your students, after taking the training, landed stellar jobs with excellent pay. Examining only the median, it is still the case that half of your students are landing jobs with salaries of less than $34,000 after taking the training. A close examination of the data is the only way of knowing which measure of central tendency best represents your findings.

There is a group of statisticians who argue that scientists should strongly consider abandoning the mean as the method of choice for measuring central tendency. Members of this camp argue that classical statistical methods as emphasized in this book work well with relatively "well-behaved" data, meaning data that don't include outliers or that are bizarrely shaped. Advocates of so-called *robust methods of description* argue that we start using measures of central tendency such the *trimmed mean* because robust measures are less influenced by outliers. A trimmed mean is computed by throwing out the "tails" of the distribution, meaning the scores that are relatively extreme, prior to the computation of the arithmetic mean. Trimmed means are essentially weighted means, with cases at the extreme ends of a distribution receiving weights of zero. For example, the 5% trimmed mean can be computed using equation 4.2 by setting the weights for the middle 90% of the scores in a sorted distribution equal to one and giving weights of zero to the remaining cases in the extreme 5% of each end of the distribution. There is an extensive literature on the use of robust measures of central tendency such as trimmed means, as well as several good books on the topic. A good starting point is Wilcox and Keselman (2003). My prediction is that in the future we will see robust statistical methods being used more frequently. The major impediment to their current use is their lack of implementation in widely-used statistical analysis programs, their relatively light treatment in standard statistical methods books (including this one), and general resistance to the use of new methodologies.

Another consideration when choosing a measure of central tendency is the level of measurement of the variable measured. For nominal-level variables, the only sensible measure of central tendency is the mode; the mean or median would have no sensible interpretation. For interval- and ratio-level variables, either the median or the mean can be used, although the mode can still be used as well. For ordinal-level variables, some controversy exists over the appropriate way of quantifying central tendency. As discussed in Chapter 2, arithmetic operations such as addition, subtraction, multiplication, and division on ordinal-level measurements are of dubious appropriateness. That would rule out the mean as a sensible measure of central tendency. However, if you are willing to ascribe or assume interval properties to an ordinal variable, then go ahead and use the mean. Whether good or bad, right or wrong, this is a common practice in the communication field and throughout the social sciences. Research by Baker et al. (1996) tells us that at least for some of the statistical procedures described in this book, little harm is done by treating ordinal data as interval.

4.3 Measures of Variation

The center of a distribution, typically described with the arithmetic mean, is an important descriptive statistic. There is another category of descriptive statistics that plays a central role in the evaluation of research findings and in the description of research results. We are often interested not only in the typical measurement in a set of measurements, but also in how spread out or different from each other the measurements in the distribution are. Sometimes important research questions involve variability in measurements. For example, if a method of preparing high school graduates for interviews is effective, it would be desirable to show that not only do people who receive training with the method get higher salaries, but that their salaries are consistently high. Or a method of reducing public speaking anxiety would be especially good if in addition to helping people make better public speeches, it also overcomes all the individual differences that produce natural variation in public speaking skill so that everyone who is familiar with the method gives good speeches. Or what if the students of one teacher vary in their performance in the class much more than students from another teacher of the same material? This suggests that one teacher might be more effective with students of all abilities than the other. The teacher with greater variability in student performance may not teach academically ill-prepared students well, so the less able students coming into the class end up learning little whereas the more able students coming in to the class end up learning well. To assess group differences in variation on some variable, we need to have a means of quantifying variation. In this section, I introduce several measures of variation.

4.3.1 The Range and Interquartile Range

The simplest measure of variation is the *range*. The range is defined as the difference between the minimum and maximum measurement in the distribution. This is a simple enough concept and needs little explanation. In the data in Box 4.1, the maximum measurement is 10 and the minimum measurement is zero, so the range is $10 - 0 = 10$. The range has an obvious limitation in that it tells us nothing about the variability of measurements in between these extremes. Two distributions may have the same range, but one may differ substantially in how the measurements vary in between these extremes. For example, consider these two sets of measurements:

$$A \qquad\qquad\qquad B$$

$$1, 2, 3, 4, 5, 6, 7, 8, 9 \qquad 3, 5, 5, 5, 5, 5, 5, 5, 11$$

The measurements in set A and B have the same range (8), but clearly the measurements in set A vary more from each other than the measurements in set B.

A conceptually similar measure of variation is the *interquartile range* (IQR). The IQR is simply the range of the middle 50% of the sorted distribution of scores. As such, it quantifies range by assessing the distance between measurements that are nearer to the center of the distribution than does the ordinary range. Observe that unlike the range, the IQR does capture the obvious differences in variability of the measurements between sets A and B. The IQR for distribution A is 4 $(7 - 3)$, whereas the IQR for distribution B is 0 $(5 - 5)$. So A is more variable using the IQR as the measure of variability as it clearly appears to be when just eyeballing the data. In the TV viewing data, the interquartile range is $3 - 1.5 = 1.5$. Verify for yourself using Table 4.1 that this is so.

4.3.2 The Standard Deviation

Although easy to grasp conceptually, the range and interquartile range are not popular perhaps because from a statistician's point of view they are a bit difficult to work with mathematically. Therefore, the development of statistical methods has tended to deemphasize these as measures of variation. There is not a large statistical theory or literature developed around range-based estimates of variability. Instead, statisticians have preferred to conceptualize variability as the difference or distance between the measurements in a distribution and the center of the distribution.

One intuitively appealing measure is the *mean deviation*, defined as

$$\frac{\sum (X - \text{Mean})}{n}$$

where the summation $(\sum)$ is over all cases in the data file. It would seem like the mean deviation would be a sensible measure of variation. However, it turns out that the mean deviation will always be zero. Recall that the mean is the arithmetic "balancing point" of the distribution. The positive deviations from the mean completely cancel out all the negative deviations. Their sum is zero, so their mean is zero. Therefore, the mean deviation is useless as a measure of variability—it is *always* zero.

But we could ignore the sign of the difference between each measurement and the mean and defined variability as the *mean absolute deviation*, as such:

$$\frac{\sum |X - \text{Mean}|}{n}$$

Although this seems sensible and it is used in some contexts, it hasn't really caught on because absolute values are difficult to work with mathematically, and there is an alternative that has been used widely in the development of statistical theory. This alternative is mathematically more appealing, although the formula may look a bit threatening. If you compute the mean *squared* difference between each measurement and the mean and then take the square root of this mean, the result is called the *standard deviation*, and it is the most widely used measure of variation in statistics and nearly all sciences, including communication. The formula implemented in most statistical computing programs such as SPSS is

$$\text{Standard Deviation} = \sqrt{\frac{\sum (X - \text{Mean})^2}{n - 1}}$$

(4.3)

It should be apparent from equation 4.3 that the more dispersed around the mean the measurements are, the larger the sum of the squared deviations from the mean will be, and so the larger the standard deviation will be. Using the data in Box 4.1, the standard deviation is computed as

$$\sqrt{\frac{(3 - 2.373)^2 + (1 - 2.373)^2 + \cdots + (2 - 2.373)^2 + (3 - 2.373)^2}{609 - 1}} = 1.332$$

Notice that the standard deviation isn't exactly the square root of the *mean* squared deviation, because the denominator in the formula is $n - 1$ not n. With large samples, the difference between using n or $n - 1$ in the computation of the standard deviation is inconsequential. For example, $(300/100) = 3$, whereas $300/101 = 2.970$. So it generally makes little difference whether n or $n - 1$ is used in the denominator of the formula. The only context in which you'd want to divide the sum of the squared deviations by n rather than $n - 1$ is if you had measurements on the *entire population* of interest. Even so, your statistical program of choice won't know whether your data are a sample rather than the entire population, and it almost certainly uses the $n - 1$ version of the formula.

The standard deviation can be interpreted as the average distance between a measurement and the mean, where we define the "distance" as the difference ignoring sign. As such, it estimates what it might seem like the mean absolute deviation estimates. True, but the standard deviation is a lot easier to work with mathematically. In the TV viewing data, the standard deviation is 1.332. So the average difference (remember, ignoring sign) between any person's response and the mean is roughly 1.332 hours.

Here is another interpretation: Recall earlier that the mean is the best guess for any measurement in the distribution, because the mean error in your guess will be zero if you use the strategy of always guessing the mean. If you ignored the sign of the error, the standard deviation estimates how far off your guess would tend to be on average. So if you guessed how a person responded by employing the "best" strategy of guessing the mean, your guess would be off by an average of 1.332 hours, plus or minus.

There is one major limitation of the standard deviation as a measure of variation. Notice from equation 4.3 that the standard deviation is essentially a kind of arithmetic mean (i.e., it is a sum divided by nearly the number of cases contributing to the sum). As such, the standard deviation is influenced by the presence of outliers in much the same way as the arithmetic mean is. So one or two extreme scores can have a big effect on the standard deviation in some circumstances. Even with this limitation, the standard deviation is widely used in communication research, and it is worth spending the effort to make sure you understand what the standard deviation quantifies.

4.3.3 The Variance

Another measure of variation that you will see discussed often is the *variance*. It doesn't need its own formula because it is simply the square of the standard deviation. Nevertheless, here it is:

$$\text{Variance} = \frac{\sum (X - \text{Mean})^2}{n - 1}$$

(4.4)

The variance has no sensible interpretation. It is the roughly the mean squared deviation between the measurements and the mean, but it is difficult to think in terms of squared deviations, so the standard deviation is the preferred measure of variation. But the variance plays an important role in statistical theory, so it can't be discounted just because it doesn't have a sensible interpretation. However, communication researchers do use the term *variance* in a generic sense to refer to variation in measurements or differences between research units on what is being measured. So a person might ask you if there is any variance in your measurement or how much variance in an outcome variable your analysis can explain, and they may or may not necessarily mean variance in a mathematical sense as defined in equation 4.4.

If all these measures of central tendency and variability seem like a lot to keep track of, keep in mind that rarely would you be doing the computations by hand. Researchers use computers to do most of their statistical calculations. Figure 4.3 presents various descriptive statistics discussed thus far as generated by SPSS. What is important is that you understand how each statistic is interpreted. Leave the computational worries to the computer.

4.4 Quantifying Skewness and Kurtosis

With the mean and standard deviation now defined, it is possible to discuss the quantification of skewness and kurtosis. Recall from section 4.1.3 that the skewness refers to the degree of asymmetry in the distribution of measurements, whereas kurtosis quantifies either the peakedness, flatness, or bimodality of the distribution, depending on your perspective. Although there are various mathematical definitions of skewness and kurtosis, two common definitions are

$$\text{skewness} = \frac{\sum (X - \text{Mean})^3}{(n - 1)SD^3}$$

(4.5)

TV hours on an average day

N	Valid		609
	Missing		1
Mean			2.373
Median			2.000
Mode			2.0
Std. Deviation			1.3317
Variance			1.7734
Skewness			1.119
Std. Error of Skewness			.099
Kurtosis			2.611
Std. Error of Kurtosis			.198
Range			10.0
Percentiles	25		1.500
	50		2.000
	75		3.000

Figure 4.3 Descriptive statistics from SPSS for the TV viewing data.

and

$$\text{kurtosis} = \frac{\sum (X - \text{Mean})^4}{(n-1)SD^4} - 3$$

(4.6)

where the summation is over all n measurements in the distribution and SD is the standard deviation of the measurements. In the TV viewing data, skewness is just over one and kurtosis about two and a half. A perfectly symmetrical distribution will have a skewness of 0. The larger the skewness in absolute value, the more skewed the distribution, and the sign of the skewness statistic quantifies the direction of the skew. The kurtosis of a distribution is often gauged relative to the normal distribution, which has a skewness of 0 based on the formula above. So kurtosis greater than zero means that the distribution is more "peaked" relative to the normal distribution, and kurtosis less than zero reflects a flatter distribution. However, as discussed in section 4.1.3, kurtosis can also be thought of as a measure of bimodality. With that conceptualization of kurtosis, a kurtosis of less than zero reflects greater bimodality. Moors (1986) shows that the smaller kurtosis, the less the distribution varies around the two points Mean $+ SD$ and Mean $- SD$.

Most good statistics programs will compute skewness and kurtosis (see Figure 4.3). Different statistics programs use slightly different formulas for skewness and kurtosis so don't be surprised to find small discrepancies in these statistics across computing programs, particularly with small samples.

4.5   Another Graphical Tool: The Box Plot

With knowledge of measures of central tendency and variability, we can now discuss a handy graphical tool known as a *box plot*. A box plot contains information about the median of a distribution, the interquartile range (IQR), the measurement interval that contains the inner 50% of measurements, and the minimum and maximum measurements in a distribution, while at the same time highlighting measurements that

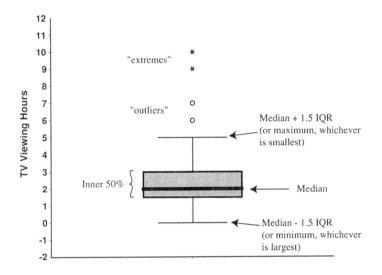

Figure 4.4 A box plot of the TV viewing data.

are unusual using certain criteria. A box plot of the TV viewing data is displayed in Figure 4.4. The figure itself is fairly self-explanatory. The dark line dividing the gray box is the median, while the upper and lower edges of the box define the end points of the ordinal middle 50% of the measurements. From the box plot, you can see that the median measurement is 2, whereas 50% of the measurements reside between 1.5 and 3. By definition, then, the interquartile range is $3 - 1.5 = 1.5$. The long horizontal lines above and below the box are set at the median plus and minus 1.5 interquartile ranges. However, if the median plus 1.5 IQRs exceeds the maximum measurement, then the upper line is placed at the maximum. If the median minus 1.5 IQRs is smaller than the minimum measurement, then the lower line is set at the minimum. The box plot also depicts the "unusual" measurements, defined as those with measurements that are more than 1.5 IQRs from the median (in either direction). Different statistical programs will depict unusual cases differently. In SPSS (which generated this figure), "outliers" in a box plot are defined as cases with measurements between 1.5 and 3 IQRs from the median. "Extreme values" are defined by SPSS as measurements more than three IQRs from the median.

4.6 Standardization

It is common in communication research to do a mathematical transformation to a set of measurements to put them in *standard* or *standardized* form. This transformation is called *standardization*. Some people refer to the process of standardization as *normalization*, although I think this is a bad choice of words because it implies that the transformation makes a set of scores normally distributed, but that is not what standardization does. When you standardize a set of measurements, you re-express the original measurements as deviations from the mean in standard deviation units, often called *standardized scores* or *Z-scores*. So if someone tells you to convert your measurements to *Z*-scores, you are being asked to standardize the measurements.

To standardize a set of measurements on a variable X, you apply the following formula to each measurement:

$$Z_X = \frac{X - \text{Mean}}{\text{Standard Deviation}}$$

(4.7)

For example, if a variable has a mean of 10 and a standard deviation of 4, a measurement of 12 in standardized or Z-score form is $(12 - 10)/4 = 0.5$. So a score of 12 is one half of a standard deviation above the mean. Similarly, a score of 4 would be one and a half standard deviations below the mean, because $Z = (4 - 10)/4 = -1.5$.

Standardization affects the mean and standard deviation (and therefore the variance) of a set of measurements. After standardization, the distribution of the Z-scores will have a mean of zero and a standard deviation of one. But the shape of the distribution is unaffected by standardization.

The standardization process can be reversed with equation 4.8:

$$X = \text{Mean} + Z_X(\text{Standard Deviation})$$

(4.8)

Therefore, if you know the mean and standard deviation of a distribution as well as how many standard deviations above or below the mean a case is, you can convert the Z-score to its original metric. For example, a Z-score of two for a measurement in a distribution with a mean of 10 and a standard deviation of three on the original metric corresponds to $10 + 2(3) = 16$.

One of the most useful applications of standardization is the aggregation of measurements of variables, each of which may be measured differently, into a single measurement. For example, suppose you wanted to quantify someone's total exposure to news media, so you ask them to report how many hours a day they watch televised news broadcasts, how many news magazines they subscribe to, how many cable news channels they receive, how many minutes a day they spend reading a newspaper, and how many times a week they access news sites on the Internet. On the surface, it might be sensible to measure media exposure for each person as the mean of the person's responses to these five questions. However, each variable is measured using different units. TV watching and newspaper reading are measured in units of time (hours or minutes), and magazine subscriptions, TV news channels, and Internet use are all counts, but of different things. And although it might not seem obvious, it is also the case that the standard deviation of this new measure of new media exposure will be determined mostly by the variable with the largest standard deviation. Often this is not desirable. But if you first standardize the measurements on the original variables prior to computing the average for each person, then the five variables are now measured on the same scale, and each will have the same standard deviation (one), meaning that the variability of the aggregate measure (the mean) will more adequately reflect the contribution of all five variables rather than the just the one with more variability.

After standardization, it is also possible to compare measurements on two variables even when they are measured on different scales. Suppose, for instance, you take a test of anxiety and a test of life satisfaction and score 105 and 65, respectively. Imagine the anxiety test has a mean of 100 and a standard deviation of 10, and the life satisfaction test has a mean of 50 and a standard deviation of 15. Standardization allows you to make the claim that you are relatively more satisfied with life than anxious, even though your score on the anxiety test is higher above the mean. Remember that you can't legitimately compare the raw score on these tests (the 105 and the 65) because they are measured on different scales—they have different means and standard deviations and the units of measurement (i.e., a single "point" on the test) can't be interpreted the same. Standardization puts the measurements on the same scale— a scale with a mean of zero and a standard deviation of one, and the unit of measurement is therefore the same. That is, a single "point" on the Z-score scale corresponds to a standard deviation from the mean. An anxiety score of 105 corresponds to a Z-score of $(105 - 100)/10 = 0.5$. A life satisfaction score of 65 converts to a Z-score of $(65 - 50)/15 = 1.0$. So you are one standard deviation above the mean on the life satisfaction test, but you are only half a standard deviation above the mean on the anxiety test. So relative to the mean and variability of scores on the tests, you are more satisfied with life than anxious.

4.7   Describing Association Between Quantitative Variables

Many of the questions communication researchers ask and the predictions that communication theories make can be framed in terms of whether or not the variables being measured in a study are related, correlated, or associated, as the examples below illustrate.

> Is greater television viewing associated with more idealistic expectations about marriage? (Segrin & Nabi, *Journal of Communication*, 2002, vol. 52, p. 250).

> The level of experienced anger in inoculation is positively associated with resistance to persuasive attacks (Pfau, Szabo, et al., *Human Communication Research*, 2001, vol. 27, p. 223).

> Intimacy is positively associated with people's use of positively-valenced strategies to manage relational uncertainty increasing events (Knobloch, *Human Communication Research*, 2005, vol. 31, p. 66).

> What is the relationship between attention to news about an institution and trust in that institution? (Moy, Torres, Tanaka & McClusky, *Communication Research*, 2005, vol. 32, p. 59).

When we talk about association, we are essentially talking about predictability, dependence, and relationship. If two variables X and Y are unrelated, uncorrelated, or unassociated, then knowledge of the value of X for a case in the data provides no information about that case's measurement on Y. If that is true, then you cannot predict Y from X. For example, if marital satisfaction (X) and length of marriage (Y) are unassociated, then knowing how long a married person has been married gives you no information about that person's satisfaction with their marriage. In contrast, if these two variables are associated, then knowledge about how long a person has been married should give you some information about how satisfied he or she is with marriage. And if education (X) and news media use (Y) are independent or unrelated, then knowing how educated a person is should provide no information about the person's media use (e.g., how much time the person spends watching TV, reading the newspaper, or reading magazines). But if education and media use are associated, correlated, or dependent, then knowing how much education a person has gives you some information about their

TV use; information that you wouldn't have if you didn't know the person's education level.

There are several numerical indices of association. In this section, I focus entirely on quantifying association between quantitative variables—variables that quantify each case on some kind of continuum. In later chapters, I discuss association between variables that are categorical (i.e., measured at the nominal level). The first measure of association discussed here is by far the most widely used, but you will see others, so I will devote some time in this section to discussion of a couple of other measures of association.

4.7.1   Pearson's Coefficient of Correlation

One popular way communication researchers quantify the relationship between two quantitative variables is with *Pearson's product-moment coefficient of correlation,* also called *Pearson's r.* The measure is named after Karl Pearson, an eminent statistician who played an important role in the development of many of the statistical methods used in communication. Pearson's r is typically used to quantify linear association (more on what I mean by "linear" later) and to test hypotheses about independence using data that are at measured at the pseudo-interval level or higher (although some argue against using it for ordinal-level data, it is commonly used for ordinal data as well). Pearson's coefficient of correlation has a rather complicated formula that can be used to compute it by hand. Few would do the computations by hand, and the computational formula is not very illuminating with respect to what Pearson's r is and how it quantifies association. Nevertheless, here it is:

$$r = \frac{n(\sum XY) - (\sum X)(\sum Y)}{\sqrt{[n(\sum X^2) - (\sum X)][n(\sum Y^2) - (\sum Y)]}}$$

(4.9)

where X and Y are the measurements on the variables being correlated, XY is the product of X and Y for each case, and the summation is over all n cases in the sample. But equation 4.9 is useless for understanding just how Pearson's r quantifies association. A different formula is bit more helpful, so I focus on it, recognizing that in the end a computer will do all the computation for you. Pearson's coefficient of correlation is conceptually defined as

$$r = \frac{\sum (Z_X Z_Y)}{n}$$

(4.10)

where $(Z_X Z_Y)$ is the product of two standardized variables: Z_X is the standardized score for a case on variable X and Z_Y is the standardized score for a case on variable Y. As always, n is the sample size, and the summation $(\sum)$ is over all cases in the data file with data on both the X and Y variables.[1] Recall from earlier (equation 4.7) that a standardized score or Z-score is an expression of the measurement relative to the mean in standard deviation units. So the formula above shows that Pearson's r is

---

[1] In a small sample, dividing the sum of the products by $n - 1$ rather than n will yield a more accurate value of r. However, rarely would you ever want to compute the correlation by hand. A computer program would use a different formula to compute the correlation that doesn't first require standardization of the variables.

essentially a mean—a mean of the product of two standardized scores on variables X and Y.

Pearson's r quantifies the *direction* and the *strength* of the relationship between two variables with a number that can range between -1 and 1. The sign of r (i.e., whether it is positive or negative) indicates the direction of the association, and the closer r is to one in absolute value (i.e., ignoring sign) the stronger the relationship. For example, suppose we quantified the political knowledge of a sample of people in some fashion as well as how frequently each person engages in political discussion. Imagine that we found that people who are below the mean on the political knowledge variable tend to be below the mean in their frequency of political discussion. If X is political discussion and Y is political knowledge, then Z_X and Z_Y would both be negative for such people, meaning that their product would be positive (because the product of two negative numbers is always a positive number). And suppose that people who are above the mean on political knowledge also tend to discuss politics more than the average. In that case, Z_X and Z_Y would both be positive for such people, meaning that their product would be positive. So if the data file tended to contain mostly two types of people, those who score relatively high on both X and Y, and those who score relatively low on both X and Y, then r would be positive, because the mean $(Z_X Z_Y)$ would be positive. Thus, a positive relationship is one where relatively low scores on one variable X tend to be paired with relatively low scores on the other variable Y, and relatively high scores on X are paired with relatively high scores on Y. In contrast, if relatively low scores on one variable tend to be paired with relatively high scores on the other, then $(Z_X Z_Y)$ would tend to be negative, so r would be negative because the mean $(Z_X Z_Y)$ would be negative. So a negative relationship between X and Y is one where relatively high scores on X tend to be paired with relatively low scores on Y, and relatively low scores on X tend to be paired with relatively high scores on Y. An absence of relationship occurs when there is no systematic relationship between pairings of scores on X and Y. In that case, there is no relationship between X and Y, r is zero, and the variables can be said to be *linearly independent* or *linearly uncorrelated*.

When a relationship is not zero, it is clear that knowledge of one variable could be used to make an educated guess about a case's score on the other variable. For example, if we knew the relationship between political knowledge and frequency of political discussion was positive, then knowing that a person discusses politics more than average allows us to make a reasonable guess that the person's political knowledge would be above average. Other examples of positive relationships include education level and annual income (the relatively more educated tend to make relatively more money), distance to work and the amount of time it takes to get to work (people who live farther from work tend to take longer to get to work), and hours spent reading the newspaper and knowledge of recent world events (people who read the newspaper more tend to know more about what is happening in the world).

In contrast, if the relationship between knowledge and discussion was negative, we'd guess that someone with less political knowledge than average would tend to discuss politics more than average. Examples of negative relationships include the age of a car and its resale value (older cars tend to be worth less), social anxiety and number of friends (socially anxious people are less likely to meet others and establish friendships), and the number of days since the last trip to the grocery store and the amount of food in the refrigerator.

To further illustrate the concept of correlation, let's consider some actual data. There has been a substantial amount of research on the effects of media on health. Both media researchers and the medical community are concerned that too much television is bad for you. Indeed, evidence shows that people who get larger daily doses of television do tend to be less healthy at least physically, using a variety of indices of health. For example, those who watch relatively more television are more likely to be overweight (Ching, Willett, Rimm, Colditz, Gortmaker, & Stempfer, 1996; Tremblay & Willms, 2003; Tucker & Bagwell, 1991).

At the beginning of this chapter, I mentioned a questionnaire that I distribute to my research methods class at the beginning of each term. Some of the questions in this questionnaire produce data that allows us to assess whether students who watch relatively more television tend to have a higher body mass. I have already discussed the TV use measure. The students are also asked on the questionnaire to indicate their weight in pounds and their height in inches. With just this information, a person's body mass index (BMI) can be computed using the formula $BMI = (700 \times \text{weight})/\text{height}^2$ (see e.g., Sparks, 2002; note that some definitions of BMI use 703 or 704.5 as the weight multiplier rather than 700). The body mass index approximates how much of a person's body weight is fat content and it is widely used in the medical community to classify people as underweight, of about the correct weight, or overweight. The students also responded to the 5–item *Television Affinity Scale*, first introduced in Chapter 2 (see Box 2.1). Recall that the *Television Affinity Scale* is a summated rating scale that is said to measure the importance that a person places on television in his or her daily life (see Rubin et al., 2004). They were also asked how many hours in a typical week they engage in some kind of fitness-related activity.

If people who watch more TV tend to have relatively more fat on their bodies, then the correlation between TV viewing and BMI should be positive. Remember a positive correlation means that people who are relatively high on one variable tend to be relatively high on the other, and those who are relatively low on one variable are relatively low on the other. With a computer, it is easy to generate the correlation between these two variables. Because it is so easy, I also requested the correlation between these variables and scores on the *Television Affinity Scale* and on the number of hours a week the respondents reporting engaging in fitness activities. The Pearson correlations between these four variables can be found in Table 4.2. As can be seen, the correlation between television viewing and body mass (located in the "BMI" row and "TV hours" column) is 0.157 in this sample. The sign is positive, reflecting the tendency for students who watch more than the average amount of television to have a higher than average BMI, as well as then tendency for those who watch less television

Table 4.2
A Matrix of Pearson Correlations

	TV hours	BMI	Fitness activity	TV Affinity
TV hours/day	1.000			
BMI	0.157	1.000		
Fitness activity	−0.044	0.055	1.000	
Television Affinity	0.508	0.138	−0.085	1.000

than the average to have a relatively lower BMI. Of course, relative is a relative term. In this case, we are talking about relative to the sample mean, not relative to all people or some larger population of students not included in this sample. From Table 4.2 you can also see that those who report television is relatively more important to their lives than do others (i.e., higher scores on the *Television Affinity Scale*) tend to have a higher body mass (Pearson's $r = 0.138$) and engage in relatively less fitness activity (Pearson's $r = -0.085$). Notice that students who report they watch relatively more television also tend to report that television is relatively more important in their lives compared to those who watch relatively less television (Pearson's $r = 0.508$). Recalling the notion of *criterion-related validity* from Chapter 2, note that this can be construed as evidence that the *Television Affinity Scale* is a valid measure of how important television is to a person.

So we've talked about how to interpret the sign of the correlation, but we've said nothing about how to interpret the *size* of Pearson's r. It is not obvious looking at the formula for Pearson's r (equation 4.10), but it is true that the larger the correlation in absolute value (i.e., ignoring sign), the greater the correspondence between the variables in how "extreme" two scores on X and Y tend to be. The stronger the correlation, the more pronounced the tendency for relatively more extreme scores on X to be paired with relatively more extreme scores on Y, and less extreme scores on X to be paired with less extreme scores on Y. One way of thinking about this is the similarity in the Z-scores for each case in the data file. The closer the correlation is to one in absolute value, the more similar each case's Z-scores are on X and Y. More formally,

$$\boxed{E(Z_Y) = r_{XY} Z_X}$$

(4.11)

For example, if a person is one standard deviation above the mean on X (that is, $Z_X = 1$), then you would expect (E) that person to be r_{XY} standard deviations above the mean on Y. Similarly, someone who is one standard deviation below the mean on X would be expected to be r_{XY} standard deviations below the mean on Y. But if the correlation is negative, then someone who is above the mean on X is expected to be $|r_{XY}|$ standard deviations below the mean on Y. So Pearson's r quantifies the degree of relative correspondence between X and Y, with the sign indicating whether the sign of the Z-scores tend to be consistent (cases above the mean on X expected to be above the mean on Y) or inconsistent (cases above the mean on X expected to be below the mean on Y).

The notion of expectation is a bit puzzling on the surface, but it is an important statistical concept. When we say that the expected value of Z_Y is $r_{XY} Z_X$, we are saying that if we had a group of people with the same Z-score on variable X, the mean of this group's Z-scores on variable Y is expected to be $r_{XY} Z_X$. So $E(Z_Y)$ is a conditional mean—the mean of Z_Y conditioned on the value of Z_X.

Here is another interpretation of the size of the association. If you square Pearson's r, you get a measure of how much of the variance in one variable can be "explained by" variation in the other (a term which is problematic in a sense because it implies that variation in one causes variation in the other, which as we will see is not necessarily true). The square of the Pearson's correlation (r^2) is called the *coefficient of determination*. For example, the correlation between hours of TV viewing per day and body mass is 0.157, meaning that the proportion of the variance between people in body mass "explained by" person-to-person variation in the how much people in this sample watch TV is $0.157^2 = 0.025$, or about 2.5%.

Communication researchers use common rules of thumb for interpreting the strength of the correlation by relying on the coefficient of determination. It is sometimes said that a "weak" correlation or weak association is one in which the variation in one variable that can be explained by the other is about 10%, which corresponds to a value of Pearson's r of about 0.30. A "moderate" correlation explains about 25% of the variation, which correspondents to $r = 0.50$. If two variables are "strongly" related, then one variable explains about 50% of the variation in the other, which translates into a correlation of about $r = 0.70$. So from Table 4.1, the relationship between hours of television viewing and body mass is weak, indeed perhaps even negligible ($r^2 = .026$), whereas the relationship between hours of television viewing and a person's self-reported television affinity is moderate in strength ($r^2 = 0.258$). Just how the coefficient of determination assesses "variance explained" will be made clearer when we talk about a statistical method called *linear regression* in Chapter 12.

These rules of thumbs for interpreting the strength of association are just that; in reality they are an oversimplification of something complex and multidetermined. Whether a relationship can be labeled as weak, moderate, or strong will depend on a lot of other things other than the mere magnitude of the association. What is "weak" to one researcher in one context may be strong to another researcher in another context. Furthermore, the strength of the association tells us nothing about practical importance. For example, even though only 2 to 3% of the variance in body mass can be explained by TV viewing habits, the medical community might construe this as high in practical importance given the negative health consequences of being overweight.

There is considerable controversy over whether Pearson's r should be squared when assessing the strength of the relationship. The coefficient of determination is literally the proportion of the variance (equation 4.4) in one variable that can be explained by the relationship between X and Y. But the variance isn't an intuitively satisfying measure of variability because it is difficult to think in terms of squared units. The standard deviation makes a lot more sense as a measure of variability, so why not articulate a relationship in terms of the proportion of the standard deviation of one variable that can be explained by the relationship? The unsquared correlation is closer to such a measure, so some argue that we should use the correlation and not its square when interpreting the strength of a relationship (see, e.g., Darlington, 1990, pp. 209–213; Beatty, 2002). Further complicating matters, these are only two of many ways of quantifying strength of association. What you do is ultimately a matter of personal preference, but the coefficient of determination is (for better or worse) widely used and you will encounter it frequently when reading the communication literature.

4.7.2   Alternative Measures of Association

So Pearson's r is nothing more than a mean of the product of two standardized variables. But as a mean, it suffers from the same limitation as the arithmetic mean as a measure of central tendency: it is highly affected by "extremes" in the distribution. Two cases that are extreme or unusual on X or Y or both can (but won't necessarily) have dramatic effects on the value of r. Although this fact has not deterred the wide use and acceptance of Pearson's r as a measure of association, it can't be completely ignored. Other measures of association are less susceptible to the influence of such unusual pairings of X and Y. Although they are not widely used by communication researchers, you should be aware of them.

Spearman's Coefficient of Correlation. A man named Charles Spearman suggested computing the correlation between two variables using their ordinal positions in the distribution instead of the actual measurements. So rather than multiplying the product of each case's Z-scores on X and Y, we first transform each case's score on X and Y into their ordinal positions in the distribution prior to standardizing and computing their product. For example, first sort the cases from high to low on X. The first case in this sorted distribution is given a value of $X_T = 1$, the next case is given $X_T = 2$, the next case is assigned $X_T = 3$, and so forth, with the case with the smallest value of X being assigned $X_T = n$. If cases are tied on X, then they are each assigned a value of X_T that corresponds to the arithmetic mean of the ordinal position for which they are tied. For example, if the second and third cases in the sorted distribution of X are the same, then they are assigned $X_T = 2.5$. This procedure is then repeated for the Y variable, yielding n scores on Y_T. Applying equations 4.9 or 4.10 the resulting data set (using X_T and Y_T rather than X and Y in the computations) yields a correlation coefficient known as *Spearman's coefficient of correlation* or *Spearman's r*. Spearman's r is less affected than Pearson's r by cases that are especially extreme on X and/or Y. Think about why this would be so. When the data are transformed into their ordinal position, no case is particularly extreme from the others in their measurement on X or Y (now defined as X_T or Y_T).

The interpretation of the sign of Spearman's r (sometimes denoted r_S) is the same as the interpretation of Pearson's r. Positive r_S means that cases that are relatively high on X tend to also have relatively high scores on Y, and negative r_S means that cases that are relatively high on X tend to be relatively low on Y. The interpretation of the size of Spearman's r is a bit more ambiguous. Larger values of r_S (ignoring sign) still reflect stronger association, but the square of r_S cannot be interpreted as a measure of the percent of variance in one variable explained by variation in the other.

Gamma. An alternative but even less widely used measure of association is *gamma*. Gamma is often used to describe correlation between ordinal variables, but it can be used to quantify correlation between variables measured at the interval or ratio level (although Spearman's or Pearson's r would usually be a better choice). Define two cases i and j as *concordant* on X and Y if $X_i > X_j$ and $Y_i > Y_j$, and define two cases as *discordant* if either (1) $X_i > X_j$ and $Y_i < Y_j$, or (2) $X_i < X_j$ and $Y_i > Y_j$. If the two cases have the same value of X or Y, define the pair as tied. Call C the number of concordant pairs of cases and D the number of discordant pairs of cases in the data. Gamma is equal to

$$Gamma = \frac{C - D}{C + D}$$

(4.12)

So gamma quantifies association in a pairwise-fashion, by quantifying how frequently pairs of cases are ordinally concordant on X and Y compared to how frequently cases are ordinally discordant. Notice that if for every pairing of cases in the data (ignoring ties), the case that is higher on X is also higher on Y, then gamma $= 1$ because $D = 0$. In contrast, if for every pairing of cases (again ignoring ties), the case with the larger X has the smaller Y, then gamma $= -1$ because $C = 0$. If it usually true that a case that is higher on X compared to other cases in the data is also higher on Y, then gamma will tend to be positive because $C > D$. But if cases that are low on X compared to other cases also tend to have values of Y that are higher, then gamma will tend to be negative because $D > C$. As with Pearson's r and Spearman's r, the closer to gamma is to 1 (in absolute value), the stronger the association.

Gamma completely ignores the absolute size of X and Y and bases the assessment of association on the relative sizes of X and Y in all possible pairwise comparisons of cases in the data on X and Y. As a result, it is largely unaffected by extremity of scores on X and Y. But the more ties there are in the data, the less informative gamma is as a measure of association, and the less useful it is as a descriptive measure of association.

Although these computations seem complicated, most good statistical programs can compute both Spearman's r and gamma so you should never have to actually do the computations yourself. When assessing the association between TV viewing and body mass, Spearman's $r = 0.15$ and gamma $= 0.12$. These are very close to Pearson's r, but this won't always be true. Although each of these measures has some intuitive appeal, neither are nearly as widely used in communication research as Pearson's r, in part because of the statistical theory of association using Pearson's r is more widely developed in the field of statistics and more widely known by communication scientists.

4.7.3   Cautions When Interpreting Correlation

Understanding Pearson's correlation, how it is interpreted, and how it should not be interpreted is very important. You will find Pearson's correlation coefficient being used throughout the communication literature. Indeed, it would be fairly difficult to find an empirical article in the field of communication that does not report some analysis that includes Pearson's r somewhere. However, it does have its limitations.

Pearson's r *Only Measures Linear Association.* Pearson's r is known as a measure of *linear association*. An association is linear if it can be described adequately with a straight line. If a relationship is not linear but instead best characterized as *nonlinear*, Pearson's coefficient can mislead you about whether and how strongly the variables are related. More detail about notion of linear and nonlinear association is provided in the next section.

Range Restriction. The size of the correlation coefficient is dependent in part on how much variability there is on the two variables being correlated. Although the correlation coefficient can be a perfectly adequate description of the relationship between two variables in a sample, it may not adequately reflect the relationship between these two variables if you had the entire population of interest available to you. The relevance of this depends on whether there is some larger population of interest that you have sampled from. We often conduct research with the goal of estimating the strength and direction of relationships in a population. To get an accurate representation of the association in the population of interest, you want to make sure that your sample is not "range restricted" on the variable or variables being correlated. By *range restricted*, I mean that the sample does not adequately represent the highs and lows in the distribution of one or both of the variables in the population. Such range restriction will tend to lower the correlation between two variables in a sample relative to the correlation in the population.

For example, it could be argued that people who watch a lot of television might be older and therefore relatively unlikely to be enrolled in an undergraduate communication research methods course. Alternatively, people who watch lots of television may be less likely to be in college. Perhaps they simply don't have the time to attend classes because they are so absorbed in the television. So the 600+ students in my data set may contain relatively fewer people who watch lots of TV than would be the case if I collected my data using a different sampling method, such as interviewing people over the phone after randomly selecting phone numbers to call. This could lower the correlation between the variables measured and produce an inaccurate inference about the strength of the relationship between TV viewing and body mass in some larger population. Very likely, the relationship would be stronger if I used a sampling method that maximized the likelihood of obtaining a sample that more accurately reflected the person-to-person variability in TV viewing than I can obtain sampling college students. Of course, if I were only interested in the relationship between TV viewing and body mass among college students, the conclusion that the relationship is weak might be perfectly reasonable, because the population of interest is naturally range restricted, and the sample may quite adequately reflect the variability in college students' television viewing habits. We only need to be concerned about the damage of range-restriction when we are interested in generalizing to a population that our sample does not adequately represent.

Correlation Does not Imply Causality. Our brains seem to be wired to think in terms of causal relationships, so much so that we often make causal claims when they aren't justified. Consider claims made by some proponents of herbal health remedies that they relieve all kinds of social and physical ills, from back pain to social phobias, stress, and anxiety. If you are feeling tense, drink a cup of Ginseng tea, and then feel less tense 30 minutes later, it seems sensible to infer that Ginseng must work. Maybe, but maybe not. Although sometimes causal claims such as this are justified, we typically don't have sufficient information necessary to make claims about causality, and we often fall victim to various fallacies in logic and biases in judgment that can lead us to believe things that just are not true (Gilovich, 1991). The tendency to interpret correlation as causation is one such bias, and it is important that you learn to recognize this bias and overcome it.

There are three criteria that must be met in order to make cause-effect claims for any research finding. The first criterion is that the cause and the effect must be correlated. If X causes Y, then it must be the case that in the presence of X (or certain scores on X), Y tends to occur (or certain scores on Y are more likely or more frequent), and in the absence of X (or certain other scores on X), Y tends not to occur (or certain other scores on Y are less likely or less frequent). Rephrased, if X and Y are causally related, then there should be some kind of association between X and Y consistent with the cause-effect relationship being claimed. It would be hard to argue that studying causes good grades if there is no correlation between how much time people study and how good their grades tend to be. If you believe that watching too much TV is bad for your health but you can't find a correlation between how much TV people report watching and measures of health (such as body mass, frequency of illness, etc.), how can you claim that excessive TV viewing causes poor health?

The second criterion is that the cause must precede the effect. If TV viewing causes poor health, then the TV viewing must precede the development of poor health. This is logically obvious, but in some communication research purportedly attempting to understand causal mechanisms this criterion is not clearly met. In studies where the presumed cause and the alleged effect are measured simultaneously, it is not obvious which variable preceded the other in the sequence of events that the researcher claims to be tapping, and there is no way of statistically disentangling the direction of causal flow. For example, we have seen that students who watch more TV tend to have a higher body mass. Although it seems sensible to argue that excessive TV viewing can increase your body mass, is it not possible that the direction of cause moves the other direction, from high body mass to greater TV viewing? For example, people who are overweight might find that viewing television is a much easier form of leisure activity than other activities, such as riding a bike, jogging, or playing tennis. Perhaps it is simply easier to sit and watch TV than it is do other things when you are overweight. So being overweight perhaps leads a person to choose to watch TV more often than someone who is not overweight would tend to choose.

Of course, it is sometimes possible to claim that the temporal sequence is met on logical grounds. For example, we know that people who are more educated tend to have more knowledge about recent political events (e.g., Delli Carpini & Keeter, 1996). Although we can't say for certain that higher education causes greater political knowledge, we can almost certainly say that political knowledge doesn't cause higher education. How can what you know now affect how much schooling you had in your past? Although an argument could be made that knowledge causes education (e.g., people with a lot of knowledge about politics might seek to learn more through formal education), this is a rather difficult story to spin convincingly and is not as parsimonious as the simpler explanation that education leads to greater knowledge through some mechanism.

Note that the two directions of causal flow described above are not mutually exclusive. Two variables X and Y are causally related *reciprocally* when X causes Y *and* Y causes X. So excessive TV viewing could lead to weight gain, but people who are overweight may be more likely to choose watching television rather than other activities because they are overweight.

Correlation is a necessary condition for claiming causality. But correlation is not a sufficient condition for claiming causality because even if two variables are correlated and the temporal sequencing criterion is met, there may be alternative explanations for the relationship other than the cause-effect explanation. Thus, the third criterion for making cause-effect claims is the elimination of plausible competing alternative explanations for the correlation. For example, there is a positive correlation in children under 12 between shoe size and vocabulary size. But we know that having big feet does not facilitate the development of a large vocabulary, and studying and learning new words will not make a child's feet bigger. The correlation is attributable to natural developmental processes. As kids age, they learn to speak and their vocabulary expands, as does their shoe size. The correlation between shoe size and vocabulary are both affected by normal human physical and mental maturation.

When two variables X and Y are correlated because they are both affected by some other variable or set of variables, we say that the correlation between X and Y is *spurious*. Two variables are spuriously associated if they share a common cause but do not causally affect each other. Might the positive relationship between frequency of TV viewing and body mass be spurious? Certainly it seems possible. For example, people acquire many beliefs, values, and habits from their parents. If a person's parents deemphasized the importance of eating healthy and getting sufficient exercise, this socialization could lead to both weight problems and a tendency to loaf in front of the television. Alternatively, a person's socioeconomic status could influence both TV viewing and body mass. The relatively less well off in society may be less able to find full-time work or may have jobs that give them more free time to watch television, while at the same their relatively low income leads them to purchase food that is less expensive but also less healthy. In later chapters, we discuss statistical procedures for assessing the viability of spuriousness as the explanation for an association between variables.

Because there are many different interpretations for a correlation between two variables, a researcher in any field needs to be careful when advocating one particular interpretation over another and realize that research design limits the kinds of interpretations one can safely make. Many of the studies you see in the communication literature are *crosssectional correlational studies.* With a crosssectional correlational design, the investigator collects a sample of people and measures them a single time on a set of variables to see how those variables are associated with each other. Such a design permits the investigator to assess only the extent to which variables are correlated, not whether they are causally related. To be sure, such research is important. Knowing that X and Y are correlated suggests that X and Y might be causally related (because causation implies correlation). This knowledge can stimulate research, and such studies can be used to test theory because theory typically predicts, describes and explains cause-effect relationships. Theories can be tested by determining if the variables in the theoretical system are correlated as the theory predicts they should be, and as they must be if there is a causal relationship between them. But by itself, correlation does not imply causation. Some correlational research designs allow the investigator to get closer to cause-effect claims, and some statistical methods discussed in later chapters can be used to rule out explanations that compete with the desired cause-effect claim the researcher might want to make.

Causality is a complicated, tangled, philosophical web. Establishing cause is a difficult scientific problem, and even if a group of scientists can gather sufficient evidence by scientific standards that X causes Y, a philosopher could take the group to task and argue that they haven't really made the case. For a good discussion of the conceptual (and some statistical) rules of causality, at least as conceptualized by scientists, see Davis (1985).

4.8 Visualizing Correlation: The Scatterplot

It is said that a picture says 1,000 words. This is probably the case for a *scatterplot*, a graphical tool used to visually display association between variables. A scatterplot depicts the relationship between two variables by representing pairs of scores on the variables in two-dimensional space. In a scatterplot, each axis represents one of the variables, and the points in the scatterplot represent each case's measurements on the two variables. Any case's score on the variables can be found by projecting the point vertically to the X axis, and horizonally to the Y axis, and reading the scores on the axes corresponding to that point. Two scatterplots depicting the relationship between television viewing and body mass, as well as between television viewing and scores on the *Television Affinity Scale* can be found in Figure 4.5.

A positive correlation will show up on a scatterplot as a distinct clustering of points along an imaginary line that progress from the lower left of the scatterplot to the upper right. This is consistent with our interpretation of the sign of Pearson's r. A positive r means that low scores on X tend to be paired with relative low scores on Y, and high scores on X are paired with relatively high scores on Y. The stronger the correlation, the clearer the clustering around this imaginary line will be on the scatterplot. On the other hand, a negative correlation will look like a clustering of points progressing from the upper left hand corner of the scatterplot to the lower right hand corner, with the strength of the correlation being reflected in how tight the clustering of the points is around this line. A weak or zero correlation will usually look like a random dispersion of points, with no clear or easily discernable pattern (but see below). Example scatterplots

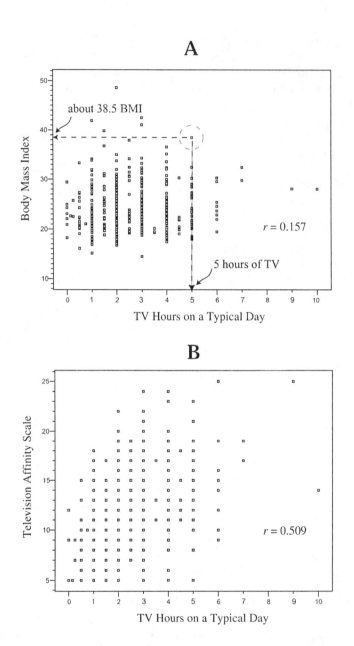

Figure 4.5 Scatterplots depicting the relationship between TV viewing frequency and body mass (A) and TV viewing frequency and television affinity (B).

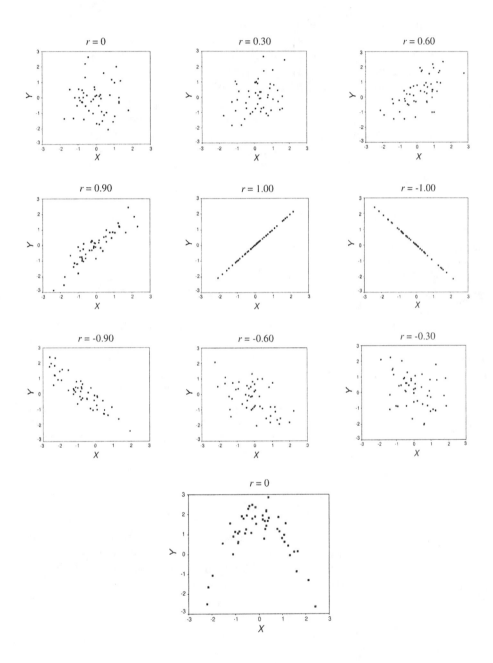

Figure 4.6 Correlations of various strengths and sizes.

reflecting correlations of different strengths and directions can be found in Figure 4.6. These scatterplots make the connection between the size of the correlation and the strength of the association clear. The stronger the association or correlation, the more line-like the points on a scatterplot will look.

One of the weaknesses of Pearson's r a descriptive tool for assessing correlation can be overcome by coupling Pearson's r with a scatterplot. Pearson's r is a measure of *linear association*. It quantifies how line-like the relationship between two variables is. There is a temptation when one finds a correlation of zero or near zero to conclude, therefore, that there is no relationship between the two variables, and thus that scores on one variable could not be used to accurately estimate scores on the other. But this is not necessarily true. Consider the scatterplot at the bottom of Figure 4.6. The Pearson correlation between X and Y in these data is zero. However, an examination of this scatterplot shows that there is a relationship between X and Y. These variables are not unrelated. There is a clear pattern in the scatterplot—relatively high scores on Y tend to be paired with relatively moderate scores on X, and relatively low scores on Y tend to be paired with relatively low or high scores on X. The problem is that Pearson's r only quantifies *linear relationship*, meaning relationships that can be described with a straight line. In contrast, our eye can pick up relationships that are best described as *curvilinear*. Using only Pearson's r as the method of assessing correlation would mislead you in this case. So the value of the scatterplot resides in its ability to depict relationships that may not be captured with a commonly used statistical index of relationship such as Pearson's r but that would be captured by the human eye.

At the same time, the eye is not often able to detect relationships that a statistical index such as Pearson's r can. Consider the two scatterplots in Figure 4.6 corresponding to correlations of 0.30 and -0.30. Looking at these scatterplots, it is not at all obvious that these data points are not just randomly distributed throughout the scatterplot. And yet we know that there is a relationship between these two variables when the relationship is quantified with Pearson's r. Our eye is unable to detect weak relationships in a scatterplot. Furthermore, our eye can also trick us into seeing a pattern in what is essentially randomness. So we should not rely on just a statistical measure of correlation such as Pearson's r or on just a visual representation such as a scatterplot. They are best used simultaneously.

4.9   Descriptively Comparing Groups

The questions that communication researchers ask and the theories and hypotheses we test are often framed in terms of comparisons. A health communication researcher might ask whether a school-based intervention to increase adolescent awareness of safe sexual practices increases the students' knowledge about sexually transmitted diseases and lowers the likelihood of engaging in risky sexual behavior. To answer this question, a researcher might examine the knowledge of high school students exposed to the intervention compared to a group of students not exposed to the intervention as well as ascertain the forms of sexual behavior they have engaged in recently. Or an interpersonal communication scholar might wonder whether married men differ from their spouses in their nonverbal sensitivity, and whether such differences are related to marital satisfaction. Or a political communication researcher might test the hypothesis that exposure to political debates increases knowledge of a political candidate's positions by determining if people who were asked to watch a debate could more accurately report the positions of candidates than those who were not given the opportunity to

A

respondent sex		N	Mean	Std. Deviation
female	TV hours on an average day	388	2.2910	1.25304
	Body Mass Index	375	22.1292	3.59652
male	TV hours on an average day	221	2.5181	1.45118
	Body Mass Index	222	25.6725	4.38599

B

			respondent sex		
			female	male	Total
weight	underweight	Count	31	3	34
		% within weight	91.2%	8.8%	100.0%
		% within respondent sex	8.3%	1.4%	5.7%
	healthy weight	Count	291	118	409
		% within weight	71.1%	28.9%	100.0%
		% within respondent sex	77.6%	53.2%	68.5%
	overweight	Count	35	71	106
		% within weight	33.0%	67.0%	100.0%
		% within respondent sex	9.3%	32.0%	17.8%
	obese	Count	18	30	48
		% within weight	37.5%	62.5%	100.0%
		% within respondent sex	4.8%	13.5%	8.0%
Total		Count	375	222	597
		% within weight	62.8%	37.2%	100.0%
		% within respondent sex	100.0%	100.0%	100.0%

Figure 4.7 Some descriptive statistics for comparing males and females.

watch a debate. All these questions are framed in terms of some kind of a comparison between groups.

Throughout this book, I address a variety of statistical methods for making such comparisons. When research questions and hypotheses focus on group comparisons, each group in the data set needs to be described statistically, and considerable insight into the differences between groups on the variables measured can be gained merely looking at how the groups differ descriptively. This is accomplished by computing one or more of the descriptive statistics described in this chapter or using one or more of the visual techniques, but analyzing each group separately.

In the research methods class data set we've been using thus far, there is a variable that codes the sex of the respondent. The data set includes 222 men (sex = 2) and 388 women (sex = 1). (Of course, these numbers are arbitrary codes and do not actually quantify anything. They are merely used to distinguish between male and female respondents in the data file). Do the men and women in this class differ in their TV viewing and body mass, and is the relationship between TV viewing and body mass different in men compared to women? And are the males more or less likely to be overweight than the females? Using the tools discussed in this chapter, you can easily answer these questions at a descriptive level. Figure 4.7, panel A, contains SPSS output from a procedure that computes several descriptive statistics for different groups in a data set. Panel B contains a *crosstabulation* of sex and a new variable coding whether the student is underweight (BMI less than 18.5), of healthy weight (BMI at least 18.5 but less than 25), overweight (BMI at least 25 but less than 30) or obese (BMI of 30 or more), using standards from the U.S. National Institutes of Health (1998). A crosstabulation is essentially a set of frequency tables, where the table for one variable is constructed conditioned on each value of a second variable. The variables in a crosstabulation can be either quantitative or qualitative, but a crosstabulation is best used with qualitative variables or quantitative variables that are discrete with only a few possible measurement values.

As can be seen in Figure 4.7, panel A, males reported watching slightly more television than did females on average, with means of 2.518 and 2.291, respectively. Males were also more different from each other in their TV viewing compared to females, as evidenced by the larger standard deviation for males (1.451) than females (1.253). Males also appear to have more fat than females on their bodies, and they are also more variable from each other on this variable compared to females. The crosstabulation (Figure 4.7, panel B) shows that the females were more likely to be underweight than males, whereas males were more likely to be overweight or obese than females. For example, 8.3% of females (31 out of 375) had a BMI less than 18.5, compared to only 1.4% of males (3 of 222). But males were more likely than females to be classified as overweight or obese. For example, 13.5% of males (30 of 222) had a BMI of at least 30 (and thus classified as obese), but only 4.8% of females did (18 of 375). Of course, these are based on self-reports of height and weight. It may be that women were more likely to underreport their weight than males. Indeed, notice that even though there are 388 females in the data set, only 375 of them are represented in the crosstabulation because 13 of them didn't report either their height or weight, meaning that they are missing on the BMI variable because it couldn't be computed. But every male provided answers to these two questions. Perhaps these females didn't report their weight because they felt they were too heavy, were self-conscious about their weight, or didn't want others to know just how much they weigh. If so, it is reasonable to speculate that females may have tended to underreport their weight or at least were more likely to do so than males. Or perhaps men are simply more likely to be overweight than women.

Although not displayed in Figure 4.7, the correlation between television viewing and BMI is positive in both the men ($r = 0.10$) and women ($r = 0.16$) in this class. In other words, whether male or female, the relationship between body mass and television viewing in this sample of college students is positive but rather weak.

4.10 Data Screening and Missing Data

The accuracy of a description about a variable or a relationship is a function of a lot of things, some out of your control and some very much in your control. For example, whether we can say that 2.373 hours is an accurate description of my students' average TV viewing depends on such things as whether they were able to accurately report about their TV viewing, whether they were honest when answering the question, whether it is sensible to expect people to know what we mean when we ask them about an "average" day, and so forth. Statistics cannot help us resolve the potential inaccuracies that result from such things as question wording or psychological processes at work when people are asked to answer questions. Nor can they make invalid measurements valid. So the accuracy of our conclusions is in part a function of aspects of the design of the research—how we measure the constructs of interest, how we obtain research units, and (if those units are people) what we are asking them to do in the study.

Given the ambiguities in interpretation resulting from decisions about research design, it is important that you don't shoot yourself in the foot by introducing a form of potential inaccuracy that is totally in your control: accuracy of the data entry. Before you conduct any kind of analysis of your data, please take my advice and first do some rudimentary *data screening*. Data screening is the process of examining a data file for errors in the data file itself. Unless the data collection process has automated the construction of the data file in some way, there is a good chance that a human being was involved in the construction of the data file that you are going to analyze, and people, including you, make mistakes. Keys on a keyboard are very close together, and none of us are perfect typists. A slip of the finger or a lapse in attention can mean that your data file contains data that should not be there. Depending on the size and frequency of such errors, the statistics you compute to summarize your data may be inaccurate, and this will affect the accuracy of your research conclusions.

There are many different approaches to data screening, some complicated and some simple. At a minimum, it is a good idea to have a statistics program generate a table containing the minimum and maximum values in the data for every variable in the data file. It is usually relatively easy to pick up data entry errors looking at these statistics. For example, suppose you were entering data from a series of questions using a 5–point response scale with response options between 1 and 5. So data for these variables in the data set should be between 1 and 5. But if a table of minimum and maximums for these variables shows a maximum of 55 for one variable and a minimum of 0 for another, then you know you made at least two data entry mistakes when entering the data for these variables. A frequency table for each of the variables could allow you to find errors more specifically, because a frequency table would tell you not only the maximum and minimum values, but also the frequency of every data value in the data set. That would allow you to determine how many data entry errors were made for each variable, so that you will know how many to look for when cleaning the data of those mistakes.

Another potential pitfall with computerized data analysis is the analysis of *missing data* as if the missing data were real. Missing data are almost inevitable when you conduct research. Data are considered missing if a case in the data file has no data for a particular variable. For example, in a multi-item survey, a person might not respond to some of the questions. You wouldn't necessarily want to discard that entire case from all analyses, because the person did respond to some of the questions. Throwing them out entirely would be inefficient. But how do you represent data in a data file when the data are missing? The standard approach is to pick some arbitrary label or number to identify a case as missing on that variable, and then tell the program that this label or code corresponds to a missing data point. For example, if a person fails to answer a question, you might code their response as -999 on that variable, or some other value that could never correspond to real data. If you use this strategy, make sure that you tell the computer that -999 corresponds to missing data (different programs have different procedures for doing this). If you don't do this, the computer will think that -999 is real data, and this will throw off all the computations and produce meaningless statistics. Trust me, it is easy to make this mistake of forgetting to tell the computer how missing data are represented, and if you are working with a group of people on a research project it is very embarrassing to discover this mistake well into the data analysis and interpretation phase of the research. I've done it more than once, and as a result, I have modified my approach to the entry of missing data by leaving a data field empty when data are missing. Most good statistical programs will allow you to leave a cell in a data matrix empty, and an empty data cell is almost universally recognized by statistics programs as "system missing." Importantly, a blank data field cannot figure into statistical computations.

Missing data have another potential effect on accuracy. We worry when a variable has missing data that there may be a reason for the missingness that is systematically related to what is being measured. For example, suppose that people who watch an extraordinary amount of television feel embarrassed about this and yet also don't want to lie. So instead of lying, they refuse to answer questions about their TV viewing. If people who watch lots of TV are more likely not to answer a question about their TV viewing, then descriptive statistics about a TV viewing variable are going to be inaccurate descriptions of the units in your data set, because heavy TV viewers are less likely to be included in the description. The proper interpretation of statistics in the presence of missing data is a complicated subject and one that I don't discuss in this book. Discussions about missing data, types of missing data, the problems that result from missing data, and strategies for dealing with missing data can be found in such sources as Allison (2002), Hertel (1976), and Roth (1994).

Throughout this book I will use a procedure of managing missing data called *listwise deletion*. I use this procedure not because it is good. Indeed, it is one of the worst methods of handling missing data in an analysis. However, it is one of the simplest, and it is also relatively common in spite of its problems. Listwise deletion means that cases that are missing data on any variable used in the construction of a statistic are excluded from any analysis involving that variable. So long as there is no systematic relationship between being missing on a variable and the value that a missing cased would have had on that variable if it were not missing, the only thing that listwise deletion does is decrease the sample size and make inferential tests lower in power than they otherwise would be in the absence of missing data. The concept of statistical power is introduced in a Chapter 8.

4.11   Introducing Some Common Symbolic Notation

As the topics in this book become increasingly more complicated, it becomes necessary to start communicating concepts symbolically. The use of symbols to represent different concepts will make it easier to represent ideas and allow me to reduce the number of words I use to express those concepts. In this final section of the chapter, I will introduce some common symbolic notation for many of the descriptive statistics introduced in this chapter.

Data are often derived by measuring members of a population obtained through some kind of sampling procedure. A *parameter* is a numerical description of an entire population, whereas a *statistic* is a numerical description of a sample. For example, if a mean is computed based on measurements from each and every member of the population of interest, this summary is referred to as a *parameter* of the population—in this case, the population mean. But if the mean is based on a sample from a population and not the entire population, the mean is then referred to as a statistic—the sample mean. In statistics, it is conventional to represent parameters symbolically with Greek letters and statistics with Roman letters. For example, the mean of a population is denoted symbolically with the Greek letter μ (pronounced "myoo"). When a mean is computed from a sample from some population, it is generally denoted symbolically with a Roman letter with a bar over it, such as $\overline{X}$ (pronounced "ex-bar") or $\overline{Y}$. This is just a convention, and the letter used is arbitrary. Furthermore, other symbols are sometimes used. For example, the letter M is used to refer to a mean in *APA Style*, a scientific presentation format widely used in communication.

Revisiting the data from the communication research methods questionnaire, if these 610 students are construed as sample from some larger population of interest (such as students at the university, or communication majors), then the mean of 2.373 might be denoted symbolically as $\overline{X} = 2.373$. But if these students were construed as the entire population of interest (i.e., all students enrolled in this course with me as the instructor at my university over the last 3 years who were willing to answer the question), then it would be sensible to denote this as $\mu = 2.373$.

The standard deviation of a population of measurements is typically denoted with the lower case Greek letter sigma (σ). When computed from a sample of a population, the Roman letter s is most often used to refer to the standard deviation, but some use the Greek letter sigma with a "hat" or "caret" over it, as such: $\hat{\sigma}$. In empirical articles published in the communication journals, the standard deviation is often abbreviated as "SD". The variance is denoted symbolically just as the standard deviation is, but with a square operator ("2") next to the symbol. So s^2 and $\hat{\sigma}^2$ are often used to denote the sample variance, and σ^2 to denote a population variance.

The correlation coefficient also gets its own symbol because it is so commonly used in research and statistical theory. A population correlation is typically denoted with the Greek letter ρ (pronounced "row"). In a sample, the Roman letter r is most often used to represent a correlation. But some reserve the use of the letter r to refer to Pearson's coefficient of correlation. I will follow this convention and use r only when I am talking about Pearson's coefficient of correlation.

So if you see a Greek letter in my notation in the following chapters, most likely I am referring to some kind of description of an entire population. However, Greek letters are sometimes used to refer not to descriptions of a population of measurements but instead to a theoretical statement of some kind that I believe to be true or am assuming is true. For example, if I were to say that men and women do not differ on average in communication anxiety, I could represent this symbolically as $\mu_{men} = \mu_{women}$. Or if I were to propose that there is no correlation between TV viewing frequency (X) and intelligence (Y), I could represent this as $\rho_{XY} = 0$.

4.12 Summary

After data collection, a researcher will typically want to describe what was found in the study. There are many ways of describing a collection of data, from graphical depictions of the data to numerical summaries of center, variation, and association. Familiarity with numerical, tabular, and visual means of describing research findings is crucial to not only the research process but also to understanding the material throughout this book.

Association is a concept that is especially important. When we do research we often focus our research questions and hypotheses on whether two variables are related to each other. Is there a systematic tendency for values on one variable to be paired with certain values on another variable? If so, we say that there is an association or correlation between the variables. But we have to be careful not to go too far in our interpretations of association by interpreting a relationship between variables as the result of some causal process. Statistical methods do not generally allow us to distinguish between causal and noncausal relationships, as this is a matter determined more by research design and logical argumentation than statistics. Nevertheless, as we will see in later chapters, statistics can be used to rule out some explanations for a relationship that interfere with our ability to infer cause.

Throughout this chapter, I emphasized the description of research results but said nothing about the ability to generalize or make inferences from those data. In Chapter 7, I begin to discuss the statistical tools used in communication for making statistical inferences, either about populations or about processes. We are not quite ready to tackle statistical inference yet because there are still a few fundamentals that need to be covered. With a solid understanding of the material from these first four chapters, you are now prepared to tackle probability, measurement theory and statistical means of quantifying reliability of measurement—topics of the next two chapters.

CHAPTER
FIVE

Fundamentals of Probability

Sports are important at many universities, but you don't have to be a university student to appreciate a good college football game. The city of Columbus, Ohio, gets energized every Saturday when the Ohio State University football team (the Buckeyes) plays, and the mood of the city changes tangibly. On the day of the game, Columbus residents hang flags with the university insignia from their porches and the highways and major streets seem to empty at game time. Of course, almost everyone in Columbus likes to believe that the Buckeyes are destined for the national title, and at the beginning of the season anything is possible. No doubt this scene is repeated in college towns throughout the nation.

When I started writing this book, the Buckeyes were 7–0 halfway through the season. Only a few college teams in the country had a midseason record this good, and the Buckeyes were perceived as a very good team that year, if not the best team in the Big Ten Conference. After all, what are the chances of a team winning 7 of the first 7 games in the season if there isn't something special about the team? Someone with training in statistics would want to know the answer to this before getting especially excited about the performance of any team, regardless of the sport.

Suppose you were to flip a coin 7 times. It is possible that you will get 7 heads in a row. It may not be very probable, but clearly it isn't impossible. Indeed, if you work through the mathematics (to be described in this chapter), it turns out that you could expect to get 7 heads in a row about once every 128 times that you flipped a fair coin 7 times. As such, we can say that the *probability* of getting 7 heads in a row when flipping a coin 7 times is 1/128, or .0078125. Using this same logic, if we assume that all football teams are equal in ability and whether team A or team B wins in any particular game is really just "chance," like flipping a coin, then the probability that the Buckeyes would win 7 of their first 7 games is .0078125. To put this probability into a different context, consider that you had a bag containing 127 red marbles and 1 blue marble. If you thoroughly shook the bag in order to scramble the marbles and then reached into the bag, the probability is .0078125 (i.e., 1/128) that the marble in your hand would be blue on the first draw from the bag. So the probability of winning 7 of the first 7 games "just by chance" is like the probability of pulling out that one blue marble on your first draw. Indeed, the probability of a 7–0 record halfway through the season seems quite small if you assume that all teams are equally good.

Is this relevant to communication science? Absolutely! Communication researchers use just such a procedure to test hypotheses and make inferences using data. In deriving this probability of 1/128, we have made the assumption that all teams are equal and whether the Buckeyes win or lose any specific game is like a coin flip—a 50:50 chance. Keep in mind that when we assume that the process is like a coin flip, we are assuming not only that the teams are equally good but also that whether a team wins or loses a given game has no effect on the likelihood of winning their next game. This assumption is required to argue that the process is akin to "chance." If this assumption is true, then we know that the probability of winning all of the first 7 games is pretty small— only .0078125. Given this, we can ask what the more reasonable conclusion is given the data available. Was it just a fluke that the Buckeyes won all 7 of their first 7 games that season, much like it would be a fluke to flip a coin 7 times and have it come up heads every time? Or, perhaps the assumption we made in deriving this probability is wrong. Maybe it is *not* true that all teams had an equal chance of winning. Instead, maybe the Buckeyes had a better chance of winning, perhaps because they were a better team than the ones they had played up to that point in the season. So we can use this probability to decide on what seems most reasonable about the process under investigation. Most statisticians would argue that a probability of .0078125 is too small for us to maintain the assumption used in generating the probability (that all teams are the same) and that the evidence is consistent with the claim that the Buckeyes are a better team than *at least one* of the teams they had played to date.[1]

In a similar way, we can make an assumption about some process or population we are studying with our research, collect some data, and then derive the probability of the result we obtained if an assumption we make about the process or population we are studying is true. The probability allows us to assess whether the data we obtained are consistent with the assumption we've made, and we can then decide whether the assumption is reasonable or should be rejected. The important point is that many decisions that we make when we do research are based on probabilities, so it is important to understand probability, the focus of this chapter. As you will see in later chapters, probability is the foundation of statistics, so an understanding of the concept of probability is fundamental to life as a successful communication scientist.

5.1 Defining Probability

Probability is about assigning numbers to the likelihood that certain events will occur, or, after the fact, assigning probabilities to the events that already did occur. Most understand at least conceptually what we mean by probability. What is the probability that you will have a car accident in the next year? Hopefully it is small. What is the probability that you will have to have surgery in the next month? Again, small we hope. What is the probability that your spouse will call you if he or she is running late from work? If you want him or her to call, hopefully the probability is relatively large. What is the probability that your favorite baseball team will make it to the World Series? Almost certain you might think, at the beginning of the season at least. Or perhaps your best friend just won the lottery. What is the probability of that happening? Pretty small, your intuition tells you.

---

[1] Incidently, the Buckeyes went undefeated that season and won the National Championship.

When you ask these questions, you are asking about the likelihood of some event happening. Your subjective judgment may be that the probability is very small, small, medium, large, or perhaps very large or even certain. And we intuitively understand that if the probability is very small, we know that the event is unlikely to happen, whereas if the probability is very large, the event is fairly likely to happen. This is our everyday use and understanding of probability. From a mathematical perspective, probability isn't much more difficult that this, but statisticians like to assign precise numbers to probabilities rather than the subjective labels that we use in our day-to-day language.

Probability can be a very daunting subject, and of all topics in mathematics, probability is the one area that can befuddle even experienced mathematicians. However, with some basic principles and a little patience, many problems in probability that seem complicated on the surface are not when you dig deeper. The key to success is staying organized in your thinking. But before discussing some of these basic principles, it is first worth defining the term *probability*. Probability has many technical definitions, but they all boil down to essentially the same basic idea. The probability of an event Y is the proportion of times that an event Y is expected to occur out of k "trials" or opportunities for the event to occur. So if the probability of Y, denoted $P(Y)$, is 0.30 then in 1000 "trials" or opportunities, you would expect Y to occur 300 times, because $(300/1000) = 0.30$.

A more specific way of conceptualizing probability is to consider how many different events are possible and how many meet certain criteria of interest. Probability is then defined as

$$\text{Probability} = \frac{\text{Number of qualifying events}}{\text{Number of possible events}}$$

(5.1)

Neither the numerator nor the denominator of equation 5.1 can be negative, and the denominator can never be smaller than the numerator. Therefore, probabilities are scaled to be between zero and one. Something with a zero probability cannot and will not happen, whereas something with a probability of one is certain to happen and always will.

Equation 5.1 is very abstract, so let's consider a few problems to see how it is used.

1. When you randomly draw a single card from a complete deck of cards that is thoroughly shuffled, what is the probability that you will draw a heart: $P(\text{Heart})$?

2. If your class contains 12 men and 18 women, what is the probability that if you select one student randomly, you select a male: $P(\text{Male})$?

3. In a class of 5 students, what is the probability that at least 2 students have the same birthday: $P(\text{at least 2 have same birthday})$?

To answer these questions, you need to know what to put in the numerator and the denominator of equation 5.1. Consider the first question. There are 52 unique cards in the typical deck (not counting the jokers), so there are 52 possible events when you draw a single card from a complete deck. Of these 52 possible events, how many would qualify as the event "drawing a heart?" Knowing that there are 4 suits (hearts, spades, diamonds, and clubs), and each suit has 13 cards (2, 3, 4, 5, 6, 7, 8, 9, 10, J, Q, K, A), then there must be 13 possible qualifying events, because there are 13 hearts in a deck of cards. So $P(\text{Heart}) = (13/52) = (1/4) = 0.25$. In our everyday language, this corresponds to a "1 in 4" chance.

Using this same logic, consider the second question. If there are 30 different students you could randomly select, then there are 30 different events possible, 1 for each student. If there are 12 men in the class, then 12 of the 30 possible random selections would yield a male student. So $P(\text{Male}) = (12/30) = (2/5) = 0.40$.

The third question is admittedly quite a bit tougher and I include it here in order to show that problems that seem complicated may not be so bad if you organize your thinking. First, to simplify the problem we will assume that birthdays are randomly scattered throughout the 365 days of the year and we will ignore leap years. This clearly isn't completely justified because births are somewhat more frequent in some months than others, and leap years do exist. Nevertheless, for the sake of simplification, we will make this assumption knowing that our answer is going to be only an approximation.

We know that there are 365 possible birthdates for the first person in the class, 365 possible birthdates for the second person, etc. Therefore (and this may not seem obvious at first), there are $(365)(365)(365)(365)(365) = 365^5 = 6,478,348,728,000$ combinations of 5 birthdays. In other words, there are about 6.5 trillion possible events, where an event is defined as a combination of 5 birthdays. For example, one event might be the 5 students having birthdays of August 12, June 18, October 24, November 2, and December 30. Any other combination of 5 birthdays qualifies as an event (including all birthdays being the same, or some being the same and some being different). We also know that $(365)(364)(363)(362)(361) = 6,302,555,019,000$ of the 365^5 combinations of 5 birthdays contain no birthdays that are the same. To appreciate why, consider that the first person could have any of the 365 possible birthdays, the second person could have any birthday except the birthday of the first person (otherwise they'd have the same birthday), the third could have any of the remaining 363 birthdays, an so forth. Therefore, the probability that in a group of 5 people, no one has the same birthday is $(6,302,555,019,000/6,478,348,728,000) = 0.973$.

But that is the right answer to the wrong question. The question is about the probability of *at least two students* having the same birthday, not the probability that none of them have the same birthday. However, the answer to the question of interest follows directly from 0.973. The probability that at least 2 of the students have the same birthday is $1 - 0.973 = 0.027$. Why? The answer stems from the fact that either you have no matches or at least one matching pair of birthdays in a group of 5 students. If you know the probability of no matching birthdays, then the probability of at least 1 matching pair of birthdays must be 1 minus the probability of no matching pairs.

5.2 Laws of Probability

As discussed above, probability can be a vexing topic even to the mathematician. The key to succeeding in the derivation of probabilities is staying organized. Some guidelines and rules of probability are also helpful. In this section, I introduce two laws of probability that will serve you well.

5.2.1 The Additive Law of Probability

The *additive law of probability* (or the additive *rule* of probability) states that the probability that *either* one of two events A and B will occur is equal to the sum of their individual probabilities minus the probability of them both occurring. Symbolically,

$$P(A \text{ or } B) = P(A) + P(B) - P(A \text{ and } B)$$

(5.2)

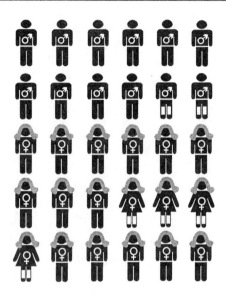

Figure 5.1 A classroom of thirty students.

Consider again the classroom with 12 men and 18 women. Suppose 10 of the men are wearing pants, and 14 of the women are wearing pants (see Figure 5.1 for a visual aid). What is the probability of randomly selecting either a man or someone wearing pants? We can answer this problem using equation 5.1 *if we are very careful.* We know there are 30 people, one of whom we will randomly select, so the number of possible events is 30. Given that there are 12 men and 24 people wearing pants, your intuition might tell you that there are $12 + 24 = 36$ qualifying events, so the probability of picking a woman or a person wearing pants is $(36/30) = 1.2$. But that can't be correct because a probability must be between zero and one. The error becomes apparent when you observe that this strategy double counts the ten men wearing pants as a qualifying event. So we have to subtract out the number of men wearing pants from the numerator of equation 5.1. There are ten men wearing pants, so the numerator becomes $12 + 24 - 10 = 26$, and the correct probability is $(26/30) = 0.867$.

Now let's derive this answer using the additive law in equation 5.2. Let A be the probability of picking a man and B be the probability of picking someone wearing pants. So $P(A) = (12/30) = 0.40$, $P(B) = (24/30) = 0.80$. From the information above we know that 10 of the men are wearing pants, so $P(A \text{ and } B) = (10/30) = 0.333$. Using equation 5.2, $P(A \text{ or } B) = 0.40 + 0.80 - 0.333 = 0.867$, which is the correct answer derived using equation 5.1.

This equation will always work, but there is a special form of the additive law of probability that applies to *mutually exclusive* events. Two events are mutually exclusive if they cannot both occur. In that case, $P(A \text{ and } B) = 0$, and the additive law reduces to $P(A \text{ or } B) = P(A) + P(B)$. Let's consider another card problem. Call event A randomly drawing a red face card from a complete deck on a single draw. Using what we know, $P(\text{Face Card}) = (6/52)$ (because there are 6 red face cards: J, Q, and K of hearts or diamonds). Call event B randomly drawing a black number card (i.e, a 2, 3, 4, 5, 6, 7, 8, 9, or 10 of either spades or clovers). We know that $P(B) = (18/52)$. In a single draw, what is the probability of picking *both* a red face card *and* a black number card, $P(A \text{ and } B)$? It could never happen in a single random draw because drawing a red face card and drawing a black number card are mutually exclusive events. No cards are both red and black. So $P(A \text{ and } B) = 0$. Therefore, by the additive law of probability applied to mutually exclusive events, $P(A \text{ or } B) = (6/52) + (18/52) = (24/52) = 0.462$. You might try deriving this answer using equation 5.1 to verify.

5.2.2   The Multiplicative Law of Probability

Another useful rule is the *multiplicative law of probability*, which states that the probability of two events A and B *both* occurring is equal to the probability of A multiplied by the *conditional probability* of B given that A has occurred. Symbolically,

$$P(A \text{ and } B) = P(A)P(B|A)$$

(5.3)

where $P(B|A)$ is the conditional probability of B given ("|") A. The A and B labels are arbitrary, so this rule can also be written as $P(A \text{ and } B) = P(B)P(A|B)$.

To illustrate this rule, let's reconsider the classroom of 30 students. What is the probability of randomly selecting a male wearing pants? If we let A be the event of randomly selecting a male and B correspond to the event of selecting someone wearing pants, then we know that $P(A) = (12/30) = 0.40$ and $P(B) = (24/30) = 0.80$. However, $P(B)$ is not relevant to the problem according to equation 5.3. What we want to know is the probability that the person selected is wearing pants given that the person selected is male, $P(B|A)$. Assuming that the person selected was male, then the probability that he is wearing pants is $(10/12) = 0.833$. This comes from the fact that 10 of the 12 men in the classroom are wearing pants—we are only considering the men in the class because we are conditioning the probability of B (wearing pants) on the knowledge that the person selected was male. So $P(B|A) = 0.833$. Therefore, the probability of selecting someone who is both male *and* wearing pants, $P(A \text{ and } B)$ is equal to $P(A)P(B|A) = (0.40)(0.833) = 0.333$ according to the multiplicative law. To illustrate that this works, consider instead using equation 5.1 to solve the problem. There are 30 people in the classroom, and of those 30 people (the number of events possible), 10 are men who are wearing pants (the number of qualifying events). So $P(A \text{ and } B) = (10/30) = 0.333$. Indeed, the multiplicative law works.

There is another form of the multiplicative probability law that is widely used in statistics. It states that if the two events A and B are *independent*, then the probability of them both occurring is equal to the product of their individual probabilities. Symbolically, the multiplicative law for independent events is expressed as such:

$$P(A \text{ and } B) = P(A)P(B), \text{if } A \text{ and } B \text{ are independent events}$$

(5.4)

But what are *independent events*? Independence is a tricky concept in probability, but it is not too difficult to master at least conceptually. Formally, two events A and B are independent if $P(B) = P(B|A)$. In words, this means that if the probability of B is the same as the probability of B given that A has occurred, then the events are independent. A classic example of independent events is the outcome of successive coin flips. If we call A the event of getting a head on the first flip and B the event of getting a head on the second flip, it should be apparent that $P(B) = P(B|A)$. The chance of getting a head on the second flip in no way is affected by whether or not you got a head on the first flip; it is the same regardless of what happened on the first flip. That is, $P(B) = P(B|A) = 0.50$. So A and B are independent events. However, randomly selecting a man (A) and randomly selecting a person with pants (B) are not independent events in the earlier problem. Why? Because $P(B) \neq P(B|A)$. We know that the probability of randomly selecting a person with pants, $P(B)$, is $(24/30) = 0.80$. But $P(B|A) \neq 0.80$. If a man was selected (A), the probability that he is wearing pants, $P(B|A)$, is $(10/12) = 0.833$.

When it is either known that two events are independent or it can be assumed that they are, then the multiplicative law of probability tells us that if some event has a constant probability $P(A)$ over k trials, then the probability of the event happening every single time (i.e., k times) is equal to $[P(A)]^k$. For example, if you flip a coin $k = 2$ times and the probability of getting a head (A) is 0.50 for each flip, then the probability of getting a head both times is $[P(A)]^2 = 0.5^2 = 0.25$. If you flip it $k = 4$ times, the probability of getting a head every time is $0.5^4 = .0625$. If you flip it 7 times, the probability of getting a head all 7 times is $0.5^7 = .0071825$. So now you see how the probability of the Buckeyes winning all 7 of their first 7 games is .0071825 if we assume that all teams are equal and who wins and who loses is like tossing a coin.

The major problem with the application of the multiplicative probability law is that it is often unknown if A and B are independent. Furthermore, you often don't have sufficient information available to determine $P(B|A)$. The example above was artificial, and I gave all the information you needed to determine $P(B|A)$. But in most real-world applications of statistics, we might have information about $P(A)$ and $P(B)$, or we can at least make some reasonable guess about those probabilities. But $P(A)$ and $P(B)$ are not sufficient to determine $P(A$ and $B)$ unless independence is known or assumed. In order to determine $P(A$ and $B)$, we need to know either $P(B|A)$ or $P(A|B)$, information that is not typically available, or we must assume that A and B are independent, an assumption that may not be warranted.

But it is possible in some circumstances to determine whether the assumption of independence is reasonable or not by considering a different way of thinking about what it means for two events to be independent. If two events are independent, then knowledge about whether or not event A has occurred should provide no information about the relatively likelihood of event B. In symbols, two events A and B are independent if $P(B|A) = P(B|\text{not } A)$, where "not A" means that A did *not* occur. So you need to ask whether $P(B|A)$ is likely to be the same as $P(B|\text{not } A)$. Consider two events: randomly selecting a male from the class in the example above (A) and randomly selecting a person taller than 6 feet (B). We know $P(A) = (12/30) = 0.40$, and suppose we knew that 6 people in class are taller than 6 feet, so $P(B) = 0.20$. What is the probability of randomly selecting a male taller than 6 feet, $P(A$ and $B)$? From the information provided, both $P(A|B)$ and $P(B|A)$ are unknown, so equation 5.3 can't be used. You might be tempted to use equation 5.4 and claim that $P(A$ and $B) = (0.40)(0.20) = 0.08$. But this application of the multiplicative probability law assumes A and B are independent events. Is this a reasonable assumption? To answer this question, ask whether the chance that the person you randomly select from the class is taller than 6 feet would depend on whether the person you selected was male (A) or female (not A). If not, then $P(B|A) = P(B|\text{not } A)$ and the events are independent. But it should be clear that the chance that the person selected is greater than 6 feet is probably different depending on whether you selected a male or female because males are, on average, taller than females. So even though you have no information about the heights of the 30 men and women in the class, it is probably safe to assume that A and B are not independent.

Therefore you can't use equation 5.4 to determine the probability that the person you randomly select is both male and taller than 6 feet. From the information provided here, this probability cannot be determined. Such is typically the case in statistics. Nevertheless, the multiplicative probability law has a variety of uses in statistics, as you will see in the next and later chapters.

5.3   Probability Distributions

In Chapter 4, I discussed distributions of data and how to graphically depict a distribution. In probability, we often talk about a related concept, the *probability distribution*. A probability distribution lists the probabilities of events in the distribution of all possible events. Consider the number of heads in 3 coin flips. There are 3 possible events when flipping a coin 3 times: no heads, 1 head, 2 heads, or 3 heads. That covers all the possibilities. To derive the probability distribution, we can easily list out the possible outcomes of 3 coin flips: HHH, THH, HTH, HHT, HTT, THT, TTH, TTT. As you can see, there are 8 possible outcomes of a sequence of three coin flips. Of these eight, only one sequence of coin flips produces no heads, so $P(0 \text{ heads}) = (1/8) = 0.125$. By the same reasoning, $P(1 \text{ head}) = (3/8) = 0.375$, because 3 of the 8 sequences includes only a single head, and $P(2 \text{ heads}) = 0.375$, and $P(3 \text{ heads}) = 0.125$. These 4 events (number of heads) and their probabilities represent the probability distribution for the number of heads in 3 coin flips. Defining X as the number of heads in 3 coin flips, the probability distribution can be represented as such:

$$P(X) = \begin{cases} 0.125 & \text{for } X = 0 \\ 0.375 & \text{for } X = 1 \\ 0.375 & \text{for } X = 2 \\ 0.125 & \text{for } X = 3 \end{cases}$$

In any probability distribution the probabilities of the events in the distribution must sum to one. Notice that is true here, as $P(0 \text{ heads}) + P(1 \text{ head}) + P(2 \text{ heads}) + P(3 \text{ heads}) = 1$.

An event can also be a measurement. For example, what is the probability distribution for the number of hours an adult living in the United States watches TV on a typical day? It would be impossible to know this without asking every adult resident of the United States. But we could estimate the probability distribution by randomly sampling, say, 1,000 people from this population. An estimate of the probability distribution could be easily derived from a frequency distribution of the observed measurements. For example, suppose just for illustration that in 1,000 people randomly sampled from the U.S. population, 20 reported that they watch no TV on a typical day, 150 reported that they watch one hour a day on the typical day, 350 report watching two hours, 200 report three hours, 150 report four hours, and 130 report five or more hours on a typical day. In that case, $P(0 \text{ hours}) \approx 0.02, P(1 \text{ hour}) \approx 0.15, P(2 \text{ hours}) \approx 0.35, P(3 \text{ hours}) \approx 0.20, P(4 \text{ hours}) \approx 0.15, P(5 \text{ or more hours}) \approx 0.13$. (The "$\approx$" symbol means approximately). So an estimate of an unknown probability distribution can be derived from a sample from that population. But it is important to remember that the estimate of a population probability distribution derived from a sample frequency distribution, such as in this example, is just that—an estimate. The accuracy of the estimate depends on the quality of the sample and its size, as will be discussed in a later chapter.

Statisticians use many different probability distributions regularly. However, there are two that have special importance in research as well as the theory of statistical inference. It is worth spending time on each.

5.3.1   The Binomial Probability Distribution

The binomial distribution is useful for describing the probability distribution for counts of events that follow a *binomial process*. A process can be said to be a binomial process if the probability of the event occurring at time t remains constant over time and is unaffected by whether the event occurred at any prior time. The coin tossing example above is an example of a probability distribution resulting from a binomial process. The probability of getting a head remains constant over time, and whether you get a head or not on any given flip is unaffected by whether or not you got a head previously. So the number of heads you get in a certain number of flips is governed by a binomial process, and the probability of getting a certain number of heads in a certain number of flips can be described with the binomial probability distribution.

The Ohio State Buckeyes win-loss record could also be considered a binomial process if you can assume that whether the Buckeyes win a given game is determined by a process similar to flipping a coin. Notice that in addition to assuming that the probability of winning is the same for each game, we are also assuming that the probability of a win is unaffected by whether or not the Buckeyes won a previous game. To a sports fan this may seem unreasonable, but nevertheless, it is an assumption that we can make—an assumption that is testable with data. If this assumption seems unwarranted, you are essentially saying that the number of wins cannot be described using the binomial probability distribution.

Binomial probabilities are computed with the binomial formula:

$$P(k) = \left(\frac{m!}{k!(m-k)!} \right) p^k (1-p)^{m-k}$$

(5.5)

where p equals the probability of the event, m is the number of trials or repetitions, and k is the number of times the event occurs. The complicated expression in parentheses quantifies the number of unique combinations of k objects that can be constructed from a set of m objects, $m \geq k$. The "!" symbol is called a *factorial*. The factorial of a number is the number multiplied by the next smallest number, multiplied by the next smallest number, and so forth, down to 1. For example $4! = (4 \times 3 \times 2 \times 1) = 24$. For convenience and by definition, $0! = 1$.

Equation 5.5 looks complicated, but it isn't too bad if you stay organized. Consider the probability distribution for the number of heads in 3 coin flips. We want to know the probability of getting zero ($k = 0$) heads in a sequence of 3 tosses ($m = 3$), assuming that the probability of getting a head is 0.5 ($p = 0.50$) for each flip. Plugging in the numbers into equation 5.5

$$P(0) = \left(\frac{3!}{0!(3-0)!}\right)0.5^0(1-0.5)^{3-0}$$

$$= \left(\frac{3 \times 2 \times 1}{1(3 \times 2 \times 1)}\right)1.0(0.5)^3$$

$$= \left(\frac{6}{6}\right)1.0(0.125)$$

$$= 0.125$$

So the probability of getting zero heads in 3 flips is 0.125. What about 2 heads in 3 flips?:

$$P(2) = \left(\frac{2!}{2!(3-2)!}\right)0.5^2(1-0.5)^{3-2}$$

$$= \left(\frac{3 \times 2 \times 1}{2 \times 1 \times (1)}\right)0.25(0.5)^1$$

$$= \left(\frac{6}{2}\right)0.25(0.5)$$

$$= 0.375$$

If you worked out all values of k from zero to three, you'd get the probability distribution that we earlier derived intuitively.

Let's use the binomial distribution to ask what the probability is of the Buckeyes winning 6 or more games in 7, assuming that all teams are equal in ability throughout the season and thus the probability of winning remains constant at 0.5 (like a coin flip). To answer this question, we need to know the probability of winning 6 games and we also need to know the probability of winning 7 games. Why? Because winning 6 games OR winning 7 games satisfies the criterion of winning 6 or more. Once we know these probabilities, we can add them up in accordance with the additive law of probability for the case of mutually exclusive events. The events are mutually exclusive because a team can't win both 6 of the first 7 and 7 of the first 7. Here we go:

$$P(6) = \left(\frac{7!}{6!(7-6)!}\right)0.5^6(1-0.5)^{7-6}$$

$$= \left(\frac{7 \times 6 \times 5 \times 4 \times 3 \times 2 \times 1}{6 \times 5 \times 4 \times 3 \times 2 \times 1 \times (1)}\right)0.015625(0.5)^1$$

$$= 0.0546875$$

and for $P(7)$:

$$P(7) = \left(\frac{7!}{7!(7-7)!}\right)0.5^7(1-0.5)^{7-7}$$

$$= \left(\frac{7 \times 6 \times 5 \times 4 \times 3 \times 2 \times 1}{7 \times 6 \times 5 \times 4 \times 3 \times 2 \times 1 \times (1)}\right)0.0078125(0.5)^0$$

$$= 0.0078125$$

So the probability of winning 6 or 7 games, $P(6 \text{ or } 7)$, is $P(6) + P(7) = 0.0546875 + 0.0078125 = .0625$.

Table 5.1

Probability Distribution for the Number of Wins in 7 Games

# of wins	$P(\#$ wins) if $p = 0.50$	$P(\#$ wins) if $p = 0.75$	$P(\#$ wins) if $p = 0.20$
0	0.0078	0.0001	0.2097
1	0.0547	0.0013	0.3670
2	0.1641	0.0115	0.2753
3	0.2734	0.0577	0.1147
4	0.2734	0.1730	0.0287
5	0.1641	0.3115	0.0043
6	0.0547	0.3115	0.0004
7	0.0078	0.1335	< 0.0001

And what about the probability of winning at least 1 game? It might seem that you'd have to do a lot of computations to answer this question. The probability of winning at least 1 game is $P(1) + P(2) + P(3) + P(4) + P(5) + P(6) + P(7)$. However, all we need to know is the probability of winning no games, $P(0)$. That probability is .0078125 from the binomial formula, or more simply from the multiplicative law of probability for independent events. Define X as the number of *losses*. In that case, we know that $P(7) = 0.5^7$. But if X is the number of losses, then the probability of 7 losses is equal to the probability of no wins if X is redefined as the number of wins. So the probability of zero wins (that is, seven losses) is equal to $0.5^7 = 0.0078125$. If you didn't zero games, then you must have won at least 1 game, so the probability of winning at least one game is one minus the probability of winning zero games (because the sum of the values in a probability distribution must sum to 1). So P(win at least one) = $1 - 0.0078125 = 0.9921875$. In other words, assuming all teams are equally good, a specific team is nearly certain to win at least one game, but from earlier computations, relatively unlikely to win six or more (again, assuming the assumption we have made is true).

So the binomial formula can be used to generate the probability distribution for the number of wins in 7 games, assuming that the outcome of each game is like a coin flip (and thereby independent with a constant probability that the team will win equal to 0.5). Of course, it can be used if we make any other assumption about the probability of winning each game, such as if the team were better than others (e.g., $p = 0.75$) or worse than others (e.g., $p = 0.20$). These probability distributions can be found in Table 5.1.

But so what? How is this useful to communication researchers? Getting a bit ahead of ourselves, researchers often use statistics to test many hypotheses in a study, and when we do this, there is always the possibility that they we be wrong at least once and make a claim that we should not make. For example, suppose that a researcher tests three hypotheses in a study but that, unknown to the researcher, in each case the hypothesis is incorrect. As introduced in a later chapter, there is a certain probability that even though a specific hypothesis is wrong, the researcher's statistical test will lead the researcher to claim that the hypothesis is correct. Suppose that the probability of incorrectly claiming a specific hypothesis being tested is correct when it is in fact wrong is 0.05 (p). Using the binomial formula, the probability distribution for the number of hypotheses correctly deemed supported that are in fact incorrect (k) in 3 tests ($m = 3$) is

$$P(k) = \begin{cases} 0.8574 & \text{for } k = 0 \\ 0.1354 & \text{for } k = 1 \\ 0.0071 & \text{for } k = 2 \\ 0.0001 & \text{for } k = 3 \end{cases}$$

From this probability distribution for the number of hypotheses incorrectly deemed supported, we can say that the probability of making at least one such mistake in this situation is $P(k > 0) = 1 - P(k = 0) = 0.143$. Some researchers would say that the probability of making at least one such mistake in a set of 3 tests is too large, and something needs to be done to bring this probability down. This is called the *multiple test problem*, and in Chapter 14, I introduce some ways of dealing with it.

5.3.2   The Normal Probability Distribution

The binomial probability distribution is known as a *discrete probability distribution*, because it is a distribution that can be used to describe the distribution of a discrete variable whose values are determined by a binomial process. Of all discrete probability distributions, the binomial distribution is probably one of the most important. Another important probability distribution is the *normal probability distribution*, or its standardized equivalent, the *standard normal probability distribution*. The normal probability distribution is a *continuous probability distribution*, in that the characteristics of the normal distribution can apply only to a continuous variable. However, it is sometimes used to describe the distribution of noncontinuous variables, although variables that are not continuous or nearly so could never be truly normally distributed.

The normal distribution is graphically depicted in Figure 5.2. The height of the line in Figure 5.2 depicts the frequency of an event, with that event being represented as the point on the number line at the bottom. The normal distribution is entirely defined by its mean (μ) and standard deviation (σ). In the case of a standard normal distribution, $\mu = 0$ and $\sigma = 1$, as discussed in section 4.6. Notice that the normal distribution is a symmetrical distribution, in that the left half of the normal distribution is a mirror image of the right half. Notice as well that most of the normal distribution is clustered near the mean. That is, a normally distributed variable will tend to have the bulk of its possible measurements near the mean. In addition, more extreme measurements on either side of the mean are increasingly unlikely in a normal distribution. As the distance from the mean increases, the relative frequency or probability of those measurements decreases. Although not technically appropriate, many people are happy to call any distribution that has this elegant "bell-shaped" appearance a normal distribution, but as we will see, a truly normal distribution has some particular features—features that may be absent from other "bell-shaped" distributions.

It is often said that the normal distribution is an amazing fact of nature, in that variables social scientists measure are very often normally distributed. Although there is some truth to the claim that many variables that communication researchers may have an interest in measuring are perhaps normal-like in appearance, in fact, very few probability distributions for things that any communication researcher measures are truly normal (c.f., Micceri, 1989). If you look closely enough, many things that appear normal are not. Even so, the normal distribution is worth becoming familiar

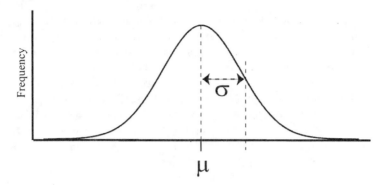

Figure 5.2 The normal distribution.

with because many things can be considered approximately normal, and the normal distribution is very important in the theory of statistical inference discussed in later chapters.

One of the features of a normal distribution is that the possible measurements for a variable that is well described with the normal probability distribution follow a particular pattern. First, in a population that is exactly normal on a particular variable, the mean, the median, and the mode of that variable are the same. Second, if a distribution is exactly normal and you know the mean and standard deviation, the *68–95–99.7 rule* (also called the *empirical rule*) allows you to determine the proportion of possible measurements that fall between particular values in the distribution (see Figure 5.3). This rule states that in a normal distribution, 68% of measurements are within 1 standard deviation of the mean, 95% are within 2 standard deviations of the mean, and 99.7% are within 3 standard deviations of the mean. This can be used to solve some interesting probability problems.

Another way of thinking about the empirical rule is that if you were to take a random sample of size $n = 1$ and measure that unit on a variable that is known to

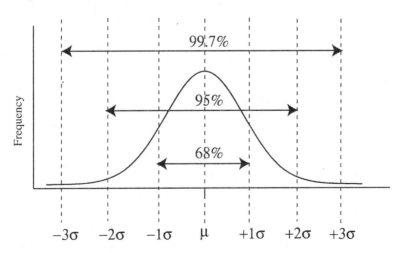

Figure 5.3 The 68–95–99.7 rule.

be normally distributed, then the probability that the measurement for that randomly selected unit will be within 1 standard deviation of the mean is 0.68, the probability it will be within 2 standard deviations of the mean is 0.95, and the probability it will be within 3 standard deviations of the mean is 0.997. In other words, almost every measurement you take will be within 3 standard deviations of the mean, and most will be within 2 standard deviations if the variable is normally distributed.

Let's apply this rule to see what it buys us. Suppose you know that in a population of interest to you scores on a measure of shyness are normal with $\mu = 120$ and $\sigma = 15$. Given this, then you know that about 68% of the people in the population are between 105 and 135 (± 1 standard deviation), 95% are between 90 and 150 (± 2 standard deviations), and nearly every person is between 75 and 165 (± 3 standard deviations). But you can go farther than this using this rule. You also know that about 84% of the people score no more than 135. How did I figure that? Think about it carefully. First, because the normal distribution is symmetrical and the median is the same as the mean, that means that 50% of the scores are below the mean of 120. We also know that 68% of the people are within one standard deviation of the mean of 120, and because the normal distribution is symmetrical, that means that half of those 68% (i.e., 34%) must be between the mean and one standard deviation above the mean. But 135 is the score that is one standard deviation above the mean. So 50% (all those below the mean) plus 34% (scores between 120 and 135) equals 84%. Thus, 84% of the people score no more than 135.

If we know that a probability distribution is normal, it is possible to determine the probability of a particular event from that distribution, or to assess the probability post hoc of some event that did occur. For example, *Interaction Involvement* is a construct introduced by Cegala (1981) to refer to the extent to which people are cognitively and behaviorally involved during conversation with others. Cognitive and behavioral involvement includes such things as paying attention when others speak, responding appropriately during conversation, and not losing oneself in one's thoughts during the conversation. Although interaction involvement can certainly vary within a person from situation to situation, it is also reasonable to construe it as a stable individual difference—some people tend to be more involved than others across conversations and interaction contexts. Suppose that scores on the *Interaction Involvement* scale are normally distributed in a population of interest to you, with $\mu = 70$ and $\sigma = 12$. If so, then the probability that someone randomly selected from this population has an interaction involvement score (X) of 82 or more is about 0.16. That is, $P(X \geq 82) = 0.16$. How so? First, ask how many standard deviations from the mean is 82. Converting 82 to a Z-score gives us the answer (recall from section 4.6 that a Z-score quantifies a case's distance from the mean in standard deviation units). If $\mu = 70$ and $\sigma = 12$, then 82 corresponds to a score a Z-score of $(82 - 70)/12 = 1$ (from Equation 4.7). From the empirical rule, we know that the probability that a measurement is one standard deviation *or more* from the mean is 0.32 (from $1 - 0.68$), and the symmetrical nature of the normal distribution means that this 0.32 probability is split equally between the two tails of the distribution. Therefore, $P(X \geq 82) = P(Z \geq 1) = 0.16$. [2] This is illustrated graphically in Figure 5.4

---

[2] As a continuous probability distribution, in theory, the probability that $X =$ any specific value is equal to zero. For example, if X is normally distributed with $\mu = 120$ and $\sigma = 15$, $P(X = 135) = 0$. Therefore, $P(X > 135) = P(X \geq 135)$. So when solving such problems, it is not necessary to distinguish between $P(X > y)$ and $P(X \geq y)$, where y is any possible value in the distribution.

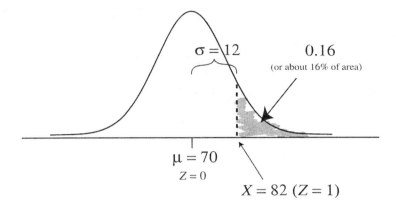

Figure 5.4 The proportion of measurements more than one standard deviation from the mean of a normally distributed variable.

With a table of normal probabilities (Appendix A) or the help of a decent statistics program, it is possible to assign very precise probabilities to events from a normal probability distribution. For example, what is the probability that any randomly selected person has a score between 49 and 82 on the *Interaction Involvement Scale* (X) if we assume the population distribution is normal with a $\mu = 70$ and $\sigma = 12$? We know that 82 corresponds to a Z-score of one, and 40 corresponds to a Z-score of $(49 - 70)/12 = -1.75$. So we need to compute the proportion of scores in the distribution that are less than one standard deviation above the mean and no more than 1.75 standard deviations below the mean. Symbolically, the problem can be phrased as such:

$$P(49 \leq X \leq 82) = P(-1.75 \leq Z \leq 1.00) = ?$$

Appendix A contains the information we need to solve this problem. The entries in the table in Appendix A are $P(X > Z)$ if X is distributed as standard normal, as a Z score is if the original variable is normally distributed. The size of the shaded area in Figure 5.5 is what we are interested in computing. What proportion of the total area under the normal distribution falls in the shaded area? There are many ways of going about this computation. Perhaps the easiest approach to is to compute the area that is not sketched in gray, and then subtract this area from one (because the proportion of measurements in the distribution *somewhere* is 1). We know already that the proportion of measurements greater than 1 standard deviation above the mean is about 0.16. So $P(Z > 1) = 0.16$. (Actually, from Appendix A, we see that the exact proportion is .1587). Now all we need to know is the area to the left of (or less than) a Z-score of -1.75. Because the normal distribution is symmetrical, we can rephrase this question by asking what proportion of the area falls to the *right* of a Z-score of $+1.75$ (in other words, that is greater than 1.75 standard deviations above the mean). That is, $P(Z < -1.75) = P(Z > 1.75)$. Appendix A tells us that the answer is about 0.04 (or 4%). It is also true that the proportion of area to the left of -1.75 (or less than 49) is about 0.04 because the normal distribution is symmetrical. Adding this 0.04 to the 0.16 we know that is greater than 82 ($Z = 1$) tells us that about 20% of the scores in this distribution are greater than 82 or less than 49. Therefore, about 80% of the scores are between 49 and 82 (because $100\% - 20\% = 80\%$). So the probability of randomly selecting someone scoring between 49 and 82 on the *Interaction Involvement*

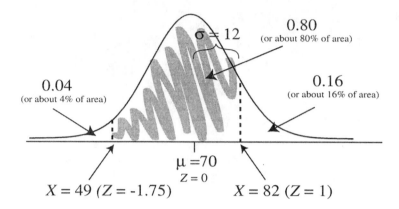

Figure 5.5 The proportion of measurements less than one standard deviation above the mean and no more than 1.75 standard deviations below the mean of a normally distributed variable.

Scale is about 0.80 assuming $\mu = 70$ and $\sigma = 12$. These normal curve problems (as they are often called) are challenging at first but once you master the use of Appendix A, they become quite simple.

An examination of Figure 5.5 reveals other ways that this problem could be solved. For example, we could first determine the proportion of people with scores greater than than 49 (that is, with $Z > -1.75$). From Appendix A, that number is about 0.96, from $1 - P(Z < -1.75)$ or $1 - P(Z > 1.75)$. Next, ask what proportion of people in the distribution have a score greater than 82 $(Z > 1)$? From Appendix A (or the 68–95–99.7 rule), that proportion is about 0.16. Therefore, the proportion of people between 49 and 82 must be about $0.96 - 0.16 = 0.80$.

Here is another question to illustrate the kinds of problems that can be solved with Appendix A. If scores on the *Interaction Involvement Scale* are normally distributed with $\mu = 70$ and $\sigma = 12$, what score defines the 95th percentile of the distribution? In other words, what *Interaction Involvement Score* does 95% of the population score less than? This problem is illustrated graphically in Figure 5.6. To answer this question, we need to know the value of Z that cuts off the upper 5% of the area under the normal distribution from the rest of the distribution. From Appendix A, we look for the entry in the table as close as we can find to 0.05. The closest Z-score is 1.64. Now, all we need to do is translate a Z-score of 1.64 back to the original metric on the *Interaction Involvement Scale*. Recalling equation 4.8, $X = \text{Mean} + Z(SD) = 70 + 1.64(12) = 89.68$. So if interaction involvement scores are normally distributed with $\mu = 70$ and $\sigma = 12$, then 95% of scores are less than about 90. A good statistics program will have built in procedures for computing normal probabilities. In SPSS, for example, the function CDF.NORMAL(X, μ, σ) will return the proportion of the area under the normal distribution less than X if the distribution of X is normal with mean μ and standard deviation σ. The IDF.NORMAL(p, μ, σ) function reverses this process, returning the value that cuts off the lower 100p% of a normal distribution with mean μ and standard deviation σ. But even though computers can do a lot of these computations for you, you should be comfortable using the table in Appendix A.

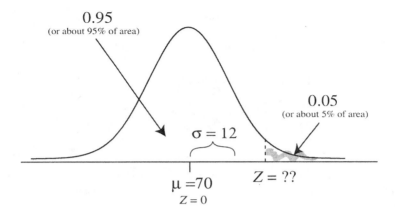

Figure 5.6 Setting up a problem to solve for percentile scores.

5.3.3   Chebychev's Theorem

It is tempting but a mistake to apply the 68–95–99.7 rule or the table in Appendix A to variables that are not normally distributed. To apply this rule or the table to the problem, you must have either the knowledge, a strong and justifiable belief, or at least be willing to make the assumption that the probability distribution of the variable is normal. For other probability distributions, the lessons described above do not apply. But there is an interesting theorem in statistics known as *Chebychev's Theorem* that will allow you to solve similar types of problems without making any assumptions whatsoever about the shape of the distribution. Chebychev's Theorem states that regardless of the shape of the distribution, the proportion of cases that fall within k standards deviations of the mean of the distribution is no less than $1 - (1/k^2)$, where k is at least 1 (the theorem does not apply for $k < 1$). So knowing the mean and standard deviation of a distribution, we can say, for example, that the proportion of cases that are within 2 standard deviations of the mean is *at least* $1 - (1/2^2) = 0.75$. And the proportion of cases that are within 3 standard deviations of the mean is at least $1 - (1/3^2) = 0.889$. So if we knew (or could approximate) the mean and standard deviation of the distribution of scores on some variable in a population of interest, we could say that the probability is at least 0.75 of randomly selecting someone within two standard deviations of the mean. This would be correct regardless of the shape of the population distribution on that variable. This is also true whether talking about samples or populations. So if you know only the mean and standard deviation of a variable in a data set, you can use Chebychev's Theorem to determine the minimum proportion of cases between certain values on that variable.

5.4   Random Variables and Expected Values

The number of heads in 3 coin flips is a *random variable*. So is the number of hours that someone randomly selected from a population reports watching TV on a typical day. And so is that person's *Interaction Involvement* score. And so is pretty much every variable that communication scientists measure. A random variable is any variable that can have two or more values, with the frequency of those possible values being defined by the probability distribution for the variable. We sometimes describe the properties of a random variable by referring to its probability distribution, if known. For example, if X is the number of heads in 3 coin flips, then we'd say X is a random variable distributed as binomial with parameters 3 and 0.5, where 3 is the number of trials and 0.5 is the probability of the event (i.e., heads). Symbolically, we say $X \sim B(3, 0.5)$, where $\sim$ means "is distributed as". If a random variable X is normally distributed with mean 15 and standard deviation 2, then we say that $X \sim \mathcal{N}(15, 2)$. More generally, the notation $X \sim \mathcal{N}(\mu, \sigma)$ refers to a random normal variable X with mean μ and standard deviation σ. Random variables can have any number of probability distributions, either known or unknown in form.

Random variables have *expected values*, often denoted with the letter E followed by something in parentheses. For example, if you were to flip a coin 3 times, about how many heads would you expect to get? If we define X as the number of heads in 3 coin flips and assume $X \sim B(3, 0.5)$, then the question can be framed as a question about $E(X)$. What is $E(X)$? The answer to this question isn't obvious, but there is an answer, and it will seem strange: $E(X) = 1.5$. What? How could you "expect" to get 1.5 heads in 3 coin flips? Indeed, it isn't actually possible to get one and a half heads in 3 flips of a coin. Nevertheless, the expected number of heads is still 1.5. The concept of expected value leads to seemingly silly but statistically justifiable statements like a person can expect to have 1.9 children in his or her lifetime. The expected value of a random variable is a concept that seems to defy both logic and intuition. Nevertheless, it is a useful concept.

The expected value of a random variable has different mathematical definitions depending on whether the variable is continuous or discrete. The definition of expected value for continuous variables requires calculus (if you are familiar with calculus, see Box 5.1 for details), so I will focus on the definition for discrete variables because the concept is a little easier to understand without a background in calculus. For a discrete random variable,

$$E(X) = \sum P(X_i) X_i$$

(5.6)

where X_i is a possible value of the random variable X, $P(X_i)$ is the probability of X_i according to the probability distribution of X, and the summation is over all i possible values of X. Let's apply the formula to the probability distribution for the number of heads in 3 coin flips. Recall that there are 4 possible events. Let $X_0 = 0$, meaning zero heads. Earlier we determined that $P(0) = 0.125$. Let $X_1 = 1$, meaning a single head. We derived earlier that $P(1) = .375$, and we also determined that $P(2) = 0.375$, and $P(3) = 0.125$. So $E(X) = 0.125(0) + 0.375(1) + 0.375(2) + 0.125(3) = 1.5$.

We could rephrase this in terms of proportions. What is the expected proportion of the number of heads in 3 flips? Let X be a random variable defined as the proportion of heads in three flips. The possible values of X are $X_0 = 0, X_1 = 0.333, X_2 = 0.667$, and $X_3 = 1$ and $P(X_0) = 0.125, P(X_1) = 0.375, P(X_2) = 0.375, P(X_3) = 0.125$. Therefore, the expected proportion of heads in 3 flips is $E(X) = .125(0) + .375(.333) + .375(.667) + .125(1) = 0.5$. Now this makes sense! The expected proportion of times that you will get heads in 3 flips is 0.50, just as you'd think it should be. And it is no coincidence that the expected number of heads is 3 times the expected proportion of heads. Indeed, for any random variable $X \sim B(n, p)$, $E(X) = np$.

This is not trivial or purely in the realm of theory. It has tremendous value because it turns out that the expected value of a random variable X is usually equal to the mean of that random variable. That is, $E(X) = \mu$. This is true for most continuous and

---

Box 5.1: Calculating the Expected Value of a Continuous Random Variable

Just as a discrete random variable has an expected value, so does a continuous random variable. However, the symbolic notation of the expected value of a continuous random variable requires calculus. The expected value of a continuous random variable X is equal to

$$E(X) = \int X f(X) dX$$

where $f(X)$ is the *probability density function* of X. The $\int$ symbol is the indefinite integral in calculus. The probability density function is a function that can be used to derive the probability that X falls between certain values in the range of possible values of X. For example, the probability density function for the normal distribution is

$$f(X) = \frac{1}{\sqrt{2\pi}\sigma} e^{-(X-\mu)^2/2\sigma^2}$$

and calculus verifies that

$$\int X \frac{1}{\sqrt{2\pi}\sigma} e^{-(X-\mu)^2/2\sigma^2} dX = \mu$$

So if you were to randomly sample a single unit from a population and measure it on a variable that is normally distributed, the expected value of that measurement is the population mean. Different continuous probability distributions have different probability density functions. But it is almost always true that the expected value of a continuous random variable is the population mean.

---

discrete distributions that you are ever likely to encounter. For example, suppose that the probability distribution of X is normal with $\mu = 10$ and $\sigma = 2$ (i.e., $X \sim \mathcal{N}(10, 2)$). Then $E(X) = 10$. This means that if we randomly selected a case from this distribution and measured it on that variable, the expected value of that measurement is μ, or 10. This is true even if μ is not a possible measurement.

Why does all this matter? As will be discussed in Chapter 7, we can apply this concept to estimating characteristics of a population from a random sample of that population, and we don't even need to know the probability distribution of the random variable in order to do so. For example, if you randomly sample from a population and measure each unit in the sample on some random variable X, the expected value of the sample mean is equal to the population mean. That is, $E(\overline{X}) = \mu$. This also applies to sample proportions, although it is helpful to use different symbols to denote the relationship between a population proportion and its expected value. Public opinion pollsters and communication researchers interested in public opinion are often interesting in estimating, for example, the proportion of people who are going to vote for a given candidate in the next election, the proportion that agree that federal government is doing a good job, or any number of other indices of people's sentiment toward political issues, government, and the like. Perhaps the pollster wants to estimate the proportion of people who are likely to vote in the next election. Let's call the population proportion π, the symbol often used to denote a population proportion (and easily confused with the number pi, also denoted as π, which is 3.1415. Unless stated otherwise, when you see the "π" symbol, assume I am referring to a population proportion and not the number pi). From a random sample, an estimate of that proportion can be derived. Call that sample estimate $\hat{\pi}$ (pronounced "pie-hat"). The sample proportion $\hat{\pi}$ has a probability distribution, and if good sampling procedures are employed, the expected value of $\hat{\pi}$ is π. That is, $E(\hat{\pi}) = \pi$. Just how this works and how we apply this important idea to the estimation of population information from a sample of a population is the topic of Chapter 7.

5.5   Summary

Communication researchers use probability all the time when testing hypotheses and making inferences from their data. The examples presented in this chapter may seem far disconnected from what communication researchers do. We rarely flip coins or draw cards from shuffled decks when doing communication research (although some of my colleagues discuss research while playing cards at academic conferences). These examples are used to illustrate some more general principles that are important for understanding the concept of probability. Comfort with the notion of probability will prove indispensable for understanding much of the rest of this book. Even though we don't draw cards or flips coins when conducting research, we often do measure random variables. We often don't know the population probability distribution for the random variables that we measure, and fortunately we don't typically need to because the concept of expected value allows us to formulate and describe statistical principles important to estimation and hypothesis testing, things that communication researchers do routinely.

CHAPTER SIX

Assessing and Quantifying Reliability

Here is a simple thought exercise. Imagine measuring a group of 100 people on any construct that might interest you, using one of the many measurement tools communication researchers have at their disposal for doing so. You might ask these 100 people to evaluate a political figure on a feeling thermometer, or request them to indicate on a 1 to 10 scale how likely they would be to buy a product after showing them an advertisement for the product, or have them respond to the *Communication Anxiety Inventory,* or provide their attitudes toward birth control by responding to a series of questions that you can use to generate a quantification of their attitude. At the end of this process, you'd have a measurement of each of these 100 participants—a set of *observed scores* or *observed measurements* quantifying each person on the construct you have measured. Now imagine repeating this a week later using these same 100 people using exactly the same procedure, resulting in another set of 100 observed scores quantifying each person on the same construct you had previously measured them on. With measurements of each person at two different times, you could determine how many of the participants responded consistently, providing you with the same observed score at both occasions. About how many of the 100 people do you think would provide a consistent response?

I leave this question unanswered, in part because there is no one correct answer, but also to show you some data resulting from just such a procedure on a slightly smaller scale. In Table 6.1, you will find the data from 15 students who took a communication research methods course from me who were asked to fill out the *Television Affinity Scale* twice, once on the first day of class and again a week later. I regularly do this exercise at the beginning of each academic term, and when I show the students a table containing their own data, they are usually quite shocked. Notice here that of these 15 students, only 4 had the same score on both occasions. When the students are probed, most admit that over a course of a week, their beliefs about the importance of television in their lives had not changed, at least as far as they are aware. And yet they responded differently the second time to these same questions, in some cases quite differently.

Perhaps these 15 students simply don't have good insight into how their own beliefs and attitudes fluctuate over time. To be sure, some of our thinking, the opinions we

Table 6.1
Television Affinity Scale Scores for 15 Students Measured Twice

							Student								
	1	2	3	4	5	6	7	8	9	10	11	12	13	14	15
Time 1	5	5	11	15	18	9	17	10	14	10	9	5	8	11	13
Time 2	5	11	12	13	17	9	17	13	16	12	8	8	9	11	12

hold, and our decisions can be influenced by small events outside of our conscious awareness. Maybe this lack of consistency is attributable to true change, but change that these students couldn't articulate or even recognize. Perhaps, but it is likely that at least some if not all of the fluctuations in measurement observed here are attributable to nothing other than "chance"—to sporadic and largely unmeasurable forces that affect the way we interpret a question at the moment it is asked, how much time we take answering it, what we happen to have on our minds at the time we have to formulate a response, and our interest in devoting the necessary cognitive energy to give a thoughtful response.

Such "chance" forces are inherent in the measurement process itself, and we cannot entirely eliminate their influence on measurement. They operate in every measurement context, even when there is no way that true change has occurred. For example, if I asked you to pace out the distance from the front door of your place of residence to the street you live on each day for a week, your measurement of the distance would probably vary from day to day, even though the true distance between your home and the street most certainly does not. Depending on how much you slept the night before, whether you had just eaten a big meal, how much of your attention you dedicate to the task itself, and whether you are wearing your boots or your slippers on a given day can affect the length of your stride, how accurately you count out the steps, and the decision as you are approaching the street where your property ends and the street begins.

If such forces operate on the measurement process as a matter of routine, then how are we to trust any of the measurements that we take on research units in our empirical studies as accurate? For instance, if these 15 students were participants in a study of mine on correlates of television affinity, how can I know what each person's "true" television affinity is knowing that their answers to my questions seem to depend on when I ask them and forces out of my control?

In theory, you can never know for certain a person's "true" score on what you are measuring. The "true" score can be thought of as the measurement that a research unit would provide to you in the absence of any of these forces that conspire to produce the kinds of variations in measurement over time depicted in Table 6.1. There will almost always be some discrepancy between the measurements you obtain (the *observed scores*) on any one occasion and the "true" scores. These discrepancies are called *measurement error*, and they are something we have to live with as researchers. But it is possible, armed with a little theory, to assess *how much* measurement error pervades a set of measurements or to assess how much measurement error a measuring instrument tends to produce. We can minimize the influence measurement error has on the scientific process by using measuring instruments that tend to produce little measurement error or by discounting research claims based on measurement procedures that probably contain lots of this random measurement error (by, for instance, not allowing studies using such methods to be published or otherwise guiding the evolution of scientific knowledge on a topic).

In this chapter, I introduce a variety of means of assessing reliability of measurement. I start by discussing the most influential theory of measurement known as *classical test theory* and show how reliability of measurement is defined under the tenets of classical test theory. This theory of measurement leads to a number of different methods and statistics used to quantify reliability of measurement of quantitative variables. But not all measurement procedures that communication researchers use yield quantitative data. Data are often categorical and result from subjective decisions that must be made about where a research unit belongs in a classification system the researcher has devised. So I end with a discussion of a variety of statistical indices used to quantify error in measurement of a different sort—error in categorization resulting from subjective perception and decision making.

6.1 Classical Test Theory

One of the most influential ways of conceptualizing measurement error is *classical test theory*. The theory has its origins in the early 1900s with work by Charles Spearman (1907, 1913), but it was popularized quite a bit later with the publication of Lord and Novick's (1968) *Statistical Theories of Mental Test Scores*. The existence of the word *test* in classical test theory can be attributed to the time and the discipline in which classical test theory was developed: psychology. In the early 1900s, the measurement of abilities and personality with a variety of psychological and mental tests that were being developed was one of the hot topics in the burgeoning field of psychology, but there was little existing theory to guide psychologists about how to measure such abilities and how to interpret the results of those measurements. Classical test theory represents an early attempt to conceptualize the measurement process. But the theory can be applied to virtually any form of measurement. Although classical test theory is slowly losing its prominence as a result of newer theories of measurement such as *generalizability theory* (Thompson, 2003b) and *item response theory* (Embretson, 1996; Embretson & Reise, 2000), it is important to understand classical test theory because many of the ways that communication researchers quantify reliability of measurement are derived from the tenets of classical test theory.

6.1.1 Partioning Measurements into Their Components

In section 2.2.1, I introduced the equation *Observed Measurement = True Score + Measurement Error*. It is handy to denote this equation symbolically as

$$\boxed{X_i = T_i + E_i}$$

(6.1)

where X_i is an observed measurement for unit i, T_i is unit i's *true score* on what is being measured, and E_i is the error in measurement for unit i. The observed measurement or *observed score* is simply the measurement that a measurement instrument being used to quantify a construct yields for case i. The measurement error, E_i, is also relatively simple to understand. It reflects the difference between the observed measurement for unit i, X_i, and unit i's true score. That is,

$$E_i = X_i - T_i$$

But what is this "true score?" The true score is one of the more difficult concepts to grasp in classical test theory, in part because it is such an abstract concept. To get a handle on this notion, try to think back to some time in your life, perhaps in school, when you felt that a score you got on a test of some kind did not reflect your knowledge or ability. Perhaps you believed your test score was too low, in that it misrepresented or underestimated your actual knowledge. Or perhaps you believe you lucked out and got a score that overrepresented what you actually know or what you could do. The score you received on the test is your observed score, X, whereas your actual knowledge or ability is your "true score", T. So the true score for unit i can be thought of as the actual amount of the construct being measured that a unit can be said to "possess." Although a researcher's measurement goal is to quantify T_i for each unit, the result of the measurement process is X_i. In the absence of anything better, X_i is used as a proxy for T_i. But $X_i \neq T_i$ unless $E_i = 0$. In other words, the correspondence between X_i and T_i is usually less than perfect, with the difference represented in equation 6.1 as E_i, the error in measurement.

In classical test theory, E_i is considered a random, unpredictable component of X_i. As illustrated earlier, repeated measurement of the same unit on the same construct using the same measuring instrument will lead to different values of X_i on each occasion even if T_i has not changed because of a variety of forces that produce measurement error. As a result of this random measurement error, X_i has a "measurement distribution," defined as the probability distribution of possible values of X_i given unit i's true score, T_i.

Before things start getting more complicated, it is worth stopping for a minute and looking at a picture that visually represents each of these three components of measurement. Figure 6.1 graphically depicts everything I have discussed thus far and some things that I have not yet discussed. The top line in the figure represents the continuum along which units vary in a quantifiable fashion on the construct being measured, from low to high. It can be thought of as the range of possible values of T_i from low values on the left to high values on the right. The normal curves depicted above this top line represent the probability distribution for X_i for 5 different units being measured. These represent the distribution of possible values of X_i given unit i's true score, T_i. So on any particular measurement occasion, each unit's observed score, X_i, can fall anywhere on the continuum underneath that unit's measurement distribution, with the probability of a particular value of X_i being represented as the height of the normal curve above the top line.

Now imagine measuring 5 units once using some method of measuring the construct of interest. The true score for unit i on what is being measured, T_i, is unobservable but its value is centered right in the middle of the measurement distribution for that unit. I have projected the 5 true scores onto the middle line in the figure to represent where these 5 true scores exist on the continuum. The 5 values of X_i on the third line represent each unit's observed score when measured on this occasion. The distance between T_i and X_i is represented with the horizontal lines with double-sided arrows on the middle line. These represent the error in the measurement of T_i on this measurement occasion by using X_i as a proxy for T_i.

$$X_i = T_i + E_i$$

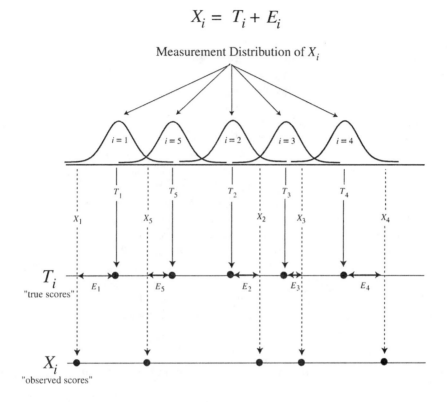

Figure 6.1 The partitioning of observed scores into true and error components.

The location of the circles on the bottom line represent the 5 values of X_i on this measurement occasion. Where these 5 circles reside on the continuum of measurement would vary at each measurement occasion for these 5 units because the errors in measurement vary randomly from measurement occasion to measurement occasion. In contrast, the location of the 5 circles representing these 5 units' true scores, T_i, would not change. They would always be located exactly where they are in this figure. So X_i is a random variable, whereas T_i is not. But if T_i remains fixed, then all of the variation in case i's observed score is governed entirely by the distribution of the measurement errors.

Classical test theory makes a number of assumptions about the measurement errors. I formally list these assumptions below and then discuss each:

(1) $E_i \sim \mathcal{N}(0, \sigma^2)$
(2) $\rho_{(E,T)} = 0$
(3) $\rho_{(E_i, E_j)} = 0$

Assumption 1 states that errors in measurement for unit i are normally distributed with mean zero and variance σ^2. Now it might seem strange to think of a single measurement error having a distribution, but remember that E_i is a random variable. For each of the i units, E_i varies from occasion to occasion. The measurement error for unit i on any single measurement occasion is simply one of many possible values of E_i that could have resulted from the measurement process for unit i. So assumption

1 states that the mean of the distribution of measurement errors for unit i is normal with mean zero. Furthermore, it states that the variance of those measurement errors is equal to some value σ^2 and that the variance of measurement errors for each unit i are all equal to this same value σ^2. Recall from section 4.3.3 that a variance is a measure of variability. It is simply the square of the standard deviation. The equality of these variances in measurement error is depicted in Figure 6.1 as normal curves that have exactly the same width for all 5 units.

An important corollary of assumption 1 is that $E(E_i) = \overline{E}_i = 0$. In words, although the random measurement errors for unit i vary from measurement occasion to measurement occasion, we expect the measurement error to be zero. So if we could repeatedly measure unit i on the construct using this measurement instrument, the average of the resulting errors in measurement would be zero.[1]

We can conceptualize X_i, T_i and E_i each as random variables. I've already described how X_i and E_i are random variables. Earlier I claimed that T_i is not, but a variable that is not random can also be construed as random variable with zero variance. That is, upon repeated measurements of unit i, the variability in unit i's true score is zero. Next, we can apply a rule in statistics that applies to the sum of random variables. It says that the expected value of a sum of random variables is equal to the sum of the expected values of those random variables (e.g., Ross, 1988). If $X_i = T_i + E_i$ (from equation 6.1) then X_i is a sum of random variables. Therefore,

$$E(X_i) = E(T_i) + E(E_i)$$

But earlier I said that the expected value of the random measurement error, E_i, is zero. Therefore,

$$E(X_i) = E(T_i)$$

But now consider this. If a unit's true score does not change from measurement to measurement, then $E(T_i) = T_i$, and so

$$E(X_i) = T_i$$

Another way of phrasing is this is that $\overline{X}_i = T_i$. That is, if you measure a unit repeatedly, over and over again, the average of the resulting observed scores would be equal to the unit's true score on what is being measured.

Assumption 2 states that the correlation between the true scores and the errors in measurement is equal to zero. So regardless of whether unit i's true score is low, moderate, or high, this provides no information about the size of that unit's measurement error. Assumption 3 states that there is no correlation between the size of the measurement errors for any two units i and j. So knowledge of one unit's measurement error gives no information about the size of any other unit's measurement error.

6.1.2   The Definition of Reliability Under Classical Test Theory

In the previous section, I illustrated how classical test theory conceptualizes measurement as an additive sum of a true score and a random measurement error. This theory leads to the expectation that a unit's observed score will be equal to that unit's true score on what is being measured, but that on any single measurement occasion, there

---

[1] If $E(E_i) \neq 0$, we say that the measurement instrument is *biased*. If the instrument has the same bias for all i units, this doesn't affect reliability. But if bias varies across the i units, it is difficult to estimate reliability. I assume in this chapter that there is no bias in measurement.

will be some discrepancy between the true score and the observed score. In other words, if we measured each unit repeatedly, we know that the average of each unit's observed measurements over time would be equal to that unit's true score because the random measurement errors will be, on average, zero.

This is nice, but in practice we don't measure each unit repeatedly. Instead, we measure each unit only once, and we don't know how large each unit's measurement error is on that single measurement occasion. Nevertheless, classical test theory gives us a means of estimating how large those measurement errors tend to be by exploiting another statistical rule. This rule states that the variance of a sum of two statistically independent random variables is equal to the sum of the variances of those variables (Ross, 1988). I already discussed that X_i and E_i are random variables, and that T_i can be construed as a random variable with zero variance. By equation 6.1, X_i is a sum of random variables, and by assumption 2 of classical test theory, T_i and E_i are independent. Therefore,

$$\sigma_X^2 = \sigma_T^2 + \sigma_E^2$$

(6.2)

I have dropped the i subscript in equation 6.2 because we are now talking about a *set* of research units rather than a single unit. On any single measurement occasion, the variance of these components are properties of the set of measurements and not the individual measurements.

Now let's imagine that we have a population of N research units and we have measured each of them on some construct, yielding N values of X_i, one for each of the N units. These N values of X_i certainly vary from each other, and that variability can be quantified as σ_X^2 using equation 4.4. These N units also vary in their true scores. Although we can't compute σ_T^2 because the values of T are unknown, the variance of those true scores does still exist. By a similar reasoning, we don't know the variance of the N measurement errors because we don't know the N values of E, but that variance still exists. In equation 6.2 we are calling this variance σ_E^2.

An important quantity in classical test theory is how much of the variance in the observed scores can be attributed to variance in the true scores. In other words, how much of the variation in X across units can be explained by variation in T across units? This amount can represented and derived as a ratio of true score variance to observed score variance. This ratio is important because it is the definition of *reliability* in classical test theory:

$$\text{reliability} = \frac{\sigma_T^2}{\sigma_X^2}$$

(6.3)

So reliability is the proportion of observed score variance that is true variation in what is being measured. This doesn't sound like the definition of reliability I gave in Chapter 2. Recall from my discussion of reliability there that reliability was a quantification of how much error exists in the measurements. But equation 6.3 does just that. Equation 6.2 tells us that the variance of the observed measurements is equal to the variance of the true scores plus the variance of the errors. Substituting equation 6.2 into the denominator of equation 6.3 yields

$$\text{reliability} = \frac{\sigma_T^2}{\sigma_T^2 + \sigma_E^2}$$

(6.4)

Remember that the measurement errors are the discrepancies between the observed scores and the true scores (equation 6.1). Larger measurement errors translate into larger error variance. So the more random error in the observed measurements, the larger σ_E^2 is. Now notice that σ_E^2 is in the denominator of equation 6.4. The larger the denominator gets, the smaller the ratio of true score variance to observed variance. But this ratio is the definition of reliability, so it follows that the larger the measurement errors, the smaller the reliability of measurement as defined by equation 6.4. Conversely, the smaller the measurement errors, the smaller the error variance, and so reliability increases. At its extreme, if the true scores and observed scores are exactly equal for every measured unit, then $\sigma_E^2 = 0$, and so reliability is 1.

This is very exciting, but we are not done yet. There is one important corollary of equation 6.4 that needs to be highlighted. Recall from section 4.7.1 that the *coefficient of determination* is the square of the correlation between variables X and Y. And remember that the coefficient of determination can be interpreted as the proportion of variance in Y that is attributable to X. This sounds a lot like how reliability is defined in classical test theory—the proportion of variability in observed scores that can attributed to variation in the true scores. Indeed, reliability is, in theory, the square of the correlation between the true scores and the observed scores. So if you take the square root of reliability, you get the correlation between the true scores and the observed scores. This makes it even clearer how reliability can be thought of as one measure of the quality of measurement. The higher the reliability of measurement, the stronger the correlation between the observed scores and the true scores. This is a desirable property to have in a set of measurements. If the measurements were only weakly correlated with the true scores, then how could you justify using the observed scores as proxies for the true scores?

6.2 Estimating the Reliability of Quantitative Measurements

Although classical test theory is an influential way of conceptualizing the measurement process, on the surface is appears useless from a practical perspective. It is important for a researcher to be able to quantify the reliability of his or her measurements, but the definition of reliability as presented in equation 6.4 is not helpful at all. The problem is that the true scores are unknown and ultimately unknowable. Therefore, the variance of the true scores (σ_T^2) cannot ever be known, so the ratio of true score to observed score variance will remain elusive. So reliability cannot be directly computed using equation 6.4.

But it turns out that this is not that big of a problem because there are ways of estimating reliability of measurement in spite of the fact that the true scores are unknown. With the guidance of classical test theory. reliability can be estimated in several ways, two of which I discuss here.

6.2.1 Estimating Reliability From Repeated Measurements Over Time

It can be shown that if the assumptions of classical test theory hold, then reliability can be estimated by measuring a set of research units twice with the measurement instrument and calculating the correlating between observed measurements over time. This correlation is equal to the reliability of measurement. More accurately, this correlation is an *estimate* of reliability, not the true reliability because each observed measurement of the same unit contains some measurement error at each time.

An estimate of reliability derived from a correlation between observed measurements over time is known as a *test-retest reliability estimate*, for obvious reasons. This method of estimating reliability requires the assumption that either there has been no change in each unit's true score over time, or if there has been some change, that the research units' true scores have all changed by the same amount. This assumption must be taken seriously. If the units' true scores have changed over time but to varying degrees, then there is no way of determining how much of the deviation from a perfect correlation between observed scores over time is due to error in measurement and how much of it is due to temporal variation in the true scores.

The longer you wait between the two measurement occasions, the more likely the research units' true scores are to have changed, but to varying degrees. Therefore, you should expect that the longer the time between test and retest, the lower the reliability estimate will be. This would argue for always minimizing the length of time between test and retest. However, if your measurement instrument is based on self-reports, such as people answering questions about themselves, the more likely they are to remember their responses from earlier if the time between measurements is brief. It is not unreasonable to expect a person to try to respond to questions about themselves consistently, and if they can remember what they told you last time you asked the question, they are likely to use that information to guide their response the second time. The result is that a test-retest estimate of reliability will tend to overestimate the actual reliability of measurement if memory for prior responses is likely to be good. So a balance must be struck between the risk of true change lowering the test-retest estimate and the possibility that respondents' memory for their earlier responses will influence their responses the second time, resulting in an overestimation of the true reliability of measurement.

The decision as to how long to wait between measurements should depend on these perceived risks. If the true scores are unlikely to change much over time or by differing amounts, then you can wait longer between test and retest. If you are measuring a construct that is likely to fluctuate a lot over time, then this dictates a shorter test-retest interval. If people are likely to remember their answers to questions you ask them, then this suggests a longer test-retest interval is in order. In my experience reading the communication literature, three to four weeks is a relatively typical time interval used for estimating reliability using the test-retest, method, but it is not unheard of to see test-retest estimates derived from test intervals as short as one week or as long as one year. Of course, there is no reason you have to commit to a single test-retest interval. If you are able to administer the measurement instrument repeatedly to the same people over multiple occasions, do so. That way, you can get estimates derived from different test-retest intervals, allowing you to determine the extent to which true scores might actually change over time, but differently for different people. And the "true" reliability is probably somewhere between the minimum and maximum estimate derived from multiple test-retest estimates.

6.2.2 Estimating Reliability From Internal Consistency of Indicator Scores

Although the test-retest method of estimating reliability is theoretically justifiable, it is often not very practical because it requires that you remeasure at least some of the units. This might be difficult or impossible. At a minimum, it is a nuisance. Fortunately, it is possible to estimate reliability of measurement using data collected at a single time, but only for *composite measures*. A composite measure is any method of measurement that produces an observed measurement for the construct by summing or averaging two or more *indicators* of the construct. An indicator of a construct is any variable whose scores can be used to estimate the construct. For example, the *Television Affinity Scale* (Box 2.1) is a 5-indicator composite measure of how important television is to a person. Each of the 5 questions is an indicator of the construct, and a person's television affinity is derived by mathematically aggregating his or her responses to these five questions into a single composite score. Composite measures that are based on the summing or averaging of a set of ordinal ratings or judgments are sometimes called *summated rating scales*. There is both an art and a science to the construction of summating rating scales. For details on summated rating scales and their design, see Spector (1992).

The estimation of reliability using the *internal consistency* method is based on a simple idea. If a research unit is relatively high on the construct being measured, then that unit's k indicator scores (where k is the number of indicators being aggregated) should exhibit a pattern consistent with that high score. Furthermore, that pattern of indictor scores should be different from the scores for a research unit that is relatively low on the construct being measured. Take the *Television Affinity Scale* as an example. Someone who believes that television is rather important to his or her day to day life should show a particular pattern of responses to the five statements. Such a person should tend to respond "agree" or "strongly agree" to statements 1, 2, 3, and 5 and "disagree" or "strongly disagree" to statement 4. Conversely, those who perceived television to be relatively unimportant to them should answer "disagree" or "strongly disagree" to statements 1, 2, 3, and 5 and "agree" or "strongly agree" to statement 4.

After the responses are numerically scored, such a consistent pattern of responses should manifest itself in relatively high intercorrelations between indicator scores. A composite measure based on k indicator scores is based on an average or sum of k observed scores, each of which contains some measurement error. Imagine generating each of the correlations between the k indicator scores. There are $k(k-1)/2$ such correlations. The strength of this pattern of the observed scores across the k items manifests itself in the size of these correlations.

The strength of these intercorrelations is governed in part by how much error in measurement exists in each indicator score. Naturally, the more measurement error in the k indicator scores, the more measurement error the composite score will have. Cronbach (1951) capitalized on the relationship between the average intercorrelation between indicator scores and the amount of measurement error in the composite measure to derive an estimate of reliability of measurement, a measure that has come to be known as Cronbach's α. Cronbach's α can be derived from either the average of the $k(k-1)/2$ correlations between the indicator scores or from the variance of the k indicator scores.[2] Because it is easier to see the relationship between reliability of the aggregated score and the average intercorrelation, we start first with *standardized alpha*, so called because it produces a reliability estimate for measurement based on the sum or average of a set of indicators that have been standardized prior to their aggregation into a single score (i.e., converted to Z-scores, which forces their variances to all be equal to 1).

---

[2] Although Cronbach has been given credit for the derivation and popularization of this measure of reliability, in fact it was derived earlier by Guttman (1945) and Kuder and Richardson (1937).

Table 6.2

Standardized α as a Function of $\bar{r}$ and k (from Equation 6.5)

	$\bar{r}$								
k	0.1	0.2	0.3	0.4	0.5	0.6	0.7	0.8	0.9
2	.182	.333	.462	.571	.667	.750	.824	.889	.947
3	.250	.429	.562	.667	.750	.818	.875	.923	.964
4	.308	.500	.632	.727	.800	.857	.903	.941	.973
5	.357	.556	.682	.769	.833	.882	.921	.952	.978
6	.400	.600	.720	.800	.857	.900	.933	.960	.982
7	.438	.636	.750	.824	.875	.913	.942	.966	.984
8	.471	.667	.774	.842	.889	.923	.949	.970	.986
9	.500	.692	.794	.857	.900	.931	.955	.973	.988
10	.526	.714	.811	.870	.909	.938	.959	.976	.989
15	.625	.789	.865	.909	.938	.957	.972	.984	.993
20	.690	.833	.896	.930	.952	.968	.979	.988	.994

Standardized alpha (α_Z) is estimated as:

$$\text{Cronbach's } \alpha_Z = \frac{k\bar{r}}{1 + (k-1)\bar{r}}$$

(6.5)

where $\bar{r}$ is the average correlation between the indicator scores (excluding an indicator's correlation with itself) and k is the number of indicators in the measurement instrument. This equation for α_Z reveals that the reliability of a composite measure is affected by both the intercorrelation between the indicators as well as the number of indicators used in the construction of the composite score. Table 6.2 illustrates this relationship. Keeping $\bar{r}$ constant (i.e., reading down a column in the table), α_Z increases as k increases. And keeping k constant (i.e., reading across a row in the table), α_Z increases as $\bar{r}$ increases.

It should be apparent why reliability increases as the average intercorrelation increases. This average intercorrelation between indicators reflects how much measurement error exists in each indicator as a measure of the construct. But why does reliability increase as the number of indicators increases? This is because the random measurement errors in the indicators are more likely to cancel each other out in the construction of the composite score as the number of indicators increases. The more random errors that are added together in the construction of the composite, the closer their average will be to zero. But this assumes that you haven't changed the average intercorrelation by increasing the number of indicators. You can't just throw in any indicator into a composite score. If the indicator you add to the pool is poor, (i.e., contain lots of measurement error) the average indicator intercorrelation will decrease, and this often will hurt the reliability of the composite more than increasing the number of indicators will help it.

If the indicators are measured on different measurement scales, you should standardize the indicator scores before the composite score is constructed and estimate reliability of the composite score using α_Z. But if the indicators are measured on the same scale (such as the same 1–5 scale as used in the *Television Affinity Scale*), so long as the variances of the observed meausurements on the indicators are not drastically different, then those observed measurements can just be added up or averaged, in which case alpha is estimated as

$$\text{Cronbach's } \alpha = \frac{k}{k-1}\left(1 - \frac{\sum s_i^2}{s_{total}^2}\right)$$

$$(6.6)$$

where s_i^2 is the sample variance of scores on indicator i and s_{total}^2 is the variance of the sum of the indicators.

Cronbach's α was derived from the assumptions of classical test theory. To meet those assumptions, the indicators must be quantitative and measured at the interval level. However, a version of α exists for composite measures constructed entirely from dichotomous indicators. This version of α is known as the Kuder-Richardson estimate, or KR–20.[3] KR–20 is named after the two psychometricians who derived it (Kuder & Richardson, 1937). KR–20 actually predates Cronbach's influential paper in which he described α. But no special formula is needed for KR–20 because it is mathematically equivalent to Cronbach's α.

Let's work through an example to illustrate these computations. The data from this study come from a telephone survey of residents of the United States. Seven hundred twenty three people were randomly selected through random digit dialing and interviewed over the phone. During the interview, the respondents were asked to provide a response to each of the statements on the *Willingness to Self-Censor Scale (WTSC)* (Hayes, Glynn, & Shahanan, in press a) The *WTSC* scale is an eight-item self-report measure of a person's willingness to express their opinion around an audience that they perceive is likely to disagree with that opinion (see Box 6.1 for the phrasing of the statements and how the *WTSC* score is constructed and Appendix E2 on the CD for a description of the data file). The statements were read out loud to the respondents, who were asked to indicate their level of agreement with each statement as it applies to them on a 1 (strongly disagree) to 5 (strongly agree) scale. Each of the eight items are used as indicators of the construct, willingness to self-censor, and with the exception of statements 4 and 8, high responses (i.e,. greater agreement) are reflective or a greater willingness to self-censor. Statements 4 and 8 are reverse worded, such that low scores on these indicators reflect a greater willingness to self-censor.

Before reliability can be computed using the internal consistency method, it is necessary to transform the responses to the reverse worded questions so that the scoring is consistent across all indicators (i.e., so that higher scores on each indicator reflect more of the construct being measured). In SPSS, the syntax[4] to accomplish this transformation would be

---

[3]The "20" in KR–20 refers to "equation 20" in Kuder & Richardson (1937).

[4]After the Windows operating system was introduced to the world, SPSS produced a Windows-based interface making SPSS a bit more user friendly than non-Windows versions. But much of the power of SPSS resides in the SPSS programming language, which you feed to SPSS through a syntax window rather than by pointing and clicking. Learning to program SPSS in syntax is a worthwhile use of your time. To get you started, you will find a document on the CD that came with this book that provides some basic SPSS commands. I encourage you to explore the SPSS language by consulting a knowledgable user or the SPSS Syntax Reference Guide published by SPSS and available through the SPSS Help menu.

Box 6.1: The *Willingness to Self-Censor Scale*

For each statement, please indicate the extent to which you strongly disagree, disagree, agree and disagree, agree, or strongly agree as it applies to you. Circle a number from 1 to 5, where 1 = strongly disagree, 2 = disagree, 3 = both agree and disagree, 4 = agree, 5 = strongly agree. Don't spend too much time on any question. Simply record your first impression.

(1) It is difficult for me to express my opinion if I think others won't agree with what I say.   1 2 3 4 5

(2) There have been many times when I thought others around me were wrong but I didn't let them know.   1 2 3 4 5

(3) When I disagree with others, I'd rather go along with them than argue about it.   1 2 3 4 5

(4) It is easy for me to express my opinion around others who I think will disagree with me.   1 2 3 4 5

(5) I'd feel uncomfortable if someone asked my opinion and I knew he or she wouldn't agree with me.   1 2 3 4 5

(6) I tend to speak my opinion only around friends or other people I trust.   1 2 3 4 5

(7) It is safer to keep quiet than publicly speak an opinion that you know most others don't share.   1 2 3 4 5

(8) If I disagree with others, I have no problem letting them know it.   1 2 3 4 5

TO COMPUTE YOUR WILLINGNESS TO SELF-CENSOR, FIRST SUBTRACT YOUR RESPONSE TO THE FOURTH AND EIGHTH STATEMENTS FROM 6. ADD THESE TWO NUMBERS TOGETHER. THEN ADD TO THIS RESULT THE SUM OF YOUR RESPONSES TO THE REMAINING STATEMENTS. YOUR SCORE SHOULD BE BETWEEN 8 AND 40.

```
compute wtsc4r = 6-wtsc4.
compute wtsc8r = 6-wtsc8.
```

The matrix of correlations between the indicator scores can be found in Table 6.3. All the entries in this correlation matrix are positive and small to moderate in size, reflecting the tendency for people to provide consistent responses to these eight statements. In other words, someone who gives a response to one statement that is above the mean tends to do so for other statements as well, and vice-versa for responses below the mean.

Table 6.3

A Matrix of Inter-Indicator Correlations (Pearson's r)

	wtsc1	wtsc2	wtsc3	wtsc4r	wtsc5	wtsc6	wtsc7	wtsc8r
wtsc1	1.000							
wtsc2	0.346	1.000						
wtsc3	0.423	0.446	1.000					
wtsc4r	0.177	0.050	0.127	1.000				
wtsc5	0.389	0.246	0.306	0.086	1.000			
wtsc6	0.432	0.338	0.374	0.073	0.361	1.000		
wtsc7	0.336	0.325	0.418	0.069	0.370	0.476	1.000	
wtsc8r	0.255	0.243	0.274	0.271	0.175	0.277	0.210	1.000

Not counting an indicator's correlation with itself (the "1.000"s on the diagonal of the matrix), there are 28 correlations in this matrix, and the average of these 28 interindicator correlations is 0.281. Applying equation 6.5 yields standardized α:

$$\alpha_Z = \frac{8(0.281)}{1 + (8 - 1)(0.281)} = 0.758$$

This estimate of 0.758 is the estimated reliability of a composite WTSC score defined as the sum or average of the 8 indicator scores *after first standardizing them* (converting them to Z-scores). That is, it is the reliability of a composite score $WTSC_Z$, where $WTSC_Z$ is defined as

$$WTSC_Z = Z_{wtsc1} + Z_{wtsc2} + Z_{wtsc3} + Z_{wtsc4r} + Z_{wtsc5} + Z_{wtsc6} + Z_{wtsc7} + Z_{wtsc8r}$$

It is good idea to define the measurement of the construct as a composite of *standardized* indicator scores if the indicators are measured on different scales or, if measured on the same scale, if the variability in the indicator scores is drastically different across indicator scores. If the indicators are measured on different scales and scores on the indicators are roughly equally variable, then a simple average or sum of the indicator scores can be used as a composite measure of the construct (after reverse coding any indicators that need to be so coded). In that case, the reliability of the composite scores can be estimated with equation 6.6. The 8 indicators of $WTSC$ are measured on the same scale (1 to 5), and examination of the standard deviations of the indicator scores (see Table 6.4) indicate they do not differ much from each other. The reliability of a simple sum (or average) of the indicator scores can be derived using equation 6.6. From the information in Table 6.4

Table 6.4

Descriptive Statistics for the *Willingness to Self-Censor Scale* Indicators

	wtsc1	wtsc2	wtsc3	wtsc4r	wtsc5	wtsc6	wtsc7	wtsc8r	Total
Mean	2.232	2.884	2.398	2.754	2.486	2.778	2.788	2.346	20.665
s	1.212	1.256	1.143	1.129	1.118	1.227	1.183	1.040	5.696
s^2	1.469	1.577	1.306	1.274	1.250	1.506	1.400	1.082	32.442

$$\alpha = \frac{k}{k-1}\left(1 - \frac{\sum s_i^2}{s_{total}^2}\right)$$

$$\alpha = \frac{8}{8-1}\left(1 - \frac{1.469 + 1.577 + 1.306 + 1.274 + 1.250 + 1.506 + 1.400 + 1.082}{32.442}\right)$$

$$\alpha = 0.760$$

So the reliability of measurement for the composite $WTSC$ variable defined as the sum (or mean) of the responses to the 8 indicators (after reverse scoring indicators 4 and 8) is estimated to be 0.760. This estimate is very close to the standardized α estimate because the differences in indicator variances (the 8 values of s^2 reported in Table 6.4) are so small. If all the indicators are measured on the same scale, typically α and α_Z will be very close to each other unless there are drastic differences in indicator variances.

Remember one corollary of the definition of reliability offered by classical test theory is that reliability can be thought of as the squared correlation between the observed and true scores. So we can say that if we could quantify each person's true score on the *Willingness to Self-Censor Scale*, the correlation between the true scores and their observed scores is estimated to be around $\sqrt{0.760} = 0.872$.

6.2.3   Reliability of Method or of Measurement?

It is common for researchers to talk about reliability as if it is a feature of a method of measurement. You might be admonished not to use an unreliable measure of your constructs or criticized on the grounds that you used a composite measure of a construct that isn't reliable. But technically, reliability is an attribute not of the method of measurement used, but the measurements that result from the use of that method (Thompson, 2003a). The same method of measurement, if used a dozen times by different researchers, yield a dozen different reliability estimates. These are not estimates of the method of measurement itself, but estimates of the reliability of the 12 sets of measurements resulting from its use.

So there is no single number that we can say is the reliability of the *Television Affinity Scale* or the *Willingness to Self-Censor Scale*. Reliability will vary, depending on who or what is being measured and under what circumstances. Therefore, the reliability estimates that others have reported when they used a measurement procedure that you used are not useful information to give to readers of your research. The fact that other researchers' measurements were reliable says nothing about the reliability of *your* measurements. For a reader of your research to evaluate the quality of your measurement, you need to provide an estimate of reliability whenever it is feasible to do so. Even if you are unable to do statistically, the burden of proof remains on you to establish that you are measuring well, even if logical argumentation is the only way to do so.

But perhaps this is semantic nitpicking to an extreme. Isn't it true that if a measurement instrument tends to produce reliable measurements then the instrument can be said to be reliable? Technically, no, but in practice, the chances of a method of measurement producing reliable measurements are better if it has done so in the past. So when selecting a method of measurement for a particular construct, it is safer to use a method that others have used and that has yielded reliable data before. If others get good reliability using a particular measurement method, there is a higher chance that you will get reliable data than if you used a different and untested method of measuring the construct. In that sense, it not unreasonable to talk about reliability as a feature of the method of measurement. Good cooks produce good food. If we praise the food as good, it seems reasonable to ascribe the good taste of the food in part to the talents of the cook. To be sure, good cooks may not *always* cook well, but the chances of getting a good meal from someone with some cooking talent are better than from someone without it. I think the same thing applies to measures of communication constructs. Good measurement procedures tend to produce good data, but not always. For this reason, you need to report the reliability of your measurements. The reliability of other researchers' measurements can be used to justify the selection of the method of measurement, but it isn't relevant to evaluating the quality of *your* data.

6.3   Reliability of Subjective Categorical Judgments

Classical test theory justifies the reliability estimates discussed thus far. But classical test theory applies only to variables measured at the pseudo-interval, interval, or ratio level. So these reliability estimators can only be used to estimate the reliability of measurement for quantitative variables. But researchers often analyze data involving variables that are categorical. For example, Dixon and Linz (2000) studied media portrayals of crime to see if televised news broadcasts tend to overrepresent the victimization of members of certain ethnic groups. The primary variables in this study were categorical—the ethnic identity of the perpetrator and the victim in news broadcasts about homicides. Johnson and Kaid (2002) studied U.S. presidential advertisements to see if "image-oriented" ads were more likely than "issue-oriented" ads to contain a fear appeal. The orientation of an advertisement and whether or not it contains a fear appeal are both categorical variables. Finally, Zhao and Gantz (2003) studied interruptions in conversations between people on television sitcoms to see if the kind of interruption (disruptive or cooperative) was related to the social status of the interruptor relative to the person being interrupted. Again, both of these variables (social status and interruption type) are categorical.

These three studies had something else in common—they all required some kind of human judgment to determine which category each research unit in the sample belonged in before the data could be analyzed. Presidential advertisements don't come labeled as issue or image-oriented, nor is there some kind of advisory in the typical political advertisement warning the viewer that they are about to be scared into acting. Interruptions do not come prepackaged in categories. They are categorized based on someone's categorization system. The form of interruption is not inherent to the communication itself—it is a label given to that communication by a human perceiver. Even something as simple as classifying the ethnicity of someone on television involves subjective judgment. People do not walk around with ethnic labels on their foreheads.

So these categorization decisions were subjective ones involving fallible human judgment. Whenever the data in a scientific study result from subjective decisions of one or more people, we immediately worry about the *reliability* of those decisions and therefore the resulting data. Remember that reliability refers to the amount of error in the measurement process. In the case of categorical variables, error manifests itself in the form of miscategorization of units into categories. So we can still rely on the true score concept by conceptualizing a unit's true score as the category into which the unit *actually* belongs rather than where a human judge *believes* it belongs. Low reliability exists when units are routinely miscategorized, meaning many categorization errors. High reliability exists when the units are by and large correctly classified.

But when the judgment is subjective, how to we define a "correct" categorization? One way of defining the correctness of a subjective categorization decision is whether it corresponds to the decisions made by other people who approach the categorization task with the same set of instructions and rules for making the decision. For example, if two people are asked to categorize a set of television advertisements into categories, we can consider the judgments reliable if they agree with each other. If they don't agree, then one or perhaps both of them are categorizing with error. But if they agree, we can assume that their judgments about category membership reflect something inherent in the unit being judged rather than the idiosyncrasies of the people doing the judging.

And this is the primary reason for worrying about agreement of subjective judgments. The scientific method dictates that the data in a study are derived by an objective and replicable process. If subjective categorization decisions turn out to be inaccurate (i.e., unreliable), then the results of a study are primarily determined by those subjective decisions rather than the features of the units being analyzed. Furthermore, subjective decisions by their nature vary depending on who makes them. Thus, the results of a study would depend highly on who was doing the categorization. If a different person or group of people were used to make decisions about category membership, then the results of the study may very well have come out different.

As Krippendorff (2004) points out, agreement is something that we measure, whereas reliability is something that we infer from agreement, and he describes several conditions necessary to make the inference from agreement to reliability. But whether you call it agreement or reliability, in order to estimate *correspondence* between subjective categorical judgments and therefore the reliability of the resulting data, it is obviously necessary to have at least two people doing the categorization, at least in the early phases of data collection. (The process of categorization is sometimes called "coding" because it involves assigning some kind of code corresponding to category membership to each unit.)

To illustrate different ways of estimating agreement in a set of categorization decisions, we'll consider a small data set derived from a study by Ford and Ellis (1998). The data here are hypothetical but similar to data they report in their article. They interviewed 26 nurses working at a midwestern hospital, asking them to recall and describe an incident in which a coworker said something supportive to them on the job. They considered three kinds of support messages: (a) instrumental support, (b) informational support, and (c) emotional support. Instrumental support was defined as a

Table 6.5

A Crosstabulation of Two Coders' Judgments of 26 Support Messages

	Coder 1		
Coder 2	Instrumental	Informational	Emotional
Instrumental	6	1	0
Informational	0	6	1
Emotional	1	2	9

message that communicated a willingness to exchange or trade time or labor. Informational support included messages that helped the nurse to improve his or her technical skill or to clarify job expectations or how the hospital functioned. Finally emotional support was defined as a message communicating empathy, trust, or acceptance of the nurse within the organization.

Ford and Ellis (1998) were interested in whether some forms of support messages are more memorable than others. Are nurses more likely to recall certain forms of support? Before answering this question, they needed to place each of the 26 memorable messages into one of the categories. This was accomplished by having two coders each read the transcripts of the interviews and independently (i.e., not working together) make a judgment as to which form of support was manifested in each message, with the requirement that each message be classified into one and only one category. This is a subjective judgment, and some information as to how consistent the judges were in their classification is pertinent to evaluating the categorization system they used, how well the coders could apply the rules and instructions they were given in order to accomplish the task, and ultimately the extent to which the categorization was done accurately and reflected the content of the messages themselves rather than just the subjective and fallible judgments of the coders.

Some hypothetical data consistent with what Ford and Ellis (1998) report in the article can be found in Table 6.5. The rows in the table correspond to the judgments of the first coder, and the columns correspond to the judgments of the second coder. For instance, 6 of the support messages both coders classified as instrumental, 6 were judged by both as informational, and both perceived 9 of the messages as providing emotional support. So the diagonals of the table represent the 21 messages that the coders classified identically. The remaining entries in the table represent the messages that the coders classified differently. For example, two of the messages the first coder judged as instrumental support but the second coder judged as emotional support. Using these data, I'll now introduce several measures that are used in communication to assess the extent to which the coders agree in their judgments. If the coders disagree, then it is difficult to argue that the messages actually manifest the content the coders claim. In other words, a different set of judges might classify the messages very differently, and so analyses of the data would vary depending on who did the coding. But if the coders agree, it is safer to assume that the category into which each message was placed reflects the content of that message, and that a different group of coders would probably have made similar judgments.

All of the measures discussed here have the property that they range from a minimum of 0 (reflecting an absence of reliability or agreement) to 1 (reflecting perfect reliability or agreement).

6.3.1   Holsti's Method

By far the simplest method of assessing agreement is Holsti's method (Holsti, 1969). This method simply counts up the number of judgments that are the same and divides this sum by the total number of judgments made. Defining F_a as the number of units (in this case, messages) judged the same by both coders, n_1 as the number of units judged by coder 1, and n_2 as the number of units judged by coder 2, Holsti's method is

$$\text{Holsti's Agreement} = \frac{2F_a}{n_1 + n_2}$$

(6.7)

Holsti's formula is general, in that it allows for the possibility that some units might be coded by only one judge (and thus, n_1 and n_2 might be different). Usually both coders would be judging each object, in which case $n_1 = n_2$. In that case, the denominator of equation 6.7 can be expressed as $2n$, where n is the number of units being judged, and Holsti's method reduces to simply the proportion of units that both judges code the same, P_a:

$$\text{Agreement proportion} = P_a = \frac{F_a}{n}$$

(6.8)

In Table 6.5, 21 messages were coded the same by the two judges, so $F_a = 21$. And each judge coded $n = 26$ messages. Applying equation 6.8, the proportion of agreement is $21/26 = 0.808$. So about 81% of the units were classified the same by the two coder. Because both judges coded all 26 messages, Holsti's method (equation 6.7) also yields 0.808.

6.3.2   Correcting for Chance Agreement: Scott's π and Cohen's κ

Holsti's method and the proportion of agreement index have been criticized on the grounds that they fails to consider that two people who were just randomly distributing the units into categories would agree sometimes, just by chance. For instance, suppose that you and I coded 100 objects into one of two categories. Rather than attending to the task, imagine that we each flipped a coin to make the decision for each object. Using the rules described in Chapter 5, we can expect that half of our judgments would be the same; 50 of the 100 units we would code the same even though we are being totally unattentive to the task and ignoring the features of the objects when doing the coding. Furthermore, the proportion of agreement will tend to be higher "just by chance" when there are fewer categories into which units can be placed. So as a measure of reliability, proportion of agreement and Holsti's method leave something to be desired.

Two commonly used indices attempt to correct the proportion of agreement measure by gauging its size relative to a measure of agreement expected by chance. Scott's π (Scott, 1955) and Cohen's κ (Cohen, 1960) are chance-corrected agreement measures (κ is the Greek letter "kappa"). They both are based on the conceptual formula:

$$\text{Chance-corrected agreement} = \frac{P_a - P_c}{1 - P_c}$$

(6.9)

where P_c is the proportion of agreements expected by chance. Using the frequency (F) of agreements rather than proportion, equation 6.9 can also be written as $(F_a - F_c)/(n - F_c)$, where F_c is the number of agreements expected by chance.

Let's dissect equation 6.9. The denominator quantifies the difference between perfect agreement and expected chance agreement. The numerator quantifies the difference between the observed agreement and chance agreement. Thus, these chance-corrected measures quantify agreement as the proportion of the difference attained between perfect agreement and chance agreement. If $P_a = P_c$, agreement and therefore reliability equals zero. Agreement and therefore reliability is greater than zero only if the proportion of agreements exceeds the proportion of agreements expected by chance (i.e., $P_a > P_c$). It is possible for agreement to be less than zero if the coders agree less than expected by chance (i.e., $P_a < P_c$). In that case, agreement (and therefore reliability) should be treated as zero.

Both π and κ define expected agreement by chance using the notion of probabilistic independence. Define p_{ij} as the probability that coder i will place an object into category j. If the two coders are working independently from each other (that is, not discussing their codings with each other or making them together), then the multiplicative law of probability (section 5.2.2) applied to independent events says that the probability that the two coders will both categorize an object into category j is the product of their individual probabilities of placing objects into category j: $(p_{1j})(p_{2j})$. So the expected proportion of judgments in agreement by chance, P_c, is

$$P_c = \sum (p_{1j})(p_{2j})$$

(6.10)

where the summation is over all j categories. In terms of frequencies, when classifying n objects into categories, the expected number of agreements for category j is $n(p_{1j})(p_{2j})$ and so the expected number of agreements by chance across all j categories is $n \sum (p_{1j})(p_{2j})$.

Although both Scott's π and Cohen's κ use the multiplicative law of probability to derive the expected agreement, they differ in how the data are used to derive the values of p_{ij}. Cohen's κ allow for the possibility that the two coders may have different probabilities of assigning a unit into category j. In contrast, Scott's π ignores the possibility of such differences and derives a common probability of categorizing an object into category j by using information from both coders to derive this common probability.

Define F_{ij} as the number of the n units coder i placed into category j. For Cohen's κ,

$$\hat{p}_{ij} = \frac{F_{ij}}{n}$$

Notice the "hat" symbol to denote this as an estimate. We can never know judge i's probability of placing a unit into category j. The best we can do is estimate that probability using information from the judges' decisions coding these 26 units at this time. Had these coders been given a different set of units to judge or were asked to judge these same 26 units at a different time, the values of F_{ij} would probably have been different, as would the estimates of p_{ij}.

Notice that $\hat{p}_{1j} = \hat{p}_{2j}$ if $F_{1j} = F_{2j}$, otherwise $\hat{p}_{1j} \neq \hat{p}_{2j}$. So when calculating Cohen's κ, each coder's estimated probability of categorizing an object into category j is respected as an estimate of a different quantity. In contrast, Scott's π constrains $\hat{p}_{1j}$ to be equal to $\hat{p}_{2j}$ by defining them both as the average of the two coders' estimated probability of classifying an object into category j. For Scott's π,

$$\hat{p}_{1j} = \hat{p}_{2j} = \frac{(F_{1j} + F_{2j})}{2n}$$

This probably sounds a bit confusing, so let's work through the computations using the data in Table 6.5. We know that the observed agreement, P_a, is 0.808. Our goal is to derive the proportion of judgments that would be expected "by chance" so that we can derive chance-corrected agreement. To compute κ we first need to derive the probability that the 2 coders would both categorize a unit as "instrumental" support, just by chance. Let's call the instrumental support message category $j = 1$. Coder 1 judged 7 of the 26 memorable message as instrumental support, so $\hat{p}_{11} = (7/26) = 0.269$. Similarly, coder 2 judged 7 of the 26 messages as instrumental support, so $\hat{p}_{21} = (7/26) = 0.269$. So assuming that the coders were working independently, the estimated probability that they would *both* judge a message as providing instrumental support is $(0.269)(0.269) = 0.072$. Continuing with this logic, let's define "informational support" as category $j = 2$ and "emotional support" as category $j = 3$. Using the same reasoning as above, $\hat{p}_{12} = (9/26) = 0.346$, $\hat{p}_{22} = (7/26) = 0.269$, $\hat{p}_{13} = (10/26) = 0.385$, $\hat{p}_{23} = (12/26) = 0.462$. Using these estimates, the estimated probability that both coders would classify a message as providing informational support just by chance is $(0.346)(0.269) = 0.093$, and the estimated probability that both would classify a message as an "emotional support" message is $(0.385)(0.462) = 0.178$. Substituting the estimated probabilities for the actual probabilities in equation 6.10, the expected agreement by chance is estimated as

$$P_c = \sum (\hat{p}_{1j})(\hat{p}_{2j}) = (0.072) + (0.093) + (0.178) = 0.343$$

and so

$$\text{Cohen's } \kappa = \frac{P_a - P_c}{1 - P_c} = \frac{0.808 - 0.343}{1 - 0.343} = 0.708$$

This example illustrates something that is typical. Correcting for chance tends to lower estimates of agreement relative to Holsti's method or the proportion of agreement, because some of the agreements are attributed to chance.

Let's now compute Scott's π. Again, we already know P_a but seek an estimate of P_c. We still rely on the multiplicative law of probability applied to independent events, but we estimate expected chance by averaging the estimated probabilities that a coder will classify a message into category j using the data from both coders. For the estimated probability that a coder will judge a message as an "instrumental," we constrain $\hat{p}_{11} = \hat{p}_{21}$ by defining them both as $[(7/26) + (7/26)]/2 = 0.269$, meaning the probability that both judges code a message as instrumental is $(0.269)(0.269) = 0.073$. In this case, the average of the probabilities across the 2 coders is the same as the individual probabilities because they both coded 7 messages as "instrumental." But not so for informational support messages ($j = 2$). Coder 1 saw 9 such messages in the 26, whereas coder 2 saw 7 informational messages, so $\hat{p}_{12} = \hat{p}_{22} = [(9/26) + (7/26)]/2 = 0.308$, and so the estimated probability that both coders judge a message as informational is $(0.308)(0.308) = 0.095$. Finally, $\hat{p}_{13} = \hat{p}_{23} = [(10/26) + (12/26)]/2 = 0.423$, so the probability that both coders perceive a message as providing emotional support is estimated as $(0.423)(0.423) = 0.179$. Putting all this together,

$$P_c = \sum (\hat{p}_{1j})(\hat{p}_{2j}) = (0.073) + (0.095) + (0.179) = 0.347$$

and so

$$\text{Scott's } \pi = \frac{P_a - P_c}{1 - P_c} = \frac{0.808 - 0.347}{1 - 0.347} = 0.706$$

In this case, κ and π are very similar. This occurs when the coders' distribution of the n units across the categories is similar, as they are here. The more discrepant the coders' distribution of the units the greater the difference between κ and π.

But this begs the question: which is the preferred method of correcting for chance? There is no simple answer to this question because it depends on what you are trying to establish with an agreement estimate. Cohen's κ is a well accepted method of correcting for chance in education and psychology, but it is not without its controversies (see, e.g., Brennan & Prediger, 1981; Potter & Levine-Donnerstein, 1999). A recent content analysis of communication journals shows that π and κ are used about equally often (Lombard, Snyder-Duch, & Bracken, 2002). This is not the place to describe the large and complicated literature about which method is better or more appropriate— to do so would require an entire or chapter or more. But a few points are worth making. First, as Krippendorff (2004) illustrates with a few numerical examples, κ seems more susceptible than π to where the disagreements in the table reside and how those disagreements are distributed across the categories. Whether this is a good or bad thing depends on your perspective, but in my judgment, an agreement estimate should not be especially sensitive to the location of the disagreements. This would lead me to prefer π over κ. Second, the units being categorized are typically only a small set of existing units that could have been categorized but were not. If those units are a random sample from a population of units, for example, it is sensible to conceptualize the *population distribution* of category membership. That is, how would the units be distributed across the categories if all existing units were available to be classified? That true distribution would determine the expected agreement by chance for any two coders selected from a pool of possible coders. Although the population distribution is unknowable, averaging the two coders' distribution seems like a sensible way of estimating that true distribution and therefore expected agreement by chance. This is what Scott's π does. Cohen's κ is more susceptible to the judgments of a coder that categorizes unlike most other coders might, because each coder's distribution is used individually to derive expected disagreement. So κ would tend to be a poorer estimator of how reliably any randomly selected pair of coders would categorize. Again, this argument would favor the use of π over κ. In practice, however, the two measures are often close so it will usually make little difference which measure you choose.

One can ask whether a method that corrects for chance agreement is better than one that does not. This is a very controversial issue. My own observations of the climate of opinion regarding this matter in the communication field is that correction for chance is a good thing and should be done when possible. However, some have argued that Scott's π and Cohen's κ overcorrect. That is, these two statistics tend

```
Run MATRIX procedure:
MEASURES OF AGREEMENT IN A CROSSTABULATION

Table Being Analyzed
   6   1   0
   0   6   1
   1   2   9

Data Codes Corresponding to Rows and Columns:
   1   2   3

Holsti          .8077
Scott pi        .7059
Kappa           .7072
Alpha           .7115
I-sub-r         .8435
```

Figure 6.2 Output from an SPSS macro that calculates agreement of two sets of categorical judgments.

to attribute a substantial amount of the agreement to chance—perhaps more than is desirable—and this makes it difficult to achieve acceptable reliability. This problem is exacerbated when the units tend to be overwhelmingly assigned to one category relative to others. For instance, perhaps category A is 9 times more frequent than category B in the population of units, and the judgments of two coders reflect this imbalance in the frequency of the categories. Using π or κ, two coders would be expected to be in agreement with each other roughly 80% of the time just by chance. Why should we assume that 80% of their agreements reflect chance rather than the two coders correctly classifying the units into their respective categories? For a good discussion of this issue, see Potter and Levine-Donnerstein (1999).

Rarely would a researcher have to compute a measure of agreement by hand. There are several specialized programs dedicated to estimating agreement of subjective decisions which can also be employed. And some commonly-used statistical programs can generate at least some of the more frequently used measures of agreement. SPSS for instance can generate κ from a crosstabulation, although it will not always generate the statistic when it seems like it should be able to because of some quirks in its programming. SPSS will not compute Scott's π, Holsti's method, or for that matter any of the other dozen or more measures of agreement that can be computed from a crosstabulation. The is unfortunate given how frequently SPSS is used by communication researhers and how often it is necessary for a communication researcher to generate one of these indices. To rectify this situation, you will find an SPSS macro in Appendix F on the CD that adds this functionality to SPSS. Figure 6.2 contains the output from this macro applied to the data in Table 6.5. As can be seen, the output corresponds to our hand computations (within expected rounding errors that are unavoidable when computations are conducted by hand). The macro also produces Krippendorff's α (Krippendorff, 2004) and Perreault and Leigh's (1989) index called I_r. Krippendorff's α is very similar to π. They will differ noticeable only when the number of units being categorized is small. For a discussion of I_r, see Perreault & Leigh (1989).

6.3.3 Using an Agreement Index

As mentioned above, we use agreement as a way of assessing reliability—how much error exists in the categorization process. So good agreement is as much a statement about the categorization process and those doing the coding as it is a statement about the quality of the data itself. When an estimate of agreement is sufficiently high, this can be used as evidence that the coders were able to do the task as instructed, that the instructions were clear, that the units fit nicely into the categorization scheme, and that the resulting data (i.e., which category does a unit belong in) are accurate.

But perfect agreement is unlikely. Two coders may generally agree and agree well, but most likely they will not always agree about where a unit belongs in the categorization system. What does a researcher do with the units that the coders disagree on? And how large does agreement have to be in order for judgments to be considered sufficiently reliable? The answer to these question depends on the stage of data generation in which the reliability estimate is being used and how many of the units were actually judged by both coders. Sometimes we use a agreement index as a means of convincing ourselves that we have given the coders a task that is doable, as a means of justifying having only a single coder complete the entire coding task, and to determine whether one or both of the coders need additional training using the categorization scheme they were given. But sometimes an agreement index is reported only to convince readers of our research that the coders were able to agree in how they classified the units, meaning that the decisions were made objectively and based on attributes of the units themselves rather than just what these particular coders perceived. I now explain the distinction between such uses of an agreement index.

Computing Agreement To Assess the Exchangeability of Coders. In many, perhaps even most studies requiring some kind of categorical coding of research units, the number of units to be coded is large. To estimate agreement, at least two coders are required to judge all the units, but this may be an inefficient way of generating the data that one needs to answer a research question or test a hypothesis. Communication researchers are not in the business of estimating agreement, and we ultimately don't care that much about agreement. What we care about is knowing which category a unit belongs in so that we can proceed with the analyses pertinent to the goals of the study when it was conceived. We could get on with this more interesting part of science more quickly if the coding task could be split up, such that two or more coders each code only some of the units. This would cut the workload substantially for each coder and streamline the research process considerably. Alternatively, if might be a lot easier if you could just use a single coder to code most or all of the units.

Indeed, such procedural simplifications are desirable. But they are justified only if it can be argued that coders are *exchangeable*. That is, does the behavior of one coder (i.e., his or her categorization decisions) essentially mimic the behavior of another? If exchangeability is satisfied, then it makes no difference which coder codes which units, as their coding decisions would be largely the same. In that case, you can give some units to one coder to categorize and some of the units to another coder. They each do half of the work they'd otherwise have to do, and the work gets done twice as fast. Alternatively, you could have one coder's judgments for a small fraction of the units serve as a reference point for evaluating the decisions of another coder. Once it is determined that one of the coders agrees with the other, then one of the coders can be dismissed as now irrelevant to the process and the remaining coder then codes all of the remaining units. Although this may not speed up the coding process, it will at least require fewer resources (e.g., less money if the coders are being paid).

The key to justifying exchangeability is the size of the agreement between two coders who are asked to code a subset of the units. So rather than having each coder code all the units, two coders first code a small fraction of the units to be coded, ideally selected randomly from the pool of units that eventually need to be coded. If agreement is sufficiently high on this sample of units, then the coders can be deemed exchangeable and the workload can either be cut in half or the coding done entirely by a single coder. So an agreement index can be used as a means of determining whether exchangeability has been satisfied. If agreement is too low, this means that the coders are not exchangeable, and it would be dangerous at this point to use the judgments of only a single coder (or multiple coders each judging a fraction of the units) when deciding which category a unit should be placed in. Low agreement can be the result of any number of things. It could be that the coders weren't paying attention to the task or otherwise didn't take it seriously, that they didn't understand the coding instructions, that the categorization system is not exhaustive of the categories that actually exist (and so the coders are having trouble fitting some units into a category), or any other number of procedural difficulties. When such disagreements arise in large number, these procedural difficulties must be overcome and agreement ultimately increased using another sample of units before coders can be deemed exchangeable.

So an agreement index can be used as a justification for streamlining the coding process, so that it can be done by only a single coder or by multiple coders. Information about agreement is for the investigator's use only, in that it is information that allows the investigator to justify splitting up the workload or using a single coder. But this information (i.e., how much agreement was achieved during the training phase) is typically reported in a research article anyway, so that readers of the research will have some sense for how the data were collected, the procedures followed, and the justification for those procedures.

Reporting Agreement as a Means of Communicating Reliability of the Data. Sometimes two coders judge all the units. This would be typical if the number of units is small or if the task is sufficiently difficult or units ambiguous enough on the dimension being coded that the judgments of two coders are deemed necessary to produce accurate data. In that case, it is possible to report the agreement between the judges across all units. But just how relevant is this information, given that disagreements will probably still exist that must be resolved before the data can be analyzed? For instance, Ford and Ellis (1998) reported Scott's π of 0.71 in their categorization of memorable support messages into the instrumental, informational, and emotional categories. When disagreements arose (and some did of course), the two coders then discussed those disagreements and made a joint decision as to the proper category for those units they perceived differently. An alternative method of resolving disagreements is to rely on the judgments of a third coder, who is used only to resolve disagreements when they occur. But why is the magnitude of agreement relevant in that case? Why not just have the two coders code together or have three coders and use "majority rule" to determine category membership?

Even when both coders code all the research units, information about agreement does provide useful information. It provides information about exchangeability, but exchangeability of a different sort. If two coders agree in their judgments, this suggests that these two coders are exchangeable not with each other, but with any other coders who could have been used. In other words, it communicates the replicability of the coding decisions and therefore the reliability of the data. If agreement is low and disagreements frequently have to be resolved with group discussion or a third coder, this suggests that a different set of coders would be relatively likely to have provided different judgments. After all, if two people are forced to agree through group discussion, they will agree, but that doesn't mean that their mutual judgment is accurate. Similarly, there will always be a majority when three people are asked to make a judgment. But that doesn't mean the majority is right. Just as it does when used during the coder training process, low agreement could reflect inherent difficulties of the task, instructions that aren't clear, or a poor categorization system. In short, low agreement brings into question the reliability of the data and ultimately the generalizability of any research findings.

6.4 How High is High Enough?

Whether you conceptualize reliability as the ratio of true score to observed score variance or agreement between judges, reliability is a good thing, and we want reliability to high. But how high does reliability need to before we can claim that our measurements are reliable, or agreement between judges sufficiently high to justify splitting up the coding task or having a single coder do most of the work? Is there a mathematical formula that tells you what reliability needs to be?

The answer is no. But science is a social, communal process, and common guidelines and rules of thumb have been offered. Unfortunately, those guidelines often conflict. Neuendorf (2001, p. 143) reviews some of these rules of thumb. One thing they do have in common is that higher is clearly better, and reliability of less than 0.70 is generally unacceptable. But for chance corrected measures of agreement, some argue that we should be more lenient in our definition of acceptable because correction for chance sometimes makes it nearly impossible to achieve agreement above 0.70. If two coders coded all the units and disagreements were resolved in some way, then 0.70 is probably high enough because those discussion will probably reduce some of the error. But if the goal is to justify using only a single coder for some or all of the units (by dismissing one coder or splitting the coding task among coders), then agreement should be higher than 0.70 in my judgement—at least 0.90, perhaps a bit lower for chance-corrected agreement. But this recommendation is no less arbitrary than any other that has been offered.

For reliability of quantitative measurements, 0.70 is generally considered the magic number. If your reliability of measurement is below 0.70, you can expect critics of your research to argue that you aren't measuring well. I personally have a hard time justifying making too much out of an analysis (my own or others) when I know that reliability of measurement is much less than 0.70. So your best strategy is to maximize the likelihood of high reliability by carefully selecting your operationalizations, using methods of measurement that are known to produce relatively little measurement error. If you find it necessary to invent your own operationalizations, be thoughtful in how you do so, and expect a critic to take you to task if you can't demonstrate that your measurements are not just or mostly random measurement error.

6.5 Summary

Few things are more important to the integrity of the scientific process than good measurement. Reliability of measurement, defined as the ratio of true score variance to observed score variance, gives us a means of quantifying how much of a set of measurements is error and how much reflects true variation between the research units on what is being measured. Classical test theory has led to the development of several means that researchers can quantify reliability of measurement when the variable being measured is quantitative. Whenever possible to do so, you should provide evidence to consumers of your research about the reliability of your measurement. It is not sufficient to report the reliability that others have reported using the measures of the constructs that you are using.

Whenever human judges must make subjective decisions about categorizing research units, reliability is typically inferred from the amount of agreement between judges in their decisions. If two judges don't agree where a set of research units belong in the categorization system being used, this suggests that their decisions reflect as much their own idiosyncratic perceptions as it does something inherent in the objects being judged. A measure of agreement can be used during the development of a categorization system and in the training of judges. Like other forms of reliability, a measure of agreement should be provided in written reports of your research so readers of your research can ascertain the extent to which the research units have been correctly classified.

CHAPTER
SEVEN

Parameter Estimation

Pick up the newspaper or turn on the television and no doubt you will read about or hear the result of one of the many polls taken daily of the public's beliefs, attitudes, values, and opinions. Claims such as "Sixty five percent of Americans approve of the way the President is handling the economy," "48% of people age 40 or over have not started saving for retirement," "54% of high school kids report that they could obtain marijuana if they wanted it" are not difficult to find in the media. If you look closely at such polls, you will notice that typically they are based on the responses of only a small fraction of the people in the population that the pollsters are making statements about. How it is possible that a researcher can make a statement about an entire population by asking questions of a small, indeed only a tiny fraction of the population of interest?

The ability to make inferences about the opinions and behavior of large groups by studying only a sample from that group stems from the theory of parameter estimation, the topic of this chapter. Parameter estimation is used for the purpose of making *population inferences*—inferences about the value of some unknown population characteristic given limited information about the population. The theory of estimation is both elegant and central to statistics. You need to understand it and understand it well.

7.1 The Theory of Estimation

Suppose you are a reporter for the *Chronicle of Higher Education* and are putting together a story on the research activity of a new Department of Communication at Anytown State University. Your goal is to provide information in your story about the mean number of publications that faculty in the department have published over the course of their careers as part of your profile on the department. Suppose there are 8 faculty members in this new department. If you were resourceful enough and had sufficient time, it might be possible for you to determine that number exactly by contacting each of the 8 faculty members, getting a copy of their curriculum vitae, and computing the mean across all $N = 8$ faculty. (Here I use capital N to denote the size of the population.) If you were able to do so, you would be able to make an unequivocal statement about the *parameter* of interest—the population mean (μ) number of publications. But it might be difficult for you to obtain this information. For example, perhaps your deadline for filing the story is looming so you don't have enough time to wait for every faculty member to respond to your request. Or perhaps you don't want to bother everyone in the department—people who are no doubt busy and have other things to do with their time. Given this constraint you might decide to prepare your report without this information. Better to report no information than incomplete information, right?

Not necessarily. Although it might be difficult to get all 8 faculty to respond to your request, you might be able to get a few of the faculty to respond if you really hound them for the information. So an alternative would be to get what information you can from a subset of the population—a sample. Rather than attempting to contact all 8 faculty members, perhaps you could contact a subset of the faculty and focus your energy on getting just those few faculty members you contact to respond to your request for information. Using the information that you get from this sample of faculty members in the department, you could make an inference about the average number of publications across *all* the faculty in the department. That is, you could use the sample mean to estimate the population mean. From this estimate, you could make a population inference—a numerical statement about the entire population (all eight faculty). Public opinion pollsters do this all the time, and armed with a little knowledge of the theory of estimation, so can you.

In Table 7.1 you will find a hypothetical data set containing the total number of publications for each faculty member at Anytown State University. According to these data, the mean number publications per faculty across the entire department is $\mu = 14$ with standard deviation $\sigma = 7.550$. Notice my use of Greek symbols here, reflecting that this is information about the entire population. (In this case, σ was computed using the version of equation 4.3 that divides the sum of the squared differences from the mean by n rather than $n - 1$ because information about the entire population is available in this table.) Of course, in practice, information about the population is not available or may be difficult or impossible to obtain, as I described above. If it were available, you wouldn't need to estimate the population mean because it would be known. I provide this information here in order to illustrate just how the process of estimation works. In a later example, we will apply the principles discussed here to a more realistic problem.

7.1.1   The Sampling Distribution

Suppose that because of time constraints, you only had enough time to collect accurate information from 3 of the faculty members (so $n = 3$, with the small letter n referring to the sample size). Although not ideal, you decide that this is better than nothing, so you will use the information from 3 of the faculty you contact. Just how would you go about deciding which 3 faculty members you will include in your sample from this population of 8 faculty? Chapter 3 discussed some of the possibilities. If your interest is in population inference, which it is here, you should use a probability sample such as a simple random sample because probability samples are the best way of insuring that no hidden biases, unconscious processes, or other things lead you to select a subset of faculty members that are not representative. For instance, suppose rather than using a probability sampling method you decided to contact the faculty members you have heard about through the media, under the assumption that they are used to talking to

Table 7.1

Publications by Communication Faculty at Anytown State University

Professor	Number of Publications
Anderson	6
Baker	10
Carter	12
Diaz	8
Edwards	14
Foster	22
Green	10
Henderson	30

the media and will be more forthcoming with the information you want. But what if the faculty members that get attention in the media tend to conduct applied research that attracts more research funds? The more research support a faculty member has, the more data they can get, and the more publications they are likely to have. So this strategy may very well lead you to overestimate the average number of publications in the population of 8 faculty.

You decide to remove yourself from the selection process and leave who you contact up to chance by conducting a simple random sample. To do so, you assign each faculty member a number 1 through 8 to identify him or her and then you have a computer randomly select $n = 3$ unique numbers between 1 and 8 to select the sample. Suppose this process leads you to include professors Anderson, Diaz, and Edwards. After some effort you manage to get a hold of each of them and obtain a copy of their C.V.s. Your variable, X, is the number of publications listed on a faculty member's C.V. For this sample of 3 faculty, the sample mean number of publications is $\overline{X} = 9.333$, with a sample standard deviation $s = 4.163$. So you include in your profile of the department that the average number of publications by members of the faculty is 9.333. Here I use Roman characters to denote the mean and standard deviation, reflecting the fact that this information comes from a sample of a population. The standard deviation isn't directly relevant right now, but I report the estimate of the standard deviation here because it is a good practice to report a measure of variability along with a measure of central tendency.

Observe that 9.333 is an underestimate of the population mean (recall that $\mu = 14$). Would you be misleading those who read your report? In some sense, yes, you would be because the population mean is not 9.333, it is 14. But you can't really be faulted for that. You didn't know the population mean. If you did, that is what you would have reported. Presumably you described how you arrived at 9.333 as your estimate, and you did honestly communicate the results from your sampling procedure. The discrepancy between your report and the truth can be attributed to nothing other than *random sampling error*. Random sampling error is error in the estimation of a parameter attributable just to the random selection process—the fact that your sample included certain members of the population rather than others merely because they were randomly selected to be included in the sample.

**Box 7.1: Deriving the Number of Combinations of k Objects
From a Population of N Objects**

In many statistical contexts, it is of interest to know how many combinations of k objects can be constructed from a set of N objects. There is a simple formula for calculating this. This combination problem is denoted symbolically as

$$\binom{N}{k}$$

which is read "N choose k" or "the number of combinations of k objects from a set of N objects." Mathematically,

$$\binom{N}{k} = \frac{N!}{k!(N-k)!}$$

where N is the number of objects in the entire set, k is the number of objects in the combination, and "!" is the factorial operation introduced in Chapter 5. For example, if there are 8 faculty in a department then there are "8 choose 3" different combinations of 3 faculty members. Applying the formula, as below, we see that there are 56 possible combinations of three faculty:

$$\binom{8}{3} = \frac{8!}{3!(8-3)!} = \frac{8 \times 7 \times 6 \times 5 \times 4 \times 3 \times 2 \times 1}{3 \times 2 \times 1(5 \times 4 \times 3 \times 2 \times 1)} = \frac{40,320}{720} = 56$$

This can also be used to determine how many possible groups of size k and $N - k$ can be created from a population of size N. For example, there are "8 choose 2" or 28 ways that 8 faculty can be placed into 2 groups of size 2 and 6. Because it is arbitrary whether we think of this as 2 groups of size $k = 2$ and $N - k = 6$ or 2 groups of size $k = 6$ and $N - k = 2$, it is therefore true that N choose k is equal to N choose $N - k$.

To illustrate random sampling error, consider what you would have included in your report if your random sampling procedure picked a different set of 3 faculty. Suppose your random selection procedure included Professors Baker, Edwards, and Henderson. In that case, your estimate would be $\overline{X} = 18$ ($s = 10.583$). A different sample of 3, such as Professors Anderson, Diaz, and Henderson, would have yielded still a different estimate: $\overline{X} = 14.667$ ($s = 13.317$). Both of these estimates of μ are different than the estimate from the original sample as well as from the actual population mean. This might seem frustrating from a practical perspective. Why should you trust any estimate from a particular random sample any more than an estimate from any other random sample? But the fickleness of a sample estimate is built into the theory of estimation and is accounted for in the estimation process.

I just illustrated that three different samples of size 3 from this population of 8 faculty members would each yield a different estimate $(\overline{X})$ of the population mean number of publications by faculty in this department (μ). A simple formula tells us that there are 56 unique combinations of 3 faculty from this population of 8 faculty, which means that there are 56 possible sample means that you can get in a sample of 3 faculty from this department (Box 7.1 describes how 56 was derived). If the sample mean number of faculty publications can vary from random sample to random sample (as we have seen it can), then $\overline{X}$ is a random variable (recall the definition

Table 7.2

The Sampling Distribution of $\overline{X}$, $n = 3$, Using the Data in Table 7.1

$\overline{X}$	Frequency	$P(\overline{X})$	Cumulative Probability
8.00	2	0.036	0.036
8.67	2	0.036	0.072
9.33	4	0.071	0.143
10.00	4	0.071	0.214
10.67	4	0.071	0.286
11.33	2	0.036	0.321
12.00	3	0.054	0.375
12.67	2	0.036	0.411
13.33	3	0.054	0.464
14.00	3	0.054	0.518
14.67	4	0.071	0.589
15.33	4	0.071	0.661
16.00	4	0.071	0.732
16.67	3	0.054	0.786
17.33	3	0.054	0.839
18.00	2	0.036	0.875
18.67	1	0.018	0.893
19.33	1	0.018	0.911
20.00	1	0.018	0.929
20.67	2	0.036	0.964
21.33	1	0.018	0.982
22.00	1	0.018	1.000

of a random variable from section 5.4). Therefore, $\overline{X}$ has a probability distribution. The probability distribution of $\overline{X}$ when taking a random sample of size 3 from this population can be generated by constructing every possible combination of 3 faculty, computing $\overline{X}$ in each sample, and then assigning to each sample mean its probability of being the sample mean obtained when randomly picking 3 faculty from the population of 8. This probability is computed as the number of samples of size three that produce that mean divided by the total number of possible samples of size three. The probability distribution for this problem, displayed in the form of a frequency table, can be found in Table 7.2.

The distribution of possible sample statistics in a sample of size n from a population is known as the *sampling distribution* of the statistic, and it is one of the more important concepts in statistical inference and the theory of estimation. In this case, the sampling distribution of interest is the *sampling distribution of the sample mean*. But any conceivable statistic has a sampling distribution, including the median, the standard deviation, a sample proportion, a sample correlation, and so forth. For instance, notice that just as the sample mean varied across the 3 samples described above, so did the sample standard deviation. So any statistic that you can compute in a sample from a population has a sampling distribution.

An examination of the sampling distribution for this problem (displayed in Table 7.2) tells us that, for example, only 21.4% of possible samples of size three from this population would produce a sample mean equal to or less than 10. This comes from the fact that only 12 of the 56 possible sample means are 10 or less. So we could say that the probability of obtaining a sample mean of 10 or less when taking a random sample of size 3 from this population is 0.214. Symbolically, $P(\overline{X} \leq 10) = 0.214$. Similarly, only 7.1% of sample means are greater than 20 (because only 4 samples out of the 56 possible produce a sample mean of more than 20), so $P(\overline{X} > 20) = 0.071$. Notice as well that only 3 samples of size 3 from this population of 8 faculty yields a sample mean *exactly* equal to the population mean of 14, but nearly three quarters of the sample means (41 out of 56) are between 10 and 18, or within about 4 publications of the population mean. So the probability of getting a sample mean within 4 publications of the population mean of 14 is $(41/56) = 0.732$, but the probability of getting a sample mean exactly equal to the population mean is only $(3/56) = 0.054$. That is, $P(\overline{X} \geq \mu - 4$ and $\overline{X} \leq \mu + 4) = 0.732$, and $P(\overline{X} = 14) = 0.054$.

What is the point of this exercise? The major point I am trying to make is that rarely will a sample mean equal the mean of the population from which the sample was derived. By the luck of the draw, the sample mean that you obtain in your research will depend on who or what was randomly included in the sample (assuming you have randomly sampled from a population, which is what the theory of estimation described here assumes). But as you will soon see, there is a certain predictable regularity to random sampling error that provides the foundation for how public opinion pollsters and other researchers can estimate characteristics of the population from only a small sample from that population.

7.1.2 Properties of the Sampling Distribution of the Sample Mean

The exercise above was purely theoretical. I showed above how a sample mean can differ from the population mean you are trying to estimate merely as a result of random sampling error. Furthermore, for any problem focused on the estimation of a population mean, there exists a sampling distribution of the sample mean, defined as the probability distribution for the sample mean when taking a random sample of size n from the population. The most effective way of illustrating these ideas was to provide a population and show you how different samples from this population yield different sample means and that the sampling distribution of the sample mean does exist and can be generated if you know each member of the population's score on the variable of interest.

But again, this was a purely theoretical exercise, and an artificial one to boot. In practice, you would almost never know the scores on the variable being measured for every unit in the population, so there is no way that you could ever generate the sampling distribution of the sample mean. Therefore, you wouldn't know whether the sample mean obtained was relatively unusual or relatively common in the distribution of possible sample means and whether you should trust your sample mean as a good estimate of μ. Furthermore, if you had information about the population, why estimate it? There would be no need to estimate μ because it would be known.

True. Typically do not have information about the entire population. But it turns out that with nothing other than a random sample from the population, we can exploit some fundamental principles in the theory of estimation to make inferences about the population mean. Importantly, we don't need to know anything about the distribution of scores on the variable in the population we have sampled from in order to use information from the sample to make a population inference about μ. This information comes from some important properties of the sampling distribution of the sample mean that you need to be familiar with in order to appreciate the elegance of the theory of estimation.

The Expected Value of the Sample Mean. Although in practice we cannot generate the sampling distribution for a sample statistic as I did in the previous example, that doesn't mean that the sampling distribution for the statistic doesn't exist. The sampling distribution of the sample mean does exist for any estimation problem, regardless of whether or not we are able to generate it as I did here. Furthermore the sampling distribution of the sample mean is a distribution, just like any distribution. It is the distribution of possible sample means when taking a random sample of a specific size from the population. As nearly all distributions do, this distribution has a mean, a standard deviation, and all the other characteristics that a distribution of numbers has.

As already discussed, Table 7.2 contains all the possible sample means when taking a random sample of size 3 from the population in Table 7.1. If you were to compute the mean of the 56 possible sample means in this sampling distribution, it turns out that the mean of this population of possible sample means is 14. The mean of the sampling distribution of the sample mean gets a special symbol: $\mu_{\overline{X}}$. So here, $\mu_{\overline{X}} = 14$. The Greek letter μ is used because $\mu_{\overline{X}}$ is population mean, in this case the population of all possible sample means when taking a sample of size 3 from this population, and the subscript $(\overline{X})$ denotes that $\mu_{\overline{X}}$ is the population mean of all possible *sample* means.

You should recognize 14 from earlier—it is the mean number of faculty publications in the population of 8 faculty: $\mu = 14$. This is an illustration of a general principle in the theory of estimation, represented symbolically in equation 7.1:

$$\mu_{\overline{X}} = \mu$$

$$(7.1)$$

Seriously, few things in the world are more exciting than equation 7.1 in my opinion. Furthermore, this is very useful information that can be exploited. The implication of this is that the "expected value" for a sample mean when randomly sampling from the population is the mean of the population. Symbolically,

$$E(\overline{X}) = \mu$$

$$(7.2)$$

When the expected value of a sample statistic is equal to the parameter it is being used to estimate, it is said that the statistic is an *unbiased estimator* of the parameter. So long as μ exists, $\overline{X}$ is an unbiased estimator of μ when taking a simple random sample from a population. So even though any sample mean you compute in a random sample from a population will likely differ from μ, it is still true that the expected value of the sample mean is the population mean. I know this sounds contradictory, but it is not. One way of thinking about this apparent contradiction is to think of the problem in this way: Any sample mean is unlikely to be exactly equal to the population mean. We've seen that this is true in this example, and it is generally true. But what if you had to guess what the sample mean was going to be before you collected any data? In earlier chapters, I pointed out that the mean of a distribution is always the best guess for any measurement in that distribution, in that the use of this guessing strategy will tend to minimize the errors in your guesses over the long run if you have no other information that you can use to improve the accuracy of your guess. By the same reasoning, your best guess for the sample mean is that it will equal the population mean, because the population mean is the sample mean's expected value. Of course, any sample mean is unlikely to be equal to the population mean, but if you expect it to be equal to the mean, than this expectation is likely to disappoint you less than any other guessing strategy that you could employ. It will tend to be least in error.

The Standard Error. I just illustrated that the mean of the sampling distribution of the sample mean is the population mean, and so the expected value of the sample mean is the population mean when randomly sampling from the population. There is also a systematic relationship between how much the possible sample means vary from each other and how variable the population is on what is being measured. Again, the sampling distribution of the sample mean is a distribution, and just like any distribution, it has variability that can be quantified. The standard deviation of the sampling distribution quantifies the average amount by which possible sample means differ from the mean of the sampling distribution. The standard deviation of the sampling distribution of the possible sample means listed in Table 7.2 is 3.684 (using n in the formula for the standard deviation rather than $n - 1$ because Table 7.2 contains every possible sample mean, not just a sample of those possible means). So the possible sample means differ from the mean of the sampling distribution by 3.684 on average. But given that $\mu_{\overline{X}} = \mu$, we can also say that the possible sample means differ by 3.684 on average from the population mean of 14. This is an important insight, as we now know how much a sample mean is expected to differ from μ, the parameter it is estimating.

The standard deviation of the sampling distribution of a statistic has a special name. It is called the *standard error* of that statistic. For the standard error of the sample mean, we use the symbolic notation $\sigma_{\overline{X}}$. The standard deviation of the sampling distribution of the sample mean, also called the standard error of the sample mean, is defined mathematically as

$$\sigma_{\overline{X}} = \sigma\sqrt{\frac{1}{n}\left(1 - \frac{n-1}{N-1}\right)}$$

$$(7.3)$$

where σ is the population standard deviation on the variable, N is the size of the population, and n is the size of the sample. Observe then that the standard error of the sample mean is determined by how variable the population is, how large the sample is, and how large the population is. In our problem, $\sigma = 7.550$, $N = 8$, and $n = 3$ (recall that 7.550 is the population standard deviation of the number of publications among all 8 faculty). Applying equation 7.3

$$\sigma_{\overline{X}} = 7.550\sqrt{\frac{1}{3}\left(1 - \frac{3-1}{8-1}\right)} = 3.684$$

which is exactly the standard deviation of the sampling distribution of possible sample means in Table 7.2.

Equation 7.3 is different from the mathematical definition of the standard error printed in most statistics textbooks because as estimation theory is typically described, the assumption is that the population is very large relative to the size of the sample. The ratio of the sample size to the size of the population is called the *sampling fraction*, defined as (n/N). In most applications, the sampling fraction is tiny. For example, the typical opinion poll is based on 1,000 or so respondents, and yet the population being sampled is usually much larger—perhaps in the millions or tens of millions. In that case, (n/N) is so close to zero that it can essentially be treated as zero. If (n/N) is very close to zero, then $(n-1)/(N-1)$ is also very close to zero. In that case, the term in parentheses in equation 7.3 is very close to one, so close to one that it can just be treated as one without doing much to damage the accuracy of the computations. Thus, it can be removed from the equation. The result is a simpler version of the standard error that applies whenever the sample size is small relative to the size of the population:

$$\sigma_{\overline{X}} = \sigma \sqrt{\frac{1}{n}} = \frac{\sigma}{\sqrt{n}}$$

(7.4)

Two important bits of information come out of a close examination of equation 7.4 (or equation 7.3). First, notice that the size of the standard error depends in part on the size of the sample, n. As the size of the sample increases, the standard error decreases. What this means is that the bigger the sample, the less a sample mean is expected to differ from the population mean. So larger samples produce more accurate estimates than smaller samples. The second thing to notice is that the standard error increases as the population standard deviation increases. So the more that members of the populations vary on the characteristic being measured, the greater the expected discrepancy between a sample mean and the population mean. What this means is that it is harder to get a good estimate of some characteristic of a population (such as its mean) when the population is relatively heterogeneous on the characteristic being measured. To overcome the effects of large variability in the population on the characteristic being measured, you need a larger sample to get a good estimate of a feature of that population.

So we know a lot about the behavior of sample means when randomly sampling from a population. We know that the expected value of a sample mean is the population mean. We also have a formula for knowing how much, on average, you would expect the sample mean to differ from the population mean. That is the standard error, defined in equations 7.3 and 7.4. But we know even more than this as a result of something called the *Central Limit Theorem*.

The Central Limit Theorem. The Central Limit Theorem says that *regardless of the shape of the population distribution on the variable measured, the sampling distribution of the sample mean converges to a normal distribution with increasing sample size.* The importance of this cannot be overstated because knowing that the sampling distribution is normal gives us a lot of new information. We typically don't know the shape of the population on the variable being measured because we don't have access to all the information about the population on that variable. But the Central Limit Theorem tells us that so long as the sample size is sufficiently large, the shape of the sampling distribution of the sample mean is approximately normal. The phrase "converges to a normal distribution" means that the bigger the sample size, the closer to a normal distribution the sampling distribution is going to be.

With the Central Limit Theorem on our side, we can now capitalize on the regularity of the normal distribution to assign probabilities of obtaining sample means of a given

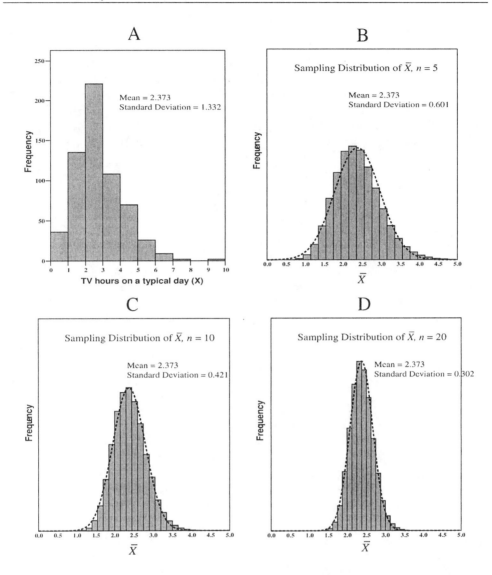

Figure 7.1 The central limit theorem in action.

size when randomly sampling from a population as well as to make reasonable guesses as to what the population mean is given information about the sample. But before describing how that is done, it is worth illustrating the Central Limit Theorem in action.

Recall that Box 4.1 contains the responses from 610 undergraduate students who took research methods from me during a three year period to the question "On an average day, about how many hours do you spend watching television?" Let's consider the group of students the entire population of interest. In that case, from Chapter 4, $\mu = 2.373$ and $\sigma = 1.332$. A histogram of this population of responses to this question is displayed in Figure 7.1, panel A. According to the Central Limit Theorem, the sampling distribution of the sample mean should be normal in its appearance, more so in larger samples, regardless of the shape of the population on the variable measured. To illustrate this, I programmed a computer to take 100,000 random samples of $n = 5$ students from the population of $N = 610$ students and compute the sample mean in each of these 100,000 samples (actually, $N = 609$ because the one student that didn't answer the question was discarded from the data). A histogram of these 100,000 sample means is found in panel B of Figure 7.1. As can be seen, the mean of these 100,000 sample means was 2.373, and the standard deviation of the 100,000 sample means was 0.601. A normal curve is superimposed over the figure with the same mean and standard deviation as these 100,000 sample means. Observe that the distribution of these sample means is close to normal, but it is not exactly normal.

I then repeated this procedure, this time taking 100,000 samples of size $n = 10$. A histogram of the sample mean for these 100,000 random samples of size 10 is displayed in panel C of Figure 7.1. Notice that the sampling distribution of the sample means looks more like a normal distribution when $n = 10$ compared to when $n = 5$. The mean of this sample of 100,000 samples was again 2.373, but the standard deviation of those sample means was smaller, at 0.421. Finally, in panel D you will see a histogram of 100,000 sample means computed in samples of size $n = 20$. Examining the correspondence between the height of the histogram bars and the normal curve superimposed over the histogram, it is clear that this distribution of sample means looks a little closer to normal than the ones in Panels B and C. The mean of these 100,000 sample means is 2.373, but the standard deviation of the sample means is smaller still, at 0.302.

The histograms in Figure 7.1 B through D do not correspond exactly to the true sampling distributions because they are based on only a subset (100,000) of all possible sample means. But because I had the computer randomly select many sample means from the set of all possible sample means, these histograms represent pretty closely what the true sampling distributions look like. An examination of these distributions illustrates the Central Limit Theorem in action, as well as the other properties of sampling distributions described earlier. The sampling distribution of the sample mean becomes increasingly more normal in its shape as the sample size increases. In addition, the mean of the sampling distribution, regardless of sample size, is indeed equal to the population mean (recall equation 7.1). Finally, observe that the standard deviation of the sampling distribution, what we called the standard error of the sample mean, also decreases as the sample size increases. This is reflected visually in the greater squashing or compression of the histogram of sample means around the mean of the sampling distribution with increasing sample size. This illustrates that when you collect a larger sample, you should expect that a sample mean will deviate less from the population mean compared to when you collect a smaller sample.

Earlier I discussed that the sampling distribution of the sample mean converges to a normal distribution as the sample size increases. At its extreme, with an infinitely large sample size, we can say that the distribution is exactly normally distributed. But with smaller samples, the distribution may not be exactly normal. There are two primary factors that determine how normal the sampling distribution of the sample mean will be—symmetry of the population distribution and sample size. The more symmetrical the population distribution on the variable being measured in the sample, the smaller the sample sizes required in order to assure that the sampling distribution is normal. So if the population is roughly symmetrically distributed, the sampling distribution of the mean will be closer to normal with a smaller sample size than if the population is asymmetrically distributed. But even with asymmetrical population distributions, the sampling distribution of the mean will become increasingly normal as the sample size increases. Just how large of a sample size is required to have confidence that the sampling distribution is normal depends on just how asymmetrical the population distribution is.[1]

7.1.3   Deriving the Probability of Obtaining Certain Sample Means

From the previous discussion, we know the following things about the behavior of sample means when sampling randomly from a population:

1. So long as the sample size is sufficiently large, the sampling distribution of the sample mean is roughly normal.

2. The mean of the sampling distribution is the population mean ($\mu_{\overline{X}} = \mu$), meaning that the expected value of any sample mean is the population mean.

3. The standard deviation of the sampling distribution is defined as in equation 7.3 (or 7.4 when the sampling fraction is small), which tells us that sample means will tend to deviate less from the population mean in larger samples.

Putting this all together, we can say that the sampling distribution of the sample mean has mean $\mu_{\overline{X}} = \mu$ and standard deviation $\sigma_{\overline{X}}$ and is normally distributed so long as the sample size is sufficiently large. Using the notation and terminology of Chapter 5, we can say that $\overline{X}$ is a random variable and

$$\overline{X} \sim \mathcal{N}(\mu_{\overline{X}}, \sigma_{\overline{X}})$$

But because ($\mu_{\overline{X}} = \mu$), we can also say that $\overline{X} \sim \mathcal{N}(\mu, \sigma_{\overline{X}})$ This regularity in the sampling distribution of the sample mean gives us a lot of power. Knowing only the population mean, the population standard deviation, the sample size, and with a little faith in the Central Limit Theorem, we can estimate the probability of obtaining means of certain sizes when sampling from the population using the methods described in Chapter 5.

For example, suppose that distribution of the Cheek and Buss (1981) Shyness index (a 13–item self report instrument used to measure how shy a person is) has mean $\mu = 32$ and standard deviation $\sigma = 8$ in a large population from which you take a random sample of size 16. What is the probability that the sample mean shyness score will be larger than 34? What about the probability of getting a sample mean less than 34? And how about the probability of getting a sample mean between 29 and 34? Symbolically, we can express these probabilities as $P(\overline{X} > 34), P(\overline{X} \leq 34)$, and $P(29 \leq \overline{X} \leq 34)$. Although it may not immediately strike you, you do already know how to find these probabilities because we solved exactly these sorts of problems in Chapter 5. To derive these probabilities, you just have to put all the pieces together.

First, the Central Limit Theorem tells us that the sampling distribution of the sample mean is roughly a normal distribution and that its mean is the population mean. So we can infer that the sampling distribution of the sample mean will be roughly normal in form and centered at 32. Second, we also know the standard deviation of the

---

[1]On the CD in Appendix F you will find an SPSS macro that can be used to illustrate these concepts better. The macro will generate multiple samples of a given size from a population you construct, compute the mean in each sample, and produce a histogram of the sample means. Using this macro, you can vary the sample size across runs and see how this affects the shape and variability of the sampling distribution of the sample mean.

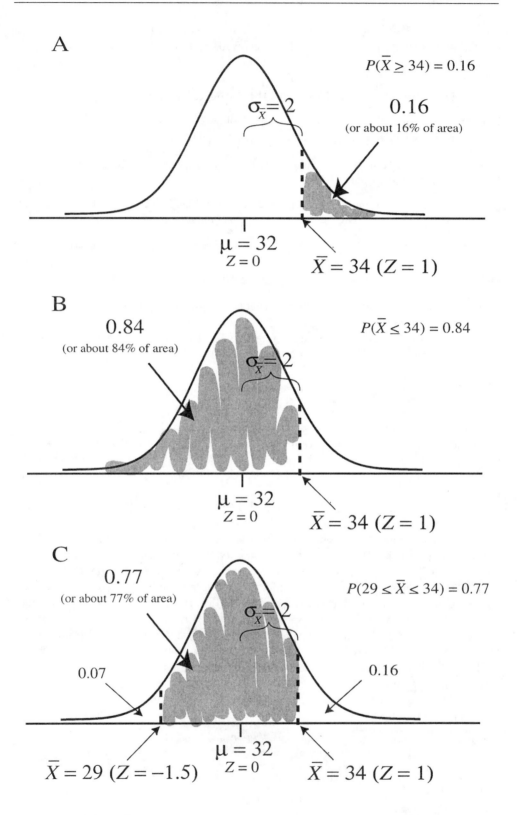

Figure 7.2 Deriving the probability of obtaining certain sample means.

sampling distribution of the sample mean, also called the standard error of the sample mean, is equal to

$$\sigma_{\overline{X}} = \frac{\sigma}{\sqrt{n}} = \frac{8}{\sqrt{16}} = 2$$

Therefore, $\overline{X} \sim \mathcal{N}(32, 2)$. So what is the probability of getting a sample mean that is larger than 34? Symbolically, $P(\overline{X} > 34) = ?$ To derive this probability, first ask how many standard deviations from the mean 34 is in the sampling distribution of the sample mean. Easy. The standard deviation of the sampling distribution is 2, so 34 is $Z = (34 - 32)/2 = 1$ standard deviation above the mean of the sampling distribution. And because we know that the sampling distribution is roughly normal in form (according to the Central Limit Theorem), we have nothing more complicated than the normal probability problem depicted in Figure 7.2, panel A.

A table of normal probabilities (Appendix A) or the 68–95–99.7 rule tells us that the proportion of area under the standard normal distribution to the right of $Z = 1$ is about 0.16. So the probability of getting a sample mean greater than 34 in a sample of size 16 from this population is 0.16. That is, $P(\overline{X} > 34) = 0.16$. By the same reasoning and method, we know that the probability of getting a sample mean of 34 or less is the proportion of area to the left of $Z = 1$ (see Figure 7.2, panel B), or 0.84. So $P(\overline{X} \leq 34) = 0.84$. And what about $P(29 \leq \overline{X} \leq 34)$? This is easy enough after converting 29 and 34 to Z-scores. We already figured out that 34 is $Z = 1$ standard deviation above the mean. It is easy to derive that 29 corresponds to a Z-score of $(29 - 32)/2 = -1.5$, so 29 is one and a half standard deviations below the mean. Panel C of Figure 7.2 represents the problem graphically, and using the standard normal table in Appendix A it is not difficult to derive that $P(29 \leq \overline{X} \leq 34) = 0.77$.

7.2   Interval Estimates

Because of their importance, it is worth repeating the following facts available to us now about the estimation process: (a) the mean of a sampling distribution of the sample mean is the population mean when randomly sampling from the population, (b) the standard error of the sample mean, defined as the standard deviation of the sampling distribution of the mean, is the population standard deviation divided by the square root of the sample size (assuming the sample is small relative to the size of the population). The standard error quantifies how much to expect the sample mean to deviate from the population mean on average, and (c) so long as the sample size is sufficiently large, the Central Limit Theorem tells us that the sampling distribution of the sample mean is normally distributed. Just how normal the sampling distribution really is depends on the size of the sample and the degree of asymmetry in the population distribution.

When we put this information together with the 68–95–99.7 rule, we can make the following statements:

1. About 68% of the time, or with probability of about 0.68, the sample mean will be within one standard error the population mean.

2. About 95% of the time, or with probability 0.95, the sample mean will be within 2 standard errors of the population mean.

3. About 99.7% of the time, or with probability of 0.997, the sample mean will be within three standard errors of the population mean.

These three points follow logically from all the information presented in this chapter, and we can make these statements because we know the sampling distribution of the sample mean is normally distributed or at least approximately so according to the Central Limit Theorem. Keep these three points in mind, because they are important in the derivation of a useful estimator μ.

7.2.1   The Confidence Interval

When the goal of a researcher is population inference, the sample mean is used as an estimator of the unknown population mean. If you were to randomly sample a population and compute the sample mean for some set of measurements in the sample, the sample mean would be your best *point estimate* of the population mean. A point estimate is a single, numerical estimate of the population parameter. So $\overline{X}$ is a point estimate of μ. But we know that any point estimate of the mean in a sample of size n from the population is almost certainly wrong—a fact I illustrated in section 7.1.1. We know that a different sample of size n or any other size would have yielded a different point estimate and that estimate would also probably be wrong. However, given what we know about random sampling and sampling distributions, we can construct a different estimate of the population mean, called a *confidence interval* or *interval estimate*. A confidence interval provides a maximum and minimum value between which you can claim the population mean probably resides.

The construction of a confidence interval relies on a simple reversal of the three points above. We know that 95% of the time, or with probability of about 0.95, the sample mean $\overline{X}$ will be within 2 standard errors of the population mean μ. This follows from the 68–95–99.7 rule discussed in Chapter 5. Then it must also be true that 95% of the time when you take a random sample from a population, or with probability 0.95, μ is within two standard errors of $\overline{X}$. So if you were to take 100 samples of a given size from a population and compute the sample mean in each sample, you'd expect that in about 95 of those samples, μ would be within 2 standard errors of $\overline{X}$. This logic can be extended to other values of the standard error other than two. For instance, 68% of the time, or with probability of about 0.68, μ is within one standard error of $\overline{X}$. And usually, 99.7% of the time, μ is within 3 standard errors of $\overline{X}$.

We almost never know the value of the population mean, μ. But we now know that about 95% of the time that a random sample of size n is taken from the population and computed, μ will be within two standard errors of $\overline{X}$. Therefore, a 95% confidence interval for μ can be derived as

$$\boxed{95\% \text{ CI for } \mu = \overline{X} \pm 2(\sigma_{\overline{X}})}$$

$$(7.5)$$

In words, the 95% confidence interval for the population mean is the sample mean plus or minus two standard errors. Suppose, for instance, you took a random sample of size $n = 16$ from a population with unknown mean but with $\sigma = 10$, and the sample mean is $\overline{X} = 20$. Then you can be 95% confident that the population mean μ is somewhere between 15 and 25. Where do these numbers come from? From equation 7.5, the lower bound on the 95 confidence interval is

$$\mu = \overline{X} - 2\sigma_{\overline{X}} = 20 - 2\left(\frac{10}{\sqrt{16}}\right) = 20 - 2(2.5) = 15$$

and the upper bound on the 95% confidence interval is

$$\mu = \overline{X} + 2\sigma_{\overline{X}} = 20 + 2\left(\frac{10}{\sqrt{16}}\right) = 20 + 2(2.5) = 25$$

The "2" in the equation 7.5 comes from the 68–95–99.7 rule, but it is just a rule of thumb. More precisely, and more generally, a c% confidence interval is defined as

$$\boxed{c\% \text{ CI for } \mu = \overline{X} \pm Z_{(100-c)/2}(\sigma_{\overline{X}})}$$

(7.6)

where c is the desired confidence and $Z_{(100-c)/2}$ is the Z-score that cuts off the upper $(100-c)/2$ percent of the standard normal distribution from the rest of the distribution.

Using equation 7.6 we can derive a confidence interval for any desired confidence. For example, to compute a 90% confidence interval for the above problem, you first need to determine the Z-score that cuts of the upper $(100-90)/2 = 5\%$ of the standard normal distribution from the rest of the distribution. Using the table of right tailed normal probabilities in Appendix A, the value of Z above which 5% of the standard normal distribution lies (i..e., right-tail proportion $= .05$) is somewhere between 1.64 and 1.65. Splitting the difference and using $Z = 1.645$, a 90% confidence for the mean would be

$$90\% \text{ CI for } \mu = \overline{X} \pm 1.645(\sigma_{\overline{X}}) = 20 \pm 1.645\left(\frac{10}{\sqrt{16}}\right) = 15.888 \text{ to } 24.113$$

For a 95% confidence interval, we used "2" in equation 7.6. But examining the normal probability table in the Appendix, you can see that for 95% confidence, the actual value of Z that cuts of the upper 2.5% of the standard normal distribution (i.e, right-tail proportion $= .025$) is not two but 1.96. But two is pretty close to 1.96, so as a rule of thumb, the use of two instead of 1.96 isn't going to get you into too much trouble.

There is considerable controversy over the correct interpretation of the confidence interval. Some people say that once a confidence interval is constructed, the probability is either zero or one that the population mean is between the upper and lower bound of the confidence interval, and so it is not accurate to say that the probability is 0.95 that μ is inside of the 95% confidence interval. However, I have no problem assigning a probability to this event. In my opinion, it is sensible to say that the probability is 0.95 that μ is in the window provided by the confidence interval, or there is a "95% chance" that μ is somewhere between the upper and lower bounds of the confidence interval. A more technically correct interpretation of a 95% confidence interval is to say that if you repeated the sampling procedure many times, computing the confidence interval for the mean each time, 95% of the confidence intervals would contain μ. But I don't like that interpretation as much because in practice we only construct a single confidence interval.

It is worth understanding how a confidence interval is derived because an understanding of the process reflects an understanding of the process of sampling error and how we can use the theory of estimation to make an informed statement about the population from the sample. In practice, however, a good statistics program will compute a confidence interval for you if you desire it. But the procedure a computer uses will be slightly different, as described next.

7.2.2   A More Realistic Approach to Interval Estimation

Until this point, I have presented estimation from a purely theoretical perspective, with some description for how to apply the theory of estimation. But I have oversimplified the process somewhat for the sake of pedagogy. If you've been paying close attention, you might have noticed something peculiar about my discussion of confidence intervals and computing the probability of obtaining certain sample means. If you goal is to estimate something about the population, how can you use this procedure if you don't have information about the population that is necessary in order to do so? For instance, to compute the standard error, you need to know the population standard deviation (σ). Remember that σ is the standard deviation of the measured variable computed using information about the *entire* population. But of course this would not typically be available to you, because your data set is unlikely to contain information about every unit in the population. And if you knew σ there is a good chance you would also know μ, and therefore there is no need to estimate μ because it would be known exactly.

For example, suppose you wanted to estimate the mean number of days that residents of the United States read the newspaper during a week. How would you estimate this? Perhaps the simplest approach would be to randomly sample U.S. residents through random digit dialing and ask each person willing to answer your question how many days a week they read the newspaper. Just such a question was included in a national poll of U.S. residents conducted in November 2003 by the Survey Research Institute at Cornell University (see Appendix E3 on the CD for a description of the variables in the data file).[2] We'll call responses to this question variable X. In a sample of $n = 628$ U.S. residents, the mean response was $\overline{X} = 4.221$ days (see Figure 7.3). This would be a sensible point estimate of μ. But how to construct a confidence interval for μ? According to the procedure outlined earlier, to compute a confidence interval for μ it is necessary to calculate the standard error ($\sigma_{\overline{X}}$) of the sampling distribution of $\overline{X}$ for a sample of size 628. However, to compute $\sigma_{\overline{X}}$, the population standard deviation of X must be known. But σ is not known and generally never is. In order to compute $\sigma_{\overline{X}}$, information about the entire population is needed, but all that is available is information from the sample of 628 people. There is no way that $\sigma_{\overline{X}}$ could ever be known for most realistic estimation problems.

It turns out that this doesn't present as big of a problem as it seems like it should. Just as we can use the sample mean $\overline{X}$ as an estimator of the population mean μ, we can use the sample standard deviation s as a point estimate of the population standard deviation σ. Importantly, s is known because it is based on the sample data. In the Cornell poll data, $s = 2.793$. Substituting s for σ in equation 7.4, we have the estimated standard error $s_{\overline{X}}$, (also denoted $\hat{\sigma}_{\overline{X}}$)

$$s_{\overline{X}} = \frac{s}{\sqrt{n}}$$

(7.7)

So in a random sample of 628 residents of the U.S., $\sigma_{\overline{X}}$ can be estimated as

$$s_{\overline{X}} = \frac{2.793}{\sqrt{628}} = 0.111$$

---

[2]Thank you to Dietram Scheufele for donating the data from this survey for this example.

Equation 7.7

		Statistic	Std. Error
Mean		4.221	.111
95% Confidence Interval for Mean	Lower Bound	4.002	
	Upper Bound	4.440	
5% Trimmed Mean		4.301	
Median		5.000	
Variance		7.799	
Std. Deviation		2.793	
Minimum		.000	
Maximum		7.000	
Range		7.000	
Interquartile Range		6.000	
Skewness		-.315	.098
Kurtosis		-1.575	.195

Equation 7.8

Figure 7.3 Descriptive statistics for the Cornell poll data.

This is an estimated standard error because the sample standard deviation of 2.793 (see Figure 7.3) is being used as a substitute for the unknown population standard deviation σ. It would seem that a $c\%$ confidence interval could then be defined as

$$c\% \text{ CI for } \mu = \overline{X} \pm Z_{(100-c)/2}(s_{\overline{X}})$$

However, in practice, this is not what is done. The problem is that the estimation of the standard error has a side effect on the estimation process. When $\sigma_{\overline{X}}$ is estimated rather than known, the sampling distribution of the sample mean is no longer best described with the normal distribution. Instead, the sampling distribution of μ follows a different distribution: the t distribution. The t distribution is very much like the normal distribution, and with a large enough sample size, the difference between the t distribution and the normal distribution is so negligible that it is convenient to think of the sample distribution of $\overline{X}$ as essentially normal. In smaller samples, however, there are some dramatic differences between the t distribution and the normal distribution. Although the t distribution is symmetrical and bell-shaped like the normal distribution, unlike the normal distribution, there are many different t distributions, each defined by its *degrees of freedom* (*df*) (see Figure 7.4). To compute the confidence interval for a mean when the standard error is estimated, you need to know the value of t that cuts off the upper $(100 - c)/2\%$ of the t distribution with $n - 1$ degrees of freedom from the rest of the t distribution. (The degrees of freedom will vary for different types of estimation problems, but when estimating a single population mean, the degrees of freedom is $n - 1$.) The confidence interval is then defined as:

$$c\% \text{ CI for } \mu = \overline{X} \pm t_{(100-c)/2}(s_{\overline{X}})$$

(7.8)

The values of t that cut off different proportions of the t distribution can be found in Appendix B. I will illustrate the use of this table first with an simple example. Recall from earlier we wanted to calculate a 95% confidence interval for a population mean based on a random sample of size 16 that yielded $\overline{X} = 20$. In the earlier problem, you were given the population standard deviation, but in reality, σ wouldn't be known.

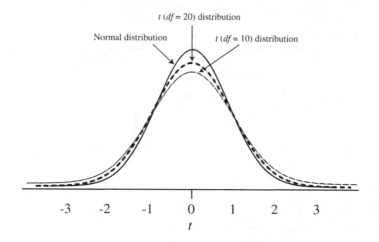

Figure 7.4 The t Distribution.

However, it could be estimated using the sample standard deviation. Suppose the sample standard deviation was $s = 9.700$. The estimated standard error of the mean, $s_{\overline{X}}$, when $n = 16$ and $s = 9.700$ is 2.425 (from equation 7.7). All that is left to know is the value of t that cuts off the upper 2.5% of the t distribution from the rest of the t distribution. When $n = 16$, $df = n - 1 = 15$, so we use the $t(15)$ distribution. Looking at Appendix B in the .025 column, $df = 15$ row, $t = 2.131$. Applying equation 7.8, the 95% confidence interval for μ is

$$95\% \text{ CI for } \mu = 20 \pm 2.131(2.425) = 14.832 \text{ to } 25.168$$

Now let's apply this to a real estimation problem. We know from the Cornell poll that 628 randomly selected U.S. residents reporting reading the newspaper, on average, 4.221 days a week with a standard deviation of 2.793. With this information, the estimated standard error of the sampling distribution of $s_{\overline{X}}$ is $(2.793/\sqrt{628}) = 0.111$ (from equation 7.7). If we want a 95% confidence interval for the mean for a sample of size 628, we need to know the value of t that cuts off the upper 2.5% of the t distribution from the rest. To do this, look under the ".025" column and then look in the 627 (which is $n - 1$) row in the df column. Notice that there is no 627 row in Appendix B. This will often happen; the needed row of the table is not there. In that case, use the closest df in the table to the actual degrees of freedom you need. Here, that is 500. The value of t in the .025 column and the 500 df row is 1.965. So the 95% confidence interval for the population mean number of days per week U.S. residents read the newspaper is

$$95\% \text{ CI for } \mu = 4.221 \pm 1.965(0.111) = 4.003 \text{ to } 4.439$$

So we can be 95% confident that the population mean is between 4.003 and 4.439 days.

At this point, you may ask yourself why we needed to bother with the t distribution. Had we used the normal distribution instead, and found $Z_{(100-c)/2}$ instead of $t_{(100-c)/2}$, the answer would have been nearly the same. Indeed, notice in Appendix B that as the degrees of freedom increases, the values of t become very close to the corresponding values of Z from the normal distribution in Appendix A. The larger discrepancies between the t and Z values occur with smaller degrees of freedom—that is, when the sample size is small. For this reason, some statistics textbooks say that if the sample size is large, just go ahead and use the normal distribution rather than the t distribution, with large being defined as $n > 30$ or so. The writers of such textbooks reserve the use of the t distribution for small sample problems. Little harm is done by using the normal distribution rather than the t distribution with large samples. However, the t distribution will produce a better and more accurate confidence interval, even with sample sizes larger than 30. And most computer programs that print a confidence interval for a mean use the t distribution when computing confidence intervals regardless of the sample size. So it is worth getting in the habit of using the t distribution rather than the normal distribution.

Of course, in reality you are unlikely to use either the t distribution or the normal distribution when generating confidence intervals because a computer program will probably be doing all your computations. I fed the Cornell poll data to SPSS and it spit out Figure 7.3 after I requested a 95% confidence interval for the mean number of days people read the newspaper. As can be seen, SPSS prints both the estimated standard error and a 95% confidence interval for the population mean. So there is little reason to have to remember exactly how these computations are done, so long as you know conceptually what a confidence interval is, understand the theory that produces it, and how it is interpreted.

7.2.3   The Relationship Between Confidence and Precision

There is an intimate connection among sample size, confidence, and accuracy of estimation. Ideally, a confidence interval is narrow. Certainly, being confident that the population mean number of days a person reads the newspaper is between 4.003 and 4.439 provides more information than being confident that it is between, say, 3.503 and 4.939. The former estimate is more precise in that it has a narrower range of possibilities. All other things being equal, a narrow confidence interval is more desirable because the estimate is more precise. However, narrowing a confidence interval typically comes at a price, either through lowered confidence or greater resource expenditure at the data collection phase. To understand how this is so, you need to spend some time looking at equations 7.7 and 7.8. An examination of these equations reveals that the width of the confidence interval is determined in part by the size of the standard error, which is determined in part by the size of the sample. As the sample size increases, everything else held constant, the standard error decreases. That is, with larger sample sizes, the average amount by which possible sample means deviate from the population mean is smaller. So with a larger sample size, a confidence interval will be narrower than would a confidence interval constructed from a smaller sample, assuming the confidence level is kept constant.

Let me illustrate this point. We saw in the example above that the 95% confidence interval for the mean newspaper use of U.S. residents from a sample of size 628 was 4.003 to 4.439 days per week. But suppose the sample size was only 50 rather than 628. Assuming the standard deviation and sample means were the same, the estimated standard error would increase to $(2.793/\sqrt{50}) = 0.395$. In a sample sample size of 50, the t statistic that cuts off the upper and lower 2.5% (and thus 5% total) of the t distribution is about 2.009 (from Appendix B). There is no listing for $df = n - 1 = 49$ but $df = 50$ is pretty close so I used that). So the 95% confidence interval would be

$$c\% \text{ CI for } \mu = 4.221 \pm 2.009(0.395) = 3.427 \text{ to } 5.015$$

Notice that the confidence interval is much wider. This is due in large part to the fact that the standard error of the sample mean in a sample of size 50 is nearly 4 times larger than in a sample of size 628. So larger sample sizes will yield more precise estimates, reflected in a narrower confidence interval.

It is also apparent from equation 7.8 and Appendix B that you can have as narrow a confidence interval as desired if you are willing to give up confidence in the accuracy of your estimation. So there is a tradeoff between precision of estimation and confidence. Suppose you wanted to be not 95% confident, but only 50% confident of the value of μ in a sample of size 628. For a 95% confidence interval, appendix B tells us that $t_{(100-c)/2} = 1.965$ and therefore the confidence interval is 4.003 to 4.439l, as discussed above. For a 50% confidence interval, $t_{(100-c)/2} = 0.675$ and so the confidence interval is narrower: 4.146 to 4.296. Therefore, all other things being equal, the width of the confidence interval gets narrower as confidence lowers. This should make some sense. The more confident you want to be that μ is in the confidence interval, the greater the range of possibilities for μ you must accept as possible. If you want more precision, you have to lower the confidence you have in the estimate if you don't change the sample size.

Equation 7.7 tells us that the standard error is also determined in part by variability in the research units on the variable being measured. And as discussed in chapter 6, variability is measurement is determined in part by reliability in measurement. A measurement instrument or procedure that is more reliable will, all other things being equal, result in less measurement variability. The smaller the between-unit variation in what is being measured, the smaller the standard error, and therefore the narrower the confidence interval. So all other things being equal, the use of a measurement procedure or instrument that is more reliable will yield narrower confidence intervals.

Here is the moral: If you want a more precise interval estimate, meaning a narrow confidence interval, you have three choices. You can make sure the sample is as large as practically feasible, because there is less sampling error in the estimation of a parameter with a larger sample size. Or you can select operationalizations of a construct that produce more reliable measurements, because higher reliability results in less between-unit variation and greater precision in estimation. Or you can reduce your confidence in the accuracy of the interval estimate.

7.2.4   Computing the Probability of a Sample Mean, Revisited

Earlier I described how to use the theory of estimation to generate the probability of obtaining a sample mean of a given size when randomly sampling from a population with a known mean and standard deviation. But of what use is this procedure if we are unlikely to ever know the mean and standard deviation of the population, two things that are required in order to implement the procedure discussed in section 7.2.1? As I described, we can get around not knowing σ by estimating it with s. However, without knowledge of μ it is impossible to know the center of the sampling distribution of $\overline{X}$, so it is therefore impossible to estimate the probability of obtaining a sample mean of a given size when sampling from the population. Nevertheless, we can compute the probability of obtaining a sample mean of a certain size if we make an *assumption* about the value of μ. If we substitute this assumed value of μ for the actual value of μ, then the probability of interest can be computed. This is the logic that underlies statistical hypothesis testing, the topic of Chapter 8.

7.2.5 Interval Estimates Derived From Samples of Convenience

Confidence intervals are a way of handling the fact that a point estimate is almost certainly wrcng when randomly sampling from a population. By providing an interval estimate rather than a point estimate, the role of sampling error in the estimation process is explicitly acknowledge and accounted for in the estimate. But the interpretation of a confidence interval, indeed, the foundation upon which it is based, assumes that random sampling error has had an opportunity to exert its effects and that its effects are well approximated by the theory of estimation described in this chapter. In other words, the theory of inference and its application to the construction of a confidence interval assumes that a meaningful population does exist and there has been an attempt at randomly sampling from that population. In the absence of these two important features of the theory of estimation, the theory of estimation does not apply, so a confidence interval has no meaning and cannot be interpreted.

As discussed in Chapter 3, when a researcher collects data using a sample of convenience, it is very difficult to articulate just what population is being sampled, and population inferences from sample information are dangerous and potentially unjustifiable. Importantly, given that the mechanism that produces random sampling error hasn't been given a chance to operate when random sampling is not undertaken, confidence intervals really have no place in the reporting of results from samples of convenience. This is important to keep in mind, because computers make it easy to generate confidence intervals. Indeed, many statistical programs will generate and print confidence intervals for statistics it computes even without you requesting it to do so. But the computer doesn't know where your data come from; it is only producing output in accordance with its programming. It is up to you to determine whether it is sensible to apply the theory of estimation as discussed in this chapter to your particular problem.

7.3 Estimating a Population Proportion

Most likely you've seen a public opinion poll reported on televised news or in your local newspaper. The goal of public opinion polling is to estimate what the public believes or thinks about something, and at the forefront of the opinion pollster's mind is population inference. The pollster wants to derive an accurate estimate of what the population thinks, but there is the obvious limitation that the pollster cannot ask everyone in the population the question or questions of interest. Instead, a random sample of the population is taken and the information extracted from each person in the sample. From what the people in the sample say, the pollster can estimate what the population thinks.

Public opinion polls are often expressed in terms of percentages or proportions because many of the questions that opinion pollsters ask require a categorical response. A common question asked near the time of an election is how you would vote if the election were held today. For example, the pollster might ask "If the election were held today, would you vote for Candidate A or Candidate B?" Responses to this question allow the pollster to estimate support for each candidate and, if taken close enough to election day, even allow the pollster to predict who is likely to win. For example, if the day before an election 55% say they will vote for Candidate A, 40% say they will vote for Candidate B, and 5% are undecided, then the pollster can be reasonably confident, if the sample size is large enough, that Candidate A is going to win the election. Exit polling works on the same principle. By asking people how they voted right after the leave their polling place, it is possible to forecast who won the election even before all the votes are counted.

The process of estimating percents or proportions does not differ from the process described for the estimation of a mean. This is because a proportion is simply a mean, so when you estimate a proportion, you are estimating a mean. This process can be made clear with the following example. Suppose in a random sample of 100 people, 45% say they are going to vote for Candidate A. So a point estimate of the population proportion who are likely to vote for that candidate is 0.45. Let's define a variable X as whether or not the person reported he or she was going to vote for candidate A. If the person says he or she is going to vote for candidate A, give that person a score of one on X. If the person says he or she is going to vote for candidate B or does not know, give that person a score of zero on X. So in this example of 100 people, the data would contains 100 cases, 45 with a score of one on X and 55 with a score of zero. What is the mean of these 100 values of 0 and 1? Add up the 100 values of X in the data and divide by the sample size, and you will find that the mean is 0.45, which is exactly equal to the proportion of people who said they were going to vote for candidate A.

Because a proportion is simply a mean of a dichotomous variable coded 0 and 1, all the rules that apply to the estimation of means apply to the estimation of proportions as well. So let's apply what we discussed earlier to the generation of a point and interval estimate for a population proportion using the Cornell poll data. One question posed to the respondents was "Do you ever go online to access the Internet or World Wide Web, or to send and receive email?" The respondents answered either yes or no. Coding a "yes" answer as $X = 1$ and a no answer as $X = 0$, $\sum X = 430$ because 430 people answered "yes." So $\overline{X} = (430/628) = 0.685$. Thus, a point estimate of the proportion of people in the U.S. who have ever accessed the internet is $\overline{X} = 0.685$. But it is more common to denote an estimate of a population proportion symbolically as $\hat{\pi}$ ("pie-hat") and the population proportion as π, so we will stick to that convention and say that $\hat{\pi} = 0.685$. The standard deviation of a dichotomous variable X coded 0 and 1 can be derived using equation 4.3, which is mathematically identical to equation 7.9 when X is a dichotomous variable coded zero and one:

$$s = \sqrt{\hat{\pi}(1 - \hat{\pi})}$$

(7.9)

In the Cornell data, $s = \sqrt{0.685(1 - 0.685)} = 0.465$.

With this information, let's now review the estimation principles discussed above but apply them to this problem. Our goal is to estimate the population proportion (π) of people who have accessed the internet and derive a confidence interval for that estimate. We've already derived the point estimate as $\hat{\pi} = 0.685$. Generalizing the principles of estimation discussed in this chapter in the context of means, we know that the expected value of the sample proportion (which remember is simply a mean) is the population proportion when randomly sampling from the population. That is, $E(\hat{\pi}) = \pi$. With a sufficiently large sample size, we know that the sampling distribution of $\hat{\pi}$ is normal or approximately so, and the standard deviation of that sampling distribution (the standard error of $\hat{\pi}$) can be estimated as $s_{\hat{\pi}} = (0.465/\sqrt{628}) = 0.019$ from equation 7.7. A confidence interval for a population proportion can be derived using

		Statistic	Std. Error
Mean		.4140	.01967
95% Confidence Interval for Mean	Lower Bound	.3754	
	Upper Bound	.4526	
5% Trimmed Mean		.4045	
Median		.0000	
Variance		.243	
Std. Deviation		.49294	
Minimum		.00	
Maximum		1.00	
Range		1.00	
Interquartile Range		1.00	
Skewness		.350	.098
Kurtosis		-1.884	.195

Figure 7.5 SPSS output from the Explore procedure.

equation 7.8. But to avoid confusion, that equation is reprinted below (equation 7.10) using the symbols for sample and population proportions to avoid confusion:

$$95\% \text{ CI for } \pi = \hat{\pi} \pm t_{(100-c)/2}(s_{\hat{\pi}})$$

(7.10)

So with 95% confidence, the population proportion of U.S. residents who have accessed the Internet is

$$95\% \text{ CI for } \pi = 0.685 \pm 1.965(0.019) = 0.648 \text{ to } 0.722$$

So we can be pretty sure that between 64.8% and 72.2% of the U.S. population has accessed the Internet.

In public opinion polls, it is very common for the pollster to report something called the *margin of error*. For example, the pollster might report that 45% ± 3% of the population is going to vote for Candidate A. The margin of error typically reported is about ± two standard errors, so if you apply the margin of error to the point estimate, what you get is a 95% confidence interval for the proportion or percent. (Technically, the margin of error is plus or minus $t_{(100-c)/2}$ standard errors for a $c\%$ confidence interval, but in practice that is usually around 1.96 or 1.97, so the margin or error can be thought of as essentially plus or minus two standard errors.) So 45% ± 3% translates into a 95% confidence interval of 42% to 48%, meaning that the population percent of people likely to vote for candidate A is between 42% and 48% with 95% confidence. In an election context, if two proportions or percents (say, e.g., the proportion who say they are going to vote for candidate A and the proportion who say they are going to vote for candidate B) are within the margin of error of each other, then it is sometimes said that the race is a *statistical dead heat*. Even though the point estimates of the proportions may differ, the presence of sampling error means that we have no reason to believe that the population proportions are different if the sample proportions are within the margin of error of each other.

What is the margin of error in our estimate of the proportion of U.S. residents who have accessed the Internet? Easy. The margin of error is 1.965(0.019) = 0.037, or about 3.7%. So according to these data, the percent of people in the United States who have accessed the Internet is $68.5 \pm 3.7\%$.

What if your are interested in estimating a proportion but the variable is not dichotomous? In the example above, a person could report either that they have or have not accessed the Internet. A person could give only one of two possible answers. But what if you wanted to estimate, for example, the proportion of U.S. residents that self-identify as Republican, yet the question as phrased allows the respondents to select a political identity from several options, such as Democrat, Republican, Independent, Green, or Libertarian? No modifications to the procedure described above are necessary. If you wanted a point and interval estimate for the proportion of people who identify as Republicans, the point estimate is simply the proportion of people who selected or volunteered "Republican" when asked, and the confidence interval derived just as described above. For instance, in the Cornell poll, 260 of the 628 respondents identified themselves as Republican. The remaining identified as either Democrat, Independent, or a member of some "other" party. Now think of this question not as a multicategorical response variable but a dichotomous one for which a person either says "Republican" or some response other than "Republican." Defining π as the proportion of the U.S. population that self-identify as Republican, $\hat{\pi} = 260/628 = 0.414$. The standard error of $\hat{\pi}$ can be derived from a combination of equations 7.9 and 7.7. From equation 7.9,

$$s = \sqrt{0.414(1 - 0.414)} = 0.493$$

and so the standard error of $\hat{\pi}$ is estimated from equation 7.7 as

$$s_{\hat{\pi}} = \frac{0.493}{\sqrt{628}} = 0.020$$

A 95% confidence interval is derived from equation 7.10 as

$$95\% \text{ CI for } \pi = 0.414 \pm 1.965(0.020) = 0.375 \text{ to } 0.453$$

The margin of error of the point estimate is $1.965(0.020) = 0.039$. So we can say that the proportion of the U.S. population that self identify as Republican is 0.414 ± 0.039 or, in percentage terms, $41.4 \pm 3.9\%$.

A computer will do all these computations for you quite easily. If the response variable held several different response codes, you'd have to create a new variable that is dichotomous. For example, in the Cornell poll data file, the variable named "Party" is set to 1 for Republicans, 2 for Democrats, 3 for Independents, and 4 for anyone who responded with something else. In SPSS, a simple command would create a new variable called "Repub" that is set to 1 for Republicans and 0 for everyone else:

```
compute repub = (party = 1).
```

A request for some descriptive statistics using the SPSS Explore procedure on variable "Repub" yields the output in Figure 7.5.

7.4 Bootstrapping a Confidence Interval

The methods of computing a confidence interval described in this chapter are based on the assumption that the sampling distribution of the sample mean can be well described with the t or normal distribution. The Central Limit Theorem justifies the use of the normal distribution in samples when σ is known, and the t distribution should be used when σ (and therefore $\sigma_{\overline{X}}$) is estimated from a sample from the population (which is almost always). However, there are circumstances when neither t nor the normal distribution are likely to adequately represent the sampling distribution of the sample mean, and the use of either of these distributions when deriving a confidence interval will yield an inaccurate interval. For example, when the sample size is small and the population from which the sample is derived is highly skewed or otherwise asymmetrical on the variable measured, the sampling distribution of the sample mean is not likely to be normally or t distributed. Indeed, the sampling distribution probably isn't even symmetrical; instead it is likely to be asymmetrical and lopsided. In such a case, the use of the t or normal distribution gives, at best, an approximation of the correct confidence interval, and not always a good approximation.

If you are happy with rough approximations, then probably little harm is done in using a theoretical sampling distribution such as the t distribution when computing a confidence interval. But what if you are not willing to assume (or simply cannot assume) that the sampling distribution of your statistic is normally or t distributed? Fortunately, there is an alternative method that can be used regardless of the actual shape of the sampling distribution of the statistic. This method is known as *bootstrapping*. Just a few years ago, bootstrapping was infeasible for most researchers because of the computational resources required. But these days, the computer on your desktop is probably fast and powerful enough to carry out the many computations required to bootstrap a confidence interval. Below I outline how to bootstrap a 95% confidence interval for a population mean or population proportion.

1. Take a sample of size n from the population of interest.

2. Take a random sample of size n with *replacement* from the original sample of size n from step 1. So if you took a sample of size 10 from the population in step 1, you'd take a sample of size 10 with replacement from that sample. When you sample with replacement, what this means is that after you randomly select a unit from your original sample, you put that measurement back into the original sample before picking the next measurement. This means that it is possible for that unit to be selected again. For example, consider a sample of size 3 from a population at step 1. If the original sample contained units with the measurements of 4, 8, and 9, a random sample of three units with replacement from the original sample might be 4, 4, and 9, or 8, 9, and 9, or even 9, 9, and 9. Even though the original sample from step 1 contains only a single unit with a 4 and a single unit with a 9, these random samples of size 3 with replacement are possible because after drawing the unit with a 4 or a 9, for example, you put those units back into the pool of units before selecting the next case to complete the sample of size 3 with replacement.

3. Compute the mean in the "resample" obtained at step 2. Call that statistic $\overline{X}^*$.

4. Complete steps 2 and 3 a total one thousand times.

5. Sort the distribution of 1000 values of $\overline{X}^*$ from steps 2 through 4 from lowest to highest.

6. Define the lower bound of the 95% confidence interval as the 25th mean in the sorted distribution of means from step 5. Define the upper bound of the 95% confidence interval as the 976th mean in the sorted distribution of means from step 5.

Bootstrapping is known as a *resampling method* of inference because it relies on a repeated resampling of the sample in order to generate the sampling distribution of the statistic. This approach to generating a confidence interval bases the computations not on the sampling distribution of the sample mean but instead on the *bootstrapped sampling distribution* of the sample mean, represented by the distribution of the values

Run MATRIX procedure:

BOOTSTRAP MEAN ESTIMATES, 1000 RESAMPLES

```
    Sample   Bootstrp   Lo95%CI   Hi95%CI        n
    4.2213    4.2224    4.0032    4.4522   628.0000
```

------ END MATRIX -----

Figure 7.6 Output from an SPSS macro that bootstraps a 95% confidence interval for a population mean.

of $\overline{X}^{*}$. The logic of the method is quite elegant and makes no assumption that the sampling distribution of the mean is normal, t distributed, or even symmetrical because it relies on an empirically derived approximation of the sampling distribution of the sample mean. Thus, this approach is especially well-suited to problems where the Central Limit Theorem cannot be trusted to adequately describe the sampling distribution, such as when taking small samples from irregularly shaped populations.

For bootstrapping to be an effective method of generating a confidence interval, you must have some faith in your sample as adequately representing the population from which the sample was derived. As always, such faith is easier to muster if you have randomly sampled from the population. But it is also important that your sample adequately represents the extremes of the population. If your population is likely to be highly skewed, for example, you want to make sure that your sample reflects that skew and contains at least a few outliers or extremes that do exist in the population, as you'd expect in a skewed distribution. You'd expect that large sample sizes would represent the population from which it was derived pretty well if proper sampling methods are employed. There is no guarantee that a small sample will adequately represent the population. But you can feel pretty confident that bootstrapping will work if your sample seems to include measurements reflecting the distribution or range of measurements you'd expect if you had a larger sample size. This is important because bootstrapping treats your sample as if it were the population. If your sample does not adequately represent the distribution of possible measurements in the population, then bootstrapping will produce an inaccurate confidence interval.

The nice thing about bootstrapping is that the approach can be used to generate an estimate of the sampling distribution of any statistic. So it is a very versatile procedure. There are many variations on bootstrapping that have been proposed (see, e.g., Efron & Tibshirani, 1998; Lunneborg, 2000; Mooney & Duvall, 1993). The method just described is known as the *percentile method* of computing a bootstrapped confidence interval. The major problem with bootstrapping is that it requires many repeated computations, making it nearly impossible to do by hand. Unfortunately, many of the widely used statistical programs do not include bootstrapping routines, making them out of the reach of many users. However, it is possible to get popular statistics program such as SPSS to generate a bootstrapped confidence interval by writing a "macro." Such a macro for SPSS can be found in Appendix F on the CD with this book. In the future, it is likely that more and more statistical programs will provide bootstrapping as an inferential tool.

This SPSS macro was used to bootstrap a 95% confidence interval for the mean number of days per week U.S. residents read the newspaper, using the Cornell poll data. The output can be found in Figure 7.6. As can be seen, the bootstrapped confidence interval is very similar (4.003 to 4.452) to what the use of the t distribution yields. The similarity between the confidence intervals in this case is attributable to the large sample size. With large sample sizes, bootstrapping and so-called normal-theory approaches to constructing confidence intervals (the other methods discussed in this chapter) tend to be very similar.

7.5 Summary

Many of the problems that communication researchers face involve the estimation of a parameter such as a population mean or a proportion from a sample from the population. The sampling distribution plays a fundamental role in the theory of statistical inference. The Central Limit Theorem gives us faith that when we sample randomly from a population, the sampling distribution of the sample mean or proportion is well approximated by a normal distribution, with the fit of this approximation governed by sample size and the symmetry of the population distribution on the variable being measured. Knowing that the sampling distribution is roughly normal, we can compute the probability of certain sample results when sampling from the population, and we can create confidence intervals that give us a lower and upper bound of values between which the population mean or proportion probably resides. But in practice, we know that the sampling distribution is better described as t distributed rather than normally distributed. When we can't trust that the sampling distribution is either t or normally distributed, we can bootstrap the sampling distribution to generate a confidence interval. The importance of these idea presented in this cannot be overemphasized because they play an extremely important role in the process of hypothesis testing, the topic of the next several chapters.

EIGHT

Hypothesis Testing Concepts

The previous seven chapters built the foundation upon which the practice of descriptive and inferential statistics is based—basic measurement concepts, describing research findings statistically, elementary probability, and the theory of estimation. With the foundation laid, we can now build the rest of the house knowing that it will not collapse. But we will add to this foundation as we progress through this book as necessary, much liking adding an addition to a house you've outgrown.

The research life of the communication scientist revolves around answering questions and testing theory related to communication processes. These questions and theories usually suggest a research hypothesis of one form or another that can be empirically tested. As discussed in Chapter 1, a hypothesis is a specific prediction about one or more expected results in a research study. Hypotheses abound in communication theory. For example, *spiral of silence theory* (Noelle-Neumann, 1993) proposes that people are more willing to censor their own opinion expression if they believe that their own opinion is relatively uncommon or losing support among the public. If so, then you would expect that if you measured a group of people's willingness to express their opinion as well as whether or the extent to which they believe others agree with that opinion, then there should be some kind of relationship between these variables. That is, those who perceive relatively more support for their positions among the public should be relatively more willing to express those opinions publicly. And according to *communication accommodation theory* (e.g., Giles, Mulac, Bradac, & Johnson, 1987), conversation partners that are attracted to each other will converge in their communication style, where convergence is defined as similarity in such things as speech rate, smiling frequency, and other forms of nonverbal expression. If we recruited a group of strangers to interact with each other in pairs and quantified their attraction to each other, we should find some relationship between how attracted the members of the dyad feel to each other and similarity in the content of their verbal and nonverbal communication, such as how quickly they speak, how frequently they smile at each other, and how much time they spend looking at each other. And the *elaboration likelihood model of persuasion* (Petty & Cacioppo, 1986) proposes that people who are highly involved in some issue, compared to those less involved, more deeply process the contents of a messages about that topic, such as a message designed to change attitudes about that topic. If so, then if we presented one of two messages to a person, one with mostly strong arguments supporting a position or one with mostly weak arguments, we should find that the one with strong arguments would produce greater attitude change but more so among receivers of the message that care about the topic compared to those who don't care about it. As these three examples illustrate, theories often suggest hypotheses that can be subjected to empirical test.

If you question whether testing hypotheses is what communication scientists regularly do, I encourage you to pick up any issue of nearly any journal that publishes communication research and look through the pages. Reaching over to my personal library and thumbing through the journals in my bookshelf, the following examples of hypotheses appear:

> Females will be more likely than males to rate pro-social advertising as memorable (Andsager, Austin, & Pinkleton, *Communication Research*, 2002, vol. 29, p. 246).

> In initial interactions, computer mediated interactants [will] deploy a greater proportion of interactive uncertainty reduction strategies (questions and self-disclosures) than [will] face to face counterparts (Tidwell & Walther, *Human Communication Research*, 2002, vol. 28, p. 323).

> Individuals presented with four interactants' unanimous opinions will manifest greater compliance than will individuals exposed to one interactant's opinion (Lee & Nass, *Human Communication Research*, 2002, vol. 28, pg. 354).

> Stories written by statehouse bureaus will more frequently use "horse race" and issue experts than will stories by newsroom-based or wire service reporters (Fico & Freedman, *Journalism and Mass Communication Quarterly*, 2001, vol. 78, p. 437).

> The frequency of web use will be positively associated with incidental exposure to news on the Web (Tewksbury, Weaver, & Maddex, *Journalism and Mass Communication Quarterly*, 2001, vol. 78, p. 537).

> Younger children who see [a] violent act that is unpunished will be more likely than those who see [a] punished action to select an aggressive solution to a hypothetical interpersonal conflict. (Krcmar & Cooke, *Journal of Communication*, 2001, vol. 51, p. 305).

> Ability to control the presentation of media content will interact with the context instability of media content viewed to have joint effects on memory recognition. (Southwell & Lee, *Journalism and Mass Communication Quarterly*, 2004, vol. 81, p. 646).

All these are examples of hypotheses that the investigators empirically tested in their research. They are specific predictions about what the researchers expected to find based on the theory, intuition, or personal curiosity that motivated the research. But not all research focuses explicitly on testing a hypothesis. Sometimes researchers ask vague questions without making specific predictions and then attempt to answer those questions by collecting data. For example,

> Does the amount of violence differ across subgenres of children's [television] programming? (Wilson, Smith, & Potter et al., *Journal of Communication*, 2002, vol. 52, p. 14).

> To what extent is online disaster relief information interactive in regard to the amount of effort web page users must exert? (Paul, *Journalism and Mass Communication Quarterly*, 2001, vol. 78, p. 739).

Will the impact of political information seeking online be moderated by computer-mediated interpersonal discussion? (Hardy & Scheufele, *Journal of Communication*, 2005, vol. 55, p. 75).

These are examples of what I called *research questions* in Chapter 1. Even though these statements are not formal hypotheses, hypothesis testing is often used when evaluating data from research focused on answering research questions rather than testing a hypothesis.

In this chapter, I describe some of the concepts that are important to understanding hypothesis testing, and then I outline the hypothesis testing procedure and apply it to testing a relatively simple hypothesis. The material in the rest of the book will build on the basic principles described here.

8.1   Hypothesis Testing Steps

Hypothesis testing involves a series of sequential steps. In this section, I describe the steps required to test a simple hypothesis statistically. In subsequent chapters of this book, I apply these concepts more specifically by describing how one would actually go about testing various hypothesis of interest.

8.1.1   Step 1: Translate the Research Hypothesis or Question into a Statistical Hypothesis

The first stage in testing a hypothesis is to translate the research hypothesis into one that can be tested statistically. I introduce the term *research hypothesis* here to distinguish it from the statistical hypotheses that you set up when conducting a hypothesis test. The distinction between the research hypothesis and the statistical hypotheses will become clearer as you read through this section.

This first phase of hypothesis testing involves translating the research hypothesis into a quantitative form given what is actually measured in the course of the research. Actually, two specific statistical hypotheses are formulated at this stage and they are pitted against each other statistically using the data available. Using methods to generate a probability from the data available, the researcher decides which of the two statistical hypotheses is the more reasonable description of reality given what is known from the data collected.

The Null Hypothesis. The null hypothesis is a statistical statement that is completely inconsistent with the research hypothesis. The null hypothesis typically takes the form of no effect, no difference, or no relationship. For example, suppose you had administered a test of communication anxiety such as the *Communication Anxiety Inventory* (see Rubin et al., 2004) to a sample of students taking a public speaking course. Perhaps your *research hypothesis* is that students that enroll in public speaking courses tend to be, on average, more anxious about communicating than some national average or "norm." Suppose that the national average on the *Communication Anxiety Inventory* is known to be 25. We will call this value of 25 the "test norm." Your *statistical null hypothesis* would be that the population mean communication apprehension score for people taking public speaking is 25 *or less*. Formally, your statistical null hypothesis, denoted symbolically as H_0, is as follows:

$$H_0 : \mu \leq 25$$

where μ corresponds to the population mean from which your sample is derived (people taking a public speaking course) and 25 is the test norm—the national average.

Notice that the statistical null hypothesis completely contradicts the research hypothesis. Recall that the research hypothesis states that students who enroll in public speaking courses are *more anxious* (and thus score higher on average) than the test norm. Thus, the statistical null hypothesis essentially articulates in statistical, symbolic form exactly the opposite of what you believe is true according to your research hypothesis.

The Alternative Hypothesis. The alternative hypothesis is a statistical statement consistent with the research hypothesis. It is and must be the logical opposite of the null hypothesis, because the null was articulated to be inconsistent with the research hypothesis. Recall that the research hypothesis was that public speaking students are *more* anxious about communication than the national norm. Framed statistically, the alternative hypothesis states that the population mean communication anxiety score for students who take public speaking is *greater than* 25. Denoted symbolically as H_a, the alternative hypothesis is

$$H_a : \mu > 25$$

If your research hypothesis is true, then the mean communication apprehension for people taking public speaking courses is larger than the population norm of 25.

The example above illustrates how to set up a directional or one-tailed hypothesis test. It is directional because the research hypothesis makes a specific prediction about how public speaking students should compare to the national average—they should be *more* anxious than that average and, therefore, score *higher* on average on the *Communication Anxiety Inventory*. But imagine that your research hypothesis was slightly different. Suppose you believed that people who enroll in public speaking courses are *different* from the norm, but you aren't sure whether they are likely to be more or less anxious than the norm. Upon reflection, either direction could be defended. People who take public speaking courses could be relatively low in anxiety about communication compared to the norm and take public speaking courses simply so that they can get better at something that they want to do and enjoy doing. Or perhaps people who are interested in public speaking are naturally outgoing, extroverted types. On the other hand, perhaps people taking a public speaking course do so because they are especially anxious and are taking the course to attempt to overcome their overwhelming anxiety.

Regardless, this research hypothesis corresponds to the following statistical alternative hypothesis:

$$H_a : \mu \neq 25$$

meaning that the population mean communication anxiety score of people who take public speaking is different from 25. The corresponding null hypothesis would be

$$H_0 : \mu = 25$$

Observe that as required, this null hypothesis completely contradicts the research hypothesis by stating that the population mean communication anxiety score for people who take public speaking courses is exactly equal to the test norm of 25. In other words, on average, public speaking students are no more or less anxious about communication than the national norm.

So the null and alternative hypotheses are specific statistical statements corresponding to the research hypothesis. This example illustrates that the specific form of the null and alternative hypotheses depends on how you phrase the research hypothesis. If you advance a specific prediction in your research hypothesis about the direction of the population parameter you are trying to estimate relative to some comparison point, then you are advancing a one-tailed or directional hypothesis. A two-tailed or nondirectional hypothesis merely states that there should be some difference between the parameter you are estimating and the comparison point, but it does not specify in advance of seeing the data just what the form of that difference is. As you will see, when we don't make a directional prediction in advance of seeing the data, the evidence against the null hypothesis has to be stronger, or the effect bigger, compared to when we make a prediction in advance of seeing the data.

8.1.2   Step 2: Quantify the Obtained Result

The next step in the hypothesis testing procedure is to quantify the obtained result of your study using some descriptive statistic that is relevant and sensitive to the research question or hypothesis. If your research hypothesis is couched in terms of an average, you might quantify your obtained result as the sample mean. If your hypothesis is phrased in terms of a percent or proportion, you'd probably quantify your result as a sample proportion or percent.

I don't have much else to say about this except that clearly the statistic that you use to quantify your result must be sensitive to and relevant to the hypothesis as framed. So, for example, if you research hypothesis states that public speaking students are more anxious than the norm *on average* in their communication anxiety, then it wouldn't be sensible to quantify your result as the proportion of students that score above 25 because your research hypothesis is articulated in terms of *average* communication anxiety and not the proportion that are above average. You might use the proportion of students that score above 25 as your statistical index of the obtained result if your hypothesis was framed differently. For example, if your research hypothesis was that more than half of the people taking public speaking are more anxious than the norm, then your null hypothesis would be $H_0 : \pi \leq .50$ and the alternative would be $H_a : \pi > .50$, where π is the population proportion of people above 25 on your chosen measure of communication anxiety (the *Communication Anxiety Inventory*. In such a case, your quantification of the obtained result should reflect the fact that your research hypothesis was articulated in terms of a proportion ("more than half"), and the proportion of people in the sample that scored above 25 would be a sensible description of the obtained result as it relates to the research hypothesis.

I presented Step 2 as if it must follow Step 1. However, in reality this isn't necessarily true. We often collect data and describe the data in some fashion first and then decide, after the fact, how exactly we are going to articulate the null and alternative hypothesis statistically. There is no requirement we first articulate the null and alternative hypothesis before we have described a data set using the variety of statistical indices available. So it is not necessarily the case that the hypothesis framing stage always precedes the quantification of the results. However, it is important to keep in mind that the legitimacy of the hypothesis testing procedure may depend on whether you have knowledge about the results of the study. For example, it would not be legitimate to test a hypothesis one-tailed if you had some kind of advance knowledge through your prior analysis of the data that the result was in the direction of the alternative hypothesis. This important idea will be described later in this chapter.

8.1.3   Step 3: Derive the p-value

Once you have collected the data, articulated the null and alternative hypotheses, and quantified the obtained result of the research in some statistical manner, then it is time to evaluate the relative plausibility of the null hypothesis in light of the data you have. This might seem strange to you, given that the null hypothesis is actually an expression of what you believe not to be true (assuming you have made a prediction). However, hypothesis testing as typically practiced in communication and other sciences is based on the process of *disconfirmation* or *falsification*. Rather than directly evaluating the alternative hypothesis, which is the statistical form of what we should find if our hypothesis or prediction is correct, we instead indirectly evaluate it through the disconfirmation or falsification of the null hypothesis. If you have set up your null and alternative hypotheses correctly and if you have reason to doubt the truth of the null hypothesis, then you must by logical extension accept the alternative hypothesis because the null and alternative hypotheses are mutually exclusive and exhaustive descriptions of reality. One of them is true, but they can't both be. So we test the alternative hypothesis, which is usually what we are interested in establishing evidence in favor of, by seeing if we have sufficient grounds based on the data available to reject the null hypothesis. We do this because the alternative hypothesis is not usually articulated specifically enough for us to directly test it. The null hypothesis, in contrast, typically provides us with a specific value (e.g., $\mu = 25$) that can be evaluated based on the data available. This will become clearer as we work through the examples in this book.

We evaluate the null hypothesis by first assuming that the null hypothesis is true and then computing the probability of the obtained result or one *even more discrepant* from the null hypothesis than what we found if the null hypothesis is in fact true. Such a probability is quantified with something called a "p-value." The p-value is the probability of the result obtained or one more discrepant from the null hypothesis than the obtained result if the null hypothesis is true. I essentially repeated this definition twice because it is such an important definition, so much so that it is worth chanting this last sentence several times out loud, posting a copy of it on your refrigerator, and requesting a friend to email you this sentence once a day until you remember it. In my experience, a failure to understand just what a p-value is causes all kinds of problems for burgeoning communication scientists. If you memorize (and of course eventually understand) this definition, you will find statistics to be a lot easier than perhaps you ever imagined it could be.

Consider, for example, that your research hypothesis is that people who take public speaking are, on average, different from the population norm of 25 on your chosen measure of communication anxiety. So the null and alternative hypotheses are $H_0 : \mu = 25$ and $H_a : \mu \neq 25$. Imagine that in sample of $n = 20$ students taking a public speaking course you found that the sample mean communication anxiety score was 26.8 with a standard deviation of 4.532. That is, $\overline{X} = 26.8$, $s = 4.532$. (Notice that I am using Roman rather than Greek characters to represent these statistics because these 20 students are not the entire population of interest. Instead, they are just a sample.) As we discussed in Chapter 7, if you had measured a different group of 20 public speaking students, no doubt the sample mean would not have been 26.8. It would have been different—maybe larger, maybe smaller, but almost certainly not 26.8. Samples of the same population will yield different sample statistics, such as $\overline{X}$, depending on who just by chance happens to have made it into the sample. Indeed, even if the null hypothesis is true, meaning that μ is equal to 25, it is reasonable to suspect that you could still get a sample mean of 26.8 or a sample mean even *more* different from 25 "just by chance"—just by the fact that your sample happens to include these 20 students rather than any other possible combination of 20 students taking public speaking.

At this stage of the hypothesis testing procedure, the goal is to determine just how likely you would be to get a sample mean as different from 25 as the one obtained if you assume that the population mean is actually 25. Framed symbolically, you need to know

$$P(\overline{X} \geq 26.8 | \mu = 25) \text{ or } P(\overline{X} \leq 23.2 | \mu = 25)$$

The "|" symbol in the expression you may recall from Chapter 5 means "conditioned on," "given that," or "assuming." Notice that two probabilities are needed here because the research hypothesis is framed nondirectionally or two-tailed. Because the research hypothesis does not state the direction of the expected result, the *p*-value needs to include the probability of getting a sample mean as different from 25 as you found in *either direction* away from 25. Remember that the *p*-value quantifies the probability of getting a result *as discrepant or more discrepant* from the null hypothesis as the result obtained. The discrepancy between the obtained result ($\overline{X} = 26.8$) and the null hypothesis ($\mu = 25$) is $26.8 - 25 = 1.8$. So any difference of at least 1.8, whether larger or smaller than 25, counts as being as discrepant or more discrepant from the null hypothesis than the obtained result. So the value of 23.2 in the second probability above stems from the fact that a sample mean of 23.2 or smaller is at least 1.8 units away from the null hypothesis but in the opposite direction from the null hypothesis than the obtained sample mean. So when testing a nondirectional research hypothesis, we want to know the probability of getting a result at least as discrepant from the null hypothesis as the one obtained in both directions away from the null hypothesis.

But what if you made a prediction in advance of seeing the data that public speaking students are, on average, *more* anxious than the norm? Then you'd frame the null and alternative hypotheses as $H_0 : \mu \leq 25$ and $H_a : \mu > 25$. Because the obtained result of $\overline{X} = 26.8$ is in the direction you expected, you'd want a slightly different probability. You still want to compute the *p*-value—the probability of the result obtained or one more discrepant from the null hypothesis than the one obtained assuming the null hypothesis is true. But because you have made a prediction about the direction of the result, the *p*-value of interest is

$$P(\overline{X} \geq 26.8 | \mu \leq 25)$$

That is, you do not consider possible results in the opposite direction from the prediction when computing a one-tailed *p*-value. In effect, by articulating a hypothesis one-tailed, you are claiming that you don't care if the result is in the direction opposite to what you expect it to be. If the possibility that public speaking students may actually be *lower* in communication anxiety than the test norm is deemed irrelevant and uninteresting to you, then you might be comfortable ignoring evidence suggesting this. This may not always be wise, and some people recommend that directional, one-tailed tests be avoided even when a specific direction can be predicted because researchers should be open to the possibility that the research findings may be exactly opposite to what was predicted. Two-tailed, nondirectional tests are more open minded, in a sense, in that evidence contradictory to the researcher's expectation in the opposite direction is deemed worthy of notice. However, as we will see, hypothesis tests framed nondirectionally require stronger evidence in order to claim that the research hypothesis is supported by the data. So the cost of being open minded is the requirement that evidence be stronger against the null hypothesis.

What if you make a directional prediction but the obtained result is in the direction opposite to what you predicted? For example, suppose your null and alternative hypotheses were $H_0 : \mu \leq 25$ and $H_a : \mu > 25$, but in the data, $\overline{X} = 22.3$. In that case, the research evidence is not consistent with the prediction, and the entire hypothesis testing procedure comes to a halt because there is no way that data that are in the direction opposite to what you predicted could ever be construed as supportive of your research hypothesis. However, you do have the option at this stage of rearticulating your null and alternative hypotheses nondirectionally and then testing those new hypotheses. The reverse is not legitimate, however. You cannot decide to change a hypothesis from two-tailed to one-tailed after seeing the obtained result. Why this is so will be made clear soon.

8.1.4   Step 4: Decide Between the Null and Alternative Hypothesis

Once the p-value is computed (using methods to be described throughout this book), the next step in the hypothesis testing procedure is to make a decision about the null hypothesis, and by extension, about the alternative hypothesis. The p-value is used in hypothesis testing as a measure of consistency between the data you have available and some assumption you are making about reality. That assumption about reality is the null hypothesis. The question you seek to answer with the p-value is whether the assumption, the null hypothesis, is reasonable given what you know from your data. More specifically, given the probability of getting the obtained result or one more discrepant from the null hypothesis as what you found in your study, you need to make a decision about which of the two statistical hypotheses the data are more consistent with. As described above, when testing a hypothesis, the null hypothesis is assumed true. Hypothesis testing is all about disconfirmation of the null hypothesis, which by logical extension leads to an acceptance of the alternative hypothesis. But if the null hypothesis cannot be disconfirmed given the data available, then it is retained as the better description of "truth."

The key to making the decision between the null and alternative hypotheses is the size of the p-value. Remember that the p-value is the probability of the obtained result or one more discrepant from the null hypothesis assuming it is true. What if the p-value is very small, meaning that if the null hypothesis is true, it would be very unlikely to get a result so discrepant from the null hypothesis "just by chance"? The simplest interpretation is that flukes do happen. In spite of the odds against it, people do win the lottery, people do get hit by lightening, and airplanes do crash. It is possible that the null hypothesis is true, and just by chance, the obtained result is very discrepant from the null hypothesis. But the simplest explanation is not necessarily the correct explanation or the best explanation.

An alternative interpretation of a small p-value is that the obtained result is not particularly unusual in a reality where the null hypothesis is false. In other words, the assumption being made about reality (framed as the null hypothesis) is simply wrong. A small probability, meaning a lack of consistency between what is known from the data and what the null hypothesis assumes leads us to reject the null hypothesis as a reasonable description of reality. Scientists prefer the most parsimonious explanation for a research finding, but only if it is consistent with the data. Chance is the most parsimonious explanation of all. But a small p-value means that the most parsimonious explanation of all, "chance," just doesn't describe the data very well so it should be rejected in favor of something better.

But how do we know if the p-value is too small? At what point do we draw the line between a rare event and a common event, a result consistent with the null hypothesis and one inconsistent with it? What criteria can we use to judge the size of the p-value and which course of action we should take, what decision we should make? The criterion used is called the *level of significance* for the hypothesis test, also called the alpha-level for the test, often simply denoted α (the Greek letter alpha). Common practice in social sciences such as communication is to use an α-level of 0.05 for determining whether or not the null hypothesis should be rejected. In other words, if the p-value is *equal to or less than 0.05*, then the researcher should reject the null hypothesis in favor of the alternative. But if the p-value is greater than .05, then the researcher "fails to reject" the null hypothesis.

More generally, if $p \leq \alpha$, then the null hypothesis should be rejected. When a p-value is less than or equal to the α-level for the test, it is said that the result is *statistically significant* at that α-level, or the α-level of significance. So someone testing a hypothesis using the .05 level (i.e., $\alpha = .05$) might claim a result is "statistically significant at the .05 level." This means that the p-value was .05 or less. So a statistically significant result is one where the investigator rejected his or her null hypothesis in favor of the alternative at the level of significance (α) used for the test.

But why did the field of communication adopt the $\alpha = 0.05$ level of significance for testing a hypothesis? Why not .04, or .10, or .025? Is there something important mathematically or statistically about 0.05? The answer is no. It is just an arbitrary guideline that has become commonly accepted and widely used throughout the sciences. In the history of statistics, a man named Ronald Fisher decided, and arbitrarily so, that 0.05 seemed small enough and with a few exceptions that guideline largely has been adopted by the science community. Scientists who think about statistical methodology for a living differ on whether the researcher should be given the latitude to choose the level of significance for his or her hypothesis test, or whether the field of study should choose it and give individual researchers little flexibility in deviating from that α-level when testing hypotheses.

Now let's take all this and extend it to the example we've been working through. Suppose that you propose the research hypothesis that students taking public speaking are more apprehensive about communication situations than the population norm. Using the *Communication Anxiety Inventory* as your measure, you argue that if your students are more apprehensive than the population norm on the measure, then the average score computed in a sample of students enrolled in a public speaking course should be greater than 25. However, you decide that you will remain open to the possibility that students of public speaking could be less anxious than the norm, so you decide to conduct a two-tailed test. So the null hypothesis and alternative hypotheses are $H_0 : \mu = 25$ and $H_a : \mu \neq 25$, where μ is the unknown population mean communication anxiety for students taking a public speaking course. You find in a sample of $n = 20$ students enrolled in a public speaking course that the sample mean is 26.8, and you compute the two-tailed probability of such a result or one more discrepant from the null hypothesis (without regard to direction, as you are doing a two-tailed test) and find that it is, say, 0.15. This p-value is larger than 0.05 (assuming you are following convention and using an α-level of 0.05 for the test), so you do not reject the null hypothesis. The result is *not* statistically significant. The sample mean of 26.8 is not different from 25 to a statistically significant degree. The data are not sufficiently inconsistent with the null hypothesis to reject it. (We haven't yet talked about how a p-value is computed, so don't worry if it seems like we are moving too fast.)

8.1.5   Step 5: Interpret the Result of the Test in Substantive Terms

Armed with your data and now having decided on the fate of the null and alternative hypotheses, it might seem like your job is done. However, you must not forget that statistics is a tool for evaluating the research hypothesis or question. The final step is to translate the results of the statistical test back into the terminology used to describe the research hypothesis. After all, we do research to answer interesting research questions or test hypotheses we have about some kind of process or phenomenon we are studying, not to conduct statistical tests. So finish the job by translating and interpreting the results of your test in substantive terms. The large p-value in the example above leads you not only to fail to reject the null hypothesis, but also to make the substantive (and more important) claim that students taking a public speaking course are no different in communication anxiety than the population as a whole. They are no more or less anxious about communication than the norm.

Keep in mind that the decisions that you make with statistical hypothesis testing are only as good as the data available. It could be that public speaking students are more anxious than the norm, but your chosen measure of anxiety is not good enough for you to detect that difference. Perhaps a different measure of communication anxiety would have produced a different result and led to a different substantive conclusion. And depending on how you obtained your sample, it is possible that the 20 students in your sample were not representative of the population of people that takes public speaking classes. If you did randomly sample from this population, this is relatively unlikely, and for this reason, random sampling is the ideal method of selecting participants for research studies. It is not clear from my description above whether or not there has was any attempt to randomly sample from some population of people taking a public speaking course, and it isn't at all clear just how we could ever randomly sample from such a population. I merely described that 20 students provided data, but I did not specify how those students were obtained. As I discuss at various points throughout this book, random sampling isn't always feasible or even desirable. Whether or not you should randomly sample depends on the kinds of inferences you are interested in making.

So hypothesis testing plays an important role in the evaluation of research findings, but its role is limited to evaluating the data available. It is up to the researcher to maximize the quality of the data through thoughtful research design strategies, such that when the p-value is computed, the substantive interpretation and conclusion about what the data are telling you can be made unequivocally.

8.2   Testing a Hypothesis About a Population Proportion

To this point I have been speaking in abstractions, and I'd now like to formalize the procedure by showing the details for testing a hypothesis, including how to compute the p-value when testing a hypothesis commonly of interest to communication researchers: a hypothesis about the value of a population proportion.

8.2.1   Testing a Nondirectional ("Two-tailed") Hypothesis

Suppose you work on the campaign staff for a city council member who is up for reelection, and you have been assigned to poll the council member's constituents to see if the constituents have a preference for raising some needed money for the city through an income tax increase or an increase in the city sales tax. So you call 200 households in the council member's voting precinct through a random digit dialing method and ask the person of voting age in the house available to take your call which of two versions of the tax he or she prefers.

Suppose you had reason to believe that the council member's constituents would favor one of the taxes more than the other, but you weren't sure whether they are likely to prefer the sales tax or the income tax. So you advance the hypothesis that they do have a preference, but you don't know and are therefore unable to say in advance which of the two tax increases they are likely to favor. From this information, you can advise your boss which tax plan he should advocate in his campaign. We now step through the procedure for testing the hypothesis that they do have a preference for one tax over the other.

Translating the Research Hypothesis into Statistical Form. Your research hypothesis is that the constituents, as a group, do have a preference, but you don't know which of the two tax alternatives the group prefers. Or maybe you don't have any intuitions about whether they have a preference, and you'd simply like to determine if they do. Either way you frame your research hypothesis (or research question, as the latter is phrased), this leads to the following null and alternative hypotheses:

$$H_0 : \pi = 0.50$$
$$H_a : \pi \neq 0.50$$

where π is the population proportion of the council member's constituents who prefer the sales tax, and the population is all people in the candidate's voting precinct. It should be fairly obvious that if the group has a preference for one form of the tax, then π must be some value different than 0.5, but if they have no preference as a group, this implies that $\pi = 0.5$. The way the research hypothesis is framed, you would want to conduct a two-tailed test because you are interested in determining if π is larger or smaller than 0.5, but with no particular preference or interest in which side of 0.5 it resides. So this completes the first phase of the hypothesis testing procedure.

Quantifying the Obtained Result. The next step is to quantify the obtained result in the sample. Because the research hypothesis is couched in terms of a proportion, we should quantify the obtained result as a proportion. Suppose that of the 200 people randomly selected from the precinct, 86 said they prefer the income tax, and 114 said they prefer the sales tax. From this information, your point estimate is that the proportion of people in the precinct that favor the income tax is (114/200) or 0.57. Denoted symbolically, $\hat{\pi} = 0.57$, read as "pi-hat," where the "hat" over the π denotes that this is a sample-derived estimate of π.

Deriving the p-value. The next step in the hypothesis testing procedure is to calculate the p-value corresponding to the obtained result. Recall that the p-value is the probability of the obtained result or one more discrepant from than the null hypothesis than the obtained result assuming that the null hypothesis is true. The obtained result, $\hat{\pi} = 0.57$, is 0.07 units away from H_0. Because the research hypothesis is framed nondirectionally, we are interested in the probability of a result of at least 0.07 from 0.50 *in either direction* assuming that the null hypothesis is true. This leads to the following probability that needs to be computed:

$$P(\hat{\pi} \geq 0.57|\pi = 0.50) \text{ or } P(\hat{\pi} \leq 0.43|\pi = 0.50)$$

Once we derive this probability, we can progress to the next step, which is making a decision about the null and alternative hypotheses.

Before deriving this probability, it is worth reviewing briefly the principle of random sampling error introduced in Chapter 7 and just why we need to derive this probability in the first place. As discussed in Chapter 7, when sampling from a population there is typically a large number of possible results (such as a sample proportion) computed on a sample of size n from that population. From sample to sample, the sample estimator (in this case, $\hat{\pi}$) will vary just by the luck of the draw from the population value as a result of *random sampling error*. The goal is to make an inference about the parameter (in this case, π) from knowledge obtained about it from the sample, keeping in mind that the estimate derived in a sample is only one of many possible sample estimates when sampling from the population. But unlike when we discussed estimation in chapter 7, in hypothesis testing, we make an *assumption* about the value of the parameter. This assumption is the null hypothesis, in this case framed as π = 0.5. Of course, we don't know what π really is, but this needn't stop us from making an assumption about what it is. Hypothesis testing is all about testing the plausibility of this assumption after the data are available. This assumption is assessed by ascertaining the likelihood, quantified as a probability, of getting a sample statistic as discrepant or more discrepant from the null hypothesis from the one obtained if the null hypothesis is true. Thus, it is the p-value that allows us to choose between the null and alternative hypothesis through the principle of falsification. If we have reason to believe that the null hypothesis is false, then we must logically accept the alternative hypothesis as the more accurate description of "reality."

As discussed in Chapter 7, although we don't know exactly what π is, we know a lot about the properties of the sampling distribution of $\hat{\pi}$. We know that the mean of this sampling distribution is centered at π. This comes from section 7.1.2 when we discussed that the mean of the sampling distribution of a mean is equal to the population mean. Because the sample proportion is a kind of mean, we can denote this symbolically as $\mu_{\hat{\pi}} = \pi$. We also know from Chapter 7 that $E(\hat{\pi}) = \pi$, so long as we haven't biased the estimator using a poor sampling strategy. So the "expected value" of $\hat{\pi}$ is the mean of the sampling distribution of $\hat{\pi}$, which is simply π. But because we are assuming that the null hypothesis is true, we are assuming that $\pi = 0.50$ and, therefore, that $E(\hat{\pi}) = 0.50$ and $\mu_{\hat{\pi}} = 0.50$.

But with the theory of estimation, we can go even further than this. Because a proportion is just a kind of mean, the Central Limit Theorem tells us that the sampling distribution of $\hat{\pi}$ is approximately normally distributed as long as the sample size is sufficiently large. Finally, remember that estimation theory also tells us something about how $\hat{\pi}$ will differ on average from its expected value. This is called the standard error of the estimator. As discussed in Chapter 7, we can estimate this standard error if we wanted to, and the equation for doing so is

$$s_{\hat{\pi}} = \sqrt{\frac{\hat{\pi}(1 - \hat{\pi})}{n}}$$

(8.1)

However, when testing a null hypothesis about the value of a population proportion, it turns out that we don't need to estimate the standard error. This is because the

p-value is a conditional probability, conditioned on the null hypothesis being true. And if the null hypothesis is true, the standard error of a sample proportion derived from a population where the null hypothesis is true is known to be

$$\sigma_{\hat{\pi}} = \sqrt{\frac{\pi_0(1 - \pi_0)}{n}}$$

(8.2)

where π_0 is the value of π assumed by the null hypothesis. This is an important distinction to keep in mind because it implies a slightly different standard error depending on whether you are making an assumption about π. If you make no assumptions about π, then the standard error of $\hat{\pi}$ must be estimated using equation 8.1. But if you make an assumption about π and therefore the center of the sampling distribution of $\hat{\pi}$, as you do when testing a hypothesis, the standard error need not be estimated because its value is known and defined as in equation 8.2. But this is one of the rare hypothesis tests where the standard error of the sample statistic is defined by the null hypothesis. Almost always the standard error of a statistic must be estimated.

Now let's put this all together. If the null hypothesis is true, then π equals 0.50 and the sampling distribution of $\hat{\pi}$ is centered at 0.50 because $\mu_{\hat{\pi}} = \pi$. That is, the expected value of $\hat{\pi}$ is 0.50 if the null hypothesis is true. But in any sample of size $n = 200$, $\hat{\pi}$ is unlikely to be equal to 0.50 even if $\pi = 0.50$ because of random sampling error. The Central Limit Theorem gives us reason to believe that the sampling distribution of $\hat{\pi}$ is normal, and if the null hypothesis is true, the standard deviation of the sampling distribution of $\hat{\pi}$, which we call the standard error of $\hat{\pi}$, is known (from equation 8.2) to be equal to

$$\sigma_{\hat{\pi}} = \sqrt{\frac{\pi_0(1 - \pi_0)}{n}} = \sqrt{\frac{0.50(1 - 0.50)}{200}} = 0.035$$

So sample means would be expected to differ from the mean of the sampling distribution by ± 0.035 on average if the null hypothesis is true. With all this known from statistical theory, we can now compute the p-value. We want to know

$$P(\hat{\pi} \geq 0.57 | \pi = 0.5) \text{ or } P(\hat{\pi} \leq 0.43 | \pi = 0.50)$$

Because the sampling distribution of $\hat{\pi}$ is normal, or at least approximately so according to the Central Limit Theorem, this probability can be derived using the standard normal distribution. To use the standard normal distribution, the obtained result needs to be converted to a *test statistic*, in this case, a Z statistic. A test statistic is a quantification of the obtained result in a form that has a well-described sampling distribution, such as the normal distribution or the t distribution. The Z statistic is nothing other than a Z-score, in that it quantifies how far the obtained result is from the null hypothesis in standard error units. Under the assumption that the null hypothesis is true, we know that the mean of the sampling distribution of $\hat{\pi}$ is π_0, which is 0.50 in this case. The Z-score is derived just as in section 4.6, but the notation is slightly different:

$$Z = \frac{\hat{\pi} - \pi_0}{\sigma_{\hat{\pi}}}$$

(8.3)

Notice that Z is just a Z-score as defined in section 4.6, in that it quantifies how far away a measurement (in this case, a set of measurements yielding the sample proportion

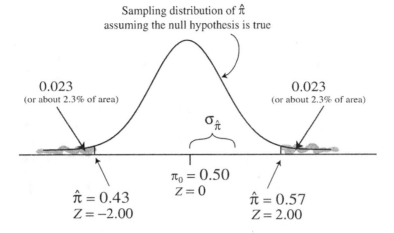

Figure 8.1 Computing the p-value is a simple normal probability problem.

$\hat{\pi}$) is away from the mean (of the sampling distribution assuming the null hypothesis, π_0, is true), in standard deviation units (where the standard deviation is defined as the standard error of $\hat{\pi}$). Applying equation 8.3 to this problem,

$$Z = \frac{0.57 - 0.50}{0.035} = 2.00$$

So 0.57 is about 2 standard errors above the mean of the sampling distribution of $\hat{\pi}$, which we are assuming under the null hypothesis is $\pi_0 = 0.50$. What is the probability of getting a sample mean at least this far away from 0.50 (in either direction, because the research hypothesis is two-tailed)? You should recognize this as a simple normal probability problem as discussed in Chapter 5. This problem is depicted graphically in Figure 8.1

The p-value for the obtained result of $\hat{\pi} = 0.57$ is the proportion of the area under the standard normal distribution in the shaded region in Figure 8.1. The table of normal probabilities in Appendix A tells us that the proportion of area to the right of $Z = 2.00$ is about .023. So if the null hypothesis is true, $P(\hat{\pi} \geq 0.57|\pi = 0.50) = 0.023$. But we also need to know $P(\hat{\pi} \leq 0.43|\pi = 0.50)$ because 0.43 deviates as far from 0.50 as does 0.57, but in the opposite direction. Using equation 8.3, a sample proportion of 0.43 corresponds to a Z-score of -2.00. The proportion of the area to the left of $Z = -2.00$ does not appear directly in Appendix A, but given the symmetry of the normal distribution, we know that $P(Z \leq -2.00) = P(Z \geq 2.00)$, the latter of which we know is 0.023. So from the additive law of probability, $P(\hat{\pi} \geq 0.57|\pi = 0.50)$ or $P(\hat{\pi} \leq 0.43|\pi = 0.50) = 0.023 + 0.023 = 0.046$. We can add these two probabilities together because these are mutually exclusive events. The sample proportion can't be both greater than 0.57 and less than 0.43. From Figure 8.1, it should be now be obvious why this p-value is called a "two-tailed" p-value.

Deciding Between the Null and Alternative Hypothesis. Having computed the p-value, the next step is to decide whether the null or alternative hypothesis is a more realistic description of the population given what is known from the sample. We know that if the population proportion is 0.50, then the probability of getting a sample proportion that deviates at least as far from 0.50 as 0.57 does in either direction is 0.046, which is slightly less than about 1 in 20 times. In other words, *if the null hypothesis is true*, then slightly fewer than 1 in 20 samples of size 200 would you get a sample proportion at least as different from 0.50 as the one obtained in this sample. You can either accept this result as a fluke and hold on to the null hypothesis as the truth about the population, or you can decide that this probability is just too small to cling to the null hypothesis as an adequate description of the population. If the latter, you'd be saying that with such a small probability, perhaps it is more reasonable to think of 0.57 or something more discrepant from 0.50 as a common occurrence when sampling from a different population—one where $\pi \neq 0.50$.

The communication science community generally doesn't leave the decision up to you and instead imposes its own standards on your decision making. Most communication scientists adopt a 0.05 level of significance (or α-level) when hypothesis testing. That is, the null hypothesis is rejected in favor of the alternative hypothesis if $p \leq .05$. If p is bigger than .05, then the null hypothesis is not rejected. Of course, you could impose your own standard if you chose to do so, but if you chose an α-level larger than .05, you would have to provide a justification for why you are parting with convention. In this case, p is indeed less than 0.05, leading to a rejection of the null hypothesis and an acceptance of the alternative hypothesis at the .05 level of significance. So the result is statistically significant. It seems that π is different from 0.50.

Note that knowing that π is different from 0.50 doesn't explictly inform us whether π is larger or smaller than 0.50. When a hypothesis is tested nondirectionally, the decision about the direction of the effect (i.e., whether π is greater or less than 0.50) does not come from the hypothesis testing procedure. The procedure only tells us that we have reason to believe that π is different from 0.50. But having rejected "chance" as the explanation for the discrepancy between the null hypothesis and the sample result, the most sensible interpretation is that $\pi > 0.50$. As will be discussed in section 8.3, it is possible that $\pi < 0.50$, but this is highly unlikely. So the hypothesis testing procedure does nothing other than allow us to rule out sampling error as the best explanation for the discrepancy between the null hypothesis and the sample result. With this explanation eliminated as implausible (because of the small p-value), we can now interpret the sample result as probably coming from a population in which $\pi > 0.50$, not one in which $\pi = 0.50$.

The Substantive Interpretation. But what does all this mean? If you were the person described in this problem, most likely your boss wouldn't be interested in all this statistical jargon. Similarly, communication scientists reading your research are not usually very interested in the specifics of the hypothesis testing procedure. Instead, they want to know what your data tell you about what you were studying. And isn't that the reason why you conducted the study in the first place—because you wanted to answer some question of interest? So answer it in English (or whatever language you are writing or speaking in), not in statistical jargon. Use statistics only as punctuation for your non-statistical interpretation of the results. So in a report to your boss (or in a journal article) you might write something like this:

> There was a preference for one version of the tax, with the majority of respondents (57%) reporting a preference for the sales tax over a new income tax, $Z = 2.00, p < .05$ two-tailed.

This interpretation deemphasizes the statistical procedure and emphasizes what the statistical analysis says about the question of interest. There is usually little need to formally talk about the specific null and alternative hypotheses being tested. People familiar with statistical methods will know what the null and alternative hypotheses were by how you framed the research question and the statistics you report in your description of the results. And people not familiar with statistical methods probably will not understand or care about these hypotheses, so why bother talking about them?

Notice that I state above that "$p < .05$." If I wanted to, I could have legitimately stated "$p = .046$." Whether you choose to report that p is less than the α-level or, instead, the exact p-value from the test or some other value that p is less than is up to you. There seems to be no standard practice in how p-values are reported, and I see no compelling reasons to adopt one standard or another. Some argue that you should report the exact p-value from the test because this facilitates a form of analysis known as *meta-analysis*, and it also allows readers of your research to use their own α-level when interpreting your results. Others argue that we should all use the same α level so there is no reason to be so specific about the p-value by reporting it exactly. Regardless, as discussed in section 8.3, p-values from hypothesis tests are only approximations, so reporting an exact p-value perhaps attaches greater precision to the p-value a hypothesis test produces than is justified.

8.2.2   Testing a Directional ("One-tailed") Hypothesis

The previous example illustrated the computation of the p-value for a nondirectional test. But what if you had reason to believe before looking at the sample result that there would be more support for the sales tax than the income tax. In that case, you could have chosen instead to test the hypothesis directionally. Thus, the null and alternative hypotheses would be $H_0 : \pi \leq 0.5$ and $H_a : \pi > 0.5$. Because π is the proportion of the councilperson's constituents that prefer the sales tax, this one-tailed research hypothesis would be confirmed if you could claim that more than half of the people prefer the sales tax.

The obtained result is unaffected by how the hypothesis is framed. The sample proportion $\hat{\pi}$ is still 0.57. In order to assess the null and alternative hypotheses, a p-value is needed. But this time, we focus the probability computations on only a part of the sampling distribution of $\hat{\pi}$. To derive this "one-tailed" p-value, first ask whether the sample result is in the direction predicted. It is here, so we can continue. Next, compute the probability of getting a sample result *at least as deviant from null hypothesis in that direction*. In other words, we want to compute $P(\hat{\pi} \geq 0.57 | \pi \leq 0.50)$. This p-value cannot be computed exactly, because the probability of getting a sample proportion of 0.57 or more depends on the value of π we assume under the null hypothesis. Unlike in the two-tailed version of the test, the null hypothesis does not specify a precise value of π and instead specifies a range of values (namely, all values less than or equal to 0.50). However, this turns out not to be a problem. To compute this probability, first assume that the π is a value as close as possible to the alternative hypothesis *but still inconsistent with it*. In this case, the value of π that is closest to the alternative hypothesis but still inconsistent with it is 0.50. Then derive the probability of the obtained result or one more discrepant than the obtained result from the assumed value of π. In other words, compute $P(\hat{\pi} \geq 0.57 | \pi = 0.50)$. This is accomplished by converting the obtained sample result to a Z statistic with equation 8.3. From the earlier problem we already know that the Z is 2.00. And we also already know that the probability of getting a sample result at least 2.00 standard errors above the null hypothesis is .023 if the null hypothesis is true (see Figure 8.1). However, this is not the p-value desired, because the actual null hypothesis is not $H_0 : \pi = 0.50$, but instead the less specific $H_0 : \pi \leq 0.50$. But it should be apparent that if π is assumed to be some value less than 0.50, then the probability of getting a sample proportion or 0.57 or larger must be less than .023 because 0.57 would be even more standard errors from the null hypothesis than when we assumed π was equal to 0.50. So the p-value must be no bigger than .023. It could be smaller. Symbolically, $P(\hat{\pi} \geq 0.57 | \pi \leq 0.50) \leq .023$. Using an α-level of .05, this leads to a rejection of the null hypothesis in favor of the alternative. It seems that, indeed, there is more support for the sales tax than the income tax.

Notice that when the direction of the result is predicted in advance and the result is indeed in the direction predicted, then the p-value is only half as big as when no prediction about the direction of the result is made. This is generally true. If the obtained sample is in the direction predicted, then the one-tailed p-value is no larger than one-half of the two-tailed p-value. This should make some sense from the multiplicative probability law discussed in Chapter 5. We know that the probability of getting a sample result at least as deviant as obtained from 0.50 in *either* direction is .046. And before the results were known, the probability that the sample result would be in the direction predicted was 0.50 (because the sample result would either be in the direction predicted or not, and those two possibilities are equally likely if the null hypothesis is true). By the multiplicative probability law, the probability of the sample result being both as discrepant or more discrepant from 0.50 (event A) AND in the direction predicted (event B) is $P(A)P(B) = (0.50)(0.046) = .023$. We can use this version of the multiplicative probability law by assuming that the size of the difference and the direction of the difference are independent events if the null hypothesis that $\pi = 0.50$ is true. This seems like a sensible assumption because knowledge as to whether or not the result is in the direction predicted provides no information about how large the difference between the sample result and the null hypothesis is. But because the null hypothesis is not $\pi = 0.50$ but instead, $\pi \leq 0.50$, we must modify this p-value by stating that the p-value is no greater than .023.

Finally, the substantive conclusion might read

> As predicted, there was a preference for the sales tax, with the majority of the respondents (57%) reporting they would prefer the sales tax over a new income tax, $Z = 2.00, p < .05$ one-tailed.

Directional hypothesis testing is only legitimate if you make your prediction in advance of seeing the obtained result. This is because the probability of the result being in the direction predicted is not 0.50 if you make your prediction after seeing the data. Typically, the "prediction" that a sensible person would make after seeing the data is that the result would be in the direction obtained. Thus, the probability of getting a result in the direction "predicted" is 1, not 0.5, if you've already seen the result. So by the multiplicative probability law, the one-tailed p-value for a prediction made after you've seen the data is just the two-tailed p-value.

One other point about one-tailed hypothesis testing is important. We've already discussed that if a result is in the direction predicted, then the one-tailed p-value is necessarily smaller than the two-tailed p-value. More specifically, it is half of the two-tailed p-value. So if a result is statistically significant two-tailed, it must be statistically significant one-tailed if it is in the direction predicted. Because the p-value is smaller when the direction of the result is correctly predicted in advance compared to when no prediction is made, this means that the difference between the obtained result and the null hypothesis need not be as large when a directional prediction is made in advance of seeing the results from the sample. To illustrate, consider this. The two-tailed p-value for the obtained result of $\pi = 0.57$ was 0.046. But suppose you predicted in advance that there would be a preference for the sales tax. What value of π would produce a one-tailed p-value of 0.046? To answer this question, you need to know the value of Z that cuts off the upper 4.6% of the standard normal distribution from the rest of the distribution. From Appendix A, that value is about 1.69. Now put 1.69 in the place of Z in equation 6.3 and isolate:

$$1.69 = (\hat{\pi} - 0.50)/(0.035)$$
$$\hat{\pi} - 0.50 = 1.69(0.035)$$
$$\hat{\pi} = 0.56$$

So when testing the null hypothesis directionally, the p-value for a sample result of 0.56 would be less than or equal to 0.046. Notice that the value of $\hat{\pi}$ that produces this p-value is closer to the null hypothesis when the test is conducted one-tailed. So smaller discrepancies from the null hypothesis will be deemed statistically significant when the researcher makes a directional prediction and conducts the test one-tailed compared to when the test is conducted nondirectionally.

But what if the obtained result is not in the direction predicted? The procedure outlined above for computing a one-tailed p-value requires that the result be in the direction predicted. If the obtained result is in the opposite direction, then the p-value is at least 0.50. No work is necessary to compute the p-value more precisely and, indeed, it could be said that the p-value is meaningless in this context because the one-tailed p-value refers to the probability of getting a result as far or farther from the null hypothesis than that obtained AND in the direction predicted. If your obtained result is in the wrong direction from the alternative hypothesis, you fail to reject the null hypothesis, period. The p-value is irrelevant.

8.3   Decision Errors, Power, and Validity

Hypothesis testing is essentially nothing more than an exercise in probability computation and decision making. The probability derived from a hypothesis testing procedure is used as an aide to making some kind of decision about a hypothesis you advance or to answer a question you propose. Ideally, the decisions we make will be correct, and the procedures commonly used by communication scientists have become common in part because they tend to produce good decisions. However, there is no guarantee that a decision will be correct, even if the hypothesis testing procedure is followed to the letter. We can't completely prevent decision errors from occurring, but we can do things to reduce the likelihood that they will occur.

8.3.1   Type I, Type II, and Type III errors

Suppose your favorite sports team wins 7 of their first 7 games of the season. Under the null hypothesis that all teams are equally good and thus who wins and who loses is really just like flipping a coin, the probability of winning all 7 games is $(0.5)^7$ or .008, from the multiplicative law of probability. This p-value of sorts might lead you to reject this assumption in favor of the more reasonable interpretation that your team is better than at least some of the teams they played. But of course it is possible even if not very probable that your team is in fact no better than any other team, and the

Status of H_0 \ Decision →	Reject H_0	Do not reject H_0
H_0 is true	Type I error	Correct Decision
H_0 is false	Correct Decision	Type II error

Figure 8.2 Possible hypothesis test outcomes.

fact that they won 7 of their first 7 games is just a fluke, like flipping a coin 7 times and it coming up heads every time. So it is possible that the decision to reject the "equal ability" assumption is the wrong decision. In rejecting that assumption, you'd be making a mistake if all teams are equally good.

Using the same reasoning, we calculated earlier that the probability of finding that 43% or fewer or 57% or more people in a random sample of 200 prefer a sales tax to an income tax is just under 0.05 if you assume that the population as a whole has no preference (i.e., they are equally split). The hypothesis testing procedure described above leads you to conclude that the population as a group does have a preferred tax (i.e., the population proportion is different from 0.50). But that doesn't mean that it is true that they *do* have a preference. It is still possible that they don't have a preference, and just by the luck of the draw, your random sample included a disproportionately large number of people that prefer the sales tax. Situations like this can and do happen in communication research, and we can do nothing to stop it from happening. Sometimes we will reject a null hypothesis (and thus accept an alternative hypothesis) that, if we knew any better, we should not reject, and sometimes we will fail to reject a null hypothesis (and thus not accept an alternative hypothesis) when we should. But sometimes, and hopefully more often than not, our decisions will be correct. We will correctly fail to reject a null hypothesis when the null hypothesis is in fact true, and we will appropriately reject a false null hypothesis when it is false.

This combination of the truth status of the null hypothesis and our decision to reject or not reject it is represented in Figure 8.2. The row classification reflects the truth status of the null hypothesis, and the column classification reflects the decision to reject or not reject the null hypothesis. Although we can never know where in this table any decision we make resides (because we don't know whether the null hypothesis is actually true or false), it is helpful to examine closely the various cells of this table to understand the kinds of decision errors that hypothesis testing can produce.

An examination of Figure 8.2 reveals that there are three distinct outcomes. One outcome is a correct decision, corresponding to either (a) the rejection of a false null hypothesis or (b) not rejecting a true null hypothesis. The other two possibilities in this table are *decision errors*. In the language of statistics, if you reject a null hypothesis that is true, it is said that you have made a *Type I error* (pronounced "type-one"). In contrast, a *Type II error* (read "type-two") occurs if you fail to reject a null hypothesis that is false. A claim that people in the council member's voting district have a preference for one of the two tax proposals when in fact they do not as a group would be a Type I error. If the constituents in the representative's voting district do have a preferred tax but you claim that they do not, you would be making a Type II error. So a Type I error is akin to the boy crying wolf, claiming that something exists when it does not, whereas a Type II error is akin to not believing the boy who cried wolf when in fact a wolf is present.

Clearly, such errors are undesirable and to be avoided. The scientific community attempts to minimize the number of Type I errors that researchers make by imposing a strict criterion on the *p*-value required to reject a null hypothesis. By requiring a *p*-value of .05 or less to reject a null hypothesis, then the probability of a Type I error in any particular hypothesis test is kept relatively low at .05. More generally, the probability of making a Type I error when conducting a hypothesis test is α, the level of significance chosen for the test. Remember that a Type I error can occur only if the null hypothesis is true. We assume when testing a hypothesis that the null hypothesis is true. If you test a hypothesis using $\alpha = .05$, then you know that the probability of incorrectly rejecting the null hypothesis if it is true is .05. So you can lower the probability of making a Type I error directly by lowering the α-level of the test and thus requiring a smaller *p*-value before you reject the null hypothesis.

But in practice, it isn't necessarily a good idea to play around with the α-level as a means of reducing the probability of a Type I error because the α-level of a hypothesis test directly affects the probability of making a Type II error. Certainly it must be true that the less willing you are to a reject a null hypothesis (by requiring a smaller *p*-value before doing so), then the more likely you are to make a Type II error by not rejecting a null hypothesis that is actually false. In statistical theory, the probability of making a Type II is some nonzero probability if the null hypothesis is false, but in practice we can't compute the probability of making a Type II error because to do so, we have to know the probability that the null hypothesis is false (or the probability that it is true). But we never know that. However, there are things that we can do to minimize this probability. For instance, we know from Chapter 7 that sample statistics such a mean or proportion tend to be closer to their true, population values with larger sample sizes. So if we want to reject a null hypothesis when it is false, we can increase the likelihood of doing so by using a larger sample size. We can also reduce the probability of a Type II error by using measurement instruments that produce reliable data. Because error in measurement increases the standard deviation of measurements and thereby increases the standard error of a statistic, the *p*-value from a hypothesis test will tend to be larger when reliability of measurement is lower. Other other things being equal, more reliable measurement yields smaller *p*-values.

Although in practice we can't compute the probability of a Type II error, we can estimate it by making assumptions. If that probability turns out to be too high when it is estimated, there are things that can be done to lower it, such as just described. The process of estimating the probability of making a Type II error is known as *statistical power analysis*, and it is best done prior to data collection when possible. The power of a statistical test is defined as the probability that the test will correctly reject a false null hypothesis. Power can be affected by the conditions of the research method (such as the sample size) as well as by the mathematical properties of the tests we use. Some statistical tests are more powerful tests than others. Ideally, we would use tests that are the most powerful, but the realities of research mean that our tests will not always be as powerful as we want them to be.

Some people believe statistical power analysis should be routinely done before collecting data. Indeed, some research funding agencies require that proposals for funding be accompanied by a power analysis. This makes a lot of sense. If a funding agency is going to give you money to conduct a study, it is reasonable for them to have some assurance that if there is some interesting result to be discovered that your statistical test will have the power to detect it. It would be a shame if their money was wasted because the statistical procedures you employed were not powerful enough to detect an effect you expect to be there in your data. In reality, power analysis is rarely done by communication researchers, perhaps because doing so requires that you make a number of assumptions that often boil down to little more than semieducated guesses about the phenomenon you are studying and the variables you intend to measure. I don't discuss statistical power analysis in this book. The standard reference work for power analysis is Cohen's (1990) *Statistical Power Analysis for the Behavioral Sciences*.

Figure 8.2 does not include on additional decision error called the *Type III error* (pronounced "Type three.") A Type III error occurs when you claim an effect (such as a population parameter) is in a particular direction away from the null hypothesis when in fact the true effect is in the opposite direction from that claim (Leventhal & Huynh, 1996). Suppose you find in some study that $\overline{X} = 25$ and you conduct a two-tailed test and reject the null hypothesis that $\mu = 20$. After rejection of the null hypothesis, it reasonable to conclude from the sample estimate $\overline{X}$ that μ is in the direction consistent with the obtained result. So if $\overline{X} = 25$ and the null hypothesis that $\mu = 20$ can be rejected in favor of the alternative that $\mu \neq 20$, it is reasonable to infer from a two-tailed hypothesis test that $\mu > 20$. This is reasonable, even though the alternative hypothesis in a nondirectional test does not explicitly state on which side of the null hypothesis the parameter actually resides.

But it is possible to correctly reject a false null hypothesis but then interpret the sample result as reflecting of a reality that is totally the opposite of reality. For example, suppose it is true that $\mu \neq 20$ and the null hypothesis that $\mu = 20$ rejected, meaning that no Type I error has been made. From the sample result of $\overline{X} = 25$ you can sensibly argue that $\mu > 20$. But what if in fact $\mu < 20$. If so, then claiming $\mu > 20$ on the grounds that $\mu \neq 20$ and $\overline{X} = 25$ is a Type III error. Type III errors are exceedingly rare, but they can't be categorically ruled out.

8.3.2   The Validity and Power of a Statistical Test

Hypothesis testing is simply an exercise in probability computation and the use of the resulting p-value to make a decision about a research hypothesis translated into a statistical form. It is more accurate, however, to refer to hypothesis testing as an exercise in probability *estimation*. A distinction must be made between the *true p-value* and the *estimated p-value*. The true p-value is the actual probability of the obtained result or one more discrepant from the null hypothesis assuming the null hypothesis is true. The true p-value cannot be known exactly. The estimated p-value, in contrast, is the p-value that a hypothesis testing procedure produces. These are not necessarily the same thing. All the hypothesis testing procedures described in this book are theoretically derived attempts at estimating the true p-value. These tests typically require assumptions—conditions that must be met in order to produce a good estimate of the p-value. For example, the test described above for testing a hypothesis about a proportion assumes that the sample size is not small. If it is used with a small sample, the resulting estimated p-value can be inaccurate. (A similar test that does not make this assumption will be discussed in a later chapter.) The less accurate the test is at estimating the p-value, the more likely you are to make a decision error because the statistical decision is based on that p-value. Some statistical tests are better than others at accurately estimating the true p-value. Not all statistical tests are good, and even otherwise good hypothesis testing procedures may perform badly in some circumstances.

Statistical tests vary in what statisticians call a test's *validity*.[1] A hypothesis testing method is considered valid if the probability of making a Type I error using the test is no greater than α, the level of significance chosen for the test. But a test might be valid in some circumstances but not in others, so it isn't totally accurate to talk about validity as a property of the test. It is possible that the p-value your test gives you is too small, meaning that the true p-value is actually larger than the p-value the test yields. A test that tends to underestimate the true p-value is called a *liberal* test. We want to avoid using liberal tests or at least avoid tests that are liberal in the conditions that we are using them. If we use a liberal test when testing a hypothesis then the probability of a Type I error is actually larger than α, meaning that we are taking a bigger risk of making a Type I error than we want to be taking and that the scientific community finds acceptable. In contrast, a test is *conservative* if it tends to produce a p-value that is larger than the true p-value. In that case, the probability of a Type I error when using the test will be less than α. A conservative test is valid because it meets the definition of validity described above. However, a conservative test will be lower in power than a less conservative test because more conservative tests are less likely to reject any null hypothesis, true or false.

The degree of liberalness or conservativeness of a test, and therefore its validity, is determined in part by whether the assumptions of the test are met when the test is applied to a given inferential problem. So liberalness, conservativeness, and validity are properties not so much of tests themselves but the interaction between the test and the conditions in which the test is used. A test may be conservative and therefore valid in some circumstances but liberal and therefore invalid in others. A test that is valid even when its assumptions are not met is called a *robust test*. Many of the tests used by communication scientists are highly robust, some are only mildly robust, and some are not at all robust. At the appropriate time, we will discuss the assumptions that various hypothesis testing procedures make and the effects of assumption violations on the validity of a test.

8.4 Hypothesis Test or Confidence Interval?

Hypothesis testing is a very widely used statistical procedure in communication science, but it is not without its controversies. Perhaps the controversy that most divides communication researchers is the value of hypothesis testing relative to confidence intervals. The most extreme advocates of confidence intervals argue that hypothesis testing is a useless statistical procedure and should be abandoned. This argument, represented in such articles as Cohen (1994) and Hunter (1997), is predicated on two perceptions of this camp: (a) all null hypotheses are false, and (b) rejection of the

---

[1]Yes, this is still another kind of validity, but a statistical test's validity has nothing to do with the kinds of validity discussed in Chapter 2. Validity is a term used in many different ways in science, and it is easy to get confused.

null hypothesis provides little information that a researcher is likely to be interested in. These arguments have been debated and discussed widely in the social science methodology and statistics literature, so it is worth spending a little bit of time talking about them.

Consider the previous example, where we asked whether the residents of a city council member's district favored one form of taxation over another. Recall that we tested the null hypothesis that $\pi = 0.50$, meaning that the constituents are equally split on whether they prefer the income tax or the sales tax. Would it ever be reasonable to assume that *exactly half* of the population prefers the income tax and half the sales tax? Most likely the population is not exactly equally split. To be sure, π might be very close to 0.50, but it almost certainly is not *exactly* 0.50. For instance, suppose there are 10,000 people in the representative's voting district. It is almost certainly not true that exactly 5,000 prefer the sales tax, and exactly 5,000 prefer the income tax. Probably the split is something different, albeit perhaps only slightly different. If you buy this argument, then you believe that the null hypothesis is almost certainly false, so why bother testing it? And if the null hypothesis is false, then it can be rejected by a hypothesis testing procedure if the sample size is sufficiently large because we can make the standard error as small as we desire by increasing the sample size. That is, a failure to reject a null hypothesis can typically be attributed only to low statistical power. Given that any null hypothesis can be rejected with a sufficiently large sample size, what value is there in testing it? Testing it provides no information, according to critics of hypothesis testing, and so hypothesis testing has no value to science.

The second argument is that the alternative hypothesis is usually so vague that accepting it provides little useful information. Continuing with this example, the null hypothesis that $\pi = 0.50$ was rejected in favor of the alternative that $\pi \neq 0.50$. So all you can say is that the population is not equally split on the income versus sales tax. To be sure, the sample result is *somewhat* informative. The fact that 57% said they prefer the sales tax suggests a preference in the district for the sales tax. But how many more prefer the sales tax? Fifty seven percent is just a point estimate that contains sampling error. By telling the council member to campaign in favor of a sales tax increase (advice motivated the results of the hypothesis test), is a campaign message espousing a sales tax going to resonate with a large majority of the constituents or only a narrow majority? If only a narrow majority, is this the best issue to campaign on? Perhaps your boss should campaign on some other issue that more certainly resonates positively with a large majority of the residents of the district.

Critics of hypothesis testing argue that confidence intervals are a better analytical tool because they provide more information than hypothesis testing provides, and they do so without making a ridiculous assumption that is certainly false. Let's calculate a 95% confidence interval for π to illustrate. We know that in a sample of size $n = 200$, $\hat{\pi} = 0.57$. From equation 8.1, the estimated standard error for the sample proportion of 0.57 is

$$s_{\hat{\pi}} = \sqrt{\frac{\hat{\pi}(1 - \hat{\pi})}{n}} = \sqrt{\frac{0.57(1 - 0.57)}{200}} = 0.035$$

Observe that we must estimate the standard error because we are not making an assumption about π as we do when testing a hypothesis. So we must use information from the sample to derive the standard error for $\hat{\pi}$. But because the standard error is estimated rather than known, we should use the t distribution to derive the confidence interval (from Chapter 7). For a 95% confidence interval we need to know the value of t that cuts of the upper and lower 2.5% (and thus 5% total) of the t distribution from the rest of the distribution. With a sample size of 200, we use the t distribution with $n - 1 = 199$ degrees of freedom. From Appendix B, this t is about 1.972. Using equation 7.10, the 95% confidence interval for π is $0.57 \pm 1.972(0.035) = 0.501$ to 0.639. So we can be pretty sure that between 50.1 and 63.9% of the residents prefer the sales tax.

Notice that 0.50 is not in the confidence interval. So we can be pretty sure that the population is not equally split, just as the hypothesis test told us. But the confidence interval provides more information than either the point estimate or the alternative hypothesis. Notice that 0.501 is in the 95% confidence interval. So as few as 50.1% prefer the sales tax but perhaps as many as 63.9%. With this information, you could tell the council member that campaigning on the sales tax is potentially dangerous because the results of the poll indicate that this is not an issue that clearly has a large majority of support. To be sure, the poll suggests that a majority do support a sales tax over an income tax but perhaps only a slim majority. That is a lot more information than hypothesis testing provides.

This is not the place to summarize decades of literature on this debate in a section of the book that does not presume that you've thought anything at all about this controversy. See Abelson (1997) or Hagan (1997) for arguments countering these criticisms of hypothesis testing. Here I offer only a few comments. First, although in some cases it is probably true that the null hypothesis is almost certainly false, to say that investigators can reject any null hypothesis with a sufficiently large sample fails to acknowledge that we are often faced with the need or desire to answer our research questions and test our predictions using what little resources we may have available. Big samples cost more than small samples in most applications (using whatever measure of resources you choose), and with smaller sample sizes, it becomes harder to distinguish between the signal (the parameter) from the noise (sampling error). Unless you truly believe with 100% confidence that your null hypothesis is false, you must accept the possibility that it *might* be true. Hypothesis testing exists so that we don't start making something out of nothing merely by collecting data, any data. If you can't confidently rule out the null hypothesis given the data that you have, then you have no license to start speculating about the implications of a true alternative hypothesis with respect to your research objectives. The fact that you (perhaps) could reject the false null hypothesis if you had enough data (a) ignores the fact that you don't have the data and you aren't sure what your sample result would be if you did, and (b) makes the whole business of science seem rather silly. Why bother collecting any data at all if our presuppositions are all that we need to make whatever claim we want to make?

Second, to be sure, confidence intervals have value, and I believe the example above makes the case for that value. However, confidence intervals have their limitations as well. As I discussed in section 7.2.5, as an inferential tool confidence intervals are useful only when the goal is population inference—making inferences about parameters using random samples from populations. But in communication, we often don't collect random samples from defined populations, and the value and meaning of a confidence interval in the absence of a random sample from a population is highly debatable. Instead, our research often focuses on theoretical predictions about the direction of the effect when we put it to the test using whatever data we can muster however derived. Is the effect zero, positive, or negative? The size of the effect may be (and often is) irrelevant. If we can argue that the effect is not zero by rejecting a null hypothesis that it is zero based on the data we have, then we have learned something about the accuracy of the theory with respect to its ability to make good predictions. We are typically interested in process inference not population inference. As I describe later in this book, we can make process inferences without random samples from populations. And we can do so without requiring a ridiculously large sample size that advocates of confidence intervals have to admit we might need to be able to rule out "chance" as the process producing the obtained result.

Whatever side of this debate you find yourself on now or in the future, it is very important to keep one indisputable fact in mind that confidence interval advocates routinely make in their arguments. When you reject H_0 in favor of H_a, in your reasoning you are ascribing more credibility to the alternative hypothesis than the null hypothesis. That is, the data suggest that the alternative hypothesis is more likely to be true than the null hypothesis. But it is easy to misinterpret and mislabel the p-value as the probability that the null hypothesis is true. *It is not!* The p-value does *not* estimate the probability that the null hypothesis is true. It is merely a measure of consistency between the data and the null hypothesis. Do not make the mistake that is often made by claiming that if p is less than .05, then the probability that the null hypothesis is true is less than 0.05. This is incorrect. Cohen (1994) discusses why this is not correct, and I encourage you to read this rather scathing criticism of hypothesis testing so that you will get a handle on just what all the fuss is about.

8.5 Summary

Hypothesis testing is so frequently done in communication research that an understanding of the procedure is essential to being able to participate as a reader and producer of research in the field. Theories make predictions about what should be found when a research study is conducted, and we use hypothesis testing to see if the prediction is confirmed in the data. Hypothesis testing is also used widely in research that is not motivated by theory because hypothesis testing allows the researcher to decide whether he or she should have faith in the finding as reflecting something real about the process or population being studied rather than as just a fluke, something you'd expect merely by such random processes as sampling error. But hypothesis testing is not without its problems. We can make mistakes when we test hypotheses, because ultimately hypothesis testing is about assigning probabilities to events, and sometimes rare events happen that produce Type I errors, and sometimes the vagaries of randomness will take a real effect and make it appear so small that we fail to detect it statistically with a hypothesis testing procedure (Type II error). Although there are criticisms of hypothesis testing, and some researchers believe hypothesis testing should be abandoned entirely, it is unlikely that hypothesis testing will go away so you need to be comfortable with the ideas and methods to be described throughout this book.

Testing a Hypothesis About a Single Mean

In Chapter 8, I introduced hypothesis testing and illustrated how to apply the concepts when testing a hypothesis about a population proportion. Throughout the rest of this book, we discuss hypothesis testing at length, starting with this chapter. As you progress through this chapter and the rest of the book, you will notice variations in the specifics of hypothesis testing. However, all hypothesis tests described in this book are governed by the same principle of *confirmation through falsification* and the use of a *p*-value for deciding between two statistical hypotheses (the null and the alternative). The procedures in this chapter focus entirely on testing hypotheses that can be phrased statistically in terms of a single mean. The wide majority of research hypotheses tested by communication researchers focus on differences between groups or the relationship between two or more variables rather information about a single measure such as a mean computed in a single sample. However, because of its simplicity, we focus first on this simple test because it serves as a good introduction to the specifics of hypothesis testing, and mastering these procedures will give you valuable practice for the more advanced problems later in this book. Having said this, one of the tests in this chapter is used quite frequently in communication science in a special form. This test focuses on a comparison of means when the data come from a "matched pairs" research design. So there is some applied value in mastering the material in this chapter as well.

9.1 The One-Sample *t* test

One topic that has inspired dozens of research studies in the field of communication is media censorship. Even in a democracy such as the United States where freedom of speech and the press is built into the laws of the country, some people nevertheless are supportive of censorship in at least some forms. One argument is that some media content (such as pornography and violence) can be harmful to others, and attitudes in favor of censorship reflect a sense that people should be protected from the deleterious effects of such content.

In 1999, Cynthnia Hoffner and her colleagues published a study in *Communication Research* on support for the censorship of television violence (Hoffner, Buchanan, Anderson, et al., 1999). They included 4 statements in a survey they administered over the phone to 253 residents of a midwestern community to assess the attitudes of the respondents with respect to censorship of violent television content. The statements read, "I support legislation to prohibit the broadcast of certain kinds of violence on television," "Any adult who wants to watch violent television should be allowed," "The government has more important things to do than regulate the violence on television," and "We should have a panel that reviews all television programming before it is allowed to be broadcast on television." Respondents were asked to indicate their agreement with each statement on a 0 to 4 scale, with a higher response indicating greater agreement (a description of the data file can be found in Appendix E4 on the CD). Each respondent's average response across the 4 questions was used as a measure of his or her attitude about censorship of television violence, with a higher response indicating greater agreement. Thus, this measure of support for censorship is what I called a *composite measure* in Chapter 6—a mathematical aggregation of two or more indicators of a construct. But notice that the second and third statements are reverse worded, in that they are phrased opposite to the first and fourth. So for statements 1 and 4, a higher response reflects a procensorship attitude, whereas for statements 2 and 3 a higher response corresponds to an anticensorship attitude. So before averaging the 4 responses to generate the attitude score, the responses to the second and third statement were transformed by subtracting them from 4. That way, higher numbers always correspond to a response reflecting a procensorship attitude. Assume that the responses to the four statements exist in a data file with variable names Q1, Q2, Q3, and Q4. In SPSS, the commands to accomplish the reverse scoring and averaging would be

```
compute q2r = 4-q2.
compute q3r = 4-q3.
compute censor = mean(q1, q2r, q3r, q4).
```

Using Cronbach's alpha, this average score was deemed a sufficiently reliable measure of *something* ($\alpha = 0.72$). Although Hoffner et al. (1999) provide no evidence that this is a valid measure of censorship attitudes, it at least has face validity (in my judgment), and the items were inspired by a previous investigator who used similar items as a measure of censorship attitudes.

A person's average response to these 4 statements is a number between 0 and 4. Clearly, this scaling of censorship attitudes to be between 0 and 4 is totally arbitrary. Had the researchers used a different response scale (such as 0 to 7, or 1 to 9, or -3 to 3), then the mean would be scaled differently. Nevertheless, it is sensible (perhaps) to consider the midpoint of the response scale (2) as the attitudinal "neutral" point. Someone who's mean is less than two has an an attitude that leans toward anticensorship, whereas someone with a mean greater than two has a procensorship attitude. So someone with a mean of 2 is sitting right on the attitudinal fence, so to speak, with either a neutral attitude or mixed feelings.

We will use this logic to test the hypothesis that residents of this midwestern community are, on average, *against* censorship of television violence. That is, if we could quantify everyone in the community using this measure, would the average censorship score be less than 2? Of course, there is no way that the investigators could have measured everyone's censorship attitude. So we are stuck trying to make an inference about this unknown population mean by relying on the sample mean. This inferential goal would be attainable only if we could muster confidence that this was a representative sample of the community of interest. To determine who was interviewed, the investigators did a form of systematic sampling of telephone numbers using the phone book for the community. But they added one to the last digit of the phone number selected so that people with unlisted numbers would have a chance to be included in the sample. This kind of sampling procedure, although not perfect, can probably be trusted as producing a relatively random sample of the community. As discussed in Chapter 3, we can never know for certain whether a sample is representative, but this form of sampling has a good chance of producing one.

The sample mean censorship attitude computed from the $n = 253$ respondents was $\overline{X} = 1.894$ with a standard deviation of $s = 0.880$. So the 253 respondents were, on average, against censorship of televised violence. But this sample mean is subject to random sampling variability. A sample mean from 253 randomly selected residents of the community will vary from sample to sample. It is possible that if everyone in the community could have been measured, the population mean would actually be higher than two (meaning procensorship). To determine whether the population mean is less than 2, we conduct a hypothesis test.

As measured here, attitude toward censorship of violent television is a quantitative variable, and we are interesting in making some kind of inference about the *population mean* censorship attitude. Statistical hypotheses tests involving the value of a mean of a quantitative variable are often conducted using the one-sample t test. The t test gets its name by its reliance on the t distribution, an important sampling distribution we first discussed in Chapter 7 in the context of confidence intervals.

9.1.1 Testing a Directional Hypothesis About a Single Mean

As discussed in Chapter 8, hypothesis testing is nothing more than an exercise in the computation and interpretation of a probability. This probability is used to make a decision between a null and an alternative hypothesis. If the probability of the obtained result or a result more discrepant with the null hypothesis (i.e., the p-value) is small, then we reject the null hypothesis in favor of the alternative. So let's implement this logic to testing the hypothesis that the population mean censorship attitude is less than 2.

Articulate the Null and Alternative Hypotheses. The first step is to translate the research hypothesis into statistical null and alternative hypotheses. The research hypothesis is that residents of this community are, on average, against censorship of violent television. The research hypothesis here is framed directionally. That is, the hypothesis as framed makes a directional prediction—that the population mean is less than 2. So a one-tailed hypothesis test is warranted. Using the logic described above, this corresponds to a statistical alternative hypothesis that the population mean of this censorship measure is less than 2. The null hypothesis is the complement of the alternative, meaning that the population mean is 2 or greater. Symbolically,

$$H_0 : \mu \geq 2$$
$$H_a : \mu < 2$$

Remember that the null and alternative hypotheses must be mutually exclusive and exhaustive. Those criteria are satisfied here. It is not possible for the population mean to be both less than 2 AND at least 2 (so they are mutually exclusive), and the null and alternative are exhaustive of the possibilities.

Quantify the Obtained Result. The next step is to quantify the obtained result. That is easy, and we have already done so. The statistical and research hypotheses are framed in terms of an average, so the obtained result should be framed as an average. In this case, we use the sample mean. As mentioned above, $\overline{X} = 1.894$.

Derive the p-value. The obtained sample mean of 1.894 is only one of many sample means that could have resulted from a random sample of 253 residents of this community. Any other random sample would produce a different mean, perhaps even one that is larger than two. The sample mean as a description of the population is subject to random sampling variability when random sampling is employed. To decide between the null and alternative hypothesis, we need to know how likely it is to get a sample mean that deviates as far or farther from the null hypothesis than the one obtained if we assume that the null hypothesis is true. Recall that this is what we called the *p*-value. It is the *p*-value that allows us to choose between the null and alternative as a better description of the population. If the *p*-value is deemed too small, then we reject the null hypothesis as an inadequate description of the population in favor of the alternative.

Because the hypothesis test is being conducted directionally, we bother deriving this *p*-value only if the obtained result is in the direction consistent with the research hypothesis and therefore the alternative hypothesis. The sample mean of 1.894 is in the direction consistent with the alternative hypothesis (i.e, it is less than 2), so we can proceed. If $\overline{X}$ was greater than two, then there would be no point in proceeding because there is no way the alternative hypothesis could be supported when the obtained result is inconsistent with it.

The probability we desire is

$$P(\overline{X} \leq 1.894 | \mu \geq 2)$$

In words, we want to know the probability of obtaining a sample mean of 1.894 or less assuming that the population mean is two or more. But recall from Chapter 8 that we can't compute this probability exactly because the null hypothesis doesn't specify a precise value for μ. Instead, it specifies a range of values (i.e., any value two or more). To circumvent this problem, we will compute a different probability and then make an adjustment once that probability is derived. So rather than computing $P(\overline{X} \leq 1.894 | \mu \geq 2)$ will will instead compute $P(\overline{X} \leq 1.894 | \mu = 2)$. This probability we can derive.

We know from estimation theory (Chapter 7) that the mean of the sampling distribution of $\overline{X}$ is μ when sampling randomly from the population and that the sampling distribution is approximately normally distributed. When we test a hypothesis about a population mean, the null hypothesis specifies what we assume the population mean is. So we assume here that the sampling distribution of $\overline{X}$ is centered on $\mu = 2$. We then determine what the probability is of getting a sample mean of 1.894 or less in a random sample of size 253 from this population if that assumption is true. This problem is denoted graphically in Figure 9.1, panel A. This probability is represented as the proportion of the sampling distribution of $\overline{X}$ in the shaded area.

We can't derive the size of the shaded area without first standardizing the problem into some kind of common metric that renders the problem solvable. This is accomplished by converting the obtained result into standard errors ($\sigma_{\overline{X}}$) from the null hypothesis. Once this conversion is done, we can rely on tables or some mathematical formulas to derive the *p*-value. Unfortunately, it would seem, we don't know how many standard errors 1.894 is from 2 because we don't know the standard error of

$\overline{X}$. However, just as we did in Chapter 7, we can estimate the standard error using equation 7.7. In this case,

$$s_{\overline{X}} = \frac{s}{\sqrt{n}} = \frac{0.880}{\sqrt{253}} = 0.055$$

Remember that the standard error of $\overline{X}$ is the standard deviation of the sampling distribution of $\overline{X}$. It quantifies how much, on average, sample means in a random sample of this size deviate from the population mean.

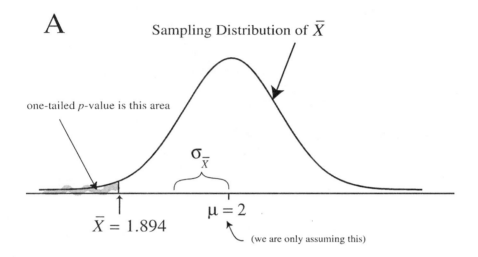

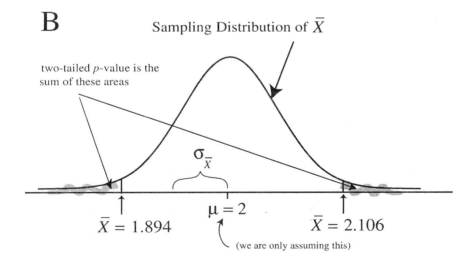

Figure 9.1 The p-value for a one- (A) and two-tailed (B) hypothesis test.

With this estimate of the standard error of $\overline{X}$ we can then *estimate* the number of standard errors 1.894 is from the assumed value of μ with the t statistic:

$$t = \frac{\overline{X} - \mu_0}{s_{\overline{X}}}$$

(9.1)

where μ_0 is the value of the population mean if the null hypothesis is true. We are assuming $\mu = 2$, so

$$t = \frac{1.894 - 2}{0.055} = -1.927$$

This means that 1.894 is 1.927 standard errors below the mean of the population if the null hypothesis is true.

Now that we know how many standard errors the obtained result is from the assumed value of the population mean, we can derive the p-value. There are two approaches to deriving it. The first approach is called the *critical value approach*. This is the method discussed in most statistical methods books, but it is probably the more complicated of the two methods and actually quite outdated. The second and more modern approach is to rely on a computer. Even though it is more complicated and a bit archaic, I will first discuss the critical value approach because it requires more thought, and at this stage it is better to get some practice thinking about the entire process rather than taking a shortcut by using a computer. As we progress through this book, we will rely on computers more and more. But if you can master the critical value approach, you are well on your way to a complete understanding of hypothesis testing.

The critical value approach is an indirect way of computing a p-value. Rather than computing the p-value directly and precisely (as we could with a computer), we instead determine the smallest number of standard errors that a sample result can deviate from the null hypothesis and still have a p-value no greater than α, the level of significance for the test (recall that α is the maximum p-value that leads to the rejection of the null hypothesis). For the one-sample t test, this smallest number of standard errors that the sample result can deviate from the null hypothesis while still being statistically significant at the α level of significance is called the *critical t* for α. If the obtained result is at least as far away from zero as the critical t value, then $p \leq \alpha$. But if the critical t is further away from zero than the obtained t value, then $p > \alpha$. This logic is presented graphically in Figure 9.2, panel A for the case of a one-tailed test in which the obtained result is in the direction predicted. (Remember that if the obtained result is not in the direction predicted away from the null hypothesis, then the null hypothesis cannot be rejected because p must be greater than α.)

These critical t values are tabled in Appendix B. We discussed the t table in Chapter 7 when deriving confidence intervals. We use the table in the same way here. We want to know the value of t that cuts off the lower $100\alpha\%$ of the t distribution in the direction predicted from the rest of the distribution, where α is the level of significance chosen for the test (typically .05 in communication research). The predicted direction was negative because the research hypothesis predicts that the population mean is less than two (in other words, the predicted value of $\overline{X}$ when converted to a t statistic is negative). Using $\alpha = 0.05$, we want the value of t that cuts off the lower $100(0.05)\%$ or 5% of the t distribution from the rest of the t distribution, as depicted in Figure 9.2, panel A.

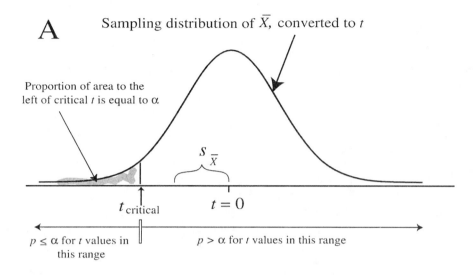

A Sampling distribution of $\overline{X}$, converted to t

Proportion of area to the
left of critical t is equal to α

$S_{\overline{X}}$

t_{critical} $t = 0$

$p \leq \alpha$ for t values in $p > \alpha$ for t values in this range
this range

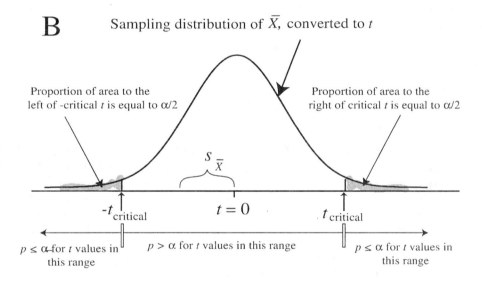

B Sampling distribution of $\overline{X}$, converted to t

Proportion of area to the   Proportion of area to the
left of -critical t is equal to $\alpha/2$ right of critical t is equal to $\alpha/2$

$S_{\overline{X}}$

$-t_{\text{critical}}$ $t = 0$ t_{critical}

$p \leq \alpha$ for t values in $p > \alpha$ for t values in this range $p \leq \alpha$ for t values in
this range   this range

Figure 9.2 The critical value approach to deriving the one- (A) and two-tailed (B)
p-value.

To get the critical value of t, we first need to know the degrees of freedom for the
problem. Recall from section 7.2.2 that there are many t distributions, each defined
by its degrees of freedom (or "df"). When testing a hypothesis about a single mean,
df is equal to one less than the sample size: $df = n - 1$. For this problem, $n = 253$,
so $df = 252$. Unfortunately, Appendix B does not have an entry for 252. So we have
no choice but to use the value of df in the table closest to 252. In this case, that value
is $df = 250$. The table tells us that the value of t that cuts of the upper 5% of the
t distribution from the rest of the distribution is 1.651. But that isn't quite what we
want to know. We want the value of t that cuts off the *lower* 5% of the t distribution,
not the upper 5%. However, the symmetry of the t distribution means that 5% of the

t distribution is less than $t = -1.651$. So the critical t value for this problem is -1.651 for $df = 252$, $\alpha = 0.05$.

With the critical t value obtained, we can now ask where the obtained t statistic lies relative to the critical t. If the obtained t is more discrepant from the null hypothesis (which corresponds to $t = 0$) than the critical t and in the direction predicted, then $p < .05$. But if the obtained t is less discrepant from the null hypothesis than the critical t or is in the opposite direction from predicted, then $p > .05$. Where does the obtained t of -1.927 fall relative to the critical t. Examining Figure 9.2, panel A, it should be apparent that -1.927 is more discrepant from the null hypothesis than the critical t and in the direction predicted. Therefore, $p < .05$.

Actually, there is one minor detail to consider. Remember that the null hypothesis was not $\mu = 2$, but $\mu \geq 2$. But all of our computations were conditioned on $\mu = 2$. In other words, what we computed above was $P(\overline{X} \leq 1.894 | \mu = 2)$. But we want $P(\overline{X} \leq 1.894 | \mu \geq 2)$ because the null hypothesis is that $\mu \geq 2$. This turns out not to be a problem if you realize that if $\mu > 2$, then the obtained result must be more even more discrepant from any other assumed value of μ that is greater than 2. Therefore, the p-value could not possibly be larger than .05 if it is less than .05 when we assume that $\mu = 2$. The claim that $p < .05$ is correct regardless of whether μ was assumed to be two or greater than two. So it is accurate to say that $P(\overline{X} \leq 1.894 | \mu \geq 2) < .05$.

Make a Decision about the Null and Alternative Hypotheses. With the p-value derived, we can now make a decision about the null and alternative hypothesis. Recall from Chapter 8 that if $p \leq \alpha$ we reject the null hypothesis in favor of the alternative hypothesis. But if $p > \alpha$, then we do not reject the null hypothesis because the data are not sufficiently inconsistent with the null hypothesis to warrant rejecting it. Sticking to convention by using $\alpha = .05$, we can reject the null hypothesis here because $p < .05$. The data suggest that the population mean is less than 2.

Interpret the Hypothesis Test in Substantive Terms. The final stage is to interpret these results in light of the original research hypothesis. Having rejected the null hypothesis that $\mu \geq 2$ in favor of the alternative hypothesis that $\mu < 2$, we can place this finding into its substantive context. If we were to write up the results of this hypothesis test, we might state that

> The evidence suggests that residents of this community hold attitudes that are against the censorship of televised violence, $t(252) = -1.927$, $p < .05$ (one-tailed), $M = 1.894$, $SD = 0.880$.

Notice that rather than focusing on the results of the hypothesis testing procedure, I interpreted this result in substantive terms and used the statistics only as punctuation for this statement. So the statement is expressed in terms of the goal of the research, not the hypothesis testing procedure, because the test is used only as justification for the claim. Few things in this world are more boring than reading a dry list of test statistics and statements about whether or not a null hypothesis was rejected. We conduct research not so that we can conduct hypothesis tests but so that we can answer questions of interest to us. So communicate the results of your hypothesis tests in substantive rather than statistical terms.

Having said this, it is expected in communication research that you tell the readers a little bit about the statistical details, such as the test statistic you used (here, the test statistic was t), the degrees of freedom when relevant ($df = 252$ here), the value of the test statistic (-1.927), and the p-value. It is desirable as well to include some descriptive statistics that are relevant. In the communication literature, it is common

---

Box 9.1: The One-Sample t test

(1) Specify the null and alternative hypotheses corresponding to the research hypothesis.

$$H_0 : \mu \geq 2$$
$$H_a : \mu < 2$$

(2) Quantify the obtained result

$$\overline{X} = 1.894, s = 0.880, n = 253$$

(3) Compute the p-value

$$t = \frac{(1.894 - 2)}{0.055} = -1.927$$

which exceeds the critical t value of -1.651, df = 252 for α = .05, so $p < .05$

(4) Make a Decision about the Null and Alternative Hypotheses

$p < .05$, so reject H_0 in favor of H_a

(5) Interpret the result in substantive terms

The evidence suggests that residents of this community hold attitudes that are against the censorship of televised violence, $t(252) = -1.927$, $p < .05$ (one-tailed), $M = 1.894$, $SD = 0.880.$.

---

to see the letter "M" to refer to a mean, and the letters "SD" to refer to a standard deviation. But remember not to focus on the hypothesis testing procedure. When possible and sensible, focus on the substantive interpretation and spare your readers the dry statistical details by using them only as punctuation for your substantive statements.

Box 9.1 summarizes these steps in the hypothesis testing procedure as applied to the one-sample t test.

9.1.2   Testing a Nondirectional Hypothesis

The previous example illustrated testing a directional hypothesis. But a research hypothesis is not always framed directionally. Often communication researchers either do not know the likely direction the effect, or they don't want to close their minds to the possibility that a result could come out exactly the opposite of what was predicted. In such cases, the hypothesis should be tested nondirectionally or "two-tailed." When conducting a two-tailed hypothesis test, the procedure is for the most part the same as when testing the effect directionally. What differs, but only slightly, is how the p-value is derived

Suppose that instead of hypothesizing that the residents of this community are against censorship of violent television, we instead hypothesized that they were not neutral, but we aren't willing to predict whether they are pro- or anticensorship. In that case, the hypothesis should be tested two-tailed. The null hypothesis is $H_0 : \mu = 2$, and the alternative hypothesis is $H_a : \mu \neq 2$. This change in the null and alternative hypotheses does not change the fact that the observed mean is 1.894 with a sample standard deviation of 0.880. So the estimated standard error remains 0.055, and 1.894 remains 1.927 standard errors below the null hypothesized value of the population mean.

What changes when the hypothesis is framed nondirectionally is the way the p-value is derived. Remember that a p-value is the probability of the obtained result or one more discrepant from the null hypothesis assuming the null hypothesis is true. When no direction is predicted in advance, we need to know the probability of getting a result as far or farther from the null hypothesis as the obtained result *in either direction* away from the null hypothesis. The probability we desire is

$$P(\overline{X} \leq 1.894 | \mu = 2) \text{ OR } P(\overline{X} \geq 2.106 | \mu = 2)$$

and this probability is depicted graphically in Figure 9.1, panel B. But where does 2.106 come from? This comes from the fact that the obtained result of 1.894 is 0.106 units away from 2 in the negative direction. The same distance from 2 in the positive direction corresponds to $\overline{X} = 2.106$.

This is not a difficult probability to derive. We know that 1.894 and 2.106 are both 1.927 standard errors away from the null hypothesis (verify for yourself that 2.106 is indeed 1.927 standard errors away from the null hypothesis, but in the positive direction). Using $\alpha = .05$, we need to know the value of t that cuts off the upper and lower 2.5% of the t distribution (and thus 5% total) from the rest of the distribution (see Figure 9.2, panel B). More generally, when we do a two-tailed test, we need to know the two values of t that cut off the upper and lower $100(\alpha/2)\%$ of the t distribution from the rest of the t distribution (yielding a total of 100α percent). The degrees of freedom remains $n - 1$, or 252 in this case. The t table in Appendix B tells us that the value of t that cuts off the upper 2.5% (in the "p = 0.025" column) of the t distribution is 1.969. (Note that we are using $df = 250$ here, the closest row in the table to the actual degrees of freedom.) The fact that the t distribution, like the normal distribution, is symmetrical tells us that the value of t that cuts off the lower 2.5% of the t distribution is -1.969. The observed value of t is less discrepant from the null hypothesis than plus or minus 1.969, so we know that the p-value must be greater .05. The null hypothesis is not rejected. Substantively, we conclude

> The residents of this community are, on average, neutral in their attitudes about censorship of televised violence, $t(252) = -1.927$, $p > .05$ (two-tailed), $M = 1.894$, $SD = 0.880$.

Observe that the hypothesis test and the substantive conclusion depends on how the research hypothesis was originally framed. As discussed in Chapter 8, one-tailed hypothesis tests can produce rejections of a null hypothesis when two-tailed tests do not, because the obtained result need not be as far from H_0 if it is in the direction predicted in advance. So if you are willing and able to take the risk of making a prediction before you have the data available, then if the finding is in the direction predicted the mathematics of statistical inference works out such that the obtained result need not deviate as from the null hypothesis to produce a statistical significant result compared to when no such advance prediction is made. Anyone can hypothesize that something will be different from something else. As a result, the evidence needs to be stronger against the null hypothesis when you don't predict in advance of seeing the result what the result will be compared to if you are willing to go out on a limb and predict the result in advance.

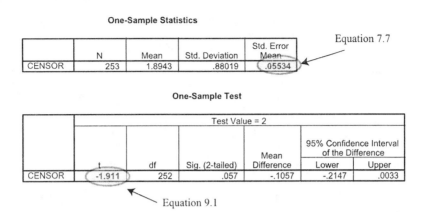

One-Sample Statistics

	N	Mean	Std. Deviation	Std. Error Mean
CENSOR	253	1.8943	.88019	.05534

Equation 7.7

One-Sample Test

	Test Value = 2					
				Mean	95% Confidence Interval of the Difference	
	t	df	Sig. (2-tailed)	Difference	Lower	Upper
CENSOR	-1.911	252	.057	-.1057	-.2147	.0033

Equation 9.1

Figure 9.3 SPSS output from a one-sample t test.

9.1.3   Conducting the One-Sample t test With a Computer

The critical value method of computing the p-value is outdated because we have computers that can estimate the p-value more precisely with much less effort. In Figure 9.3 you will find the output from SPSS for a one sample t test. I told SPSS that the "test value" was 2. This value of 2 comes from the null hypothesis. As can be seen, SPSS provides the obtained mean and standard deviation, as well as the estimated standard error of $\overline{X}$. The obtained t value is listed as -1.911, which differs from the t value we computed by hand only because we carried out the computations to only the third decimal place, whereas SPSS is carrying it out to the 16th decimal place or more. The t statistic listed in the output is more accurate. The p-value is displayed under "Sig. (2-tailed)" SPSS is telling us that the p-value for a two-tailed test of the null hypothesis that $\mu = 2$ is equal to .057.

But what if we wanted a one-tailed test of the null hypothesis that $\mu \geq 2$ against the alternative that $\mu < 2$? SPSS doesn't give us the one-tailed p-value. What do we do? The answer is to simply cut the two-tailed p-value in half, *but only if the obtained result is in the direction predicted.* We can do this because the sampling distribution of t is symmetrical. The two tailed p-value of .057 tells us that 5.7% of the t distribution lies more than 1.911 standard errors from the mean, ignoring sign. So we know that one half of 5.7% = 2.85% of the t distribution lies beyond -1.911 (with the other 2.85% residing beyond $+1.911$). In other words, the probability of getting a sample mean that is at least 1.927 standard errors less than 2 is no greater than 0.029 if the null hypothesis that $\mu \geq 2$ is true.

Marginally Significant? According to SPSS, if we were conducting a two-tailed hypothesis, the null hypothesis should not be rejected because $p > .05$. But isn't 0.057 close enough? Do we have to stick to 0.05 or can we consider any p-value close to the standard α-level of 0.05 as statistically significant? This is a controversial question. Some argue that given that the $p \leq .05$ rule is arbitrary, we shouldn't be such sticklers for detail by requiring that the p-value be .05 or less. Instead, any p-value that is "sufficiently close" to 0.05 should be all that is required to reject the null hypothesis. Still others argue that scientists must be consistent and follow shared rules that were established to protect one's field from making claims that aren't warranted. The only way that scientific discovery can be trusted is if we all follow the same rules. Still others take the middle position and refer to a p-value that is close to the point of rejection but not quite as "marginally significant." The term "marginally significant" is often used to refer to results with p-values between .05 and .10. Whether this concept is reasonable depends on your perspective. I cannot tell you what to think, but you should be aware that some people treat the .05 criterion as flexible, others adhere to it religiously, and still others strike a compromise between the two through the use of the concept of "marginally significant."

My personal feelings about this are mixed. On the one hand, the concept of a marginally significant result is to some extent inconsistent with the logic of hypothesis testing. A decision has to be made to either reject the null hypothesis or not. What does "marginally significant" mean with respect to that decision? In my experience reading the communication literature, a marginally significant result is often interpreted as if it is statistically significant. But if you are going to treat "marginally significant" results as statistically significant, why not be honest about it up front and make it clear that you are actually using $\alpha = 0.10$ as your level of significance and not $\alpha = 0.05$. But on the other hand, hypothesis testing methods such as the one-sample t test yield only an *approximation* of the p-value, not the true p-value. To strictly adhere to a 0.05 criterion ignores the fact that the p-value is itself only an estimation.

9.1.4   Statistical Assumptions

The accuracy of the p-value from the one sample t test depends on how well the sampling distribution of the mean can be described with the t distribution. The theoretical development of the t distribution as applied to testing the value of a single mean was based on the assumption that the population from which the sample is derived is normally distributed on whatever is being measured. So technically, the t test makes the assumption that the population is normally distributed on what is being measured. The one-sample t test also makes the assumption of independence of observations. The observations can be considered independent if the value of one measurement relative to the mean gives you no knowledge about the likely value or values of the other measurements in the sample relative to the mean. Independence might be violated if you included identical twins in the sample, or perhaps a couple that were husband and wife, or perhaps people who just lived in the same household. Identical twins, married people, and even brothers and sisters tend to be very similar to each other in a lot of ways. Knowing, for example, that one member of the household was against censorship gives you reason to suspect that other people in the house are probably against it as well.

The extent to which the assumptions of a hypothesis test are met can affect either the validity or power of the hypothesis test. When the assumptions of a test are violated, the p-value may not be accurate. It turns out, fortunately, that the one sample t test is fairly robust. Recall from Chapter 8 that a robust test is one that is valid even when the assumptions of the test are violated. When sampling from nonnormal populations, you can rest well knowing that the sampling distribution of the sample mean can still be well approximated by the t distribution in many circumstances, so the p-values are unlikely to be adversely affected by violations of the normality assumption (but see Wilcox & Keselman, 2003, for a different perspective). This is not necessarily true for small samples, however, if the population distribution is very asymmetrical and highly skewed. In such a case, the sampling distribution of the sample mean is probably not well-approximated with a t distribution. In that case, alternative methods are available, such as bootstrapping (described below).

The one-sample t test is not robust to violations of independence. This assumption must be taken seriously, as violating it can have profound effects on the accuracy of the p-value and therefore any resulting decision about the null and alternative hypotheses.

9.1.5   Large Versus Small Samples

Many statistics textbooks discuss large sample and small sample versions of this test. For small samples, the test is conducted just as I described here. For large samples, typically defined as $n > 30$, some statistical methods book authors argue that the t distribution is so close to the normal distribution that it is safe to treat the sampling distribution as normal and thus compute the critical values or p-values using the normal distribution. Although no major damage is done using this rule, I do not follow this practice and nor do most statistical programs. I suggest you avoid it as well. Get in the habit of treating the sample mean as t distributed even when the sample size is large.

The problem with the use of the normal distribution for determining the p-value is that for sample sizes between 30 and 100 or so, the sampling distribution of the mean most certainly is *not* normal whenever you have to estimate the standard error using the sample standard deviation. However, if you know the population standard deviation and thus don't need to estimate the standard error of the sampling distribution of the sample mean, it is perfectly appropriate to treat the sampling distribution of the mean as normal rather than t distributed. So the decision to use the normal distribution versus the t distribution for computing the p-value should be based on whether or not the standard error of the sample mean is being estimated (usually it is) rather than on the size of the sample.

9.1.6   Confidence Intervals

As discussed in Chapters 7 and 8, there is quite a stir in the methodology literature about the relative merits of hypothesis testing versus parameter estimation with a confidence interval. Advocates of the confidence interval approach to statistics argue that confidence intervals provide more information about the possible range of values of the population mean than does a hypothesis test, so confidence intervals should be the method of choice for making inferences. It is true that rejection of the null hypothesis only tells us that the value of the parameter being estimated is likely not equal to the null hypothesized value(s). Hypothesis testing does not give information about the likely value of the population mean except in a very rough sense. Also in favor of confidence intervals, you can actually test a hypothesis using a confidence interval. The null and alternative hypotheses are set up just as if one is conducting a hypothesis test. But rather than computing the p-value assuming the null hypothesis is true, you compute a 95% confidence interval around the sample mean as an interval estimator of the population mean. If the value of the population mean assuming the null hypothesis is true lies outside of the confidence interval and the likely values of the population mean as expressed by the confidence interval are in the direction predicted, then you can reject the null hypothesis at $\alpha = .05$ in favor of the alternative hypothesis. So a hypothesis about a single mean can be tested using either the procedure described here or by constructing a confidence interval around the sample mean.

Observe in Figure 9.3 that the SPSS output for a one-sample t test does include a 95% confidence interval for the difference between the null hypothesis and the sample mean. To understand what SPSS is doing here, imagine subtracting 2 from each person's censorship score. Then construct a 95% confidence interval for the mean of this new variable using the procedure described in Chapter 7. If zero is not in the confidence interval, you can reject the null hypothesis that $\mu = 2$ at $\alpha = .05$ two-tailed. Notice in the output in Figure 9.3 that zero is inside the confidence interval, so the null hypothesis that $\mu = 2$ cannot be rejected two-tailed at the .05 level of significance.

9.1.7   Bootstrapping the p-value

Recall from Chapter 7 that the sampling distribution of the sample mean is not always normal, t distributed, or even symmetric. In particular, when taking a small sample from a very asymmetric or highly skewed population, the sampling distribution of the mean is irregular in shape and certainly not like the normal or t distribution (see Mooney & Duvall, 1998, for examples). But the computation of the p-value using the one-sample t test assumes that the sampling distribution of the sample mean is shaped like the t distribution. When this assumption is violated, the p-value may not be accurate, and that is a bad thing given that the decision about the null and alternative hypotheses is based on the p-value. The best solution to this problem is to generate the sampling distribution of the mean empirically through bootstrapping and then compute the p-value based on the bootstrapped sampling distribution of t . This is a computationally-intensive procedure that requires a computer.

The procedure is very similar to the procedure described in Chapter 7. First, compute the obtained t statistic just as if you were computing an ordinary one sample t test. Call this value t. Next, subtract the null hypothesized value of the mean from every observation in the sample. For example, the null hypothesized value of the population mean in the problem we've been considering in this chapter is 2. So we would subtract 2 from every composite censorship attitude score in the data. Next, take a "resample" of size n with replacement from the original sample (where n is the original sample size), and compute a new value of t using equation 9.1. Call this t^*. Repeat this resampling from the original sample a total of 1,000 times, computing t^* in each resample. The two-tailed p-value is defined as the proportion of values of t^* from the resampling procedure, ignoring sign, that exceed the original value of t in absolute value. This is the bootstrapped estimate of the two-tailed p-value. If you were interested in a one-tailed p-value, you'd want to know the proportion of values of t^* that exceed t in the direction obtained (assuming that the obtained result was in the direction predicted).

This method of computing the p-value makes no assumptions at all about the shape of the population distribution on whatever is being measured, so it can be confidently used in a sample from any population regardless of the sample size. However, it is computationally tedious and very few statistical programs used by communication researchers include bootstrapping methods for computing a p-value.

9.2   Comparing the Means of Paired Responses

In the previous section, I introduced the one-sample t test for testing a hypothesis about the value of a population mean. Although understanding the logic of the test is important, the fact is that this test, at least in the form described above, is not widely used. This is because communication research often revolves around questions about comparisons between groups of people or between measurements over time. But there is a version of the one-sample t test that is widely used for a particular category of research designs.

9.2.1   The Paired-Samples t test

Consider a scenario where a single sample of participants is measured at 2 different times on the same variable, between which each person in the sample is asked to engage in some kind of task. For example, the participants might watch a political advertisement, or they may watch a certain TV show between the two measurement periods. Is it often of interest to know whether there has been any change between the 2 times on the variable being measured. Such a research design is called a *single-group pretest posttest design* (Shadish, Cook, & Campbell, 2002). Or consider comparing 2 research units that are paired through some kind of social connection, like mother-daughter, husband-wife, or boss-subordinate, with the goal of seeing whether the 2 units differ from each other on average on some variable. Such a research design is called a matched-pairs design. For example are husbands more argumentative than their wives? To conduct this study, you might administer Infante and Rancer's (1982) *Argumentativeness Scale* to 30 husband-wife pairs and test whether the mean argumentativeness score for husbands is different from the mean for the wives. We can test a hypothesis about the size of the average difference between measurements that are paired in some fashion with the *dependent groups t test*, also called the *paired t test*, or the *matched-pairs t test*. The name comes from the matching or pairing of the measurements. Each measurement in the data is paired or matched with another measurement in the data. For example, in the single-group pretest posttest design, a person's measurement at time 1 is paired with his or her measurement at time 2. In the matched pairs design such as described above, the husband's measurement on the argumentativeness scale is paired with his wife's measurement on the same variable. Although the test goes by a different name when analyzing data from such designs, as you will see, this test is nothing more than a one-sample t test on the mean of a difference score.

Every four years the United States elects a new president or reelects the incumbent president. A month or two before the election, the two candidates verbally spar in the form of one or more debates. These debates are carried live on national television, and most of the major network stations and cable news channels broadcast them. During the debates the candidates are given questions by one or more moderators, who allow only a minute or two for the candidate to respond. The goal of these debates is to allow the electorate to hear each candidate's position on various issues and to see how well they can make their case and defend their positions—an important characteristic of any leader.

Of course, mass and political communication researchers take great interest in the debates and conduct research examining their effects on voters' perceptions of the candidates. The election held in the year 2000 was no exception. A group of researchers at the University of Pennslyvania's Annenberg School of Communication conducted a massive study in the months prior to and shortly after the 2000 election and made their data available in the form of a book (Romer, Kenski, et al., 2004). The investigators randomly sampled residents of the United States by random digit dialing and asked them a series of questions about the election, their media use, evaluation of the candidates, and so forth. Some of the respondents were participants in a *panel*. A

Table 9.1

Pre- and Postdebate Candidate Evaluations

		Predebate (X_1)	Postdebate (X_2)	Change ($X_1 - X_2$)
Bush	M	62.960	62.451	0.509
($n = 225$)	SD	32.438	30.672	19.699
Gore	M	51.324	53.218	−1.893
($n = 226$)	SD	37.024	34.254	16.801

panel is a group of measured two or more times on the same variables, with the goal of assessing how their responses change over time or may be affected by events that transpired between interviews.

Some members of a panel were twice asked to evaluate Al Gore (the Democratic nominee) and George Bush (the Republican nominee). They were first asked to provide their evaluation before the debate that aired on October 3, 2000. Their evaluations were provided to the interviewer in response to the question "On a scale of zero to 100, how would you rate George Bush?" They were instructed that a response of zero reflects a very unfavorable evaluation, 100 reflects a very favorable evaluation, and 50 represents the middle point, meaning neither favorable nor unfavorable. These respondents were then asked the same question when recontacted after the debate had aired. They were also asked at this point whether they had viewed the debate. Using data from this panel, we can assess if the respondents' general evaluations of the two candidates for president changed after the broadcast of the presidential debate on October 3. To answer this question, I included respondents in the analysis below who (a) were first contacted no earlier than one week prior to October 3, (b) were contacted the second time no later than one week after October 3, and (c) reported that they watched the entire debate. So the two evaluation were given no later than two weeks apart but close to the date of the debates, and the analysis does not include anyone who did not watch the debate in its entirety.[1]

The means and standard deviations to these questions at each time point can be found in Table 9.1. As can be seen, there was a change in the evaluations of Al Gore following the debate. He was perceived somewhat more positively by these respondents after the debate compared to before. But George Bush was perceived somewhat more negatively after the debate compared to before, but only slightly so.

Let's call variable X_1 a respondent's evaluation of a candidate before the debate and variable X_2 a respondent's evaluation of that same candidate after the debate. The entries in the first two columns of Table 9.1 are the sample means and standard deviations of these two variables, $\overline{X}_1$ and $\overline{X}_2$, for each candidate. This is a random sample of U.S. residents, so $\overline{X}_1$ and $\overline{X}_2$ can be thought of as estimates of their respective population means μ_1 and μ_2. If we were able to find everyone in the country who watched the debate and ask them these questions both before after the debate, then

---

[1]The Annenberg data are proprietary so I do not provide them with the CD that comes with this book or on the book's web page. Instructions for generating the data file for this analysis can be found in Appendix E5 on the CD.

$\mu_1 = \mu_2$ if the debates did not affect evaluations of the candidate on average. But if the debates did affect such evaluations on average, then it would be true that $\mu_1 \neq \mu_2$. Rephrased differently, if a candidate's performance in the debate did not affect viewers' evaluations of the candidate, then $\mu_1 - \mu_2 = 0$. But if the debates had some effect on perceptions, then $\mu_1 - \mu_2 \neq 0$. If the performance had a beneficial effect, then $\mu_1 - \mu_2 < 0$, whereas $\mu_1 - \mu_2 > 0$ if performance had a detrimental effect on evaluations.

Both μ_1 and μ_2 are unknown, and therefore so too is $\mu_1 - \mu_2$. But we can estimate μ_1 and μ_2 using $\overline{X}_1$ and $\overline{X}_2$. However, given that each of these sample estimates is subject to random sampling variability, it follows that the difference between $\overline{X}_1$ and $\overline{X}_2$ will also vary from random sample to random sample. So it is possible that even if the debate had no effect whatsoever, "just by chance" the difference between the sample means might be some value other than zero. Indeed, even if $\mu_1 - \mu_2$ is equal to zero, it is highly unlikely that $\overline{X}_1 - \overline{X}_2$ will be equal to zero. In fact, it is almost certain that this difference will be something other than zero, just by chance. To assess whether μ_1 and μ_2 are the same or different, we can conduct a hypothesis test.

We are interested in determining if exposure to the debates changes people's evaluations of the candidate on average. Because no specific prediction is being advanced about what effects that exposure might have (i.e., whether evaluations improve or decline), the research hypothesis is framed nondirectionally. The null and alternative hypotheses are

$$H_0 : \mu_1 = \mu_2$$
$$H_a : \mu_1 \neq \mu_2$$

or, equivalently,

$$H_0 : \mu_1 - \mu_2 = 0$$
$$H_a : \mu_1 - \mu_2 \neq 0$$

A decision between the null and alternative hypotheses can be made using a paired-samples t test. As I explain below, this test is nothing other than a one-sample t test on a difference score, so you already know everything you need to know to conduct this test.

To understand how this is a simple problem about the value of a single population mean, consider that each person is asked to provide his or her evaluation twice, between which they viewed the debate. If the debate had no effect on the person's evaluation, then you would expect that, on average, the difference between each person's evaluations at the two time points would be zero. But if the debate had some effect on the person's evaluation, then the difference between the pre and post evaluations should be, on average, different from zero. We can create a new variable, let's call it D, that quantifies the difference between each person's predebate (X_1) and postdebate (X_2) evaluation. That is, $D = X_1 - X_2$. Let's call the population mean difference μ_D. We don't know μ_D, but from a random sample, we can estimate it with the sample mean difference, $\overline{D}$. We can now rearticulate the null and alternative hypotheses as

$$H_0 : \mu_D = 0$$
$$H_a : \mu_D \neq 0$$

Let's now apply what we covered in section 9.1. For evaluations of George Bush, the obtained result is $\overline{D} = 0.509$, $s = 19.699$, $n = 226$. This information allows us to estimate the standard deviation of the sampling distribution of $\overline{D}$ using equation 7.7:

$$s_{\overline{D}} = \frac{s}{\sqrt{n}} = \frac{19.699}{\sqrt{226}} = 1.310$$

One-Sample Statistics

	N	Mean	Std. Deviation	Std. Error Mean
D	226	.5088	19.69912	1.31037

One-Sample Test

	Test Value = 0					
				Mean	95% Confidence Interval of the Difference	
	t	df	Sig. (2-tailed)	Difference	Lower	Upper
D	.388	225	.698	.50885	-2.0733	3.0910

Figure 9.4 SPSS one-sample t test output comparing pre- and postdebate evaluations of George Bush.

So in a random sample of 226 people, sample difference would expect to vary from the mean of the sampling distribution of $\overline{D}$ by about 1.310.

If the null hypothesis is true, then the mean of the sampling distribution of $\overline{D}$ is 0, so the obtained sample difference is (from equation 9.1)

$$t = \frac{\overline{D} - \mu_0}{s_{\overline{D}}} = \frac{0.509 - 0}{1.310} = 0.388$$

standard errors from the null hypothesis. What is the two-tailed probability of getting a sample mean 0.388 standard errors or more away from the null hypothesis if the null hypothesis is true? We can ask whether the obtained t of 0.388 exceeds the critical value of t for $df = 226 - 1 = 225$, or we can use a computer. I'll do both this time. There is no row in Appendix B for $df = 225$, so we'll use $df = 200$. Because we are conducting a two-tailed test, we look under the "p = 0.025" column and find that the critical t values for $df = 200$ and $\alpha = 0.05$ are ± 1.972. The obtained t statistic is not more discrepant from zero than the critical t, so $p > .05$ (refresh your memory for this reasoning by examining Figure 9.2 panel B).

SPSS output from a one-sample t test comparing the pre and post-debate evaluations of George Bush can be found in Figure 9.4. Notice that SPSS displays all the information we just derived manually above, as well as a more precise estimate of the two-tailed p-value. We see that the p-value is 0.698, well above the $p = .05$ criterion. So we fail to reject the null hypothesis. The substantive conclusion is

> Those who viewed the Gore-Bush debate did not change their evaluations of George Bush following the debate. Although his predebate evaluation was on the favorable side ($M = 62.960, SD = 32.438$), it was also favorable after the debate ($M = 62.451, SD = 30.672$) and not discernably different from before, $t(225) = 0.388, p = 0.698$.

I will leave it up to you to test whether the debates had an effect (either positive or negative) on evaluations of Al Gore. You should find $t(224) = -1.690, p > .05$, leading to a failure to reject the null hypothesis of no difference between the evaluations pre and post debate. The debate did not, on average, change people's evaluations of either candidate. You can conduct this test manually using the information provided in

Table 9.1. To conduct the test by computer, you'll have to purchase Romer et al. (2004), where the data files can be found.

An Alternative Approach. In my opinion, the comparison of the means from paired responses is most easily understood as a test comparing the average difference score to the null hypothesis. The average difference $(\overline{D})$ between pairs of measurements is equal to the difference between the means of the paired variables, $(\overline{X}_1 - \overline{X}_2)$, and rejection of the null hypothesis that μ_D is equal to zero leads to the inference that $\mu_1 \neq \mu_2$. A mathematically equivalent approach is to directly quantify how far $\overline{X}_1 - \overline{X}_2$ deviates from the null hypothesis by expressing the obtained difference between the means in standard error units of that difference. The standard error of $\overline{X}_1 - \overline{X}_2$ can be estimated with equation 9.2 as

$$s_{(\overline{X}_1 - \overline{X}_2)} = \sqrt{[s_1^2 + s_2^2 - 2(r_{X_1 X_2})s_1 s_2]/n}$$

(9.2)

where s_1 and s_2 are the standard deviations of X_1 and X_2 and $r_{X_1 X_2}$ is the correlation between X_1 and X_2. A t statistic is then calculated as

$$t = \frac{\overline{X}_1 - \overline{X}_2}{s_{(\overline{X}_1 - \overline{X}_2)}}$$

(9.3)

and the p-value derived using using the t distribution with $n-1$ degrees of freedom. Using the data from the pre- and postdebate evaluations of Bush, $s_1 = 32.438$, $s_2 = 30.672$, and $r_{X_1 X_2} = 0.807$. Plugging the numbers into equation 9.2,

$$s_{(\overline{X}_1 - \overline{X}_2)} = \sqrt{[32.438^2 + 30.672^2 - 2(0.807)32.438(30.672)]/226} = 1.309$$

and from equation 9.3

$$t = \frac{62.960 - 62.451}{1.309} = 0.388$$

Notice that this is the same t statistic as we derived using the one-sample t test (Figure 9.4). Because the degrees of freedom remains $n-1 = 225$, the p-value is the same, as is the statistical decision. It appears that among people who viewed the first debate, evaluations of George Bush did not change on average following the debate.

Most statistical programs can accomplish the paired samples t test using either of these approaches. SPSS output corresponding to this approach can be found in Figure 9.5.

9.2.2   Paired-Sample Inference From Nonrandom Samples

Let's work through another example examining the same question but using a different data set and slightly different methodology. Benoit, McKinney, and Stephenson (2002) were interested in seeing if televised presidential debates influence viewers' perceptions of the candidates, such as their honesty, trustworthiness, and experience. This study was conducted during the 2000 presidential primary season. To conduct the study they asked a sample of students to evaluate Bill Bradley, who was running for the Democratic nomination for vice-president, on a variety of personality characteristics (e.g., honest)

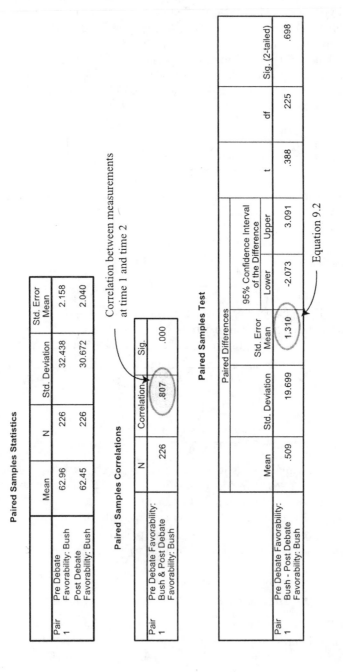

Figure 9.5 SPSS paired samples *t* test output comparing pre and postdebate evaluations of George Bush

on a 1 (not at all) to 9 (highly) scale. A week later, the students were recruited to a lab and were shown a videotape of one of the debates between then vice president Al Gore and Bill Bradley. Immediately after watching the debate, the students again rated Bill Bradley on the same personality characteristics they had previously evaluated him on prior to seeing the debate. Of interest to the researchers, among other things, was whether the students' evaluations of Bill Bradley after viewing the debate were different, on average, from the evaluations they provided before viewing the debate.

The data for responses to the "honesty" characteristic are displayed in Table 9.2. The data under the "predebate" column are the ratings given to Bill Bradley prior to seeing the debate (variable X_1), and the numbers under the "postdebate" column are the ratings of Bill Bradley made by the same people after having viewed the debate (variable X_2). The difference between each participant's evaluation of Bradley before and after the debate is listed in the "Pre - Post" column. (These data are made up here, but the basic findings reported below are consistent with what Benoit et al. reported in their article.)

As can be seen in Table 9.2, Bill Bradley was rated as more honest on average after the debate ($M = 6.850$) than before the debate ($M = 5.950$). This difference between the means of $5.950 - 6.850 = -0.900$ corresponds to the mean of the difference between variables X_1 and X_2. But X_1 and X_2 are both random variables, and therefore so is the difference between them. Most likely, in a different sample of size 20, the mean difference would not be -0.900. It would probably be something else. Indeed, there exists a sampling distribution of the difference between X_1 and X_2, and it is possible that this sampling distribution is centered at 0. If it is centered at zero, this would imply that the evaluations of Bill Bradley were unaffected by the debate.

Recall that the research question was whether the evaluations would be different, on average, after viewing the debate. From the previous example, logic would suggest that we could frame the null hypotheses as $H_0 : \mu_D = 0$, where μ_D is the population mean difference between X_1 and X_2 and D is defined as $X_1 - X_2$. The alternative hypothesis would be $H_a : \mu_D \neq 0$. To test the hypothesis, we need to know the probability of getting a mean difference ($\overline{D}$) as far away from 0 as the obtained difference of -0.900, "just by chance" if in fact viewing the debates has no effect on the evaluation of the candidates.

If we simply applied the principles from earlier and used the paired-samples t test, the obtained mean difference of $\overline{D}$ is -0.900 and the standard error of $\overline{D}$ can be estimated as

$$s_{\overline{D}} = \frac{s}{\sqrt{n}} = \frac{1.774}{4.472} = 0.397$$

meaning that the average amount you'd expect the sample mean to deviate from the population mean is 0.397 just by "chance," where "chance" is defined as random sampling error. This means that the obtained sample mean of -0.900 is

$$t = \frac{\overline{D} - \mu_D}{s_{\overline{D}}} = \frac{-0.900 - 0}{0.397} = -2.267$$

standard errors from the null hypothesis. The negative sign for t means that the obtained sample mean is 2.267 standard errors *below* the null hypothesis. The table of critical values of t in Appendix B tells us that the critical t for $\alpha = .05$ two tailed is ± 2.093 for $df = n - 1 = 19$. The obtained t exceeds the critical t, so we can reject the null hypothesis of a zero average difference in favor of the alternative hypothesis

Table 9.2

Twenty Evaluations of Bill Bradley Before and After Debating Al Gore

	Predebate X_1	Postdebate X_2	Pre–Post $(X_1 - X_2)$
	5	6	−1
	8	6	2
	8	9	−1
	9	9	0
	4	7	−3
	9	7	2
	7	6	1
	4	6	−2
	6	6	0
	3	5	−2
	8	7	1
	9	8	1
	3	5	−2
	7	9	−2
	6	6	0
	7	7	0
	3	6	−3
	3	6	−3
	5	9	−4
	5	7	−2
M	5.950	6.850	−0.900
SD	2.164	1.309	1.774

that the evaluations pre- and postdebate are different on average. Our substantive conclusion might be

> Bill Bradley was evaluated as significantly more honest after the partic-
> ipants viewed the debate ($M = 6.85$) compared to prior to viewing the
> debate ($M = 5.95$), $t(19) = 2.267, p < .05$ two-tailed.

There is a slight problem with this logic. But before dealing with this, first let's consider whether we can we conclude from these results that the change in evaluation was caused by the viewing of the debate. At first it might seem that such a conclusion is reasonable, but after reflecting on this, it should be clear that we can't be certain of this. A week of time did pass between the initial evaluations and the second evaluations. Perhaps the change is attributable not to viewing the debate but instead to something else that happened during that week. For example, perhaps during the week Bradley initiated an advertising campaign that emphasized his moral character. Or perhaps he received an endorsement that week from an important and well respected political figure. Or perhaps, etc., etc. In short, any other thing that happened that week could be what affected the perceptions of the participants, not the debate itself. This is an inherent problem in a single-group pretest-posttest design such as this. This study cannot conclusively tell us whether it was the viewing of the debate that caused the change over time, because anything that happened between the pre- and posttest measurement occasions could be responsible for any change (see, e.g., Shadish, Cook, & Campbell, 2002, for a discussion of the problems with the single-group pretest posttest design).

Let's return to my logical objection to the use of the paired samples t test. This application of this test to data from a nonrandom sample leaves a lot to be desired, at least conceptually. The mathematics of sampling distributions, which is ultimately what is used to derive the p-value, presumes random sampling from a population. What can happen "by chance" is defined as the sampling distribution of $\overline{D}$, with variability around the null hypothesis being attributed to random sampling error. But the students in this study were not randomly sampled from any particular population. They were just students that presumably were conveniently available to the researcher. There is no basis for making a population inference from this sample result. You could not say, for example, that the population mean change in honesty evaluations would be about 0.900 scale units after viewing the debate, plus or minus some amount provided by a confidence interval. To make such a statement, you'd have to randomly sample from the population of interest, or at least make the strong argument that your sample is representative of the target population. Given that no population can be reasonably defined here, even if a random sample had been collected, it isn't clear what such a statement would mean.

But in this study, population inference was not the goal. Instead, the researchers were simply interested in seeing if a group of students would, on average, change their evaluations of Bradley after seeing the debate. If the students do change their evaluations, this suggests that debates can affect people's perceptions of the candidate. The goal was *process inference*. The researchers did not care at all about whether the obtained difference of 0.900 is a good estimation of how large the difference is in some broader population. And it is a good thing they didn't care because the method of recruiting participants leaves much to be desired if that was the goal. Instead, the researchers were interested in whether viewing debates influences people's perceptions of the debaters. So process inference and not population inference was the objective of the study.

However, this still doesn't get us around the problem produced by using the sampling distribution to evaluate the obtained result and derive the p-value. The sampling distribution of the mean difference is used to generate the p-value, but the notion of a sampling distribution at least as discussed thus far is predicated on the existence of random sampling error. But there has been no random sampling in this study, so there can be no random sampling error. Fortunately, we can justify the use of the paired samples t test in this situation indirectly by showing a different method of generating the p-value that does not presume random sampling tends to produce a similar p-value to the t test: *the permutation test* for paired samples.

Let's assume that the debate had absolute no effect on these students' evaluations. Furthermore, assume that each student's 2 evaluations of Bill Bradley are the evaluations that he or she would have given regardless of the order in which they were taken. In that case, the first student's rating of 6 following the debate could be thought of as having been just as likely to have been the evaluation given prior to the debate.

Table 9.3

Eight Permutations of the Ratings for the First 3 Cases in Table 9.2

Permutation		Student 1	Student 2	Student 3
1	Predebate	5	8	8
	Postdebate	6	6	9
2	Predebate	5	8	9
	Postdebate	6	6	8
3	Predebate	5	6	8
	Postdebate	6	8	9
4	Predebate	5	6	9
	Postdebate	6	8	8
5	Predebate	6	8	8
	Postdebate	5	6	9
6	Predebate	6	8	9
	Postdebate	5	6	8
7	Predebate	6	6	8
	Postdebate	5	8	9
8	Predebate	6	6	9
	Postdebate	5	8	8

Similarly, that student's predebate evaluation of 5 was just as likely to have been given following the debate. So for the first student in the data file, a predebate score of 5 and a postdebate score of 6 would have been just as likely as a predebate score of 6 and a postdebate score of 5. This same logic can be applied to all 20 students in the data file.

Now ask how many unique reorderings of 20 pairs of pre- and postdebate evaluations are possible? We know that for student 1, there are 2 possible orders of pre and post debate evaluations (5,6 and 6,5). For student 2, there are also two (8,6 and 6,8). For student 3, there are also two (8,9 and 9,8). So there would be 8 different possible reorderings of the first 3 students' data. To illustrate why, consult Table 9.3, which displays these possible reorderings or "permutations" of the first 3 students' data. Notice, for instance, the permutation 1 differs from permutation 2 only in the order of measurements for student three, which are reversed compared to permutation 1. And permutation 6 differs from permutation 1 in the order of measurements for both student 1 and student 3.

Table 9.4

The Permutation Distribution of the Sample Paired Mean Difference

$\overline{D}$	Frequency	$P(\overline{D})$	Cumulative Probability
−1.600	18	< 0.001	< 0.001
−1.500	80	< 0.001	< 0.001
−1.400	272	< 0.001	< 0.001
−1.300	768	0.001	0.001
−1.200	1792	0.002	0.003
−1.100	3712	0.004	0.006
−1.000	6960	0.007	0.013
−0.900	11888	0.011	0.024
−0.800	18880	0.018	0.042
−0.700	27984	0.027	0.069
−0.600	38928	0.037	0.106
−0.500	51200	0.049	0.155
−0.400	63744	0.061	0.216
−0.300	75392	0.072	0.288
−0.200	84912	0.081	0.369
−0.100	91120	0.087	0.455
0.000	93280	0.089	0.545
0.100	91120	0.087	0.631
0.200	84912	0.081	0.712
0.300	75392	0.072	0.784
0.400	63744	0.061	0.845
0.500	51200	0.049	0.894
0.600	38928	0.037	0.931
0.700	27984	0.027	0.958
0.800	18880	0.018	0.976
0.900	11888	0.011	0.987
1.000	6960	0.007	0.994
1.100	3712	0.004	0.997
1.200	1792	0.002	0.999
1.300	768	0.001	1.000
1.400	272	< 0.001	1.000
1.500	80	< 0.001	1.000
1.600	16	< 0.001	1.000

$$\mu_{\overline{D}} = 0.000$$

It can be shown that there are $2^{20} = 1,048,576$ sets of 20 pre- and postdebate evaluations that can be generated by reordering the evaluations within each student. So with these 40 measurements (20 honesty evaluations obtained pre and postdebate), there are $1,048,576$ possible differences between 20 the pre- and postdebate evaluations. More generally, if there are n pairs of measurements, then there are 2^n possible sets of paired measurements that differ from each other only in the order of the pairings.

Each set of possible orderings of two variables X_1 and X_2 has associated with it a difference between the means of those two variables, $\overline{X}_1$ and $\overline{X}_2$. Defining $\overline{D}$ as $\overline{X}_1 - \overline{X}_2$, that means that with n pairs of measurements, there are 2^n values of $\overline{D}$ that can be generated as a result of reordering the pairs. Table 9.4 shows the possible values of $\overline{D}$ and how often they occur in this set of 1,048,576 possible sets of 20 pairs. The distribution listed in Table 9.4 is very much like a sampling distribution, except that it reflects not all possible statistics obtained through random sampling but instead through *permutation* of the order of the pre and post-debate evaluations. As such, it is called the *permutation distribution* of the mean difference.

Observe in Table 9.4 that the mean of the possible mean differences resulting from reordering the pre- and postdebate measurements is zero. So the expected value of $\overline{X}_1 - \overline{X}_2$ over 20 predebate and postdebate measurements is zero if a random process was determining, within each case, which evaluation the participant provided first and which he or she provided second. To evaluate whether the obtained mean difference can be attributed to such a random process, we can ask how many of the 1,048,576 possible reorderings of the pre- and postdebate evaluations yield a mean difference of at least 0.900 in either direction (remember the obtained result is -0.900 and there was no prediction about the direction of the difference, so the test is two-tailed). From Table 9.4, we see that there are $11,888 + 6,960 + 3,712 + 1,792 + 768 + 272 + 80 + 16 = 25,488$ possible mean differences that are -0.900 or smaller, and the same number of mean differences were possible in the opposite direction (0.900 or greater). So if the pre- and postdebate evaluations were just randomly ordered, then the probability of getting a mean difference as large as 0.900 between pre- and postdebate evaluations in either direction is $(25,488 + 25,488)/1,048,576 = 0.049$. This is a bona-fide p-value and it is smaller than $\alpha = .05$, leading us to reject the null hypothesis of *random ordering* of pre- and postdebate measurements and conclude that the pre- and postdebate evaluations are not just randomly ordered. Instead, there seems to be a systematic ordering, such that the postdebate evaluations tend to be different, on average, than the predebate evaluations.

There are two important lessons here. First this test, called a *permutation test*, does not require us to assume a random sample from a population. The permutation test conceptualizes chance in a paired measurement design such as this as a random ordering of the paired evaluations. Rejection of the null hypothesis of random ordering of measurements justifies a conclusion that there is some systematic ordering, which we can use to justify a claim in this case that "chance" is not a very plausible explanation for the obtained difference between the means. That is, a random ordering of the scores would rarely produce a mean difference as large as obtained in the study itself.

Second, and very important, notice that the p-value from this permutation test is not much different than the p-value resulting from the paired-samples t test. The t test gave a two-tailed p-value of less than .05, as did the permutation test. Usually these two methods will produce a similar p-value, so the paired samples t test and the paired-samples permutation test will tend to produce the same statistical decision. This justifies the use of the paired samples t test as a means of evaluating "chance" as the most plausible explanation for the average difference between two measurements absent some kind of random sampling from a defined population. So even if the units are not derived from a random sampling plan, the paired-samples t test can be used to evaluate the null hypothesis of random ordering of paired measurements against the alternative hypothesis of systematic ordering of the pairs of measurements. But, in the absence of random sampling from a specified population, population inference is unwarranted. So no claim can be made that this result applies to some broader population of people not included in the study. The inference is restricted to the *process* producing the obtained result in these 20 research participants. But as discussed above, process inference is often the goal in communication research, so this apparent limitation of nonrandom sampling isn't much of a limitation at all.

This method of hypothesis testing has been around since the early part of the 20th century (see, for example, Fisher, 1935, pp. 44–48; Siegel, 1956, pp. 88–92), but as an approach to statistical inference, it was computationally impractical until very recently because of the number of computations that are required to derive the p-value. Oddly, given the advancement of computing power since then, most statistical programs that enjoy wide use by communication researchers still have not implemented permutation tests even though the speed of your desktop computer can easily handle the computations. However, anyone with a little computer programming skill can write a program to conduct this test, and there are some decent programs available that can conduct this and related tests. NPSTAT is one program that is capable of conducting this test. It can be downloaded off the internet for free and can be found by any decent internet search engine. Another more modern program, written by David Howell (*Resampling Statistics*), also freely available on the Internet, can conduct this test. For more complete discussion of permutation tests, see Edgington (1995) or Lunneborg (2000).

9.3   Summary

In this chapter, I introduced the one-sample and paired-samples t test. These tests are used to test a hypothesis about a single mean or the average difference between paired measurements. As described here the tests assumes random sampling from a population with the goal of statistical generalization from sample to population. In the absence of random sampling, it is harder to justify the use of this test. However, the test can be used to approximate inferential methods such as the paired-samples permutation test, which doesn't presume random sampling from a population. As always, in the absence of random sampling, one is not in a position to make population inferences. But as the example in section 9.2.2 illustrates, this is not necessarily a problem because communication researchers are often more interested in process inferences than they are in population inferences.

These are some of the simpler hypothesis testing procedures available to communication researchers. Understanding how these tests work, their conceptual basis, and how to implement them in your research is important for its own sake. But it is also important to understand these tests because their conceptual basis is shared with other more complicated statistical tests, some of which I introduce in the next chapter.

TEN

Comparing Two Independent Groups

The research process often focuses on comparisons. Communication theories and the hypotheses they generate frequently predict how two groups will differ from each other. These groups may be defined by sex or education (e.g., people with or without a college education) or perhaps how much they use the Internet (a little versus a lot). Or the groups may be artificially created for the purpose of the study, such as whether they are asked by a researcher to spend 30 minutes reading a print or an online version of the *Los Angeles Times*. Or the researcher may make predictions about how two different stimuli (such as two TV programs or two persuasive messages) might affect a person's thoughts, attitudes, opinions, memory, or behavior differently.

A quick glance through some recent volumes of the communication literature reveals that communication researchers often advance hypotheses focused on such differences between people, conditions, or stimuli. For example,

> Online news readers will recognize fewer international, national, and political news topics than will print news readers (Tewksbury & Althaus, *Communication Research*, 2000, vol. 77, p. 457).

> Females will be more likely than males to rate pro-social advertising as memorable (Andsager, Austin, & Pinkelton, *Communication Research*, 2002, vol. 29, p. 250).

> Liars will show fewer movements, slower speech rate, more pauses, more speech disturbances, and a longer latency time than truth tellers (Vrij, Akehurst, Soukara, & Bull, *Human Communication Research*, 2004, vol. 30, p. 11).

> Soft-money-sponsored issue-advocacy advertisements in political campaigns exert greater influence on attitudes about candidates than candidate-sponsored positive or contrast ads (Pfau, Holbert, Szabo, & Kaminski, *Journal of Communication*, 2001, vol. 52, p. 303).

> Stories leading newscasts are more likely to be structurally balanced than stories run inside newscasts (Carter, Fico, & McCabe, *Journalism and Mass Communication Quarterly*, 2002, vol. 79, p. 45).

The latter two examples illustrate that the groups may not be people, but instead categories of objects, such as news stories or advertisements. In this chapter, I overview some of the more commonly used statistical methods for assessing differences between two groups. The methods described in this chapter are applicable to data collection procedures that produce measurements at the pseudo-interval level or higher (see Chapter 2 if you need to review levels of measurement). As you will see as you work through this chapter, some of the computational aspects of the tests are more intense than in previous chapters. However, keep in mind that most of the computations are done by computer, so your time is best devoted to understanding the conceptual basis of these tests rather than their mathematical derivations. Focus on the story rather than the words.

10.1 The Independent Groups t test

In the previous chapter, you were introduced to the one-sample t test for testing a hypothesis about the value of a population mean. There is a version of the t test used to test the null hypothesis that two population means are the same against the alternative hypothesis that the two means are different. That is,

$$H_0 : \mu_1 = \mu_2$$
$$H_a : \mu_1 \neq \mu_2$$

The parameters μ_1 and μ_2 refer to the population means for group 1 and group 2, respectively. In the case of a directional test, the alternative is that one of the means is larger than the other, with which mean is larger being predicted in advance of seeing the data (e.g., $H_a : \mu_1 > \mu_2$) and the null is that the mean predicted to be larger is in fact not larger (e.g., $H_a : \mu_1 \leq \mu_2$).

During the 2004 U.S. Presidential campaign, numerous political actions groups ran television ads trying to sway a highly divided electorate to vote for one candidate over another. Someone who runs a political action group might be profoundly interested in knowing if there are differences between Republicans and Democrats in how much TV they watch on average. If Democrats and Republicans differ in how much time they spend in front of the television, then they may differ in how easy they are to target through TV advertising. To illustrate how to determine whether Democrats and Republicans differ on average in their TV viewing frequency, we will consider data from a poll conducted by the Center for Survey Research at The Ohio State University (see Appendix E6 on the CD for information about the data file).[1] The Center randomly selected residents of Ohio using random digit dialing to complete a telephone survey. Included in the survey was a question asking the respondents how many hours of TV they watch on a typical day. They were also asked to identify which political party they identify with. Three hundred and forty six respondents identified themselves as either a Republican ($n = 178$) or a Democrat ($n = 168$). To simplify notation, let's call the Democrats group 1 and the Republicans group 2. The sample mean and standard deviation on responses to the TV viewing question for the two groups were $\overline{X}_1 = 3.607$, $s_1 = 2.524$, $\overline{X}_2 = 2.507$, $s_2 = 1.943$. So the Democrats in this sample watched more TV on a typical day than the Republicans. Democrats also appeared to be more variable around their group mean than did Republicans. So Democrats in this sample differ from each other in how much TV they watch more than the Republicans differ from each other.

Using the mean as a representation of "typical" TV viewing for each group, we will test the research hypothesis that Democrats and Republicans differ on average

---

[1] Thank you to Jerry Kosicki for allowing me to use these data.

in how much TV they watch. The null hypothesis is $H_0 : \mu_1 = \mu_2$ (or equivalently, $H_0 : \mu_1 - \mu_2 = 0$) and the alternative hypothesis is $H_a : \mu_1 \neq \mu_2$ (or equivalently, $H_a : \mu_1 - \mu_2 \neq 0$). From the obtained result, we estimate that Democrats watch a little more than one hour of TV than Republicans on a typical day. That is, $\overline{X}_1 - \overline{X}_2 = 1.101$. But it should come as no surprise that the two sample means differ. Both and $\overline{X}_1$ and $\overline{X}_2$ are random variables. They will differ from sample to sample and, therefore, so will the difference between the two sample means, $\overline{X}_1 - \overline{X}_2$. Indeed, if the null hypothesis is true, we know that the chance of getting two sample means that are *exactly* the same is very small. Random sampling error will produce a discrepancy between the difference between two means in a sample and the true mean difference in the population. The sample mean difference, $\overline{X}_1 - \overline{X}_2$, has a sampling distribution just as any descriptive statistic computed from a sample from a population (or populations in this case). Different random samples of the same size will produce different estimates of the difference between the population means.

Applying the lessons of Chapter 7, the expected value of $\overline{X}_1 - \overline{X}_2$ is $\mu_1 - \mu_2$. And if the null hypothesis is true, meaning $\mu_1 = \mu_2$, then the sampling distribution of $\overline{X}_1 - \overline{X}_2$ is centered at zero, meaning $E(\overline{X}_1 - \overline{X}_2) = 0$. So if the null hypothesis is true, we would expect the difference between the two sample means to be equal to zero, but at the same time we know that random sampling error will produce discrepancy between the sample mean difference and its expected value. As with any hypothesis test, we need to know the probability of getting a difference between the sample means as large as the difference obtained in the sample or larger if we assume that the null hypothesis is true.

The most commonly used method of generating this probability is the *independent groups t test*. But before progressing with a discussion of this test, it is necessary to get a handle on what is meant by the term "independent groups." Two groups can be considered independent if two conditions are met. First, membership in one group must imply nonmembership in the other group. So a case in the data file can contribute data to one and only one group. This criterion is met in this example because a person is never classified in the data as both Democrat and Republican. If someone were in both groups, then that person's TV viewing data would show up twice in the data set, and that would be a violation of independence of groups. The second requirement is a bit more vague, but it is important. There must be no natural social linkage or connection between any two cases in the data set classified into different groups that might lead to you expect similarity in their measurements on the outcome variable. This is most easily illustrated with an example that violates independence. Suppose you were interested in the TV viewing habits of husbands and wives with different party affiliations. So you seek out couples with different party affiliations and ask the man and the woman how much TV they watch on an average day, with the goal still of seeing if Democrats and Republicans differ in how much TV they watch. In this case, there would be a social connection between pairs of cases classified into different groups. The groups cannot be considered independent and it wouldn't be appropriate to conduct an independent groups t test comparing the mean TV viewing of Democrats and Republicans. The *dependent groups or matched pairs t* test. would be more appropriate, introduced in Chapter 9.

One way of determining if your data pass this second test of independence is to ask whether it would be meaningful to compute the difference in the response between any two cases in different groups and have that difference be interpretable or meaningful. With the example just presented, you can imagine that it might be meaningful to compare the TV viewing habits of the husband compared to the wife. So the groups can't be considered independent. In the TV viewing example, we are safe because in assuming independence because there is no social connection as far as I am aware between respondents to the poll who are classified into different groups. It would not be meaningful to compute the difference in TV viewing between any two respondents who placed themselves in different parties because the people in the sample are just strangers to each other. That is, the difference in TV viewing between any specific Republican and any specific Democrat in the sample wouldn't have any sensible interpretation. So the groups can be considered independent.

There are three widely available variants on the independent groups t test for testing a hypothesis about two independent group means. Although one of them is by far the mostly commonly used, I argue here that the less widely used alternative really is better and should be used much more often than it currently is. A third alternative is widely discussed in "how-to" books on using popular statistics programs as well as in some textbooks, but I argue below that this third approach has little value and may as well be abandoned.

As was the case with the one-sample t test discussed in Chapter 9, the goal is to derive a p-value for the obtained difference between the sample means assuming a true null hypothesis. To do this, we convert the obtained sample mean difference to departure from the null hypothesis in standard error units.

10.1.1 The Pooled Variance Approach

The most commonly employed method of comparing group means requires the "pooling" of the sample variances of each group in order to estimate the standard error of the mean difference. Recall from section 4.3.3 that a variance is just the square of the standard deviation, and it is important in the estimation of the standard error of a sample mean. This approach first requires the computation of a pooled estimate of the variability in the outcome variable, defined as

$$s^2_{pooled} = \frac{(n_1 - 1)s_1^2 + (n_2 - 1)s_2^2}{n_1 + n_2 - 2}$$

$$(10.1)$$

where s_1^2 is the sample variance of the outcome variable in group 1, s_2^2 is the sample variance of the outcome variable in group 2, and n_1 and n_2 are the sample sizes. This pooled variance estimate is simply a weighted average of each of the individual group variances, with each group weighted by one less than the number of cases in each group. Using the data from the Ohio poll,

$$s^2_{pooled} = \frac{(168 - 1)6.371 + (178 - 1)3.775}{168 + 178 - 2} = 5.035$$

This pooled variance represents the variance of the number of hours of TV watched by respondents, combining information from both Republicans and Democrats into the estimate. With this pooled variance estimate calculated, the standard error of the sample mean difference is estimated as

$$s_{(\overline{X}_1 - \overline{X}_2)} = \sqrt{\frac{s^2_{pooled}}{n_1} + \frac{s^2_{pooled}}{n_2}}$$

$$(10.2)$$

Applying equation 10.2 to the the TV viewing data,

$$s_{(\overline{X}_1 - \overline{X}_2)} = \sqrt{\frac{5.035}{168} + \frac{5.035}{178}} = 0.241$$

So the average amount by which we would expect the difference between two sample means computed from two independent groups of size 168 and 178 to vary from each other just by random sampling error is 0.241. Remember that the standard error is just the standard deviation of the sampling distribution of the statistic, in this case, the sample mean difference, $\overline{X}_1 - \overline{X}_2$.

Once the estimate of the standard error is derived, the obtained sample mean difference is converted to a test statistic with a known sampling distribution. The test statistic is t, defined as

$$t = \frac{(\overline{X}_1 - \overline{X}_2) - (\mu_1 - \mu_2)_0}{s_{(\overline{X}_1 - \overline{X}_2)}}$$

(10.3)

where $(\mu_1 - \mu_2)_0$ is the population mean difference assumed under the null hypothesis. In this case, the null hypothesis is $\mu_1 = \mu_2$, so $(\mu_1 - \mu_2)_0 = 0$. Applying equation 10.3 to our data,

$$t = \frac{(3.607 - 2.506) - 0}{0.241} = 4.568$$

So the sample mean difference of $3.607 - 2.506 = 1.101$ is about 4.6 standard errors above the expected value of the sample mean difference if the null hypothesis is true. The t statistic is no different conceptually than the t statistic for the one-sample t test from Chapter 9. Examining equation 10.3, the numerator quantifies the difference between the obtained result and the null hypothesized value of the difference between the population means, and the denominator is the estimated standard error of the difference.

We need to know the probability of getting a t statistic as large or larger than 4.568, ignoring sign (because the test is two-tailed), if the null hypothesis is true. Symbolically, we seek to derive

$$P(\overline{X}_1 - \overline{X}_2 \geq 1.101|\mu_1 - \mu_2 = 0) \text{ OR } P(\overline{X}_1 - \overline{X}_2 \leq -1.101|\mu_1 - \mu_2 = 0)$$

This p-value cannot be derived easily without a computer. However, we can approach the problem differently by asking what values of t cut off the upper and lower 2.5% of the t distribution (and thus 5% in total) from the rest of the distribution, thus allowing us to determine whether p is equal to or less than 0.05. This "critical value" of t for $\alpha = .05$ can be found in Appendix B. The degrees of freedom (df) for the independent groups t test using the pooled variance approach is $n_1 + n_2 - 2$. In this case, $df = 168 + 178 - 2 = 344$. Although most t tables don't have degrees of freedom listed for 344, we can approximate from the table in Appendix B that the critical t for a two-tailed test at $\alpha = .05$ is somewhere between 1.96 and 1.97. It doesn't make any difference which of these two values we choose because regardless, the obtained t of 4.568 clearly exceeds this critical t so we reject the null hypothesis, $p < .05$. Indeed, the obtained t exceeds the critical t for $\alpha = .001$ as well, so we could claim $p < .001$. The substantive interpretation is

---

**Box 10.1: The Independent Groups t test
(Pooled Variance Approach)**

(1) Specify the null and alternative hypotheses corresponding to the research hypothesis.

$$H_0 : \mu_{Democrats} = \mu_{Republicans}$$
$$H_a : \mu_{Democrats} \neq \mu_{Republicans}$$

(2) Quantify the obtained result

$$\overline{X}_{Democrats} = 3.607, s = 2.524, n = 168$$
$$\overline{X}_{Republicans} = 2.506, s = 1.943, n = 178$$

(3) Compute the p-value

$$t = \frac{(3.607 - 2.506) - 0}{0.241} = 4.568$$

which exceeds the critical t value of 1.97, df = 344 for $\alpha = .05$, so $p < .05$

(4) Make a decision about the null and alternative hypotheses

$p < .05$, so reject H_0 in favor of H_a

(5) Interpret the result in substantive terms

Ohio Democrats watch more television on a typical day than do Ohio Republicans, $t(344) = 4.568, p < .05$ two-tailed, $M_{Democrats} = 3.607$ hours (SD = 2.524), $M_{Republicans} = 2.506$ (SD = 1.943).

Ohio Democrats watch more television on a typical day than do Ohio Republicans, $t(344) = 4.568, p < .001$ two-tailed, $M_{Democrats} = 3.607$ hours $(SD = 2.524)$, $M_{Republicans} = 2.506$ $(SD = 1.943)$.

A summary of this hypothesis testing procedure can be found in Box 10.1.

But in practice we wouldn't bother doing all these computations manually because a good computer program will take care of all the work for us. Figure 10.1 shows the SPSS output from this test. SPSS actually displays two t test results. The pooled variance approach is listed in the row labeled "Equal variances assumed." We see that the t value that SPSS computes is the same as our computations by hand, within rounding error. Notice that SPSS provides additional information as well. Under "Sig. (2-tailed)" is the actual p-value. As described in Chapter 9, we wouldn't say that $p = 0.000$, because we know the probability of obtaining a mean difference as large as the obtained just by chance can't possibly be zero. The ".000" is the result of rounding the output to the nearest third decimal place. We can say that $p < .0005$, however, because if the p-value was between .0009 and .0006, then SPSS would have rounded the p-value in the output to .001.

The statistical theory that tells us that the t statistic from the pooled variance approach follows the t distribution with $n_1 + n_2 - 2$ df is based on the assumption that each of the two populations (in this case, Republicans and Democrats in Ohio) are equally variable on the outcome variable (i.e., $\sigma_1^2 = \sigma_2^2$). This assumption is called *homogeneity of variance* or *equality of variance*, and whether this assumption is met

Group Statistics

	Do you usually think of yourself as	N	Mean	Std. Deviation	Std. Error Mean
On an average day, about how many hours do you personally watch television?	DEMOCRAT	168	3.6071	2.52422	.19475
	REPUBLICAN	178	2.5056	1.94340	.14566

Independent Samples Test

		Levene's Test for Equality of Variances		t-test for Equality of Means						
									95% Confidence Interval of the Difference	
		F	Sig.	t	df	Sig. (2-tailed)	Mean Difference	Std. Error Difference	Lower	Upper
On an average day, about how many hours do you personally watch television?	Equal variances assumed	10.295	.001	4.563	344	.000	1.1015	.24140	.62672	1.57633
	Equal variances not assumed			4.529	313.536	.000	1.1015	.24320	.62302	1.58003

Equation 10.2

Pooled variance approach t test

Welch-Satterthwaite approach t test

Equation 10.4

Equation 10.5

Figure 10.1 SPSS output for the independent groups t test.

can affect the accuracy of the p-value and therefore the accuracy of the statistical decision about the null hypothesis. Many statistics books describe the pooled variance approach as robust to violations of the homogeneity of variance assumption, meaning that even when this assumption is violated, the p-value the test gives will be pretty accurate. But in fact the test is not as robust as is often claimed. There are real world conditions where you should not trust the results of this test. Namely, if the population group variances are in fact different by a ratio of more than about 2 to 1, there are differences in group sample size, and especially (though not necessarily) if these two conditions are combined with nonnormality in the outcome variable, then this t test can yield a very poor approximation of the p-value (Boneau, 1960; Hayes & Cai, in press; Murphy, 1976; Stonehouse & Forester, 1998). In some situations the test can be very liberal, yielding a p-value that is far smaller than the true p-value, and this produces an inflation in the Type I error rate. In other words, the probability of a Type I error may be greater (perhaps substantially) than the level of significance (α-level) chosen for the test. This tends to occur when the sample sizes are different and the smaller group has the larger variance. In other situations, the test can be very conservative, meaning low in power. This tends to occur when the group when the smaller sample size has the smaller variance. Because of these problems with the pooled variance approach, I do not recommend this approach, although it is commonly used by communication researchers (and other social sciences as well).

10.1.2   The Welch-Satterthwaite Approach

A second approach that is implemented in most statistical packages but not used nearly as much as it should be is based on a different method of estimating the standard error of the sample mean difference and then estimating the correct degrees of freedom to use when generating the p-value from the t distribution. This approach is sometimes called the *Welch t test* or the *Welch-Satterthwaite t test* in honor of the statisticians that contributed to it (Satterthwaite, 1946; Welch, 1937). With this approach, the standard error of the mean difference is defined as

$$s_{(\overline{X}_1 - \overline{X}_2)} = \sqrt{\frac{s_1^2}{n_1} + \frac{s_2^2}{n_2}}$$

(10.4)

Applying equation 10.4 to the Ohio poll data,

$$s_{(\overline{X}_1 - \overline{X}_2)} = \sqrt{\frac{6.371}{168} + \frac{3.775}{178}} = 0.243$$

The t statistic is still computed using Equation 10.3, which in these data yields,

$$t = \frac{(3.607 - 2.506) - 0}{0.243} = 4.531$$

This t statistic is so close to the t statistic using the pooled variance approach because the sample sizes for the two groups are very similar. The larger the differences in the two sample sizes or the more different the sample variances, the more different these two t statistics will tend to be. The elimination of the pooling of the variances removes the assumption that the populations sampled are equally variable on the outcome (TV viewing in this case). So one can apply this test regardless of whether the group variances are the same or different. The other difference between this test and the pooled variance approach is in how the degrees of freedom is computed. The degrees of freedom for this test is derived with a rather scary looking formula:

$$df = \frac{\left[(s_1^2/n_1) + (s_2^2/n_2)\right]^2}{[(s_1^2/n_1)^2/(n_1 - 1)] + [(s_2^2/n_2)^2/(n_2 - 1)]}$$

(10.5)

In the Ohio poll data,

$$df = \frac{[(6.371/168) + (3.775/178)]^2}{[(6.371/168)^2/(167)] + [(3.775/178)^2/(177)]} = 313.53$$

When reporting the degrees of freedom for the Welch-Satterthwaite approach, you can round to the nearest integer if you want.

Although equation 10.5 looks daunting, the fact that computers do all the work for you means this test no more complicated than the pooled variance approach. The SPSS output for the Welch-Satterthwaite t test is provided in Figure 10.1 in the row labeled "Equal variances not assumed." Here, the two-tailed p-value is still less than .0005, resulting in a rejection of the null hypothesis in favor of the alternative.

Although the results of the two approaches are the same here, this won't always be true. The Welch-Satterthwaite approach is by far better than the pooled variance approach described earlier. It tends to produce a more accurate p-value across a wider variety of circumstances than does the pooled variance method, and I recommend that you use it rather than the pooled variance approach even if you have no reason to suspect that the population variances are unequal (see, for example, Gans, 1981; Hayes & Cai, in press; Moser & Stevens, 1992; Moser, Stevens, & Watts, 1989; Stonehouse & Forrester, 1998; Zimmerman, 2004).

10.1.3 The Conditional Decision Rule

A third approach is a combination of the first two approaches with an additional hypothesis test required to implement it. The pooled variance approach assumes homogeneity of variance. In contrast, the Welch-Satterthwaite approach makes no assumption about the equality of the population group variances. The conditional decision rule states that you should choose between these two approaches by first formally testing the equality of the group variances. If the homogeneity of variance test leads you to claim that the group population variances are equal, then you should base your test of the hypothesis that the group means are equal on the pooled variance approach. However, if the homogeneity of variance test leads you to believe that the group population variances are different, then use the Welch-Satterthwaite approach to test the equality of the means.

Most statistical programs will print a test of homogeneity of variance along with the independent groups t test output. SPSS, for instance, prints the outcome of Levene's test (Levene, 1960), as can be seen in Figure 10.1. Levene's test and other variance equality tests are discussed in section 10.2, and I save a detailed discussion of this test until later. For now, you need to know only that Levene's test is a test of the null hypothesis that $\sigma_1^2 = \sigma_2^2$ (variance equality) against the alternative that $\sigma_1^2 \neq \sigma_2^2$ (variance inequality). Rejection of the null hypothesis leads you to conclude that the group variances are unequal in the population from which the sample was derived, which would lead you to use the Welch-Satterthwaite t test to test the equality of the group means. If the null hypothesis of equal group variances is not rejected, then you'd use the pooled variance t test to these the null hypothesis that the group means are the same.

In these data, Levene's test results in a rejection of the null hypothesis that Democrats and Republicans are equally variable in how much TV they watch (because the p-value for Levene's test is less than .05). Democrats in Ohio seem to differ from each other more than Ohio Republicans differ from each other in how much they watch TV on a typical day. So according to the logic of the conditional decision rule, you'd use the Welch-Satterthwaite approach to test for differences between the population means.

Although the logic of the conditional decision rule makes some intuitive sense, it turns out to offer very little in terms of accuracy of the test of the hypothesis that the group means are the same. Several researchers have examined this rule and all have concluded that a much simpler and equally accurate approach is to just use the Welch-Satterthwaite approach in all circumstances and not worry about whether the variances are equal or not because the Welch-Satterthwaite t test seems to perform well under many different circumstances (Gans, 1981; Hayes & Cai, in press; Moser & Stevens, 1992; Moser, Stevens, & Watts, 1989; Zimmerman, 2004). So my advice is to stick to the Welch-Satterthwaite t test and don't worry so much about the homogeneity of variance assumption except in certain circumstances discussed next. Nevertheless, there is value to testing for differences in group variance, as I discuss in section 10.2.

10.1.4   The Behrens-Fisher Problem

For a long time statisticians have been aware that variance inequality can produce all kinds of problems when it comes to testing differences between group means. This has been named the *Behrens-Fisher problem* and it has been widely studied (e.g., Pfanzagl, 1974; Scheffe, 1943; Welch, 1937). The Welch-Satterthwaite t test is one of the simpler methods available to deal with the problem, and it deals with it reasonably well in most circumstances you are likely to confront. However, even it is invalid in some circumstances. When all of the following conditions are met, even the Welch-Satterthwaite t test can produce an inaccurate p-value and thus an increased likelihood of a decision error: (a) very large differences in group variance, (b) very large differences in sample size, (c) the smaller group has the larger variance and (d) extreme nonnormality of the outcome variable. When all four conditions are met, very few widely available statistical tests can validly test the null hypothesis that two groups have the same mean. That is, in these conditions the probability of a Type I error is generally greater than the α-level (although the Welch-Satterthwaite t test seems to be less affected by the Behrens-Fisher problem than the pooled variance approach, which again suggests it should be used routinely). When these conditions are met, all three approaches described above test the vaguer null hypothesis that the distribution of the outcome is identical in the two populations, rather than the more specific null hypothesis that the group means are the same. There are other so-called nonparametric statistical methods that test the hypothesis of the equality of distributions that are often recommended when the assumptions of the t test are violated, such as the Mann-Whitney U test. I don't discuss these methods in this book. They are rarely used by communication researchers, and they don't offer many advantages over the more versatile Welch-Satterthwaite t test.

This is not to say that there are no alternatives available to deal with the Fisher-Behrens problem. For example, a method proposed by Mielke & Berry (1994) seems to work reasonably well (see, e.g., Hayes & Cai, in press). However, these alternatives are not implemented in most statistics programs, they are computationally tedious, and they are rarely used by scientists in any field.

10.1.5 Violations of the Normality Assumption

As already discussed, the pooled variance approach to testing the equality of means is not particularly robust to violations of homogeneity of variance when the sample sizes are unequal. The Welch-Satterthwaite t test is superior in that it does not assume homogeneity of variance. Both tests were mathematically derived by their inventors based on the assumption that the outcome variable is normally distributed in the population(s) sampled. Fortunately, both tests are quite robust to violations of this assumption when *only* this assumption is violated. Even when the distribution is nonnormal, both tests will perform reasonably well. However, the joint violation of nonnormality and equality of variance can produce big problems in the pooled variance approach. So the normality assumption is not particularly important unless nonnormality is combined with the other 3 conditions described in section 10.1.4.

Although the independent-groups t test reasonably robust to violations of normality assumption, nonnormality can reduce the power of the test. Specifically, power can be reduced when there are a few unusual measurements in the outcome variable distribution. Such unusual measurements are common with some outcome variables used by communication researchers, such as response latencies (i.e., how long it takes to provide a response to a stimulus or a question). The distribution of response latencies tends to be positive skewed, sometimes severely so. The proper analysis of highly skewed variables such as response latencies is controversial. Some recommend a mathematical transformation of the outcome variable prior to analysis. Possible transformations include the natural logarithm $[X' = ln(X)]$, the square root $(X' = \sqrt{X})$, or the inverse transformation $(X' = 1/X)$. An alternative is *truncation*, where the researcher makes an a priori decision to throw out measurements more than a certain number of standard deviations away from the mean prior to analysis. Transformation and truncation can reduce the impact of cases with large estimation errors on hypothesis tests and increase statistical power.

However, there are problems with transformation as well. First, the selection of transformation is often arbitrary, and there is no clear guidance for determining which transformation is best. Second, two analysts with similar data but that who choose a different transformation can end up with different parameter estimates, standard errors, confidence intervals, statistical decisions, and so forth. Third, there is something rather inelegant and unappealing about modifying one's data to fit the assumptions of the analytical tool rather than choosing an analytical tool that is better suited to the process that generated the data. Truncation suffers from the same problem of arbitrariness and difficulty in deciding what the proper truncation point should be. At a minimum, research results that are based on an arbitrary truncation or transformation prior to analysis should be replicated before they are trusted, particularly if the outcome of the analysis depends substantially on the choice of transformation or truncation point. For some guidance on the use of transformations see Carroll & Ruppert (1988) and Cohen, Cohen, West, and Aiken (2003, p. 244–246). Ratcliff (1993) and Ulrich &

Miller (1994) discuss transformation and truncation methods as applied to the analysis of response latencies.

10.1.6   Confidence Intervals for the Mean Difference

The independent groups t test is used to test a hypothesis about the difference between two population means. Rejection of the null hypothesis that there is no difference is important, but it leaves open the question as to how large the population difference is. We confronted this same ambiguity in Chapters 8 and 9, and we resolved the ambiguity in part by computing a confidence interval. We can do the same thing here using an identical procedure. A $c\%$ confidence interval for the mean difference is derived using equation 7.8, with a few changes to reflect the fact that the parameter of interest is a population mean difference rather than simply a population mean:

$$\boxed{c\% \text{ CI for } \mu_1 - \mu_2 = (\overline{X}_1 - \overline{X}_2) \pm t_{(100-c)/2}(s_{\overline{X}_1 - \overline{X}_2})}$$

(10.6)

For example, a 95% confidence interval for the difference between Democrats and Republicans in how much they watch TV on a typical day is

$$95\% \text{ CI for } \mu_1 - \mu_2 = (3.607 - 2.506) \pm 1.968(0.243) = 0.623 \text{ to } 1.579$$

using the Welch-Satterthwaite standard error estimate and 1.968 is the t value that cuts off the upper and lower 2.5% (and thus 5% total) of the t distribution with 313 degrees of freedom. So we can be pretty sure that the true difference between the average TV viewing of Democrats and Republicans in Ohio is somewhere between about 0.623 and 1.579 hours. As can be seen in Figure 10.1, a program such as SPSS does all the work for us and produces the same confidence interval we computed manually above, within expected rounding error.

Notice that SPSS will produce confidence intervals using information from both the pooled variance standard error and the Welch-Satterthwaite standard error.

10.1.7   Bootstrapping Confidence Intervals and p-values

It is also possible to bootstrap the sampling distribution of the mean difference using the same procedure as described in Chapter 7 to derive a 95% confidence interval. We might want to bootstrap when the distribution of the outcome variable is highly skewed because the t distribution may not adequately describe the sampling distribution of the mean difference in such a case. You need the help of special software to do this though. To bootstrap the sampling distribution, you sample from each group with replacement, with the sample size in each resampled group being equal to the original sample sizes, n_1 and n_2. In this resample of the original data, you compute the mean difference. Repeat the procedure so that you have 1,000 sample mean differences, each resulting from a resample of the original data with replacement. Then, sort these 1,000 mean differences from low to high. The lower limit of the 95% confidence interval is defined as the 25th mean difference in this sorted list of mean differences, and the upper limit is the 976th mean difference in the list.

Bootstrapping can also be used to generate a p-value for the hypothesis of no difference between the means and it does not require the assumption that the mean difference follows a particular sampling distribution such as the t distribution. When the outcome variable is highly skewed, bootstrapping is a good way of approximating the p-value because it doesn't require any assumptions about the shape of the sampling distribution, which may not be t distributed in such a case. To bootstrap a p-value, you first compute a test statistic such as the difference between the means or the t statistic (preferably using the standard error estimate from the Welch-Satterthwaite approach). Call this statistic θ ("θ" is the Greek letter "theta", pronounced "thay-tuh"). You then transform each score on the dependent variable (X) such that both groups have exactly the same mean in the sample. This is accomplished with the following equation:

$$X^* = X - \overline{X}_i + \overline{X}$$

where $\overline{X}_i$ is the mean of the case's group on X and $\overline{X}$ is the overall mean X ignoring which group the case belongs to (see e.g., Efron & Tibshirani, 1998). After this transformation, both group means will be equal to $\overline{X}$. Then take a bootstrap resample of this new data set of values. This resample is generated by taking a sample of size n_1 with replacement from the values of X^* for group 1 as well as a sample of size n_2 with replacement from the X^* values for group 2. In the resulting data set for each resample, compute the same test statistic θ as you computed in the original data set. Call this statistic θ^*. Repeat this resampling procedure a total of 1000 times, yielding 1,000 values of θ^*. These 1,000 values of θ^* represent the bootstrapped resampling distribution of the test statistic. The two-tailed p-value is defined as the proportion of values of θ^*, ignoring sign, that are at least as large as θ, ignoring sign. Symbolically,

$$p = \frac{\#(|\theta^*| \geq |\theta|)}{1000}$$

```
Run MATRIX procedure:

***** BOOTSTRAP TWO GROUP MEAN DIFFERENCE *****

Obtained Results
                Mean         SD           n
group 1       3.6071      2.5242      168.0000
group 2       2.5056      1.9434      178.0000

Obtained Mean Difference (Mean 1 - Mean 2)
      1.1015

BOOTSTRAP 95% CONFIDENCE INTERVAL FOR DIFFERENCE
      Lo95%CI      Hi95%CI
        .5785       1.5838

BOOTSTRAP P-VALUES
  2-tail p      .0050
  Right-p       .0050
  Left-p        .0000
```

Figure 10.2 SPSS macro output for bootstrapping the sampling distribution of the mean difference.

If the mean difference is in the direction predicted in advance of seeing the data, then the one-tailed p-value is defined as the proportion of values of θ^* that are more extreme from 0 and in the same direction as θ.

Bootstrapping is versatile in that it be used to generate a p-value for any test statistic that you choose to represent the effect of interest. See Efron and Tibshirani (1998) for details. The problem with this approach to computing p-values is that few if any statistical programs used by communication researchers do bootstrapping. But a little programming skill is all that is necessary to conduct this test in whatever programming language you desire. A macro written in the SPSS language to bootstrap a confidence interval for a mean difference as well as the p-value can be found in Appendix F on the CD with this book. The output from this macro applied to the Ohio poll data can be found in Figure 10.2. As can be seen, the 95% confidence interval for the mean difference is 0.5785 to 1.5838. A test of the null hypothesis that $\mu_1 = \mu_2$ can be rejected in favor of the alternative that $\mu_1 \neq \mu_2$, with a p-value of .005. This test makes no assumptions about the shape of the sampling distribution of $\overline{X}_1 - \overline{X}_2$, nor does it assume that the Democrats and Republicans are equally variable in how much TV they watch.

10.1.8 Effect Size

The confidence interval provides more information than does a p-value about the difference between the means. Whereas a statistically significant difference tells us that the population mean difference is different from zero, a confidence interval provides a window of possible values of the population difference, the size of which is determined by the confidence we want to have that the population mean difference is actually in the window. It is also common to express the difference between means using a measure of *effect size*. Effect size can be quantified in many ways. The two discussed here can be thought of as "standardized measures," in that they are not expressed in terms of the original metric of measurement.

Eta-squared. Eta-squared (symbolically denoted η^2) quantifies the proportion of the variance in the dependent variable that is explained by group membership. As such, it is much like the coefficient of determination introduced in Chapter 4 in that it is a variance-explained measure of association. Eta-squared can be derived from the t statistic and degrees of freedom for t:

$$\boxed{\eta^2 = \frac{t^2}{t^2 + df}}$$

(10.7)

You could use the t statistic and degrees of freedom from either the pooled variance or Welch-Satterthwaite method, although η^2 is typically discussed and computed using the statistics from the pooled variance method. Using the pooled variance t and df also produces a value of η^2 that is consistent with other definitions of η^2 I give in later chapters. From the computer output in Figure 10.1, $t = 4.563$ and $df = 344$. Plugging the numbers in

$$\eta^2 = \frac{4.563^2}{4.563^2 + 344} = 0.057$$

So we can say that whether a person identifies themselves as a Republican or as a Democrat accounts for about 5.7% of the variance in TV viewing frequency. Using the same standards as we applied to the coefficient of determination, this is a rather small effect. For reasons described in Chapters 13 and 14, η^2 tends to overestimate the proportion of variance explained by group membership in the population. The bias in large samples is typically tiny, however. An alternative variance-explained measure without this bias is provided in Chapter 14.

The square root of η^2 can be interpreted like a correlation. In this case, the square root of 0.057 is about 0.239. In fact, if you calculated Pearson's correlation between the TV viewing frequency and a dichotomous variable coding whether a person is a Democrat or a Republican, you would find that $r_{XY} = 0.239$.

The Standardized Mean Difference. With only two groups, it is possible to quantify effect size in terms of how different the two means are in standard deviation units. Hedge's g accomplishes this, defined as

$$g = \frac{\overline{X}_1 - \overline{X}_2}{\sqrt{s^2_{pooled}}}$$

(10.8)

where s^2_{pooled} is defined as in equation 10.1 (see Rosenthal, Rosnow, & Rubin, 2000). Plugging the numbers in,

$$g = \frac{3.607 - 2.506}{\sqrt{5.035}} = 0.491$$

meaning that the two means differ by about about half a standard deviation. The computation of Hedge's g in this fashion assumes that the groups are equally variable on the dependent variable in the population(s) sampled. The sign of g can be negative, but the sign is usually removed before g is reported.

Eta-squared and Hedge's g are intimately connected. In fact, η^2 can be derived from g using equation 10.9 (Rosenthal et al., 2000):

$$\eta^2 = \frac{g^2}{g^2 + [4\ df/(n_1 + n_2)]}$$

(10.9)

where n_1 and n_2 are the sample sizes for groups 1 and 2 and df is the degrees of freedom from the pooled variance t test.

The proper quantification of effect size is a controversial area in statistics. For more detail, see Rosenthal et al. (2000) or Richardson (1996).

10.2 Testing for Group Differences in Variability

Recall from Chapter 3 that the measure of variability or spread of a distribution of measurements typically used by communication researchers is the standard deviation or its squared equivalent, the variance. These measures of variability quantify the extent to which measurements in a sample are dispersed around the mean. The larger the standard deviation (or variance), the more variable the measurements are around the mean. In inferential statistics, variability is often conceptualized as a nuisance to reduce or eliminate as much as possible. All other things being equal, the more variable the research units in a data set on the things measured, the wider confidence intervals tend to be, and the larger p-values from inferential tests tend to be. And if the means of two groups are being compared, differences in the variability of the groups can produce problems with the pooled variance t test and, in at least some circumstances, even the Welch-Satterthwaite t test.

But group differences in variability can itself be interesting and perhaps even the primary focus in a study. Consider, for example, the finding from section 10.1 that Ohio Democrats are more variable in how much TV they report watching than Ohio Republicans. Why is that? What factors or processes, be they personality, attitudinal, or lifestyle, make Republicans more homogeneous than Democrats in their TV viewing habits? Or suppose you found in an experiment that people randomly assigned to read a newspaper for 30 minutes a day for a week were less variable in how much knowledge they possessed about current events after a week than people randomly assigned to watch a national news broadcast for 30 minutes a day. This might suggest that newspapers have a homogenizing effect on the public, reducing individual differences in knowledge about the world. Or you may find in a study of public speaking methods that one method tends to produce greater consistency in students' speeches compared to other methods, with consistency quantified as the standard deviation in quality judgments given by a group of objective judges of the speeches. So group differences in variability can be an interesting phenomenon and can provide clues about the process in operation independent of what is learned looking at mean differences.

A mean is a descriptive statistic with a sampling distribution. We know that from random sample to random sample from a population, a sample mean will vary from its population value. The standard deviation and variance also have this property. The variability you find in any sample is not the "true" variability in the population. It is just an estimate of variability and is subject to the same forces of random sampling error as is the mean. What this means is that if two groups have different variances in a sample, that doesn't mean that this difference in variability exists in the population. It is unlikely that two variances will be exactly equal in a sample, even if they are equal in the population. To make the claim that an observed difference between two standard deviations or variances reflects something in the population rather than just random sampling variability, you need a statistical test. In this section, I will describe two methods of comparing the variability of two populations. I will also briefly discuss a third only to point out its defects and suggest that you not use this often-used but deficient method. This section only begins to touch the surface of all the existing tests of variance equality. There are dozens of them. The two that I focus on here have the quality that they are quite easy to understand and can be easily computed by hand or by a statistical program.

The two tests described here are designed to test the null hypothesis that two independent groups are equally variable on some outcome variable. Like a test of mean differences, these tests can also be conducted directionally if you have a specific advance prediction that one group should be more variable than the other.

10.2.1 Levene's Test

In section 4.3, I discussed the mean absolute deviation as a potential measure of variability in a distribution of scores. Although this measure seems sensible, it is not widely used in statistics. However, it is used in Levene's test, one of the variance equality tests implemented in some statistical programs. Recall that the mean absolute deviation quantifies variability as the mean difference between a measurement and the mean, ignoring the sign of the difference. The larger the mean absolute difference, the more spread out around the mean the measurements in the distribution. It makes intuitive sense that if two groups differ in variability, then they should have different mean absolute deviations. Levene's test (Levene, 1960) is no more than a t test on the difference between two mean absolute deviations.

To compute Levene's test, you transform each case's measurement on the outcome, X, to the absolute deviation between X and $\overline{X}$ for the case's group. That is,

$$X' = |X - \overline{X}_j|$$

where $\overline{X}_j$ is the group mean for the group (j) in which the case belongs. For example, recall from section 10.1 that Democrats report watching an average of 3.607 hours of TV on a typical day. So each Democrat's TV viewing measurement is transformed to $X' = |X - 3.607|$. Using the same reasoning, each Republican's TV viewing measurement is transformed to $X' = |X - 2.506|$. So X' quantifies the distance between a respondent's reported TV viewing and the mean viewing of the people in that respondent's political party. If Democrats and Republicans are equally variable in how much TV they watch, then the mean of their values of X' should be the same, within expected sampling error. Remembering that group 1 is the Democrats and group 2 is the Republicans, $\overline{X}'_1 = 1.884, s = 1.673, n = 168$ and $\overline{X}'_1 = 1.335, s = 1.389, n = 178$. A t test comparing these mean absolute deviations using the pooled variance approach serves as a test of the null hypothesis that $H_0 : \sigma_1^2 = \sigma_1^2$ against the alternative $H_0 : \sigma_1^2 \neq \sigma_1^2$. Using equations 10.1, 10.2, and 10.3, $t(344) = 3.208, p < .05$. So the null hypothesis is rejected in favor of the alternative hypothesis. It appears that Democrats in the state of Ohio are more variable than Ohio Republicans in how much TV they watch.

Some programs (such as SPSS) will conduct this test and display it in its t test output (see Figures 10.1 and 10.3). However, notice that the statistic listed for Levene's test is not t but instead F. F is an important sampling distribution that I introduce in Chapter 13. But when only two variances are being compared, F from Levene's test in SPSS is simply the square of t. Indeed, observe from Figure 10.1 that that $3.208^2 = 10.291$, which is what SPSS gives within rounding error.

10.2.2   The Brown-Forsythe Test

Recall from Chapter 3 that one problem with the mean as a measure of central tendency is its susceptibility to the influence of extreme cases in a distribution. Part of the problem with Levene's test is its use of the group mean in quantifying a case's deviation score X'. When the distribution of the outcome is highly skewed, these means can be moved considerably in the direction of the skew, and this affects the validity of Levene's test. Brown and Forsythe (1974) proposed a method of testing variance equality that is identical to Levene's test, with one major exception. Rather than constructing the deviation scores as distance from the mean for the group, this test uses the distance from the group *median*. The median is less susceptible to the influence of extreme measurements in a distribution than the mean and this yields a variance equality test that has better statistical properties. Namely, the Brown-Forsythe test is less likely to produce a Type I error than Levene's test and thereby lead you to conclude that two groups differ in variance when they do not. Other than this minor modification in the computation of the distance scores, the computation of the Brown-Forsythe test is identical to Levene's test.

Unfortunately, few statistical programs available or in wide use implement the Brown-Forsythe test. But is fairly easy to get SPSS to do this test with a little programming. This is accomplished by creating the X' scores in the command syntax and then requesting an independent groups t test comparing the mean distance from the median between the two groups. In the TV viewing example, the median TV viewing for Democrats (identified in the data with the value "1" on the PARTY variable) is 3.00, and the median for Republicans is 2.00 (with Republicans identified in the data with PARTY = 2). With this information, the following SPSS commands create a new variable called XP (for "X-prime") that is the distance between each person's TV viewing response and the sample median TV viewing for members of that person's political party.

```
if (party = 1) xp = abs(tvhrs-3).
if (party = 2) xp = abs(tvhrs-2).
```

The mean distance from the median for Democrats is 1.800 ($s = 1.869$) and for Republicans, the mean distance from the median is 1.258 ($s = 1.562$). So in the sample, Democrats in Ohio differ from their own median more than do Republicans in Ohio. An independent groups t test comparing each party's mean distance from the median using the pooled variance approach provides a test of the null hypothesis that the groups are equal in variability. Using equations 10.1, 10.2, and 10.3, the independent groups t test with XP (defined above) as the dependent variable gives $t(344) = 2.918, p < .05$, leading to a rejection of the null hypothesis. The larger mean distance from the median for the Democrats suggests that Democrats vary more in how much TV they watch compared to Republicans. So in this case, the Brown-Forsythe test agrees with Levene's test.

The literature suggests that the Brown-Forsythe test is better than Levene's test, in that it keeps the probability of a Type I error rate at or less than the level of significance (α) chosen for the test better than does Levene's test (Conover, Johnson, & Johnson, 1981). So I recommend that you use the Brown-Forsythe test when possible. This is not to say that Levene's test is useless. Because Levene's test is computed by many statistical packages, including SPSS, it is a little bit easier to use and probably little harm is done using it. But if Levene's test yields a p-value near .05, I recommend that you do another comparison of the variances using the Brown-Forsythe test. If the two tests produce different decisions, then treat the decision using the Brown-Forsythe test as the correct one.

There is one important caveat to consider. Whereas Levene's test can be construed as a test of *variance* equality, the Brown-Forsythe test can be construed as a more generic test of equality of *dispersion*. This is a technical point but worth acknowledging. Wilcox (2002) notes that the expected value of the average squared distance from the median is not necessarily σ^2. Therefore, the Browne-Forsythe test does necessarily test the null hypothesis that $\sigma_1^2 = \sigma_2^2$. Instead, it tests the null hypothesis that $\zeta_1^2 = \zeta_2^2$, where ζ (the Greek letter "zeta") is defined as the average squared distance from the median. To be sure, ζ^2 and σ^2 are very similar, but they aren't the same. Specficially, ζ^2 and σ^2 differ in skewed populations. Thus, the Brown-Forsythe test can be construed as a test of variance equality only if the populations sampled are symmetrically distributed on the variable being measured.

10.2.3   The F-ratio Test: A Test to Avoid

There is another variance equality test discussed in many statistics textbooks and statistics software manuals and that many statistical programs conduct. This test is based on a ratio of the largest to the smallest sample variance. This ratio, defined as

$$F = \frac{s^2_{largest}}{s^2_{smallest}}$$

has a known sampling distribution if the null hypothesis that the population variances are equal is true. The sampling distribution used to compute the p-value is called the F distribution, which will be introduced in Chapter 13. Although this test is widely implemented in statistical programs and was once recommended, most statisticians now advocate against its use. I don't recommend that you use this test because it assumes normality in the population distributions of the variable and is *not* robust to violations of this assumption. As a result, the probability of an incorrect decision about the equality of the population variances using this test can be and often will be much higher than the level of significance used for the test. I mention this test only so that you will be aware of this serious shortcoming and stay away from it.

10.3   Comparing Two Groups from Nonrandom Samples

Let's consider another example to further explore methods of comparing two group means. Throughout this section we will rely on some hypothetical data motivated by a study by Tewksbury and Althaus (2000), who investigated how exposure to online versus print versions of a newspaper might differentially affect how much information people learn about current events in the world. In this study, 16 university students volunteered to participate in a study they were told was about learning from the news. Their participation was recruited through a sign up sheet posted in the classroom where an Introduction to Mass Media course was being taught. In exchange for their participation, they were given extra credit in the course. Half of the students were recruited individually to a laboratory containing a room laid out much like you'd see the typical family room in any house, with a couch, coffee table, recliner, and a television set. These students were given a print copy of the *New York Times* and were asked to read it for 30 minutes. After the 30 minute period, the students were given a test on what they learned reading the *New York Times*. This test contained a series of questions that asked the students whether they had seen a particular article in the paper, and if so, to write a sentence or two summarizing what the article was about. There were 15 such questions pertaining to 15 public affairs articles in the paper (defined as a story about national or international events or politics), and a question was scored as correct if the student stated that he or she not only recalled reading the article but could also correctly summarize the article. So each student's recall score could be any value between 0 and 15. The other half of the students completed an identical procedure, except rather than reading the print version of the newspaper, they were given a laptop computer connected to the Internet and were asked to read the online version of the *New York Times*. These students were also given a test of their learning of the content after 30 minutes. The content of the two versions (online versus print) were identical. The only difference between the two versions of the *New York Times* was in the presentation form (online versus print). Which version of the *New York Times* a student received in the study was randomly determined. This random assignment was accomplished by creating a random sequence of eight ones and eight twos prior to the beginning of the study. When a participant arrived at the laboratory, they were assigned to the condition represented by the next number in the sequence (1 = print, 2 = online). So after 16 participants, 8 would have been assigned to the print version and eight to the online condition.

In the language of science, this research design is referred to as an *experiment*. In an experiment the researcher determines, usually through some kind of randomization procedure such as random assignment, which of two or more different versions or "conditions" of the experiment each participant is assigned to. Experiments are great for assessing cause-effect relationships because, if well designed, we know that any differences on the dependent variable between the people assigned to different conditions of the experiment can be attributed only to whatever independent variable was manipulated in the experiment. In this case, the dependent variable is learning of the news, measured as the number of articles the participant could correctly recall. The manipulated independent variable was the form of the news (print vs. online). Of interest in this experiment was whether the form of the news media affects how much people learn from the media.

Causal inferences of this sort can be made in well designed-experiments even in the absence of random sampling. Whereas random assignment affords causal inferences, random sampling affords population inferences. Ideally, both random assignment and random sampling are a part of the design of any communication study. In that case, both causal and population inference can be made. But experimentalists often don't collect random samples. As discussed below, this isn't necessarily a problem so long as the researcher understands the constraints that nonrandom sampling produces on the inferences that can be made.

The data from this experiment are presented in Table 10.1. These data are made up for the purpose of this example, but the basic results reflect what Tewksbury and Althaus found in their study. Treating the print condition as group 1 and the online condition as group 2, the results are as follows: $\overline{X}_1 = 4.875, s_1 = 1.458, \overline{X}_2 = 2.875, s_2 = 0.991$. So the students who received the print version of the *New York Times* recalled more stories on average than the students who received the online version of the Times, with the students in the print condition being somewhat more variable in their recall than students in the online condition of the experiment.

The key question is whether the difference between the means can be attributed to the version of the newspaper the students read, or can we reasonably attribute the obtained difference to "chance." Thinking about this a bit, it seems that this problem is considerably different than in the previous example. In the previous example, we had a random sample from two defined groups: Democrats living in Ohio, and Republicans living in Ohio. Assuming the null hypothesis is true, the obtained difference between Democrats and Republicans in how much TV they watch is the result only of random sampling error—the luck of the draw resulting from randomly selecting the 346 residents that ultimately provided data to the researcher. But in this example, there has been no random sampling of any kind. The 16 students were not a random sample of students, nor were they a random sample of any population whatsoever. The sample was obtained by requesting volunteers through a sign up sheet posted in the lecture theater of an Introduction to Mass Media course at the university the students attended. So can we legitimately use the independent groups t test to assess whether the difference in learning can reasonably be attributed to "chance" when there was no opportunity for random sampling variability to exert its effect on the obtained difference?

Group Statistics

	Experimental Condition	N	Mean	Std. Deviation	Std. Error Mean
Number of Items Correct	print	8	4.8750	1.45774	.51539
	online	8	2.8750	.99103	.35038

Independent Samples Test

		Levene's Test for Equality of Variances		t-test for Equality of Means					95% Confidence Interval of the Difference	
		F	Sig.	t	df	Sig. (2-tailed)	Mean Difference	Std. Error Difference	Lower	Upper
Number of Items Correct	Equal variances assumed	1.100	.312	3.209	14	.006	2.0000	.62321	.66334	3.33666
	Equal variances not assumed			3.209	12.332	.007	2.0000	.62321	.64618	3.35382

Figure 10.3 SPSS *t* test output from the news learning study.

Table 10.1
Data File from the News Learning Study

Group	Recall
2	3
2	3
1	5
2	1
1	4
2	3
2	3
2	4
2	2
1	4
1	4
1	8
2	4
1	6
1	4
1	4

For now let's not worry about this detail and proceed as we discussed in section 10.1. Tewksbury and Althaus (2000) reasoned that the manner in which online versions of a paper are laid out (with nonlinear links to different sections and stories) may enhance the likelihood that a reader will skip around and read only articles that interest him or her. In contrast, readings of the print form of the paper must work through the paper page by page, making it more likely that the reader will come across (and read) articles related to a diverse range of topics including those that may not have been immediately interesting to the reader. Such a process would be supported if people who read the print version of the news learn more of its content than those who read the online version of the same paper, and that is just what they hypothesized. Quantifying learning as the mean recall score in each group, the statistical hypotheses are $H_0 : \mu_1 \leq \mu_2$ and $H_a : \mu_1 > \mu_2$ From the SPSS independent groups t test output in Figure 10.3, $t = 3.209, df = 12$ (or 14 if you follow the practice of using the pooled variance approach, which I don't generally recommend but in this case it doesn't matter because the sample sizes are equal). The *two-tailed* p-value is .007. But because the researchers specified in advance the direction of the result expected and the result was in fact in the direction predicted, the two-tailed p-value can be cut in half to derive the one-tailed p-value. So the one-tailed p-value is .0035. In other words, the probability of getting a mean difference as large as two points favoring the print group is quite small "just by chance" if we assume that the population means are the same. The p-value is less than 0.05, so the null hypothesis should be rejected in favor of the alternative. There is a statistically significant difference between the two means. Substantively, we might say

Those who read the print form of the *New York Times* learned significantly more about public affairs stories ($M = 4.875, SD = 1.458$) than those who read the online version of the same paper ($M = 2.875, SD = 0.991$), Welch $t(12) = 3.209, p < .01$.

But enough pretending. These students are not a random sample of students, or people, or anyone. The t test described in section 10.1 is founded on the theory of inference based on random sampling from a specific population and that deviations from the null hypothesis are attributable to random sampling error (assuming the null hypothesis is true). A small p-value, according to this model of inference, leads us to reject the null hypothesis in favor of the alternative that the population means differ. But is it justifiable to use such a test when there has been no random sampling from a specified population? Random sampling variability never had an opportunity to exert its influence on the result because there was no random sampling from any population that we can unambiguously identify.

The most common solution to this apparent dilemma is to just ignore the fact that the t test was designed for an entirely different problem and pretend as if the sample is a random one. As they should, communication researchers typically do acknowledge that a sample is not random by discussing limitations on the generalizability of findings from a convenience sample like this. In other words, the absence of random sampling would lead a researcher to be very cautious in his or her attempts to generalize these findings to some larger population or group not represented in the study. But rarely do researchers acknowledge that random sampling error never had an opportunity to exert its influence on the result, a potentially great oversight because the t test is based on a model of inference driven by random sample-to-sample variability in study results.

Arguments are often made that nonrandom sampling is inconsequential because experiments are not usually conducted with the purpose of population inference in mind, like public opinion polls typically are. Instead, the purpose of experimentation is usually causal inference (Frick, 1998; Mook, 1983; Sparks, 1995). Of interest is not some population real or imagined, but whether the manipulation had an effect on the dependent variable, as quantified by the mean difference. We make the assumption under the null hypothesis that the manipulation had no effect on the dependent variable. If this assumption is true, we would expect no difference between the means. Define μ_1 as the mean recall score for a hypothetical population of people that could have participated in this study and randomly assigned to the print condition, and define μ_2 as the mean recall score for a hypothetical population of people that could have been in the study and randomly assigned to the online condition. If the form of newspaper has no effect on learning, then both of these means would be the same. As such, any group of 8 participants that could have been assigned to the print condition would be expected to be the same, on average, in their recall as any group of 8 participants that could have been assigned to the online condition. If we can reject this assumption by ascertaining that the probability of obtaining a mean difference as large as that found is too small, then we can argue that if the study was otherwise well designed, the manipulation must be responsible for the difference obtained and not some "chance" process like random variability in sample means attributable to who participated in the study. If we had a sensible explanation for the process that would produce this effect, then we can generalize about the process at work. In other words, the explanation offered prior to collecting the data for why the means should differ is given some support when the means do in fact differ by more than "chance" can explain. And if the process is at work producing the mean difference observed in a sample of 16 participants, it is sensible to suggest that this process could have a similar effect on other people, or it could be at work in the "real world" outside of the confines of the laboratory and the specific experimental situation constructed to test the explanation or theory. So it is the process that we are making inferences about, not some population, either real or hypothetical (c.f., Mook, 1983). Of course, there could be other reasons that the means are different other than the outcome of some process you claim is operating. Whether those alternative explanations are plausible depends on whether the design of the study allows them to be plausible. A well designed experiment will rule out alternative explanations in advance, leaving only the desired explanation as the most plausible one.

There is still something about this justification that on the surface seems problematic, however, and that is that the mathematics underlying the computation of the p-value in the t test is based on a random sampling model of chance—that the discrepancy between the null hypothesis and the obtained results is attributable to just *random sampling error*. Given that there has been no random sampling, how can we be sure that the p-value is a sensible index of the discrepancy between the obtained result and the null hypothesis?

A solution to this apparent dilemma is to consider an alternative conceptualization of chance not based on random sampling from a population—the *random assignment model* of chance. As you will see, this alternative and arguably more appropriate conceptualization of chance when applied to the analysis of experiments will usually produce a similar p-value as the independent groups t test does. As such, it legitimizes the use the t test as an approximation to the p-value that a test based on the random assignment model of chance would produce. So let's spend some time considering this model.

10.3.1 The Random Assignment Model of Chance

The random assignment model of chance is based not on the outcome of the random sampling process but on the random *assignment* process. This model assumes under the null hypothesis that the manipulated variable (in this case, print vs. online media) has no effect whatsoever on the response variable. If this assumption is true—if the manipulation in fact had no effect on learning as measurement—the measurement that you obtained from each and every participant in the experiment is the measurement that you would have obtained from each participant regardless of which condition each participant had been assigned to. And under this assumption, the obtained mean difference is not the result of the effect of the manipulation but merely the outcome of the random assignment process. Under this assumption, each possible random assignment of the measurements into two groups of size n_1 and n_2 has associated with it a mean difference, and any of those mean differences were equally likely to have been the obtained result in the study. If this assumption is true, the result you obtain in an experiment is merely the result of the random assignment of the units of measurement into two groups of size n_1 and n_2. Thus any random assignment of scores to two groups of these sizes will produce a difference of some magnitude (or zero magnitude) "just by chance."

To illustrate what I mean by this, consider the data in Table 10.2. In panel A of this table are the data from Table 10.1, showing a difference of $\overline{X}_1 - \overline{X}_2 = 2.00$ questions favoring the print group. Now let's assume for a moment that the manipulation of newspaper format had no effect on the outcome variable, meaning the learning measurements obtained from each and every participant are the same learning scores that would had been obtained from each and every participant regardless of which condition each person was assigned to. If this assumption is true—meaning that the manipulation of media form had no effect whatsoever—then the configuration of data in panel B was just as likely to have occurred as the configuration of data in panel A. Panel B was created by randomly assigning the 16 learning scores in panel A into two groups of size eight each. Observe that in panel B the mean difference is $\overline{X}_1 - \overline{X}_2 = -0.25$. In this configuration of the data, the online group answered more questions correctly on average. Panel C is the result of repeating this process, randomly reallocating the measurements in panel A into two groups of size 8. In Panel C, the difference is neither 2 nor 0.25, as in panels A and B, but instead $\overline{X}_1 - \overline{X}_2 = -1.00$. So this random assignment of the 16 learning scores into two groups yielded yet a different mean difference. Again, under the assumption that the manipulation had no effect, the arrangement of the data in panel C was just as likely as the arrangement of the data in Panels A and B.

So the obtained result, represented in panel A, can be thought of as just one of many different ways this study could have come out if we assume that the manipulation had no effect on the number of questions each participant correctly answered on the test. If this assumption is true, the outcome in panels B and C also could have occurred merely as the result of randomly assigning these 16 participants into 2 groups of size 8. Of course, these are only three of the possible ways that the random allocation could have occurred. Using the formula from Box 5.1 in Chapter 5, we can determine that the number of unique ways of reassigning these 16 scores into 2 groups of size 8 is "16 choose 8" or $16!/(8!8!)$, which is 12,870. So there are 12,870 different ways that this study could have come out given the 16 measurements available, if we assume that only random assignment is responsible for the mean difference observed.

I used a program called NPSTAT (available for free online) to generate all 12,870 possible combinations of these 16 scores into two groups of size eight. The program then computed the mean difference for each of these 12,870 combinations, and a frequency distribution of the mean difference for all these combinations can be found in Table 10.3. This frequency distribution is much like a sampling distribution of the mean difference. Remember that a sampling distribution of the mean difference is the distribution of all possible sample mean differences when taking a random sample of size eight from two populations. The distribution displayed in Table 10.3 is called the *randomization distribution of the mean difference*. It represents the possible mean differences when randomly assigning these 16 scores into 2 groups of size 8.

If you were to generate the mean of all possible mean differences in Table 10.3, you'd find that the mean is zero. This is consistent with our intuition that if format of the news had no effect and the resulting difference was the result of only random assignment, you'd expect there to be no difference between the means.

So what can we do with this information? Let's use it to test the assumption we've made about the process producing the result we found—that the obtained difference is the result of only random assignment variation. If it is the case that the form of the newspaper (i.e., in print or online form) has no effect on learning and the obtained difference is attributable only to the random assignment process, then we'd expect no difference between the means in the two groups. That is, $E(\overline{X}_1 - \overline{X}_2) = 0$. In this study, the print group correctly answered two questions more on average than did the online group (i.e, $\overline{X}_1 - \overline{X}_2 = 2.00$). What is the probability of getting a difference of two or more favoring the print group if the obtained difference reflects only the random

Table 10.2 The Obtained Result (A) and Two Possible Study Outcomes (B and C) Resulting From the Random Reassignment of 16 Units and Their Obtained Measurements into 2 Groups of Size 8

A		B		C	
Print	Online	Print	Online	Print	Online
4	3	3	4	4	3
4	3	4	3	4	3
8	1	1	8	1	8
6	3	6	3	3	6
5	4	4	5	5	4
4	3	4	3	4	3
4	4	4	4	4	4
4	2	4	2	2	4
$\overline{X} = 4.875$	$\overline{X} = 2.875$	$\overline{X} = 3.750$	$\overline{X} = 4.000$	$\overline{X} = 3.375$	$\overline{X} = 4.375$

assignment process? From the randomization distribution in Table 10.3, we can see that the probability of getting a difference of two or more favoring the print group is $21/12,870 = .00163$ just by random assignment of the 16 people into two conditions. This value of .00163 can be thought of as a bona-fide one-tailed p-value of the test of the null hypothesis that the obtained difference of two favoring the print group is the result of random assignment only. Because $p < .05$, we can reject this null hypothesis in favor of the alternative hypothesis, which is that the obtained difference is the result of something other than random assignment. We can't say what that process is using the outcome of a statistical test, but when an experiment such as this is designed well and competing alternative explanations can be confidently ruled out, then it is reasonable to infer that the obtained difference is attributable to the manipulation—in this example, the form of the media the participants were given in the study. So we have reached the same conclusion that the independent groups t test gives, but we made no random sampling assumption using this method. Notice as well as that the one-tailed p-value is not much different from the one-tailed p-value that SPSS gives for the independent groups t test for these data. Recall that the one-tailed p-value from the t test was .0035, in contrast to this method's p-value of .0016.

The statistical test we just employed is called a *randomization test*. The idea of the randomization test has been around for a long time, but randomization tests haven't caught on much outside of the mathematics field. It goes without saying, therefore, that randomization tests are not widely used in communication research, but in my opinion they should be used more often because they are not grounded on the assumption of random sampling like the t test is. It is based on a totally different conceptualization of chance—chance as random assignment variation. This makes the test conceptually and philosophically quite appealing because it better matches the methodology

Table 10.3
The Randomization Distribution of $\overline{X}_1 - \overline{X}_2$

$\overline{X}_1 - \overline{X}_2$	Frequency	$P(\overline{X}_1 - \overline{X}_2)$	Cumulative Probability
−2.000	21	0.002	0.002
−1.750	147	0.011	0.013
−1.500	336	0.026	0.039
−1.250	575	0.045	0.084
−1.000	840	0.065	0.149
−0.750	1079	0.084	0.233
−0.500	1304	0.101	0.334
−0.250	1394	0.108	0.443
0.000	1478	0.115	0.557
0.250	1394	0.108	0.666
0.500	1304	0.101	0.767
0.750	1079	0.084	0.851
1.000	840	0.065	0.916
1.250	575	0.045	0.961
1.500	336	0.026	0.987
1.750	147	0.011	0.998
2.000	21	0.002	1.000

typically used for recruiting participants in experimental research—convenience or volunteer sampling. But as I've illustrated here, the independent groups t test can be used as a reasonable approximation to the p-value that a randomization test would give. Mathematicians have demonstrated analytically that this will usually be the case (Baker & Collier, 1955; Fisher, 1966; Hoeffding, 1952; Scheffe, 1959). This justifies the use of the independent groups t test to the analysis of experimental data in the absence of random sampling (see Reichardt & Gollub, 1999, or Lang, 1996, for different justifications). The sampling distribution generated from a process that assumes random sampling from a population closely approximates under a true null hypothesis what a randomization distribution resulting from random assignment of measurements into groups looks like. Thus, the p-values will tend to be similar, as will the statistical decisions that result. There are some exceptions to this, but this is an advanced topic not pursued in this book. Edgington (1995) and Lunneborg (2000) provide a more thorough treatment of randomization tests.

It is important to keep in mind that in the absence of random sampling, the researcher has no basis for making a population inference away from the obtained data to some specified population. That is, there is no statistical basis for making that claim that in some larger population, the difference between those who read the newspaper online versus in print form is around 2 units. This is true regardless of whether you use the t test or a randomization test when analyzing your data using a nonprobability sample. Even if we could make such a statement, it would be meaningless and trivial, because these populations are purely hypothetical, and who cares how many more questions one hypothetical group can answer relative to another hypothetical group on some artificial knowledge test constructed by a researcher? In the experiment, a world has been created in which some people are exposed to the news in print and some online. But this is a world that exists only in the laboratory. No population exists from which these 16 people, or any 16 people for that matter, could ever be considered representative.

But as I've argued above, most communication researchers analyzing data from experiments aren't concerned about population inference as much as they are about process inference. If the study is designed well and alternative explanations can be ruled out, rejection of the null hypothesis that the obtained mean difference is attributable to only random assignment variability leads to the inference that the difference is attributable to the form of the newspaper the participants were given. Of course, the exact process producing the difference is not provided by the statistical test—it only tests the "chance" explanation (in this case, the random assignment process). But studies are usually designed to test a specific process that the investigator believes is at work. Rejection of random assignment variation as the explanation for the mean difference suggests that the process at work producing the difference might be the process the researcher claims. Whether the process is in fact what the researcher claims is not something that can statistics can establish—only good design and good logical and theoretical argumentation can be used to establish what the process is.

10.3.2 Inference Without Random Sampling or Random Assignment

In this chapter, I introduced two models by which two sample means can vary from each other "just by chance." The random sampling model of chance is based on the notion that random samples from a population will produce discrepancies between $\overline{X}_1 - \overline{X}_2$ and $\mu_1 - \mu_2$ that result from random sampling error. The random assignment model of chance, in contrast, attributes differences between $\overline{X}_1 - \overline{X}_2$ to the random assignment process. Different random assignments of the obtained measurements into two groups of size n_1 and n_2 will produce differences between sample means even if the manipulated variable has no effect whatsoever on the outcome variable measured. Whereas the random sampling model assumes that a sample was derived randomly from an indentifiable population, the random assignment model requires only that the units were randomly assigned into groups.

But what should an investigator do who has neither randomly sampled from a population nor randomly assigned units into groups? Is statistical inference possible? Some say no. This camp of people (see, e.g., Bakan, 1966; Merton, Reader, & Kendall, 1957; Morrison & Henkel, 1969; Selvin, 1957) argue that statistical inference requires some kind of realistic and applicable model of chance, but in the absence of random assignment or random sampling, no model of chance exists that can be applied to one's data and so description of the data is all that is possible. In short, a p-value derived from either of these models has no sensible interpretation without random assignment or random sampling, and inference about both processes and populations is impossible. If true, this would seem problematic and even unnerving given how frequently communication scientists conduct research and compare groups in a sample that originate neither from random sampling nor random assignment. If inference is not possible, if p-values are meaningless, what have we been doing all these years reporting statistical tests in studies of this sort?

Let's put this debate into some kind of context. Suppose I wanted to know whether males and females differ in how important television is to their day-to-day lives. Perhaps I had some kind of theoretical basis for predicting that they differ, or perhaps I am just curious. Now recall Chapter 4, in which I discussed a questionnaire that I regularly distribute to undergraduate students at The Ohio State University who enroll in my research methods course. That questionnaire contains, among other things, the 5-item *Television Affinity Scale* as well as a question that asks the respondent to identify his or her sex. Using these data (see Appendix E1 on the CD), I discover that the sample means are not the same: The mean for the 220 males who responded to the questions is 11.996 (SD = 4.322), whereas for the 388 females who provided data, the mean is 11.307 (SD = 4.238). According to a two-tailed independent groups t test using the random sampling model of chance, $t(448) = -1.902$, $p > .05$ using the Welch-Satterthwaite approach. So I can claim based on this evidence that males and females to not differ in how important television is to their daily lives.

If I did this, I could be criticized in a number of ways. First, regardless of the outcome of the test, clearly I would have no basis for inferring anything about males and females in general merely from a sample of college students. Although there are a number of ways that I could attempt to counterargue that criticism, none are particularly convincing. For example, I could argue that I am interested in generalizing my results to students at my university. But that isn't a very good counterargument because this population is trivial, and who knows if students who take this class are representative of students at OSU. I could narrow my population still further and argue that my students represent students who take this class, or perhaps communication majors. Maybe, but again, who knows whether this class is representative of all students who take my class or of communication majors. Furthermore, the population is even more trivial now. But maybe I could say I want to make inferences about just the students taking my class *during the time period of data collection*. The standard criticism would be that statistical inference has no meaning in this context because I have a *census* of that population (Bakan, 1966; Merton, Reader, & Kendall, 1957; Morrison & Henkel, 1969; Selvin, 1957). The means are what they are. Sampling error does not exist (random or otherwise) when the sample consists of the entire population. No inference from sample to population is needed when the entire population is in one's data set.

A second grounds for criticism is my failure to randomly sample from a specific population, so there is little basis for applying a probabilistic model that assumes I have. It is clear that I can't apply the random assignment model because these students obviously were not randomly assigned to be males and females. But I might argue that I can apply the random sampling model by treating this sample as a random sample from all students who take my class both current and future, thereby negating the criticism that my sample constitutes a census. Thus, the population is specified, and I can pretend like the sample is random. But pretend all I want, the fact is that the sample is *not* random. Thus, I have no theoretical basis for applying the random sampling model of chance to the data. So the p-value is meaningless, and so is any kind of inference.

I don't believe this is true. I think it is possible to generate a test of a meaningful null hypothesis about the source of differences between groups even in the absence of random sampling and random assignment, but the nature of the inference is different still from what the random sampling and random assignment models yield. To understand how, consider this simple thought exercise. Imagine that I write down each male respondent's score on the *Television Affinity Scale* on a separate sheet of paper. Each male in the sample gets his own sheet of paper, so in a sample of 220 males who responded to the *Television Affinity Scale*, I'd have 220 sheets of paper, each with a number corresponding to that male's *Television Affinity Scale* score. Imagine I do the same thing for the female responses, producing 388 sheets of paper each with a single number on it. Now suppose I stacked these two sets of papers on top of each other, yielding a stack of 608 sheets of paper, with the top 220 sheets being the male responses and the bottom 388 being the female responses. Next, I leave the office for the day, carrying these sheets of paper in my arms, with the intention of calculating the mean difference when I arrive home, remembering that the 220 on top are the males and the bottom 388 are the females. But suppose that when walking to my car across campus, a big gust of wind comes along and blows all the sheets of paper out of my arms, scattering them across the quad outside of my office building. In a panic, I run around picking up each piece of paper, but by the time I am done, the sheets of paper are hopelessly scrambled, and I have no way of knowing which responses are the males and which are the females.

Imagine that I went ahead and calculated two means anyway, one from the top 220 responses on the top of my scrambled pile, and the other from the bottom 388 responses of this pile. Let's call that mean difference $\overline{D}'$. Now one more twist on this scenario. Suppose that, unknown to me, my research assistant had already entered the data into a computer, so an electronic file exists that had the responses of the males and females to these questions, and so the mean male response and the mean female response can be recovered. We know from above that the difference between these two means, $\overline{X}_{male} - \overline{X}_{female}$, is 0.689. The following question is worth answering: What is the probability that, ignoring sign, $\overline{D}'$ is at least as large as 0.689? I'll describe why the answer to this question is useful in a minute.

Now let's suppose that males and females don't differ in how they respond to the *Television Affinity Scale*. I have no idea whether this is true or not. All I have is the responses of 220 males and 388 females. But I can assume that this is true, and if this assumption is correct, then any of the scores in my data could have come from a male or a female with equal probability. In other words, I'd have no way of determining from any response whether that response was more or less likely to come from a male or female. The implications of this are important. What this means is that the mean difference between men and women calculated in the data my research assistant typed into the computer is no more informative about differences between males and females than is $\overline{D}'$, the difference I derived using the scrambled stack of papers. Both 0.689 and my calculated value of $\overline{D}'$ would be an equally likely mean difference when 220 males and 388 females are asked to respond to the questions on the scale. And if the wind happened to be blowing in a different direction, or if I waited five minutes before starting to pick up the papers, I would have ended up with a different scrambled stack and a different value of D'. But that value of $\overline{D}'$ is also no more informative about differences between men and women than is the obtained sample mean difference of 0.689.

If my assumption that males and females don't differ in their television affinity (as measured here) is true, then you would expect that two sample means would be equal to each other, so their difference would be equal to zero. I don't know whether the obtained difference of 0.689 is a better summary of how males and females tend to respond than any value of $\overline{D}'$ generated merely by randomly scrambling the scores up. But now let's assume that the obtained difference of 0.689 reflects the fact that men and women do in fact differ in their television affinity. In other words, it reflects the reality that males tend have higher scores than females. If I knew this to be true, then if I saw a relatively high score in my data, it would be reasonable for me to guess that this responses more likely came from a male than a female. In other words, I would know that responses to this scale are not randomly distributed across males and females. Instead, there is a systematic tendency for males to have larger scores than females.

How can we distinguish between these two possible realities—the possibility that the mean differences reflect differences in how males and females respond to the questions versus the possibility that they respond the same? We can make the distinction by asking what the probability is of getting a mean difference of at least 0.689 (in either direction) "just by chance," where we define chance as a random process pairing *Television Affinity* measurements to males and females. If you think of the dispersion of the papers across the quad as the outcome of random process (i.e., the wind randomly scattering the papers around), then my early question makes sense: What is the probability that $\overline{D}'$ is at least as large as 0.689? If that probability is very small, we could argue that the original pairing of *Television Affinity Scale* measurements to groups that produced the data obtained is not like a random process (like the wind scattering the papers to the wind). But if the probability is fairly large, then this means that the obtained mean difference looks a lot like a random pairing process would tend to produce.

At least in theory, we can generate this probability using the same logic that we used to generate a *p*-value for the randomization test introduced in section 10.3.1. If the process pairing *Television Affinity Scale* measurements to males and females is a random process, then the obtained mean difference is only one of many mean differences that would result from the random allocation of these 608 measurements into two groups of size 220 and 388. Each of these pairings results in a sample mean difference. The probability of interest is the proportion of sample mean differences in this set of *possible* mean differences that is at least as large as the obtained mean difference of 0.689, ignoring sign for a two-tailed test.

If you had a powerful computer, you could probably generate this probability. But consider this: How many ways can 608 numbers (the 608 measurements on the *Television Affinity Scale* in the data available) be placed into two groups of size 220 and 388? From Box 7.1, that number is 608!/(220!388!). But this number is so large that my computer crashed trying to calculate it exactly. The exact number isn't important because even if we could calculate it, it would take practically forever for today's computers to generate all the possible mean differences that could result from separating 608 scores into two groups of size 220 and 388. But we can't generate the probability without doing this.

No so fast. Because we can't generate all possible mean differences that could be produced with these 608 scores, we can't generate the desired probability *exactly*, but we can *estimate* this probability by *randomly sampling* from the possible mean differences that random pairing of these 608 measurements to groups would produce. We simply randomly reassign the 608 scores into two groups of size 220 and 388, calculate the resulting mean difference, and repeat this over and over again. We only need to repeat this process 5,000 times or so to get a good estimation of the probability. Computer programs exist to do this. A program I published (Hayes, 1998) can accomplish these computations (also see the RANDGRP macro in Appendix F on the CD, introduced later in Chapter 14), as can others freely available on the Internet such as Resampling

Statistics or NPSTAT. Using NPSTAT with 5000 random pairings, the estimated probability of getting a mean difference of 0.689 merely by randomly redistributing the 608 scores into two groups of size 220 and 388 was calculated as 0.054.

Now what do we do with this? This can be interpreted as a p-value for the test of the null hypothesis that a random process pairing of *Television Affinity* measurements into groups is responsible for the mean difference obtained in this sample. Rejection of this null hypothesis would lead to the inference that there was some kind of a systematic process producing the obtained mean difference—a process such as a different between how men and women respond to the questions in the scale. In this case, the estimated p-value is not less than 0.05, so the null hypothesis is not rejected. There is no evidence that, in these 608 respondents, there is any systematic process at work leading men and women to differ in how they respond. The data are consistent with a random process.

But notice that this decision is the same decision that would have resulted by using the independent groups t test. This will tend to be true. So the independent groups t test can be used to test the null hypothesis of a random pairing process against the alternative of a systematic pairing process. There is no need to use a fancy program to generate the p-value and make an inference as to whether the process producing the observed data is random or systematic.

10.4   Thinking Clearly About Inference

In this chapter, I have presented three conceptualizations of chance when applied to evaluating the difference between the means of two groups measured on the same variable. Assuming a true null hypothesis, the random sampling model attributes variation between two sample means to random sampling variability. Rejection of the null hypothesis allows the researcher to make an inference about the population means. The random assignment model conceptualizes chance variation in sample means as the result of randomly assigning each unit in the study to one of two conditions, assuming that the experimental manipulation had no effect on the outcome variable. Rejection of the null hypothesis that the obtained difference is attributable to random assignment of units into groups allows for the inference that, absence any other compelling alternative explanation, something about manipulation of the independent variable caused the difference between the observed means. The random pairing model of chance attributes the obtained result to a random process pairing the outcome and independent variable. Rejection of this null hypothesis leads to the inference that some kind of systematic process is producing the obtained difference between the means. But generalization cannot be made beyond those units to a broader population when the research units are derived through a nonprobability sampling method (such as convenience sampling). However, generalizations about the process producing the difference in the sample are warranted.

These models are not mutually exclusive. For example, it is possible to both randomly sample from a population and then randomly assign sample units into conditions. Rejection of the null hypothesis that the population means are equal allows for both an inference about the causal effect of the manipulation and also the generality of that causal effect to the population of units rather than just those units in the study.

The most common model applied to the comparison of group means is the random sampling model. It is this method that you will see reported in the communication literature. Although in theory it is applicable only to the comparison of groups derived from random samples from a defined population, I have shown here that it can also be used to estimate the p-value that the random assignment model will produce when applied to the same data, even when the units in the study are not randomly sampled from a population. Inference is about the process producing the obtained difference between the means (a causal process or just random assignment?) but not about populations. If neither random sampling nor random assignment are part of the design, the random sampling model will tend to produce the same decision as a test of the null hypothesis of a random process pairing the outcome variable to the groups.

In the absence of random sampling from a population, generalizability of a research findings is determined by replication. But even when samples are collected randomly from a population, the generalizations of a research finding away from those who provided the data to the research applies only to the population sampled. If the population sampled is only one of perhaps many interesting populations, only replication of the study in one or more of those populations can establish whether the original research finding is a general one or whether it applies only to the population originally sampled.

10.5   Comparing Two Independent Proportions

Sometimes communications researchers are interested in examining if two groups differ on an outcome that is dichotomous, meaning one that can have only one of two possible values. Examples include whether or not a person is willing to be interviewed by a reporter, whether a news story makes it on to the local television news broadcast, whether a person used a contraceptive last time he or she had sex, or whether a defendant on trial is convicted or acquitted. In studies with such outcome measures, research questions and hypotheses are sometimes framed as differences in proportions. For example, are men more willing than women to be interviewed by a reporter? Suppose you had a reporter approach people and see if they agreed to be interviewed for a local TV news broadcast. If men and women are equally willing to be interviewed, this implies that in a sample of men and women, the proportion of men agreeing to be interviewed should be the same as the proportion of women who agree. The analysis of categorical outcomes such as this requires different procedures than those discussed in this chapter. Although the comparison of proportions certainly seems like it belongs in this chapter, I instead place a discussion of these methods in Chapter 11, where I describe the problem in terms of association and statistical independence.

10.6   Summary

In this chapter, I introduced several common methods for comparing two groups. By far the most popular of these tests is the independent groups t test, used to compare two independent population means based on estimates of these means from a sample. There are several strategies for comparing two groups means, and I argue here that although the pooled variance approach is most commonly used, the Welch-Satterthwaite approach is superior in terms of keeping Type I rates at acceptable levels across the largest variety of situations. Although the pooled variance approach assumes equality of variance, there seems to be little benefit to conditioning the choice of these two tests on the outcome of a variance equality test, as the Welch-Satterthwaite test works quite well even when the population variances are not the same. I also introduced the randomization test for comparing means in an experiment, a test that does not presume random sampling from a population. The fact that the randomization test and the

p-value from a t test tend to agree so closely justifies the use of the t test to samples of convenience in experiments. When the groups being compared come from neither a random sample nor constructed through random assignment, there is considerable controversy over whether either of these models should be applied and what a p-value means. I have justified the use of the randomization model even in this circumstance and argued that the p-value from the population model of inference can be used as an approximate test of the null hypothesis of a random mechanism pairing the independent and outcome variables. But it is important to remember that statistical inferences about some larger population cannot be made from samples of convenience or other nonprobability samples. However, processes at work that produce a study outcome can be studied with samples of convenience. It is these processes that often interest researchers as much or more than does statistical generalization from a sample to a population.

Researchers pay less attention to group variances than to group means, but tests of equality of variance are worth conducting routinely because differences in variance can suggest how some process or phenomenon is operating differently in the two groups, and this can lead to new hypotheses and explanations for how and why groups differ on some outcome variable. Some statistics programs routinely print Levene's test as part of its standard t test output, but the literature suggests that Levene's test can lead to incorrect statistical decisions when the distribution of the outcome is not normal. The Brown-Forsythe test is preferred. Researchers should avoid the common strategy of forming a ratio of the largest to smallest variance advocated by some statistics texts, as this test assumes normality of the population and is not robust to violations of this assumption.

ELEVEN

Some Tests for Categorical Variables

The last several chapters introduced ways of statistically testing hypotheses couched in terms of a mean or difference between means. Sometimes communication researchers are interested not in a mean but instead on how a set of research units are distributed across a set of categories. For example, communication theories and research hypotheses often make predictions about how people's responses to questions should be distributed across a set of response options, how frequently certain categories of objects (e.g., types of television shows) are found in a population (all prime time network television broadcasts) or the choices that people make in response to a question or their preference for an object out of a set of objects presented to them. Or, as discussed in the last chapter, sometimes communication researchers are interested in comparing two groups on an outcome measure that is dichotomous, such as responses to a yes/no question or whether or not a person chooses to purchase a product, agrees with a message, or talks to someone about a problem they are having, for example. Such questions can be tested by assessing whether two nominal variables (e.g., group membership and the yes/no decision) are statistically independent. The tests described in this chapter all share the feature that they focus on the analysis of frequencies. We start by determining how to test whether the distribution of a categorical variable conforms to an expectation or deviates from that expectation.

11.1   Testing a Hypothesis About a Frequency Distribution

Dixon and Linz (2000) were interested in assessing whether televised news stories of crime in a community overrepresent the frequency by which people in certain ethnic groups are victims of crime and underrrepresent the victimization of other ethnic groups. They suspected that there was some kind of ethnic or racial bias in crime reporting, and to test this hypotheses, they did a content analysis of randomly selected televised news broadcasts in Los Angeles over a 20-week period. They coded televised news stories of homicides with respect to the ethnic category of the victim (White, Black, Latino, "Other"). In a random sample of 139 televised news stories about homicide in the Los Angeles area, the victim was White in 60 of the stories

(43%), Black in 32 of the stories (23%), Latino in 26 of the stories (19%) and of some other ethnic group in the remaining 21 stories (15%).

From these data, it is clear that victims of homicides who make the local televised news are more likely to be White. It is tempting to conclude that news reporting is biased, in that White victims of homicide seem to make the news more than victims from the other three groups. However, such a conclusion would be premature at this point. Remember that these frequencies are observations from a random sample of televised news broadcasts. Just like a sample mean can vary from sample to sample, so will the frequencies of any nominal variable. In this sample, a White person was the homicide victim in 60 of the 139 stories included in the samples. It is very unlikely that in a different random sample of 139 homicide stories that a White person would be a victim in 60 of them. Most likely, the number would be something different from 60—perhaps 42, perhaps 82, perhaps 59, or perhaps any other number between 0 and 139. Thus, the number of White homicide victims in a random sample of 139 homicide stories is a random variable. This same logic can be applied to all ethnic categories. So a frequency distribution is subject to random sampling variability, just as is a sample mean.

Let's now reconceptualize this problem as one of estimation of *relative frequencies*. Sixty of 139 televised homicide stories were about a White victim. Given that this is a random sample of televised news stories broadcast in the Los Angeles area during the period of study, we can reasonably estimate that the proportion of televised homicide news stories in the population that include a White victim is around 0.432. Let's call the population proportion π_W, with the subscript denoting a White victim. Of course, we don't know π_W, but we do have a sample derived point estimate of it: $\hat{\pi}_W = 0.432$. Similarly, there exists the population proportions π_B, π_L, and π_O corresponding to the population proportion of televised news stories about homicide where the victim was Black, Latino, or a member of some other ethnic group. We don't know these proportions either, but from the data, we have point estimates of them: $\hat{\pi}_B = (32/139) = 0.230$, $\hat{\pi}_L = (26/139) = 0.187$, $\hat{\pi}_O = (21/139) = 0.151$. As they should, these four sample estimates sum to one, reflecting the fact that these 4 categories are exhaustive of the possibilities. That is, a victim was either White, Black, Latino, or a member of some other group.

These estimated proportions are characteristics of the sample and useful as point estimates of the population. But we know that from sample to sample, these estimated proportions will vary due to random sampling variability. This sample-to-sample variability in these estimates, random as it is, can be described mathematically. As a result, hypotheses about the population proportions can be tested statistically.

11.1.1 Testing the Hypothesis of Equal Relative Frequencies

Information from the sample suggests that televised news stories about homicide are more likely to describe the homicide of a White victim than either a Black, Latino, or person of some other ethnic background, with such broadcasts accounting for 43% of televised news stories about homicide. It is possible that, just by chance, this sample happened to include many more stories about White victims than victims of other ethnic groups. That is, perhaps in the population of news broadcasts in Los Angeles, all four of the population proportions are equal and the obtained differences can be attributed to nothing other than chance random sampling variability. To assess this possibility, we need a statistical test.

The statistical test is known as the χ^2 (pronounced "kie-squared") *goodness of fit test*. The named of the test is based on the statistic and sampling distribution used to compute the p-value—the chi-squared distribution—and the fact that the test is designed to assess how well a set of expectations fits the observed frequencies. The χ^2 distribution can be used in a number of ways. In this case, we will use it to determine if N members of a population are equally distributed across a set of k categories, with any apparent differences in the category frequencies in a sample of size n attributable only to random sampling variability. More precisely, we will use it to test the equality of the population proportions. So if there are k categories, then the null hypothesis is, in general terms:

$$H_0 : \pi_1 = \pi_2 = \cdots = \pi_k$$
$$H_a : \text{at least two of the population proportions are not equal}$$

We could denote the alternative hypothesis symbolically, although in my experience this invites confusion, so I will stick with the verbal rather than symbolic version of the alternative hypothesis.

In this example, the null and alternative hypotheses are

$$H_0 : \pi_W = \pi_B = \pi_L = \pi_O$$
$$H_a: \text{at least two of the proportions are not equal}$$

It is tempting but not correct to denote the alternative as $H_a : \pi_W \neq \pi_B \neq \pi_L \neq \pi_O$. This is incorrect because it is possible for both the null and alternative hypothesis to be false when the alternative is phrased this way. For example, suppose that $\pi_W = 0.20$, $\pi_B = 0.20$, $\pi_L = 0.30$, $\pi_O = 0.30$. It is clear in this case that the four proportions are not the same but H_0 and H_a are both false. As such, H_a framed in this way cannot qualify as an alternative hypothesis because the null and alternative hypotheses must be mutually exclusive and exhaustive.

To test the null against the alternative hypothesis, we follow the same steps as in previous chapters, although the specifics of the method must be modified to reflect the fact that the hypotheses are about a distribution of frequencies rather than about a mean or a difference between means. After the null and alternative hypotheses are articulated, then the obtained result must be quantified. The obtained result is the sample proportions, which as discussed above are $\hat{\pi}_W = 0.432$, $\hat{\pi}_B = 0.230$, $\hat{\pi}_L = 0.187$, $\hat{\pi}_O = 0.151$. We then need to calculate the probability of getting sample proportions that deviate as far or farther from the null hypothesis than the obtained proportions do assuming that the null hypothesis is true. If the population proportions are all equal, then with $k = 4$ categories, the population proportions must be $\pi_W = 0.25$, $\pi_B = 0.25$, $\pi_L = 0.25$, and $\pi_O = 0.25$. More generally, if there are k categories, then the population proportions corresponding to the null hypothesis are all $1/k$. Of course, even if these are the population proportions (meaning that the null hypothesis is true), it is unlikely that in any random sample from this population the sample proportions will be exactly equal to their population values. Indeed, the sample proportions in this example are all descriptively different from 0.25. But are the differences more than you would expect just by chance (i.e., random sampling variability) if you assume the null hypothesis is true? To answer this question, we need to compute a p-value. The p-value is derived by computing a test statistic called the χ^2 statistic. It is defined as

$$\chi^2 = \sum \frac{(O_j - E_j)^2}{E_j}$$

(11.1)

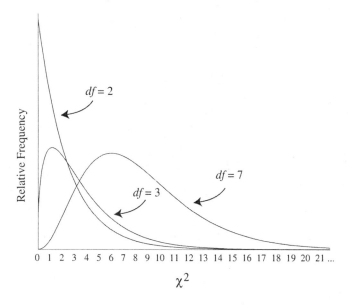

Figure 11.1 The χ^2 sampling distribution.

where O_j is the observed frequency of cases in category j, E_j is the expected frequency of cases in category j if the null hypothesis is true, and the summation is over all k categories. To apply this formula, it is necessary to convert the null hypothesis proportions into expected frequencies. But this is fairly easy. In a sample of size n, the expected number of cases in each of the k categories is n/k if the null hypothesis is true. So in a random sample of $n = 139$ homicide stories, if the null hypothesis is true, then you'd expect to find $(139/4) = 34.75$ homicide stories with a White victim, 34.75 stories with a Black victim, 34.75 stories with a Latino victim, and 34.75 stories with a victim from some other ethnic group. Let's call these expected frequencies E_W, E_B, E_L, and E_O. The observed frequencies are the actual number of observations in each category in the sample. So for the victim data, $O_W = 60$, $O_B = 32$, $O_L = 26$, $O_O = 21$. Applying equation 11.1

$$\chi^2 = \frac{(60 - 34.75)^2}{34.75} + \frac{(32 - 34.75)^2}{34.75} + \frac{(26 - 34.75)^2}{34.75} + \frac{(21 - 34.75)^2}{34.75} = 26.209$$

This obtained χ^2 of 26.209 quantifies the discrepancy between the observed frequencies and the expected frequencies assuming a true null hypothesis. On the one extreme, χ^2 will be zero if the observed and expected frequencies are exactly equal. This will occur if the sample proportions and the corresponding population proportions under the null hypothesis are exactly equal (because in that case, the numerator of each term above would be zero, so the sum of the terms would be zero). At the other extreme, if all the cases in the sample are in only one of the categories, then χ^2 will be at its maximum possible value. So the greater the observed frequencies differ from the expected frequencies, the larger χ^2 will be because the numerators of the terms above will be relatively large relative to the denominators. It should also be apparent that because the observed frequencies are all random variables, then χ^2 is also a random variable when randomly sampling from the population.

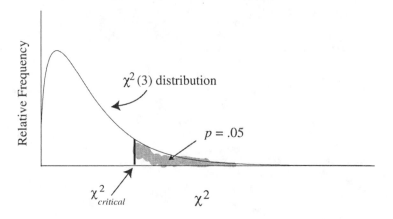

Figure 11.2 The critical χ^2 value for $\alpha = .05, df = 3$.

Having now quantified the discrepancy between the observed frequencies and the expected frequencies, the next step is to determine the probability of obtaining such a large χ^2 when randomly sampling from a population where the null hypothesis is true. This p-value is calculated by determining the proportion of possible values of χ^2 in the sampling distribution of χ^2 that exceed the obtained χ^2. Like the t distribution, the χ^2 sampling distribution is a family of distributions defined by their degrees of freedom. But unlike t, the χ^2 distribution is not a symmetrical distribution. For small degrees of freedom, the χ^2 distribution is very skewed, with the extent of skew decreasing as the degrees of freedom increases (see Figure 11.1). When testing a hypothesis about a frequency distribution or set of proportions, the relevant degrees of freedom is defined as $df = k - 1$, where k is the number of categories. In this example, $k = 4$, so we would compute p using the $\chi^2(3)$ distribution, where the number in parenthesis is the degrees of freedom. This p-value can be computed easily with a computer, or you can consult a table of critical values of χ^2 to determine if p is less than the α-level for the test (as always, usually 0.05 is used). This critical value (represented graphically in Figure 11.2) can be found in Appendix C. Using this table, p is equal to or less than .05 if the obtained χ^2 statistic of 26.209 exceeds the critical value for $\alpha = .05$. By looking under the $p = .05$ row, $df = 3$ column, the critical value of χ^2 is 7.815. This means that only 5% of obtained χ^2 statistics would be expected to be as large or larger than 7.815 if the null hypothesis is true. The obtained χ^2 is clearly larger than this, so p is less than .05. A closer look at Appendix C show that the obtained chi-square is larger than the critical χ^2 for α as small as .001, so we can claim that the p-value is even less than .001.

An alternative to the use of the χ^2 table in Appendix C is to have a computer program compute the p-value directly. SPSS output for this problem can be seen in Figure 11.3 panel A. The p-value, listed under "Asymp. Sig.", is ".000." SPSS is rounding the p-value to the nearest third decimal place in this output. From this output, we can claim that p is no bigger than .0005. It would be incorrect to say that $p = 0$, because clearly it is possible to get a χ^2 value at least as large as the obtained χ^2 of 26.209. If it were not possible, then how is it that such a χ^2 value was obtained in this sample? Whenever you see a computer program print out something like "$p = .000$" the correct interpretation is that p is very small, and certainly smaller than .05. This is a nondirectional p-value because the alternative hypothesis is nondirectional. In general, whenever $k > 2$, a goodness of fit test is inherently nondirectional because of the way the null and alternative hypotheses are defined with this test.

With the p-value computed, the next step is to use this information to make a decision about the null and alternative hypotheses. Using $\alpha = .05$, we would reject the null hypothesis because p is less than .05. As a result of this rejection, we must accept the alternative hypothesis that at least two of the population proportions differ.

A

VICTIM

	Observed N	Expected N	Residual
White	60	34.75	25.25
Black	32	34.75	-2.75
Latino	26	34.75	-8.75
Other	21	34.75	-13.75
Total	139		

Test Statistics

	VICTIM
Chi-Square[a]	26.209	← Equation 11.1
df	3
Asymp. Sig.	.000

a. 0 cells (.0%) have expected frequencies less than 5. The minimum expected cell frequency is 34.8.

B

VICTIM

	Observed N	Expected N	Residual
White	60	18.1	41.9
Black	32	38.9	-6.9
Latino	26	75.1	-49.1
Other	21	7.0	14.1
Total	139		

Test Statistics

	VICTIM
Chi-Square[a]	158.995	← Equation 11.1
df	3
Asymp. Sig.	.000

a. 0 cells (.0%) have expected frequencies less than 5. The minimum expected cell frequency is 7.0.

Figure 11.3 SPSS output from two goodness of fit tests.

We end the process with the substantive conclusion, which might read something like this in written form:

> Televised news broadcasts of homicide in the Los Angeles area presented stories about victims of different ethnicities in differing frequency. In 139 randomly selected news stories, the victim was White in 43% of the stories, Black in 23% of the stories, Latino in 19% of the stories, and of some other ethnic group in the remaining 15% of the stories, $\chi^2(3) = 26.209$, $p < .0005$

Finding the Source of the Rejection. It seems from the results of this test that there are many more homicide stories about White victims that would be expected if televised news stories about homicide represent victims of different ethnicities in equal proportion. It is also apparent that there are somewhat fewer stories about Black, Latino, and victims of some other ethnic group than expected. It is sometimes desirable to ascertain which of the categories are deviating from their expected values more than just sampling error would tend to produce just by chance. This is accomplished by computing the *standardized residual* for each category. The standardized residual is defined as

$$Z_j = \frac{O_j - E_j}{\sqrt{E_j}}$$

(11.2)

The values of Z_j are bona-fide Z-scores, in that they quantify how each frequency deviates from its expected value in standard error units if the null hypothesis is true. To determine whether a category's observed frequency is different from the expected value to a statistically significant degree, a two-tailed p-value for each standardized residual can be computed using the standard normal distribution. Using equation 11.2 and Appendix A, $Z_W = 4.283$, $p < .0001$; $Z_B = -0.467$, $p > .05$; $Z_L = -1.484$, $p > .05$; $Z_O = -2.332$, $p < .05$. So it appears that the rejection of the null hypothesis is attributable to the much larger than expected number of White victims and the much smaller than expected number of victims that are neither White, Black, or Latino on televised news broadcasts of homicide. The frequencies for Black and Latino victims do not differ from their expected values to a statistically significant degree.

11.1.2 Testing the Fit of Observed Frequencies to Any Expectation

The preceding analysis indicates that Los Angeles news broadcasts of homicide do not represent the ethnicity of victims of homicide in equal proportion. But on reflection it should be apparent this cannot be used as evidence for the claim that there is some kind of racial or ethnic bias in news programming. As Dixon and Linz (2000) correctly note, it would not be at all surprising to find more televised news stories of White homicide victims than other groups if white people are more likely to be victims of homicide in Los Angeles. Indeed, it would be rather odd to find that such broadcasts represented the ethnicities of the victim in equal proportion if there are differences in the frequency in which people of different ethnicities are murdered in Los Angeles. In other words, perhaps it is unreasonable to use 34.75 as the expected frequency for all categories in this test. Perhaps we should use expected frequencies that are sensitive to the actual distribution of the ethnic backgrounds of homicide victims in Los Angeles.

Fortunately, Dixon and Linz (2000) were able to obtain information about how frequently people of various ethnicities are murdered in Los Angeles. Such information is compiled by the California Department of Justice at the county level. According to their statistics, in all homicides in Los Angeles and Orange counties, a White person was the victim in 13% of them, a Black person was the victim in 28% of them, a Latino was the victim 54% of the time, and in the remaining 5%, the victim was of some other ethnic group. From this information, we can derive a set of expected frequencies that are sensitive to the actual homicide rates in Los Angeles. Define Ω_W as the population proportion of homicides in Los Angeles and Orange County where the victim was White (Ω is the Greek letter "Omega"), and define Ω_B, Ω_L, and Ω_O as the corresponding population proportions for Black, Latino, and other ethnic groups respectively. According to population statistics from the California Department of Justice, $\Omega_W = 0.13$, $\Omega_B = 0.28$, $\Omega_L = 0.54$, and $\Omega_O = 0.05$. If the news broadcasts of homicide were representing victims in proportion to their frequency in the population, then this implies that $\pi_W = \Omega_W$, $\pi_B = \Omega_B$, $\pi_L = \Omega_L$, $\pi_O = \Omega_O$. (Remember that earlier we defined π_j as the population proportion of news broadcasts about homicide with a member of ethnic group j as the victim). But if the broadcasting misrepresents the victimization rate of different ethnic groups, then this implies that the population proportions are different from these values. So the null and alternative hypotheses are

$$H_0 : \pi_W = 0.13, \pi_B = 0.28, \pi_L = 0.54, \pi_O = 0.05$$
$$H_a : \pi_W \neq 0.13 \text{ or } \pi_B \neq 0.28 \text{ or } \pi_L \neq 0.54 \text{ or } \pi_O \neq 0.05$$

According to the null hypothesis, if the population proportion of news broadcasts depicting a White homicide victim is equal to 0.13, then in a sample of 139 news broadcasts of homicide, you would expect $0.13(139) = 18.07$ of them to be about a White victim. Using this logic for all 4 categories, if the null hypothesis is true, then the expected frequencies are $E_W = 18.07$, $E_B = 38.92$, $E_L = 75.06$, $E_O = 6.95$. To test the null hypothesis, we quantify the discrepancy between the observed and expected frequencies with the χ^2 statistic:

$$\chi^2 = \frac{(60 - 18.07)^2}{18.07} + \frac{(32 - 38.92)^2}{38.92} + \frac{(26 - 75.06)^2}{75.06} + \frac{(21 - 6.95)^2}{6.95} = 159.00$$

This is substantially larger than the critical χ^2, $df = 3$, for $\alpha = .05$, as well as for $\alpha = .001$ (see Appendix C), so we can reject the null hypothesis and accept the alternative (see Figure 11.3, panel B for SPSS output for this problem). So televised news broadcasts about homicide in Los Angeles do not represent the actual victimization rates of members of different ethnic groups. We can further probe this finding by converting the observed frequencies to standardized residuals with equation 11.2: $Z_W = 9.849$, $p < .0001$; $Z_B = -1.106$, $p > .05$; $Z_L = -5.666$, $p < .0001$; $Z_O = 5.329$, $p < .0001$. So it seems that televised news stories about homicide tend to overrepresent the victimization of Whites and members of "other" ethnic groups while underrepresenting the victimization of Latinos relative to their frequency of homicide in the Los Angeles area. Blacks, on the other hand, seem to be represented as victims on televised homicide news stories in roughly equal proportion to their victimization in the Los Angeles area.

11.1.3   Statistical Assumptions

As discussed in Chapter 8, hypothesis testing procedures are mathematical approaches to estimating the true p-value for the obtained result in order to make a decision of some kind. The quality of this estimation and therefore the correctness of your decision about the null and alternative hypothesis depends on the assumptions of the test being met. If the assumptions are violated, the test can be either liberal or conservative, depending on the form of the assumption violation. The primary assumption of the goodness of fit test is that a case in the sample must be assigned to one and only one of the k categories. A violation of this important assumption can invalidate the test, meaning that the resulting p-value will be an underestimate of the true p-value, and this inflates the probability of making a Type I error.

It has also been said that the χ^2 goodness of fit test is a *large sample test*, meaning that it is appropriate to use the χ^2 distribution to compute the p-value only if the sample is sufficiently large. However, just what qualifies as sufficiently large is not at all clear. Related to this assumption, some have argued that in order for the test to produce an accurate p-value, the minimum expected frequency should be no smaller than five. Notice that SPSS provides information in the output about the smallest expected frequency (Figure 11.3). These two assumptions are closely related, in that the smaller the sample size, the more likely that at least one of the expected frequencies will be smaller than five. So if you believe in the importance of this assumption, you'd be hesitant in trusting the p-value if you have one or more expected frequencies smaller than five.

Statisticians have looked carefully at the conditions under which the χ^2 goodness of fit test is likely to perform poorly using the Monte-Carlo method. In a Monte-Carlo study, a researcher creates artificial populations through mathematical simulation where the null hypothesis is known to be true and then repeatedly takes random samples from that population, applying the test to each sample. The performance of the test is gauged by how often the test falsely rejects the null hypothesis (which the researcher knows to be true because he or she created the populations mathematically so that the null hypothesis is true). Various Monte-Carlo studies suggest that the χ^2 goodness of fit test actually performs pretty well even when the sample size is small and there are categories with expected frequencies smaller than 5. There are many rules of thumb for determining whether a sample size is sufficiently large to trust the results of this test. Koehler and Larntz (1980) provide a rule of thumb that applies when k (the number of categories) is at least 3 and the smallest expected frequency is at least 0.25. In that case, they suggest that a sample size can be considered sufficiently large if the sample size (n) is at least 10, and n^2/k is at least 10. In this example, $k = 4$ and $n = 139$, so both of these criteria are satisfied.

11.1.4   Alternative Tests for the $k = 2$ Case

In Chapter 8, I introduced the Z test for testing a hypothesis about a single population proportion. Recall in that section that 200 residents of a city council member's voting district were randomly selected to participate in a poll and were asked whether they would prefer an income tax or a sales tax increase. Of interest was whether the residents of the voting district, as a group, had a preference or whether they were equally split on this issue. Defining π as the population proportion of residents that prefer the sales tax, we tested the null hypothesis that $\pi = 0.5$ against the alternative that $\pi \neq 0.5$ and rejected the null hypothesis, $Z = 2.00, p < .05$. We can use the χ^2 goodness of fit test to test the null hypothesis that $\pi_{sales} = \pi_{income}$ income against that alternative that $\pi_{sales} \neq \pi_{income}$. If the null hypothesis is true, then in a random sample of size 200 you'd expect that 100 respondents would report a preference for the sales tax and 100 would report a preference for the income tax. In other words, $E_{sales} = 100$,

$E_{income} = 100$. The observed frequencies, on the other hand, were $O_{sales} = 114$, $O_{income} = 86$. Calculating χ^2 using equation 11.1,

$$\chi^2 = \frac{(114 - 100)^2}{100} + \frac{(86 - 100)^2}{100} = 3.920$$

For $k = 2$ categories, the critical χ^2 for $df = k - 1 = 1$ is 3.84 for $\alpha = .05$. The obtained χ^2 just barely exceeds the critical value, so $p < .05$.

These are mathematically equivalent tests. For the special case where $k = 2$, the Z test for a population proportion will provide the same result as the χ^2 test of goodness of fit. Notice that the critical χ^2 value for $df = 1$, $\alpha = .05$ is 3.84, which is equal to the square of 1.96—the value of Z that cuts off the upper and lower 2.5% (and thus 5% total) of the standard normal distribution from the rest of the distribution. So either test can be used. They will produce the same decision.

The Exact Binomial Test. As discussed in section 11.1.3, the goodness of fit test is generally construed as a "large sample" test, meaning that it will produce more accurate p-values in larger samples. When the sample is very small, it is not a good idea to use the χ^2 distribution to test hypotheses about a frequency distribution. And because the χ^2 goodness of fit test and the Z test on a population proportion are mathematically identical, it follows that the Z test should not be used for small samples. Agresti and Finlay (1997) argue that when $k = 2$, the sample size can be considered sufficiently large for the Z or χ^2 test if it is at least $10/\pi_{min}$, where π_{min} is the smallest of π_0 and $1 - \pi_0$, and where π_0 is the null hypothesized value of the population proportion. But when $k = 2$, there is a method that works for even very small samples. This test relies on the binomial probability distribution called the *exact binomial test on a proportion*. When testing the null hypothesis that a population proportion π is some specific value, the exact binomial test should be used when the sample size is less than $10/\pi_{min}$.

Let's continue with the example from Chapter 8, where you were asked to imagine that you were working for a person running for city council. Perhaps because of financial or time constraints, you were unable to obtain a large random sample of residents of the voting district. Instead, you obtained a small random sample of 12 residents of the district and invited them to the campaign headquarters for a focus group. You ask these 12 residents which of the two taxes they would prefer if they had to choose. Suppose that of these 12, 8 stated a preference for the sales tax and four stated a preference of the income tax. You could provide a point estimate of the population proportion of residents that prefer the sales tax ($\hat{\pi} = 0.67$), as well as a confidence interval for that proportion. But 12 is rather small sample size, and there is reason to be concerned that the sampling distribution of $\hat{\pi}$ might not be normal or even t distributed (recall that the Central Limit Theorem states only that the sampling distribution becomes normal as the sample size increases). For the same reason, it wouldn't be wise to apply the Z test if you couldn't have faith that the sampling distribution of Z is normal.

We can get around these worries by employing the binomial distribution to derive the p-value. Suppose you are interested in determining if residents of the voting district have a preference for one form of the tax. So $H_0 : \pi = 0.50$ and $H_a : \pi \neq 0.50$. Using the logic of the goodness of fit test, if the null hypothesis is true, then you'd expect that in a sample of size 12, 6 would state a preference for the sales tax and six for the income tax. The observed number of residents that preferred the sales tax was eight. If we denote our random variable X (the number that state a preference for the sales tax), then $X = 8$. This represents a deviation of 2 from the expected value assuming the null hypothesis is true. The two-tailed p-value can be derived by determining $P(X \geq 8|\pi = 0.50)$ or $P(X \leq 4|\pi = 0.50)$. X is random variable of course, because its value would vary in a sample of size 12 from sample to sample.

If the residents of the voting district don't have a preference as a group, then you'd expect that any randomly selected person from the voting district would state that they prefer the sales tax with probability of 0.50. Similarly, the probability that any randomly selected person would state they prefer the income tax would also be 0.50. Consider an "event" the act of randomly selecting someone that prefers the sales tax. We know that the probability of the event is 0.50 if the null hypothesis is true. In a sample of size 12, there are 12 "trials," and the probability of the event we can assume would be constant over all 12 trials. Thus, from Chapter 5, $X \sim B(12, 0.5)$. To determine the exact p-value, use equation 5.5. In this case, $m = 12$, $k =$ the number of people who state they prefer the sales tax, and $p = 0.50$.

The easiest way to derive the two-tailed p-value is to compute $P(X = 5)$, $P(X = 6)$, and $P(X = 7)$, add up these probabilities, and then subtract this sum from 1. This would produce $P(X \geq 8|\pi = 0.5)$ or $P(X \leq 4|\pi = 0.50)$. Here are the computations:

$$P(5) = \left(\frac{12!}{5!(12-5)!}\right) 0.50^5(1-0.50)^{12-5} = 792(0.50)^5 0.50^7 = 0.193$$

$$P(6) = \left(\frac{12!}{6!(12-6)!}\right) 0.50^6(1-0.50)^{12-6} = 924(0.50)^6 0.50^6 = 0.226$$

$$P(7) = \left(\frac{12!}{7!(12-7)!}\right) 0.50^7(1-0.50)^{12-7} = 792(0.50)^7 0.50^5 = 0.193$$

So $P(X \geq 8|\pi = 0.5)$ or $P(X \leq 4|\pi = 0.5) = 1 - (0.193 + 0.226 + 0.193) = 0.388$. This leads to a failure to reject the null hypothesis. From this sample of size 12, there is no reason to believe that the residents of the voting district have a preference for one tax over the other. This is an exact p-value, not an estimate as the Z or χ^2 test yields, this test does not require any faith in the Central Limit Theorem in order to employ it, and this test will work with any sample size. Of course, as the sample size increases, the number of computations increases substantially. In a large sample, it is easier to employ the Z test from Chapter 8 or the χ^2 goodness of fit test.

11.1.5   Testing Goodness of Fit for Process Inference

Throughout this section, I have described the goodness of fit test as one focused on making inferences about the size of or differences between population proportions from a sample frequency distribution. To do this, it is necessary to collect some kind of random sample from the specified population. Such random sampling affords the ability to make population inferences. However, this test can be used to make other kinds of inferences when the sample is not obtained randomly. For instance, suppose that you work for an advertising agency that is designing a magazine advertisement for a soft drink company. The graphic designers and marketing experts in the advertising firm develop three different magazine advertisements, and you are interested in knowing which of the three advertisements will be most likely to grab the attention of people. To determine this, you recruit 150 people to come to the firm's office and participate in a series of focus groups. You recruit participants from a list of people who have agreed to participate in marketing research being conducted by the advertising firm in exchange for chances to win cash prizes and other goodies through a lottery system.

The people on the list are sent an email requesting their participation, and people who agree to participate are given a time to come to the firm for their focus group meeting. During the focus groups, each participant is shown the three advertisements and asked to select which of the three advertisements they find the most attention grabbing.

Your goal is to determine which ad is most attention grabbing. Suppose that 72 of the participants select advertisement A, 48 select advertisement B, and 30 select advertisement C. Thus, you estimate that more people are likely to notice and attend to advertisement A. In the language and symbols of statistics focused on population inference, $\hat{\pi}_A = (72/150) = 0.48$, $\hat{\pi}_B = (48/150) = 0.32$, and $\hat{\pi}_C = (30/150) = 0.20$ You might test the null hypothesis that $\pi_A = \pi_B = \pi_C$ against the alternative that at least two of these proportions differ in order to determine whether the obtained differences in the proportions can be attributed to random sampling variability. If the null hypothesis is true, then you'd expect 50 people to select advertisement A, 50 to select advertisement B, and 50 to select advertisement C. Using equation 11.1 or a computer program,

$$\chi^2 = \frac{(72-50)^2}{50} + \frac{(48-50)^2}{50} + \frac{(30-50)^2}{50} = 17.760$$

which is much larger than the critical value of χ^2, $df = k - 1 = 2$, for $\alpha = .05$. So it seems that "chance" cannot be invoked as a sensible explanation for the obtained differences in the frequencies. There appears to be a clear preference for advertisement A over the others. From this information, you might direct the purchasing department to acquire advertising space for advertisement A.

On the surface, it would seem that employing this test in this kind of situation does an extreme injustice to the statistical theory upon which the test is based. These 150 are by no means a random sample from any population that can be clearly articulated. As such, how can one even begin to think about the sample proportions as somehow estimating a population parameter? And given that there has been no random sampling, how sensible it is to employ a test that construes chance-driven deviation from the null hypothesis as the result of random sampling variability? Random sampling variability has never been given a chance to exert its effect on the obtained result.

All is not lost because there is a different way of thinking about chance by conceptualizing each participant's choice between A, B, and C as being driven by a process that could be described as either *random* or *systematic*. For example, perhaps participants had no particular thoughts or feelings leading them to make one selection or another, so they in effect just picked one of the advertisements randomly because they were asked to make a selection. This would be a chance process. A systematic process, on the other hand, might be some kind of mental strategy where the participants spent time looking at the three advertisements, considered their features, how attractive and attention grabbing they were, and generated a decision based on this mental process. Or it might be a much less interesting systematic process, like the participants tending to select the first advertisement they see. We can use the χ^2 goodness of fit test to determine how well the data fit what would be expected if people were just randomly selecting an advertisement. If the data do not fit such expectations well, the random process explanation can be rejected in favor of the explanation that there was some kind of systematic process at work leading the participants to select one advertisement in greater numbers than others.

We don't need a special test to distinguish between the random and systematic process explanations. The random process leads one to expect that in a sample of 150 participants, each advertisement should get nominated 50 times. Of course, random processes are just that, so it is unlikely that people's random responses would exactly produce an even distribution of stated preferences across the 3 advertisements, just like flipping a coin 50 times is unlikely to produce exactly 25 heads and 25 tails. The p-value, as a measure of consistency between the obtained frequencies and what a random process would lead the researcher to expect, can be used to determine how probable the difference between the obtained and expected frequencies is if you assume that people were just randomly picking an advertisement. The χ^2 distribution can be used to generate that p-value. Rejection of this null hypothesis of a random process leads you to claim that the process generating the obtained frequency distribution is the result, at least in part, of some kind of *systematic* process. So the resulting inference is a process inference. In the absence of random sampling from a population, it would not be wise to make a statistical generalization, such as "in the population of readers of this magazine, 48% would have found advertisement A more attention grabbing." But who cares? You just want to know which ad was most preferred so that a decision can be made about which advertisement to run. Knowing that the preference for advertisement A could not be attributed to just random responding is important and useful information to have because it puts your selection of advertisements on some kind of solid scientific footing.

Of course, you do not know whether readers of the magazines the ad is going to be run in would have the same preferences. For this reason, it would have been wise to obtain the participants from a pool of likely readers of the magazine. But even so, if the things that lead the 150 participants to prefer magazine A in relatively large numbers are likely to have the same effect on people who read these magazines (such as color features, font size, etc), it is probably safe to assume that readers of the target magazines will be more attracted to advertisement A than they would have been to the other advertisements. If you aren't confident that such processes would be at work in people who will actually be exposed to the advertisement, then which of the advertisements the actual magazine readers will find most attention grabbing remains anyone's guess.

11.2   Association Between Two Categorical Variables

In Chapters 4 and 5, I introduced the concepts of association and independence. Two variables X and Y are said to be *associated* or *dependent* if certain values on X are paired more frequently with certain values of Y. For example, if two variables are *positively associated*, this means that relatively high scores on X tend to paired relatively frequently with relatively high scores on Y, and relatively low scores on X tend to be paired more frequently with relatively low scores on Y.

In Chapter 4, I focused entirely on association between quantitative variables. However, we are often interested in quantifying and testing for association between variables that are categorical. For instance, a researcher might want to know whether an advertisement that advocates the importance of regular screening for a particular type of cancer is more effective in getting people to take the test when it emphasizes the peace of mind it brings relative to when it attempts to scare the person in to acting. If the outcome variable is measured as whether or not the person took the test within 6 months of hearing the message, then both of the variables are categorical. Or a researcher might want to know whether males are more likely than females to agree to a request when they are told whether or not their friends agreed relative to when they are not so told. Again, both variables in this case are categorical.

11.2.1   Testing for Independence in a 2×2 Crosstabulation

Johnson and Kaid (2002) examined whether the use of a fear appeal in presidential advertisements was related to the type of advertisement—issue or image-oriented. In other words, when presidential advertisements are constructed, is there some kind of a systematic association between whether the ad focuses on issues versus the image of the candidate and whether or not fear is induced as a motivator for action? In case you are not familiar with the term, a fear appeal is a message designed to incite some kind of worry or fear in the audience, often by warning of some kind of negative consequence if the position or behavior advocated in the advertisement is not adopted. For example, an advertisement might mention that taxes will increase if the candidate's opponent wins or that national security will be weaker and terrorism more likely if the candidate is not elected to office.

To conduct their study, Johnston & Kaid obtained 1,213 advertisements from the University of Oklahoma's archive of advertisements used by candidates running for President of the United States. Presidential candidates between 1952 and 2000. The archive does not contain all advertisements ever run in a U.S. Presidential election, and with no reason to assume that this archive is not basically representative of the types of ads that have ever been run, it is sensible to construe this as a random sample of the population of advertisements. They coded each advertisement to see whether a fear appeal was used. Of the 1,213 advertisements coded, 264 of them contained a fear appeal and 949 did not. They also coded each advertisement with respect to whether it was primarily an issue-oriented advertisement or an image-oriented ad. They defined an issue-oriented ad as one that focused on some kind of specific policy or proposed policy, or discussed some general concern about an issue such as the environment, employment, and so forth. Image-oriented ads were defined as those that focused primarily on the personality characteristics of the candidate. Their coding yielded 429 image-oriented ads and 784 issue-oriented ads.

With two characteristics coded in each advertisement (issue vs. image and fear appeal vs. no fear appeal), it is possible to place each advertisement in a crosstabulation as in Table 11.1. This is a "2 × 2" (pronounced "two by two") crosstabulation because the rows and columns are based on two categories each. This table shows that 60 of the 1,213 advertisements were image-oriented fear appeal based ads, 204 were issue-oriented fear appeal ads, 369 were image-oriented without a fear appeal, and 580 were issue-oriented without a fear appeal. So are fear appeals more or less likely in image-oriented ads compared to issue-oriented ads, or they about equally frequent in both types of advertisements? In other words, does a candidate's use of a fear appeal depend on whether the advertisement is an issue or an image-oriented ad?

A first glance at the table shows that there are many more issue-oriented ads with a fear appeal than there are image-oriented ads with a fear appeal (204 versus 60). It might seem like fear appeals are more common in issue-oriented ads. However, this isn't the relevant comparison because there are many more issue-oriented ads than there are image-oriented ads. Indeed, notice that there are also more issue ads without a fear appeal than there are image ads without a fear appeal. So the differences between these frequencies reflect nothing more than the larger number of issue-oriented ads in the sample.

Table 11.1

A Crosstabulation of Ad Type and Use of a Fear Appeal

| | Ad Type | | |
Fear Appeal	Image	Issue	Total
Yes	60	204	264
No	369	580	949
Total	429	784	1213

The relevant comparison is to examine the proportion of issue-oriented ads that contain a fear appeal and compare that to the proportion of image-oriented ads that contain a fear appeal. Define $\pi_{\text{fear}|\text{image}}$ as the proportion of image-oriented ads in the population of presidential advertisements that contain a fear appeal, and define $\pi_{\text{fear}|\text{issue}}$ as the proportion of issue-oriented ads in the population that contain a fear appeal. We don't know these population proportions, because the archive does not contain all U.S. presidential advertisements. The 1,312 ads that Johnston and Kaid examined are just a sample from the population of all ads. But from this sample, we can calculate point estimates of the proportions as

$$\hat{\pi}_{\text{fear}|\text{image}} = 60/429 = 0.140$$
$$\hat{\pi}_{\text{fear}|\text{issue}} = 204/784 = 0.260$$

So 14% of image-oriented ads in the sample contained a fear appeal and 26% of issue-oriented ads in the sample contained a fear appeal. From these data, it seems that fear appeals are more common in issue-oriented ads than they are in image-oriented ads. But you wouldn't expect these two proportions to be equal in a random sample of advertisements. It seems possible that the use of fear appeals could be equally common in issue ads and image ads, and the obtained difference is the result of random sampling variability. To determine whether the use of a fear appeal actually does depend on whether the advertisement is an issue or image ad, we need to conduct a statistical test.

Before discussing this test, let's review the concept of independent and dependent events from Chapter 5 because we will need these concepts to completely understand how this test works. Recall that two events can be considered independent if knowledge of whether or not one event occurred gives you no information about whether or not the other event occurred. Probabilistically, if we define event B as randomly selecting a fear appeal ad from the population of presidential advertisements and event A as randomly selecting an issue-oriented ad, then independence implies that $P(B|A) = P(B|\text{not } A)$. In other words, the probability that a randomly selected ad contains a fear appeal is the same regardless of whether that ad is an issue-oriented or image-oriented ad: $P(\text{fear}|\text{issue}) = P(\text{fear}|\text{image})$. Thus, independence in a 2×2 crosstabulation implies equality of conditional probabilities.

If the proportion of ads with a fear appeal is the same for both issue-oriented and image-oriented ads, then knowledge of whether an advertisement is issue or image-oriented would give you no information about whether or not the ad contains a fear appeal. So whether or not the ad contains a fear appeal and the type of ad it is (issue or image-oriented) can be thought of as independent events. This implies that $\pi_{\text{fear}|\text{image}} = \pi_{\text{fear}|\text{issue}}$. But if the use of a fear appeal and the type of ad are dependent events, this suggests that these proportions are different: $\pi_{\text{fear}|\text{image}} \neq \pi_{\text{fear}|\text{issue}}$. In that case, the likelihood or probability that a randomly selected advertisement contains a fear appeal depends on whether the ad is an issue- or image-oriented ad.

In a 2×2 table, the test of independence can be framed in two different ways. In its simplest form, the null hypothesis and alternative hypotheses are

H_0: the two variables are statistically independent
H_a: the two variables are statistically dependent

From the preceding discussion these are equalivalent to the following null and alternative hypotheses:

$$H_0 : \pi_{\text{fear}|\text{image}} = \pi_{\text{fear}|\text{issue}}$$
$$H_a : \pi_{\text{fear}|\text{image}} \neq \pi_{\text{fear}|\text{issue}}$$

How might we go about testing this hypothesis? There are several ways we could do this, but by far the most common method is the χ^2 test of independence. To understand how this test works, imagine you randomly selected an advertisement from the population of advertisements. What is the probability that the randomly selected advertisement is an issue-oriented ad? We don't know the answer to this question, but the data in Table 11.1 can be used to estimate this probability. In this sample, 784 of the 1213 ads were issue-oriented, so a reasonable estimate of the probability of selecting an issue-oriented advertisement is (784/1213) or 0.646. So our estimate of P(issue-oriented) is 0.646. Using the same logic, we can estimate that the probability that a randomly-selected advertisement contains a fear appeal is (264/1213) = 0.218. Applying these computations to all of the possible events yields

$$P(\text{issue-oriented}) = (784/1213) = 0.646$$
$$P(\text{image-oriented}) = (429/1213) = 0.354$$
$$P(\text{fear appeal}) = (264/1213) = 0.218$$
$$P(\text{no fear appeal}) = (949/1213) = 0.782$$

The multiplicative law of probability from section 5.2.2 tells us that if two events are independent, then the probability of both events occurring is equal to the product of the individual probabilities. Using the multiplicative law, if the type of ad (issue or image) and whether it contains a fear appeal (yes or no) are independent, what is the probability that a randomly selected advertisement will be both issue-oriented and contain a fear appeal? Image-oriented without a fear appeal? By the multiplicative law of probability, these probability can be estimated as:

$$P(\text{issue-oriented AND fear appeal}) = 0.646(0.218) = 0.141$$
$$P(\text{issue-oriented AND no fear appeal}) = 0.646(0.782) = 0.505$$
$$P(\text{image-oriented AND fear appeal}) = 0.354(0.218) = 0.077$$
$$P(\text{image-oriented AND no fear appeal}) = 0.354(0.782) = 0.277$$

It is important to keep in mind that these probabilities are derived from the assumption that the events are independent. We don't actually know if they are. But if we *assume* that they are independent, then we can justifiably calculate these probabilities as we did.

With these probabilities estimated, we are now in a position to determine what the crosstabulation would be *expected* to look like if the null hypothesis of independence is true. If the probability of any randomly selected ad is both issue-oriented and contains a fear appeal is 0.141, then in 1,213 randomly selected advertisements, you'd expect to find that $0.141(1213) = 171.033$ of those ads would be issue-oriented fear appeal advertisements. By the same reasoning, you'd expect that $0.505(1213) = 612.565$ of 1,213 randomly selected ads would be issue-oriented ads without a fear appeal. This logic can be used to derive the expected number of image-oriented ads without a fear appeal and image-oriented with a fear appeal.

This works, but the computation of these expected frequencies actually introduces a lot of rounding error into the computations when done this way. It is better to use the frequencies in the table to generate these expectations. Using the table of frequencies rather than these probabilities, the expected number of issue-oriented advertisements with a fear appeal is equal to the number of fear-oriented ads multiplied by the number of issue-oriented ads divided by the total number of ads in the sample. More generally, if the row and column variables are independent, then the expected frequency for each cell in a crosstabulation is equal to

$$E(\text{row AND column}) = \frac{F(row)F(column)}{n}$$

(11.3)

where $F(row)$ is the frequency of cases in that row of the table, $F(column)$ is the frequency of cases in that column of the table, and n is the total number of cases in the table. Using this rule, it is easy to derive that if we assume independence between the orientation of the ad and whether it contains a fear appeal, then the expected frequencies in this crosstabulation are

$E(\text{issue-oriented with a fear appeal}) = (784)(264)/1213 = 170.631$
$E(\text{image-oriented without a fear appeal}) = (429)(264)/1213 = 93.369$
$E(\text{issue oriented with a fear appeal}) = (784)(949)/1213 = 613.369$
$E(\text{image-oriented without a fear appeal}) = (429)(949)/1213 = 335.631$

Figure 11.4, panel A provides both the observed frequencies ("count") and these expected frequencies ("expected count") together in the same crosstabulation. Notice that the *conditional proportions* computed with the expected frequencies assuming the null hypothesis is true are the same (i.e., the proportion of ads with a fear appeal conditioned on the type of ad). That is, using the expected frequencies rather than the observed frequencies, we see that the proportion of image-oriented ads with a fear appeal is $93.369/429 = 0.218$, and the proportion of issue-oriented ads with a fear appeal is $170.631/784 = 0.218$.

As can be seen in Figure 11.4, the observed number of advertisements in each cell of the crosstabulation do not equal the expected frequencies. But we'd be surprised if they were exactly equal. Each of the observed frequencies is subject to the vagaries of random sampling. They will vary from sample to sample. So even if the null hypothesis of independence is true, there is likely to be some discrepancy between the observed and expected frequencies. The question is whether the obtained discrepancies between the expected and observed frequencies are large enough for us to reject the null hypothesis of independence.

In the previous section we saw how the χ^2 statistic quantifies the discrepancy between a set of frequencies and the expected values of those frequencies assuming a true

A

FEAR * ADTYPE Crosstabulation

			ADTYPE		
			image	issue	Total
FEAR	fear appeal	Count	60.00	204.00	264.00
		Expected Count	93.37	170.63	264.00
	no fear appeal	Count	369.00	580.00	949.00
		Expected Count	335.63	613.37	949.00
Total		Count	429.00	784.00	1213.00
		Expected Count	429.00	784.00	1213.00

Equation 11.3

B

Equation 11.1

Chi-Square Tests

	Value	df	Asymp. Sig. (2-sided)	Exact Sig. (2-sided)	Exact Sig. (1-sided)
Pearson Chi-Square	23.584[b]	1	.000		
Continuity Correction[a]	22.882	1	.000		
Likelihood Ratio	24.871	1	.000		
Fisher's Exact Test				.000	.000
Linear-by-Linear Association	23.564	1	.000		
N of Valid Cases	1213				

a. Computed only for a 2x2 table

b. 0 cells (.0%) have expected count less than 5. The minimum expected count is 93.37.

Figure 11.4 SPSS output from the χ^2 test of independence.

null hypothesis. This statistic is useful in this circumstance as well. We still define the χ^2 statistic as in equation 11.1, which in these data is equal to

$$\chi^2 = \frac{(60 - 93.369)^2}{93.369} + \frac{(204 - 170.631)^2}{170.631} + \frac{(369 - 335.631)^2}{335.631} + \frac{(580 - 613.369)^2}{613.369} = 23.584$$

The degrees of freedom for this test of independence in a 2×2 crosstabulation is 1 (a general formula for calculating the degrees of freedom will be introduced later). Appendix C shows that the critical value of χ^2 with 1 df is 3.84 for $\alpha = .05$. The obtained χ^2 of 23.584 is larger than the critical value, so the null hypothesis is rejected in favor of the alternative hypothesis at $p < .05$. Indeed, the obtained χ^2 is larger than the critical χ^2 for $\alpha = .001$, so $p < .001$. The type of advertisement and the use of a fear appeal are not independent. Symbolically, $\pi_{fear|image} \neq \pi_{fear|issue}$. The substantive conclusion my between written as such:

In political advertisements run by candidates for U.S. President, fear appeals were more common in issue-oriented ads (26%) than in image-oriented ads (14%), $\chi^2(1) = 23.584, p < .001$.

The SPSS output for this problem can be found in Figure 11.4, panel B. As can be seen, the SPSS output is consistent with all our hand computations, and the more precise p-value is $p < .0005$.

The χ^2 statistic quantifies discrepancy between the observed and expected frequencies without regards to direction of the discrepancy. As a result, the p-value from the χ^2 test of independence is inherently two-tailed. If you make a prediction as to the direction of the difference between the proportions in advance of seeing the data and the results are in the direction predicted, you can justifiably cut the two-tailed p-value in half to derive the one-tailed p-value. However, this is sensible only in a 2×2 table. In crosstabulations of larger dimensions, a hypothesis about the association cannot be framed and tested directionally because of the way that the χ^2 statistic quantifies departure from independence.

SPSS also provides a number of other statistics in its output for testing association in a crosstabulation, only one of which we discuss here. The p-value listed next to "Fisher's exact test" in the SPSS output is the p-value for a randomization test, which is conceptually the same as the randomization test described in Chapter 10. This p-value for Fisher's exact test is the proportion of possible crosstabulations that you can construct with 264 fear appeal ads, 949 no fear appeal ads, 429 image-oriented ads, and 784 issue ads that have a χ^2 value equal to or greater than the obtained χ^2 value of 23.584. This p-value does not presume random sampling from a population of advertisements as the mathematics underlying the generation and use of the χ^2 distribution for this problem does. It is often interpreted as a test of *random association* in a crosstabulation table, meaning that it tests the null hypothesis that the ad type and whether or not a fear appeal is used are just randomly paired in the data. With large samples, the p-value for Fisher's exact test will be very similar to the p-value for the χ^2 statistic. With small samples, the χ^2 distribution may not accurately describe the distribution of χ^2 when the null hypothesis is true, so if the sample size is small, Fisher's exact test should be used instead. The similarity in their p-values with larger samples justifies the use of the χ^2 statistic even in the absence of random sampling, although when there is no random sampling, the researcher has no grounds for population inference.

11.2.2 Quantifying Strength of Association in a 2×2 Table

The χ^2 test of independence only tells us that the two variables are related. It tells us nothing about the strength of the association. How to quantifying strength of association in a crosstabulation is controversial. Entire books have been written on the topic, and there exists strong disagreements between very smart people about how to do so. Furthermore, even if we could agree how to best quantify association, there are many different ways of doing so depending on whether one of the variables is construed as a dependent variable or whether one is simply looking to quantifying association without concern for each variable's role in some kind of causal system.

In Chapter 4, I introduced Pearson's coefficient of correlation and its square, the coefficient of determination. Although I introduced these two concepts in the context of quantifying association between quantitative variables, they are useful as measures of association in a 2×2 crosstabulation as well. To calculate Pearson's r in a 2×2

table, pick any two arbitrary numbers to code the two categories of variable X. Do the same for variable Y. For example, we might code issue-oriented ads as $X = 1$, image-oriented ads as $X = 0$, ads with fear appeals as $Y = 0$, and ads without fear appeals as $Y = 1$. So an image-oriented ad with a fear appeal would be coded $X = 0$, $Y = 0$, and so forth. Then calculate Pearson's correlation between X and Y with equation 4.9 or with a computer program. The resulting number is called the "phi" coefficient (pronounced as "fie" or "fee," and denoted symbolically as ϕ). But given that the sign (but not the size) of this coefficient will depend on the arbitrary numbers used to code the categories, the sign of phi is sometimes removed before it is reported as a measure of association. The equation below actually removes the sign for you.

$$|\phi| = \sqrt{\frac{\chi^2}{n}}$$

(11.4)

where χ^2 is the χ^2 statistic quantifying departure from independence in the 2×2 table. In this example,

$$|\phi| = \sqrt{\frac{23.584}{1213}} = 0.139$$

The ϕ coefficient is closely related to a more general measure of association in a crosstabulation known as Cramer's V, described later. In fact, in a 2×2 table, ϕ and V will be the same in absolute value.

Ignoring sign, the coefficient is bound between zero and one, with zero reflecting an absence of association or complete independence, and one reflecting perfect association. The square of ϕ can be interpreted in the same way that the coefficient of determination is interpreted. It quantifies the proportion of variance that the two categorical variables "share." But this interpretation is a bit ambiguous and difficult to make sense of intuitively.

A more intuitively satisfying measure of association in a 2×2 table is the *odds ratio*. An *odds* is much like a probability, except that unlike a probability, an odds is not constrained to be between zero and one. To understand an odds, consider you place your hand into a bag containing 1 blue marble and 3 red marbles and draw out a single marble. Whereas the probability of drawing the blue marble is $1/4 = 0.25$, the *odds* of doing so are $1/3 = 0.33$. Recall from equation 5.1 that the denominator of a probability is all possible events. So there are 4 possible events (because there are four marbles), and only one qualifies as qualifying event. But to calculate odds, you put the number of nonqualifying events in the denominator of equation 5.1:

$$\text{Odds} = \frac{\text{Number of qualifying events}}{\text{Number of nonqualifying events}}$$

(11.5)

Let's use equation 11.5 to generate some odds. Considering the 1,213 presidential advertisements, what is the odds that any randomly selected advertisement from this set of 1,213 is an image-oriented ad? Easy. There are 429 image-oriented ads, and the remaining 784 are issue-oriented ads. So the odds of randomly selecting an image-oriented ad from the set is $(429/784) = 0.547$. Similarly, the odds of randomly selecting an ad with a fear appeal from the set is $(264/949) = 0.278$. When the odds is greater than one, then the event is more likely to occur than not. But when the odds are less than one, then the event is less likely to occur than not. Therefore, when odds = 1, the event is just as likely to occur than not. It should be clear, therefore, that an odds of one translates to a probability of 0.50.

An odds ratio is simply a ratio of odds. Consider this: In these data, the odds that a randomly selected issue-oriented ad contains a fear appeal is $(204/580) = 0.414$. Notice that I am conditioning the computation of this odds on the advertisement being issue-oriented. Thus, 0.414 is a *conditional odds*. And the odds that a randomly selected image-oriented ad contains a fear appeal is $(60/369) = 0.163$. The ratio of these conditional odds is $(0.414/0.163) = 2.540$. So the odds that an ad contains a fear appeal is about two and a half times higher if it is an issue-oriented ad relative to when it is an image-oriented ad.

In the data the odds ratio is 2.540. We don't know what the odds ratio is in the population of all U.S. Presidential campaign advertisements. But if the data are construed as a random sample from a population of all advertisements, this odds ratio of 2.540 can be interpreted as a point estimate of the odds ratio in the population of advertisements. Of course, this point estimate of the odds ratio is subject to random sampling variability. But the χ^2 test of independence allows us to reject the null hypothesis that the population odds ratio is one. Note that an odds ratio of one would occur only if the odds of the event (an ad containing a fear appeal) is the same regardless of whether it is an image or issue-oriented ad. In other words, an odds ratio of one corresponds to complete independence between the two variables. So rejection of the null hypothesis that the variables are independent using the χ^2 test leads necessarily to a rejection of the null hypothesis that the population odds ratio is one.

11.2.3   An Alternative Test: The Z test for Independent Proportions

There is an alternative version of a test of association in a 2×2 table that is sometimes used by communication researchers, but I only briefly describe it here. It is a reasonably valid test if the sample size is large. Just how large the sample must be depends on a number of factors. This approach is much like independent groups t test, in that the test statistic is a quantification of the difference between the two independent proportions expressed in terms of the standard error of the difference. The test statistic is

$$Z = \frac{\hat{\pi}_1 - \hat{\pi}_2}{\sqrt{[\hat{\pi}_1(1 - \hat{\pi}_1)/n_1] + [\hat{\pi}_2(1 - \hat{\pi}_2)/n_2]}}$$

(11.6)

where $\hat{\pi}_1$ is the estimated conditional proportion in group 1, $\hat{\pi}_2$ is the estimated conditional proportion in group 2, and n_1 and n_2 are the sample sizes of the two groups. In this case, group 1 is the group of 429 image-oriented ads, and group 2 is the group of 784 issue-oriented ads, and $\hat{\pi}_1$ and $\hat{\pi}_2$ are the proportion of advertisements with a fear appeal in the image and issue-oriented groups, respectively. Plugging the numbers in,

$$Z = \frac{0.140 - 0.260}{\sqrt{[0.140(1 - 0.140)/429] + [0.260(1 - 0.260)/784]}} = -5.232$$

The p-value for Z is derived from the standard normal distribution in Appendix A. So the p-value is the proportion of the area under the normal distribution more extreme than -5.232 (in either direction for a two-tailed test, or in the predicted direction if the obtained difference is in the direction predicted for a one-tailed test). This is a very small proportion, and certainly far less than 0.05, leading to a rejection of the null hypothesis that the π_1 and π_2 are equal in favor of the alternative that they are different.

Although this test is not directly implemented in many statistical programs, Z can be computed using the independent groups t test available in most statistical packages. The outcome variable should be coded 0 and 1 to represent the two groups. Then execute a t test. Z will be equal to the Welch-Satterthwaite t statistic, which will be printed in most statistical packages labeled as the t statistic that does not assume equal variances. Because the t distribution is nearly indistinguishable from the normal distribution when the sample size is large, the p-value from the Welch-Satterthwaite test will typically be very close to the p-value using the normal distribution.

The denominator of equation 11.6 serves as an estimate of the standard error of the sample difference in proportions. If the sample is derived from random sampling of the population, this standard error can be used to calculate a meaningful $c\%$ confidence interval for the population difference:

$$c\% \text{ CI for } \pi_1 - \pi_2 = (\hat{\pi}_1 - \hat{\pi}_2) \pm t_{(100-c)/2} \sqrt{\frac{\hat{\pi}_1(1 - \hat{\pi}_1)}{n_1} + \frac{\hat{\pi}_2(1 - \hat{\pi}_2)}{n_2}}$$

(11.7)

These computations are too laborious to attempt by hand, so I suggest you use a computer program. As discussed above, we can use the output from the Welch-Satterthwaite t test to derive the Z test results. Most programs will simultaneously print a confidence interval as well. Submitting the data in Table 11.1 to SPSS yields $Z = 5.243$, $p < .0005$ and a 95% confidence interval for $\pi_{\text{fear|issue}} - \pi_{\text{fear|image}}$ of 0.075 to 0.165.

11.2.4   Another Example With a 3×2 Crosstabulation

The 2×2 table is the simplest and smallest possible crosstabulation in which you can test for independence. But the test of independence described previously can be used on a table of any row and column dimensions. The computations do not change at all by changing the number of rows or columns in a table, although the number of required computations increases. Of course, this is of no consequence because a computer will typically be used to do the computations. Consider the 3×2 crosstabulation in Figure 11.5, panel A. These data come from Zhao and Gantz (2003), who coded 435 conversation interruptions observed on prime time television shows broadcast on the major networks between March and July of 2000. Each interruption was coded with respect to the form of interruption (disruptive or cooperative) and the status of the interrupter relative to the person being interrupted. They defined a "disruptive interruption" as one where the interruption served the function of expressing disagreement with or rejection of something the speaker said, disconfirmation of something the speaker said, or to change the topic. A "cooperative interruption" was defined as one that expressed agreement or understanding, requested clarification, or communicated interest. The status of the relationship was defined as "positive" if the person doing the interrupting was of higher social status than the speaker (e.g., a father interrupting his daughter or a boss interrupting a subordinate), "negative" if the interrupter was of lower social status (e.g., a daughter interrupting her mother), or "neutral" if the interactants were, in the situation being presented, of equal status.

As can be seen in Figure 11.5, panel A, the majority of the interruptions were classified as disruptive (329 out of $435 = 75.6\%$ or 0.756 expressed as a proportion). And a slight majority of the interruptions occurred between conversational partners of neutral status (241 of $435 = 55.4\%$ or 0.554 in terms of a proportion). None of this is particularly relevant to the researchers' objective, however. They hypothesized that the form of the interruption would depend on the status of the interrupter relative to the speaker. The null and alternative hypotheses are

H_0: form of interruption and status of the interrupter are independent.
H_a: form of interruption and status of the interrupter are dependent.

But because one of the variables has only two possible categories, it is possible to articulate the null hypothesis in terms of population proportions. So the null and alternative hypotheses can be framed equivalently as

$H_0 : \pi_{\text{disruptive|positive}} = \pi_{\text{disruptive|neutral}} = \pi_{\text{disruptive|negative}}$
$H_a :$ at least two of these proportions are different

In the 435 interruptions coded in the sample, $\pi_{\text{disruptive|positive}} = 0.834$ (121 out of 145), $\pi_{\text{disruptive|neutral}} = 0.701$ (169 out of 241), $\pi_{\text{disruptive|negative}} = 0.796$ (39 out of 49). So it appears from these data that disruptive interruptions are less likely when the interaction partners are of neutral (equal) status. But this is just a sample—arguably a reasonably random one of interruptions that occur on prime time sitcoms. To test whether the form of interruption and the status of the interrupter are independent in the population (of prime time sitcoms broadcast on the major networks), we need to determine the probability of getting sample proportions as different from each other as the ones obtained here. To do so, we quantify discrepancy from independence using the χ^2 statistic. From equation 11.3 and assuming independence, the expected frequency for disruptive interruptions from a positive status interrupter is $329(145)/435 = 109.667$, and the expected frequency for cooperative interruptions is $106(145)/435 = 35.333$. The expected frequencies for the remaining cells assuming independence can be found in Figure 11.5, panel A. The discrepancy between the observed and expected frequencies assuming the null hypothesis of independence is true is quantified with the χ^2 statistic:

$$\chi^2 = \frac{(121 - 109.667)^2}{109.667} + \frac{(24 - 35.333)^2}{35.333} + \cdots + \frac{(39 - 37.059)^2}{37.059} + \frac{(10 - 11.940)^2}{11.940} = 9.190$$

which exceeds the critical χ^2 of 5.991 for $df = 2$ and $\alpha = .05$ (see Appendix C). The degrees of freedom comes from a formula that applies to a test of independence in any table with r rows and c columns is

$$\boxed{df = (r - 1)(c - 1)}$$

(11.8)

This table has 2 rows and 3 columns, so $df = (2-1)(3-1) = 2$. Because the obtained χ^2 exceeds the critical χ^2 for $\alpha = .05$, the null hypothesis of independence can be rejected, $p < .05$. SPSS or another computer program would yield a more precise estimated p-value of .01 (see Figure 11.5). From this test, we can conclude substantively that

Although disruptive interruptions were more common than cooperative interruptions, disruptive interruptions occurred with differing frequency depending on the status of the interrupter, $\chi^2(2) = 9.190$, $p < .05$.

A

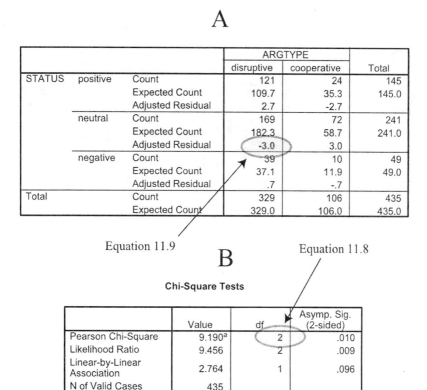

			ARGTYPE		
			disruptive	cooperative	Total
STATUS	positive	Count	121	24	145
		Expected Count	109.7	35.3	145.0
		Adjusted Residual	2.7	-2.7	
	neutral	Count	169	72	241
		Expected Count	182.3	58.7	241.0
		Adjusted Residual	-3.0	3.0	
	negative	Count	39	10	49
		Expected Count	37.1	11.9	49.0
		Adjusted Residual	.7	-.7	
Total		Count	329	106	435
		Expected Count	329.0	106.0	435.0

Equation 11.9

B

Equation 11.8

Chi-Square Tests

	Value	df	Asymp. Sig. (2-sided)
Pearson Chi-Square	9.190[a]	2	.010
Likelihood Ratio	9.456	2	.009
Linear-by-Linear Association	2.764	1	.096
N of Valid Cases	435		

a. 0 cells (.0%) have expected count less than 5. The minimum expected count is 11.94.

Figure 11.5 SPSS output from a χ^2 test of independence between interruption type and status.

Claiming that two variables in a crosstabulation are dependent is akin to claiming that the conditional distribution of one variable varies across the categories of the second variable. In our interpretation of this test we have focused on the comparison of the conditional proportion of disruptive interruptions, conditioning on the status of the interrupter. But an alternative interpretation is also possible. We could also focus the interpretation of the nonindependence by conditioning on the type of interruption. So we could claim that the distribution of the status of the interrupter for disruptive interruptions is that same as the distribution of the status of the interrupter for cooperative interruptions. Observe that among all 329 disruptive interruptions, 37% were from a positive status interrupter, 51% were from a neutral status interrupter, and 12% were from a negative status interrupter. The distribution of the status of the interrupter is different, however, for the cooperative interruptions. Of the 106 cooperative interruptions, 23% were from positive status interrupters, 68% were from neutral status interrupters, and 9% were from negative status interrupters. The claim that status and interruption type are dependent is the same as claiming that these conditional distributions are different from each other to a statistically significant degree.

Probing the Source of Dependency. When this test of independence is applied to a table with dimensions greater than 2×2, rejection of the null hypothesis of independence doesn't tell you that much. We can legitimately claim from this analysis that the form of the interruption is related to the status of the interrupter relative to the speaker, but that is about it. Can we be more specific than this? We can, by computing the *adjusted residual* in each cell. The residual for a cell in the table is the difference between the observed and expected frequency in a cell assuming independence. The adjusted residual standardizes this residual relative to its expected variability if the null hypothesis is true with the following formula:

$$Z_{ij} = \frac{O_{ij} - E_{ij}}{\sqrt{E_{ij}[1 - (F_i/n)][1 - (F_j/n)]}}$$

(11.9)

where Z_{ij} is the adjusted residual for the cell defined by the ith row and j^{th} column of the table, F_i is the number of cases in row i and F_j is the number of cases in column j. For example, the adjusted residual for the positive, disruptive interruptions cell $(i = 1, j = 1)$

$$Z = \frac{121 - 109.667}{\sqrt{109.667[1 - (145/435)][1 - (329/435)]}} = 2.68$$

The adjusted residual has a sampling distribution that is approximately normal. So it is possible to attach a two-tailed p-value to each adjusted residual using the standard normal distribution (Appendix A). This p-value can be used to determine whether the observed frequency is deviating from its expected frequency more than random sampling variability would tend to produce. An adjusted residual greater than 1.96 in absolute value is deemed larger than would be expected by chance (because 1.96 is the critical value for $\alpha = 0.05$ two-tailed). Applying equation 11.9 to all cells in the table, the adjusted residuals are: positive-disruptive, $Z = 2.685$, $p < .01$; positive-cooperative, $Z = -2.685$, $p < .05$; neutral-disruptive, $Z = 2.982$, $p < .01$; neutral-cooperative, $Z = -2.982$, $p < .01$; negative-disruptive, $Z = 0.685$, $p > .05$; negative-cooperative, $Z = -0.685$, $p > .05$. So the dependencies are driven by a larger than expected number of disruptive arguments from a positive status interrupter (and thus a smaller than expected number of cooperative arguments from a positive interrupter) and a smaller than expected number of disruptive arguments from a neutral interrupter (and thus a larger than expected number of cooperative arguments from a neutral interrupter).

An alternative approach is to collapse the larger table into one or more theoretically or practically interesting 2×2 tables. For example, the researchers explicitly hypothesized that disruptive interruptions would be more common in positive status interrupters than in negative status interrupters. If you delete the neutral row from Table 9.3 and test for association in the resulting 2×2 table, $\chi^2(1) = 0.337$, $p > 0.05$. This test disconfirms that hypothesis, as there was no statistically significant relationship between interruption type and status in this reduced table. Doing a similar test deleting the positive row column yields $\chi^2(1) = 1.800$, $p > .05$, and when deleting the negative status row, $\chi^2(1) = 8.601$, $p < .01$. So it seems that the nonindependence in the table is driven by the relatively smaller number of disruptive arguments from neutral status interrupters (70%) relative to positive status interrupters (83%)

11.2.5   Testing for Independence in Larger Tables

I have focused my discussion of testing for independence in a crosstabulation by applying the χ^2 test of independence to relatively small tables—either a 2×2 or a 3×2
table. But this test can be applied to a table with any number of row and columns.
The derivation of the expected frequencies in each cell of the table is the same, as is the
computation of χ^2 and the p-value. Rejection of the null hypothesis of independence
implies that there is some a relationship between the categorical variables—that they
are statistically dependent. For example, suppose you crosstabulated 1000 randomly
selected college-educated people on two variables: their college type (3 categories: 2-
year junior college, 4-year public university, 4-year private university) and the source of
news they select as their "primary" source (6 categories: newspaper, late-night national
network news, early-evening national network news, Internet, local televised news, or
"other"). The result would be a 3×6 crosstabulation. A test of independence would
assess whether there is a relationship between the type of college the person attended
and the person's primary source of news. Rejection of the null hypothesis of independence implies that a person's primary source of news depends on the type of college
the person attended. From equation 11.8, this test would be based on a χ^2 statistic
with $df = (r - 1)(c - 1) = (3 - 1)(6 - 1) = 10$. But as discussed above, rejection of
this null hypothesis would not be very informative, so it would be necessary to probe
the source of the nonindependence using the procedure just described.

11.2.6   Quantifying Association in a Table of Any Size

As noted earlier, there are many ways of quantifying association between categorical
variables, but a treatment of even a small fraction of them would require a highly
technical and lengthy discussion. I introduce only one here, Cramer's V, because it
can be applied to tables of any size and is a *symmetrical measure*, in that it makes no
difference which variable, if either, is construed as the dependent variable in a causal
system linking the two variables together. For a detailed discussion of alternative
measures of association for a crosstabulation, consult Agresti (1990), Everitt (1977),
Goodman and Kruskal (1979), or Liebertrau (1983).

Cramer's V is widely used as a measure of strength of association between categorical variables. It is defined as

$$V = \sqrt{\frac{\chi^2 \, min(r, c)}{n}}$$

$$(11.10)$$

where χ^2 is the value of χ^2 from a test of independence and $min(r, c)$ is the smaller of
two values: the number of rows in the table and the number of columns. For instance,
in a 3×4 table, $min(r, c)$ is 3, and in a 6×4 table, $min(r, c)$ is 4. Using the data from
section 11.2.4, $\chi^2 = 9.190$, $n = 435$, and $min(r, c) = 1$, so

$$V = \sqrt{\frac{9.190(1)}{435}} = 0.145$$

Cramer's V has no simple interpretation, except that the larger V, the stronger the
association. If the association is perfect, $V = 1$, whereas $V = 0$ when the variables are
statistically independent.

11.3   Summary

The χ^2 distribution is one of many sampling distributions used in inferential statistics, and it has many different uses. In this chapter we used the χ^2 statistic to test a variety of different hypotheses involving categorical variables. We first discussed how to test a hypothesis about the distribution of a categorical variable. The goodness of fit test is useful for determining whether several responses or objects are equally distributed across a number of categories or whether they distribute themselves consistent with some kind of expectation. This statistic is also used to assess the discrepancy between a crosstabulation of frequencies and what that crosstabulation should look like if the two categorical variables are statistically independent. Rejection of the null hypothesis of independence leads to the inference that the two categorical variables are statistically related, dependent, or associated. Association between variables is one of the more common statistical forms that a research hypothesis takes, and we will explore additional means of testing for association in several of the upcoming chapters.

CHAPTER

TWELVE

Simple Linear Regression

In several chapters of this book, I have discussed the concepts of independence and association between events and variables. In Chapter 4, I introduced Pearson's coefficient of correlation (r) as a measure of association between two quantitative variables. Chapter 5 included a discussion of the multiplicative law of probability, which can be used to derive the probability of two events both occurring. At that point, I introduced a special form of the multiplicative law for independent events, defining two events as independent if the occurrence of one event has no influence on the likelihood of the other event occurring or that knowledge about whether an event occurred or not provides no new information about the likelihood of the second event occurring. In Chapter 11, I discussed the χ^2 test of independence for categorical variables. In that context, two categorical variables can be said to be independent if the relative frequency distribution of one variable is the same across the categorical levels of the other variable.

If two variables X and Y are associated or correlated, meaning that they are not independent, then this gives you some ability to estimate Y from X or X from Y using information about the relationship between X and Y. But if X and Y are independent, information about a case's measurement on X carries no information about that case's measurement on Y. In that case, there is no point in trying to use information about X to estimate Y. For example, in Chapter 4, we saw that there was a relationship between peoples' perceptions of how important television is to their lives and how frequently they watch television. Recall that students who scored relatively high on the *Television Affinity Scale* reported that they watched relatively more TV than students who scored relatively low on the scale. We quantified this relationship with Pearson's coefficient of correlation and found $r = 0.51$. So we could use information about a person's score on the *Television Affinity Scale* to estimate how much TV he or she watches. But there was little or no association between how frequently students in this sample reported watching TV and how often they reported engaging in fitness activity. The two variables were for the most part linearly independent. The relationship was so close to zero ($r = -0.04$) that it would seem fruitless to try to estimate a person's daily fitness activity from their TV viewing frequency.

The extent to which knowledge of one variable gives you information about the values of some other variable is powerful statistical knowledge. In the next several chapters, I will focus on a statistical technique known as *linear regression* as a means of exploiting that information and using it to test hypotheses. In this chapter, I introduce some of the fundamental principles of linear regression. An understanding of the principles of linear regression is fundamental to an appreciation of the versatility of regression described in later chapters and, indeed, to virtually any kind of analysis involving multiple variables. So we spend considerable time in this chapter focusing on the conceptual basics of linear regression.

Starting with this chapter and continuing throughout the rest of this book, we will rely heavily on a data set from the American National Election Study (NES). The NES is an ongoing telephone and face-to-face survey of the U.S. population conducted every two years just prior to and just following every federal election. It is used widely by political scientists, political communication, and public opinion scholars to test hypotheses and theory and to understand what influences the American electorate. It is a rich data set collected over many years that has inspired hundreds of research studies. As we work through the next several chapters, I will introduce new variables as they become relevant to our purpose. A description of the variables in the data set I am using can be found in Appendix E7 on the CD, along with some SPSS code to extract the data from a data file that can be downloaded from the NES web page (http://www.umich.edu/~nes/). And on the web page for this book (http://www.comm.ohio-state.edu/ahayes/smcs/) you will find the data file resulting from the application of the commands in Appendix E7 on the CD.

Included in the NES study from the 2000 federal election was a series of questions asking participants to recall information about the candidates for president and vice-president of the United States (Al Gore, Joe Lieberman, George W. Bush, and Dick Cheney) as well as other political figures. For example, participants were asked if they knew which state each of the candidates lived in, their religious affiliations, and their political orientation (liberal vs. conservative). They were also asked if they knew each candidate's position on a variety of social issues (e.g., gun control, defense spending). Another set of questions asked the respondent to identify the office of several prominent political figures (e.g., Tony Blair, Janet Reno). A total of 22 such questions were asked, and answers were coded as either correct or incorrect. The total number of questions answered correctly will be used as our operationalization of the respondent's *political knowledge*, with possible scores ranging between 0 and 22. How to best measure political knowledge is a controversial area in political science and political communication, but we will ignore this debate (see, e.g., Delli Carpini & Keeter, 1993; Mondak, 1999; Robinson, Shaver, & Wrightsman, 1999). Whether this is a valid measure of political knowledge is open to argument, but we can at least say that the data are relatively reliable. As discussed in Chapter 6, with 22 indicators of political knowledge we can estimate reliability using Cronbach's α or $KR - 20$ (the equivalent of α for dichotomous indicators). In these data, $\alpha = 0.82$. The average political knowledge score for the 343 respondents was 11.222 with a standard deviation of 4.452.

The source of a person's political knowledge has been and continues to be a hot topic of research in political communication. Where does political knowledge come from? On the surface, the answer would seem obvious. People have little direct access to politicians and the places where political decisions are made, and thus the major source of information about political figures and events must be from the media, such as newspapers and the television. But these forms of media are not the only sources of information about politics. People also discuss politics with each other, and thus some of our political knowledge likely comes from discussions that we have with friends, family and neighbors. The internet has recently added an additional lens through which the happenings of politics can be viewed. Many news organizations have web pages, so people who don't tune into news broadcasts or subscribe to a newspaper can still access a wealth of information about current political events. The Internet has also merged interpersonal communication with electronic communication, and web "blogs" and chat rooms can be potential sources of information about politics.

Decades of research has established the existence of a "knowledge gap" between the relatively poor, uneducated members of society and the relatively wealthy and educated segment (Kwak, 1999; McLeod & Perse, 1994; Tichenor, Donohue, & Olien, 1970; Viswanath & Finnegan, 1996). This knowledge gap applies to many domains of knowledge, but political knowledge is one area that has received substantial research attention. When you look at evidence from research in a number of different disciplines, measures of socioeconomic status such as education tend to be positively correlated with how much factual knowledge people possess about people and events in politics, as well as basic civics knowledge such as how government operates (see, e.g., Delli Carpini & Keeter, 1996; Verba, Schlozman, & Brady, 1995). Many explanations for the tendency for the less educated to be less politically knowledgeable have been offered, such as differential access to media, the tendency of the less educated to be less interested in political affairs, and a weaker aptitude for processing information and learning from media.

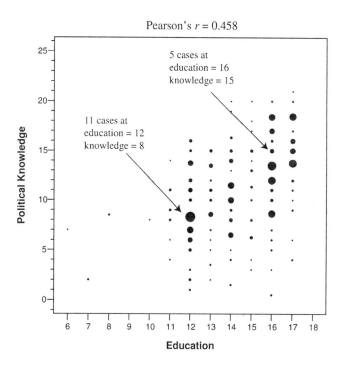

Figure 12.1 A scatterplot depicting the relationship between education and political knowledge.

But you don't have to take the existence of a positive relationship between education and political knowledge on faith. The NES includes a question asking the respondent to indicate the highest grade he or she completed. The maximum possible response coded in the data was 17, indicating someone with more than an undergraduate college education. Among the 343 respondents in the data, the mean number of years of education was 14.286, with a standard deviation of 2.096. Using this as a reasonable (albeit imperfect) measure of education, the correlation between our measure of political knowledge and education is indeed positive in the NES data, Pearson's $r = 0.458$. A graphical depiction of this relationship is depicted in Figure 12.1 in the form of a scatterplot. This scatterplot looks slightly different than the plots I presented in Chapter 4 in that the points in the plot vary in size here. The size of the point in the scatterplot is used to depict the *number* of cases in the data set that reside at that location in the scatterplot. The larger the point, the more cases with that pair of measurements on the two variables. As can be seen, there does appear to be a tendency for people who completed relatively more schooling to have relatively more political knowledge.

We will use this relationship to begin our discussion of *simple linear regression*. A linear regression analysis will seem at first to provide little new information from what a correlation coefficient provides, but as we dig deeper into linear regression, you will see that it also provides additional information that you don't get from Pearson's r.

12.1   The Simple Linear Regression Model

Linear regression is a means of estimating the value of a quantitative outcome variable from another quantitative or dichotomous variable by using information about the relationship between the two. When you conduct a regression analysis, usually you have some reason to think of one of the variables, the Y variable, as the outcome or end product of some kind of process that links a second variable X to Y. Traditionally, the Y variable is called the *outcome*, *criterion*, or *dependent* variable. The X variable, in contrast, is the *predictor* or *independent* variable. In regression analysis, the X variable is used to estimate the outcome variable and is sometimes conceptualized as somehow "influencing" Y, either through some causal process or some other indirect mechanism. However, regression analysis does not itself allow us to assess causality formally because it is simply a means of assessing and describing association mathematically. Regression cannot tell the researcher whether the relationship between the outcome and the predictor is causal. That is a research design issue, not a statistical one. The two variables may not be causally related, but that doesn't mean you can't conduct a regression analysis, because regression analysis is simply a means of assessing correlation and quantifying association.

We will define *simple linear regression* as a procedure for generating a mathematical model estimating the outcome variable Y from a single independent or predictor variable, X. The resulting model is often called a *regression model*, and we use the term *simple* to mean that there is only a single X variable in the model. In Chapter 13, I introduce *multiple linear regression*, where there can be more than one X variable. The goal of simple linear regression is to generate a mathematical model of the relationship between X and Y that "best fits" the data or that produces estimations for Y from X that are as close as possible to the actual Y data. I will frequently use the term "model" to refer to a regression model. Fitting a regression model to a data set is sometimes called *generating a model*, *running a regression*, or *regressing Y on X*.

12.1.1 The Simple Regression Line

You probably can recall from high school mathematics that any straight line can be represented with a mathematical equation. Figure 12.2 displays a number of lines in two-dimensional space, along with their equations. A linear equation is defined by two pieces of information: the *Y-intercept* and the *slope*. The Y-intercept is the value of Y when $X = 0$, and the slope quantifies how much Y changes with each one-unit increase in X. Consider the equation in Figure 12.2 defined as $Y = 3.5 + 0.5X$. The first number in this equation is the Y-intercept. Notice that if you set X to 0 and do the math, then $Y = 3.5$, because $Y = 3.5 + 0.5(0) = 3.5$. And as can be seen in the figure, when $X = 0$, the line crosses the Y axis at 3.5. Also observe that with each increase of one unit in X, Y increases by 0.5. For example, when $X = 3$, the equation gives $Y = 3.5 + 0.5(3) = 5$, and when $X = 4$, $Y = 3.5 + 0.5(4) = 5.5$. So a one unit increase in X results in a change of 0.5 in Y. The change in Y as a function of a one-unit increase in X is called the *slope* of the line. So the slope of this equation, the second number in the formula, is 0.5. Simple regression is all about finding the intercept and slope that best describes the linear relationship between X and Y in the data.

Formally, the simple regression model looks like this:

$$Y_i = a + bX_i + e_i$$

(12.1)

Equation 12.1 might look confusing but it is actually quite simple. It states that case i's Y value (such as a person's political knowledge score) can be defined in terms of three components. The first component, represented as a, is called the *regression constant*. Although it has an important interpretation, in regression analysis, it usually not given much attention. The second component, bX_i, quantifies how the predictor variable X is related to Y mathematically. The value of b is called the the *regression coefficient* or

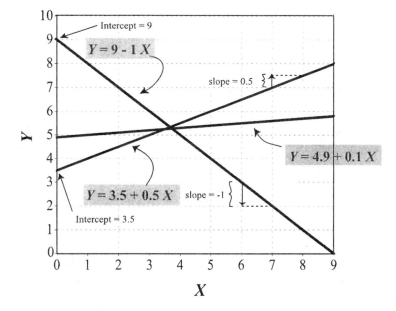

Figure 12.2 Three linear equations and their graphical representations.

regression weight for the predictor variable. It is determined in part by size of the the relationship between X and Y in the data. The value of b tells us how much "weight" should be given to case i's X value in deriving case i's "expected value" of Y. The final component, e_i, is case i's *error*, also called the *residual* or *error in estimation*. This is the part of case i's value on the Y variable that is not accounted for by the relationship between X and Y. It is whatever is left over after generating an estimate of case i's Y value given knowledge of case i's X value and the relationship between X and Y in the data. The i subscripts for Y, X, and e indicate that each case in the data set has its own value of Y, X, and its own residual or error. The absence of a subscript for a and b indicate that these are not values that are unique to each case in the data file. Instead, they are characteristics of the data set as a whole.

The residual component for each case is generally conceptualized as random in size and sign. In other words, it is treated as random "noise" in Y, meaning variation in Y that cannot be attributed to the relationship between X and Y. Whether it actually is totally random and unpredictable is another question. It may be that the residual components are related to some other variable related to Y but not available in the data or available in the data but not included in the regression model. The residuals will play an important role in linear regression, and I'll discuss their important role when it becomes relevant to do so. For now, let's just ignore the residual and rewrite the regression model in the following form:

$$\boxed{E(Y_i) = \hat{Y}_i = a + bX_i}$$

(12.2)

Equations 12.1 and 12.2 are similar, but in equation 12.2 the residual term has been removed and the Y has been replaced with $\hat{Y}$. This $\hat{Y}$ is called the *fitted, estimated, expected, predicted,* or *modeled* value of Y from the regression model, and pronounced "why hat." (Take your pick which term you prefer. I prefer "estimated" and so I'll tend to use that.) This equation illustrates that each value of X in the data has associated with it an estimated Y, with that value being determined by the regression constant (a) and the regression weight (b). This expected value of Y can be thought of as the expected mean Y for a group of cases that all have the same value of X.

Notice from equation 12.2 that two cases that have the same value of X must have the same value of $\hat{Y}$. But equation 12.1 illustrates that they may not have the same value on Y because each case has its own residual component, e_i. The only information contained in equation 12.2 that can be used to distinguish between cases with respect to their values of $\hat{Y}$ are b and their scores on the X variable. Because cases in the data file vary on X, they will differ on $\hat{Y}$ as a function of the size of b. Two cases that differ by one unit on X will differ by b units on $\hat{Y}$, meaning that they are "expected" to differ by b units on Y as well. If b is positive, the case that is one unit higher on X will be b units higher on $\hat{Y}$. If b is negative, the case that is one unit higher on X will be b units lower on $\hat{Y}$.

At the beginning of this chapter, I mentioned that if two variables Y and X are correlated, then you can use information about X to estimate Y. Simple linear regression analysis formalizes this estimation process. How this works is best illustrated by taking a look at some computer output from a simple linear regression analysis estimating a person's political knowledge from their education level. The SPSS output from just such a regression using the NES data can be found in Figure 12.3. Looking at the section of the output labeled "Unstandardized Coefficients," under "B" you can find the regression constant (a) and the regression weight for education (b). From this

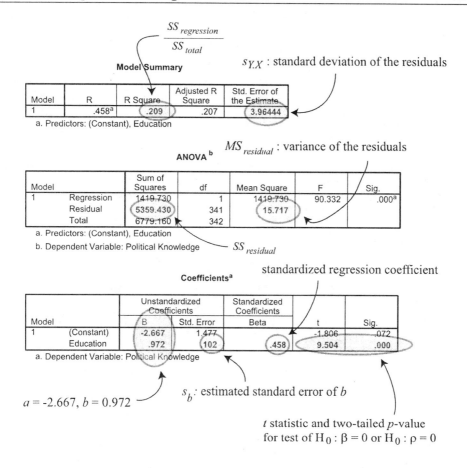

Figure 12.3 SPSS output from a simple linear regression analysis.

output, $a = -2.667$ and $b = 0.972$, so the linear regression equation estimating political knowledge (Y) from education (X) is

$$\hat{Y}_i = -2.667 + 0.972(X_i)$$

The regression coefficient of 0.972 tells us that two people who differ by 1 unit in education are estimated to differ by 0.972 units in political knowledge. The "units" are in terms of the original units of measurement. So a one-unit difference in education corresponds to people who differ by one year in their highest grade completed, and the unit of political knowledge is the number of questions answered correctly on the knowledge test the respondents were given. Because the regression coefficient is positive, we can say that if two people differ by one unit in their education, the person who has one more year of education is estimated to have answered 0.972 *more* political knowledge questions correctly. The regression constant, a, is -2.667 and tells us that for someone who never went to school (i.e., $X = 0$), that person is expected to have answered -2.667 questions correctly. This is obviously silly, and I will discuss later some of the dangers of "extrapolation away from the data" that give rise to such a nonsensical interpretation of the regression constant in this circumstance.

With the regression equation determined, we can now take a close look at how it produces $\hat{Y}$. In Table 12.1 you will find X and Y for several cases in the NES data set.

Table 12.1

Generating $\hat{Y}$ and Components from the Regression Model

i	X_i	Y_i	$\hat{Y}_i$	$Y_i - \hat{Y}_i$	$(Y_i - \hat{Y}_i)^2$	$(\hat{Y}_i - \overline{Y})^2$	$(Y_i - \overline{Y})^2$
1	13	8	9.969	−1.969	3.877	1.570	10.381
2	14	12	10.941	1.059	1.121	0.079	0.605
3	14	11	10.941	0.059	0.003	0.079	0.049
4	16	13	12.885	0.115	0.013	2.766	3.161
5	12	14	8.997	5.003	25.030	4.951	2.778
.	.	.	.	.	.	.	.
.	.	.	.	.	.	.	.
339	17	14	13.857	0.413	0.171	6.943	7.717
340	14	5	10.941	−5.941	35.295	0.079	38.713
341	13	3	9.969	−6.969	48.567	1.570	67.601
342	13	15	9.969	5.031	25.311	1.570	14.273
343	12	10	8.997	1.003	1.006	4.951	1.493

$$SS_{residual} = 5359.430$$
$$SS_{regression} = 1419.730$$
$$SS_{total} = 6779.160$$

Applying the regression equation from above produces the values of $\hat{Y}$ in the fourth column. For example, consider case $i = 4$. Applying the regression equation to case 4's education score $(X = 16)$ yields

$$\hat{Y}_4 = -2.667 + 0.972(16) = 12.885$$

For case 340, a person who reported completed 14 years of education, the regression equation yields

$$\hat{Y}_{340} = -2.667 + 0.972(14) = 10.941$$

So someone with 16 years of education is expected to correctly answer 12.885 of these questions, whereas someone with 14 years is expected to answer only 10.941 of them correctly. These expected values of Y can be construed as the expected mean number of questions answered correctly among a group of people with the same education level. So if we had lots of people who reported having completed 16 years of education, this regression model estimates that the mean political knowledge of this group, operationalized here with this 22 item political knowledge test, would be 12.885.

Just as a line in two-dimensional space (as in Figure 12.2) can be represented with a mathematical equation, an equation of the form $\hat{Y} = a + bX_i$ can be represented visually as a line. The least squares regression line we just derived in the NES data is superimposed over a scatterplot in Figure 12.4. As we discuss next, there is no other line that can be drawn through this scatterplot that better describes the linear relationship between education and political knowledge in these data when a popular criterion for defining "best" is used.

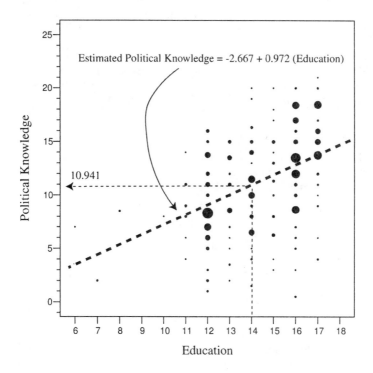

Figure 12.4 A graphical depiction of the linear regression equation.

12.1.2 The Least Squares Criterion

This is all very well and nice, but how does the computer go about deciding on the regression constant and the regression coefficient?[1] Why $a = -2.667$ and $b = 0.972$? Why not $a = 1.033$ and $b = 0.235$? Or $a = 0.453$ and $b = 0.510$? The answer is that the two values chosen by the computer are the "best", in that they best fit the data, or best describe the linear association between education and political knowledge. But this doesn't directly answer the question. What makes these values any better than any other two values that presumably one could use to generate an estimate of political knowledge from a person's education level? The answer is that it depends on how you define "best." There are many different criteria that could be used to judge how well this line fits the data, but the most frequently used method is called the criterion of *least squares*. Linear regression based on the least squares criterion is sometimes referred to as *ordinary least squares regression*, or *OLS regression*. There other ways we could define best other than using the least squares criterion, but we will stick to the least squares criterion in this and subsequent chapters. According to the least squares criterion, the best fitting linear regression equation minimizes the *sum of the squared residuals*. To understand this criterion, let's discuss residuals a bit more.

---

[1] It is possible to derive a and b without the assistance of a computer. The procedure for doing so is described in Box 12.1

Box 12.1: Calculating a and b the Hard Way

Although computers make the computation of the least squares regression line easy, it is possible to generate the regression constant and regression coefficient knowing only the correlation between X and Y, and some basic descriptive statistics about the variables. The regression coefficient is equal to

$$b = r_{XY}\frac{s_Y}{s_X}$$

where r_{XY} is the Pearson correlation between X and Y and s_X and s_Y are the sample standard deviations for X and Y respectively. In the NES data, $r_{XY} = 0.458, s_X = 2.096, s_Y = 4.452$, and so

$$b = 0.458\frac{4.452}{2.096} = 0.972$$

Once b is derived, a is computed as

$$a = \overline{Y} - b(\overline{X})$$

In these data, $\overline{Y} = 11.222$ and $\overline{X} = 14.286$, so

$$a = 11.222 - 0.973(14.286) = -2.664$$

which agrees with computer computation within expected rounding error.

According to equations 12.1 and 12.2, $Y_i = a + bX_i + e_i$ and $E(Y_i) = \hat{Y}_i = a + bX_i$. Substitution of equation 12.2 into equation 12.1 yields

$$\boxed{Y_i = \hat{Y}_i + e_i}$$

$$(12.3)$$

Equation 12.3 says that each case's Y measurement is the sum of the estimated Y from the regression model and that case's residual. Rearranging equation 12.3

$$\boxed{e_i = Y_i - \hat{Y}_i}$$

$$(12.4)$$

which illustrates clearly that the residual is the difference between a case's measurement on Y and what the regression equation estimates that case's Y should be given the linear relationship between X and Y.

Given that $\hat{Y}$ is determined by a and b, it follows that if we changed a and b, $\hat{Y}$ would change for every case in the data, and therefore so too must e_i. So any two values for a and b will generate different values of $\hat{Y}_i$ and e_i for each case. But regardless of which values of a and b are used, $\hat{Y}_i$ is not likely to be exactly equal to Y_i for every case in the data.

Column 5 in Table 12.1 lists the residuals for each case resulting from the application of the linear regression equation $\hat{Y} = -2.667 + 0.972(X)$, and a graphical representation of the residual component of Y can be found in Figure 12.5[2]. A positive residual means that the model underestimates a case's Y measurement, whereas a negative residual

---

[2]To reduce the clutter in Figure 12.5, many of the data points are eliminated from this scatterplot.

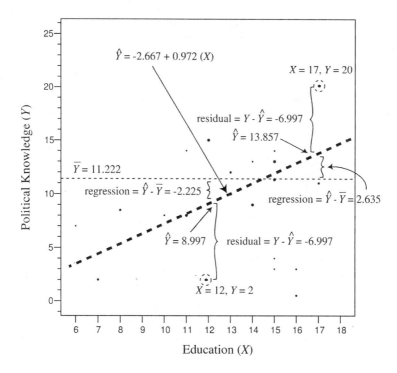

Figure 12.5 The regression and residual components of Y.

means the model overestimates it. Notice that the estimate is pretty close to cases 3 and 4 but pretty far off for cases 5 and 341. The positive residual for case 5 means that the model underestimates that person's political knowledge. Although that case correctly answered 14 questions correctly, the regression model estimates that he or she was expected to have answered 8.997 questions given the relationship between education and political knowledge in the data, a difference of $14 - 8.997 = 5.003$. In contrast, case 341 answered far fewer questions correct than the regression model estimates he or she should have given the relationship between education and political knowledge.

It is largely inevitable that there will be *some* discrepancy between $\hat{Y}_i$ and Y_i. No regression model computed from real data perfectly fits the data. But it should be clear that if a model fits well, the residuals it generates should be close to zero. So a good fitting model yields residuals near zero, and a bad fitting model yield residuals that are very far from zero. The key to finding the best fitting linear model is finding the values of a and b than make the residuals as close to zero as they possibly can be. There are a number of ways that this could be done, but the least squares criterion goes about it by minimizing the *sum of the squared residuals*, $SS_{residual}$, defined mathematically as

$$SS_{residual} = \sum (Y_i - \hat{Y}_i)^2$$

(12.5)

where the summation is over all cases in the data contributing to the regression analysis. In least squares regression, there is only a single, unique set of values of a and b that minimize $SS_{residual}$, and those are the values that a statistical program that does regression using the least squares criterion will produce. Although this might not seem sensible at first, it is if you think about it. If the regression model perfectly fits the data, then all the residuals will be equal to zero, and so $SS_{residual}$ will also be equal to zero. The greater the discrepancy between $\hat{Y}$ and Y across the data set as a whole, the larger $SS_{residual}$ will be. So $SS_{residual}$ can be thought of as a measure of *lack of fit.* The larger $SS_{residual}$ is, the *worse* the regression model fits the data.

But why the sum of the squared residuals? Why not minimize the sum of the residuals without squaring them first, or why not just minimize the average of the residuals? There are two answers to this question. First, the math tends to be easier when the squared residuals are minimized rather than something else. This does not mean that there aren't other sensible measures of best fit. It simply means that the method of least squares has turned out to be very useful and easy to work with mathematically, so it has won the favor of statisticians and therefore researchers. The second answer is that the process of minimizing the sum of the squared residuals at the same time *does* minimize the sum of the unsquared residuals. Indeed, the least squares criterion ensures that the sum of the unsquared residuals is *zero.* But if it is true that the sum of the unsquared residuals is zero, then it must be true that the mean residual is also zero. So the least squares criterion is very sensible. The best fitting regression line is the one that makes the mean residual equal to 0! This is important. *In least squares linear regression, the mean of the residuals will always be zero.*

The squared residuals for some of the cases in the NES data that the least squares regression model produces can be found in Table 12.1, column 6. The sum of these squared residuals is displayed at the bottom of that column. As you can see, when a and b are set to -2.667 and 0.972, respectively, $SS_{residual} = 5359.43$. No other two values of a and b yield a smaller $SS_{residual}$ in these data. Most statistical programs also print the sum of the squared residuals in a section of the regression output (see Figure 12.3).

12.1.3   The Standard Error of Estimation

How far off will the estimations of Y be on average? That is, on average, how much do $\hat{Y}_i$ and Y_i differ? As described above, the mean of the residuals is equal to zero, and this will always be true in regression using the least squares criterion. When talking about average error in estimation, statisticians often ignore the sign of the error. When you ignore the sign, the average difference between $\hat{Y}$ and Y computed across all cases in the analysis is called the *standard error of estimation* or the *standard error of prediction.* This is somewhat of an unfortunate name, given that the term "standard error" is generally used in statistics in reference to a sampling distribution. It might be easier to distinguish between the concepts if you think of the standard error of estimation as the standard "error of estimation" rather than the "standard error" of estimation. Regardless, the standard error of estimation is the standard deviation of the residuals. It is roughly the average amount by which $\hat{Y}_i$ and Y_i differ, ignoring sign. The standard error (often denoted symbolically as $s_{Y.X}$) is defined as

$$s_{Y.X} = \sqrt{\frac{\sum(\hat{Y}_i - Y_i)^2}{df_{residual}}} = \sqrt{\frac{SS_{residual}}{df_{residual}}}$$

(12.6)

where $df_{residual}$ is the *residual degrees of freedom.* In simple regression, the residual degrees of freedom is always equal to two less than the sample size ($n - 2$) and will be displayed on all regression computer outputs. Applying the numbers from the NES data,

$$s_{Y.X} = \sqrt{\frac{5359.430}{343 - 2}} = 3.964$$

This value is also displayed on the SPSS regression output in Figure 12.3. The interpretation is that the average discrepancy between a person's actual political knowledge score in the data (Y) and the amount of political knowledge the model estimates ($\hat{Y}$) for a person given his or her education is 3.964. However, the standard error of estimation it isn't *exactly* an average, in the same way that the standard deviation is not exactly an average, because $SS_{residual}$ is being divided by a number slightly smaller than n.

The standard error of estimation is closely related to another statistic that will be important at various points in this book, the *mean squared residual*, or $MS_{residual}$. The mean squared residual is the *variance* of the residuals and is defined simply as the residual sum of squares divided by the residual degrees of freedom. It is also the square of the standard error of estimation; that is, $MS_{residual} = s_{Y.X}^2$.

In the previous section, I described how the least squares criterion minimizes $SS_{residual}$. If the value of a and b generated using the least squares criterion minimize the sum of the squared residuals, then it must also be true that they minimize the standard error of estimation. No values of a and b would produce a smaller standard error of estimation.

12.1.4 The Standardized Regression Equation

Regression and correlation are interrelated statistical concepts. In this section, I intend to illustrate the intimate connection between correlation and regression by showing that Pearson's coefficient of correlation is the least squares regression weight in a regression model estimating Y from X after Y and X are standardized.

Recall from section 4.6 that a set of measurements is standardized by converting each measurement into deviations from the mean in standard deviation units. The resulting measurements are often called Z-scores. Standardization yields a new variable with a mean of 0 and a standard deviation of 1. Standardization does nothing else to the measurements. The distributions have the same shape, for instance, and Pearson's correlation between two variables that have been standardized remains the same as the correlation between the unstandardized variables. So the correlation between education and political knowledge is $r = 0.458$, regardless of whether the correlation is computed using the original (or "raw") data or the standardized data. Calling the standardized political knowledge variable Z_Y and the standardized education variable Z_X, let's run a regression estimating Z_Y from Z_X. The best fitting least squares regression model is:

$$\hat{Z}_Y = 0 + 0.458(Z_X)$$

Most computer programs that conduct regression analysis will print the regression coefficients from a regression on the standardized variables. For example, in Figure 12.3 you can see that SPSS lists the *standardized regression coefficient* under the label "Standardized Regression Coefficients: Beta." Different programs will label the standardized coefficients differently, and even the same program might change its labeling from version to version.

A linear regression equation generated from standardized predictor and outcome variables is called a *standardized regression equation*, for obvious reasons. Notice that the regression constant here is 0, and that will always be true in a standardized regression equation. So we can drop it from the standardized regression equation and rewrite the standardized regression equation as

$$\hat{Z}_Y = 0.458(Z_X)$$

Observe that standardized regression coefficient, which I will denote as $\tilde{b}$ to distinguish it from the unstandardized regression coefficient, is exactly equal to Pearson's r. So the standardized simple regression equation can be written in either two forms:

$$\boxed{E(Z_Y) = \hat{Z}_Y = \tilde{b}Z_X}$$

(12.7)

or

$$\boxed{E(Z_Y) = \hat{Z}_Y = r_{XY}Z_X}$$

(12.8)

where r_{XY} is the Pearson correlation between X and Y.

Let me briefly digress a bit by talking a little about notation. The symbols that I have been using thus far are not standard in the literature, but looking through the numerous books available on regression analysis as well as the communication journals, it is apparent that there is little consistency in how people symbolically denote standardized and unstandardized regression weights as well as the regression constant. Some people use the Greek letter beta (β) to refer to the unstandardized regression weight and the Greek letter alpha (α) to refer to the regression constant. Others use the Roman letters b and a, as I have. Still others use β to refer to the standardized regression weight. Further confusing things, the standard in statistics is to use Greek letters to refer to population parameters and Roman letters to refer to sample statistics. So the use of β to refer to the sample regression weight (either standardized or unstandardized) goes against this convention. However, communication researchers often use the Greek letter β to refer to sample regression coefficients in their tables and figures and may or may not specify whether these estimates are standardized or unstandardized. I have tried to get around this problem by sticking to this Roman versus Greek convention. So the Roman letter b in this book refers to a regression weight computed in a sample using the unstandardized data, and the Greek letter β will refer to the unstandardized *population* regression weight, something I have not yet introduced. Exhausting all the possibilities, I needed to make up a new symbol for the sample standardized regression weight, which I am denoting here as $\tilde{b}$. Making things even more confusing, computer programs vary in how they label the regression coefficients, depending on whether they are standardized or unstandardized.

Back to business. In section 12.1.1, I defined the regression coefficient b as the expected difference in $\hat{Y}$ between two cases who differ by one unit on X. That same interpretation can be applied to $\tilde{b}$. The standardized regression coefficient is the expected difference in $\hat{Z}_Y$ between two cases who differ by one unit on Z_X. But the predictor and outcome variables are in standardized units now. So two cases who differ by one unit on Z_X differ by one standard deviation on X. The standardized regression equation tells us that two cases who differ by *one standard deviation* on X are estimated to differ by $\tilde{b} = r_{XY}$ units on Z_Y, meaning $\tilde{b} = r_{YX}$ *standard deviations* on Y.

In simple regression, the standardized and unstandardized regression coefficients are related to each other by equations 12.9 and 12.10:

$$b = \tilde{b} \left(\frac{s_Y}{s_X} \right)$$

(12.9)

$$\tilde{b} = b \left(\frac{s_X}{s_Y} \right)$$

(12.10)

Equations 12.9 and 12.10 illustrate that if Y and X are both standardized, then $b = \tilde{b}$ because the standard deviation of a standardized variable is one (i.e., $s_Y = 1$ and $s_X = 1$).

Notice from equations 12.7 and 12.8 that when Z_X equals zero, so does $\hat{Z}_Y$. Remembering that a Z-score of zero corresponds to the mean, we can say that a case that is at the mean of X is expected to be at the mean of Y. So the standardized regression line, if depicted graphically, must pass through the point $Z_X = 0$ and $\hat{Z}_Y = 0$. This is sensible and reflects that fact that someone who is average on a predictor of Y should be about average on Y as well. Furthermore, this is true regardless of the size of the correlation between X and Y and does not depend on the variables being standardized first; someone who is average on X is expected to be average on Y, independent of the magnitude of the relationship between X and Y and regardless of whether the data are represented in standardized or unstandardized form. So in an unstandardized regression equation, the estimate for a case at $X = \overline{X}$ is the mean of the outcome variable, $\overline{Y}$, and the regression line will always pass through the point $\overline{X}$ and $\overline{Y}$.

12.1.5   Variance Explained by a Regression Model

In section 4.7.1 I introduced the square of Pearson's r as the *coefficient of determination*, defined as the proportion of variance in one variable that can be explained by variation in the other. In this I chapter I substantiate this interpretation of r^2.

In a regression model, a regression equation is generated to estimate Y from X using information about how X and Y are related to each other. If X and Y are not related to each other, X can't be used to estimate Y, and our best estimation for Y is $\overline{Y}$. Similarly, if we didn't know a case's X value, we couldn't use it to estimate Y, regardless of whether or not X and Y were related to each other. In such a case, our best guess for Y for any case in the data set is $\overline{Y}$. So in the absence of any information about X or if X and Y are uncorrelated, the best guess for any case's score on Y is always $\overline{Y}$.

If we didn't know a person's education, the best estimate of a person's political knowledge in these data is the mean political knowledge score of 11.222. The mean has this special property, in that it is always the best guess, meaning that over many many guesses, guessing the mean will produce the smallest average error in those guesses. But suppose you did know a person's education. Knowing a person's education, you can use that information to adjust your guess for that person's political knowledge away from the mean. For example, if we knew the person had completed 15 years of education, we would adjust our estimate of political knowledge for that person from 11.222 upward to $\hat{Y} = -2.667 + 0.972(15) = 11.913$. This adjustment is justified on the grounds that there is a relationship between education and political knowledge, a relationship described with the linear regression model. This difference between $\hat{Y}_i$ and $\overline{Y}$ is known as the *regression component* of Y_i and represents how far away from $\overline{Y}$ a case's $\hat{Y}$ falls. A graphical representation of the regression component of Y can be found in Figure 12.5

Earlier I defined the residual component as the amount the actual value of Y differs from what the best fitting linear regression model estimates. So, using simple regression, we can break any individual score on Y into three components, represented with the equation:

$$Y = \text{mean} + \text{regression} + \text{residual}$$

The three components are (a) the mean of Y, which is the same for all cases in the data set, (b) the regression component, defined as the adjustment of the estimation of Y away from $\overline{Y}$ given knowledge of X, and (c) the *residual* component. Doing the math, you will find that the following equation holds:

$$\boxed{Y_i = \overline{Y} + (\hat{Y}_i - \overline{Y}) + (Y_i - \hat{Y}_i)}$$

(12.11)

Let's play around with this equation. First, after subtracting $\overline{Y}$ from both sides, the result is

$$Y_i - \overline{Y} = (\hat{Y}_i - \overline{Y}) + (Y_i - \hat{Y}_i)$$

Now, let's square both sides of the equation. From high school algebra, you get something ugly:

$$(Y_i - \overline{Y})^2 = (\hat{Y}_i - \overline{Y})^2 + 2(\hat{Y}_i - \overline{Y})(Y_i - \hat{Y}_i) + (Y_i - \hat{Y}_i)^2$$

This equation expresses the square of the difference between the actual Y measurement for a case in the data and $\overline{Y}$ as a function of the other components in the regression. If you add these squared differences across all cases in the data file, what you'd find is that this equation holds:

$$\sum(Y_i - \overline{Y})^2 = \sum(\hat{Y}_i - \overline{Y})^2 + 2\sum(\hat{Y}_i - \overline{Y})(Y_i - \hat{Y}_i) + \sum(Y_i - \hat{Y}_i)^2$$

Although not apparent from anything we've discussed thus far, it turns out that in the mathematics of regression $\sum(\hat{Y}_i - \overline{Y})(Y_i - \hat{Y}_i) = 0$. So the equation above reduces to

$$\sum(Y_i - \overline{Y})^2 = \sum(\hat{Y}_i - \overline{Y})^2 + \sum(Y_i - \hat{Y}_i)^2$$

What this equation says is that the sum of the squared deviations between the Y scores and $\overline{Y}$ (called the *total sum of squares*) is equal to the sum of the squared deviations between the estimated scores for Y and the $\overline{Y}$ (called the *regression sum of squares*) plus the sum of the squared deviations between the actual Y scores and the estimated Y scores (the *residual sum of squares*). Symbolically,

$$\boxed{SS_{total} = SS_{regression} + SS_{residual}}$$

(12.12)

The squared total, regression and residual components can be found for some of the cases in the NES data file in Table 12.1, and their sum across all 343 cases in the data file is at the bottom of the table. In these data, $SS_{total} = 6779.16$, $SS_{regression} =$

1419.73, and $SS_{residual} = 5359.43$. These sums of squares are are also displayed in the SPSS output in Figure 12.3. Indeed, observe that in accordance with equation 12.12, $6779.16 = 1419.73 + 5359.43$.

Notice that SS_{total} quantifies variability in Y around $\overline{Y}$. Indeed, observe that it is actually the numerator of the formula for the variance given in Chapter 4 (see equation 4.4). Furthemore, $SS_{residual}$ quantifies variability in Y that cannot be accounted for by the relationship between X and Y. It is the sum of the squared errors and thus represents discrepancy between the actual Y values and what the regression model estimates for Y given knowledge of X. What is left over is the variance in Y that the regression model accounts for—that is attributable to the relationship between X and Y: $SS_{regression}$. If SS_{total} quantifies variance in Y and $SS_{regression}$ quantifies the adjustment made to estimates of Y given the relationship between X and Y in the data, then the proportion of the variance in Y around $\overline{Y}$ that is accounted for by the relationship between X and Y must be the ratio of the regression sum of squares to the total sum of squares. This ratio is known as R^2. Symbolically,

$$R^2 = \frac{SS_{regression}}{SS_{total}}$$

(12.13)

So R^2 is the proportion of variance in Y explained by the regression model. But notice that R^2 is also equal to the coefficient of determination, r_{XY}^2. Using a similar reasoning, you should be able to deduce that the proportion of variance in Y *not* explained by X is equal to $SS_{residual}/SS_{total} = 1 - R^2$.

One logical derivation from this is important. As previously discussed, the least squares criterion minimizes $SS_{residual}$. If the regression constant and regression coefficient are the values that minimize $SS_{residual}$, then it is also true that they must *maximize* $SS_{regression}$ and therefore R^2 because SS_{total} is unaffected by the values of a and b.[3]

12.1.6   More on Residuals

We would hope that if we practiced a sport a lot, we'd improve. Indeed, it is probably safe to say that practice causes improvement. Consider distance running. If we practice running, we can run farther, and if we practice enough, we might even reach near the limit of human capability. Now, entertain this hypothetical situation. Let's take two 30 year-old men of about equal weight and height and ask them to run as far as they can before they simply must stop. Matt has been running long distances fairly regularly for much of his life. Furthermore, Matt is very health conscious, watches what he eats, and he works out regularly. In contrast, Erik hasn't done much running since high school, and he isn't as lean as he used to be. Not surprisingly, Matt runs much farther than Erik when we ask them to compete against each other. From this, we conclude that Matt is a better runner than Erik. In some sense this is true, and this is a perfectly logical and reasonable conclusion. In absolute terms, Matt can run farther. But in some ways this isn't a fair comparison. Matt obviously had a big advantage because he has been practicing running all his life and he is in much better shape than Erik. Would Erik look so bad if we compared him to people who haven't done much running? Perhaps Erik actually can run much farther than people like himself,

---

[3]SS_{total} is a property of Y, not the predictors of Y. In any regression model estimating Y, regardless of which variable or variables are used to estimate Y, SS_{total} remains the same.

while Matt actually doesn't run so well when compared to people like himself—people who have been running all their lives and are in good physical condition? If so, then maybe we can say that Erik is a *better* runner than Matt and that if Erik was given the practice that Matt has had, Erik would actually run a greater distance than Matt.

One of the wonderful things about regression is that it gives us a method for comparing Matt and Erik on equal footing. How? Use the residuals! Remember that residuals are deviations from what would be predicted from knowledge about the relationship between the outcome and the predictor variable. By looking at their residuals, you can compare two people on outcome measure even if they differ on a variable known to be related to that outcome.

Consider this example. In the NES data there are two people with a political knowledge score of 14 (actually, there are many more than 2, but I want to only focus on two of them). One of these respondents, call him Jim, didn't complete high school, having apparently dropped out after 11th grade according to his response. Another of these respondents, call him Bill, not only completed high school but also has some advanced education given he reported having completed 17 years of school. In an absolute sense, Jim and Bill are equal in their political knowledge as measured here. Relatively speaking, however, given that Jim didn't complete high school, it could be argued that Jim is more politically knowledgeable, or at least differs from Bill in some important way that leads him to be more politically knowledgeable than you'd expect him to be. How so? We know that there is a relationship between education and political knowledge such that people who are more educated have greater political knowledge. From the regression equation, given Jim's level of education you'd expect him to have a political knowledge score of only about 8.025 (from $-2.667 + 0.972 \times 11$). So he correctly answered almost 6 questions more than you'd expect from someone with 11 years of education. But Bill is right where a person with at least 17 years of education would be expected to be given the relationship between education and political knowledge in these data (because $E(Y) = -2.667 + 0.927 \times 17 = 13.857$).

So linear regression gives us a new way of conceptualizing deviation and difference—as differences from what would be predicted from knowledge about a variable related to the outcome. Residuals can be thought of as a new measure of Y that has been purified of the influence of X or adjusted for the relationship X and Y. This adjustment of Y given the relationship between X and Y gives us tremendous power as data analysts. For example, suppose that people working in a particular company who do essentially the same job have drastically different salaries, and it happens to be the case that the women seem to be the ones with the lower salaries. If the company was sued by the women for sexual discrimination, its attorney might advance the argument that people who perform equally get paid equally, and the differences in their salaries are attributable to differences in their performance. Indeed, it may be true that there are substantial individual differences in performance quality, and that the company rewards good performance equitably. If performance could be measured, you could generate a regression equation estimating salary from performance. We know that the residuals in this regression will average zero. But what if the women had lower average residuals, meaning that their salaries were lower than the regression model estimated they should be given their performance. In that case, the attorney's argument breaks down, because even after adjusting for differences in performance, the women tend to have lower salaries then the men on average.

An additional property of residuals needs to be emphasized. As discussed above, the residual can be thought of as a new measure of Y purified of its relationship with X.

This interpretation is justified on the grounds that the correlation between the residual components of Y and the predictor variable X is zero. *This will always be true in a simple linear regression using the least squares criterion.* And because $\hat{Y}$ is perfectly correlated with X (because it is simply a linear transformation of X), it follows that the residual component of Y is uncorrelated with $\hat{Y}$ as well.

12.1.7   The Dangers of Extrapolating Away From the Data

Regression can be used to estimate the unknown from the known. With information about the relationship between political knowledge and education, you could estimate a person's political knowledge given information about his or her education, even if that person didn't provide data in this study, and you could do so more accurately than if you guessed the mean. However, there is a danger in this exercise. The minimum and maximum education levels reported in this study are 6 and 17, respectively. What if you wanted to estimate the political knowledge of someone who never went to school at all? According to the regression equation, such a person's estimated political knowledge would be $\hat{Y} = -2.667 + 0.972(0) = -2.667$. In this instance, the regression equation yields a score outside of the bounds of possible values of the political knowledge variable. Because there is no one in the study with such a small amount of education, there is no information upon which to make a sensible estimation because such people never provided us information that could be used in generating the regression equation. And remember that the maximum reported education level was 17. In the measurement scheme, 17 was the quantification for education for anyone who reported *at least* 17 years of education. So a score of 17 collapses information about people who are highly educated into a single measurement, and it makes no distinction between people with 17 years of education and, say, 25 years. So you wouldn't want to use this regression equation to infer that someone with 25 years of education would be estimated to score $-2.667 + 0.972(25) = 21.633$.

My point is that there is risk in applying a regression equation to units not in the sample who fall much outside the minimum and maximum values of the predictor variable in the data used to generate the regression equation. The regression equation is the result of a mindless, computational exercise that a computer engages in. A statistical program just crunches the numbers and spits out the information. It is up to you to use the information the computer gives you in a sensible manner.

12.2   Population Inference in Linear Regression

Thus far I have been describing regression as a descriptive procedure. The linear regression equation is the "best" description of the linear relationship between X and Y, in that in minimizes the sum of the squared deviations between what the model estimates for Y from X and the actual Y measurements. The linear regression equation yields estimates for Y given the relationship between X and Y, and the regression coefficient b quantifies how two cases who differ by one unit on X are expected to differ on Y. But often we want to know more. When the goal of the research is population inference, we want to know whether the relationship observed in the sample accurately reflects something about the population from which the sample was derived. As always when making population inferences, we assume in the discussion that follows the sample was collected randomly from the population. Additional assumptions of the statistical tests described here are outlined in section 12.2.4.

12.2.1   Testing a Hypothesis About the Population Regression Weight

Suppose that there is no relationship between education and political knowledge of U.S. residents, and you knew this to be the case. If so, then knowing how educated a person is provides no information about a person's political knowledge. Therefore, even if you knew a person's education level, you should disregard it when generating an estimate of that person's political knowledge. It should receive no weight in your estimation. In that case, your "intuitive" regression equation should look something like

$$E(Y) = \hat{Y} = a + 0(Education) = a$$

The value of 0 for b in this equation reflects the fact that you are disregarding a person's education when estimating his or her political knowledge score, as you should if there is no relationship between political knowledge and education. Instead, you would consistently estimate the same number for everyone. Recall that in the absence of any other information, the best estimate for any person's political knowledge would be the mean. Assuming you had an estimate of the population mean, then your intuitive regression equation would set a to $\overline{Y}$ and so

$$\hat{Y} = \overline{Y}$$

But Suppose now that you had the entire population available to you so that you were able to quantify each person's political knowledge and you knew everyone's highest grade completed. If there is no relationship between education and political knowledge in the population, then the least squares regression equation estimating political knowledge from education in the population would be:

$$\hat{Y} = \mu + 0(Education)$$

where μ is the population mean political knowledge as measured here. This population equation can be written generically as

$$\boxed{\hat{Y} = \alpha + \beta(X)}$$

(12.14)

In this example, X = Education, $\alpha = \mu$, and $\beta = 0$ if education and political knowledge are unrelated in the population. Greek letters are used in equation 12.14 because these reflect a regression model using data from the entire population rather than from a sample of that population. Of course, you will could never know the population regression equation relating political knowledge to education except in the rare circumstance in which information about the entire population is available on the variables you are measuring. Instead, you typically have only a sample measured on X and Y and an estimate of α and β, the sample regression constant and regression coefficient, which we have been denoting as a and b.

The population regression coefficient β carries information about the expected difference in political knowledge between two people who differ by one year in education. As discussed above, if there is no relationship between political knowledge and education in the population, then $\beta = 0$. But in a sample, it is unlikely that b, the sample-based estimate of β, will be exactly equal to zero even if $\beta = 0$. Random sampling error will produce discrepancies between b and β regardless of the true value of β.

It is often of substantive interest to ask whether your sample comes from a population where $\beta = 0$, or whether it come from a population where $\beta \neq 0$. There is no way to tell for certain, but you can test the assumption that $\beta = 0$ with a hypothesis test using what you know about b. Rejection of the null hypothesis that $\beta = 0$ implies that $\beta \neq 0$ and, by extension, that there is some nonzero relationship between political knowledge and education in the population sampled. That is, if you can conclude that $\beta \neq 0$ then you can conclude that there is linear relationship between X and Y.

Like any sample statistic, b has a sampling distribution, reflecting the distribution of possible values of b when taking a random sample of size n from a population in which the population regression weight is β. Using information about b as well as how much b is expected to differ from β as a result of random sampling error, we can test any desired hypothesis about the size of β in the population.

When testing a hypothesis about the value of β, we follow all the same steps outlined in previous chapters. First, we quantify the effect of interest. Second, we specify the null and alternative hypotheses. Third, we convert the effect to a statistic with a known sampling distribution. Next, we compute the probability of getting an obtained result as discrepant or more discrepant from the null hypothesis as the one obtained. Fifth, we make a decision about the null hypothesis based on this probability. Finally, we translate the result of the hypothesis testing procedure into a substantive conclusion.

The first step is done already. In our sample, b is the quantification of the relationship between education and political knowledge. In the sample of 343 people, $b = 0.972$. The relationship is positive, reflecting the fact that people with relatively more education are estimated to have relatively more political knowledge.

We will set up the hypothesis test nondirectionally by asking whether there is a relationship between education and political knowledge. As discussed above, if there is no such relationship, this implies that in the population, the regression weight for education is zero. The alternative would be its logical complement: that the population regression weight is not zero. Symbolically, the statistical null and alternative hypotheses are

$$H_0 : \beta = 0$$
$$H_a : \beta \neq 0$$

The next step is to convert the obtained result to a statistic with a known sampling distribution. If the assumptions of linear regression are met (discussed in section 12.2.4), the standard approach is to convert b into a t statistic by dividing b by an estimate of the standard error of b:

$$t = \frac{b - \beta_0}{s_b}$$

(12.15)

where β_0 is the null hypothesized value of β and s_b is an estimate of the standard error of b. The standard error of b quantifies how much, on average, b is expected to deviate from β when taking a random sample of size n from the population and estimating the simple linear regression model.[4] If the assumptions of OLS regression are met, the standard error can be estimated as

$$s_b = \sqrt{\frac{s_Y^2(1 - r_{XY}^2)}{(n-2)(s_X^2)}}$$

(12.16)

where s_X^2 and s_Y^2 are the variances of X and Y respectively, and r_{XY}^2 is the squared correlation between X and Y. From the data, $s_X^2 = 4.392, s_Y^2 = 19.822$, and $r_{XY}^2 = 0.458$. Plugging the numbers in,

$$s_b = \sqrt{\frac{(19.822)(1 - 0.458^2)}{341(4.392)}} = 0.102$$

which using equation 12.15 produces a t statistic of

$$t = \frac{0.972 - 0}{0.102} = 9.529$$

Although this looks computationally tedious, these computations are produced in the output generated by most statistics programs capable of conducting linear regression, as in Figure 12.3. The minor difference in the t statistic between the output and our hand computations is attributable to rounding error in hand computations. The computer is more accurate, so we will use $t = 9.504$ as the obtained t statistic.

The next step is to generate a p-value for the obtained result. We want to know the probability of getting a b of 0.972 or more discrepant (in either direction) from zero if we assume the null hypothesis that $\beta = 0$ is true. To do this, we look at whether the obtained t exceeds the critical t for the chosen α-level, just as we have throughout the previous chapters. But t with how many degrees of freedom? In linear regression, the degrees of freedom for the regression weight is $df_{residual}$, the *residual degrees of freedom*. In *simple* linear regression, $df_{residual} = n - 2$, which is $343 - 2 = 341$ here. Using the t table in Appendix B, the critical t is between 1.966 and 1.968. We'll use 1.967. The obtained t is much larger than 1.967 (ignoring sign because the test is being conducted two-tailed), so the null hypothesis is rejected in favor of the alternative. Indeed, the obtained t of 9.504 is larger than the critical t for $\alpha = 0.001$ as well, so we can say that $p < .001$. The null hypothesis that $\beta = 0$ should be rejected in favor of the null hypothesis that $\beta \neq 0$, with the logical leap from the obtained result that β is probably greater than 0. The substantive conclusion is

> From a linear regression estimating political knowledge from the highest grade completed, people with more education had higher political knowledge, $b = 0.972$,
> $t(341) = 9.504, p < .001$.

Of course, we don't have to bother with all this because a good statistical program like SPSS will print the p-value for you. In Figure 12.3, you can see that the p-value is less than .0005, leading you to reject the null hypothesis that $\beta = 0$ at $\alpha = .05$ (or .01, or even .001).

---

[4]Some statistics books use β_0 to refer to the population regression constant. It is easy to get confused when you switch between books that use different symbolic notation

A one-tailed test could be conducted using the same procedure used in previous chapters by first asking whether the result is in the predicted direction, and if so, assessing the probability of getting such an extreme result in that direction. Because of the symmetry in the t distribution, the one-tailed p-value can be computed by cutting the two-tailed p-value in half, but only if the obtained result is in the direction predicted in advance of seeing the data.

12.2.2 Confidence Intervals for β

Rejection of the null hypothesis that $\beta = 0$ leads to the inference that there is a nonzero linear relationship between education and political knowledge. It is possible to be more precise by constructing a confidence interval for β. The procedure for computing a $c\%$ confidence interval for β is the same as a $c\%$ confidence interval for μ described in Chapter 7. A $c\%$ confidence interval for β can be estimated as

$$\boxed{c\% \text{ CI for } \beta = b \pm t_{(100-c)/2}(s_b)}$$

(12.17)

Applying equation 12.17, we can be 95% confident that if the entire population were measured on education and political knowledge as operationalized here, β in the best fitting linear regression model would be $0.972 \pm 1.968(0.102)$, or between 0.771 and 1.173.

12.2.3 Reframing Inference In Terms of the Population Correlation

The regression weight estimating Y from X is only one way of quantifying linear association between two variables. As you know, association can also be measured as the Pearson's correlation between X and Y. Just as we can imagine having the entire population available and computing β, we can imagine having the entire population and quantifying association using Pearson's r, symbolically represented with the Greek letter ρ (rho, pronounced "row"). If the null hypothesis is true that $\beta = 0$, this implies that $\rho = 0$. Rejection of the null hypothesis that $\beta = 0$ implies that $\rho \neq 0$, so no separate inferential procedure is necessary to test the null hypothesis that $\rho = 0$. Nevertheless, relationships are often quantified using Pearson's correlation and hypotheses about relationship are often framed in terms of correlations, so it is worth describing the procedures for making inferences about ρ using information from a sample. In all examples in this section when I use the term "correlation," I am referring to correlation quantified using Pearson's method.

Testing $H_0 : \rho = 0$. By far the most common null hypothesis tested is that the correlation is zero in the population from which the sample was derived. This is an important null hypothesis, because ruling out $\rho = 0$ in the population allows one to claim that the two variables are not independent. As when testing a hypothesis about a mean, the differences between means, or a population regression weight, we have to acknowledge that based on the vagaries of random sampling, the obtained correlation r is unlikely to be exactly equal to the population value of the correlation, ρ. Just by chance, random sampling error in the estimation of ρ from a random sample will produce discrepancies between r and ρ. Just like a sample mean, a sample correlation has a sampling distribution that describes the distribution and relative frequency of certain sample values of r when sampling randomly from the population. The question is, like with all hypothesis testing, whether the obtained value of r in the sample deviates too far from the value of ρ assumed under the null hypothesis. If the probability of the deviation between r and the assumed value of ρ is too small, we reject H_0 in favor of the alternative.

So the research hypothesis of no *linear* association between X and Y corresponds to the following null and alternative hypotheses:

$$H_0 : \rho = 0$$
$$H_a : \rho \neq 0$$

If the null hypothesis is true, then the t distribution can be used to derive the probability of the obtained r or an r more discrepant from the null hypothesis that $\rho = 0$ assuming the null hypothesis is true. The conversion of r into t is accomplished with the following formula:

$$t = \frac{r}{\sqrt{(1 - r_{XY}^2)/(n-2)}}$$

(12.18)

where the denominator in equation 12.18 is the estimated standard error of r. In the NES data, the sample correlation between political knowledge and education is $r_{XY}^2 = 0.458$, and $n = 343$, so

$$t = \frac{0.458}{\sqrt{(1 - 0.458^2)/341}} = 9.514$$

Observe that this is the same t value obtained when testing the null hypothesis that $\beta = 0$. The p-value can be computed directly by computer or indirectly using the critical value approach. The relevant t distribution for generating the critical t is the t distribution with $n - 2$ degrees of freedom. This is the same as $df_{residual}$ from simple linear regression, so the critical t value is the same as when testing the null hypothesis that $\beta = 0$ (within rounding error). Therefore, the p-value is the same, and the same statistical decision is made. Here, $p < .001$ (by computer or critical value), so the null hypothesis is rejected in favor of the alternative. The fact that the sample correlation is positive leads to the inference that the population correlation ρ is larger than zero.[5] Our substantive conclusions is

> People who are relatively more educated tend to be more politically knowl-edgeable, $r(341) = 0.458, p < .001$.

The number in parentheses is the degrees of freedom. The degrees of freedom is not always reported, but there should be sufficient information in the description of a study for you to determine the degrees of freedom if you needed to.

Had we predicted in advance that the correlation would be positive, then it could have been sensible to articulate the null and alternative hypotheses as $H_0 : \rho \leq 0$ and $H_a : \rho > 0$. Because the result is in that predicted direction, we can justifiably cut the two-tailed p-value in half. As always, if the result is significant two-tailed, it is significant one-tailed if the obtained result is in the direction predicted.

Confidence Intervals for ρ. The calculation of a confidence interval for ρ is considerably more complicated than for β. The complication stems from three facts about the sampling distribution or r that are not true about the sampling distribution

---

[5]This procedure cannot be used to test a null hypothesis other than $\rho = 0$. For example, you could not use this method to test the null hypothesis that $\rho = 0.3$ against the alternative that $\rho \neq 0.3$.

of b: (a) correlations are bound between -1 and 1 and therefore so is the sampling distribution of r, (b) the sampling distribution of r is not symmetrical if $\rho \neq 0$, and (c) the standard error of r depends on the value of ρ. These facts complicate the procedure used to calculate a confidence interval for a correlation compared to when generating confidence intervals for other statistics such as a population mean or regression coefficient.[6]

To calculate a confidence interval, the first thing that needs to be done is to convert the sample correlation r to a statistic that has come to be known as *Fisher's Z* using a formula known as *Fisher's r-to-Z transformation*:

$$Z_r = 0.5 \ln \left(\frac{1+r}{1-r} \right)$$

(12.19)

where "ln" is the natural logarithm. Fisher's Z is also called the *hyperbolic arctangent* of r in trigonometry, and some trigonometric calculators will have a button for the hyperbolic arctangent. In these data, the sample correlation between education and political knowledge is 0.458, so

$$Z_r = 0.5 \ln \left(\frac{1 + 0.458}{1 - 0.458} \right) = 0.495$$

If r has a sampling distribution, so too must Z_r. However, unlike the sampling distribution of r, the sampling distribution of Z_r has no upper or lower bound, it is approximately normal (and therefore symmetrical), and it's standard deviation does not depend on the size of ρ. The standard error of Z_r is simply $\sqrt{1/(n-3)}$. So in a sample of size $n = 343$, the standard error of Z_r is $\sqrt{1/340} = 0.054$.

A $c\%$ confidence interval for Z_ρ (the population correlation converted to Fisher's Z) is derived as

$$c\% \text{ CI for } Z_\rho = Z_r \pm Z_{(100-c)/2} \sqrt{\frac{1}{(n-3)}}$$

(12.20)

where $Z_{(100-c)/2}$ is the Z-score that cuts off the upper $(100 - c)/2$ percent of the standard normal distribution from the rest of the distribution (Appendix A). From Appendix A, that Z-score is 1.96 for $c = 95$. So the 95% confidence interval for Z_ρ is $0.495 \pm 1.96(0.054)$, or 0.389 to 0.601.

We are not done yet, however, as this is the 95% confidence interval for Z_ρ, not ρ. To get the confidence interval for ρ, we need to undo Fisher's r-to-Z transformation on the upper and lower bounds of this confidence interval. This reversal is accomplished with the following formula:

$$r = \frac{e^{2Z_r} - 1}{e^{2Z_r} + 1}$$

(12.21)

---

[6]On the CD in Appendix F you will find an SPSS macro that will generate a graphical representation of the sampling distribution of the sample correlation. The macro will generate multiple samples of two variables X and Y from a population with a specified ρ_{XY}, compute r_{XY} in each sample and produce a histogram of these sample correlations. Using this macro, you can vary the sample size as well as the population correlation across runs and see how this affects the shape and variability of the sampling distribution of r_{XY}.

where "e" is the number 2.718. Applying equation 12.21 to the lower and upper bounds of the confidence interval for Z_ρ yields the lower and upper bounds of the confidence interval for ρ:

$$\text{Lower} = \frac{e^{2(0.389)} - 1}{e^{2(0.389)} + 1} = \frac{1.177}{3.177} = 0.370$$

and

$$\text{Upper} = \frac{e^{2(0.601)} - 1}{e^{2(0.601)} + 1} = \frac{2.327}{4.327} = 0.538$$

So we can be 95% confident that the population correlation between political education and political knowledge as operationalized here is between 0.370 and 0.538.

12.2.4   Statistical Assumptions

In previous chapters, I discussed how almost all statistical procedures make assumptions. For statistical tests, we often make assumptions about the population from which the sample was derived. For other procedures such as correlation and regression, we also make assumptions about the nature of the relationship between the predictor and the outcome as well as the errors of estimation resulting from the best-fitting least-squares linear model. Understanding these assumptions is important to knowing how much trust you can have in your analysis and the inferences you attempt to draw from the analysis.

It is important to make a distinction between a *primary* and a *secondary* assumption in regression. Consistent with Darlington's (1990) use of the terms, a primary assumption is one that, if violated, affects the meaning that one can place on the statistics produced by a regression analysis. A secondary assumption is one that if violated does not change the meaning of the statistics but doing so may affect the accuracy of the population inferences that one makes.

Linearity. As Darlington (1990) discusses, linear regression (and therefore the analysis of correlation using Pearson's r as the measure) has only one primary assumption, and that is the assumption of linearity. Violation of linearity jeopardizes the interpretation of the information contained in a regression analysis. Pearson's r quantifies the linear association between X and Y. As discussed in Chapter 4, a violation of linearity jeopardizes the interpretation of a correlation. We desire to interpret the magnitude of the correlation as a measure of the strength of the association. But it only quantifies the strength of the *linear* association. Two variables may be correlated but not linearly. So the size of the correlation can only be interpreted as the strength of the correlation if one is willing to assume that the relationship is linear. Similarly, the simple regression weight b quantifies how two people who differ by one measurement unit X are expected to differ on Y. The person lower on X is expected to differ by b measurement units on Y. Notice that this interpretation is not conditioned on that person's value of X. It is assumed to apply regardless of the value of X. But if the relationship between X and Y is nonlinear, then the expected difference in Y between two people who differ by one measurement unit on X *depends on* the starting value of X. Thus, b has no sensible interpretation if the relationship between X and Y is not linear.

Fortunately there are means of determining whether the assumption of linearity is reasonable. One of the simplest methods is to construct a scatterplot of the relationship between X and Y. Strong nonlinearity is often apparent in a scatterplot. It is sometimes helpful when visually searching for nonlinearity to plot the residuals on the

Y-axis rather than the actual Y values. Such a scatterplot is sometimes called a *detrended scatterplot*. In a detrended scatterplot, nonlinearity will show up as a tendency for residuals with the same sign to be clustered together in the scatterplot. Other forms of nonlinearity will show up as a different pattern of clusterings of the residuals with similar signs.

The major problem with assessing linearity visually is that it is sometimes difficult to tell looking at a scatterplot (whether or not detrended) whether there is a nonlinear relationship. Especially if the relationship is weak, it may be very hard to eyeball a scatterplot and detect a nonlinear relationship. Similarly, our eye (or our expectations) may trick us into seeing nonlinearity that isn't actually present in the data. There are more rigorous ways of testing for nonlinearity statistically, but I save a discussion of that for Chapter 13.

Conditional Normality of the Errors in Estimation. Imagine that you had the entire population available to you and you could generate $\hat{Y}$ for every unit in the population. In that case it is possible to imagine that you could generate the distribution of errors in estimation at each $\hat{Y}$ value. OLS regression assumes that the errors in estimation are normally distributed at each and every value of $\hat{Y}$. Normality of the estimation errors in the population is a secondary but not a primary assumption. If the errors in the estimation of Y from X are not conditionally normally distributed, this has no effect on the interpretation of b (or r), because normality of the residuals is not a primary assumption of linear correlation and regression. But violations of normality of the estimation errors can in some circumstances affect the tests of significance and the width of confidence intervals.

There are various visual ways of testing the plausibility of this assumption by analyzing the residuals in the sample. One visual approach is just to eyeball a histogram or other kind of display of frequencies of the residuals and see if the residuals tend to follow a roughly bell-shaped, normal-like distribution. Although this does not specifically test the assumption, it is unlikely that the assumption is seriously violated if such a histogram of the residuals has a normal-like appearance. A second approach is to construct a *normal-probability plot* available in most good statistical analysis programs. A normal-probability plot graphs the implied Z-score for a case's standardized residual assuming the distribution is normal against its actual Z score in the data. A *standardized residual* is the residual divided by the standard error of estimation. For example, the smallest score in a distribution of 20 scores should have a standardized residual of -1.65, because according to the normal distribution, only 1 in 20 scores would have a Z-score of -1.65 or less. If the distribution of the residuals is normal in the population, then a scatterplot of the implied Z versus the actual Z scores should follow a straight line. The problem with both of these approaches is that they require subjective judgment.

An alternative approach is to conduct a formal test of the normality of the distribution. The null hypothesis is that the distribution of estimation errors is normal, and the alternative hypothesis is that they are nonnormal. Each standardized residual (Z) is converted to the probability that any randomly selected residual would be as large or larger than Z in either direction away from zero if you assume that the residuals are normally distributed in the population. If the standardized residual is called Z in the SPSS file, then the following SPSS command will generate this probability:

```
compute p = 2*(1-CDF.NORMAL(abs(z),0,1)).
```

The resulting variable will contain this probability. For example, a case with a standardized residual of 1.96 or -1.96 would have a p-value of 0.05 because only 5% of the residuals in the population should have a standardized residual larger than 1.96 in absolute value. Once these probabilities are calculated, you then multiple all of these probabilities by the sample size, n. The resulting numbers are called *Bonferronicorrected probabilities* (more on this in Chapter 14). If any of the Bonferroni-corrected probabilities are less than 0.05, then you can reject the null hypothesis that the errors in estimation are normally distributed. An alternative test is the Kolmogorov-Smirnov test. This test is available in SPSS and other good programs but I do not discuss it here. See, for example, Siegel (1956).

It is a common but incorrect belief that ordinary least squares regression assumes that both the outcome and the predictor variables are normally distributed. In fact, least squares regression makes no assumption whatsoever about the distribution of the predictor variable. It makes no difference how the predictor variable is distributed, as inferences are unaffected by the distribution of the predictor. Additionally, the assumption of normality applies to the conditional errors in estimation, not to the predictor variable itself.

Research on the performance of linear regression when the normality assumption is violated suggests that the hypothesis tests for b (and therefore r) are fairly robust to violations of error normality (e.g., Edgell & Noon, 1984; Hayes, 1996). Recall from Chapter 8 that a robust statistical test is one that tends keep Type I error rates at the desired level even when its assumptions are violated. So even if the normality assumption is violated, hypothesis tests on b and r tend not to be substantially affected. However, this is not always true. *Extreme* nonnormality can affect the Type I error rate of the hypothesis tests and the accuracy of confidence intervals. If you are worried that you might be rejecting a null hypothesis that you perhaps shouldn't because of a violation of this assumption, I suggest using a permutation test, as described above and in the next section. A permutation test on b makes no assumption about the shape of the distribution of errors and is valid regardless of the shape of that distribution.

Although error nonnormality tends to have relatively little effect on Type I error rates, extreme nonnormality of the error can reduce the power of hypotheses tests in regression. A transformation of the outcome variable can sometimes reduce the power loss the results from extreme nonnormality of the residuals, but as discussed in Chapter 10, transformations should be used with caution. For some guidance on the use of transformations in regression, see Carroll and Ruppert (1988) and Cohen, Cohen, West, and Aiken (2003, p. 244–246).

Homoscedasticity. Another secondary assumption of regression is that the conditional estimation errors are equally variable for all values of $\hat{Y}$ in the population. This assumption is known by the tongue-twisting name of *homoscedasticity.* A simple eyeball test of the homoscedasticity assumption is to plot the residuals against the predicted values. What you would be looking for is evidence that the residuals tend to be spread around the regression line in the vertical direction by about the same amount for all values of $\hat{Y}$. Evidence of heteroscedasticity would look like a tendency for the errors to be systematically larger (in absolute value) at certain $\hat{Y}$ values. Figure 12.6 depicts a few example forms of heteroscedasticity and how they might appear in a scatterplot of residuals against $\hat{Y}$ values.

The problems with this "eyeball" test of homoscedasticity are its subjectivity and that it is useful only for detecting obvious departures from homoscedasticity. An alternative approach to testing for homoscedasticity is to compute the Pearson correlation between $\hat{Y}$ and the *absolute value* of the residuals in the sample. If the residuals tend to be more variable at large or small values of $\hat{Y}$, then the correlation between Y and the absolute value of the residuals will tend to be positive or negative. A test of the hypothesis that the population correlation between $\hat{Y}$ and the absolute value of the residuals can be used as a formal test of the null hypothesis that the homoscedasticity assumption is met. However, this test cannot detect some kinds of violations of the homoscedasticity assumption. There are several more precise tests of homoscedasticity (e.g., Breusch & Pagan, 1979), but they are computationally complicated and not available in most of the popular statistical programs that communication researchers use. See Fox (1991) for a discussion of some of these tests

The homoscedasticity assumption is much more important than the normality assumption. Research on the performance of the hypotheses tests described above for b (and r) show that violations of the homoscedasticity assumption can have substantial effects on the performance of these tests (e.g., Edgell & Noon, 1984; Hayes, 1996; Kowalski, 1972; Long & Erwin, 2000; Rasmussen, 1989). If the errors in estimation are not equally variable across all values of $\hat{Y}$, then the errors are said to be *heteroscedastic*. Heteroscedasticity can produce p-values for hypothesis tests that are either too small or too large compared to the true p-value. Similarly, heteroscedasticity can affect the width of confidence intervals, producing confidence intervals that are either too wide or too narrow. The problem with heteroscedasticity is that it produces estimates of the standard error of b (or r) that are either too large or too small, depending on the

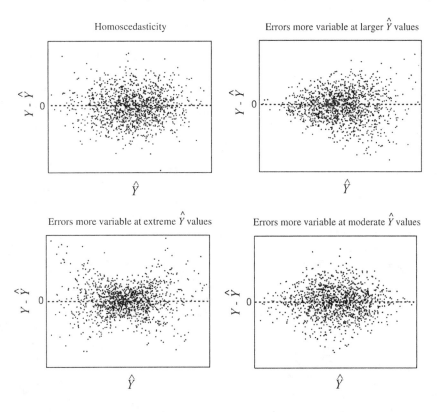

Figure 12.6 Some examples of homoscedasticity and heteroscedasticity.

Run MATRIX procedure:

Criterion Variable
 PKNOW

HC3 Heteroscedasticity-Consistent Regression Results

	B(OLS)	SE(HC3)	t	P>|t|
Constant	-2.6674	1.3613	-1.9594	.0509
EDUC	.9722	.0959	10.1419	.0000

------ END MATRIX -----

Figure 12.7 Output from an SPSS macro for OLS regression using the HC3 standard error estimator.

form of heteroscedasticity. Because the standard error figures directly into the computation of t as well as the computation of the confidence interval for β or ρ, this means that the confidence intervals will be wrong, and the p-values from hypothesis tests poorly estimated, meaning that decisions about the null hypothesis are more likely to be incorrect.

It is nearly impossible to determine if violations of homoscedasticity in your data are likely to adversely affect the accuracy of a specific hypothesis test and confidence interval. Perhaps the simplest approach to dealing with this problem is to conduct hypothesis tests and construct confidence intervals using a *heteroscedasticity-consistent* standard error estimator. There are several approaches to this, all of which are quite complicated mathematically (see Long & Erwin, 2000). The best method is known in the statistics literature as HC3. Unfortunately, few statistical programs have built-in procedures for computing an HC3 standard error estimate for the regression coefficients in an OLS regression model, the exception being STATA. But it is possible to get more widely used programs such as SPSS to conduct hypothesis tests in regression using HC3, and a macro for doing so can be found in Appendix F on the CD. The output from this macro applied to the NES data can be found in Figure 12.7.

The HC3 estimate of the standard error of b in these data is 0.0959, yielding a t statistic of 10.1419. This is actually larger than the t statistic using the ordinary standard error, meaning that the p-value from the use of HC3 is smaller. This test does not assume homoscedasticity, and given that the results are the same as when using the standard error that assumes homoscedasticity (the original output in Figure 12.3), we can safely say that if the homoscedasticity assumption is violated in the original analysis, it isn't drastically affecting the inference.

Because heteroscedasticity can affect the accuracy of the inferences a researcher makes from a regression analysis, I suggest that you routinely check to see whether the use of HC3 produces a different decision about β or a dramatic and substantively different confidence interval. If it does not, then you can rest well knowing that the validity of your statistical inferences are not being compromised by heteroscedasticity. But if the results differ, trust the results from the use of HC3 more.

Independence of Estimation Errors. An additional secondary assumption of regression is the assumption of independence of estimation errors. What this means is that the estimation errors are unrelated to each other. This assumption might be violated in studies where, say, friends are participating together each of whom provides a score on Y, or where participants in a study are allowed to talk to each other during the procedure prior to obtaining the measurement on Y, or when the Y data are the result of measurements of the same unit on multiple occasions (such as over time). This is an important assumption, and violating it can have negative effects on the accuracy of the p-value from traditional hypothesis tests (Hayes, 1996; Kenny & Judd, 1986; Zimmerman, 2002; Zimmerman, Williams, & Zumbo, 1993). This is a topic far too advanced for this book. For guidance on how to test for and deal with various forms of violations of independence, consult Beck (2001), Fox (1991), Griffin & Gonzales (1997), Luke (2004), Kenny, Mannetti, Pierro, Livi, & Kashy (2002), or O'Connor (2004) .

12.3 Inference in Nonrandom Samples: The Permutation Test

In many studies you see in the communication literature, the population model of inference underlying the hypothesis tests we've discussed in this chapter is of questionable appropriateness. These tests assume under the null hypothesis that discrepancy between the obtained result (quantified as either b or r) from the null hypothesis is attributable to random sampling error. But suppose that your data came from a convenience sample, perhaps of students taking a large lecture course at a university rather than from a random sample of U.S. residents. Communication research based on nonrandom samples is common, indeed routine, and researchers usually test hypotheses about relationships between variables using the procedures described thus far even though there has been no random sampling from a specific population. Fortunately, there is an alternative method of deriving a p-value that is not based on the notion that variation between the obtained result and the null hypothesis is driven by random sampling error. Although with nonrandom samples the kinds of generalizations that are possible are more limited, this does not matter nearly as much as it might seem, depending on your research objectives.

In Chapter 10, I introduced the randomization test for comparing two group means, where the p-value for the difference between two means obtained in a sample is calculated by enumerating all the possible differences that random assignment of scores into two groups could create. The obtained mean difference is then evaluated and the p-value computed in reference to this randomization distribution. There is a conceptually similar test that can be used to test the null hypothesis off *random association* between two variables when the relationship in the data is quantified with Pearson's r or the simple regression weight estimating Y from X.

To conduct this test, you create a reference distribution for evaluating the obtained result by calculating all possible values of some statistic θ you are using to quantify the result that you could get if you assume that the X and Y data are just randomly paired together in your sample. Depending on your purpose, you might define θ as Pearson's r or the simple regression weight b. To generate this distribution, you create all possible pairings of X and Y measurements in the data and compute θ in each of these arrangements of the data. The null hypothesis tested is that X and Y are *randomly paired* or *randomly associated*, or that the process linking the X and Y data is a random one, against the alternative hypothesis that they are not randomly paired, or that the process linking X and Y in your data is *systematic*. The p-value is defined as the proportion of values of θ in the distribution of possible values of θ given the data available that are as extreme or more extreme from zero that the obtained outcome. If that p-value is small, you reject the null hypothesis of random pairing and argue that the X and Y variables are not just paired together as a result of a random or "chance" process. Instead, there is some kind of systematic association between X and Y in the data reflecting a systematic (i.e., "nonchance") process.

Consider a simple data set with only 4 cases, with each case measured on an X and Y variable, with the measurements (X,Y) for the 4 cases being (2,4), (4,5), (6,8), and (7,7). You could define your obtained result (θ) as either Pearson's r or the simple regression weight b. It makes no difference which you use, and the outcome of the test is not affected by which of these 2 statistics is used to quantify the association between X and Y in the data. For this example, we'll define θ as the simple regression weight, b. In this data set, the simple regression weight estimating Y from X is 0.746. With 4 observations, it can be shown that there are 24 different ways of pairing the X and Y data together (see Table 12.2), each of which has a simple regression weight corresponding to the relationship between Y and X in that permutation of the measurements. Notice in Table 12.2 that the mean of these 24 possible values of b is zero. So given the data available (the four values of X and the four values of Y), it is sensible to say that if X and Y are just randomly associated, then any of these 24 values of b are equally possible given the data available, and if the process linking X and Y in the data was the result of a random process, then the expected value of b is zero.

To test the null hypothesis of random association, you need a p-value. That p-value can be computed as the proportion of possible simple regression weights given the data available that are more extreme from zero than the obtained b (in either direction for a two-tailed test or in the obtained direction for one-tailed test if the result is in the direction predicted). Looking at Table 12.2, you can see that of the 24 possible values of b, 4 are at least as far away from 0 as the obtained b of 0.746. So the two-tailed p-value is $4/24 = 0.167$. Using $\alpha = 0.05$ as the decision criterion, the null hypothesis of random association cannot be rejected. In other words, the obtained result can be attributed to a random process linking X and Y, rather than a nonrandom or systematic process.

For this *permutation test of random association*, we computed the p-value without relying on the assumption that the observations were randomly selected from a population. However, as discussed in previous chapters, we have no basis for making a population inference when there has been no random sampling from a specific population. So we cannot say anything about a population regression weight (β) from the results of this test when it is applied to a nonrandom sample. Furthermore, a confidence interval would have no meaning. Generalizations away from the obtained data cannot be made on statistical grounds. Instead, you have to ask whether you would have reason to doubt that the results you obtained in your sample would be different if you had a different group of participants, either randomly selected or not. There is often no easy answer to this question as it depends on lot on the topic of investigation and the methodological details of the study. Replication is probably the best means of generalizing when a study result is derived from a nonrandom sample. If the result replicates using a different group of participants that are different in potentially important ways from the original group of participants, and even better when the investigator is someone other than you, then you can be more confident that the finding is generalizable. Generalizability is as much an empirical question as it is a statistical one.

On the surface it might seem like a permutation test of random association is practically infeasible. In this simple example based on a sample of size 4, there are only 24 possible permutations of the data, and so it is fairly easy to derive the permutation distribution of b. The number of possible permutations of the X and Y measurements

Table 12.2

An Example Permutation Distribution of r and b

	Case #	1	2	3	4		
	X (Obtained)	2	4	6	7	r_{XY}	b
Permutation							
1	Y(Obtained)	4	5	8	7	0.906	0.746
2	Y	5	4	8	7	0.741	0.610
3	Y	5	8	4	7	0.082	0.068
4	Y	8	5	4	7	−0.412	−0.339
5	Y	8	4	5	7	−0.247	−0.203
6	Y	4	8	5	7	0.412	0.339
7	Y	4	8	7	5	0.247	0.203
8	Y	8	4	7	5	−0.412	−0.339
9	Y	8	7	4	5	−0.906	−0.746
10	Y	7	8	4	5	−0.741	−0.610
11	Y	7	4	8	5	−0.082	−0.068
12	Y	4	7	8	5	0.412	0.339
13	Y	4	7	5	8	0.659	0.542
14	Y	7	4	5	8	0.165	0.136
15	Y	7	5	4	8	0.000	0.000
16	Y	5	7	4	8	0.329	0.271
17	Y	5	4	7	8	0.823	0.678
18	Y	4	5	7	8	0.988	0.814
19	Y	8	5	7	4	−0.659	−0.542
20	Y	5	8	7	7	−0.165	−0.136
21	Y	5	7	8	4	0.000	0.000
22	Y	7	5	8	4	−0.329	−0.271
23	Y	7	8	5	4	−0.823	−0.678
24	Y	8	7	5	4	−0.988	−0.814
				Mean		0.000	0.000

in a sample of size n is $n!$ (notice that $4! = 4 \times 3 \times 2 \times 1 = 24$). With a sample of size 10, the number of permutation increases dramatically to $10! = 3,628,800$. That is a lot of values of b to compute, but a computer could fairly easily handle it, and there are programs that can conduct a permutation test such as this in a sample of size 10 fairly quickly. But 10 is still a pretty small sample size. Increasing the sample size to 15 results in an explosion in the number of permutations of the data possible to over 1.3 *trillion*. Even a fast computer would take a while to generate all the possible values of b in a sample of only 15. With sample sizes much bigger than that, forget about it. Even today's modern computers would take far too long to compute just one p-value!

Fortunately, it is not necessary to generate all possible permutations to conduct a permutation test. Instead, if the number of possible permutations is large, a computer algorithm can randomly sample from the possible permutations and compute the p-

value using only the permutation distribution generated through the random sampling of the possible values of b. Good accuracy in the estimation of the p-value can be obtained by sampling only 5,000 or so of the possible permutations. When a p-value is based on a random sample of the possible permutations, the test is called an *approximate permutation test*. There are some free programs available on the Internet that can conduct this test (such as NPSTAT and Resampling Statistics). But SPSS and most of the other statistics packages used by communication researchers cannot conduct permutation tests, although the times are changing quickly and it is probably just a matter of time before the major software developers start including permutation routines in their programs. Until then, SPSS users can rely on the macro in Appendix F on the CD that conducts an approximate permutation test.

To illustrate this macro, let's determine whether there is a relationship between how many hours of TV people watch and their body mass index. We'll answer this question using the data from my communication research methods course. Recall that this is a sample of convenience, in that I made no attempt to randomly sample from any particular population when collecting these data. Instead, I simply used students in my classes over the last several years. In these data, the correlation between TV viewing frequency and body mass index (BMI) is $r = 0.156$, and the simple regression weight estimating BMI from TV viewing is $b = 0.506$. Using the methods described in sections 12.2.1 and 12.2.3, the p-value for these results is about 0.0001. But these methods of generating the p-value are based on the assumption that a random sample has been collected from a specific population and that, under a true null hypothesis, discrepancy between the null hypothesis and the obtained result is attributable to just random sampling variation. Clearly that model of chance is hard to justify here. But we can compute a p-value through data permutation using the macro. The output of this macro can be found in Figure 12.8. For this output, I requested that SPSS

```
Run MATRIX procedure:

Variables: DV = bmi IV = tv

Obtained Results
                   r        b
  Obt            .1568    .5059
  se(Obt)        .0405    .1308
  sig(two)       .0001    .0001

Approximate Permutation Test Results
                 prob
Two-tail        .0002
>= Obt          .0002
=< Obt          .9999

Number of Permutations:
  10000

------ END MATRIX -----
```

Figure 12.8 Output from the SPSS permutation test macro.

generate 10,000 random permutations of the X (TV viewing hours) and Y (body mass index) pairs. From this output, the two-tailed permutation test p-value is 0.0002. So the null hypothesis of random association between TV viewing and body mass can be rejected. There seems to be some kind of systematic association between these two variables.

When I introduced the randomization test to compare two groups in Chapter 10, the similarity between the p-value produced from the randomization test and the independent groups t test was used to justify the use of the independent groups t test in nonrandom samples. This justification was based on the fact that the two tests typically yield the same statistical decision, so the independent groups t test could be used to derive an approximation of the p-value that a randomization test would give. The same logic applies when computing a p-value for a correlation coefficient or simple regression weight through data permutation. The use of the t distribution will tend to produce a p-value that is very similar to what a permutation test will produce. So the methods based on the t distribution described in sections 12.2.1 and 12.2.3 give a good approximation of the p-value from a permutation test and will tend to yield the same statistical decision about whether X and Y are associated in the data more than a random process would tend to produce. But without random sampling from a population, population inferences are unjustified, regardless of which method you use.

As computers have gotten faster, tests based on data permutation are being discussed and recommended more and more often. For a discussion of permutation tests in greater detail, see Edgington (1995) and Lunneborg (2000).

12.4   Detecting Influential Cases

Recall from chapter 4 that the mean and the standard deviation suffer from the limitation that they are affected by extreme or unusual cases. One or two especially large or especially small values on the variable being measured can drastically affect both the mean and the standard deviation. I described in Chapter 4 how Pearson's r is just a kind of mean and therefore it is also susceptible to the influence of extreme cases in the data set. And because linear regression has such strong similarities to Pearson's r as a means of describing and testing for association, it makes sense that linear regression is not immune to the influence of extreme cases. When doing any kind of analysis, it is important to be sensitive to the fact that such extreme cases may distort the results of your analysis, sometimes substantially, leading you to incorrect conclusions about the relationship between the variables.

12.4.1   Distance, Leverage, and Influence

A case that substantially affects any of the terms in a regression model (i.e., the constant or the regression weight) has high *influence* on the analysis. Of course, all cases in a data file have some influence on the results, but some cases more than others, and sometimes one or two cases will have substantially more influence than others. Influence can be quantified, but before discussing how to quantify influence, a few other terms need to be introduced. Influence can be thought of as a combination of *leverage* and *distance*. Leverage refers to how unusual a case's score is on the predictor variable. Cases that are high in leverage are unusual on the predictor variable, but a case high in leverage may or may not have high influence. Each case in a regression analysis has a leverage value. Different statistical programs compute leverage slightly differently, so I won't provide a mathematical definition of leverage here. Distance, in contrast, refers to how far a case's Y value deviates from $\hat{Y}$. Distance is much like a residual, but there are many different mathematical definitions of distance so I won't provide one here. Influence is generally a combination of high leverage and high distance. A case that is high in influence will be unusual on the predictor variable and will tend to have a large distance (either positive or negative). However, it is not necessarily true that an influential case will have a large distance because an influential case can affect a regression model so much that it lowers its own distance to a point that its distance does not stand out as unusual.

Figure 12.9 graphically illustrates these concepts. The dotted line in each panel of Figure 12.9 displays the best fitting linear regression line estimating Y from X, and the solid line displays the regression line if the case represented with the hollow square is deleted from the data. Panel A illustrates that a case that is unusual on Y may have very little influence if it is not unusual on X. The case represented with the hollow square is low in leverage (because it is not extreme or unusual on X) but high in distance (because Y is very discrepant from $\hat{Y}$ from a model that excludes that case). Notice that the regression constant and the slope of the regression line are barely affected when this case is included in the regression analysis. Therefore, it is low in influence. Although the correlation is reduced somewhat, it is still statistically different from zero. Panel B illustrates that a case that is unusual on X, and therefore high in leverage, may not be an influential case. The regression line and the correlation are almost identical with and without the case with high leverage in the regression analysis. Panel C shows a case with high leverage, moderate distance, and high influence. The regression equation differs dramatically when that case is included in the regression analysis, and the correlation drops considerably. Panel C also illustrates how an influential case can shrink its own residual (and therefore its distance). The residual from the regression that includes the high leverage case is not especially large because the case pulls the regression line toward it. But its residual from the regression line excluding it is quite substantial.

12.4.2 Influence as Change in the Model When a Case is Excluded

There are many different strategies and statistics that are floating around the statistics literature for detecting cases that might be exerting high influence in a regression analysis. The strategy that I am suggesting here is only one of many possible, but I believe its simplicity makes it easy to understand and apply, so long as you have a good statistics program that can compute the statistics I advocate here.

Above I mentioned that an influential case will typically have high leverage, and including it will substantially alter the regression equation and potentially the tests of significance for terms in the regression model that are of interest to you. One way of screening for cases that are potentially (but not necessarily) influential is to compute the leverage for each case in the analysis. Different statistical programs quantify leverage for each case slightly differently. It is easy to ask SPSS to compute the leverage statistic and add a variable to the data file containing each case's leverage in the analysis. For a simple regression in SPSS, the leverage statistic will range between 0 and 1 and will have a mean of $1/n$. A potentially influential case will have a leverage statistic that is substantially different from the mean. There are many different ways of determining how different is "substantially" different, but usually these high leverage values can be spotted easily with a quick glance through the data file without any kind of fancy

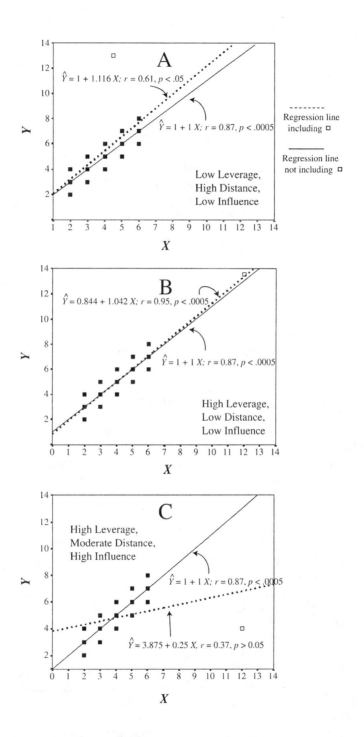

Figure 12.9 Combinations of leverage, distance, and influence.

mathematics or statistical tests. Simply sort the cases from high to low in the data set on the leverage statistic and take a look at the leverage for the cases in the first few rows in the sorted data file. If one or more of the first few leverage statistics look substantially larger than the ones that follow, then those cases are high in leverage. In panels B and C, for instance, the case represented with the hollow square has a leverage value of 0.625. Most of the remaining cases have leverage values in the range of .02 to .07. So this case clearly has substantially higher leverage than the other cases. But as panel B in Figure 12.9 shows, a case high in leverage may not be influential.

One of the most intuitively satisfying measures of influence is the $dfbeta$ statistic. Each case in a regression analysis has as many $debeta$ values as there are parameters being estimated in the regression model. In simple regression there are two parameter estimates, the constant (a) and the regression coefficient (b), so each case has two $dfbeta$ statistics, $dfbeta(a)_i$ and $dfbeta(b)_i$. A $dfbeta$ statistic quantifies how each regression parameter estimate (i.e., a and b) is changed by including case i in the regression analysis. Formally,

$$dfbeta(a)_i = a - a_i$$

$$(12.22)$$

$$dfbeta(b)_i = b - b_i$$

$$(12.23)$$

where a_i and b_i are the regression constant and regression coefficient, respectively, when case i is removed from the analysis. For example, in the data in Panel C of Figure 12.9, the regression model excluding the case represented with the hollow square (call it case $i = 1$) is $Y = 1 + 1(X)$, so $a_1 = 1$ and $b_1 = 1$. When that case included in the analysis, the model is $Y = 3.812 + 0.25(X)$. So for that case, $dfbeta(a)_1 = 3.812 - 1 = 2.812$ and $dfbeta(b)_1 = 0.25 - 1 = -0.75$, meaning that a increases by 2.812 and b decreases by 0.75 when that case is included in the analysis. Influential cases will have one or more values of $dfbeta$ that are very extreme relative to the $dfbeta$ statistics for the other cases. They can be spotted by sorting the data file by the absolute value of the $dfbeta$ statistic you are focusing on from high to low. The extreme $dfbeta$ values will be at the top of the data file after this sorting, and you'd be looking for cases with $dfbeta$ statistics that are clearly extreme relative to nearby cases.

Another way of examining the $dfbeta$ statistics is to display for each case in the data file what a and b would be if that case was excluded. From the discussion above, $a_i = a - dfbeta(a)_i$ and $b_i = b - dfbeta(b)_i$. For cases with low influence, a_i and b_i should be close to a and b, whereas for cases with high influence, a_i and/or b_i will be very different from a and b.

In practice, most researchers would have substantially more interest in $dfbeta(b)$ than in $dfbeta(a)$ because $dfbeta(b)$ quantifies how the regression coefficient is changed, and it is b and its test of significance that is usually of substantive interest to the researcher because it is directly related to the relationship between X and Y observed in the data. Because one or two influential cases can substantially change b, it follows that the presence of those cases might substantially affect the standard error of b and tests of significance for b. So influential cases can not affect both the regression weight and the substantive conclusion about whether X and Y are related to each other.

But what do you do if you find an influential case? The temptation might be to just delete it, but that may not be a good strategy. Before making that decision, it is a good idea to see if the case's influence is attributable to some kind of data entry error. It is all too easy to enter data incorrectly, and sometimes influential cases are the result of simple human error. If data entry error isn't responsible, the decision to delete or not delete has to be made with caution. If the substantive conclusions resulting from the regression analysis are unchanged, even if one or more of the regression coefficients is changed somewhat, then it makes little difference whether or not you include the case. An argument could be made for excluding the case because its presence may yield a misrepresentation of the best regression model. However, potential critics may feel uncomfortable with your decision to exclude the case just because it is strange in some way, and if the results are substantively the same with it included, that argues in favor of keeping the case in the data. If the substantive conclusion is substantially changed (if, for example, a statistically significant effect is attributable only to the presence of one or two influential cases, or if deleting a case makes an effect that was significant become nonsignificant), then you have a real dilemma on your hands. You and only you can tell what best represents the real finding in your research and how that finding should be reported. There is always the option of collecting additional data. An influential case's influence can be weakened if additional data fall into a pattern consistent with the analysis that excludes that case, and that gives you more justification for excluding that case as not representing the people or process under investigation. If you do decide to delete one or a few influential cases, you are obligated to inform the readers of your research about your decision and how you justified the decision.

The measurement of influence and the detection of cases that might be distorting a regression analysis is far more complicated than I have presented here. There are many different approaches that circulate in the statistics literature. A good introductory discussion of this interesting topic can be found in Fox (1991).

12.5 Summary

In this chapter, I introduced the simple linear regression model. The goal of simple linear regression is to develop a mathematical model of the relationship between two variables. There is much overlap between the information contained in a simple linear regression analysis and Pearson's r. For example, the test that $\beta = 0$ is mathematically identical to the test that $\rho = 0$, and the standardized regression coefficient $\tilde{b}$ is equal to r. The main advantage of linear regression analysis over simple correlation is its ability to disentangle two of the primary components of each Y measurement: the part attributable to the relationship between Y and X, and the part that X does not account for. The latter component—the residual—can be used as a new quantification of Y that has been "purified" of the relationship between Y and X. This process of purifying or "partialing out" the influence of one variable on another is very important in multiple regression, the topic of the next chapter.

Multiple Linear Regression

In Chapter 12, we saw that there are individual differences in how much people know about people in politics and the positions political figures hold on social issues. The fact that people who are more educated tend to have more political knowledge raises some interesting questions. Is the relationship due to the role of education in producing a citizenry that is better able to learn information? Is it that more educated people process political information in a deeper way? Are they better able to make connections between events and people that enhances their memorability?

Of course, political communication scholars know that education is only one of many predictors of political knowledge. For instance, people who take a greater interest in politics tend to know more about current political events and people, as do people who watch more television news, subscribe to the newspaper, or browse internet news cites. People also vary in how much they talk about politics with family, friends, workmates, and neighbors, and such discussion perhaps can also serve as a source of political information.

Many of these predictors of political knowledge are interrelated, so it is difficult to know what is really responsible for the relationship between any of these variables and political knowledge. For example, is the relationship between education and political knowledge attributable to the role education plays in helping people to acquire the skills needed to process and make sense of the complexities of the political process, or is it just that educated people tend to watch more televised news, a primary medium for the communication of political events? Or perhaps educated people take more interest in politics and so pay more attention to political information collected through any number of sources.

Although no statistical technique can be used to answer such questions unequivocally, the method discussed in this chapter is tremendously useful at helping the researcher to tease apart, discount, or empirically support some explanations over others. In this chapter, we extend the simple regression model by adding additional predictor variables to a regression model. When more than one variable is used as a predictor in a regression model, the model is known as a *multiple regression model*. Multiple regression is one of the more widely used statistical techniques in communication science. It would be difficult to find an issue of any of the major empirical journals in communication that does not contain a multiple regression analysis within its pages. Multiple regression is used in virtually every area of communication research, including health communication, communication technology, public opinion, interpersonal communication, and mass communication. Knowledge of multiple regression is, without a doubt, fundamental to being able to read and understand the communication literature.

There are at least four common uses of multiple regression in communication research, and you are likely to see each of these uses frequently as you read the communication literature. The first use of multiple regression discussed in this chapter is to assess the contribution of a set of predictor variables in explaining variability in an outcome variable. As we discussed in Chapter 12, the R^2 statistic indexes the proportion of variance in Y explained by variation in X. As such, in simple regression R^2 is just the square of Pearson's r. But this statistic can also be used to assess the contribution of several variables in explaining variation in Y when all those variables are considered simultaneously. For example, how much of the variability in evaluations of a political figure can be explained by individual differences in news exposure, such as reading the newspaper, watching televised news broadcasts, and browsing online news sites? Multiple regression can be used to answer this question.

The second use of multiple regression is to examine the relationship between a predictor variable and the outcome variable after "controlling for" their interrelationships with one or more additional predictor variables. For example, do the discussions we have with people about politics influence our evaluation of a political figure? If such discussions can influence our perceptions of politicians, then you would expect that a person's evaluation of a certain political figure (such as the president of the United States) would be related to how frequently they report discussing politics. If no such relationship exists, it would be hard to argue that discussion plays any role in how political figures are perceived. Perhaps you have developed a means of quantifying a person's evaluation of a political figure on a continuum from negative to positive, and you found the people who discuss politics more frequently perceive a particular politician more positively, or perhaps more negatively. This suggests that discussion might affect people's evaluations of political figures. However, this isn't particularly compelling evidence because there are alternative explanations; namely, the relationship could be *spurious* because both variables might both be affected by some third variable or set of variables. In this chapter we will discuss how to use multiple regression to discount (or support) spuriousness association as an explanation for a relationship between two variables.

Third, multiple regression can be used to assess different models of a process that produces a correlation between two variables. For instance, income and political knowledge tend to be correlated, such that those with higher income tend to know more about current political events and people. What is the process that links income and knowledge? One possibility is that income produces greater news exposure, which in turn leads to greater knowledge. Perhaps people who have more money can afford more sources of media such as newspapers, magazines, cable television, and access to fast internet connections allowing them to browse internet news sites. Such greater exposure to media naturally produces greater knowledge given that the news media is a major source of information about political affairs. People with less income may be less able to afford the diversity of media available, so they would get less exposure to information about public affairs. If such a process were at work, we can say that media exposure *mediates* the relationship between income and knowledge. Multiple regression can be used to assess the consistency of the data with such an explanation.

Fourth, multiple regression can be used to assess how the effect of variable X on Y might vary as a function of some other variable W. For example, maybe news exposure influences evaluations of political candidates only among people who are not interested in politics. People with an interest in politics may process political information deeply and be less influenced by the content of the news media, content which often includes the personal opinions of pundits and other things that are irrelevant to people who follow politics closely. People with less interest in politics may process political information with less effort and be more susceptible to being influenced by the statements that they hear on television about a political candidate made by people who offer personal opinions rather than facts. If such a process were at work, we could say that political interest *moderates* the relationship between media use and the evaluation of political figures. Testing for moderation using multiple regression is discussed in Chapter 16.

13.1   The Multiple Regression Model

The multiple regression model looks similar to the simple regression model, except that the multiple regression model contains more than one predictor variable:

$$Y_i = a + b_1 X_{1i} + b_2 X_{2i} + b_3 X_{3i} + \ldots + b_k X_{ki} + e_i$$

(13.1)

where X_{1i} is case i's measurement on predictor variable X_1, X_{2i} is case i's measurement on predictor variable X_2, and so forth, up through variable X_k, where k is the number of variables being used to estimate Y. So in the multiple regression model, each case's measurement on the outcome variable is defined as the additive sum of a regression constant plus the sum of k predictor variables each weighted by its own regression coefficient. In multiple regression, there are k values of b (one for each predictor variable) called *partial regression weights* or *partial regression coefficients*. Anything left over is the residual (e_i). As in simple regression, the values of X and Y are specific to the individual cases in the analysis and thus differ for each case, whereas the regression constant and the partial regression weights are characteristics of the regression model and do not vary across cases. Also, as in simple regression, the error is thought of as a random in size and sign. It is the part of Y unaccountable for by the predictor variables in the model.

It is convenient to drop the residual term and rewrite equation 13.1 in terms of the estimated or expected Y value:

$$E(Y) = \hat{Y}_i = a + b_1 X_{1i} + b_2 X_{2i} + b_3 X_{3i} + \ldots + b_k X_{ki}$$

(13.2)

where $\hat{Y}_i$ is case i's estimated Y. Just as in simple regression, the multiple regression model assumes that the dependent measure is quantitative in nature and measured at the interval or ratio level, and that the predictor variables are either quantitative and measured at either the pseudo-interval level or higher, or dichotomous. But communication researchers often conduct a multiple regression analysis of an outcome variable that is quantitative but only ordinal or pseudo-interval. In many circumstances, probably not much harm is done in analyzing ordinal outcome data using OLS regression. There are methods that are more appropriate for the regression analysis of ordinal outcome variables that you should eventually familiarize yourself with (see section 13.6.7).

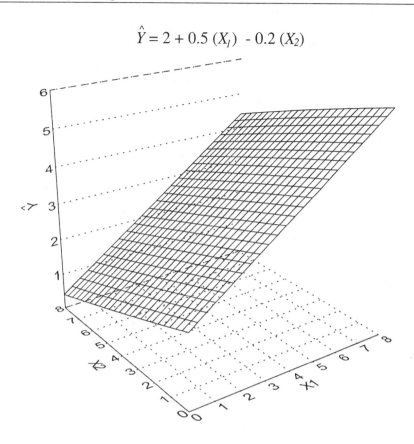

$$\hat{Y} = 2 + 0.5\,(X_1)\ -\ 0.2\,(X_2)$$

Figure 13.1 A three-dimensional regression plane.

In simple regression, the regression equation is a description of the relationship between X and Y that can be characterized visually and described mathematically as a line. In multiple regression, the result is still a regression equation, but rather than being a line, it is best conceptualized as a regression *surface*. For example, consider a multiple regression model of the form $\hat{Y} = 2 + 0.5(X_1) - 0.2(X_2)$. This regression equation will produce a $\hat{Y}$ value as a function of both X_1 and X_2. Figure 13.1 represents this regression equation visually. As can be seen, when there are two predictor variables the regression equation yields a regression plane, with the $\hat{Y}$ from the regression model residing somewhere on this plane in three-dimensional space. It becomes difficult to visually represent or even cognitively conceptualize what the regression surface would look like with more than 2 predictor variables. With k predictor variables, the regression surface requires $k+1$ dimensions in space to represent it visually, something very difficult to imagine much less illustrate when $k > 2$.

The "best fitting" multiple regression model can be found using the same least-squares criterion as is used in simple least squares regression. The mathematics of regression yields a regression model with a regression constant and k partial regression coefficients that minimize the sum of the squared residuals across the entire data set. But when there is more than one predictor variable, there are a number of statistics that a multiple regression analysis produces, all of which relate to different research or statistical questions. For example, the partial regression weights quantify a variable's "unique" relationship with Y. And it is possible to ask if two or more variables, when considered together, enhance the accuracy of the regression model compared to a model that excludes them. This is accomplished by comparing R^2 statistics from different regression models. But we will start first with the simplest application of multiple regression: Quantifying and testing for association between a single dependent variable and two or more predictor variables considered simultaneously.

13.2 Quantifying and Testing for Multivariate Association

Is there a relationship between political knowledge and demographics, such as age, income, education, and sex? In other words can you predict how much a person knows about current events and people in politics from things like their age and how much money they make? And just how much of the between-person variability in political knowledge can be explained by demographics? In this section we will address these questions still relying on the NES data set introduced in Chapter 12. In addition to the highest year of education completed, respondents to the NES survey were also asked the year they were born, their household income in thousands of dollars, and whether they are male or female. From the year a person was born, the person's age can be derived by subtracting his or her year of birth from 2000 (the year the study was conducted). We will code the person's sex dichotomously as either male (1) or female (0). Finally, a question on the survey asked the respondents to indicate their income using a series of categories, such as $10,000 to $20,000, $20,001 to $30,000, etc. In this data set, income is quantified as the midpoint of the income interval selected, in thousands of dollars. For instance, a measurement of 25 represented a reported income of between 20 and 30 thousand dollars.

13.2.1 R^2 as an Index of Multivariate Association

A first stab at answering these questions might be to look at the correlations between these demographic variables and political knowledge. The correlations, quantified with Pearson's r, are displayed in Figure 13.2.

		Political Knowledge	Age	Years of Education	Sex (Male = 1, Female = 0)	Household income (in $1000s)
Political Knowledge	Pearson Correlation	1	.105	.458	.302	.334
	Sig. (2-tailed)	.	.052	.000	.000	.000
	N	343	343	343	343	343
Age	Pearson Correlation	.105	1	-.091	.053	-.059
	Sig. (2-tailed)	.052	.	.092	.326	.280
	N	343	343	343	343	343
Years of Education	Pearson Correlation	.458	-.091	1	.129	.343
	Sig. (2-tailed)	.000	.092	.	.017	.000
	N	343	343	343	343	343
Sex (Male = 1, Female = 0)	Pearson Correlation	.302	.053	.129	1	.143
	Sig. (2-tailed)	.000	.326	.017	.	.008
	N	343	343	343	343	343
Household income (in $1000s)	Pearson Correlation	.334	-.059	.343	.143	1
	Sig. (2-tailed)	.000	.280	.000	.008	.
	N	343	343	343	343	343

Figure 13.2 A matrix of correlations between demographics and political knowledge (from SPSS).

Examining the matrix of correlations, it seems clear that there is a relationship between political knowledge and demographics. This correlation matrix from SPSS displays not only the correlations but also the p-values for the test of the null hypothesis that $\rho = 0$. With the exception of age, all of the correlations are statistically significant at $p < .0005$, meaning that the null hypothesis that the population correlation between that demographic variable and political knowledge is zero can be rejected two-tailed. For age, the p-value doesn't quite get as low as 0.05, but it is pretty close. From these results, we can conclude that people with more political knowledge tend to be more educated and make more money (or at least live in a home with people who, collectively, make more money), and males tend to be more politically knowledge then females (more on the relationship between gender and knowledge in a minute). Depending on how much you insist that the p-value must be no greater than .05 to reject the null hypothesis, you could either conclude no relationship between age and political knowledge or "marginally significant" evidence that the correlation is positive. In section 13.5 we will see that the relationship between age and political knowledge is better described as *curvilinear*, so Pearson's r does not adequately describe this relationship.

Although this answers the first question (Can you predict knowledge from demographics?), it does not answer the second question (How much person-to-person variability in knowledge can be explained by demographics?). One way of answering this second question might have occurred to you. Knowing that the proportion of variance in Y that is explained by X is just the square of Pearson's r, couldn't we square each of the 4 correlations between demographics and knowledge and then add up these squared correlations to calculate how much of the variance in political knowledge is explained by demographics? If you did this, you would find that the proportion of variance explained is $0.011 + 0.210 + 0.091 + 0.112 = 0.424$. Although this strategy seems sensible, 0.424 is too large. Usually, adding up the squared correlations between the outcome variable and each of the predictors will overestimate the proportion of variance in the outcome variable attributable to the *set* of predictor variables. The problem with this strategy is that it fails to take into account that the demographic variables are intercorrelated with each other, and thus you are double counting the contribution of one or more of these demographics by adding up the squared simple correlations. For example, notice that education and income are positively correlated. Those with relatively more education also reported relatively higher household income ($r = 0.343, p < .0005$). So some of the variability in political knowledge attributable to education also can be attributed to income. As a result, the sum of the squared simple correlations will tend to overestimate how much variability is attributable to the set of predictors.

To better conceptualize the interpretational difficulties that intercorrelation between predictors produces, consider the following example. Suppose the CEO at a large organization argues that men are better project managers on the grounds that when men are assigned to projects, they tend to complete the projects faster and under budget compared to when females are assigned to manage a project. However, suppose that in this company, men have higher average salaries. A woman could argue that the manager's sex has nothing to do with performance. Instead, perhaps it is men's greater salary that leads to better performance. That is, men who are paid more appreciate more their value to the company, are more motivated to perform well, and have more to lose if they fail. Perhaps, the argument goes, if women were paid equally to men, they would be equally motivated to perform well and would do so. This is entirely plausible, but without more information it is impossible to know whether it is salary or sex that is driving differences in managerial performance because they are intercorrelated. By the same reasoning, it is difficult to unambiguously attribute variations in political knowledge to income or education when the two are correlated with each other. There is no way to know which variable is driving individual differences in knowledge. But as you will see soon, it turns out multiple regression provides a partial escape from this interpretational ambiguity.

Before discussing the correct procedure for determining the amount of variance in political knowledge that can be explained by demographics, I want to digress briefly by commenting on one of the correlations in Figure 13.2. The correlation between sex (1 = male, 0 = female) and political knowledge is 0.302. The positive sign reflects the fact that females in this samples had a lower average political knowledge score than did males ($M_{males} = 12.622$, $SD = 4.380$, $n = 164$; $M_{females} = 9.939$, $SD = 4.130$, $n = 179$). The females were coded 0 and the males were coded 1 on the sex variable, so the positive correlation makes sense; relatively high scores on sex (i.e., being male) are paired with relatively high scores on the political knowledge variable, and relatively low scores on sex (i.e., being female) are paired with relatively low knowledge scores. Of course, the coding of males as 1 and females as zero is totally arbitrary. If the female code was larger than the male code, then correlation would be negative, but the magnitude of the correlation would be unaffected by this recoding. Indeed, any two arbitrary numbers could be used to code males and females and the strength of the correlation would not change.

Pearson's correlation quantifies how predictable a variable is from the values of another variable. What if you were to estimate a person's political knowledge from whether or not they were male by regressing political knowledge on sex? If you did so, the regression equation would be $\hat{Y} = 9.939 + 2.683(Sex)$. So $b = 2.683$ and it is statistically different from zero, $t(341) = 5.839, p < .0005$. From the significance test, we can reject the null hypothesis that $\beta_{sex} = 0$, and the value of b tells us that that the relationship between gender and political knowledge is positive. From Chapter 12, this should come as no surprise given that the test that $\beta = 0$ is mathematically equivalent to the test that $\rho = 0$. Indeed, if you calculated the t statistic for Pearson's r using equation 12.18, you would find that $t = 5.850$ which is same t statistic that the simple regression gives for b (within rounding error). But also notice something else. The regression weight of 2.683 is exactly equal to the difference between the two means. That is, $M_{male} - M_{female} = 12.622 - 9.939 = 2.683$. And the regression constant is 9.939, which is the mean political knowledge for females. Finally, an independent groups t test using the pooled variance formula (which recall from Chapter 10, I don't advocate, but I have to use here to illustrate a point I am going to make below) yields $t(341) = 5.839, p < .0005$, which is the same t statistic that the regression gave. All these analyses seem to lead to the same conclusion. They must be mathematically related.

I am trying to make three points. My first point is that it is entirely appropriate to calculate the correlation between a dichotomous X and some quantitative outcome variable Y. Second, testing the null hypothesis that the population correlation is zero is equivalent to conducting an independent groups t test using the pooled variance approach discussed in Chapter 10. So rejecting the null hypothesis that $\rho = 0$ when X is dichotomous is equivalent to rejecting the null hypothesis that the two population means are the same. Third, both of these are equivalent to a simple regression predicting the outcome from the dichotomous variable that codes group membership.

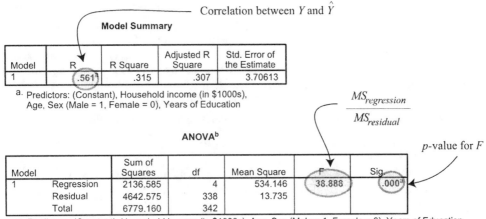

Correlation between Y and $\hat{Y}$

Model Summary

Model	R	R Square	Adjusted R Square	Std. Error of the Estimate
1	.561[a]	.315	.307	3.70613

a. Predictors: (Constant), Household income (in $1000s),
Age, Sex (Male = 1, Female = 0), Years of Education

$\dfrac{MS_{regression}}{MS_{residual}}$

ANOVA[b]

p-value for F

Model		Sum of Squares	df	Mean Square	F	Sig.
1	Regression	2136.585	4	534.146	38.888	.000[a]
	Residual	4642.575	338	13.735		
	Total	6779.160	342			

a. Predictors: (Constant), Household income (in $1000s), Age, Sex (Male = 1, Female = 0), Years of Education
b. Dependent Variable: Political Knowledge

Coefficients[a]

Model		Unstandardized Coefficients		Standardized Coefficients	t	Sig.
		B	Std. Error	Beta		
1	(Constant)	-4.446	1.574		-2.825	.005
	Age	.042	.014	.139	3.061	.002
	Years of Education	.807	.103	.380	7.877	.000
	Sex (Male = 1, Female = 0)	1.952	.407	.219	4.794	.000
	Household income (in $1000s)	.020	.005	.181	3.754	.000

a. Dependent Variable: Political Knowledge

Figure 13.3 SPSS output from a multiple regression estimating political knowledge from age, education, sex, and household income.

When group membership is coded 0 and 1, as it is here, the regression coefficient quantifies the difference between the group means, and the hypothesis test that $\beta = 0$ tests the null hypothesis that the group means are the same. These are all mathematically equivalent approaches and answer the same conceptually equivalent questions. *But this is only true when the categorical predictor variable is dichotomous.* When a predictor variable is categorical but has more than two categories, you cannot sensibly compute the simple correlation between 3 or more group codes and the outcome variable and interpret it as the relationship between category membership and the outcome variable. However, as you will see in the next chapter, it is possible to compute a measure of association between a categorical variable and a quantitative variable by coding the groups in a particular way.

Now back to the original problem. How much of the person-to-person variability in political knowledge can be explained by demographics? To answer this question, we run a multiple regression model estimating political knowledge from the four demographic variables. The output from a multiple regression analysis is displayed in Figure 13.3. From the SPSS output, the best fitting multiple regression model is

$$\hat{Y} = -4.446 + 0.042(Age) + 0.807(Education) + 1.952(Sex) + 0.020(Income)$$

Just as was the case in simple regression, the regression constant and these 4 regression coefficients minimize the sum of the squared residuals. No other combination of coefficients would produce a smaller $SS_{residual}$ than this combination.

With this mathematical description of the relationship between demographics and political knowledge, we could derive how many questions any person with a combination of demographics would be expected to answer correctly. For example, a 45 year old ($Age = 45$) male ($Sex = 1$) with a high school education ($Education = 12$) and a household income of \$55,000 ($Income = 55$) would be expected to answer about

$$\hat{Y} = -4.446 + 0.042(45) + 0.807(12) + 1.952(1) + 0.020(55) = 10.180$$

questions correctly. And a 35 year old ($Age = 35$) woman ($Sex = 0$) with 16 years of education ($Education = 16$) and an income of \$75,000 ($Income = 75$) is estimated to answer about

$$\hat{Y} = -4.446 + .042(35) + 0.807(16) + 1.952(0) + 0.020(75) = 11.436$$

questions correctly.

Imagine applying this regression equation to all 343 cases in the NES data set. This would produce 343 values of $\hat{Y}$ that would be paired with 343 values of Y, the actual number of questions answered correctly. I did this and computed the correlation between the $\hat{Y}$ and Y values. The correlation was 0.561. Notice that this correlation is listed on the output in Figure 13.3 as "R". This is the *multiple coefficient of correlation* or simply the *multiple correlation*. It quantifies the correlation between the estimates the regression model yields for each case and the actual measurement on the outcome variable. This can be interpreted like Pearson's r, meaning that if you square R, you get the proportion of the total *variance* in the outcome variable that the predictors in the model explain. This is listed in the output under "R-square." Just as in simple linear regression, R^2 is the ratio of the regression sum of squares to the total sum of squares:

$$R^2 = \frac{SS_{regression}}{SS_{total}} = \frac{2136.585}{6779.160} = 0.315$$

So we can say that these four demographic variables explain about 31.5% of the person to person variation in political knowledge, when we quantify "variation" as the variance (equation 4.4). Rephrased, the proportion of variance in political knowledge attributable to age, sex, education, and income is 0.315. The proportion remaining unexplained is

$$1 - R^2 = 1 - \frac{SS_{regression}}{SS_{total}} = \frac{SS_{residual}}{SS_{total}} = \frac{4642.575}{6779.160} = 0.685$$

meaning 68.5% of the variance cannot be attributed to these four demographic variables. This 68.5% remaining is either random variability that cannot be explained by anything, or it is systematic variability that can be explained by something other than the 4 demographics in the regression model.

This might seem confusing. But remember from Chapter 12 that SS_{total} quantifies person-to-person variation around $\overline{Y}$ using a particular (and admittedly arbitrary) measure of variation: the sum of the squared difference between Y and $\overline{Y}$. SS_{total} is much like the variance—in fact, it is exactly $n - 1$ times the variance. And $SS_{regression}$ quantifies the part of that total variation around $\overline{Y}$ that is the result of the relationship between the predictors and Y. The ratio of these two quantities gives us the proportion of the total variation in the outcome variable attributable to the relationship between the outcome variable and the set of predictors.

Finally, remember that the least squares method selected the constant and regression coefficients such that $SS_{residual}$ is as small as it possibly can be. But because $SS_{total} = SS_{regression} + SS_{residual}$, it follows that the least squares method also maximizes $SS_{regression}$ and therefore R^2. But given that $\sqrt{R^2} = R$, it follows logically that the least squares criterion must also maximize R, the correlation between $\hat{Y}$ and Y. No other combination of 4 regression coefficients for these 4 predictor variables (plus the regression constant) will produce a larger correlation between $\hat{Y}$ and Y.

13.2.2   Average Estimation Error

The standard error of estimate, also minimized by the least squares criterion, can be computed using equation 12.6 as

$$s_{Y.X} = \sqrt{\frac{SS_{residual}}{df_{residual}}} = \sqrt{\frac{4642.575}{338}} = 3.706$$

meaning that the average discrepancy between Y (the respondent's actual political knowledge score in the data) and $\hat{Y}$ (what the model estimates) is 3.706, ignoring the sign of the error. Observe that the residual degrees of freedom, $df_{residual}$ is no longer $n-2$, as it is in simple regression. In multiple regression, the residual degrees of freedom is $n - k - 1$, where k is the number of predictor variables in the regression model. In this model, $k = 4$ and $n = 343$, so $df_{residual} = 343 - 4 - 1 = 338$.

The squared multiple correlation, R^2, has been defined as the proportion of variance in the outcome variable attributable to the predictor variables in the model, and so $1 - R^2$ is the proportion of variance *not* attributable to the predictor variables. So the variance of the component of the outcome not attributable to the predictor must be

$$(1 - R^2)s_Y^2$$

which is $MS_{residual}$, the variance of the residuals. So the standard error of estimation can also be defined as

$$s_{Y.X} = \sqrt{(1 - R^2)s_Y^2} = \sqrt{MS_{residual}}$$

(13.3)

13.2.3   Population Inferences About Multivariate Association

We are often interested in making population inferences from a sample, something that is possible only when the sample is randomly selected from the population of interest. In this example it was, so it makes some sense to ask whether there is reason to believe that these demographics, as a set, are related to political knowledge in the population from which the sample was derived. The multiple correlation (or its square) quantifies the relationship between these four demographics and political knowledge in this sample. But it is possible that in the population from which the sample was derived there is in fact no relationship between demographics and political knowledge. If there is no such relationship, this is equivalent to saying that the population multiple correlation, R, is zero. Because there is no useful Greek equivalent of the capital letter R, I will use $\mathcal{R}$ to refer to the population multiple correlation. This is also equivalent to saying that in the population, the partial regression weights for the 4 demographics are all zero, meaning that there is no relationship between *any* of these four demographic variables and political knowledge in the population from which the sample was derived. Think about why this is so. We can imagine that there exists a true population regression model that best estimates a person's political knowledge from these four demographic variables in the entire population. If the entire population were available, this regression model would like like this:

$$\hat{Y} = \alpha + \beta_{age}(Age) + \beta_{education}(Education) + \beta_{sex}(Sex) + \beta_{income}(Income)$$

If all four of these demographic variables are unrelated to political knowledge, then that means that the best fitting population regression model should completely disregard information about a person's age, education, sex, and income. This information would be disregarded mathematically if and only if $\beta_{Age} = 0, \beta_{Education} = 0, \beta_{Sex} = 0$, and $\beta_{Income} = 0$. In that case, there would be no relationship between demographics as a set and political knowledge in the population, meaning that $\mathcal{R} = 0$. So testing the hypothesis that $\mathcal{R} = 0$ is equivalent to testing the hypothesis that all four partial regression weights are zero in the population.

Just like any statistic computed in a sample, R has a sampling distribution and therefore so too does R^2. If the null hypothesis is true, it is unlikely that R (and therefore R^2) will be zero. In fact, the probability that R will be zero is 0 because of the way that regression works. In order for R to be exactly zero in a sample, all k partial regresssion weights must be exactly zero, something that is next to impossible. The sampling distribution of R is driven by the fact that each of the k values of b in a multiple regression model will fluctuate around their population values, β, in different samples of size n from the population. But in most studies we usually have only a single sample from the population of interest. A multiple regression analysis based on a different group of 343 respondents would have produced different values of b, which when combined to generate $\hat{Y}$ would produce a different value of R and therefore R^2. Even if all k of the βs are zero in the population, the values of b in the sample are not all going to be exactly zero, and as a result, R is not going to be zero. So R has a sampling distribution that is affected by random sampling error, just as does any descriptive statistic computed on a random sample from a bigger population. And so too does R^2.

To test the hypothesis that there is no relationship between demographics and political knowledge, we need to derive the probability of getting a value of R as large or larger as obtained in a random sample of 343 people if there is no relationship between these 4 demographics and political knowledge in the population. The hypothesis testing steps are the same as before. First, we quantify the effect. That is done: $R = 0.561$. Next, we set up the null and alternative hypotheses. The null hypothesis and alternative hypotheses are

$$H_0 : \mathcal{R} = 0$$
$$H_a : \mathcal{R} > 0$$

or, equivalently,

$$H_0 : \mathcal{R}^2 = 0$$
$$H_a : \mathcal{R}^2 > 0$$

which is also equivalent to

$$H_0 : \beta_{age} = \beta_{education} = \beta_{sex} = \beta_{income} = 0$$
$$H_a : \text{at least one of } \beta_{age}, \beta_{education}, \beta_{sex}, \beta_{income} \text{ is not zero}$$

Next, a p-value needs to be derived. This p-value is derived by first transforming the obtained result to a statistic with a known sampling distribution. That statistic is the F statistic, defined as

$$F = \frac{df_{residual} R^2}{k(1 - R^2)}$$

(13.4)

Notice that F is a function of both the number of cases in the data file (which is closely related to $df_{residual}$), the number of predictors in the regression model (k), and the size of the multiple correlation (R). In these data and using the information in Figure 13.3,

$$F = \frac{338(0.315)}{4(1 - 0.315)} = 38.858$$

Although not apparent from equation 13.4, F is ratio of variance in the regression components of Y to variance in the residual components of Y. The variance of these components are constructed by dividing the sum of squares for each component by their respective degrees of freedom:

$$F = \frac{SS_{regression}/df_{regression}}{SS_{residual}/df_{residual}} = \frac{MS_{regression}}{MS_{residual}}$$

(13.5)

From Figure 13.3, $MS_{regression} = 534.146$ and $MS_{residual} = 13.735$, so $F = 38.889$, which agrees with equation 13.4 within rounding error. As you would expect, all these computations are handled by computer software. This F ratio is listed in the SPSS output in Figure 13.3. Because SPSS is doing the computations with higher precision that we can do by hand, we will consider the F ratio to be 38.888.

When the null hypothesis is true, the these variances will be about the same, meaning that the expected value of F if the null hypothesis is true is about 1 (not exactly 1, but close).[1] But it is unlikely to be 1 in any sample even if the null hypothesis is true. To decide between the null and alternative hypotheses, we need to know the probability of getting such a large F in a sample of size 343 with 4 predictors if the null hypothesis is true.

Before discussing how this is done, let's first talk a bit about the F sampling distribution. The F distribution is like the t distribution because it is a family of distributions. But unlike t, each F distribution is based on two kinds of degrees of freedom: the numerator degrees of freedom ($df_{numerator}$) and the denominator degrees of freedom ($df_{denominator}$). In the context of regression, $df_{numerator}$ is also called the *regression degrees of freedom* ($df_{regression}$) and $df_{denominator}$ is the *residual degrees of freedom* ($df_{residual}$). The F distribution looks a lot like the χ^2 distribution, and is in fact closely related to it. Its shape is governed largely by the numerator degrees of freedom. The larger $df_{numerator}$, the closer the F distribution is to a normal distribution. When $df_{numerator}$ is small, the F distribution is highly skewed.

We use the F distribution much like we use the t, χ^2, and normal distributions in the context of hypothesis testing: to generate a p-value. Define $F_{critical}$ as the

---

[1] If the null hypothesis is true, $E(F) = df_{residual}/(df_{residual} - 2)$.

value of F that cuts off the upper $100\alpha\%$ of the F distribution from the rest of the distribution. Define $F_{obtained}$ as the obtained F statistic for the study result. In this analysis, $F_{obtained} = 38.888$. To get the p-value, we can ask whether $F_{obtained}$ is at least as large as $F_{critical}$ for a given α level for the test. If so, we can say that $p \leq \alpha$. Or we can have a computer derive the proportion of the area under the F distribution to the right of $F_{obtained}$. This proportion is the p-value for the study result. A table of critical values of F for $\alpha = 0.05$ can be found in Appendix D1 (Appendix D2 displays the critical values for $\alpha = 0.01$). This table tells us the value that $F_{obtained}$ must exceed in order to claim that $p \leq 0.05$. The critical value of F can be found at the intersection of the numerator and the denominator degrees of freedom. We already defined the residual (or denominator) degrees of freedom as $n - k - 1$. The regression (or denominator) degrees of freedom is simply k, the number of predictor variables. From the table of critical values of F for $\alpha = 0.05$, the critical F is around 2.402 for $df_{numerator} = 4$, $df_{denominator} = 338$. The obtained F is well above this critical value, meaning that $p < .05$.[2]

But very few researchers would generate a p-value in this way using a table of critical values because computer programs can do these computations and produce the p-value more precisely. From the SPSS output in Figure 13.3, the p-value is listed as .000, which means that the p-value is less than .0005. So the null hypothesis can be rejected, $p < .0005$. We conclude that $\mathcal{R} > 0$ and so $\mathcal{R}^2 > 0$. Rephrased in terms of the population regression weights, the null hypothesis that all four partial regression weights are zero in the population can be rejected. All the population regression weights are not zero.

13.2.4   Adjusted R^2

Can we conclude that in the population, these 4 demographics explain 31.5% of the variance in political knowledge? Not quite, because R^2 is actually a *positively biased estimator* of the proportion of variance in the outcome variable explained in the population by the predictors in the model. A positively biased estimator is one that tends to overestimate the parameter it is designed to estimate. As a positively biased estimator, the squared multiple correlation will tend to be larger than the proportion of variance in Y explained by the predictors in the population. The extent of this bias is related to sample size. All other things being equal, the larger the sample, the smaller the bias. The bias is attributable to the fact that the least squares criterion tends to produce a regression model that fits the sample better than it will fit a different sample or the population as a whole—something called *overfitting the data*. If the population regression weights were known, then the squared correlation between $\hat{Y}$ and Y in the population will tend to be lower than R^2.

A statistic called *adjusted R^2* compensates for this bias in R^2. It is defined as

$$\text{adjusted } R^2 = 1 - \frac{MS_{residual}}{MS_{total}}$$

                                                                          (13.6)

where $MS_{residual}$ is defined as above and MS_{total} is the total variability in Y, defined as SS_{total}/df_{total} and df_{total} is $n - 1$. From information in Figure 13.3,

$$\text{adjusted } R^2 = 1 - \frac{13.735}{19.822} = 0.307$$

---

[2]Because the table does not contain a df_{denom} row of 338, I am using 300 instead.

Adjusted R^2 can be interpreted as the estimated proportion of variance in Y that can be explained by the set of predictor variables using the *population* regression coefficients and regression constant, which are of course unknown. In these data, adjusted R^2 is not much different from R^2, illustrating that in large samples of this size, the bias in R^2 is quite small.

Having rejected the null hypothesis that $\mathcal{R} = 0$, we can now claim that the demographic variables in the model, when considered as a set, are related to political knowledge. If we were to write up the results of this analysis, we might write something like this:

> There is a relationship between demographics and political knowledge, with demographics explaining about 31% of the variance in political knowledge, $F(4, 338) = 38.888, p < .0005$, adjusted $R^2 = 0.307$

The numbers in parentheses following F are the regression and residual degrees of freedom, respectively.

In my substantive conclusion I reported adjusted R^2. If you are trying to make a population inference, then it makes more sense to report adjusted R^2 than R^2. But in practice, communication researchers seem to use R^2 and adjusted R^2 interchangeably. Given that the bias in R^2 is quite small with even moderate sample sizes, it generally doesn't make much difference which you report.

13.3 Partial Association

The previous section focused on the use of multiple regression for estimating and making inferences about how much of the variance in an outcome can be explained by a set of predictor variables. In such an analysis, the researcher's focus is typically on R or R^2 with little or no emphasis placed on the regression coefficients or their interpretation. For this reason, I did not discuss the interpretation of the regression coefficients. But these coefficients are rich in meaning. Each regression coefficient quantifies the *partial relationship* between the corresponding predictor variable in the regression model and the outcome, *statistically controlling for* its interrelationship with the other predictors in the model. The size of these regression coefficients and their tests of significance are often the primary interest in a multiple regression. Before discussing in detail how they are interpreted, we need to spend a little time talking about what it means to *control* for something.

13.3.1 Experimental Versus Statistical Control

You probably are already familiar with the concept of *experimental control*. In an experiment, the researcher manages the situation or stimuli that participants in the study are exposed to and randomly assigns participants into one of two or more versions of those situations or stimuli prior to assessing the outcome variable. For example, a researcher of media effects might randomly assign people to read either an online or print version of a newspaper for 60 minutes (the independent variable). After the exposure period elapses, the outcome variable is measured, such as how many questions about recent political events the participants can answer correctly. If people assigned to different conditions learn different amounts of information and the experiment was otherwise well designed, then the researcher is in a good position to argue that variations in the independent variable caused difference between the experimental conditions on the outcome variable. Recalling the criteria of causality discussed in Chapter 4, at least two of the three criteria are satisfied: temporal sequence and correlation. The temporary sequencing criterion is satisfied because the presumed cause (which form of media the person was randomly assigned to) preceded the presumed effect (learning) in time. There is no way that how much a person learned during the exposure period could possibly affect which condition the person was assigned to when participants are randomly assigned to experimental conditions. And showing a difference between the two conditions in how much the participants learned satisfies the correlation criterion: If two variables are causally related, then they must be correlated.

But there is a third criterion that the researcher needs to deal with: ruling out of plausible alternative explanations. Experiments that are well designed allow the researcher to make stronger statements about cause-effect relationships than are possible using other research designs. Experimentation is all about experimental control, and good experimental design requires that the researcher think about the possible alternative explanations for a result that he or she expects to find before collecting any data so that those alternative explanations can be ruled out by designing the experiment so that they are not plausible. For example, if the online and print forms of the newspaper had different content, then that may be responsible for any difference in political learning between people assigned to different conditions, not the form of the media itself. So the researcher would want to control for differences in content by making sure that the online and print forms of the newspaper have identical content. Or if the participants assigned to the online condition did their browsing while sitting at an uncomfortable desk while those assigned to the print form got to read the paper in a comfortable recliner, then any differences between the conditions could be attributable to this subtle but perhaps important third variable that is perfectly correlated with the intended manipulation. So the researcher would want to make sure that the physical conditions of the experiment and the environment in which it occurs do not vary for people assigned to different conditions. The purpose of experimental control is to maximize the *internal validity* of the experiment. An experiment is internally valid if the only thing that differs between the various conditions in the experiment is the variable being intentionally manipulated by the researcher. This allows us the researcher to claim more confidently that any differences between the groups on the dependent variable are due to the variable being manipulated in the experiment and nothing else.

There are many occasions where experimental control isn't possible. A classic example is research on the relationship between television violence and aggression. The evidence seems to suggest that excessive exposure to televised violence leads to violent behavior. But there are alternative explanations circulating. Perhaps children raised by parents with aggressive tendencies learn aggressive behavior from their parents, who also are less likely to prohibit their children from watching violent television shows. Ideally we would conduct an experiment in which we experimentally control how much violent television children are exposed to during their childhood. Half of the children in the study could be assigned to a violent TV condition, and the other half assigned to the nonviolent TV condition. The children in the violent television condition would be exposed to a long series of violent shows over a period of years, and the participants in the nonviolent condition would be prevented from watching any violent TV. Later, perhaps when the children are in their teens, their aggressive tendencies could be measured in a number of ways. If the children assigned to the violent TV condition were more aggressive later in their lives, it would be hard to explain this without invoking some kind of causal argument linking television violence to aggression. But clearly this kind of a study couldn't be done for ethical as well as practical reasons. The best we can do are short term violence exposure experiments, but such studies probably do not adequately represent the long-term, cumulative exposure to violence that is necessary to detectably affect behavior.

Experimental control often isn't possible for other reasons. Frequently, the data to be analyzed have already been collected, and thus it isn't possible to change the manner in which the data were collected. This would be common when analyzing data from a government statistics file, from city records, or from any other source other than you, the investigator. In such situations, although experimental control isn't possible another form of control is—*statistical control*. When we statistically control for something, we are essentially removing its influence from the analysis mathematically by quantifying the relationship between two variables of interest with a measure of *partial association*.

13.3.2 Mechanisms That Can Produce Association Between Two Variables

There is a debate in the political communication literature about whether people learn about politics through political discussion. The two-stage model of media effects would argue that political learning does occur through discussion. According to this model, some people learn about current events through the media, who then transmit that information to others through discussion. So even if you don't watch televised news, read the newspaper, or regularly browse the Web for news, you still acquire information about political events by talking about politics with people who are informed by the media.

If people learn about politics from interpersonal discussion, you'd expect there to be a relationship between the frequency in which a people engage in political discussion and how much knowledge they have about current political events and people. That is, people who engage in relatively more political discussion should have relatively higher political knowledge than people who engage in relatively less political discussion. But if discussion does not result in the learning of political information, then frequency of interpersonal discussion should be unrelated to political knowledge. In other words, information about how much political discussion a person engages in should provide no information about a person's relative amount of political knowledge.

The National Election Study regularly includes a question asking respondents how many days in the last week prior to the interview that they talked about politics with family or friends. Responses vary between 0 (no days) to 7 (every day). We will assume that people who report talking about politics more often in the week prior to the phone interview probably also tend to talk more about politics in general, so responses to this question will be used as the operationalization of how frequently a person engages in political discussion. In the NES data, $M = 4.831, SD = 2.547$. (Although this mean may seem rather high, this question was asked after the 2000 election, and the 2000 election was probably one of the more controversial and widely-discussed elections in the history of the United States. As such, this measure of political knowledge probably overestimates how frequently people tend to discuss politics outside of the context of the controversial year 2000 election.)

In the NES data, the correlation between political knowledge and political discussion is $r = 0.365, p < .0005$. From a simple linear regression predicting political knowledge (Y) from discussion,

$$\hat{Y} = 8.142 + 0.637(Discussion)$$

So two people who differ by one day in their political discussion are expected to differ by 0.637 in the number of questions answered correctly. The positive relationship tells us that the person who discusses politics more frequently is expected to be more politically knowledgeable.

Although the statistical interpretation of the the correlation and simple regression coefficient estimating knowledge from discussion is simple enough, what it means about the process linking political knowledge and discussion is not at all clear. In Figure 13.4, I graphically depict five possible processes that would produce a relationship between two variables X and Y. In diagrams of this sort, a straight unidirectional arrow is used to depict the direction of causal flow.

The top two diagram depicts a process in which discussion about politics (X) directly causes greater knowledge (Y). For instance, perhaps people learn about current political events and people by talking to political knowledgable people. But it could also be that people are less likely to talk about politics if they aren't informed (the straight unidirectional path from Y to X in the second diagram). In other words, you may be disinclined to talk about politics with people if you feel like you don't have up-to-date knowledge on current political events. We can't distinguish between these two possibilities in the NES data set because it is impossible to establish the temporal sequence. Even if we could, we could still say only that the relationship *may be* causal; the existence of the relationship by no means justifies a causal claim by itself.

Another causal mechanism that can produce association between two variables is *mediation*. A relationship between X and Y is said to be mediated if their association is attributable to an intervening variable that is affected by X and that, in turn, affects Y. The intervening variable is called a *mediating variable* or a *mediator variable*. For example, political discussion may not directly cause an increase in political knowledge, as suggested earlier. It could be that discussion about politics prompts people to attend to the news media more as a means of preparing for future discussions about politics. As a result of that increased attention to news media, people learn more about current events and people in politics. In this example, attention to news media is the mediating variable in the causal sequence of events linking political discussion to political knowledge. Although multiple regression can be used as a means of assessing the plausibility of a mediational hypothesis, I save a discussion of mediation until Chapter 15.

But there are plausible alternative explanations other than a causal explanation for the relationship between two variables. For example, perhaps the relationship between political discussion and political knowledge is *spurious* and attributable to individual differences in how often people read the newspaper. Perhaps newspaper use leads to political knowledge through exposure to information, while at the same time people who read the newspaper might be more likely to interact with other people about *anything* they might have read in the newspaper, such as how their favorite team performed in a game, the construction of a new shopping mall in town, or a recipe they saw in the food section. Such discussions, once started, might eventually evolve into discussions about politics. So newspaper use (W) may causally affect both political discussion and knowledge. Such a process would produce a correlation between discussion and

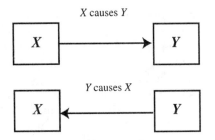

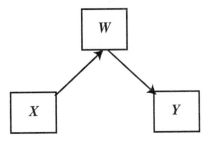

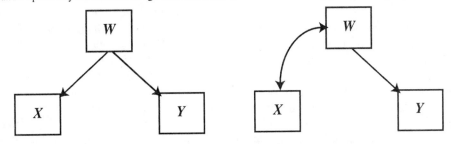

Figure 13.4 Some processes that can produce a relationship between X and Y.

knowledge, but it would be a spurious association due to them both being affected by the same causal variable—newspaper use.

Finally, two variables may be *epiphenomenally related*. An epiphenomenal relationship between X and Y exists if X is related, but not necessarily causally so, to a third variable W that *is* causally related to Y. In diagrams such as at the bottom of Figure 13.4, correlation that is not postulated necessarily to be the result of a causal process is typically represented with the curved bidirectional arrows between variables. For instance, frequency of newspaper use may cause individual differences in political knowledge (the arrow linking W and Y). If people who read the newspaper also just happen to discuss politics more frequently but not necessarily *because* they read the newspaper more (the curved, bidirectional arrows linking W and X), this can produce an epiphenomenal relationship between political discussion and knowledge. Indeed, anything related to newspaper use could be correlated with political knowledge, but perhaps only epiphenomenally.[3]

---

[3]Another mechanism that can produce association between two variables is *mediation*. I introduce mediation in Chapter 15.

The pattern of relationships between newspaper news use, political discussion, and political knowledge are consistent with these latter two possibilities. The NES survey also included a question asking the respondents to indicate how many days in the last week they read the newspaper. On average, the respondents reported having read the newspaper about three and a half days ($M = 3.545, SD = 2.822$). Furthermore, greater newspaper use was associated with greater political knowledge ($r = 0.312, p < .0005$), and people who read the newspaper more frequently also reported discussing politics more frequently ($r = 0.174, p < .01$). So it may be that the relationship between political discussion and political knowledge is spurious, resulting from the fact that greater newspaper use causes both greater discussion and greater political knowledge. Or the relationship could simply be an epiphenomenon of the fact that people who read the newspaper more tend to learn more about political events, and those same people also just happen to discuss politics more frequently (for whatever reason). However, it could be that political discussion does indeed result in the learning of political information. The pattern of correlations does not allow us to distinguish between any of these explanations. We need something more.

13.3.3   Measures of Partial Association

How can we tell whether or not two variables are spuriously or epiphenomenally associated? The answer to this question is found in an understanding of statistical control and measures of *partial association*. Two variables X and Y that are partially associated are correlated even after accounting for or removing their shared relationship with a third variable or set of variables. This process of removing what X and Y have in common with a variable or set of variables W is known as *statistical control*. The process of statistically controlling for a variable W prior to assessing the association between X and Y is also called *partialing out* W from the relationship. Thus, you often hear or read about reports of the relationship between two variables X and Y after partialing out or statistically controlling for some third variable W or set of variables, say Z, W, and V. The variables being partialed out of the relationship are often called *covariates*.

Recall from Chapter 12 that the residuals in a regression model can be conceptualized as measures on the outcome variable that are "purified" of the linear relationship between it and the predictor variable, and the Pearson correlation between the residuals and the predictor variable in a simple regression will always be zero. To measure partial association between X and Y controlling for W, new measures of X and Y must be created that are both purified of variable W and therefore uncorrelated with W.

This process is probably best illustrated by actually doing it manually. The question to be answered is whether the relationship between political discussion and political knowledge might be spurious or epiphenomenal, resulting from their shared association with newspaper use. To answer this question, we first create new measures of political discussion and political knowledge that are purified of their relationship with newspaper use. To partial out newspaper use from political discussion, we run a regression predicting political discussion (X) from newspaper use (W) and calculate the residuals from this regression. In the NES data, the best fitting simple regression model is

$$\hat{X} = 4.275 + 0.157(W)$$

I will use the notation $e_{A.B}$ refer to the residuals in a regression predicting variable A from some other variable B. So the residuals from the regression estimating political discussion from newspaper use are calculated as

$$e_{X.W} = X - [4.275 + 0.157(W)]$$

For example, someone who discusses politics twice a week and reads the newspaper five days a week would have a residual of

$$e_{X.W} = 2 - [4.275 + 0.157(5)] = 2 - 5.060 = -3.060$$

Such a person discusses politics about 3 days a week *less* than you would expect from someone who reads the newspaper 5 days a week. The mathematics of regression ensures that values of $e_{X.W}$ are linearly uncorrelated. That means that you cannot predict whether a person's political discussion, now defined as $e_{X.W}$, is high or low from how much he or she reads the newspaper. But you can say that people who discuss politics more than expected given their newspaper use will have positive values of $e_{X.W}$ and those discuss politics less than expected given their newspaper use will have negative values of $e_{X.W}$

To partial out newspaper use from political knowledge, we regress political knowledge (Y) on newspaper use. The best fitting simple linear regression model is

$$\hat{Y} = 9.474 + 0.493(W)$$

The residuals from this regression result in a new measure of political knowledge uncorrelated with newspaper use:

$$e_{Y.W} = Y - [9.474 + 0.493(W)]$$

People who have more political knowledge than expected given how much they read the newspaper have positive values of $e_{Y.W}$, and people who have less political knowledge than expected have negative values of $e_{Y.W}$.

Here comes the most important thing to understand about the concept of statistical control. If the relationship between political discussion and political knowledge is attributable to them both being affected by newspaper use (spurious association) or by the shared relationship between political discussion and newspaper use (epiphenomenal association), then there shouldn't be any relationship between $e_{X.W}$ and $e_{Y.W}$. But if these new measures of political discussion and political knowledge are related to each other, then there is no way that the association can be attributed to newspaper use, because that part of the process producing the association between knowledge and discussion has been partialed out of the relationship. If political discussion leads to political knowledge, or having more knowledge leads you to discuss politics more, then there should still be some relationship between political discussion and political knowledge, now measured as the residuals after partialing out newspaper use. That is, there would still something left in the new measure of political knowledge ($e_{Y.W}$) that can be explained by variation in the new measure of political discussion ($e_{X.W}$). Rephrased yet again, people who discuss politics relatively more than expected from their newspaper use should have more knowledge than expected from their newspaper use. In short, the residuals should be correlated.

Because of the importance of understanding this logic, it is worth going over it one more time in a slightly different manner. Suppose we restricted the analysis to people

Coefficients[a]

Model		Unstandardized Coefficients		Standardized Coefficients	t	Sig.
		B	Std. Error	Beta		
1	(Constant)	.000	.216		.000	1.000
	e(X.W)	.559	.086	.332	6.494	.000

a. Dependent Variable: e(Y.W)

Figure 13.5 SPSS output from a simple regression estimating residual political knowledge from residual political discussion, partialing out newspaper use

who read the newspaper two days a week. This group of people would vary in their political knowledge, and they would also vary in their political discussion. If discussion leads to knowledge, or knowledge to discussion, then there should be a relationship between these two variables in this group of people. If such a relationship exists, there is no way you could argue that the relationship is either spurious or epiphenomenal due to the their shared relationship with newspaper use, because everyone in this group reported the same level of newspaper use. This logic could be applied to any group of people defined by any level of newspaper use. But multiple regression allows us to examine this relationship between Y and X, conditioning on all values of W, through the process of partialing or statistical control. We don't need to do this kind of selective analysis because the process of statistically controlling for political interest essentially equates everyone on newspaper use mathematically.

In Figure 13.5 you will find SPSS output from a simple regression estimating $e_{Y.W}$ from $e_{X.W}$. The standardized regression coefficient (which remember from Chapter 12 is equivalent to the Pearson correlation when there is only a single predictor in the regression model), tells us that the correlation between the residuals is 0.332. The unstandardized regression coefficient gives the estimated difference in political knowledge between people who differ by one unit in political discussion after partialing out the relationship between these two variables and newspaper use. The relationship between the residuals is positive ($b = 0.559, r = 0.332$) and statistically different from zero. Even after statistically controlling for individual differences in news use, people who discuss politics more frequently tend to be more politically knowledgeable. Thus, the tendency for people who discuss politics more to have more political knowledge cannot be exclusively the result of newspaper use affecting both knowledge or discussion, and it cannot be an epiphenomenon of a noncausal relationship between newspaper use and political knowledge. If it were, then there should be no relationship between $e_{X.W}$ and $e_{Y.W}$.

The correlation between these residuals is called the *partial correlation* between political knowledge and political discussion, controlling for newspaper news use. The partial correlation can be interpreted just as as Pearson's r is interpreted. It indexes the strength of the association between two variables after statistically controlling for a third variable or set of variables. The square of the partial correlation can be interpreted as the proportion of variance in Y that is not explained by W that can be uniquely explained by X. I know this sounds confusing. This interpretation of the squared partial correlation will be clarified later in the chapter.

The regression weight predicting the knowledge residuals from the discussion residuals is also a measure of partial association, called a *partial regression weight*. It quantifies how two people who differ by one unit in how frequently they discuss politics are estimated to differ in their political knowledge after controlling for differences between them in their newspaper use.

One common interpretation of partial regression weights and partial correlations is based on the concept of "equating." To equate something means to make them equal. If we were to restrict the analysis to a group of people who read the newspaper the same amount, then the partial regression weight of 0.559 can be interpreted as the estimated difference in political knowledge between two people who differ by one unit in their political discussion but read the newspaper with equal frequency. The partial correlation quantifies the correlation or strength of the association between political knowledge and political discussion in this group of people equated in their newspaper use.

This seems like a lot of work. Do we have to do all these regressions and compute all these residuals to get a measure of partial association? Fortunately, we do not. The process of generating a multiple regression equation to estimate political knowledge from both newspaper use and political discussion will produce these measures of partial association. In Figure 13.6 you will find SPSS output from such a multiple regression. The regression equation predicting political knowledge from newspaper use (W) and political discussion (X) is

$$\hat{Y} = 7.082 + 0.405(W) + 0.559(X)$$

The multiple correlation is about 0.444 and statistically different from zero, $F(2, 340) = 41.695, p < .0005$. About 20% of the variance in individual differences in political knowledge can be explained by differences in political discussion and newspaper use. But this really isn't relevant because this says nothing about the partial association between political discussion and political knowledge controlling for newspaper use. That information is contained in the partial regression equation and the tests of significance for the regression coefficients. Notice that the regression weight for political discussion is 0.559, which is exactly the same value as the regression weight predicting the residual political knowledge from residual political discussion after controlling for newspaper use (Figure 13.5). So multiple regression has greatly simplified the task of quantifying partial association. There is no need to actually generate the residuals and then estimate one set from the other. Multiple regression does it all for you in one fell swoop.

Some statistics programs will print the partial correlation in the output from a multiple regression. In the SPSS output, the partial correlations are listed under the word "Partial" in the output. Notice that the partial correlation between political knowledge and political discussion is 0.332, just as we computed earlier. Had I not asked SPSS to print the partial correlation, or if you were doing the analysis with a program that can't print the partial correlation, it is possible to generate it with some hand computation using the t statistic for political discussion. The partial correlation (pr) between a predictor variable and a dependent variable, controlling for all other predictors in a regression can be derived from equation 13.7:

$$|pr| = \sqrt{\frac{t^2}{t^2 + df_{residual}}}$$

(13.7)

Model Summary

Model	R	R Square	Adjusted R Square	Std. Error of the Estimate
1	.444a	.197	.192	4.00145

a. Predictors: (Constant), Political Discussion, Newspaper Use

ANOVAb

Model		Sum of Squares	df	Mean Square	F	Sig.
1	Regression	1335.204	2	667.602	41.695	.000a
	Residual	5443.956	340	16.012		
	Total	6779.160	342			

a. Predictors: (Constant), Political Discussion, Newspaper Use

b. Dependent Variable: Political Knowledge

regression constant and partial regression weights

Coefficientsa

Model		Unstandardized Coefficients		Standardized Coefficients	t	Sig.	Correlations		
		B	Std. Error	Beta			Zero-order	Partial	Part
1	(Constant)	7.082	.507		13.980	.000			
	Newspaper Use	.405	.078	.257	5.206	.000	.312	.272	.253
	Political Discussion	.559	.086	.320	6.484	.000	.365	.332	.315

a. Dependent Variable: Political Knowledge

Test of H$_0$: partial $\beta = 0$ (also tests null hypothesis that population partial correlation and population semipartial correlation equals zero)

Simple correlations between predictor and outcome

Partial correlations between predictor and outcome, controlling for the other predictors

Semipartial correlations between predictor and outcome, controlling for the other predictors

Figure 13.6 SPSS Output from a multiple regression estimating political knowledge from newspaper use and political discussion.

From Figure 13.6, the t statistic for political discussion is 6.484, and $df_{residual} = 340$, so

$$|pr| = \sqrt{\frac{6.484^2}{6.484^2 + 340}} = 0.332$$

Using this equation, the sign of the partial correlation is lost. But the sign of pr is just the sign of the t statistic. If t is negative, pr is negative. If t is positive, pr is positive.

With equation 13.8 the partial correlation between Y and X controlling for W can be derived using only the simple correlations between the variables rather than the t statistic from a multiple regression:

$$pr = \frac{r_{XY} - r_{XW}r_{YW}}{\sqrt{(1 - r_{XW}^2)(1 - r_{YW}^2)}}$$

(13.8)

In the NES data, $r_{XY} = 0.365, r_{XW} = 0.174$, and $r_{YW} = 0.312$. Applying equation 13.8,

$$pr = \frac{0.365 - (0.174)(0.312)}{\sqrt{(1 - 0.174^2)(1 - 0.312^2)}} = 0.332$$

The Semipartial (or "Part") Correlation. There is a third measure of partial association that is useful and provides slightly different information about the partial relationship between two variables controlling for a third. This measure is called the *semipartial correlation*, or *part correlation*, often symbolized as sr. The semipartial correlation between outcome variable Y and predictor variable X controlling for W is the correlation between Y and the residuals from a regression estimating X from W. Unlike the partial correlation between Y and X controlling for W, W is not partialed out of the outcome variable. As with the partial correlation, you need not actually compute these residuals and correlations manually if you have a good regression program. In Figure 13.6, the semipartial correlations are listed under the "Part" column. This output shows that the semipartial correlation between political knowledge and political discussion, controlling for newspaper use, is 0.315.

Although a good statistical program will print the semipartial correlation, it can be computed with information contained in any regression output with equation 13.9:

$$|sr| = \sqrt{\frac{t^2(1 - R^2)}{df_{residual}}}$$

(13.9)

where t^2 is the square of the t statistic for the partial regression coefficient and R^2 is the squared multiple correlation estimating Y from X and W. This formula will produce the correct absolute value for the semipartial correlation but it may not produce the correct sign. The correct sign of the semipartial correlation is the sign of the t statistic for that predictor in the regression model. So if t is negative, the semipartial correlation is negative. If t is positive, the semipartial correlation is positive. Using this equation, the semipartial correlation is

$$|sr| = \sqrt{\frac{6.484^2(1 - 0.444^2)}{340}} = 0.315$$

The semipartial correlation is most often interpreted after squaring it. The squared semipartial correlation between Y and X controlling for W can be interpreted as the proportion of the total variance in Y uniquely explained by X. The square of the semipartial correlation between knowledge and discussion controlling for newspaper use is 0.099, So we can say that about 9.9% of the *total* variance in people's political knowledge can be uniquely explained by individual differences in political discussion, controlling for newspaper use.

13.3.4 Partial Versus Semipartial Correlation

Looking at Figure 13.6, you can see that 0.099 is closer to zero than the squared simple correlation between discussion and knowledge, which is $0.365^2 = 0.123$. So 12.3% of the total variance in political knowledge can be attributed to political discussion, but only 9.9% of the total variance an be *uniquely* attributed to political discussion after controlling for newspaper use. But the squared partial correlation is $0.332^2 = 0.110$, meaning that 11% of the variance in political knowledge not explained by newspaper use can be uniquely explained by political discussion.

Wow, this sounds confusing. But it is worth completely understanding the distinction between the partial and semipartial correlation, so let's spend some time distinguishing between them. The distinction can be clarifed with the use of a *Venn diagram*, found in Figure 13.7. In a Venn diagram, the variance of each variable is represented by the area in the circle corresponding to that variable, and the variance that two variables *share* is represented by overlap in the circles.

In a Venn diagram, it is convenient to conceptualize the variance of a variable as arbitrarily set to be equal to 1, as if the variables had been standardized. In that case, then the sections where two circles overlap represent the *squared* simple correlation between those two variables. So the squared simple correlation between X and Y is represented by A + B, the squared simple correlation between X and W is B + E, and the squared multiple correlation estimating Y from X and W is A + B + C. So in a Venn diagram, the larger the overlap between two variables, the larger the correlation between those variables. Two variables that do not overlap are uncorrelated. Given these rules, the variability that X and Y share is A + B, and partialing X out of Y is akin to removing A + B from the total area A + B + C + D, leaving only C + D as the remaining variance in Y. Similarly, partialing out W from Y is represented here as the removal of B + C from the total variance of Y, leaving A + D as the variance remaining in Y.

Before progressing it is worth introducing some new notation to simplify presentation of some concepts. The notation θ_{ABC} will refer to a correlation (θ) of some kind (such as a multiple correlation or a partial correlation) involving three variables A, B, and C. The first letter in the sequence will refer to the outcome variable, and all letters that follow refer to predictor variables. So, for example, R_{YXW} refers to the multiple correlation estimating Y from X and W, and r_{YW}^2 is the squared correlation between Y and W. By definition, $R_{YXW} = R_{YWX}$, and $r_{YX}^2 = r_{XY}^2$. If a period "." is inserted between two variables, then all variables that follow are being statistically controlled. For example, $pr_{YW.X}$ is the partial correlation between Y and W controlling for X, where Y is the outcome variable, and $sr_{YX.W}^2$ is the squared semipartial correlation between Y and X controlling for W.

In Figure 13.7, the squared semipartial correlation between Y and X controlling for W ($sr_{YX.W}^2$) is equal to A/(A+B+C+D). It is the proportion of the total variance in Y uniquely shared with X. When I say "uniquely," I mean that the overlap between X and Y defined as A shares nothing with W. Similarly, the squared semipartial correla-

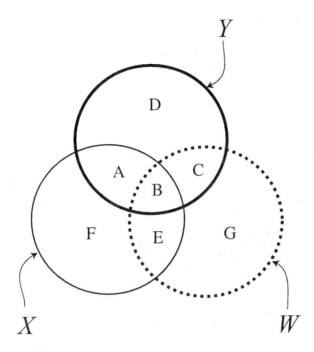

If the area of each circle is defined as equal to 1, then

$$r^2_{YX} = A + B \qquad sr^2_{YX.W} = A \qquad pr^2_{YX.W} = A / (A + D)$$

$$r^2_{YW} = B + C \qquad sr^2_{YW.X} = C \qquad pr^2_{YW.X} = C / (C + D)$$

$$r^2_{XW} = B + E$$

$$R^2_{YXW} = A + B + C = r^2_{YX} + sr^2_{YW.X} = r^2_{YW} + sr^2_{YX.W}$$

Figure 13.7 A Venn diagram illustrating the relationship between simple, partial, and semipartial correlation.

tion between Y and W controlling for X ($sr^2_{YW.X}$) is represented as C /(A+B+C+D). But remember that we are defining the total area of a circle as 1, so A + B + C + D = 1. Therefore, $sr^2_{YX.W}$ = A and $sr^2_{YW.X}$ = C.

In contrast, recall that with a partial correlation, the variable being controlled statistically is removed from both the predictor *and* outcome variable. The partial correlation between Y and X controlling for W measures the association between what is left of Y and what is left of X, after partialing out W from both. So in the Venn diagram, the squared partial correlation between Y and X controlling for W ($pr^2_{YX.W}$), is A /(A + D). That is, it is the proportion of what is left in Y after partialing out W from Y that is uniquely shared with X. Rephrased differently, the squared partial correlation between Y and X controlling for W is the proportion of variance in Y that cannot be attributed to W that can be uniquely attributed to X. Using the same logic, the squared partial correlation between Y and W controlling for X ($pr^2_{YW.X}$) is C /(C

+ D). It is the proportion of variance in Y that cannot be attributed to X that can be uniquely attributed to W.

A close examination of Figure 13.7 reveals that the squared multiple correlation estimating Y from X and W ($R^2_{YXW} = A + B + C$) is equal to the square of the correlation between Y and X ($r^2_{YX} = A + B$) plus the squared semipartial correlation between Y and W controlling for X ($sr^2_{YW.X} = C$). That is,

$$R^2_{YXW} = r^2_{YX} + sr^2_{YW.X}$$

By a similar logic,

$$R^2_{YXW} = r^2_{YW} + sr^2_{YX.W}$$

It is also apparent that

$$R^2_{YXW} \leq (r^2_{YX} + r^2_{YW})$$

If $r^2_{XW} > 0$ and r^2_{YX} and r^2_{YW} are both greater than 0, then R^2_{YXW} will typically be less than $(r^2_{YX} + r^2_{YW})$ because the sum of the squared simple correlations double counts the area represented as B. But if either X or W are uncorrelated with Y or if X and W are uncorrelated with each other, then R^2_{YXW} is typically equal to $r^2_{YX} + r^2_{YW}$.[4]

An even closer examination of Figure 13.7 reveals that

$$pr^2_{YX.W} = \frac{sr^2_{YX.W}}{1 - r^2_{YW}}$$

Because $1 - r^2_{YW}$ is almost always less than 1 but never greater than 1, it follows that

$$pr^2_{YX.W} \geq sr^2_{YX.W}$$

The distinction between the semipartial and partial correlation is probably one of the most difficult things to master in multiple regression, and it will take some practice to do so. The semipartial correlation is usually not interpreted without squaring it. After squaring it, it is used as measure of how much of the total variance on an outcome variable can be attributed uniquely to a specific predictor variable. It is also used as a means of quantifying how much additional variance a predictor variable explains, above and beyond what is explained by the other predictors in a multiple regression model. The partial correlation, in contrast, is *usually* not squared before interpreting it, and it is used as a "corrected" correlation between two variables after removing the influence that a third variable has on both. However, there is a measure of effect size introduced in Chapter 14 called *partial* η^2 that can be interpreted as a squared partial correlation, but I don't generally recommend its use.

13.3.5   The Standardized Partial Regression Coefficient

If the predictor and outcome variables are all standardized prior to analysis, the regression model is sometimes called the *standardized regression model*, and the regression coefficients referred to as *standardized partial regression coefficients*. Many statistics

---

[4]There are some circumstances in which $R^2_{YXW} > r^2_{YX} + r^2_{YW}$. For example, using the NES2000 data, in an OLS regression estimating political knowledge (Y) from local television news exposure (W) and national network news exposure (X), $R^2_{YXW} = 0.061$, and yet $r^2_{YX} = 0.027$ and $r^2_{YW} = 0.009$ and so $R^2_{YXW} > r^2_{YX} + r^2_{YW}$. For additional examples of such phenomena, called *complementarity* or *suppression*, see Hamilton (1987) and Darlington (1990, p. 153-155).

programs routinely report the regression coefficients in both standardized and unstandardized form. From Figure 13.6, the standardized regression equation estimating political knowledge from newspaper use and political discussion is

$$\hat{Z}_{knowlege} = 0.257(Z_{newspaper\ use}) + 0.320(Z_{discussion})$$

In a standardized regression equation, the constant is always zero.

The interpretation of the partial regression coefficients is much the same as the interpretation of the unstandardized coefficients, except that a one-unit difference in a predictor is interpreted as a standard deviation rather than in terms of the original metric. So controlling for newspaper use, two people who differ by one standard deviation in political discussion are expected to differ by 0.320 standard deviations in political knowledge, with the person who discusses politics more frequently estimated to have higher political knowledge.

Standardized regression coefficients tend to be reported more frequently in the communication literature than unstandardized regression coefficients, a pattern I would like to see reversed. As discussed in sections 13.6.5 and 16.3.8, some people prefer standardized coefficients because, it is claimed, they allow for comparisons of the relative importance of predictor variables in estimating the outcome, they are comparable across studies that differ in design and the measurement procedures used, and they can be used to compare the effect of one variable on the outcome across subsamples. But none of these claims are unconditionally true. Furthermore, standardized regression coefficients for dichotomous predictors such as a person's sex are meaningless. So long as you provide sufficient details about the measurement procedures in the description of your research methodology, unstandardized coefficients facilitate interpretations of variation in the outcome variable attributable to each predictor in a way that can be compared across studies using the same measurement procedure and across subsamples in the same data set. Furthermore, the reporting of standardized coefficients at the expense of unstandardized coefficients makes it difficult to interpret moderated multiple regression models, introduced in Chapter 16. Although I and others prefer the reporting of unstandardized coefficients, not everyone shares this preference. Probably the safest strategy is to report both the unstandardized and standardized coefficients when writing about your research, so that you will satisfy people from both camps.

13.3.6 Inference for Measures of Partial Association

In multiple regression based on a random sample from a population of interest, the t statistic and p-value for a partial regression weight are used to test the null hypothesis that the population partial regression weight (partial β) is zero against the alternative that it is different from zero (for a two-tailed test). Just as in simple regression, the t statistic is defined as the partial regression weight divided by its standard error. In multiple regression, the standard error for the partial regression weight for predictor j is estimated as

$$s_{b_j} = \sqrt{\frac{MS_{residual}}{n(s_j^2)(1 - R_j^2)}}$$

(13.10)

where s_j^2 is the sample variance of predictor variable j and R_j^2 is the squared multiple correlation estimating predictor variable j from the other predictor variables in the regression model. The estimated standard error of the partial regression weight for political discussion can be derived knowing that $s^2_{discussion} = 6.486$ and $R^2_{discussion} = 0.030$ as[5]

$$s_{b_{discussion}} = \sqrt{\frac{16.012}{343(6.486)(1 - 0.030)}} = 0.086$$

When the sample partial regression coefficient of 0.559 is divided by its standard error, this yields a t statistic of

$$t = \frac{0.559}{0.086} = 6.500$$

This statistical test is printed by all good regression programs (as in Figure 13.6 from SPSS, which agrees with this computation within expected rounding error). The p-value is computed using the t distribution with $df_{residual}$ degrees of freedom. From Appendix B, this t statistic exceeds the critical value for $\alpha = 0.05$, two-tailed, so the null hypothesis can be rejected. The computer tells us that $p < .0005$. So controlling for newspaper use, people who discuss politics more frequently tend to be more politically knowledgeable. The substantive interpretation might be phrased as such:

> If political discussion leads to greater political knowledge, then the relationship between how frequently one talks about politics and political knowledge should be positive. It was, $r = .365, p < .0005$. The alternative explanation that this relationship can be attributed to the tendency for newspaper use to promote both discussion and knowledge is not consistent with the data. In a multiple regression predicting political knowledge from both newspaper use and political discussion, the relationship between discussion and knowledge remained positive and statistically significant even after controlling for newspaper use, $b = .559$, partial $r = .332, t(340) = 6.484, p < .0005$.

In this summary, I did not include information about the multiple correlation because the size and significance of the multiple correlation is not particularly relevant to the question as to whether the relationship between political discussion and political knowledge exists even after controlling for political interest. However, it is not uncommon for communication researchers to report R^2 anyway.

What if you wanted to reframe the inference in terms of the population partial correlation or semipartial correlation? You can go ahead and do so, but there is no additional test needed. The test that the population partial regression weight is zero is mathematically identical to the test that the population partial correlation is zero. If the null hypothesis that the partial population regression weight equals zero 0 is rejected, then the null hypothesis that the population partial correlation equals zero should also be rejected, as should the null hypothesis that the population semipartial correlation is zero.

Observe in Figure 13.6 that SPSS prints all the measures of partial association as well as a hypothesis test for the newspaper use variable as well. Everything said about estimating and testing for partial association between political discussion and political knowledge applies to the interpretation of the newspaper use variable as well. The partial regression weight for newspaper use is 0.504, and the null hypothesis that the population partial regression weight for newspaper use equals zero should be rejected, $t(340) = 5.206, p < .0005$. Two people who discuss politics the same amount but who differ by one day in their newspaper use are expected to differ by 0.504 units in their

---

[5]In this example, because there is only one additional predictor (newspaper use), R^2_i is simply the square of the correlation between newspaper use and political discussion.

political knowledge. The positive partial regression weight means that the person who reads the newspaper more frequently is expected to have greater political knowledge. The partial correlation between newspaper use and political knowledge is $pr = 0.272$. This is the same as the correlation between the residuals estimating newspaper use from political discussion and the residuals estimating knowledge from political discussion.

In this example, there were only two predictor variables. But the lessons here are general ones and apply when there are more than two predictors. For example, we could have assessed the partial correlation between political discussion and political knowledge after controlling for political interest, age, gender, education, and income simply by including these demographic variables in the multiple regression model as well.

Having now discussed the meaning of these measures of partial association, we can go back to the analysis of demographic predictors of political knowledge (section 13.1) and interpret the partial regression coefficients in the multiple regression estimating political knowledge from age, sex, education, and income (see Figure 13.3). As can be seen, each demographic variable is significantly related to political knowledge even after controlling for all the other demographic variables in the model. For example, in a group of people of the same gender, age, and income, people who differ by one year of education are expected to differ by 0.807 units in their political knowledge. And men have higher political knowledge then women, even after controlling for gender differences in education, age, and income. The regression analysis leads us to estimate that men, on average, are expected to correctly answer about 1.952 more questions than women.

13.3.7 Confidence Intervals for Measures of Partial Association

Being able to claim that the partial relationship is not zero can be very important. Theories can be validated or refuted on the grounds that a relationship that the theory predicts should be nonzero is in fact nonzero. So null hypothesis testing does have an important role to play in research. But there are some contexts where it might be even more informative to be able to make more precise statements about the size of the partial relationship in the population. Confidence intervals provide more information, and it doesn't hurt to report confidence intervals whenever you have randomly sampled from some population with the goal of making a population inference. Indeed, some people argue that such confidence intervals should be routinely reported. But when a sample is not derived from a random sampling plan from a defined population, confidence intervals have no meaning.

All of the measures of partial association discussed can be converted into confidence intervals. For the partial regression coefficient, a $c\%$ confidence interval for partial β can be derived in the usual way as

$$\boxed{c\% \text{ CI for partial } \beta = \text{partial } b \pm t_{(100-c)/2}(s_b)}$$

(13.11)

where the t value comes from the t distribution with $df_{residual}$ degrees of freedom. So the 95% confidence interval for the partial β estimating political knowledge from political discussion, controlling for newspaper use, is $0.559 \pm 1.968(0.086)$, which is 0.390 to 0.728.

When computing a confidence interval for a partial correlation or semipartial correlation, use the procedure described in section 12.2.3. However, the standard error for that correlation after converting it to a Z with Fisher's r-to-Z transformation is $\sqrt{1/(df_{residual} - 1)}$ rather than $\sqrt{1/(n - 3)}$.

13.3.8 Assumptions for Statistical Inference and Detecting Influential Cases

Just as in simple regression, the inferential tests discussed in sections 13.3.6 and 13.3.7 contain certain mathematical assumptions that must be at least approximately met in order for the p-values and confidence intervals to be interpreted as desired and to maximize the accuracy of inference. And a case or two in an analysis can affect one or more of the partial regression coefficients more so than others, and it is worthwhile to identify those cases if they exist.

Assumptions for Accurate Inference. In the previous section, I illustrated how the partial correlation in a multiple regression analysis is the correlation between two sets of residuals, and the partial regression weight is the regression weight estimating the outcome variable residuals from predictor variable residuals, partialing out the covariate from each. Given this, it follows that all the statistical assumptions that apply to inferential tests in simple regression discussed in section 12.2.4 apply to tests involving measures of partial association in multiple regression. For example, in a multiple regression estimating Y from X and W, the test that $\beta_X = 0$ assumes that the residuals from a regression estimating the residuals in estimation of Y from W from the residuals estimating X from W are normal, homoscedastic, and independent. That is a lot to digest, but if read the previous sentence slowly with the material from the previous section in mind, it will make sense. Any of the techniques described in section 12.2.4 can be used to test these assumptions. Some statistical programs facilitate this process through the generation of a *partial scatterplot*, which is a scatterplot of the residuals. The "eyeball" tests can be applied to a partial scatterplot to assess the assumptions of homoscedasticity or normality, as can the more rigorous statistical methods discussed in that section.

Significance tests for the regression coefficients tend to be relatively robust to violations of the normality assumption but not the homoscedasticity assumption. Recall that heteroscedasticity affects standard errors, and the standard errors from OLS regression output that most computer programs produce are likely to be too large or too small when the homoscedasticity assumption is violated. For that reason, it is worth using the HC3 standard error estimator discussed in Chapter 12 if you have any reason to believe that the heteroscedasticity assumption is violated. But as Long and Erwin (2000) note, even if you have no reason to question the assumption of homoscedasticity, it is worth using HC3 as a matter of routine when conducting a multiple regression analysis. To do so, you can use the macro in Appendix F on the CD with this book to reassure yourself that any heteroscedasticity that might exist is not affecting the accuracy of your inferences about partial association. The output from this macro for a regression estimating political knowledge from newspaper use and political discussion can be found in Figure 13.8. Notice that the standard errors differ slightly from those in Figure 13.6, but not so much so that the t statistics and p-values are drastically affected.

Influential Cases. A case in a multiple regression analysis can exert influence on one, many, or all of the partial regression coefficients. In the context of multiple regression, a case's leverage is defined as atypicality in its *pattern* of predictor variable measurements. A case may be atypical on one predictor but not on another, or it

Run MATRIX procedure:

Criterion Variable
 pknow

HC3 Heteroscedasticity-Consistent Regression Results

	B(OLS)	SE(HC3)	t	P>|t|
Constant	7.0819	.4864	14.5604	.0000
npnews	.4054	.0802	5.0521	.0000
pdiscuss	.5594	.0849	6.5863	.0000

------ END MATRIX -----

Figure 13.8 Output from an SPSS macro for OLS regression using the HC3 standard error estimator

may be atypical on several predictors. Such cases may have high influence on one regression coefficient but not on others. As such, an influential case may drastically alter parts of the regression equation but not other parts of it. A case's influence in multiple regression can still be assessed with the *dfbeta* statistic,, and good statistics software makes it easy to generate these statistics. When looking for influential cases, you can use the same strategy as described in Chapter 12, but of course there are more *dfbeta* statistics for each case to consider in multiple regression—one for each regression coefficient as well one for the regression constant.

The testing of assumptions and detection of influential cases in multiple regression is a topic that can fill an entire book. For a good introduction, see Fox (1991).

Violations of Random Sampling. The inferential methods discussed in this chapter are based on the population model of inference. This model is useful for making inferences about parameters (such as the population partial βs) from a random sample of a population. But communication researchers often conduct multiple regression analysis on data not derived from any kind of random sampling plan. At various points throughout this book, I have offered alternative models of inference that do not assume random sampling, such as randomization and permutation tests. These methods produce p-values with a model that does not gauge "chance" using random sampling error as the benchmark for evaluating discrepancy between the obtained result and the null hypothesis. No population inferences are warranted in the absence of random sampling.

Applying the logic of the permutation test to regression models with multiple predictors is somewhat controversial in the statistics literature. The controversy revolves around just what to permute when deriving the permutation distribution of a statistic (such as a partial regression weight) under the assumption of *random partial association* between a predictor and an outcome. In a permutation test in simple regression (see section 12.3), the Y measurements are permuted over the X measurements to derive the permutation distribution of the simple regression weight under the null hypothesis of random association between X and Y. A simple extension of this method to multiple regression would be to permute Y across units in a multiple regression and estimate the model in each permutation, keeping the predictor values unpermuted across units. But as Kennedy (1995) discusses, this approach is unsatisfying because it does not adequately test the null hypothesis of partial random association, which is often the primary goal of researchers using multiple regression.

As discussed earlier, partial regression weights can be framed in terms of a regression of residuals on residuals. Given this, it makes sense that permutation tests for partial random association can be undertaken by permuting residuals across residuals. For example, define X' as the residuals from a regression estimating political discussion from newspaper use, and define Y' as the residuals from a regression estimating political knowledge from newspaper use. The permutation test discussed in section 12.3, permuting Y' across X', can be used to test the null hypothesis of partial random association between political knowledge (Y) and political discussion (X), controlling for newspaper use, against the alternative hypothesis of partial systematic association (see Kennedy, 1995).

Most of the time, such a permutation test on residuals will produce a p-value very similar to what the use of the t distribution will produce using the method described in section 13.3.6. So the p-value from the t distribution can be used as a good approximation to the p-value from a permutation test of partial random association. But when the data are derived from a nonrandom sampling plan, the rejection of the null hypothesis of partial random association does not allow for a population inference about partial β. Instead, it allows only for an inference about whether the partial relationship can be attributed to random process rather than a nonrandom one. But this is perfectly satisfying for most reseachers (Frick, 1998; Mook, 1983), because ruling out a random process gives one license to interpret the obtained result as reflecting some kind of a systematic process linking the predictor to the outcome, controlling for the other predictor variables in the model, rather than just a chance mechanism (such as a random pairing of the predictor and outcome).

13.4   Setwise Partial Association and Hierarchical Regression

It is often of interest to communication researchers to know whether a *set* of variables is associated with an outcome after controlling for one or more covariates. For example, is "communication," defined as a set of variables quantifying media use and interpersonal discussion, related to political knowledge after controlling for political interest and demographics? If so, how much of the variance in political knowledge can be uniquely attributed to "communication?" To answer this question, we need a measure of how much variability in political knowledge a set of variables explains independent of, or partialing out a second set of variables.

Let's make this more concrete. Suppose we operationalize "communication" as people's responses to a series of questions about how often they read the newspaper, how often they watch local and national network televised news broadcasts, how often they talk to people about politics, and how often they listen to political talk radio. The 2000 NES study includes such questions. We have already talked about the measurement of political discussion and newspaper use. The respondents were also asked how many days in the last week they watched the national network news on TV, how many days in the last week they watched local *early* TV news broadcasts, and how many days in the last week they watched the local *late* TV news broadcasts. Responses could range from 0 to 7 days. Local televised news use was operationalized in the data analysis below as the respondent's mean response to the last two questions. To measure political talk radio exposure, the participants were asked how often he or she listens to political talk radio, and how much attention to he or she pays to it (as opposed to having it on the radio but not really listening). Responses to both questions about political talk radio were made on a 1 to 4 scale. The average response to these two questions was used in the analyses below (such that a higher average reflected greater exposure to political talk radio). Finally, respondents were also asked to indicate how often they follow local or government affairs. Responses were made on a 1 to 4 scale, where $1 =$ hardly at all, $2 =$ only now and then, $3 =$ some of the time, and $4 =$ most of the time. We will use this as an operationalization of political interest.

Unlike the example presented in the previous section, in this case there are several variables rather than just two. The measures of partial association described above are useful for quantifying the relationship between a single predictor and the outcome, controlling for one or more additional predictor variables. But to assess the joint contribution of *two or more* variables in explaining variance in an outcome after partialing out one or more covariates, we need a means of quantifying *setwise partial association*.

13.4.1 Setwise Partial and Semipartial Correlations

Two measures of setwise partial association are the *setwise semipartial correlation* and the *setwise partial correlation*. Both of these are typically interpreted after squaring them. The setwise squared semipartial correlation is often symbolically denoted as ΔR^2, read as "delta R-squared" or "change in R-squared." Another common notation is SR^2. SR^2 is calculated by fitting two regression models and comparing their R^2 statistics. The squared setwise partial correlation is not as widely-used, but its computation is relatively straightforward. I will symbolize the setwise squared partial correlation as PR^2.

The procedure to estimate and test hypotheses about setwise partial association is typically referred to as *hierarchical regression analysis* because the investigator essentially builds a regression model in a hierarchical fashion, giving the variables to be controlled priority in explaining variability in the outcome prior to entering the set of variables for which the setwise partial association is desired. But this should not be confused with *hierarchical linear modeling*, which is a different statistical technique you might also read about occasionally in the communication literature.

Before discussing how these measures are derived, it is worth spending some time getting a conceptual grasp on what they are measuring by using a Venn diagram (see Figure 13.9). In the previous section, X and W were single variables. But they need not be. Let's call W the *set* of variables defined as age, education, income, gender, and political interest, and let's call X the *set* of variables defined as local televised news use, newspaper news use, exposure to national network news, interpersonal discussion about politics, and exposure to political talk radio. Y is still the number of questions correct on the political knowledge test. Defining the sum of A, B, C and D to be equal to 1, the proportion of the total variance in political knowledge that can be explained from all nine of these variables simultaneously is R^2_{YXW}, which is A + B + C. In the diagram, B + C is R^2_{YW}, the squared multiple correlation estimating political knowledge from demographics and political interest. And A + B is the squared multiple correlation estimating political knowledge from communication, R^2_{YX}. But A + B it is not the proportion of the total variance in political knowledge *uniquely* attributable to communication because the variability in political knowledge defined as B is accounted for in part by political interest and demographics (W) and in part by communication (X). The only part of the variance in political knowledge that can be *uniquely* attributed to communication is A, so A is the setwise squared semipartial correlation between communication and political knowledge controlling for demographics and political interest, $SR^2_{YX.W}$. But remember that a squared semipar-

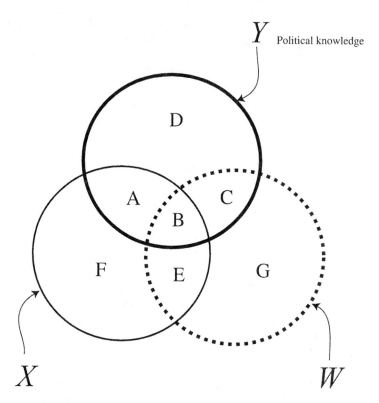

Figure 13.9 A Venn diagram depicting the relationships between sets of variables.

tial correlation quantifies the proportion of *total* variance in Y uniquely attributable to X, whereas the squared partial correlation between Y and X quantifies the proportion of the variance in Y remaining after partialling out W that is uniquely attributable to X. So $PR^2_{YX.W}$ is defined as A / (A + D).

13.4.2 Calculating SR^2 and PR^2

The computation of the setwise squared semipartial correlation $SR^2_{YX.W}$ is relatively simple. Notice in the Venn diagram that if R^2_{YXW} is equal to A + B + C, and R^2_{YW} is equal to B + C, then A, the quantity desired, must be equal to $R^2_{YXW} - R^2_{YW}$. Therefore,

$$\boxed{SR^2_{YX.W} = R^2_{YXW} - R^2_{YW}}$$

(13.12)

So to calculate the setwise squared semipartial correlation between communication (X) and political knowledge (Y) controlling for political interest and demographics (W), we need to calculate these two R^2 statistics. The first step is to compute R^2_{YW}

by fitting a regression model predicting knowledge from political interest and demographics. The best fitting least squares regression model is

$$\hat{Y} = -4.167 + 0.009(Age) + 0.548(Education) + 1.460(Sex)$$
$$+0.019(Income) + 1.859(Political\ Interest)$$

and the R^2 for this model is 0.422. So demographics and political interest explain a tad over 42% of the variance in political knowledge.

In the Venn diagram, 0.422 is the area B + C. We want to know A. To get A, we need to compute R^2_{YXW}, which is the squared multiple correlation from a regression estimating political knowledge from demographics, political interest, and the five communication variables. That regression model is

$$\hat{Y} = -2.967 + 0.003(Age) + 0.449(Education) + 1.414(Sex) + 0.014(Income)$$
$$+1.405(Political\ Interest) + 0.264(Discussion) + 0.052(Network\ TV\ News)$$
$$+0.184(Newspaper\ Use) - 0.205(Local\ TV\ News) + 0.313(Talk\ Radio)$$

with an R^2 of 0.465. So all 10 ten of these variables explain 46.5% of the variance in political knowledge. From equation 13.12

$$SR^2_{YX.W} = 0.465 - 0.422 = 0.043$$

meaning that communication uniquely explains about 4.3% of the total variance in political knowledge after controlling for demographics and political interest. You can see why SR^2 is sometimes referred to as a measure of *incremental variance explained* and called the "change in R^2." It is the increment in the variance accounted for by the addition of the five communication variables to the first regression model.

What about the setwise squared *partial* correlation for X, $PR^2_{YX.Z}$? Earlier we defined A in the Venn diagram as $SR^2_{YX.W}$ and A / (A + D) as $PR^2_{YX.W}$. A close look at Figure 13.9 shows that A + D is equal to $1 - R^2_{YW}$. This is the proportion of the total variance in political knowledge not attributable to demographics and political interest. And we know that A = $SR^2_{YX.Z}$. So the setwise squared partial correlation between Y (political knowledge) and X (communication) controlling for W (demographics and political interest) must be

$$PR^2_{YX.W} = \frac{SR^2_{YX.W}}{1 - R^2_{YW}}$$

(13.13)

Plugging the numbers from above into equation 13.13 yields

$$PR^2_{YX.W} = \frac{0.043}{1 - 0.422} = 0.074$$

This can be interpreted as the proportion of the total variance in political knowledge that is not attributable to demographics and political interest that can be uniquely attributed to communication.

13.4.3   Inference for Measures of Setwise Partial Association

Earlier we saw that proportion of the total variance that a set of predictor variables X uniquely explains in an outcome variable Y after controlling another set of variables W

can be assessed by determining how much R^2 changes when X is added to a regression model that already contains variables W. This change in R^2 is the setwise squared semipartial correlation between Y and X controlling for W ($SR^2_{YX.W}$). Because of the way that regression works, R^2 is certain to increase somewhat as more and more predictors are added to a regression model, even if those predictors are unrelated to the outcome in the population. This is because in a sample, the correlation between any predictor or set of predictors and the outcome is unlikely to be *exactly* zero. As a result, just by chance sampling variability, R^2 will increase as the complexity (i.e., the number of predictors) of a model increases.

We often want to know whether the incremental variance in Y explained by predictor set X is statistically different from zero after controlling for predictor set W. In other words, does a regression model estimating Y from X and W explain significantly more of the total variance in Y than does the regression model that includes just W? This is akin to asking whether the population setwise squared semipartial correlation for the X variable set is different from zero. Symbolically, we want to test the null hypothesis that

$$H_0 : \mathcal{SR}^2_{YX.W} = 0$$

against the alternative hypothesis

$$H_a : \mathcal{SR}^2_{YX.W} > 0$$

Just as does any statistic, $SR^2_{YX.W}$ has a sampling distribution. We want to derive the probability of the obtained "change in R^2" or a larger change if the null hypothesis is true. This is accomplished by converting the obtained SR^2 to a statistic with a known sampling distribution from which the p-value can be computed. The statistic is F, defined as

$$F = \frac{df_{residual} SR^2_{YX.W}}{m(1 - R^2_{YXW})} \tag{13.14}$$

where m is the number of variables in predictor set X and $df_{residual}$ is the residual degrees of freedom in the regression model estimating Y from both X and W. The residual degrees of freedom for this model is defined as $n - m - k - 1$, where n is the sample size and k is the number of variables in variable set W. In this analysis, $n = 343$, $k = 5$, $m = 5$, $SR^2_{YX.W} = 0.043$, and $R^2_{YXW} = 0.465$, so

$$F = \frac{332(0.043)}{5(1 - 0.465)} = 5.336$$

Assuming that the null hypothesis is true, F follows the F distribution with $df_{numerator} = m$ and $df_{numerator} = df_{residual}$. From Appendix D, the critical value for $F(5, 332)$ is about 2.244 using $\alpha = .05$. The obtained F of 5.336 exceeds this, as well as the critical value for $\alpha = 0.01$. So the null hypothesis is rejected. Communication explains a statistically significant amount of variance in political knowledge controlling for demographics and political interest. This might be written up as such:

In a hierarchical multiple regression, demographics and political interest were entered in the model at the first step, and the five communication variables at the second step. After controlling for political interest and demographics, communication explained an additional 4.3% of the variance in political knowledge, $\Delta R^2 = 0.043, F(5, 332) = 5.336, p < .01$

These computations are easy enough to do by hand, if not somewhat annoying to do so. Fortunately, a good statistical program will do all the work for us. Figure 13.10 displays computer output from a hierarchical regression analysis from SPSS. Note that in a hierarchical regression analysis, the variables entered at the beginning get first dibbs at explaining variance in the outcome. Variables entered at the next stage then get their chance to explain whatever variance they can uniquely explain after the variables entered first have sucked out whatever variance they can explain in the outcome variable.

This output contains information from two regression models, as well as information about the difference between the two models. Model 1, the first model, is the regression model estimating political knowledge from political interest and demographics. The second model contains these same predictors but also the five communication variables. The top of the output contains the summary information about each of the models, such as R, R^2, and adjusted R^2, but it also contains a test of the null hypothesis that the change in population $R^2 = 0$ between models 1 and 2. Notice in the "Model Summary" section of the SPSS output, in the Model 2 row, there are statistics labeled "R-square change", "F-change", and "Sig. F-change". The R square change statistic is the difference between R^2 for model 2 and the R^2 for model 1, which we defined as $SR^2_{YX.W}$ for the communication variables, F change is the F statistic from equation 13.14 (within rounding error), and Sig. F change is the p-value for the change in R^2 after the communication variables are entered at step 2. So there is no need to do these computations by hand if you know how to get your statistical program to do it for you.

13.4.4 Interpreting Regression Statistics for the Predictor Variables

When assessing setwise partial association, researchers usually focus on the incremental increase in R^2 after a set of variables is added to a regression model. But the regression coefficients and their tests of significance can be interpreted using the same rules described in section 13.3.3. Looking at Figure 13.10, the regression coefficients, partial correlations, and semipartial coefficients in the model 1 output quantify the partial association between political knowledge and each of the demographics, controlling for political interest and the other demographic variables, as well as between political knowledge and political interest controlling for all the demographic variables. The partial association measures in model 2 for political interest and demographics control not only for each other, but also all of the communication variables in the model. Furthermore, the measures for each of the communication variables represent the partial association between that communication variable and political knowledge, controlling for demographics, political interest, and all the other communication variables.

Notice that the partial association measures for demographics and political interest differ between the two models. This is no surprise; indeed, it is totally expected. In the first model, the communication variables are not statistically controlled in the measures of partial association, whereas in the second model the measures of partial association between political knowledge and demographics and political interest control for the communication variables. So the measures of partial association in model 1 are based on a different set of statistical control variables.

It is often of interest to know the proportion of variance that a *single* predictor (X) uniquely explains in an outcome variable, controlling for a set of additional variables (call it set W). This proportion of variability explained could be calculated using the

Increase in R^2 resulting from the addition of the set of variables added in the second step. This is equal to the sample squared setwise semipartial correlation for this variable set.

Test of null hypothesis that population setwise squared semipartial correlation (for the set of variables added in the second step) is equal to 0.

Equation 13.14

Model Summary

Model	R	R Square	Adjusted R Square	Std. Error of the Estimate	Change Statistics				
					R Square Change	F Change	df1	df2	Sig. F Change
1	.650a	.422	.414	3.40950	.422	49.234	5	337	.000
2	.682b	.465	.449	3.30485	.043	5.336	5	332	.000

a. Predictors: (Constant), Interest in Politics, Household income (in $1000s), Sex (Male = 1, Female = 0), Age, Years of Education
b. Predictors: (Constant), Interest in Politics, Household income (in $1000s), Sex (Male = 1, Female = 0), Age, Years of Education, Local News Exposure, Political Talk Radio Exposure, Political Discussion, Newspaper Use, National Network News Exposure

Coefficients

Model		Unstandardized Coefficients		Standardized Coefficients	t	Sig.	Correlations		
		B	Std. Error	Beta			Zero-order	Partial	Part
1	(Constant)	-4.167	1.448		-2.878	.004			
	Age	.009	.013	.030	.681	.496	.105	.037	.028
	Years of Education	.548	.100	.258	5.494	.000	.458	.287	.227
	Sex (Male = 1, Female = 0)	1.460	.380	.164	3.844	.000	.302	.205	.159
	Household income (in $1000s)	.019	.005	.171	3.859	.000	.334	.206	.160
	Interest in Politics	1.859	.235	.371	7.898	.000	.523	.395	.327
2	(Constant)	-2.967	1.480		-2.005	.046			
	Age	.003	.014	.010	.218	.827	.105	.012	.009
	Years of Education	.449	.100	.211	4.486	.000	.458	.239	.180
	Sex (Male = 1, Female = 0)	1.414	.373	.159	3.794	.000	.302	.204	.152
	Household income (in $1000s)	.014	.005	.125	2.799	.005	.334	.152	.112
	Interest in Politics	1.405	.251	.280	5.586	.000	.523	.293	.224
	Political Discussion	.264	.077	.151	3.417	.001	.365	.184	.137
	National Network News Exposure	.052	.082	.031	.635	.526	.165	.035	.025
	Newspaper Use	.184	.072	.117	2.547	.011	.312	.138	.102
	Local News Exposure	-.205	.095	-.101	-2.158	.032	-.098	-.118	-.087
	Political Talk Radio Exposure	.313	.151	.090	2.075	.039	.270	.113	.083

a. Dependent Variable: Political Knowledge

Figure 13.10 SPSS output from a hierarchical multiple regression estimating political knowledge first from demographics and political interest, and then adding communication.

procedure described in section 13.4.2. That is, the additional variance in Y explained by adding variable X to a model already containing variable set W can be quantified as $SR^2_{YX.W} = R^2_{YWX} - R^2_{YW}$. However, it can be shown that if X is only a *single* predictor (as opposed to a set of predictors), $SR^2_{YX.W}$ is equal to the squared semi-partial correlation for X in the the model that includes both X and W, and its test of significance is given in all standard regression output as the t statistic for variable X.

For example, let's define W as demographics, political interest, and all the communication variables except exposure to local TV news, and X as local TV news exposure. According to the method described above, we can estimate the proportion of variance uniquely attributed to local TV news exposure as

$$SR^2_{YX.W} = R^2_{YWX} - R^2_{YW} = 0.465 - 0.458 = 0.007$$

So exposure to local TV news uniquely explains just under 1% of the variance in political knowledge after controlling for demographics, political interest, and the other 4 communication variables.

But we actually don't need to calculate R^2_{YW} to derive this. Instead, all we need to do is to conduct a multiple regression estimating Y from X and W. The output in Figure 13.10, model 2, is this model. When X is a single variable, the square of the semipartial correlation for X is the increase in R^2 uniquely attributable to X. From Figure 13.10, the semipartial correlation for local TV news exposure is -0.087, which when squared yields 0.007. This increase in R^2 of 0.007 is statistically different from zero, $t(332) = 2.158, p < .05$.

One interesting point about this analysis is worth pointing out. Although local TV news use uniquely explains just under 1% of the variance in political knowledge, notice from the partial regression coefficient (and the sign of the partial and semipartial correlations) that the partial relationship is *negative*. Two people who are of the same age, education, sex, income, and who watch the national network news, listen to political talk radio, read the newspaper, and discuss politics equally often but who differ by one day in their frequency of watching local TV news are expected to differ by 0.207 units in political knowledge. The person who watches more local TV news is expected to have *less* political knowledge. I'll leave it up to you to speculate on the meaning of this interesting result.

13.5   Modeling and Testing for Nonlinearity

We have been talking about linear regression. From the name, you would assume that linear regression would not be useful for modeling curvilinear relationships because curves are, by definition, not lines. You may recall from high school math that a curve can be expressed as a mathematical equation. Consider the equations represented graphically in Fig 13.11. These equations look much like the regression equations that we have been discussing, in that Y is generated as a function of one or more variables, each weighted by some number. And yet the relationship between X and Y is obviously not linear for any of these functions. It turns out we can fit curves with linear regression, depending on how we use the information contained in the predictor variables. In this section, I will only discuss the *quadratic regression model*, a special form of a curvilinear relationship because it is perhaps the simplest form of curvilinear model estimated in communication research.

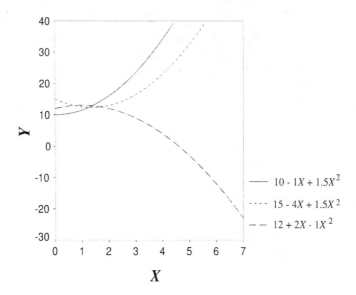

Figure 13.11 A set of quadratic functions

13.5.1   The Quadratic Regression Model

A quadratic relationship between any variable X and Y can be described with a quadratic regression model of the form

$$\hat{Y} = a + b_1(X) + b_2(X^2)$$

$$(13.15)$$

Notice that this model has two predictors, X as well as the square of X. So in the quadratic model, a variable is used as a predictor twice, once in its original form, and again after squaring it. This squaring of a predictor variable allows for the fitting of a curvilinear relationship between X and Y. A quadratic regression model should include both the square of the variable and the original variable as well. In no circumstance that I can think of would you want to exclude X from the model while including X^2. If X should be given no weight in estimating Y, then the regression analysis will give it no weight. Excluding X from the regression model is like forcing its regression coefficient to be zero, which may not be appropriate. Let the analysis decide how X should be weighted.

Before describing the quadratic model in more detail, it is worth asking why we would ever want to do this. There are two primary reasons. First, as discussed in Chapter 12, linearity is a primary assumption of regression. If the relationship between Y and X (or between Y and X controlling for W in multiple regression) is not linear, then the regression coefficient cannot be interpreted sensibly. This is because if the relationship between X and Y is curvilinear, then the estimated difference in Y between two cases who differ by a single unit on X depends on the two values of X. As a result, there is no single number that can be used to represent the estimated difference in Y as a function of a one unit difference in X. Second, some communication theories argue that a relationship between two variables is not linear, and in order to test the theory, it is necessary to see whether a curvilinear model such as the quadratic model fits better than a model that assumes the relationship is linear. For example, the number of times a commercial is presented and one's attitude toward the product being advertised is often conceptualized as a curvilinear relationship. As you are exposed more and more to an advertisement, you often come to like the product more through familiarity. But at some point, you get sufficiently irritated by seeing the commercial yet again that your attitude begins to become more negative, and the more additional advertisements you see for the product, the more you end up disliking the product. Other examples of curvilinear relationships in communication research are discussed by Albarracin and Kumkale (2003), Comstock, Rowell, and Bowers (1995), Eveland (1997), Hirsch (1980), Picard (1998), and Solomon and Williams (1997).

To illustrate the application of a quadratic model, consider the relationship between political knowledge and age. In the NES data set, the best fitting simple regression equation estimating political knowledge (Y) from age is

$$\hat{Y} = 9.783 + 0.032(Age)$$

but the coefficient for age just misses accepted standards for rejection of the null hypothesis that the population regression weight is zero, $t(341) = 1.953, p = 0.052$. The squared multiple correlation is 0.011, meaning that about 1% of the variance in political knowledge in this sample is explained by age. But consider the best fitting quadratic regression model:

$$\hat{Y} = 5.551 + 0.226(Age) - 0.002(Age^2)$$

where Age^2 is the square of a person's age. In this model, $R^2 = 0.025$, which represents an increase in the variance explained of $0.025 - 0.011 = 0.014$. The regression coefficient for Age^2 in this model quantifies the amount of curvature in the relationship between age and political knowledge. Rejecting the null hypothesis that $H_0 : \beta_{Age^2} = 0$ is akin to saying that there is some curvilinearity in the relationship between age and political knowledge in the population. In this model, b_{Age^2} is statistically different from zero, $t(340) = -2.242, p = .026$. From section 13.4.4, this is akin to the test of the null hypothesis that the increment in $\mathcal{R}^2 = 0$ when the square of age is added to the population regression model. We can reject that null hypothesis too.

It is difficult to interpret the nature of the relationship between X and Y in a quadratic regression model, so it is best to plot $\hat{Y}$ as a function of X to get a visual picture of the relationship, along with the best fitting regression line. Such a plot can be found in Figure 13.12, along with the best fitting linear and quadratic regression models. The quadratic model estimates that political knowledge is relatively lower among the younger and older in the population relative to those in the middle of life. Perhaps the relatively younger are less interested in political affairs or are too busy establishing their careers to pay much attention to politics and so are less likely to absorb political information from the mass media. In contrast, the older people in the population might be less able to recall information they've recently seen on the news as a result of maturational deterioration in memory. To be sure, there are many possible explanations for this curvilinear relationship.

In a quadratic regression model the strength of the relationship between X and Y is quantified as the proportion of variance in Y attributable to both X and X^2 together. In this example, the proportion of variance in political knowledge attributable to age is not 0.011 (from the simple linear regression model) but instead 0.025 (from the quadratic regression model). The proportion of the variability in political knowledge attributable to the curvilinear component of the relationship between X and Y is the difference between R^2 for models with and without X^2, or, equivalently, the squared semipartial correlation for X^2. So of the 2.5% of the variance in political knowledge attributable to age, $0.025 - 0.011$ or about 1.4% of that variance is attributable to the curvilinear component. Notice, however, that in a quadratic regression model R^2 does not indicate whether the relationship is increasing or decreasing with X (or perhaps both), because R^2 is always positive. To assess the sign of the relationship, it is necessary to look at a plot of $\hat{Y}$ against X, as in Figure 13.12. It may be the case that one cannot put a sign on the relationship, because whether the relationship is positive or negative may depend on the intervals of X that you focus on.

13.5.2   Interpreting the Coefficients in a Quadratic Regression Model

In a quadratic model of the form $\hat{Y} = a + b_1(X) + b_2(X^2)$, it is tempting to interpret b_1 as the linear component of the relationship between the predictor and the outcome. However, that is not entirely correct. The regression coefficient for X, b_1, does not quantify the positiveness versus negativeness of the relationship. It can be shown with some simple calculus that b_1 is the *instantaneous rate of change in Y* when $X = 0$. So b_1 is a conditional effect in a quadratic regression model in that it quantifies how Y is changing as a function of changes in X when $X = 0$. In trigonometric terms, b_1 is the slope of the line tangent to the curve at the point $X = 0$. It easy to create examples where b_1 is negative even though Y is generally increasing (rather than decreasing) as X increases.

In the quadratic model above, the coefficient for *Age* of 0.226 is statistically different from zero. But we cannot interpret this to mean that there is a positive linear

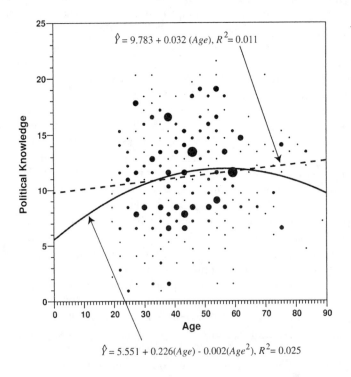

$$\hat{Y} = 9.783 + 0.032\ (Age),\ R^2 = 0.011$$

$$\hat{Y} = 5.551 + 0.226(Age) - 0.002(Age^2),\ R^2 = 0.025$$

Figure 13.12 Modeling a curvilinear relationship with linear regression.

relationship between age and political knowledge. Instead, it reflects the conditional relationship between X and Y at $Age = 0$. Obviously, the coefficient for Age has no useful interpretation in this example. Not only is there no one in the sample with an age even close to zero, but how sensible would it be to interpret the rate of change in knowledge as a function of age among newborns?

What does b_2 represent? It can be shown that b_2 quantifies both the steepness versus shallowness of the bend in the relationship as well as whether the relationship curves upward or downward. The larger b_2 in absolute value, the tighter the curve. If b_2 is positive, then the curve bends upward, whereas if b_2 is negative, the curve bends downward

This simple quadratic model can easily be extended to include additional predictor variables simply by adding them to the regression model. For example, we could have included demographics as well as newspaper news use in the quadratic regression model by including them as predictors of political knowledge in the regression model. In that case, the coefficient for the square of age would quantify its partial curvilinearity, controlling for the other predictor variables in the model.

13.6   Miscellaneous Issues in Multiple Regression

We have only scratched the surface of multiple regression. I could go on and on, but this chapter has to end somewhere. However, multiple regression is a theme that will permeate most of the rest of this book. I end this discussion of multiple regression temporarily by addressing a variety of miscellaneous issues that you must be aware of when conducting and interpreting a multiple regression analysis.

13.6.1   A Reminder About Causality

Remember that a multiple regression analysis simply takes data and produces statistics and test of significance. The proper interpretation of those statistics is the responsibility of the user. Even experienced scientists mistakenly believe that because multiple regression gives us a means of statistically controlling for those variables that provide alternative explanations and compete with the desired causal interpretation for a relationship between X and Y, we can say that X and Y are causally related because those alternative explanations have been ruled out statistically (see, e.g., Goertzel, 2002). However, whether or not two variables are causally related can only be determined through proper research design or convincing logical or theoretical arguments, not statistics. Multiple regression allows you to demonstrate that or test whether variables are associated after controlling for other variables. But whether or not one can conclude that the correlation is a causal one is not a question that multiple regression can answer unless the research design affords causal conclusions. Thus, although I have made statements in some of the examples above that might imply causality and have even used causal language now and then, in fact such statements are not warranted if the data collection does not allow us to determine whether the partial associations are causal. For example, the fact that there is a relationship between political discussion and political knowledge even after controlling for education, income, political interest, and other things does not imply that the more you discuss politics the more you will know about politics as a result. It does mean that these other variable are not producing the association spuriously or epiphenomenally. That is important information to have as an investigator, and for this reason multiple regression is a very useful procedure in spite of its apparent limitation that it still doesn't allow us to get at causal relationships.

13.6.2   Number of Cases Required for a Regression Analysis

How many cases should you have in a data set before conducting a multiple regression analysis? This question focuses on how large a sample should be in order to have significance tests of sufficient power, meaning that if the null hypothesis is false, there's a good chance that you will able to reject it. There are numerous opinions on this issue. One of the most common recommendations is that there should be anywhere between 20 and 50 cases per predictor variable. But such a recommendation isn't much help. For instance, if you have 4 predictor variables, popular opinion would thus suggest somewhere between 80 and 200 cases, which is a rather wide range of opinion. Although such ratio rules are quite common, they oversimplify the issue, and in fact there is no general rule that applies except that more is better. Indeed, Darlington (1990) argues that more important than the ratio of cases to predictors is the absolute number of cases, and Green's research (Green, 1991) on estimating required sample size to attain a given level of power is consistent with Darlington's recommendation.

When the interest is in detecting a statistically significant R^2 value, generally you need fewer cases than when the interest is in a specific measure of partial association. But even then, the exact number will depend on such things as how large of an association (multivariate or partial) is expected or worthy of detecting, and how intercorrelated the predictor variables are. Thus, there really are no specific guidelines that apply to all problems a researcher is likely to confront. For most research problems, I am uncomfortable when conducting a relatively simple multiple regression analysis to base the analysis on fewer than 50 cases, and as the number of predictor variables increases, the number of cases necessary increases as well. I'm more comfortable with at least 100 for simple studies involving no more than a couple of predictor variables. As the analysis increases in complexity, I attempt to add to this base figure of 100.

As a general rule, always try to maximize your sample size given the resources available (resources such as time, money, and research personnel), and realize that any analysis, not just multiple regression, becomes very difficult to trust when it is based on a small sample size. Small samples tend to produce results that won't replicate because the analysis is capitalizing on the idiosyncrasies of the few cases in your data.

13.6.3   Multicollinearity

I've heard more than one researcher claim that multiple regression can be used only when the predictor variables are statistically independent. Nothing can be further from the truth. In fact, if the k predictor variables are mutually uncorrelated, a multiple regression offers nothing over a set of k simple regressions estimating the outcome from each of the predictors separately. The beauty and strength of multiple regression is its ability to tease apart the unique contributions that two or more interrelated predictors make in explaining variation in an outcome variable. However, there are limits to how intercorrelated predictor variables can be before the system starts to break down. When the predictor variables in a multiple regression are highly correlated, they are said to be *collinear* or *multicollinear*. At its extreme, if one of the predictor variables is perfectly predictable from the other predictors (either individually or as a set), the predictor variable set is said to be *singular*, and a regression program will fail to produce a solution.

Multicollinearity is a term that can be used to describe either a single predictor variable or the set of predictors as a whole. The multicollinearity of a predictor variable is measured by a statistic called the variable's *tolerance*. Imagine a regression estimating predictor variable j from the other $k-1$ predictor variables in the regression model. From this regression, you could compute R_j^2, which measures the proportion of variance in predictor variable j explained by the other predictor variables. Variable j's tolerance, T_j, is defined as $1 - R_j^2$ and is interpreted as the proportion of variance in predictor variable j that is unique or unrelated to the other predictor variables:

$$\boxed{T_j = 1 - R_j^2}$$

(13.16)

Each variable in a regression model has its own tolerance statistic. Good statistical programs can display each variable's tolerance, if requested to do so. If your preferred program does not, you can generate the tolerance for each variable simply by estimating R_j^2 as described above.

Although there are no good hard and fast rules for determining when one should be particularly concerned about multicollinearity, a couple of guidelines should be kept in mind. First, high tolerance is better than low tolerance. Tolerance is a measure of how much variance in a predictor variable is unique to that variable or not related to or predictable from the other predictor variables. Low tolerance implies high multicollinearity. High tolerance implies low multicollinearity. The higher the tolerance, the less that predictor variable shares with the other predictor variables in the model, and the easier it is to detect true partial associations between the outcome and that variable. The lower the tolerance, the more that variable has in common statistically with the other variables in the analysis, perhaps because they are measuring conceptually similar things or things that are difficult to distinguish between analytically.

Second, multicollinearity lowers the power of tests of significance for measures of partial association and increases sample-to-sample variation in those measures. If predictor variables are highly related to each other, it is difficult to tease apart their unique relationships with a dependent variable. What this means is that tests of significance for measures of partial association may lead to nonsignificance, even though each variable when considered alone is highly related to the dependent variable to a statistically significant degree. The lower power that results from multicollinearity is attributable to the higher standard errors for the regression coefficients. Notice that the equation for the standard error of the partial regression coefficient for predictor j (equation 13.10) includes $1 - R_j^2$ in the denominator. The role of tolerance in the size of the standard error for predictor variable j can be seen more easily by rewriting equation 13.10 as

$$\boxed{s_{b_j} = \sqrt{\frac{1}{T_j}} \sqrt{\frac{MS_{residual}}{n(s_j^2)}}}$$

(13.17)

Remember that the standard error quantifies expected sample to sample variability in a statistic. As the relationship between variable j and the other predictors increases, tolerance decreases, and so $s_{b(j)}$ increases. So the regression coefficients will vary more from sample to sample when the predictor variables are highly correlated. The stronger the correlation between variable j and the other predictors, the more wildly partial b_j will fluctuate around partial β_j from sample to sample.

The inverse of a variable's tolerance ($1/T_j$) is called the variable's *variance inflation factor*, or VIF. So the larger the intercorrelation between predictor variable j and the other predictors (meaning lower tolerance), the larger VIF_j. Equation 13.10 can be written yet again as

$$s_{b_j} = \sqrt{VIF_j} \sqrt{\frac{MS_{residual}}{n(s_j^2)}}$$

(13.18)

This expression of the standard error of b_j illustrates that the variance inflation factor quantifies just how much larger the standard error of a partial regression coefficient is as a result of the intercorrelation between the predictors. More specifically, $\sqrt{VIF_j}$ quantifies the factor by which the standard error of b_j increases as a result of the intercorrelation between the predictor variables. The baseline for comparison is the the standard error of b_j if predictor variable j was uncorrelated with the other predictors. For example, a tolerance of 0.5 translates into a VIF of 2, meaning that the standard error of b_j is $\sqrt{2} = 1.414$ times larger than it would be if variable j was uncorrelated with the other predictors.

Equations 13.17 and 13.18 illustrate that caution should be exercised when deciding which variables to include in a multiple regression analysis. The glory of multiple regression is its ability to statistically control variables and test hypotheses involving variables that are interrelated. But if the variables are too highly related, problems are introduced. There is not much that can be done to eliminate the problem produced by multicollinearity. It is a reality of research that some predictor variables are going to be intercorrelated and that makes it more difficult to attribute variability in an outcome to one variable or the other. But multicollinearity, if it exists, will not necessarily adversely affect standard errors and therefore hypothesis tests for every predictor in a regression analysis. For example, consider that an outcome variable Y is being estimated by three variables, X, W, and Q. If W and X are highly correlated with each other but uncorrelated with Q, then W and X are collinear with each other but not with Q. The intercorrelation between W and X will have little or no effect on standard errors or tests of significance for W.

There are some rules of thumb circulating for deciding when you should be concerned about multicollinearity based on the size of a variable's tolerance or variance inflation factor. None of these guidelines are particularly useful in my opinion. But if you look at the relationship between tolerance and standard error inflation that occurs as as a result of multicollinearity, it is clear that although multicollinearity can be a problem in some circumstances, it has to be rather high (and therefore tolerance rather low) before standard errors are dramatically affected. Figure 13.13 graphically depicts this relationship. Remember that the square root of VIF quantifies the factor increase in the standard error of the partial regression weight that results from multicollinearity. Although any correlation between predictor variable k and the other predictors begins to inflate the standard error of predictor j, it isn't until the tolerance hits 0.25 (i.e., $R_j^2 = 0.75$) that the standard error is doubled. Although a doubling of the standard error can drastically reduce power in small samples or when a partial relationship is small, in large samples, researchers often have power to burn as a result of the power that a large sample size buys. So although multicollinearity is a bad thing to be sure, it is nearly unavoidable, and its presence need not incite panic.

Although multicollinearity reduces the power of statistical tests of partial association for individual predictors in a regression model, intercorrelations between variables

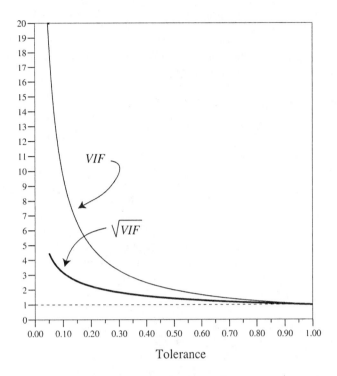

Figure 13.13 The relationship between predictor variable intercorrelation and standard error inflation.

that define a predictor variable set do not affect tests of significance for measures of setwise partial association between an outcome variable and that set. For instance, in the example presented in section 13.4.1 we tested whether "communication" (variable set X) was significantly associated with political knowledge (Y) after controlling for political interest and demographics (variable set W). In that example, "communication" was a set of communication-related predictor variables and its partial association with political knowledge was quantified as $SR^2_{YX \cdot W}$. Even though the 5 communication variables in the set were statistically intercorrelated, the power of the test of the null hypothesis of no setwise partial association between communication and political knowledge would not have been affected by the intercorrelation between these communication variables. However, power would have been reduced by intercorrelations between any of the communication variables and any of the variables in variable set X (demographics and political interest).

13.6.4 Selecting Predictor Variables to Include in a Regression Model

Given the damage that can be done to an analysis by including predictor variables in a model that are very highly correlated, the next question becomes, "Which variables should be in a model?" That is, how can you tell whether or not you should include a variable in a regression model? The answer to this question is deceptively simple. A variable should be in a regression model if it makes sense for it to be there. The variables that you do and do not include in a regression model should be based on a consideration of what question or questions you are trying to answer. If you want to know if a relationship between X and and some outcome variable Y persists after controlling for W, then you certainly should have W as well as X in the model. But if no one would argue that the relationship between X and Y is difficult to interpret without controlling for W, then why bother controlling for it? In such a case, there is no harm done by not including W in the model.

The beauty of multiple regression lies in its ability to tease apart spurious or epiphenomenal associations from associations attributable to other phenomena (such as causality). But just because a partial association is significant, this doesn't mean that the association is "real" in any sense. It is always possible that you haven't controlled for something important, and that had you done so, the partial association of interest to you would be dramatically different. Not including important variables in a regression is called *underspecification*. So you should include relevant variables when trying to statistically control, but you need not include variables that have no reason for being there.

In short, regression models should generally be constructed for a reason. Multiple regression is most useful when the variables that are in a model serve some function with respect to better illuminating some process or finding. Decisions about whether or not a variable serves a function are better made when the investigator has good experience and knowledge in the field being investigated, and when there is a clear purpose for the analysis. But including irrelevant variables or variables that you simply *want* to control may not do any harm, particularly if the sample size is large. But realize that including too many predictors, particularly ones that are not relevant to the primary goals of the study, can produce problems with multicollinearity if the "irrelevant" predictor variables are highly correlated with the predictor variables you are most interested in. Furthermore, you should not include lots of highly redundant measures of the same construct in a regression model if you are interested in questions about partial association involving that construct. Doing so will increase multicollinearity, produce instability in the estimates of partial association, and lower the power of hypothesis tests involving that construct.

Stepwise Variable Entry. There is a method of generating regression models that allows the investigator to wash his or her hands of the ambiguity in variable selection. The procedure is known as *stepwise regression*. In a stepwise regression, a model is built by a statistical software program based on the statistical relationships between the independent and dependent variables. Using this procedure, a regression model starts with only a constant. At the first step of the model building phase, the computer enters the predictor variable into the model that is most highly correlated with the outcome variable. Based on the remaining variables, the computer adds the variable that increases R^2 the most and to a statistically significant degree. If predictor variable or variables already in the model become statistically nonsignificant once this new variable is added, those predictor variables are removed from the model. This process continues until none of the remaining variables that have yet to be entered would increase R^2 to a statistically significant degree. Thus, this process is like hierarchical regression, except that a computer rather than the investigator determines the order of variable entry.

Although this procedure is common, it is also misunderstood. In my opinion, there are few benefits to this kind of multiple regression. I advocate a model building strategy where theory or predictions guide the decisions about what variables to include in a regression model. Stepwise procedures are largely atheoretical and exploratory, wreak havoc with Type I error rates, and can miss a lot of interesting phenomena. This does not imply that exploratory analyses serve no useful function. They certainly do. But stepwise regression tends to produce solutions that capitalize on chance relationships in a data set, and thus stepwise procedures often produce less replicable findings. But if you are simply exploring a data set and only want to include variables in a model that show statistically significant partial associations with the outcome variable, stepwise regression is perfectly appropriate. However, my personal personal belief is that solutions stemming from stepwise regression should be replicated to make sure that they are not due simply to chance associations that this method of variable selection will tend to pick out more frequently than other methods. An alternative is to build the model in a stepwise fashion using half of the data and then fit the resulting model to the other half—a procedure called *crossvalidation*. It is surprising how much different the best fitting model generated in one half of the data will look when it is reestimated on the second half.

13.6.5   The "Relative Importance" of Predictor Variables

There are occasions where one might be interested in which variable in a regression model is *most important* in explaining variation in the dependent variable. I use the word "important" here in a statistical sense, not in a theoretical or practical sense. For example, are individual differences in newspaper use more important in explaining variation in political knowledge compared to, say, individual differences in viewing of national network televised news broadcasts? Multiple regression gives us a means, in part, of answering this question, although how to quantify importance of a predictor is highly controversial.

You might be tempted to use the unstandardized partial regression weights as measures of importance and say that those with larger weights (in absolute value) are more important. For instance, in the regression model estimating political knowledge from demographcis only (Figure 13.3), you can see that the partial regression weight for age is twice as large as the partial regression weight for income, but of the four demographic predictors, the weights for sex and education dwarf the weights of income and age. You might claim that sex is the most important demographic predictor (of the 4 included in this model), followed by education, age, and income.

The problem with the use of the unstandardized regression coefficient as a measure of importance is that it is scale bound. For example, the unit of measurement for income is thousands of dollars whereas the unit of measurement for age is years. These are inherently noncomparable units of measurement, so regression weights cannot be sensibly compared. Furthermore, the partial regression weight for variable i itself depends on the unit of measurement chosen for that variable. For instance, the partial regression coefficient for income of $b = 0.020$ means that two people of the same education, sex, and age but who differ by one thousand dollars in their income are expected to differ by 0.020 units on the political knowledge measure. But what if income were quantified in tens of thousands of dollars rather than thousands of dollars? In that case, the regression coefficient for income would be 0.200, which then makes income more important than age. Similarly, the use of 0 and 1 for coding males and females is totally arbitrary. We could have used 0 for females and 5 for males, and that would change the coefficient for sex from 1.952 to 9.760. We can't use a statistic that is influenced by measurement decisions such as scaling as a measure of importance.

It might seem that we could eliminate this problem by standardizing the variables so that each observation on each variable is measured in terms of standard deviations from the variable's mean. Recall from Chapter 12 that the standardized regression coefficient quantifies the regression weight estimating the outcome from the predictor after both are standardized. In multiple regression, the standardized regression coefficients represent the partial regression weights estimating the outcome from the predictors assuming *all* variables are standardized. So the standardized regression equation estimating political knowledge from demographics is (from Figure 13.3)

$$\hat{Z}_Y = 0.139(Z_{Age}) + 0.380(Z_{Education}) + 0.219(Z_{Sex}) + 0.181(Z_{Income})$$

Because the variables are measured on the same scale after standardization (all variables have a mean of zero and a standard deviation of 1), differences in the units of measurement across variables don't influence the size of the standardized partial regression weights, and the partial regression weights will be unaffected by changes in the unit of measurement (such as years to days, dollars to cents, or how a dichotomous variable is coded). Using the standardized regression weights, education is most important, followed by sex, income, and age.

Although some people advocate the standardized partial regression weight as a measure of importance (e.g., Hunter & Hamilton, 2002), it has some serious problems as well. A standardized regression weight for predictor i is interpreted as the number of standard deviations on the outcome that two cases are expected to differ who are one standard deviation apart on predictor variable j but who are equal on all the other predictors in the model. As Darlington (1990) points out, when the predictors are highly intercorrelated, it may be difficult to imagine that two such units could actually exist. In addition, the standardized regression weights are model dependent. That is, the relative size of the standardized partial regression weights will depend on what other variables are being used as predictors. This is not a problem for an investigator interested in rank ordering the relative importance of the predictors in the context of only those predictors. But suppose one investigator estimates Y from variables A, B, C, and D, but another investigator estimates the same Y variable from variables A, B, E, F, and G. It may be the case that variable A is highly important in one investigator's model but not in the other. This would be expected because the size of a standardized partial regression weight (as well as other measures of partial association) depends on which variables are being statistically controlled. And even if the two investigators are using the same predictors, if the two investigators are doing an analysis on two different samples of research units, the standardized regression coefficients will differ from each other as a result of differences in the variability of one or more of the variables across the two samples (because the unit of measurement for a standardized variable is one standard deviation). So the standardized regression coefficients cannot be used to compare the importance of variables across regression models that are based on different predictors, nor can they be used compare the same model from different samples of research units (such as different samples of people) unless you can assume that the variances of the predictor and outcome variables do not vary across across samples. For a detailed discussion of some of the problems with standardized coefficients as measures of importance, see Kim & Mueller (1976), Kim & Ferree (1981).

Although there are many measures of relative importance that are in part justifiable, I tend to prefer the squared semipartial correlation because it has *ratio* qualities (c.f. Darlington, 1990). For example, if one variable has a squared semipartial correlation of 0.4, and another variable has a squared semipartial correlation of 0.2, we can say that the first variable uniquely explains twice as much variance in Y as the second variable (of course, controlling for each other). The standardized regression weights don't have this nice property. In practice, if one is interested merely in the rank order of the variance explained, then using the standardized regression weights will tend to lead to the same rank order as using the squared semipartial correlations. However, the squared semipartial correlation still suffers from noncomparability across models based on different predictors, or across samples when the predictor and/or outcome variables differ in variability across samples (Linn & Werts, 1969).

How to measure the relative importance of predictors in a regression model is a highly controversial topic. Many of the differences in opinion revolve around how to conceptualize and quantify "importance." For instance, not everyone agrees that judgments of importance should be based on variance accounted for measures such as the squared semipartial correlation. Perhaps we should focus instead on reduction in estimation error, for example. Some argue that the simple unsquared correlation should be used in some circumstances (Beatty, 2002; Darlington, 1990), or the product of the standardized regression weight and the simple correlation between that predictor and the outcome (Darlington, 1968), or just the simple correlation, ignoring the interrelationship between the predictors. A relatively new procedure called *dominance analysis* (Azen & Budescu, 2003; Budescu, 1993) is an interesting way of conceptualizing relative importance. In a dominance analysis, the relative importance of predictor A over predictor B is gauged by first generating all $2^{(k-2)}$ possible regression models from k predictors that contain at least A and B. For instance, with 5 predictors (A, B, C, D, and E), there are $2^{(5-2)} = 8$ possible regression models that contain A and B (AB, ABC, ABD, ABE, ABCD, ABCE, ABDE, and ABCDE). Each of these 8 regression models has a squared semipartial correlation for both A and B. Once these regression models and squared semipartial correlations are computed, A is deemed to be completely dominant over B if the squared semipartial correlation for A is always larger than the squared semipartial correlation for B. For details on this procedure, see Azen and Budescu (2003).

13.6.6 The Effects of Measurement Error

Hard as we may try, we will never perfectly measure the constructs we study. There will always be some mismatch between what we intend to be measuring and what we actually measure. And even if we measure validly, there nevertheless will almost always be some error in our measurement, such that case i's observed measurement on variable X does not correspond precisely to case i's true score on that variable. Recall from Chapters 2 and 6 that the discrepancy between the observed and true scores is quantified with an index of *reliability*. To the extent that there is some discrepancy between the observed scores and true scores, reliability is less than one. When there is no correspondence between observed and true scores, reliability is zero.

When assessing the association between two variables X and Y (using Pearson's r or a simple regression weight), measurement error in either X or Y tends to lower the statistical power of inferential tests of the relationship between X and Y, but it does not bias r or b as a measure of the association. In other words, in a random sample from a population in which the null hypothesis of no association is true, we can expect r or b to be 0, regardless of the reliability of measurement of X and Y. But hypothesis tests will be lower in power than they would be if the variables were measured without error. The reduction in power is caused by an increase in the standard error of the statistic that results from error in measurement. The lower the reliability of measurement of X

or Y, the larger the standard error of r or b and so, all other things being equal, the smaller the t statistic and the larger the p-value in inferential tests.

But the same cannot be said of measures of partial association. Error in measurement of predictor variables in multiple regression can bias measures of partial association. Even if there is no partial association between X and Y controlling for W in the population, the expected values of $pr_{YX.W}$, $sr_{YW.W}$, and partial b for X are not zero if W is measured with error. This means that hypothesis tests for a predictor are invalid when variables that are being statistically controlled are measured with less than perfect reliability.

An example will illustrate this. Suppose that the population correlations between the true scores of three variables are as follows: $\rho_{XY} = 0.35$ $\rho_{XW} = 0.50$, $\rho_{WY} = 0.70$. From equation 13.8, the partial correlation between X and Y controlling for W is

$$\rho_{YX.W} = \frac{0.35 - (0.50)(0.70)}{\sqrt{(1 - 0.50^2)(1 - 0.70^2)}} = \frac{0}{0.618} = 0$$

Imagine that X and Y were measured perfectly (i.e., reliability = 1), but that W was measured imperfectly, with reliability of 0.80. It can be shown that if the population correlation between any two variables X and W is ρ_{WX} when both are measured without error, then the correlation between X and W when one or the other is measured with error is equal to ρ_{XW} times the square root of the product of the reliabilities of X and W.[6] Therefore, the population correlation between X and W when W is measured with reliability of 0.80 is equal to $0.50\sqrt{(1)(0.8)} = 0.447$, and the population correlation between W and Y is equal to $0.70\sqrt{(1)(0.8)} = 0.626$. Therefore, the population partial correlation between Y and X controlling for W measured with reliability 0.80 is

$$\rho_{YX.W} = \frac{0.35 - (0.447)(0.626)}{\sqrt{(1 - 0.447^2)(1 - 0.626^2)}} = \frac{0.070}{0.698} = 0.100$$

So the introduction of measurement error into W has produced a nonzero partial correlation between X and Y controlling for W even though the population partial correlation is zero between the true scores. This is a general phenemenon and applies to any measure of partial association, such as the partial regression weight and the semipartial correlation. If a measure of partial association between predictor variable i and Y is a biased measure when a covariate is measured with error, then a hypothesis tests using that measure of partial association between i and Y is invalid. In other words, if the null hypothesis is true, then the probability of a Type I error is greater than α when a covariate is measured with error.

Given that communication researchers almost never measure with perfect reliability, this suggests that multiple regression should not be used to test hypotheses about partial association. However, I think this would be going too far. First, it is usually true that the outcome variable is measured with error as well. Reliability in the measurement of Y will tend to lower the power of statistical tests of partial association. This reduced power can counteract the inflated Type I error rate that measurement error in a covariate produces. Second, there is nothing inherently wrong with using an invalid test so long as well all recognize the test is invalid, agree that this is acceptable, and stick to the same criterion for deciding whether or not to reject the null hypothesis. The consequence is that the discipline will be making more Type I errors across the

[6]This is a reexpression of the formula for correcting a correlation for attenuation due to measurement error. See Nunnally, 1978, p. 220.

discipline than perhaps we realize. But if we can live with that, then we shouldn't worry too much about it. The usefulness of multiple regression as a data analytic tool far outweighs the relatively small cost of the estimation bias that measurement error produces in some circumstances.

13.6.7 Categorical, Ordinal, and Bounded Outcome Variables

The extent to which the assumptions of OLS regression are met determines the validity and power of hypothesis tests that an OLS regression model yields. Although assumption violations need not produce a problem for accurate inference, there are some instances in which the assumptions of OLS cannot possibly be met because of the nature of the outcome variable. For instance, not all outcome variables of interest to communication researchers are quantitative, and yet OLS regression requires the outcome to be numerical and measured at the interval level or higher. Sometimes we are interested in examining the relationship between a variable or set of variables and an outcome that is *categorical*. Examples include whether or not a person is willing to be interviewed by a reporter (Baldassare & Katz, 1989), whether a news story makes it on to the local television news broadcast (Gant & Dimmick, 2000), which types of media people use most frequently or prefer (Van Eijck & Van Rees, 2000), use of a contraceptive (Kincaid, 2000), or whether a defendant on trial is convicted or acquitted (Bruschke & Loges, 1999). For categorical outcomes, the interest is typically estimating the probability of category membership as a function of one or more predictors and interpreting the coefficients from the model. Probabilities are constrained to be between 0 and 1, and yet nothing about the estimation of an OLS model requires that $\hat{Y}$ be bounded in this fashion. As a result, the model can yield $\hat{Y}$ values that are outside of the range of possibility and regression coefficients that have questionable meaning. Furthermore, the relationship between a predictor of a categorical outcome and the probability of category membership is typically nonlinear rather than linear, making OLS regression inappropriate. Finally, the errors in the estimation of probabilities are often neither normal nor homoscedastic, two assumptions that OLS regression makes.

Relatively simple extensions of multiple regression apply to the analysis of dichotomous (i.e., an outcome variable that can take only one of two values) or multicategorical dependent variables. *Logistic regression* can be used and in much the same way as ordinary least squares regression, except that it is designed to assess the relationship between a set of predictors and a dichotomous dependent variable. *Multinomial logistic regression* requires just one additional conceptual leap beyond logistic regression that the user must master in order to successfully analyze multicategorical dependent variables. Readers interested in more detail on the analysis of a categorical outcome from a set of one or more predictor variables (that can be either quantitative, categorical, or a mixture) should consult one of several good (although sometimes technical) treatments of the analysis of categorical response variables, such as Hosmer and Lemeshow (2000), Long (1997), Menard (2001), Pampel (2000), or Wright (1995). In addition, Denham (2002) discusses the analysis of categorical responses in the context of communication research and provides several examples from the communication literature. Although some researchers employ *discriminant function analysis* when their outcome variable is categorical, it has some unrealistic assumptions and limitations that make it a less-than-ideal analytical choice (see e.g., Hosmer & Lemeshow, 2000; Press & Wilson, 1978)

An outcome variable might be quantitative but still not best analyzed with an OLS regression model. For instance, self-report measures of attitudes or behavior are sometimes single-item questions requiring an ordinal-level response of some kind (such as *strongly disagree* to *strongly agree*, or *never* to very *frequently*). Such response scales often also constrain the response to relatively few options, as the omnipresent 5–point Likert scale does. It is common for communication researchers to analyze such outcomes using multiple regression by assuming that the response scale has interval qualities. Whether this is legitimate is debatable. Although it is sometimes not unreasonable to assume an ordinal variable has interval properties, data from such response scales usually still cannot meet the assumptions of OLS regression because the errors in estimation are necessarily discrete and (therefore nonnormal). Furthermore, when an outcome variable is bounded on the upper and/or lower end (as most ordinal response scales are), the assumption of homoscedasticity becomes less plausible, as such bounds tend to compress response variation differently depending on the value of the predictor(s) or $\hat{Y}$. Finally, an OLS model of a discrete, ordinal variable can produce estimations that are outside of the lower or upper bound of measurement.

Although it is difficult to assess the extent to which these problems are affecting an analysis, and in some circumstances these possible problems are fairly inconsequential, it makes more sense to me to use an analytical method such as *probit regression* or *ordinal logit regression* to model such outcomes because they are explicitly designed for this purpose. These methods yield models that are conceptually similar to OLS regression models and can be used to test many of the same statistical hypotheses, although the mathematics of the methods alters the interpretation of the coefficients. A good (albeit a bit technical) introduction to these methods can be found in Borooah (2002), Liao (1994), and Long (1997). Scott, Goldberg, and Mayo (1997) provide a good nontechnical overview.

An outcome variable can be quantitative and measured at the interval level but still not best analyzed with OLS regression. An example would be a "count" outcome—an variable that is measured by counting things up. For instance, political communication researchers often build regression models estimating political knowledge, much as I did in this chapter, operationalizing political knowledge as the number of questions that a person can correctly answer about a political candidate or candidates. So long as (a) the number of things being counted is fairly large and (b) the average count is not near the lower or upper end of the measurement scale, little harm is typically done by modeling such variables with OLS regression and interpreting the coefficients and hypothesis tests as I have done here. But often the distribution of counts is highly skewed and clustered toward the lower or upper bound of the measurement scale. For instance, scholars of political participation often define participation as the number of political behaviors a person reports having engaged in recently. Sometimes the list of behaviors the participants is given to choose from is short in length (perhaps 5 items or less), and the individual behaviors exhibited by relatively few people. So measurements of 0 or 1 on the outcome variable predominate the data. It is difficult in such situations to justify the use of OLS regression for many of the same reasons we can question OLS analysis of probabilities or ordinal variables. The bounded, discrete nature of the outcome variable makes it unreasonable to apply a method that makes assumptions that are certainly not met. For count variables that are highly skewed with measurements clustered mostly toward the upper or lower bound of the measurement scale, *Poisson regression* or *negative binomial regression* is the preferred strategy (Liao,

1994; Long, 1997). A good and relatively nontechnical introduction can be found in Gardner, Mulvey, and Shaw (1995).

Having said all this, I think it is easy to become paralyzed as a data analyst by focusing too much on whether the assumptions of a statistical method are perfectly met. I've never analyzed a data set knowing unequivocally that the conditions of the statistical test employed are satisfied. For instance, in order for the normality of errors assumption to be met, the outcome variable must be measured at the interval or ratio level and *continuous and unbounded*. But truly continuous measurement is relatively rare. A mathematical model of an outcome variable using OLS regression or any similar method can never be more than an approximation. All models are wrong in some sense, either because important variables have been excluded from the model or because the data do not meet the assumptions of the method used to build the model. Our statistical methods can, at best, approximately model a process that is probably too complicated to be modeled perfectly or, for that matter, even completely understood (MacCallum, 2003). Approximations are about the best we will ever be able to do. So I see no reason to lose sleep over the application of OLS regression to data that OLS regression was not designed to analyze so long as you can muster the faith that the analysis and your qualitative interpretation of your study results are not going to be completely inappropriate or wrong. However, I think it is a mistake for us not to think carefully about our data when choosing how to analyze it and instead act as creatures of habit by reflexively pulling multiple regression out of the toolbox whenever a research question or hypothesis focuses on questions of partial association between variables. I believe that we should use the most appropriate analytical method that is both feasible and available. Many of the methods I've advocated in this section are a bit more complicated than OLS regression, but I think their greater complexity is not a good excuse for failing to use them when they are better suited to the data you have. By all means, master multiple regression, but use that knowledge as a foundation you can build upon to acquire these skills when you are ready.

13.7 Summary

This is one of the longest chapters in the book and for good reason. Multiple regression is one of the more widely used statistical methods in communication science. Understanding how it is used and what it is used for are essential to making sense of the communication literature and being able to participate in the discipline. So I spent more time describing the details of multiple regression analysis than you would tend to find in comparable books on statistical methods. But the length of this chapter is also influenced by the versatility of the method. Multiple regression is a "general data analytic system" (Cohen, 1968) in that many of the methods described in this book reduce down to a form of regression. For example, we saw in this chapter that the independent groups t test comparing two means is nothing other than a simple regression. To understand how these forms of analysis can be represented with regression, it is necessary to have a good grasp on the details of regression. In the next several chapters, I introduce the analysis of variance and covariance. And I show throughout these chapters that analysis of variance and covariance can be represented as a regression model, and that measures of effect size widely discussed and used in the analysis of variance and covariance are actually measures of association and partial association. So we are not done talking about regression. It will continue to be a theme throughout the next several chapters.

FOURTEEN

Single Factor Analysis of Variance

Throughout the last several chapters we've been examining the correlates of political knowledge. We discovered that not only can you predict political knowledge from a variety of demographics and communication variables but that most of these variables uniquely contribute to explaining individual differences in political knowledge. With the exception of gender, all the predictor variables we have considered thus far have been quantitative in that they quantify individual variations on some variable, such as how frequently a person discusses politics or how often a person's watches the national network news. Even a dichotomous variable such as gender can be thought of as a crude measure of quantitative dimension, such as a person's biological maleness (1 = lots, 0 = none). But what about a *multicategorical* variable—a categorical variable with several categories—such as a person's political affiliation? Some people are Democrats, others are Republicans, and still others identify with no party or some other political group such as the Green party. There is no sensible way that people can be quantified on a variable such as political affiliation because, by its nature, political affiliation is not a quantitative dimension along which people vary. At yet we still may be interested in determining whether people who identify with different political parties vary in some way, such as how much they know about politics.

As this example illustrates, predictors of some outcome variable of interest are not always quantitative. Indeed, there are many occasions in communication research when the independent variable or variables of interest are categorical. For example, Armstrong and Chung (2000) conducted an experiment examining the effects of TV interference on learning of new information. They asked college students to read a newspaper story either in the presence or absence of a televised distractor (a popular television show) and then assessed their recall of the information in the story either in the presence of absence of a televised distractor that was either similar to or different from the distraction during the learning phase. The students were randomly assigned to one of 6 conditions in this experiment. Thus, the independent variable could have one of 6 different levels or values, depending on the condition of the experiment that the researcher assigned the student to. This variable is not quantitative by any means. It is strictly a nominal or categorical variable. For example, in one condition, the TV program was on during the reading of the story but not during the test. In another condition, the TV program was not on during the reading of the story but it was on during the test. This is a qualitative, categorical manipulation of the independent variable (presence vs. absence of distraction and when that distraction was present).

An experiment such as this is a good example of a situation in which an independent variable being used to explain some kind of outcome variable (such as learning of news content) is categorical. But there are other kinds of categorical variables that communication researchers *observe* rather than *manipulate*, with the emphasis on seeing how people that fall into different categories vary on an outcome variable. For example, Rimal (2001) classified people into four groups based on how much they felt they were at risk for developing a cardiovascular disease and how much confidence they had in their ability to prevent becoming a victim of cardiovascular disease. They also assessed these people with respect to how much they talked about health-related issues with others in the past week. Their analysis focused on whether the four groups defined by their combination of perceived risk and perceived confidence differed on average from each other in how much they talked to others about health-related issues. In this study, the categorical variable was not a manipulation, as was the case in Armstrong and Chung (2000), but a naturally occurring dimension. Other categorical variables that are often used to predict or explain some dependent variable include a person's ethnicity, religion, the political party a person belongs to, or any other conceivable individual difference that manifests itself as category or group membership rather than as a score on some quantitative dimension.

In this chapter, we discuss statistical methods focused on assessing whether a set of groups, on average, differ on an outcome variable. These groups may be naturally existing groups defined by such dimensions as gender, religious affiliation, or political party affiliation. Or they may be experimentally generated groups, such as several experimental conditions and a control condition. The procedure described in this chapter is known as *analysis of variance* (often abbreviated as ANOVA from ANalysis Of VAriance). However, as will be shown toward the end of the chapter, analysis of variance is just a special case of multiple regression. I only discuss "oneway" or "single factor" analysis of variance in this chapter. Single factor analysis of variance differs from other kinds of analysis of variance in that the groups are presumed to differ on only a single dimension or *factor* of interest in the analysis, such as a person's political party affiliation, his or her ethnic group, or which one of several levels of a single manipulated variable a person is assigned to in an experiment.

14.1 Analysis of Variance

The goal of analysis of variance is to determine if two or more groups differ from each other on some outcome variable on average, where the average is defined as the arithmetic mean. When conducting any study and you've measured two or more groups on some outcome variable, there is almost certainly going to be some difference between the group means. Two or more groups may be equal on the variable in the population from which a sample was derived, but it is unlikely that in the sample the group means will be exactly equal. Sampling variability will produce some discrepancy between two or more means in a study. Similarly, even if some kind of experimental manipulation of a variable has absolutely no effect on people in a study, it is unlikely that two or more groups exposed to different levels of an experimental manipulation will be exactly equal on the outcome variable on average. When we conduct an analysis of variance, we are determining whether the groups differ from each other by more than "chance" would tend to produce. That is, do the groups really differ on the dependent variable in some systematic way, or can the observed differences be easily explained as the result of "chance." There are different mechanisms that produce "chance" outcomes, as I discuss later.

In analysis of variance, the null hypothesis is that k group means are the same in the population from which the sample was derived, and the alternative is that they are not the same. Symbolically,

$$H_0 : \mu_1 = \mu_2 = \ldots = \mu_k$$
$$H_a : \text{at least two } \mu \text{ are different}$$

where k is the number of groups being compared. We can think of these k groups as either subpopulations of a single common population from which the sample was derived, or as k distinct populations. Either way you conceptualize the groups, the null and alternative hypotheses are the same.

14.1.1   Partitioning the Outcome Variable into its Sources of Variation

ANOVA is literally the analysis of variance, in that it focuses on the relative size of two forms of variability in the data: (a) variability in the dependent variable attributable to group differences and (b) variability that is not attributable to group differences. To understand these sources of variation and what they quantify, it is worth discussing how you can partition the measurements on an outcome variable into these sources of variation. Throughout this section, we will continue to rely on data from the 2000 National Election Study. In addition to the measure of political knowledge used throughout the last few chapters, participants were asked to identify themselves as either a Democrat, a Republican, or as identifying with some other political party. Of the $n = 343$ respondents, 141 identified themselves as Democrats, and the mean political knowledge of these self-identified Democrats was 11.418. We will refer to the Democrats as group 1, so $\overline{Y}_1 = 11.418, n_1 = 141$. One hundred forty seven respondents called themselves Republicans, and the mean political knowledge of these Republicans was 11.816. Let's call the Republicans group 2, so $\overline{Y}_2 = 11.816, n_2 = 147$. The remaining 55 respondents identified with neither the Democratic nor the Republican party. Their mean political knowledge as 9.128, so $\overline{Y}_3 = 9.128, n_3 = 55$.

In analysis of variance, each case's measurement on the outcome variable Y can be broken into three distinct components, as represented by the following equation:

$$\boxed{Y_{ij} = \overline{Y} + (\overline{Y}_j - \overline{Y}) + (Y_{ij} - \overline{Y}_j)}$$

$$(14.1)$$

where Y_{ij} is case i's measurement on the dependent variable and case i is a member of group j, $\overline{Y}$ equals the outcome variable mean, and $\overline{Y}_j$ equals the outcome variable mean for group j.

The first component in this formula, $\overline{Y}$, is often called the *grand mean* and it is the same for all cases in the data set. It is simply the mean of Y computed using every case in the data. In these data, $\overline{Y} = 11.222$, the mean political knowledge computed across all 343 respondents in the study. The second component $(\overline{Y}_j - \overline{Y})$ represents the difference between the mean of Y for the group the case is in and the grand mean. The final component $(Y_{ij} - \overline{Y}_j)$ quantifies how that case's Y measurement differs from the mean for the group that the case is a member of.

Table 14.1
Partitioning Variability in Y Into Components

i	Group (j)	Y_{ij}	$\overline{Y}_j$	$\overline{Y}$	$(Y_{ij} - \overline{Y})^2$	$(\overline{Y}_j - \overline{Y})^2$	$(Y_{ij} - \overline{Y}_j)^2$
1	1(Democrat)	8	11.418	11.222	10.381	0.038	11.683
2	1	13	11.418	11.222	3.161	0.038	2.503
3	1	8	11.418	11.222	10.381	0.038	11.683
.	.	.	.	.	.	.	.
.	.	.	.	.	.	.	.
140	1	3	11.418	11.222	67.601	0.038	70.863
141	1	10	11.418	11.222	1.493	0.038	2.017
142	2(Republican)	12	11.816	11.222	0.605	0.353	0.034
143	2	11	11.816	11.222	0.049	0.353	0.666
144	2	14	11.816	11.222	7.717	0.353	4.770
.	.	.	.	.	.	.	.
.	.	.	.	.	.	.	.
287	2	5	11.816	11.222	38.713	0.353	46.458
288	2	15	11.816	11.222	14.273	0.353	10.138
289	3 ("Other")	6	9.127	11.222	27.269	4.389	9.778
290	3	10	9.127	11.222	1.493	4.389	0.762
291	3	6	9.127	11.222	27.269	4.389	9.778
.	.	.	.	.	.	.	.
.	.	.	.	.	.	.	.
342	3	19	9.127	11.222	60.497	4.389	97.476
343	3	1	9.127	11.222	104.489	4.389	66.048

$$SS_{total} = 6779.160$$
$$SS_{between} = 298.698$$
$$SS_{within} = 6480.462$$

In Table 14.1 I show a part of the data file sorted by party identification. Consider the first row in Table 14.1. We'll call this respondent case #1 ($i = 1$) and refer to her as "Alice." Alice identified herself as a Democrat ($j = 1$), and she got eight questions correct on the knowledge test ($Y_{11} = 8$). From equation 14.1, Alice's score of 8 can be broken up into three components. The first component is how respondents in this study tended to do on the knowledge test on average, ignoring which political party the person identified with. This is the grand mean, $\overline{Y}$. The second component is how respondents like Alice, her fellow Democrats, tended to differ from this grand mean. The third component is how Alice's score is different from the mean for Democrats. Plugging the numbers in:

$$
\begin{aligned}
Y_{ij} &= \overline{Y} + (\overline{Y}_j - \overline{Y}) + (Y_{ij} - \overline{Y}_j) \\
8 &= 11.222 + (11.418 - 11.222) + (8 - 11.418) \\
8 &= 11.222 + 0.196 + -3.418 \\
8 &= 8
\end{aligned}
$$

Because the grand mean carries no information about either group or individual differences, it serves no useful function in terms of partitioning sources of variation. So let's subtract the grand mean from both sides of equation 14.1. The result is

$$(Y_{ij} - \overline{Y}) = (\overline{Y}_j - \overline{Y}) + (Y_{ij} - \overline{Y}_j)$$

(14.2)

Equation 14.2 says that each case's Y measurement, expressed now as deviation from the grand mean, contains two components. The first component is how that case's group mean differs from the grand mean $(\overline{Y}_j - \overline{Y})$. The second component is how that case differs from the mean of the group the case belongs to $(Y_{ij} - \overline{Y}_j)$. Thus, Alice's deviation from the grand mean is $8 - 11.222 = -3.222$, which means that her political knowledge score is 3.222 points below the grand mean. This component of Alice's score, called the *total* component, itself contains two components. The first of these two components, called the *between-groups* component, quantifies how Alice's group (Democrats) differ from the grand mean. The second component, the *within-group* or *error* component, is how Alice's political knowledge score differs from the mean political knowledge of Democrats. So a case's deviation from the grand mean is the sum of a between-group component and a within-group component. For Alice,

$$
\begin{array}{ccccc}
(8 - 11.222) & = & (11.418 - 11.222) & + & (8 - 11.418) \\
-3.222 & = & 0.196 & + & -3.418 \\
-3.222 & = & -3.222 & &
\end{array}
$$

Notice that each of these components is a quantification of variation. How Alice differs from the grand mean (-3.222) is a combination of how Alice's group varies from the grand mean (0.196) and how Alice varies from her group mean (-3.418). Equation 14.2 can be applied to every case in the data, and the math will work out every time.

14.1.2   Total, Between-, and Within-Group Variability in Y

In the previous section I apportioned one case's Y measurement, expressed as a deviation from the grand mean, into two nonoverlapping components. This can be done for each case in a data set. So if there are n participants in a study, there are n total components (one for each participant), as well as n between-groups components and n within-groups components. Of course, the n total components are not going to be all the same, nor will the n between-groups components, nor will the n within-groups components. They will vary from each other. We can derive a measure of how much they vary from each other by adding up all n of each of these components after first squaring them. If you do so, the following equation holds:

$$\sum(Y_{ij} - \overline{Y})^2 = \sum(\overline{Y}_j - \overline{Y})^2 + \sum(Y_{ij} - \overline{Y}_j)^2$$

(14.3)

In analysis of variance, these n components after they are squared and summed over all n cases are called the *total sum of squares* (SS_{total}), the *between-groups sum of squares* ($SS_{between}$), and the *within-groups* or *error sum of squares* (SS_{within} or SS_{error}), respectively. So equation 14.3 can be written as

$$SS_{total} = SS_{between} + SS_{within}$$

(14.4)

where

$$
\begin{array}{rcl}
SS_{total} & = & \sum (Y_{ij} - \overline{Y})^2 \\
SS_{between} & = & \sum (\overline{Y}_j - \overline{Y})^2 \\
SS_{within} & = & \sum (Y_{ij} - \overline{Y}_j)^2
\end{array}
$$

In Table 14.1, I provide the squared components for several case in the data file. Observe that when you add up each of these squared components across all n cases in the data file (see the bottom rows of the table), it is indeed true that $SS_{total} = SS_{between} + SS_{within}$. That is, $6779.160 = 298.698 + 6480.462$

So SS_{total} quantifies variation of Y around $\overline{Y}$, whereas $SS_{between}$ quantifies variation of the sample means $(\overline{Y}_j)$ around $\overline{Y}$. Now let's stop a minute, step back, and observe something important. Imagine for a moment that you had everyone in the population available to you, and you could ask everyone these 22 political knowledge questions. After you did so, you could divide them up into Republicans, Democrats, and "Others" and calculate the three population means: μ_1, μ_2, and μ_3. You would also be able to compute the population grand mean, μ. Now imagine computing $SS_{between}$ using data from the entire population:

$$
\text{population } SS_{between} = \sum (n_j)(\mu_j - \mu)^2
$$

where the summation is over all k groups. If the null hypothesis is true, it should be apparent that $SS_{between}$ would have to be equal to zero, right? It would be zero because all k values of μ_j would be equal to a common value μ, so $(\mu_j - \mu)^2 = 0$ for all k groups. However, if the null hypothesis was false, then $SS_{between}$ would be greater than zero.

But this isn't ever going to happen. Instead, in research we are stuck dealing with samples. The problem is that even if the null hypothesis is true, $SS_{between}$ is most certainly not going to be zero in a sample. In order for $SS_{between}$ to be zero in a sample, the three sample means would have to be *exactly* equal. But even if the null hypothesis is true, it is highly unlikely that the three sample means will be exactly equal to zero. Given that $SS_{between}$ cannot be less than zero, if follows that in any sample, $SS_{between}$ is almost certain to be greater than zero. Nevertheless, $SS_{between}$ remains a statistic that is sensitive to the difference between the means. Larger discrepancies between the sample means will translate into a larger $SS_{between}$. And because $SS_{total} = SS_{between} + SS_{within}$, it follows that larger discrepancies between sample means translates into a smaller value of SS_{within}.

14.1.3 The F ratio

From the previous discussion, we know that even if the null hypothesis is true, $SS_{between}$ is unlikely to be zero in any sample, and that it will be some positive number. The key to testing the null hypothesis is to determine how likely it is to obtain a $SS_{between}$ as large or larger as observed in the sample assuming the null hypothesis is true. In short, we need a p-value. To compute this p-value, we need to convert the obtained value of $SS_{between}$ to one with a known sampling distribution. The sampling distribution that works relatively well is the F-distribution. The conversion of $SS_{between}$ to F is accomplished with a fairly simple formula:

$$
\boxed{F = \frac{SS_{between}/df_{between}}{SS_{within}/df_{within}}}
$$

$$(14.5)$$

where $df_{between}$ and df_{within} are the *between-groups* and *within-groups* degrees of freedom, respectively. Equation 14.5 is a ratio of between-group variability to within-group variability, as we defined these concepts earlier. But it is a ratio of between and within group variability *per degrees of freedom*. In single factor analysis of variance, $df_{between} = k - 1$, and $df_{within} = n - k$, where n is the total sample size.

The ratio of a sum of squares relative to degrees of freedom has a special name in analysis of variance. Such a ratio is called a *mean square*. Defining the *mean square between groups* as

$$MS_{between} = \frac{SS_{between}}{df_{between}}$$

(14.6)

and the *mean square within groups* as

$$MS_{within} = \frac{SS_{within}}{df_{within}}$$

(14.7)

then equation 14.5 can be rewritten as

$$F = \frac{MS_{between}}{MS_{within}}$$

(14.8)

An examination of equations 14.5 and 14.8 shows that this F ratio is related to the size of the difference between the sample means. In any sample of k groups with total sample size n distributed among the k groups, the larger the discrepancies between the sample means, the larger $SS_{between}$ will be, the smaller SS_{within} will be, and therefore the larger F will be. So the F ratio can be used to quantify the size of the difference between the k means in the sample.

In the NES data, we can calculate F relatively easily from the information contained in Table 14.1. From that table, $SS_{between} = 298.698$ and $SS_{within} = 6480.462$. There are $k = 3$ groups, and the total sample size is $n = 343$, so $df_{between} = k - 1 = 2$ and $df_{within} = 343 - 3 = 340$. Plugging these numbers into equations 14.5 to 14.8,

$$F = \frac{298.698/2}{6480.462/340} = 7.836$$

It can be shown (and I'll elaborate in the next section why) that if the null hypothesis is true, $E(F) \approx 1$. But in any sample, F is unlikely to be one even if the null hypothesis true. When taking a sample of total size n from k populations with the same mean (or k subpopulations with the same mean from a single common population), F will differ from sample to sample. So F has a sampling distribution, just as does t, χ^2, Z, and any other test statistic we've used thus far to test a hypothesis. As with any hypothesis test, we need to calculate the probability of getting an F-ratio as large as obtained in the sample or larger assuming the null hypothesis is true in order to decide between the null and alternative hypotheses. To generate this p-value, we can derive the critical value for F for a given α level, or we can use a computer to derive the p-value more precisely. As discussed in Chapter 13, the F distribution is a family of distributions defined by a numerator and denominator degrees of freedom. In a single factor ANOVA, $df_{numerator} = df_{between}$, and $df_{denominator} = df_{within}$. From Appendix

Political Knowledge

	N	Mean	Std. Deviation
democrat	141	11.4184	4.34603
republican	147	11.8163	4.24267
other	55	9.1273	4.72995
Total	343	11.2216	4.45220

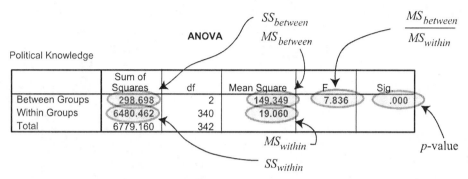

ANOVA

Political Knowledge

	Sum of Squares	df	Mean Square	F	Sig.
Between Groups	298.698	2	149.349	7.836	.000
Within Groups	6480.462	340	19.060		
Total	6779.160	342			

Robust Tests of Equality of Means

Political Knowledge

	Statistic[a]	df1	df2	Sig.
Welch	6.910	2	145.303	.001

a. Asymptotically F distributed.

Figure 14.1 SPSS output from a single factor ANOVA.

D1, the critical F for rejection of the null hypothesis using $\alpha = 0.05$, $df_{numerator} = 2$ and $df_{denominator} = 340$ is about 3.026. The obtained F of 7.836 exceeds this, so the null hypothesis is rejected. The substantive conclusion:

> People who self-identify as Democrats, Republicans, or neither differ in their political knowledge, $F(2, 340) = 7.836, p < .05$, with means of 11.418, 11.816, and 9.127, respectively.

Lots of work, I know. Fortunately, any decent statistics program can conduct all the computations for you and even provide a more precise p-value. Output from a single-factor ANOVA from SPSS corresponding to this data set can be found in Figure 14.1. All the information we computed by hand is available in the output, so there is no need to do all this manual computation.

14.1.4 Underlying Statistical Theory

In the previous section I claimed that the expected value of F is about one if the null hypothesis is true. I will now clarify why this is so. To do so, let's go back to imagining we had the entire population available to us. If we did, we could compute

$$\tau = \sum [n_j(\mu_j - \mu)^2]$$

(14.9)

where the summation is over all k groups. It should be apparent that if the null hypothesis is true, then τ must be equal to zero, because in that case all group means $\mu_j = \mu$. But if the null hypothesis is false, τ must be greater than zero.

If we assume that the k groups are equally variable around their respective means on the outcome variable, we can calculate a single number to quantify the *within-group variance*, defined as

$$\sigma^2 = \frac{\sum(Y_{ij} - \mu_j)^2}{N}$$

(14.10)

where N is the total population size (that is, the sum of the sizes of the k groups being compared) and the summation is over all i members of the population, each of whom is a member of some group j. It is sensible to use a single number σ^2 as a quantification of within-group variance only if we can assume that the k subpopulations are equally variable around their mean. If we can't make that assumption, there is no single σ^2 but instead k different within group variances, one for each group. It should be apparent that the size of σ^2 is independent of whether the null hypothesis is true or false, because nowhere in equation 14.9 is there anything that reflects how much the group means differ from each other. Instead, σ^2 is sensitive only to how much members of each group differ from their respective group means.

It can be shown that when taking k random samples of size n_j from k groups with common within-group variance σ^2, then MS_{within} (equation 14.7) is an unbiased estimator of σ^2, and $MS_{between}$ (equation 14.6) is an unbiased estimator of

$$\sigma^2 + [\tau/(k-1)]$$

But in the special case where the null hypothesis is true, $\tau = 0$. In that case, $MS_{between}$ and MS_{within} estimate the same quantity (σ^2). So if the null hypothesis is true, the ratio of $MS_{between}$ to MS_{within} (the F ratio) is expected to be about one.[1] But if the null hypothesis is false, $MS_{between}$ estimates σ^2 plus something additional, with that additional thing being a function of the difference between the population group means. The larger the difference between the population means, the larger the ratio of $MS_{between}$ to MS_{within} will tend to be.

14.1.5 Statistical Assumptions of ANOVA

The goal of any hypothesis test is to make a decision a between a null and alternative hypothesis. The decision between the two hinges on the p-value, so it is important to know that we can trust the p-value that a hypothesis test gives. Like virtually every statistical test, the mathematics that leads to the use of the F distribution to generate the p-value carries with it a variety of assumptions, and a violation of these assumptions can invalidate the test.

Like the independent groups t test using the pooled variance method, ANOVA makes the assumptions that the population or populations from which the sample was derived are normally distributed on the outcome variable, the the groups are equally variable on the outcome variable in the population or populations sampled, and all observations are statistically independent. ANOVA as described here is robust to all but extreme forms of nonnormality, but not to violations of variance equality or independence. Methods for testing the important assumption of variance equality are

---

[1]More precisely, $E(F) = df_{within}/(df_{within} - 2)$ if the null hypothesis is true.

discussed in Chapter 10, so I do not discuss them here. Although my discussion of these tests focused on the $k = 2$ case, these tests have equivalent versions for $k > 2$. For example, to test the null hypothesis that that the k group variances are the same in the population, you could apply the transformations described in sections 10.2.1 (Levene's test) or 10.2.2 (the Brown-Forsythe test) and then conduct an analysis of variance on the resulting scores. A significant p-value from the resulting ANOVA suggests a violation of the assumption of equal population variances. However, recall from Chapter 10 that I advocated that you not assume equality of variance when comparing two groups means and instead use the Welch-Satterthwaite t test in all circumstances, regardless of whether there is evidence that the assumption of equal variances is met. The Welch-Satterthwaite test does not require equality of variance and it tends to perform best across a variety of situations. It follows that I would (and do) argue against using the standard ANOVA F ratio to test the null hypothesis when $k = 2$ and instead test the null hypothesis with the Welch-Satterthwaite t test.

The problem with violations of the assumption of equality of variance across groups is that the resulting p-value may be a poor estimation of the true p-value, and this can produce a decision error. The nature of this lowered estimation accuracy is attributable to the null hypothesis that is actually tested when groups differ in variance. Although the ANOVA is used to test the null hypothesis that two or more population means are equal, the F ratio is sensitive to more than just differences in the sample means. It is also sensitive to differences in variability within groups. If you can't assume the variances equal, then you can't interpret analysis of variance as a test of the equality of population means. By making the assumption of equal variances, we can more confidently attribute a large F ratio and small p-value to differences in group means. But we can't just assume anything we want and not worry about the consequences of violating those assumptions. If the variances differ between groups, the null hypothesis being tested with ANOVA is the equality of the population distributions on the outcome variable. Rejection of this null hypothesis tells us nothing about the nature of those differences—it could be differences in mean, differences in variance, differences in shape, or any combination of these.

Given the interpretational ambiguity that a violation of the assumption of variance equality produces, what should you do? There are two courses of action. The first course is to test for variance equality to determine whether the assumption is reasonable. Levene's test, the Brown-Forsythe test, and others can be used for this purpose. For example, to conduct the Brown-Forsythe test, we would convert each case's political knowledge measurement to absolute deviation from the case's group median. In the NES data, the variable called *party* codes political party group (1 = Democrat, 2 = Republican, 3 = Other) and *pknow* is the political knowledge measurement. The following SPSS code will produce the transformation:

```
if (party = 1) knowt = abs(pknow-11).
if (party = 2) knowt = abs(pknow-12).
if (party = 3) knowt = abs(pknow-9).
```

An ANOVA using *knowt* as the outcome variable leads to a nonsignificant F-ratio, $F(2, 340) = 0.413, p = 0.662$, meaning there is no evidence that the equality of variance assumption is violated. If the F ratio from the Brown-Forsythe test was statistically significant, then the p-value from ANOVA may be inaccurate, meaning you might be more likely to make a decision error.

The other course of action is to use a test to compare the population means that does not assume equality of the group variances. I believe it is probably safer to apply a different statistical test of the ANOVA null hypothesis that doesn't assume equality of variance. There is a test that is mathematically identical to the Welch-Satterthwaite test when $k = 2$ but that can also be used when there are more than two groups. This test is called the *Welch F test* and it is essentially a multiple group version of the Welch-Satterthwaite t test. Simulation research shows that the Welch F test does tend to produce a more accurate p-value and therefore keeps the probability of a Type I error close to α even the groups are not equally variable. This test is computationally complicated, and I refer you to Welch (1951) if you are interested in the details.

Fortunately, a good program like SPSS will conduct the Welch F test. Figure 14.1 shows that the Welch F statistic is 6.910, $p = 0.001$. So even if we don't assume variance equality and use the Welch F test, we would reject the null hypothesis of equality of means. I do recommend that you at least double check the results of the regular ANOVA F by conducting the Welch F whenever possible. If the two give conflicting results, trust the Welch F test more.

14.1.6   Revisiting the Pooled Variance t test

In chapter 10 we entertained data from a study examining the effect of media form on learning. Eight participants in this study were randomly assigned to read an online version of the *New York Times* over a 5-day period, and the another eight were randomly assigned to read a print version of the *New York Times*. After 5 days, both groups took a test to see how much they learned about public affairs. We conducted an independent groups t test and ruled out "chance" as the explanation for the obtained difference, $t = 3.209, p = .006$, with means of 2.875 and 4.875 for the online and print versions of the experiment, respectively (see Figure 10.3). Could we have tested the null hypothesis that the two groups learned the same amount on average using ANOVA? Indeed we could have. An ANOVA on the data in Table 10.1 yields $F(1, 14) = 10.299, p = 0.006$. Observed that the p-value from the ANOVA is .006, just as the two-tailed t test gives. So analysis of variance has produced the same decision about the null hypothesis as the independent groups t test. Furthermore, but not nearly as obvious, observe that $F = t^2$. The t statistic from the pooled variance approach was 3.209, which when squared equals about 10.299, which is the F ratio from the analysis of variance. This will always be true when comparing only two group means. The independent groups t test using the pooled variance approach will give the same result as analysis of variance assuming equality of variance, because they are mathematically equivalent tests.

14.1.7   Quantifying Effect Size

In previous chapters we talked about significance tests versus confidence intervals. Significance tests allow a researcher to evaluate the consistency between the obtained result and an assumption about the population or effect in the population. In contrast, a confidence interval both allows you to determine if the effect (for example, the difference between means) is likely to be zero as well as construct a window of the likely values of the effect in the population. In ANOVA, there is no such thing as a confidence interval for the difference between more than 2 means. However, it is possible to estimate how much of the variance between research units on the outcome variable is attributable to the groups in which the units belong. Some journals in communication require that researchers report an estimate of effect size, so it is worth understanding how effect size is estimated.

The simplest measure of effect size is η^2 (eta-squared), defined as

$$\eta^2 = \frac{SS_{between}}{SS_{total}}$$

(14.11)

This statistic quantifies the proportion of variance in the outcome variable attributable to group membership and can be interpreted much like a squared correlation is interpreted. Eta-squared is conceptually equivalent to R^2 in a multiple regression context and it is useful as a description of variance explained in the sample. But it is a biased measure of effect size in the population. Even if the null hypothesis is true, $SS_{between}$ will be greater than zero in a sample (because almost never will the group means be exactly equal in a sample) and so $SS_{between}$ will almost always be larger than zero. The smaller the sample the larger the bias. The concept of bias is predicated on the notion of the "true" effect size. If you had access to everyone in the population and could categorize them with respect to their political party identification (Republican, Democrat, or Other) and quantify their political knowledge with this measure, it would be possible to derive the "true" effect size for political party membership. The true effect size can be thought of as the effect size you would get if you had data for the entire population.

Two other measures attempt to estimate this true effect size and do so with greater precision than does η^2. ϵ^2 (epsilon-squared) has several equivalent forms that you might see in the literature:

$$\epsilon^2 = 1 - \frac{MS_{within}}{MS_{total}} = \frac{SS_{between} - (k-1)MS_{within}}{SS_{total}}$$

(14.12)

ϵ^2 is also a proportion of variance accounted for measure and is conceptually equivalent to adjusted R^2 in regression. An alternative is known as ω^2 (omega-squared) and is based on a slightly different mathematical approach. The formula is

$$\omega^2 = \frac{SS_{between} - (k-1)MS_{within}}{SS_{total} + MS_{within}}$$

(14.13)

In any sample, $\eta^2 \geq \epsilon^2 \geq \omega^2$. Using the information contained in Figure 14.1, the effect sizes quantifying the relationship between political party identification and political knowledge are

$$\eta^2 = \frac{298.698}{6779.160} = 0.044$$

$$\epsilon^2 = 1 - \frac{19.060}{19.822} = 0.038$$

$$\omega^2 = \frac{298.698 - (3-1)19.060}{6779.160 + 19.060} = 0.038$$

So between 3.8% and 4.4% of the variance in political knowledge can be explained by political party identification, depending on which measure of effect size you use. Most communication researchers would interpret this as a rather small effect.

Given these different options, which measure of effect size should you use? The logic of η^2 is somewhat inconsistent with the way the estimation of the F ratio is derived, and it is known that R^2 (which is conceptually the same as η^2) is an overestimate of the proportion of variance in the outcome variable attributable to the predictors in the population. But as a purely descriptive measure, there nothing wrong with it. If you are interested in making inferences about the size of the effect in some group other than your sample (such as in a bigger population), I recommend the use of either ϵ^2 or ω^2, and it really doesn't matter which. Unfortunately, most statistical programs do not report either of these measures of effect size, but they sometimes report η^2. However, with the formulae above, you can compute any of these measures by hand without too much difficulty or hassle. As the example above illustrates, with large samples the differences between the three measures will be small.

The measurement of effect size is a controversial topic. For example, in a special methodological issue of *Human Communication Research* there are two articles that report conflicting advice on how to quantify effect size (Beatty, 2002; Levine & Hullet, 2002), and my discussion hasn't helped matters. A good starting place for those of you interested in measures of effect size is Maxwell, Camp, and Arvey (1981), where the three measures of effect size I describe here are compared. In the end, most journals that require a measure of effect size don't specify a preference for one versus the other. So long as you report something, you are probably better off than if you report nothing. This is not to say that it doesn't matter at all which measure you use. But if you go beyond the typical practice of reporting only a p-value when interpreting the results of an ANOVA, you will have satisfied a substantial number of the critics of hypothesis testing and the tendency for communication researchers to focus mostly on p-values when interpreting statistical tests.

14.1.8   Why Not Multiple t tests?

Analysis of variance allows us to compare several group means to each other. But why do we need a separate test to do this? We already have a statistical test that can be used to compare two independent means to each other—the independent groups t test discussed in Chapter 10. Why can't we just conduct three t tests, first comparing Republicans to Democrats, then Republicans to those who identify as neither Republican nor Democrat, and then Democrats to those who don't identify as either? The problem with this approach is that even if all three of these means are equal in the population, the probability of incorrectly claiming that they are not all the same is going to be higher than α when you conduct multiple t tests. Define the *omnibus null hypothesis* as the null hypothesis tested with analysis of variance—that all k population means are equal. By conducting multiple t tests to test the omnibus null hypothesis using the α level of significance for each test, the probability of incorrectly rejecting the omnibus null hypothesis is greater than α.

But why is that? The answer comes from elementary probability and the rules discussed in Chapter 5. First, recognize that as we do more and more hypothesis tests, the probability of rejecting a true null hypothesis increases. There is no way around this. Flukes do happen, and you'll get a difference between the sample means "just by chance," leading you to reject a null hypothesis that is in fact true. The more hypotheses you test in a study, the greater the chances of making such a mistake. At its extreme, if a study involves lots of comparisons between the means of many groups, the probability of finding at least one "false" difference between two groups can be close to one.

Let's put this intuition into more formal language using the multiplicative probability law. Recall that the multiplicative probability law says that if two events are independent, then the probability of the two events both occurring is equal to the product of the probabilities of each event. This law generalizes to more than two events. For example, if three independent events A, B, and C have probabilities of occurring equal to $P(A)$, $P(B)$, and $P(C)$, then the probability of them *all* occurring is $P(A \text{ and } B \text{ and } C) = P(A)P(B)P(C)$. Now let's apply this law to conducting multiple t tests. Let's assume that the omnibus null hypothesis is true. So Democrats (group 1), Republicans (group 2), and "Others" (group 3) in the population sampled have the same political knowledge on average. That is, $\mu_1 = \mu_2 = \mu_3$. Now consider the null hypothesis $\mu_1 = \mu_2$ tested with an independent groups t test. We know that the probability of incorrectly rejecting this null hypothesis if it is true is .05 when using $\alpha = .05$ as the level of significance for the test. Therefore, the probability of correctly *not* rejecting the null hypothesis if it is true is equal to $1 - \alpha = .95$. So if the *omnibus null hypothesis* is true (i.e., $\mu_1 = \mu_2 = \mu_3$), the probability of correctly claiming that $\mu_1 = \mu_2$ is 0.95. We can apply this same logic to the other two mean comparisons. If the omnibus null hypothesis is true, the probability of correctly not rejecting the null hypothesis that $\mu_2 = \mu_3$ using the independent groups t test at $\alpha = 0.05$ is $1 - 0.05 = 0.95$, as is the probability of correctly not rejecting the null hypothesis that $\mu_1 = \mu_3$. Therefore, the probability of correctly not rejecting *all three null hypotheses* with the independent groups t test, assuming all three are true, is equal to the product of these three probabilities: $(0.95)(0.95)(0.95) = 0.857$. That means that the probability of incorrectly rejecting *at least one* of the null hypotheses assuming they are all true is one minus the probability of correctly failing to rejecting all of them, which is $1 - 0.857 = 0.143$. But if you rejected even one of the null hypotheses tested with the independent groups t test, then you *must* reject the omnibus null hypothesis. So by conducting multiple t tests using $\alpha = 0.05$ for each test, the probability of incorrectly rejecting the omnibus null hypothesis that *all* the means are equal is not $\alpha = .05$ as we generally desire when testing a null hypothesis, but considerably more than that.

This logic is not exactly correct because these three hypothesis tests are not statistically independent. But even if we correct for this nonindependence, we can say that when we test g true null hypotheses using $\alpha = .05$ for each of the g tests, the probability of incorrectly rejecting *at least one of them* is between α and $g\alpha$, where α is the level of significance used to test each null hypothesis (Ryan, 1959). Here, $g = 3$, so the probability of making at least one Type I error in this set of tests is somewhere between .05 and .15.

The probability of making at least one incorrect rejection of a true null hypothesis when conducting multiple hypothesis tests is known as the *familywise Type I error rate* (Keppel, 1991) or the *experimentwise Type I error rate* (Ryan, 1959, 1960). I prefer the term *familywise* because "experimentwise" implies that the study is an experiment, which it may not be. Formally, the familywise Type I error rate (α_{FW}) when a constant level of significance (α) is used to reject the null hypothesis in each of the g hypothesis tests is

$$\boxed{\alpha \leq \alpha_{FW} \leq g\alpha}$$

(14.14)

It should be clear from equation 14.14 that as g increases, the familywise Type I error rate increases dramatically. For example, with $k = 5$ groups, there are $5(4)/2 = 10$ t tests (5 choose 2 from Chapter 7, Box 7.1) that you would need to conduct to compare all groups to each other. When $k = 5$, $g = 10$, so the familywise Type I error rate may be as high as 0.50. This is an unacceptable Type I error rate by most scientific standards.[2]

The increase in the Type I error rate that results from multiple hypothesis tests is known as the *multiple test problem* or *Type I error inflation*, and methods of dealing with this problem fill the statistics literature. Analysis of variance gets around the multiple test problem by conducting a single test of the omnibus null hypothesis. In so doing, it keeps the Type I error rate when testing the omnibus null hypothesis at α.

14.1.9   Inference with Nonrandom Samples

My discussion of ANOVA thus far has been focused on population inferences. The National Election Study is based on a random sample of residents of the United States. Such random sampling affords the ability to make population inferences using information in the sample. The F distribution is driven in that case by random sampling variability—F ratios differ from sample to sample when the null hypothesis is true because of the random nature of the participant selection process. Although it is not uncommon for research focused on comparing naturally existing groups to be based on random samples, it is at least as common in communication science if not more so for the groups to be artificially created by the researcher, and the sample derived through convenience sampling rather than some kind of random sampling plan (e.g., Potter, Cooper, & Dupagne, 1993; Rossiter, 1976). Experimentation, a frequently used research method in communication, is an example. In an experiment, the researcher manipulates the levels of the independent variable and randomly assigns people into the levels of that manipulation prior to measuring a variable that the manipulation is expected to affect. Almost never is there an attempt by the researcher to recruit participants for an experiment through some kind of random sampling plan. But this does not present a problem for the use of analysis of variance, although the lack of random sampling does change the nature of the inference. I illustrate this in much the same way that I justified the use of the t test to compare group means from an experiment in Chapter 10, by showing that analysis of variance will usually produce the same statistical decision that a method based on an alternative method of conceptualizing chance—the randomization test. Other justifications are possible (e.g., Lang, 1996), but I believe an understanding of the randomization test makes it crystal clear just what we are testing when we apply analysis of variance to experimental data.

A study by Sundar (2000) on multimedia effects on information processing represents well the experimental research method as it has been applied to questions about communication. The literature on the relationship between media modality, multimodality, and information processing is conflicting. Some literature suggests that learning is improved by presenting information in multiple modalities, whereas other literatures suggests that the same information presented simultaneously in multiple forms can lead to information overload and reduced learning. Sundar (2000) asked how different modes on information presentation on the Web (e.g., text, video, audio), as well as how various combinations of modes on a web page relate to such variables

---

[2]Because a probability cannot be greater than one, the maximum value for α_{FW} is set to 1 if $g\alpha > 1$.

LEARN

	N	Mean	Std. Deviation
text	12	8.0833	2.02073
text+picture	12	8.3333	2.30940
text+audio	12	6.3333	2.01509
text+picture+audio	12	6.4167	1.31137
text+video	12	5.7500	1.71226
Total	60	6.9833	2.11124

ANOVA

LEARN

	Sum of Squares	df	Mean Square	F	Sig.
Between Groups	63.567	4	15.892	4.383	.004
Within Groups	199.417	55	3.626		
Total	262.983	59			

Robust Tests of Equality of Means

LEARN

	Statistic[a]	df1	df2	Sig.
Welch	3.783	4	27.177	.014

a. Asymptotically F distributed.

Figure 14.2 SPSS ANOVA output from the Sundar (2000) study.

as learning, web page evaluation, and overall experience with the site. He created five web pages each of which contained the same three news stories. The web pages varied in the modes of information presentation. One of the web pages (the "text" condition) contained the content only in textual form. The second web page (the "picture" condition) contained the same text content but each story also included a photograph relevant to the content. The third page (the "audio" condition) contained the same content as the text condition but it also included an audio download for each story. The fourth page (the "picture + audio" condition) was a combination of the picture plus audio conditions, with the text for each story accompanied by a photograph and an audio download. The last page (the "video" condition) combined text with a picture and a video download containing story relevant video. The participants were 60 undergraduate students enrolled in communication courses who were willing to participate in exchange for extra course credit. They were randomly assigned to browse one of the five web pages for 15 minutes with instructions to make sure they read each of the three news stories. After browsing the page, the participants were given a 12–item multiple choice test that was used to quantify their learning of information in the stories.

Appendix E8 on the CD describes a data set corresponding to this experiment. These data are not the actual data from the study but, when analyzed, they yield the same basic results as Sundar (2000) reported in Table 1 of his article. The precise results are not important for the purpose of this section, but the output from an ANOVA using SPSS is presented in Figure 14.2. What is important is a comparison of two different methods of analyzing these data. Sundar (2000) conducted an analysis of variance comparing the mean learning of participants across the 5 conditions. In these data, $F(4, 55) = 4.383, p = .004$. If we were to interpret this result just as the

ANOVA in the previous example was interpreted, we'd reject the null hypothesis that $\mu_{text} = \mu_{picture} = \mu_{audio} = \mu_{picture+audio} = \mu_{video}$ and claim that these five population means are not the same. However, it isn't at all clear just what the populations are here and therefore what population means these sample means are estimating. The participants in the study were not obtained through any kind of random sampling plan, so there is little statistical basis for making an inferential leap from these participants to some broader population. And because Sundar (2000) made no attempt to randomly sample from any population, random sampling error did not get an opportunity to exert its effect on the study-to-study variation in outcomes that the F sampling distribution is supposed to represent, at least as described in the previous example. So is it reasonable to derive the p-value for F using the F distribution?

It is, and here is why. In experiments, our focus is on causal or process inference, not population inference. We want to know whether variations in the manipulated variable are responsible for differences between the groups on the outcome variable. But recall from Chapter 10 that even if we assume that the independent variable has no effect whatsoever on the outcome variable, we will still find some differences between the group means. Assume that the measurement on the outcome variable that each participant provides to the data set is the measurement that each would have provided regardless of which condition he or she was assigned to. This is akin to assuming that the manipulation had no effect at all on the outcome variable. If this assumption were true, random assignment variability will just by itself produce different study outcomes (i.e, different F ratios). If Jim had been assigned to condition A rather than condition B, Joan to condition C rather than B, Alex to condition A rather than C, and so forth, then a different mean difference would have been obtained, as would a different F statistic. So the "chance" mechanism producing study to study variation is the random assignment process rather than random sampling variation.

With computers, the right software, or a little programming skill, it is relatively easy to determine the probability of the obtained difference between the means or a pattern more discrepant from equality if we assume that random assignment variability is the sole mechanism producing the obtained result. This is accomplished by producing every possible random reassignment of the n participants and their corresponding scores on the outcome variable into k groups of size $n_1, n_2, \ldots, n_k$ and deriving the F ratio (or some other statistic we desire) for each of those possible study results. The p-value is then defined as the proportion of possible random assignments that produce an F ratio at least as large as the F ratio actually obtained in the study.

The one problem with this approach is the potentially massive number of such possible random reassignments. The number of ways of randomly reassigning n measurements into groups in this manner is defined mathematically as

$$\left(\frac{n!}{n_1! n_2! \ldots n_k!} \right)$$

where $n!$ is defined as in Chapters 5 and 10 as $n(n-1)(n-2)\ldots(1)$. In the data set corresponding to the Sundar (2000) study, $n = 60$, and these 60 participants were assigned randomly into 5 groups of equal size, so $n_1 = 12$, $n_2 = 12$, $n_3 = 12$, $n_4 = 12$, and $n_5 = 12$. From the expression above, the number of possible ways this study could have come out (i.e., the number of possible F ratios given the 60 learning scores obtained) assuming that the manipulation had no effect is $60!/(12!12!12!12!12!)$, or about 3.3×10^{38}. That's 33 followed by 37 zeros, and that is a big number! Although computers are fast and getting faster every year, we'd nevertheless have to wait a long time to get the p-value. So this approach is computationally infeasible, or so it would seem.

But it actually *is* feasible to do something very similar. Rather than enumerating all possible F ratios resulting from random assignment, why not just randomly sample from the possible random assignments? This is easy to do if you have the software or good programming skills. You can randomly sample from the possible random reassignments by just randomly scrambling the 60 Y scores, reassigning them randomly to groups (in this case, groups of equal size because in the original study, the groups were of equal size) and computing F. Repeating this many times (say, between 1,000 and 10,000—the more the better) you end up with what is called the *approximate randomization distribution of F*. The p-value for the obtained result is then approximated as the proportion of F ratios in the approximate randomization distribution that are equal to or exceed the obtained F, including the obtained F itself. So the approximation randomization distribution must include the obtained F ratio. Therefore, if you have $(m-1)$ scramblings of the data file in the approximate randomization distribution, resulting in m values of F (because you include the obtained F in that distribution) the p-value for the obtained F ratio can be no smaller than $1/m$.

Using an SPSS macro included in Appendix F on the CD (a earlier version was published in Hayes, 1998), I computed this *approximate randomization test* using this data set. I requested 5,000 "randomizations" of the data file and resulting F ratios (which actually yielded only 4,999 because the actual random assignment of scores from the study counts as one of the permutations). In the resulting approximate randomization distribution of F, only 26 F ratios were equal to or larger than the obtained F ratio of 4.383. So the p-value for the obtained result is approximately $26/5000 = 0.0052$ by this test (see Figure 14.3). But notice that this approximation of p is very close to the p-value that the analysis of variance produced (which was 0.004). The p-value from a randomization test will usually be very close to the p-value that analysis of variance produces—something this example illustrates and that mathematical arguments also support (Baker & Collier, 1955; Hoeffding, 1952; Scheffe, 1959). This justifies the use of analysis of variance to rule out "chance" as the explanation for the difference between the means in an experiment even when there has been no random sampling from any population or populations that can be defined. Indeed, Ronald Fisher, the man who invented analysis of variance, argued that ANOVA can be considered a valid test because it tends to agree with the decision that a randomization test yields. So randomization tests are really the "purest" means of statistical inference for experimental data. ANOVA is just a fast way of approximating what a randomization test would produce.

But let's not forget that random sampling from populations is still the only way to make a solid argument for population inference. In the absence of random sampling, we cannot generalize the results of this study to all people or some other vague population. But so what? That wasn't the purpose of the study. The goal was process and causal inference, not population inference. From these results, Sundar could argue that different combinations of formats in a multimedia web page *can* influence learning of information on the page. Generalization is restricted to the process producing the effect, not a population. Statistical generalization away from the data can be accomplished by replication. If the same results are found in replications using different participants, this can be used to build the case that the result is a generalizable phenomenon—one that is not restricted to only those people that participated in the study.

```
Run MATRIX procedure:

Group Statistics
              n         Mean
       12.0000      8.3333
       12.0000      8.0833
       12.0000      6.3333
       12.0000      6.4167
       12.0000      5.7500


Approximate Randomization Test Results
            F       p-value
      4.3830         .0052


Number of randomizations requested
   5000


------ END MATRIX -----
```

Figure 14.3 SPSS macro output for a randomization test equivalent of a single factor ANOVA.

In section 10.3.2, I introduced the logic of a test of the null hypothesis of random pairing of an outcome variable to two groups in the absence of random sampling *and* random assignment. An analogous approach can be used to the test a null hypothesis of random pairing of an outcome variable to groups when $k > 2$. The same macro in Appendix F on the CD for the randomization test can be used to test this null hypothesis against the alternative that a systematic process is producing the obtained result. But because the p-value from this program will tend to be similar to the p-value from ANOVA, this means that ANOVA can be used to test the null hypothesis of a random process pairing the outcome to groups. But as with the randomization test, in the absence of random sampling from a population, inferences are restricted to the process producing the obtained result. No population inferences can be made.

14.2   Pairwise Mean Comparisons

Analysis of variance shares its status with multiple regression as one of the more widely-used statistical procedures in communication science. However it is an inherently vague test. Rejection of the null hypothesis tested with analysis of variance leads one to conclude only that k means are statistically different from each other by more than chance can explain, but it does not specify precisely which means differ from which. If one has no particular predictions with respect to which means should differ, this is perfectly fine, and analysis of variance yields at least some useful information. However, frequently an investigator conducts a study with a specific purpose in mind that specifies precisely which means should differ. Analysis of variance rarely tests the specific hypothesis that the researcher is interested in testing, and this contradicts good data analysis practice—a statistical test should be sensitive to the question of interest.

Inherent in this criticism of ANOVA is an important assumption: the researcher has made a prediction about which means will differ from which. Rarely does a theory that motivates communication research not make such specific predictions, but there are some contexts in which the researcher may genuinely not have any predictions or expectations. For example, the goals of a research project are sometimes framed in terms of research questions rather than specific hypotheses. If no specific predictions are made in advance, ANOVA can be a sensible analysis strategy and the null hypothesis that ANOVA tests is *perhaps* worth testing (although in section 14.5.3 I suggest that ANOVA isn't necessarily useful even then). Nevertheless, the researcher is still left with only a vague conclusion when the omnibus null hypothesis is rejected. All that can be said is that at least two of the means do differ from each other. More information is typically desired, and almost always more information is subsequently sought. Which means differ from which? In this section, I outline some strategies for answering this question.

14.2.1   The Multiple Test Problem Resurfaces

In section 14.1.8 I argued that ANOVA avoids the multiple test problem that plagues a set of $k(k-1)/2$ possible t tests comparing group means by testing the omnibus null hypothesis with a single test in one fell swoop. The more hypothesis tests that you conduct, the more likely that you will make at least one Type I error in the set. By comparing all means to each other simultaneously using ANOVA, you can keep the Type I error rate for testing the omnibus null hypothesis equal to a specified α level.

If the omnibus null hypothesis is rejected, the researcher typically will then ask which means differ from which. If there are no specific predictions made in advance and no guiding principles that leads one to focus on particular differences over others, then a sensible strategy is to conduct all possible comparisons between the means. Each of these comparisons is called a *pairwise comparison*, and the goal of conducting these pairwise comparisons is to determine which means differ from which to a statistically significant degree. However, each and every one of the $k(k-1)/2$ tests still entail a risk of Type I error, just as any hypothesis test does. So many different methods of conducting all possible pairwise comparisons have been proposed in the statistics literature to deal with Type I error inflation when conducting all possible pairwise comparisons.

There are two basic strategies that you might consider employing when conducting these comparisons. One strategy, often called *Fisher's protected t*, is to conduct all of the $k(k-1)/2$ possible t tests comparing each mean to each other mean, *but only following a statistically significant analysis of variance*. The logic of Fisher's protected t is that a statistically significant F from ANOVA tells the researcher that at least two of the means differ from each other, so the researcher has earned the license to go in and find where the differences are without worrying about Type I error inflation. After all, the familywise Type I error rate is based on the assumption that the omnibus null hypothesis is true. But if you have reason to believe it is not true, then the familywise error rate becomes inconsequential and irrelevant.

This logic, although sensible on the surface, actually doesn't work that well in practice. If the omnibus null hypothesis is true, then conducting all possible t tests only if the F from ANOVA is statistically significant at $p \leq \alpha$ will keep the familywise Type I error rate at α. However, when the omnibus null hypothesis is *false*, the Fisher protected t method can still produce Type I error inflation in the set of all $k(k-1)/2$ possible t tests. So if you are worried about falsely rejecting a true null hypothesis when conducting these follow-up tests, you should not employ Fisher's protected t method because the probability of making at least one Type I error in this set of $k(k-1)/2$

pairwise comparisons is not necessarily kept at α or less. Ryan (1980) provided an extreme but convincing example where $k = 10$ and only one of means is larger than the other 9 in the population, the remaining 9 of which are all the same. Although the ANOVA F might be significant, it is highly likely that at least one of the 36 comparisons between the 9 means that are actually equal in the population will be statistically significant if some kind of correction for multiple tests is not applied.

So the second and preferred strategy is to acknowledge that it is still possible to make a Type I error in subsequent tests even if the F from ANOVA is statistically significant. So you if you are concerned about Type I error inflation, you should employ some kind of statistical method to keep the familywise Type I error rate at an acceptable level. Any time that you conduct multiple hypothesis tests, you run a new risk of making a Type I error, and the more tests you do, the more likely that at least one of them will produce a Type I error. This is true regardless of whether the F from an ANOVA is statistically significant. The solution is to correct for multiple comparisons in the follow up tests. Unfortunately there are dozens of tests designed to reduce the problem of Type I error inflation when conducting pairwise comparisons and very little clear guidance on just which to use in any given situation. These tests go by such names as the *Newman-Keuls* method, *Tukey's HSD test*, *Tukey's b*, *Dunnett's test*, *Duncan's multiple range test*, and so forth, and so on. There is a large and confusing literature on these various approaches to conducting pairwise comparisons. Rather than spending any time discussing these methods, I refer you to such overviews as Klockars and Sax (1986), Jaccard, Becker, and Wood (1984), Carmer and Swanson (1973), Keppel (1991), or Games, Keselman, and Rogan (1981). The major problem with these methods is that they tend to assume equal group sample sizes or equality of variance, two assumptions that I don't particular like and that I think one need not make in order to deal with the multiple test problem effectively. Personally, I prefer not to employ any of these methods (actually, there is one that I like, described later) and instead rely on a simple although slightly conservative approach described next.

14.2.2   The Bonferroni Correction

According to probability theory, if an event will occur with a constant probability α, the probability that the event will occur at least once over g trials is no greater than $g\alpha$. So if you do 6 hypothesis tests using $\alpha = 0.05$, the probability that you will make at least one Type I error in the 6 tests is no greater than $6(.05) = .30$, and thus the probability of making no Type I errors is at least $1 - 0.30 = 0.70$. According to this logic, if you want to keep the probability of making at least one Type I error no higher than a specific value (α_{FW}) across all g tests, then a test should be deemed statistically significant only if $p \leq (\alpha_{FW}/g)$. For example, if you conduct 4 statistical tests and want to make sure you make no Type I errors in the set with a probability no less than .95, then this can be accomplishing by using $\alpha = .0125$ as your criterion for rejecting the null hypothesis for each test. This is because the probability of making at least one Type I error is no more than $.0125(4) = 0.05$ and thus the probability of making no Type I errors in this set is no smaller than $1 - 0.05 = 0.95$.

This procedure is the simple form of the *Bonferroni correction* to α. In section 14.1.8, I defined α_{FW} as the *familywise Type I error rate*—the probability of making at least one Type I error in a set of hypothesis tests. Define α_{PC} (for "per-comparison") as level of significance used for each of tests (i.e., the largest p-value that would lead to a rejection of the null hypothesis for that test). In all discussions of hypothesis testing thus far, α_{PC} has been set to 0.05, The multiple test problem refers to the fact that by using $\alpha_{PC} = .05$ for each and every hypothesis test, then α_{FW} will be some value larger than .05. The Bonferroni correction to α requires that if you want to maintain α_{FW} at a certain value across a set of g tests, then α_{PC} should be set to α_{FW}/g. This procedure works for both *independent and dependent* statistical tests. Notice, however, that is is possible for $g\alpha$ and thus α_{FW} to be greater than 1, which isn't sensible given that a probability can't be greater than one. In such a situation, it is better to think of α_{FW} simply as "large."

A mathematically equivalent variant of the Bonferroni correction to α is the *Bonferroni correction to the p-value*. This correction involves multiplying the p-value for each test by the number of tests conducted. If the p-value for any specific comparison is still less than your desired α_{FW} after multiplying each p-value by the number of tests conducted, then you can reject the null hypothesis for that comparison.

A more complex but slightly more accurate procedure that applies to statistically independent hypothesis tests is to set α_{PC} not to α_{FW}/g but instead to

$$\boxed{\alpha_{PC} = 1 - (1 - \alpha_{FW})^{\frac{1}{g}}}$$

(14.15)

as your criterion for each test. So if you wanted to keep the familywise Type I error rate across $g = 4$ tests at .05, then instead of rejecting the null hypothesis for each test using $p = .0125$ (which is .05/4), use $p = .0127$. In most applications, the difference between the simpler and this slightly more complex (but more accurate) version of the Bonferroni correction (sometimes called the Sidak method) is negligible. In practice it rarely matters which of these two versions you use, although the more complicated approach represented with equation 14.15 is slightly more powerful.

To apply the Bonferroni correction, either request it using your statistical program if available or conduct all possible t tests between the means and multiply each p-value by g, the number of tests being conducted. If the p-value after this multiplication remains less than your desired α_{FW}, then reject the null hypothesis tested with that specific t test. The problem with this approach is that as k increases, the number of possible pairwise comparisons (g) increases considerably, and the Bonferroni correction becomes increasingly less powerful for detecting a difference between means. But the simplicity of the method makes it a strong competitor to the many existing methods for reducing the Type I error inflation that occurs when conducting all possible pairwise comparisons.

14.2.3 Holm's Sequential Rejection Method

A related but slightly less conservative approach goes by several names: *Holm's sequential rejection method, Bonferroni layering,* or *Ryan's method* (see, e.g., Darlington, 1990; Holm, 1979). This method is very similar to the Bonferroni method, except that greater correction is applied to the smaller p-values. To apply this test, first rank order the comparisons by the size of their p-values from smallest to largest. Then multiply the smallest p-value by g, the number of tests being conducted. If this Bonferroni corrected p-value is less than your desired α_{FW}, reject the null hypothesis and proceed to the next smallest p-value. This next smallest p-value you multiply by $g - 1$ and again compare this p-value to α_{FW}. Continue with this procedure until the corrected p-value is larger than your desired α_{FW} for the first time. At that point you stop and fail to reject the null hypothesis for all remaining comparisons. For example, suppose your

Table 14.2
All Pairwise Comparisons Using Different Corrections for Multiple Tests

| | | | | | | Two-tailed p-value | | | |
Group i	Group j	$\overline{Y}_i$	$\overline{Y}_j$	t	Uncorrected	Simple Bonferroni	Bonferroni Layering	Games-Howell
Text	Picture	8.083	8.333	−0.282	0.780	1.000	1.000	0.998
Text	Audio	8.083	6.333	2.124	0.045	0.450	0.225	0.245
Text	Audio+Picture	8.083	6.417	2.397	0.027	0.270	0.189	0.159
Text	Video	8.083	5.750	3.052	0.006	0.060	0.054	0.042
Picture	Audio	8.333	6.333	2.260	0.034	0.340	0.204	0.196
Picture	Audio+Picture	8.333	6.417	2.500	0.023	0.230	0.184	0.136
Picture	Video	8.333	5.750	3.113	0.005	0.050	0.050	0.039
Audio	Audio+Picture	6.333	6.417	−0.120	0.906	1.000	1.000	1.000
Audio	Video	6.333	5.750	0.764	0.453	1.000	1.000	0.938
Audio+Picture	Video	6.420	5.750	1.071	0.297	1.000	1.000	0.819

study had 4 groups, you were conducting all of the 6 possible pairwise comparisons, and the p-values for the 6 t tests were, in order of increasing p, .0004, .003, .02, .12, .25, .67. Applying this method, the corrected p-values for the first three comparisons would be .0024, .015, and .08. So the first two comparisons are statistically significant using a desired α_{FW} of .05. We stop at the third because the correction at this stage produces a nonsignicant p-value, so all subsequent comparisons are deemed not statistically significant.

Bonferroni layering will tend to be more powerful than either the simple or complex version of the Bonferroni correction described previously. Like all the other Bonferroni methods discussed here, this is a versatile procedure in that it can be used to keep α_{FW} at a desired level for *any* set of hypothesis tests, not just tests involving pairwise mean comparisons.

14.2.4 The Games-Howell Method

These Bonferroni-based methods are satisfying in how simple they are. But they can be conservative compared to some alternatives. There is a good method for conducting all possible comparisons between k means that is less conservative because it doesn't correct the p-values quite as much as the Bonferroni methods while still keeping good control over the Type I error rate across the set of g tests. Known as the *Games-Howell* method, it has been recommended as better compared to other commonly used tests for pairwise comparisons because it does not assume equal sample sizes and equal variances across the groups (Jaccard, Becker, & Wood, 1984). The Games-Howell method involves conducting all possible t tests using the Welch-Satterthwaite approach described in Chapter 10, but the value of t required to reject the null hypothesis is modified to keep α_{FW} at a specified level. Details of the computations are available in Games and Howell (1976).

Table 14.2 contains the results of these different pairwise comparison approaches for the Sundar (2000) data analyzed in section 14.1.9. There were 5 groups in this study, and so there are $5(5-1)/2 = 10$ possible pairwise comparisons.

As can be seen, 6 of the 10 t tests (using the Welch-Satterthwaite approach) yield a statistically significant difference between the means prior to correcting for the multiple test problem. The simple Bonferroni correction to the p-values yields only one significant difference (between the video and picture conditions). Bonferroni layering leads to the same conclusion. But both of these methods tend to be slightly conservative. The Games-Howell method is less conservative and produces two statistically significant comparisons (video vs. picture and video vs. text). This conclusion is consistent with Sundar's (2000) analysis, in which he used a different pairwise comparison method. There is no way of knowing which is the "correct" finding, of course, because of the probabilistic nature of hypothesis testing and the fact that we can never know which of the null hypotheses are true and which are false. Unfortunately, the literature on pairwise comparisons isn't particularly helpful in choosing which of these methods is the best way of conducting these comparisons.

14.2.5 Using a Pooled Error Term

My discussion of pairwise comparisons is a bit unorthodox relative to comparable sections in other statistics books. But those books are not entirely consistent with each other. When you read the communication literature, you will come across a variety of different approaches that communication researchers have used to correct for multiple tests when conducting all possible pairwise comparisons. From what I can tell, which test a researcher uses seems to be rather arbitrary, and there is usually little information provided in the article that allows the reader to discern why the researcher chose to use a particular test rather than another. Most likely the choice was based on what that particular investigator was taught, or what book he or she used to guide the analysis. Given the large number of approaches that are circulating in the statistics literature, it shouldn't be surprising that there is little uniformity in the methods that researchers use. The approaches I have described above are how I think about the problem, but not everyone will agree with my approach. I believe that the Games-Howell method and the two Bonferroni methods are the simplest to understand and apply and make the fewest assumptions, and for those reasons I think these strategy are sensible.

Nevertheless, I feel obligated to discuss one thing that alternative methods (not discussed in this book) have in common. In my discussion of pairwise comparisons and in the results presented in Table 14.2 all the t tests were conducted using the data from only the participants that are members of the groups being compared. The standard error of the difference and the resulting p-values were derived using the Welch-Satterthwaite approach discussed in Chapter 10. So the standard error is estimated using only the variability in the mean difference attributable to the 24 participants involved in the comparison conducted. But this is not typical practice. More common is to derive the standard error of the difference using a measure of variability in Y within groups based on information provided by *all* units in the data, regardless of whether those units are members of the two groups being compared. This is entirely sensible if you are willing to assume equality of variance on the outcome variable. In this case, the standard error of the difference between any two sample means $\overline{Y}_i$ and $\overline{Y}_j$ is estimated as

$$
s_{(\overline{Y}_i - \overline{Y}_j)} = \sqrt{MS_{within}\left(\frac{1}{n_i} + \frac{1}{n_j}\right)}
$$

(14.16)

Notice that equation 14.16 is the same as equation 10.2, substituting MS_{within} as the pooled variance estimate (s_p^2 in equation 10.2). The ratio of the sample mean difference to the standard error derived using equation 14.16 is t distributed on df_{within} degrees of freedom if the null hypothesis that $\mu_i = \mu_j$ is true, as is the assumption that all k population variances are equal. Degrees of freedom for t increase by using MS_{within} to derive the standard error rather than calculating the standard error using only the variances of the groups that contribute to the comparison. This produces a test that is more powerful than the methods described in this chapter, but valid only if the assumption of variance equality is met. For the same reasons I gave in Chapter 10, I don't recommend pooling variances when comparing two means, as there is no reason to assume equality of variance and the consequences of this assumption not being met are potentially severe when a pooled variance estimate is used in this context (Boneau, 1960; Hayes & Cai, in press). But be aware that most statistical programs use equation 14.16 in their routines for conducting all possible pairwise comparisons between means. SPSS is one of the exceptions that does allow you to request tests that do not assume equality of variance or equal sample sizes, such as the Games-Howell method. [3]

---

[3] As of the publication of this book, SPSS does have an implementation of the simple Bonferroni and the Sidak methods, but the corrections to the p-value are based on tests that use a pooled error term.

14.3   Focused Contrasts

The previous discussion of pairwise comparisons is predicated on the assumption that you have no particular interest in specific comparisons involving two or more means but instead are interested in doing all of the possible pairwise comparisons in search of *something, anything* that is statistically significant. However, communication researchers often have reasons to expect that certain means differ from others, or that a set of groups that are conceptually similar in some way will differ from one or more groups that are conceptually different. Typically, those hypotheses require considerably fewer comparisons to test than all possible pairwise comparisons. Suppose, for example, that Sundar was interested in comparing "traditional print media format" on the web to "nonprint format." (He was not and did nothing like I describe here. I use this only as an example.) Print media has for the most part always contained either text or text and pictures, whereas other media formats such as television, radio, and the internet include modes of information transmission that don't exist in print media. The text and picture conditions are conceptually like print media, whereas the remaining three conditions all contain features that print forms of media do not share. So an interesting set of comparisons would be to compare the learning of participants in one of the print media format conditions to learning by participants in one of the other three conditions. Comparisons within these formats would not be conducted because they aren't relevant to the question. So rather than doing all of the 10 possible pairwise comparisons, only 6 need be conducted (text vs. audio, text vs. audio+picture, text vs. video, picture vs. audio, picture vs. audio+picture, picture vs. video). But the number of necessary comparisons could be reduced even further to one by creating two new groups. The first group contains everyone in either the text or the picture conditions, and the second group contains everyone else. A single test comparing these two means to each other would test whether print vs. nonprint formats produce differences in learning.

Such comparisons between means are called *focused contrasts* because they are focused on testing a specific question or hypothesis rather than the much vaguer question about which of the k group means differ. There are two main approaches that can be employed when conducting focused contrasts. I outline each of these approaches below and talk about some of their strengths and weaknesses.

14.3.1   Focused t tests

The simplest approach is to do the contrasts of interest by conducting one or more t tests comparing the relevant groups. The primary advantage of this *focused t test* approach is that it is very simple to understand, and most readers of your research would understand exactly how you conducted the comparisons. It can also be more powerful than conducting all possible comparisons. As described above, only 6 t tests are necessary to compare each of the print media forms to the nonprint forms. Using the simple Bonferroni method, you'd set α_{PC} to .0083 and reject the null hypothesis for each comparison only if $p \leq .0083$ (which is .05/6) rather than $p \leq .005$ (which is 0.05/10). But this approach can yield conflicting results. For example, in the Sundar (2000) study this approach yields statistically significant differences between either of the print media forms compared to the video form, but not compared to any of the other nonprint forms of media.

An alternative focused t test would rely on a slightly different approach by acknowledging that although participants assigned to either of the print media format conditions did experience slightly different stimuli, they are conceptually identical. They experienced a web page that, for all intents and purposes, could have been printed from the web and read like a newspaper. Similarly, the participants assigned to one of the three nonprint media formats all experienced something conceptually the same— their experience involved more than just reading the text and looking at the pictures. They got an experience that was unique to nonprint forms of media. So why not collapse the text and picture groups into a single condition, and collapse the remaining groups into a second condition, and then just compare the two resulting sample means with a single independent groups t test? In this case, the nonprint media format resulted in less learning than the print media formats, Welch $t(42) = 3.952, p < .0005$, with means of 6.17 and 8.21, respectively. (Note: the degrees of freedom is 42 rather than 58 because the Welch-Satterthwaite approach is being used.)

14.3.2 Contrast Coefficients

A popular approach for conducting focused contrasts is the use of *contrast coefficients*. These coefficients are numbers that are used to construct a weighted combination of the means. The contrast then tests whether this weighted combination is different from zero. This method is widely implemented in statistical packages and used by communication scientists, but there are some cautions that must be exercised when it is used, cautions I describe shortly.

To conduct a contrast using contrast coefficients, a weighted linear combination of the group means is created, with the weights being selected so that the test yields the desired contrast. The resulting linear combination has a standard error associated with it, and the ratio of the linear combination divided by its standard error is distributed as t if the null hypothesis is true and the assumptions of the test are met. So there are three basic steps: (a) construct the linear combination of means corresponding to the contrast, (b) compute the standard error of the contrast, and (c) compute the p-value for the ratio of the linear combination to its standard error.

The linear combination, arbitrarily designated as δ, is defined as

$$\delta = \sum \lambda_j \overline{Y}_j$$

(14.17)

where the summation is over all k groups, λ_j is group j's *contrast coefficient*, and $\overline{Y}_j$ is the sample mean for group j. *Assuming equality of the group variances on* Y, the standard error of δ can be estimated as

$$s_\delta = \sqrt{MS_{within} \sum \frac{\lambda_j^2}{n_j}}$$

(14.18)

where MS_{within} is the within-groups mean square from an ANOVA comparing all means to each other and n_j is the sample size for group j. If the null hypothesis is true, the ratio δ/s_δ is distributed as t on df_{within} degrees of freedom. The square of t is also distributed as F on $df_{numerator} = 1$ and $df_{denominator} = df_{within}$. Because $df_{numerator} = 1$, such contrasts are sometimes called *single df contrasts*.

But what are these contrast coefficients? Table 14.3 lists a few example contrast coefficients for a study involving 4 groups, and what those coefficients correspond to

Table 14.3

Some Example Contrasts and Their Corresponding Contrast Coefficients

Contrast Coefficients				Original Groups in Contrast Grouping		
Group 1	Group 2	Group 3	Group 4	1	2	Contrast
1	−1	0	0	1	2	$\delta = \overline{Y}_1 - \overline{Y}_2$
1	0	0	−1	1	4	$\delta = \overline{Y}_1 - \overline{Y}_4$
1/2	1/2	−1/2	−1/2	1, 2	3, 4	$\delta = \left(\frac{\overline{Y}_1 + \overline{Y}_2}{2}\right) - \left(\frac{\overline{Y}_3 + \overline{Y}_4}{2}\right)$
1/2	1/2	−1	0	1, 2	3	$\delta = \left(\frac{\overline{Y}_1 + \overline{Y}_2}{2}\right) - \overline{Y}_3$
1	−1/3	−1/3	−1/3	1	2, 3, 4	$\delta = \overline{Y}_1 - \left(\frac{\overline{Y}_2 + \overline{Y}_3 + \overline{Y}_4}{3}\right)$

in terms of the comparison actually being conducted. Focused contrasts in k group designs are always based on only two "contrast groupings," although each of the two contrast groupings may be a combination of several groups from the study (such as in the third, fourth, and fifth examples in Table 14.3). For example, in the fourth row of Table 14.3, the two contrast groupings are (1) the combination of groups 1 and 2, and (2) group 3.

There are many different rules you could apply for constructing contrast coefficients depending on your objective and the hypothesis you want to test, but here are the four to keep in mind. If you follow these rules carefully, you should have no trouble determining what the contrast coefficients should be for any desired contrast. The first rule is to make sure that the contrast coefficients in the first contrast grouping are all positive, and the coefficients in the second contrast grouping are all negative. Which contrast grouping is "first" and "second" is arbitrary. Second, groups that are not placed in any contrast grouping should be given a coefficient of zero. Third, set the contrast coefficients in each contrast grouping to the reciprocal of the number of groups in that contrast grouping (the reciprocal of a number is 1 divided by that number). So in the fifth contrast in Table 14.3, there is only group in contrast grouping one, so its coefficient is just 1/1 or 1. The second contrast grouping contains 3 groups, so the coefficients for the groups in that contrast grouping are set to 1/3. But following rule one, those contrasts are set to −1/3 rather than 1/3. If you follow these three rules, you will automatically meet the fourth rule, and that is that the sum of all the contrast coefficients should be equal to zero. That is, $\sum \lambda_j = 0$.

There is nothing magical about these coefficients except that they conform to the four rules above. Once the contrasts coefficients are set, they can be modified by multiplying every coefficient by a constant. For example, the coefficients in the fourth row of Table 14.3 could have been 3, 3, −6, and 0 (all coefficients multiplied by 6). It makes no difference because outcome of the test won't be affected by this transformation of the coefficients.

This sounds rather complicated. But with a little practice it turns out to be fairly easy to figure out what the coefficients should be to produce a desired contrast. Continuing with the Sundar (2000) study as an example, let's set up the contrast coefficients comparing the mean learning of participants in the text or picture condition to the mean learning of participants in the other three conditions. So contrast grouping 1 is the text and picture conditions (2 groups), and contrast grouping 2 is the audio, audio+picture, and video conditions (3 groups). By the first rule, we'll make the coefficients for the text and picture conditions positive and the remaining coefficients negative. There are 2 groups in contrast grouping 1, so the coefficients for the text and picture conditions are both 1/2. But there are 3 groups in contrast grouping 2, so the coefficients, combined with rule 1, are all $-1/3$. We have satisfied the first three rules, so we must have also met the fourth rule. Indeed, these 5 coefficients do sum to 0. If we apply equation 14.17, then the contrast is

$$\delta = \sum \lambda_j \overline{Y}_j = (1/2)\overline{Y}_{text} + (1/2)\overline{Y}_{picture} - (1/3)\overline{Y}_{audio} - (1/3)\overline{Y}_{audio+picture} - (1/3)\overline{Y}_{video}$$

A little algebraic manipulation shows that this contrast is equal to

$$\delta = \left(\frac{\overline{Y}_{text} + \overline{Y}_{picture}}{2} \right) - \left(\frac{\overline{Y}_{audio} + \overline{Y}_{audio+picture} + \overline{Y}_{video}}{3} \right)$$

In words, these coefficients define a contrast between the mean of the text and picture conditions and the mean of the other three conditions. Plugging the numbers in,

$$\delta = (1/2)(8.083) + (1/2)(8.333) - (1/3)(6.333) - (1/3)(6.417) - (1/3)(5.750) = 2.041$$

So the difference between the means of the contrast groupings is 2.041 in favor of the print format grouping. From the ANOVA, MS_{within} is 3.626. Assuming equality of variance in learning across the groups, the standard error of the contrast can be estimated using equation 14.18 as

$$s_\delta = \sqrt{3.626 \left(\frac{(1/2)^2}{12} + \frac{(1/2)^2}{12} + \frac{(-1/3)^2}{12} + \frac{(-1/3)^2}{12} + \frac{(-1/3)^2}{12} \right)} = 0.500$$

and so $t = 2.041/0.500 = 4.082$. This is greater than the critical t for $df = df_{within} = 55$, $\alpha = 0.05$ (which is about 2.01 from Appendix B). So we reject the null hypothesis that the format of the information presented has no effect on learning from the Web. It appears that people learn less when the format of the information includes elements not found in traditional print media, such as an audio or video stream.

This is a lot of work! Fortunately, these computations can be conducted by a good statistics program. Figure 13.2 contains the relevant sections from SPSS output corresponding to this contrast. The statistics we just computed above can be found in the row labeled "Assume equal variances." The SPSS output agrees with our hand computations within expected rounding error.[4]

The estimate of the standard error of the contrast is based on the assumption that the k groups are equally variable on the outcome measure. If this assumption doesn't

---

[4]Because SPSS requires that noninteger coefficients be represented in decimal form, it was necessary for me to add 0.01 to the last contrast coefficient to meet the requirement that they add up to 1. One way around this burp in the implementation of the method is to use a different set of coefficients that will produce a mathematically identical test. For example, you can verify for yourself that the following set of contrast coefficients would produce the same result: 3, 3, -2, -2, -2.

ANOVA

LEARN

	Sum of Squares	df	Mean Square	F	Sig.
Between Groups	63.567	4	15.892	4.383	.004
Within Groups	199.417	55	3.626		
Total	262.983	59			

Contrast Coefficients

	COND				
Contrast	text	text+picture	text+audio	text+picture+audio	text+video
1	.5	.5	-.33	-.33	-.34

Contrast Tests

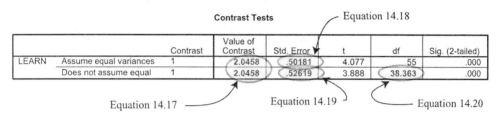

		Contrast	Value of Contrast	Std. Error	t	df	Sig. (2-tailed)
LEARN	Assume equal variances	1	2.0458	.50181	4.077	55	.000
	Does not assume equal	1	2.0458	.52619	3.888	38.363	.000

Equation 14.18 · Equation 14.17 · Equation 14.19 · Equation 14.20

Figure 14.4 Output from a focused contrast test in SPSS.

seem reasonable (or you simply don't want to make it) you can use a different estimate of the standard error that doesn't assume equality of group variances (and there usually is little reason to make this assumption when tests are available that don't require it). The estimated standard error without assuming equality of variance is

$$s_\delta = \sqrt{\sum \frac{s_j^2 \lambda_j^2}{n_j}}$$

(14.19)

where s_j^2 is the variance of the outcome variable for group j and the summation is over all k groups. Like the Welch-Satterthwaite approach to the independent groups t test, a different degrees of freedom is required to produce an accurate p-value. The formula is messy but it works:

$$df = \frac{[\sum(s_j^2 \lambda_j^2/n_j)]^2}{\sum[(s_j^2 \lambda_j^2/n_j)^2/(n_j - 1)]}$$

(14.20)

Using the group standard deviations reported at the top of Figure 14.2 and the contrast coefficients above, $s_\delta = 0.526$ and so $t = 2.041/0.526 = 3.880$. The p-value is derived using the t distribution with 38.36 degrees of freedom, or by comparing the obtained t to the critical t for $df = 38$. SPSS does all these computations for us (see Figure 14.4) and shows a p-value of less than 0.0005.

A Caution When Group Sample Sizes are Different. Although the application of this method seems complicated, most good statistics programs implement this method, so it actually is easy to apply it in your own research. Nevertheless, there is reason to prefer the simpler t test method over the contrast coefficients method in at least some circumstances. Using the coefficients method, the computation of the contrast does not consider the fact that the groups that define a contrast grouping may differ substantially in size. If the group sizes are different, the t test approach and the method of contrast coefficients can produce quite different results because they are based on different mean comparisons. Because the 5 groups in this example are all the same size (all $n_j = 12$), the two approaches closely agree here. But consider a different example. Using the NES data, suppose we wanted to compare the mean political knowledge of Republicans compared to a contrast grouping that includes the Democrats and those who affiliate with neither party. Recall from section 14.1.1 that $\overline{Y}_{Democrat} = 11.418$, $\overline{Y}_{Republican} = 11.816$, and $\overline{Y}_{Other} = 9.128$, yielding

$$\delta = (-1/2)(11.418) + (1)(11.816) + (-1/2)(9.128) = 1.543$$

which is exactly equal to the mean of the Republicans in the sample minus the arithmetic mean of the means of the Democrats and "Other" groups. But if you were to instead construct a new group that combines the Democrats and Other groups into a single group, the mean of this group (which contains 196 respondents) is 10.776. The difference between the mean knowledge of Republicans and the mean of this combined group is $11.816 - 10.776 = 1.040$. So the obtained difference between the means differs depending on which method of analysis you choose. In this example, the contrast coefficients approach is based on a larger observed mean difference than the focused t test approach. This is because the group of respondents that identify themselves as neither Democrat nor Republican is much smaller in size, but it is given equal weight in the computation of the sample mean for the second contrast grouping when the contrast is formed with contrast coefficients. So the contrast coefficients approach gives all groups equal weight in the construction of the contrast, whereas the focused t test approach weights each group by its sample size. This would be defensible if the differences in sample size reflect the result of the sampling strategy rather than real differences in the relative sizes of the groups in the populations being compared.

This problem with the use of *unweighted* contrast coefficients can be eliminated by constructing *weighted* contrast coefficients instead. Define n_{g_j} as the sum of the sample sizes for the groups that reside in group j's contrast group. Still defining δ as

$$\delta = \sum \lambda_j \overline{Y}_j$$

a weighted contrast is based on contrast coefficients of

$$\lambda_j = -\frac{n_j}{n_{g_j}}$$

for groups in contrast group 1 and

$$\lambda_j = \frac{n_j}{n_{g_j}}$$

for groups in contrast group 2. If a group j is not used in the construction of a contrast, set $n_j = 0$.

Using this procedure, we can construct a weighted contrast comparing the average political knowledge of a group defined as the Democrats ($j = 1$) and "Others" ($j = 3$) to the Republicans ($j = 2$). Contrast group 1 is the Democrats ($\overline{Y}_1 = 11.418, n_1 = 141$) and "Others" ($\overline{Y}_3 = 9.128, n_3 = 55$) and contrast group 2 is the Republicans

$(\overline{Y}_2 = 11.816, n_2 = 147)$. For the Democrats, Republicans, and "Others", respectively, $n_{g_1} = 141 + 55 = 196, n_{g_2} = 147, n_{g_3} = 141 + 55 = 196$, and so

$$\lambda_1 = -\frac{141}{196}$$

$$\lambda_2 = \frac{147}{147}$$

$$\lambda_3 = -\frac{55}{196}$$

Using these weighted contrast coefficients,

$$\delta = -\frac{141}{196}(11.418) + \frac{147}{147}(11.816) + -\frac{55}{196}(9.128) = 1.040$$

with standard error equal to 0.473 using equation 14.19. This difference of 1.040 is indeed the difference between the two group means if you recoded the three groups into two (now with samples sizes of 196 and 55)

In SPSS, we could generate this contrast with the command

```
oneway pknow by party
/contrast -0.7193877 1 -0.2806123.
```

The result for the line in the SPSS output corresponding to the test that does not assume variance equality will be very close to but not exactly equal to the result for the Welch-Satterthwaite t test setting up the problem as a focused t test. In my judgment it makes more sense to weight by sample size rather than give all groups equal weight, so the use of weighted contrast coefficients or a focused t test would be preferred whenever there are more than trivial differences in the sample sizes of the various groups being combined into contrast groups.

Notice that if the group sample sizes are equal, this method yields the same contrast coefficients as does the method introduced earlier.

14.3.3 Scheffe's Test

I emphasized the use of focused contrasts as a means of testing *a priori* predictions about an expected pattern of means. "A priori" has several different meanings, two of them being "not derived from experience" and "derived from hypothesis or theory." But contrasts often suggest themselves *a posteriori* meaning "based on observation." Once the data are available and the group means computed and known, new comparisons may suggest themselves that seem worth conducting. For example, if a study with 4 groups results in two means that seem very different from the other two, the investigator might be interested in knowing whether a comparison between a contrast grouping including those two means and a second grouping that combines the remaining two is statistically significant. The investigator may not have had an a priori reason to conduct this contrast. Instead, the contrast suggested itself only a posteriori after looking at the data and observing the pattern of means.

Patterns are fairly easy to find in nearly anything if we look closely enough, and it is easy to spin a logically coherent story to explain those patterns. The problem is that the human brain is good at seeing patterns where there are none. If you held 10 coins in your hand and dropped them simultaneously to the floor, some of the coins will land close to each other but others far away. This is something you will have trouble *not* noticing. And yet your intuition is that where the coins land relative to each other is essentially random. There is no need to speculate on why some coins land near to each other and others far away. Similarly, we know that k sample means are unlikely to be exactly equal to each other even if the populations from which the samples were derived have the same mean. And random assignment of people into experimental conditions will just by itself produce k means that are descriptively different even when the independent variable has no effect on the outcome variable. But random variability between means often doesn't appear random to the brain. Our brains, trying to see order in chaos, pick out patterns and our curiosity as scientists starts the process of speculation. Why are some of the means similar to each other and others very different?

Looking at a set of means in search of contrasts that seem worthy of conducting implicitly involves lots of comparisons being conducted simultaneously. We may observe, for example, that means A and B are similar to each other, while means C, D, E, and F appear more similar to each other than they do to A and B. Notice the number of comparisons that have to be conducted in your head to pick out this apparent pattern. Given our ability to find patterns in randomness, and the number of implicit comparisons that such pattern discovery involves, any contrast that suggests itself after seeing the data requires a rather serious correction to the inferential process to compensate for our tendency to see patterns in randomness.

Scheffe (1953) devised a test that is well suited to testing contrasts that suggest themselves to a researcher only after scanning a table of means. Recall that a focused contrast can be converted to a t statistic and therefore to an F statistic using the function $F = t^2$. Scheffe showed that if all means are equal, differing from each other in the sample by just "chance," then 95% of all possible contrasts will have a F statistic no greater than $(k-1)(F_{critical})$ where $F_{critical}$ is the value of F that cuts off the upper 5% of the F distribution with $df_{numerator} = k - 1$ and $df_{denominator} = n - k$. This fact can be used to test the significance of any contrast or set of contrasts you construct after seeing the data, with the comfort of knowing that the probability of making at least one Type I error in the set of contrasts is no greater than 0.05. For example, in the Sundar study, $k = 5, n = 60$. The obtained value of δ for a contrast can be converted to a t statistic as described in section 14.3.2 and then transformed to an F ratio as $F = t^2$. That contrast is declared statistically significant only if that F statistic is at least $(5 - 1)(2.557) = 10.228$, where 2.557 is the value of F that cuts off the upper 5% of the $F(4, 55)$ distribution (see Appendix D1).

Suppose, for instance, we wanted to know whether the contrast comparing learning in the video condition to the average of the learning for the remaining 4 conditions is statistically significant, but we decided that this contrast was worth testing only after noticing that the video condition had the smallest mean. The contrast coefficients for the 5 conditions would be $1/4$, $1/4$, $1/4$, $1/4$, and -1 for the text, picture, audio, audio+picture, and video conditions respectively. Using equations 14.17 and 14.19, $\delta = 1.542, s_\delta = 0.569, t = 2.711, F = 7.350$. This F is not greater than 10.228, so the contrast is declared not statistically significant using $\alpha = .05$.

Scheffe's test is very versatile, and it can be used to keep the familywise Type I error rate at .05 for any set of contrasts, including any set of pairwise comparisons. Its two weakness are its tremendous conservativism and its assumptions of equality of group variances and equality of group sample sizes. The conservativism of the test is warranted when it is used as just described because of our tendency to see patterns in randomness that leads us to conduct a contrast that is selected for testing because the difference appears to be large and thus worth testing. But it should not be used for conducting a priori hypothesis tests because of its low power. The mathematics of the test is based on the assumption of equality of variance and equality of group sample sizes, and its validity is questionable when these assumptions are violated.

14.4 ANOVA as a Special Case of Multiple Regression

Researchers often associate analysis of variance with experimental research focusing on demonstrating cause-effect relationships, whereas multiple regression is used for the analysis of data from correlational studies. However, statistical procedures are stupid as to the origins of the data and the kinds of inferences they afford. The inferences that one can reach with a statistical test depend mostly on the method of data collection. Here, I will illustrate that when you conduct an ANOVA, you are just doing multiple regression. The distinction researchers make between the two methods as a function of the research design is an artificial one.

14.4.1 Coding a Categorical Variable for a Regression Analysis

Recall from section 13.2.1 that if we were to generate a regression model estimating a variable Y from a dichotomous predictor variable X that codes which of two groups a case belongs to, then the regression weight for that dichotomous predictor will be the difference between the means of the two groups, and the test that the regression weight is statistically different from zero tests the null hypothesis that the group means differ only by a "chance" mechanism, such as sampling variability.

Now let's extend this to the analysis of a categorical predictor variable with more than 2 categories. Earlier we did an analysis of variance to test the null hypothesis that Democrats, Republicans, and people who identify with neither party are equally knowledgeable politically, on average. We rejected the null hypothesis, $F(2, 340) = 7.836, p < .0005$. We can test the same null hypothesis that is tested with ANOVA in multiple regression by representing k groups with a set of $k - 1$ *dummy variables*. A dummy variable is a dichotomous variable with two possible values, typically 0 or 1. We use these dummy variables to code which group a case belongs to. So with $k = 3$ political party groups, we need $k - 1 = 2$ dummy variables to code a person's political party identification. Let's call these two dummy variables *Demo* and *Repub*, for Democrats and Republicans, respectively. For all Democrats in the data, we will set *Demo* to 1 and *Repub* to 0. For all Republicans, we set *Repub* to 1 and *Demo* to 0. Finally, for those who identify with neither group, we set *Demo* and *Repub* both to 0. This procedure, called *dummy coding*, is a common way to code a categorical variable in multiple regression, but it is not the only way. See, for example, Darlington (1990) for other ways of coding group membership.

It might seem strange to you that we use only $k - 1$ dummy variables and not k dummies to represent k groups. Only $k - 1$ dummy variables are necessary because the apprent missing dummy variable contains no additional information about group membership. In this example, it might seem that the people who don't identify with either party are not represented with this coding scheme. However, this group is represented as $Demo = 0$ and $Repub = 0$. So an additional dummy code set to 1 for this group and 0 otherwise would be redundant with information already contained in the *Demo* and *Repub* dummy variables. The group that gets no dummy code is called the *reference group* or *reference category*.

14.4.2   Testing the Omnibus Null Hypothesis Using Regression

What if there is no relationship between political party identification and political knowledge in the population from which this sample was derived? If this is so, then you would expect that if you had the entire population available and fit a multiple regression model estimating political knowledge from *Demo* and *Repub*, then the population multiple correlation $\mathcal{R}$ would be zero. Rephrased, the best fitting regression model should give no weight to both *Demo* and *Repub* when estimating a person's level of political knowledge, because information about which group a case belongs to would provide no information about that case's level of political knowledge. Mathematically, the population multiple regression model would look like

$$\hat{Y} = \mu + \beta_{Demo}(Demo) + \beta_{Repub}(Repub)$$

where μ is the population mean political knowledge, $\beta_{Demo} = 0$ and $\beta_{Repub} = 0$. So this population regression model would generate the population mean for every person, regardless of their political identity. But if the political parties differ on average in their political knowledge, then at least one of the regression coefficients, β_{Demo} or β_{Repub}, should be different from zero, meaning that $\mathcal{R}$ should be different from zero.

Of course, we never have the entire population available, but we can still estimate the regression equation using the sample data. In the data file, party identification is held in a variable named "party" with values 1 (Democrat), 2 (Republican), and 3 ("Other"). The SPSS commands below create the dummy variables:

```
compute demo = (party = 1).
compute repub = (party = 2).
```

The output from a multiple regression estimating political knowledge from *Demo* and *Repub* using the NES data is displayed in Figure 14.5. As can be seen, $R = 0.210$, $R^2 = 0.044$, adjusted $R^2 = 0.038$. So around 4% of the variance in political knowledge can be attributed to these two dummy variables coding group membership.

Recall from Chapter 13 that the test that $\mathcal{R} = 0$ is equivalent to the null hypothesis that the population regression weights for all predictors are equal to zero. So if Democrats, Republicans, and "Others" differ in their political knowledge, on average, this implies that $\beta_{Demo} = 0$ *and* $\beta_{Repub} = 0$. Rejection of this null hypothesis implies that at least one of the population partial regression weights is different from zero, meaning that these three groups differ, on average, in their political knowledge.

From Figure 14.5, the null hypothesis that $\mathcal{R} = 0$ in the population can be rejected, $F(2, 340) = 7.836, p < .0005$. Notice the striking correspondence between the outputs in Figures 14.1 and 14.5. For instance, $SS_{regression} = SS_{between}$ and $SS_{residual} = SS_{within}$. And because $df_{regression} = df_{between}$ and $df_{residual} = df_{within}$, it follows that $MS_{regression} = MS_{between}$ and $MS_{residual} = MS_{within}$. Therefore, the ANOVA and R have the same F ratio and p-value. This is no coincidence, because analysis of variance is simply a special form of multiple regression where the predictor variables are dummy variables coding group membership. They are mathematically equivalent. The test that $\mathcal{R} = 0$ from a multiple regression is the same as the test from analysis of variance that all the group population means on the dependent variable are the same, differing from each other by just "chance." And as discussed in section 14.1.7, R^2 from

Model Summary

Model	R	R Square	Adjusted R Square	Std. Error of the Estimate
1	.210[a]	.044	.038	4.36580

a. Predictors: (Constant), repub, demo

ANOVA[b]

Model		Sum of Squares	df	Mean Square	F	Sig.
1	Regression	298.698	2	149.349	7.836	.000[a]
	Residual	6480.462	340	19.060		
	Total	6779.160	342			

a. Predictors: (Constant), repub, demo

b. Dependent Variable: Political Knowledge

Coefficients[a]

Model		Unstandardized Coefficients		Standardized Coefficients	t	Sig.
		B	Std. Error	Beta		
1	(Constant)	9.127	.589		15.505	.000
	demo	2.291	.694	.254	3.301	.001
	repub	2.689	.690	.299	3.897	.000

a. Dependent Variable: Political Knowledge

Figure 14.5 Regression analysis estimating political knowledge from party affiliation.

the multiple regression can be thought of as a measure of effect size equivalent to η^2 in ANOVA, and adjusted R^2 is equivalent to ϵ^2

14.4.3 Interpreting the Regression Model

From Figure 14.5, the best fitting regression model estimating political knowledge from political party self-identification is

$$\hat{Y} = 9.127 + 2.291(Demo) + 2.689(Repub)$$

But what do these regression weights mean? Their meaning is most easily illustrated by seeing what the model estimates for each group:

$$\text{Democrats}: \quad \hat{Y} = 9.127 + 2.291(1) + 2.689(0) = 11.418$$
$$\text{Republicans}: \quad \hat{Y} = 9.127 + 2.291(0) + 2.689(1) = 11.816$$
$$\text{Neither}: \quad \hat{Y} = 9.127 + 2.291(0) + 2.689(0) = 9.127$$

Notice that the regression model reproduces the group means (recall that $\overline{Y}_1 = 11.481$, $\overline{Y}_2 = 10.816$, and $\overline{Y}_3 = 9.127$). Remember that the least squares regression criterion minimizes $SS_{residual}$. Therefore, the $\hat{Y}$ values that minimize the sum of the squared deviations between the actual Y values and those estimates are the means of the groups.

The partial regression weights for each of the dummy variables in the regression model quantify the difference between the mean Y for the reference group and the mean Y for the group that dummy variable codes. For example, *Demo* codes Democrats.

The regression weight for *Demo*, b_{Demo}, is 2.291, which is exactly equal to the difference between the mean political knowledge of those who define themselves as neither a Democrat nor a Republican and the Democrats ($11.418 - 9.127 = 2.291$). The test of significance for b_{Demo} tests whether the difference between the population mean political knowledge of Democrats and the population mean political knowledge of people who identify with neither party is equal to zero (i.e., $H_0 : \mu_{Demo} - \mu_{Other} = 0$, $H_a : \mu_{Demo} - \mu_{Other} \neq 0$ or, equivalently, $H_0 : \beta_{Demo} = 0$, $H_a : \beta_{Demo} \neq 0$). By the same logic, the regression coefficient for *Repub*, b_{Repub}, quantifies the mean difference in political knowledge between Republicans and those who identify with neither group ($11.816 - 9.127 = 2.689$), and the test of significance tests whether this difference is statistically different from zero in the population (i.e., $H_0 : \mu_{Repub} - \mu_{Other} = 0$, $H_a : \mu_{Repub} - \mu_{Other} \neq 0$, or, equivalently, $H_0 : \beta_{Repub} = 0$, $H_a : \beta_{Repub} \neq 0$). Finally, notice that the regression constant ($a = 9.127$) is the mean of the reference group; in this case, those who identify with neither of the major political parties. This should make sense as it is the value that the regression model predicts when all dummy codes equal zero. Although not very interesting in this context, the test of significance for the regression constant tests whether the mean of the reference group is statistically different from zero in the population ($H_0 : \mu_{Other} = 0$, $H_a : \mu_{Other} \neq 0$).

It makes no difference which group is coded as the reference group. But it is often desirable to construct the dummy variables so that the reference group is a natural or meaningful control group (in an experiment) or some other meaningful baseline group. That way, by running a regression estimating the outcome variable from the dummy codes, you get not only a test that all the means are the same, but also a set of $k - 1$ tests comparing each group mean to the baseline group.

14.5   Some Controversies in the Comparison of Multiple Groups

This chapter illustrates that even though users of analysis of variance have a similar goal—understanding the nature of group differences—there are many different approaches to accomplishing that goal. With a method as widespread as analysis of variance, it is no surprise that methodologists have devoted a lot of energy to the development of specialized tools for comparing means, either in pairwise or contrast form. When a lot of people are thinking about the same problem, there are bound to be differences in opinion and controversies about just how to approach and solve the problem. In this section, I articulate what amounts to nothing more than just my opinions about some of the more general controversies surrounding the multiple test problem and whether analysis of variance is a useful test in the first place. No doubt there are many who would disagree with my perspectives.

14.5.1   Planned Versus Unplanned Comparisons: To Correct or Not?

My discussion of pairwise comparisons and focused contrasts makes a distinction that is similar to but not the same as the distinction between *planned* and *unplanned* comparisons. Unplanned comparisons refer to comparisons between groups that the investigator had not anticipated doing before the study was conducted but that seem worth doing after the data are available and group means known. Planned comparisons, by contrast, refer to specific comparisons between the means that the researcher anticipated doing before the data were collected. They are comparisons that are motivated by the research questions, the hypotheses, or the theories the researcher is testing. It is conceivable that all possible mean comparisons may have been planned. Furthermore, a focused contrast may have suggested itself only after the researcher looked at the table of means. So focused comparisons need not have been planned.

I make this distinction because some believe that whether a comparison was planned or not affects whether some kind of multiple test correction is required prior to interpreting the results of the test. According to this camp of thinkers, we should be less worried about Type I error inflation when conducting a series of comparisons that we had planned on doing all along than we should when we are just mining the data in search of something that is statistically significant. There is some logic to this position. If I have 10 groups of people that I was comparing on some variable Y, there are $10(9)/2 = 45$ possible pairwise mean comparisons. The probability that there will be at least one statistically significant comparison even if the population means are the same is rather large. Some kind of compensation for the fact that many hypothesis tests are being conducted probably is warranted. However, suppose that in addition to doing all possible comparisons, I had planned on comparing group 1 to 2 and the mean of groups 3 and 4 combined to the mean of group 5. It makes some sense that I should be less concerned about Type I error inflation as a result of doing that specific comparison because the probability of a difference just by chance for that specific comparison I wanted to do before I had any data or saw the results is smaller than the probability of finding a difference in at least one of the 45 pairwise comparisons. Rephrased differently, you understandably wouldn't be particularly impressed if I threw five dice across a table and at least 2 of them came up a 6. But you might be *very* impressed if I singled out two of the dice in advance and correctly forecasted that those two in particular will come up 6 when I throw the 5 dice. Or if I played the lottery every day, it wouldn't be particularly surprising if I won something once. But it would be surprising if I was able to successfully predict the precise day that I was going to win something. If our goal is to minimize the number of times we claim there is an effect (such as a difference between means) when there isn't, we should want to exert more control over that error rate when we are just searching for *something, anything* (e.g., 2 of the 10 means differ) than if we are searching for something specific.

The extreme form of this position is that no multiple test correction is required for planned comparisons. Although I am willing to accept that we can justifiably worry less about the multiple test problem for a series of planned comparisons, I do not believe that we should not be concerned about the inflated Type I error rate that will result when multiple tests are conducted, even if they are all planned. Whether a set of comparison is planned or not, if you do several hypothesis tests, the chances of making at least one Type I error increases, period.

One possible middle ground, advocated by Rosenthal and Rubin (1984), is to employ separate corrections for planned and unplanned comparisons or comparisons with different interest value to the researcher. For example, suppose in a study of 4 groups you had two specific focused contrasts you were interested in doing because they are directly relevant to a prediction a theory you are testing makes. You also figure you may as well do all possible comparisons because there might be other differences that you don't anticipate and that the theory doesn't predict should be there but may still be present in the data and worth discovering. In that case, you might partition the desired familywise error rate into 2 categories, reserving, say, 0.025 for the focused contrasts and 0.025 for all possible comparisons. Then employ a Bonferroni correction factor of 6 for the pairwise comparisons and a separate Bonferroni correction of 2 for the 2 planned comparisons. So the p-value required to reject the null hypothesis for each of the planned comparisons would be set to $0.025/2 = 0.0125$, and the required p-value for the pairwise comparisons would be $.025/6 = 0.0041$. So both the planned and unplanned comparisons would be conducted with greater power than if you applied a Bonferroni correction of 8 to the entire set of 8 tests.[5] And the probability of at least one Type I error is held at $1 - [(0.9875)(0.9875)(0.9959)^6] \approx .05$.

This example makes it clear that conceptualizing comparisons as planned or unplanned may not be a good distinction to make. You might plan on doing all possible comparisons as well as focused contrasts. Yet your plan in doing all possible comparisons is just to fish the data pond and see if you catch something. This is a very different motivation than your motivation for conducting the focused contrasts, which are directly relevant to the purpose of your study. Those comparisons and what they reveal are fundamental to your goals when you decided to conduct the study, unlike all possible comparisons, which are just an attempt to find something interesting and worth talking about. Maybe it is better to think of comparisons and contrasts in terms of their interest value to you, or their importance to your research goals. Those comparisons and contrasts that are directly relevant to why you conducted the study can justifiably be treated more leniently with respect to control of the Type I error rate than those comparisons that are less important to you, or that aren't motivated by particular questions, theories, or predictions that you had in mind when you conducted the study.

14.5.2   Are We A Bit Fickle About The Multiple Test Problem?

This is the first chapter in which I have formally discussed the multiple test problem. The problem and various approaches to dealing with it evolved and were popularized in the context of comparing group means, and so it makes sense that I have waited until this chapter to discuss it. When you read the literature in communication, you are more likely to find discussions of the multiple test problem and the manners by which researchers deal with it in the context of an analysis focused on exploring group differences. You will almost never find such a discussion in the context of multiple regression, and it isn't at all obvious why not. If there are k predictors in a regression model, then the typical output from a multiple regression program will contain at least k hypothesis tests. Assuming none of the predictors is related to the outcome after controlling for the other predictors, the probability of making at least one Type I error in this set of k hypothesis tests is not .05 but larger than that. Yet no one talks about the multiple test problem in multiple regression, and no one corrects the p-values in a multiple regression for multiple tests. Similarly, it is not uncommon for a communication researcher to present a matrix of correlations in a research paper along with the p-values for each correlation. In a matrix of correlations between k variables, there are $k(k-1)/2$ correlations and p-values. That is a lot of hypothesis tests being conducted simultaneously, yet you almost never see a researcher correct those p-values to compensate for multiple tests. But the multiple test problem is just as real there as it is when comparing group means.

My point is in part to bring to your attention how fickle we are about the multiple test problem, but also to point out that this is a problem that pervades the scientific process. When we analyze data, we often conduct multiple hypothesis tests. Regardless of the nature of the data and the questions that we are asking, and regardless of whether

---

[5]We are assuming here that the focused contrasts are not contained within the set of 6 pairwise comparisons.

the tests are planned or unplanned, the more tests that are conducted, the more likely we are to find a p-value less than .05 just by chance. In other words, the probability of making at least one Type I error increases anytime you conduct more than one hypothesis test. If you choose to correct for multiple tests in any of these contexts, the Bonferroni family of methods described above can be used, because the logic of these methods applies to any set of tests, not just tests involving means.

This brings up an interesting philosophical issue. If Type I errors are bad and to be minimized, why do we only correct for multiple tests in a single study, but not across studies? A research paper may have 2 studies in it. The investigator might correct for multiple tests in each study independently, but not in the entire set of 2 studies. If the goal is to minimize Type I errors, it isn't obvious why, for example, a Bonferroni correction should not include all the hypothesis tests in the paper and not just those in a particular study. But why stop there? A researcher typically conducts multiple studies in a year. Shouldn't he or she correct for all hypothesis tests conducted that year? If the goal is to minimize Type I errors, it isn't obvious why not. Continuing this logic, why doesn't the entire field of communication correct for all tests done by anyone in a given area (such as mass communication) or during a given year across the entire field, or even the entire field's history. And why stop there? Why not correct for all hypothesis tests ever done in the history of communication science. Such questions are worth asking, but I will not attempt to answer them here. Darlington (1990, p. 263-267) discusses these issues, so I refer you to him as well as a special colloquy on the multiple test problem in the journal *Human Communication Research* in 2003.

14.5.3   Do We Really Need ANOVA?

If you've been following this chapter carefully, you might have noticed a bit of circularity in this entire process. The use of analysis of variance was justified on the grounds that doing all possible t tests inflates the Type I error rate across the set of tests. By conducting a single test of the omnibus null hypothesis with analysis of variance, the probability of incorrectly rejecting a true omnibus null hypothesis is kept at α. But rejection of this null hypothesis is not very informative, so follow up tests need to be conducted to determine which means differ from which. The more such follow up tests that are conducted, the greater the risk of a Type I error in this set of tests, so some kind of multiple test correction is required to keep α_{FW} at an acceptable level. But then why bother with ANOVA in the first place? All possible comparisons with a correction for Type I error inflation can be used to test the same null hypothesis that ANOVA tests. If any two means are deemed statistically significant when conducting all pairwise comparisons, then the omnibus null hypothesis that ANOVA tests must perforce be rejected. Again, why bother with the ANOVA in the first place (see Wilcox, 1987, and Howell, 1997, for similar sentiments)? You may as well just start with all possible comparisons using a method that keeps the Type I error rate across the set to a satisfactory level (such as the Games-Howell method or one of the Bonferroni procedures) and end up with both specific information about which means differ and a decision about the omnibus null hypothesis.

This same logic can be applied to focused contrasts. These contrasts are formed because they directly test a hypothesis of interest. There is no logic in requiring a significant F from analysis of variance, a test which doesn't directly test the hypothesis of interest, prior to employing a test that does. Thus, you might consider foregoing the analysis of variance entirely and proceed directly to the test that is relevant to the hypothesis you are actually interested in testing. If those specific tests do not reveal anything of interest, then conduct the analysis of variance to see if at least the omnibus null hypothesis can be rejected.

14.6   Summary

Communication science often focuses on comparisons between groups—groups that are either naturally occurring (such as racial or ethnic groups, marital status, or political party membership) or artificially created by the researcher (in experiments). The t test is well suited to the comparison of two groups means, but analysis of variance is typically used to compare the means of more than two groups. However, rejection of the null hypothesis that three or more group means are equal provides very little information. Researchers typically seek more information about the nature of those differences. The problem is that the discovery of those differences typically requires multiple hypothesis tests which raises the risk of concluding that an apparent difference is real that is just as easily attributed to chance. Statisticians have developed methods of lowering the risk of such decision errors over a set of hypothesis tests. But methods that focus on all possible pairwise comparisons between a set of k means entail many more hypothesis tests than the researcher may need to conduct in order to test the hypothesis that the study was designed to test. The result of conducting so many additional tests is that each test may be conducted with lower power compared to an alternative analytical strategy that focuses only on specific comparisons of interest to the researcher. When specific predictions are advanced in a research study, or when the research is guided with a clear purpose or goal in mind, a much smaller set of focused contrasts can typically be constructed to precisely test those predictions or illuminate a process that the researcher is most interested in. But a strong argument can made that rather than testing whether k means differ with ANOVA prior to probing the nature of those differences, the researcher could instead go right to those focused contrasts and forego the analysis of variance entirely.

How to comparing means is a controversial one. Not everyone agrees that a correction for multiple tests is necessary, and some would argue that a nonsignificant result from an analysis of variance should stop the business of comparing means in its tracks because the researcher has no evidence that any of the means are statistically different from each other. Where you stand on these controversies is something that only you can decide for yourself.

At the beginning of this chapter we found statistically significant differences in the political knowledge of people who differ in their political affiliations or self-definitions. What causes such differences? Do the differences found tell us something about how people with different political leanings attend to information about politics, or their ability to process political information they receive from the media? For example, if political knowledge comes largely from attending to the media, perhaps the difference between these three groups can be attributed to differences in their media use. If so, then this would suggest that these group differences would not exist among a group of people who differed in their political affiliation but not in their media use. To test this possibility, we can statistically control for group differences (if any) in media use prior to assessing group differences in political knowledge. The procedure to accomplish this is known as *analysis of covariance*—the focus of the next chapter. But just as analysis of variance is nothing other than a special form of multiple regression, so too is analysis of covariance.

FIFTEEN

Analysis of Covariance: ANOVA With Statistical Controls

In the previous chapter, I introduced analysis of variance, a statistical procedure frequently used to test whether two or more group means are statistically different. In the field of communication and other social sciences, the groups being compared are often created by the researcher in an experimental context. One of the methodologically elegant features of an experiment is its ability to roughly equate a set of groups on all individual differences that might be related to the dependent variable through the random assignment of the study participants to the experimental conditions. Because the participants in an experiment are assigned to groups at random, we know that the groups of people assigned to different experimental conditions will be, on average, roughly equivalent on all variables except the manipulated independent variable—the variable which is under the control of the researcher—prior to the beginning of the study.

However, there are many situations where is impossible to randomly assign participants to groups. For example, it would be impossible to study gender differences or the effects of personality by randomly assigning people to male and female groups or to be extroverts or introverts. For other reasons, sometimes random assignment simply isn't feasible, practical, or ethical. This can be a problem when interpreting the results of an analysis of variance because it makes the source of group differences on the outcome variable ambiguous. For example, in Chapter 14 we found that Democrats, Republicans, and people who self-identify with neither party differ from each other, on average, in their political knowledge. One might want to speculate about how differences in political ideology and attitudes affect political knowledge. Perhaps identification with one of the two major parties leads to a greater exposure to politics through various communication channels, such as the mass media or political discussion. People who identify with neither party perhaps aren't as interested in the day to day affairs of government and choose to spend their available time and cognitive energy focusing on things other than keeping abreast on and discussing the happenings of government.

Perhaps. However, it is also entirely possible that differences between these 3 groups in their political knowledge have nothing to do with interest in politics and media exposure. Any other conceivable difference between people with different political leanings could account for this difference. For instance, perhaps people who are less educated don't even know what it means to be a Democrat or Republican, and so they say something else when asked what they consider themselves politically. And people who are less educated may simply have fewer of the cognitive skills required to make sense of, interpret, and therefore recall information about politics. Such an explanation could account for knowledge differences between people who identify with different political groups without invoking some kind of process driven by political attitudes or exposure to political information.

When people cannot be randomly assigned to groups, the only way of dealing with competing explanations for a difference between groups on the outcome variable of interest is to ask if the differences between the groups exist on that variable even after statistically controlling for group differences on variables that can be used to explain the differences observed. For instance, differences in education can't be responsible for differences in knowledge if the three groups differ in political knowledge even after statistically controlling for group differences in education. Whether observed differences between groups exist independent of other third variables can be assessed with a procedure called *analysis of covariance* (ANCOVA). But ANCOVA is useful even in well conducted experiments in which the random assignment procedure nearly guarantees that the groups will be equal on all variables other than the variable being manipulated. Variation on the dependent variable can usually be attributed to more than just the experimental manipulation. Using the Sundar (2000) study from the previous chapter as a case in point, many factors other than the form of information transmission (i.e., text, audio, video, etc.) can affect how much people learn when browsing online news sites. Experience with the World Wide Web, for example, could affect how fluently people move through the Web and therefore how many learnable bits of information they come across. But in the analysis of variance, variation in the outcome variable attributable to anything other than the independent variable is treated as if is unpredictable individual differences. That unaccounted for variation ends up in the quantification of within-group variability, MS_{error}. It is possible to reduce MS_{error} and therefore increase the power of analysis of variance by statistically removing variation in the outcome variable attributable to things other than the manipulated variable. Analysis of covariance, through the statistical control process, can accomplish this if you had the foresight to measure those things likely to be related to the outcome variable.

ANCOVA is often introduced using the same logic as my presentation of analysis of variance in Chapter 14, by partitioning variation in the outcome variable Y into its components. Eventually I will do that. But I am going to part company with many of my colleagues interested in design and analysis by focusing my discussion of analysis of covariance mostly in terms of its properties as a special form of multiple regression and show how analysis of covariance is accomplished in multiple regression.

15.1 Analysis of Covariance as Multiple Regression

Recall from section 13.4 that we can assess the partial contribution of a set of variables X in explaining variation in some outcome variable Y, controlling for one or more other variable(s) W by running a hierarchical multiple regression predicting Y first from W, and then adding the set of X variables of interest to the model. The change in R^2 and the test of significance of this change is interpreted as the incremental increase in variance in Y explained by X controlling for W. Using this logic, we can determine whether k groups differ from each other on average on the outcome, statistically controlling for other variables that the groups may also differ on. As you will see, this is accomplished by defining X as a set of $k - 1$ dummy variables coding group membership and then conducting a hierarchical multiple regression analysis, first entering W into the model and then entering X.

15.1.1   Conducting an ANCOVA With Regression

We'll start the discussion of ANCOVA with a simple example, ascertaining whether differences in the political knowledge of Democrats, Republicans, and those who identify with neither party is attributable to group differences in the frequency of political discussion. Looking at the data, the explanation that differences in political discussion could be driving the knowledge differences found in Chapter 14 seems very plausible. People with relatively more political knowledge do tend discuss politics more frequently ($r = 0.365, p < .0005$). Furthermore, there is evidence that Democrats, Republicans, and "Others" differ in their frequency of political discussion, $F(2, 340) = 3.874, p < .05$, such that those who identify with neither of the two major political parties do report less frequent political discussion on average ($M = 4.182$) compared to Democrats ($M = 4.674$) and Republicans ($M = 5.225$).[1] So perhaps the group differences in political knowledge observed can be attributed to group differences in political discussion. To assess this possibility we can rephrase the question as such: After controlling for political discussion, does party identification explain any variation in political knowledge? In other words, can the estimation of people's political knowledge be improved with information about their political affiliation after taking into account how much they discuss politics? If so, this suggests that differences between the three groups cannot be attributed to differences in how much they discuss politics.

This question can be answered with a hierarchical regression analysis. Political discussion functions in this analysis as a *covariate*. First we need to quantify the proportion of variance in political knowledge (Y) that can be explained by individual differences in political discussion (W). This relationship can be quantified as R^2_{YW} (or simply r^2_{YW} given that there is only one predictor in this model). Next, we need to quantify how much of the variance in political knowledge can be explained by both political discussion *and* political identification. This is quantified as R^2_{YWX}, where X is a set of two dummy variables coding group membership, as discussed in section 14.4. Using the strategy described there, let's create one variable (*Demo*) set to 1 for the Democrats and 0 for everyone else, and another variable (*Repub*) set to 1 for the Republicans and zero for everyone else. We'll leave the remaining group uncoded as the reference group (*Demo* = 0, *Repub* = 0).

The goal is to determine if R^2_{YWX} is larger than R^2_{YW} more than "chance" can explain, under the null hypothesis that people from different parties don't differ in their political knowledge after accounting for group differences in political discussion. Figure 15.1 shows SPSS regression output from a hierarchical multiple regression. As can be seen, $R^2_{YW} = 0.133$ (from the "model 1" summary) and $R^2_{YWX} = 0.161$ (from the "model 2" summary). Therefore, $SR^2_{YX.W} = \Delta R^2 = 0.028$, and this incremental increase in R^2 is statistically different from zero, $F(2, 339) = 5.589, p = .004$ (from the

---

[1] Regardless of which method you use to compare Others to Republicans and Democrats, the differences between these pairs of means are statistically significant, without or without a multiple test correction

Model Summary

Model	R	R Square	Adjusted R Square	Std. Error of the Estimate	Change Statistics R Square Change	F Change	df1	df2	Sig. F Change
1	.365[a]	.133	.130	4.15181	.133	52.280	1	341	.000
2	.401[b]	.161	.153	4.09703	.028	5.589	2	339	.004

a. Predictors: (Constant), Political Discussion
b. Predictors: (Constant), Political Discussion, demo, repub

ANOVA[c]

Model		Sum of Squares	df	Mean Square	F	Sig.
1	Regression	901.173	1	901.173	52.280	.000[a]
	Residual	5877.987	341	17.237		
	Total	6779.160	342			
2	Regression	1088.814	3	362.938	21.622	.000[b]
	Residual	5690.346	339	16.786		
	Total	6779.160	342			

a. Predictors: (Constant), Political Discussion
b. Predictors: (Constant), Political Discussion, demo, repub
c. Dependent Variable: Political Knowledge

Coefficients[a]

Model		Unstandardized Coefficients B	Std. Error	Standardized Coefficients Beta	t	Sig.
1	(Constant)	8.142	.481		16.919	.000
	Political Discussion	.637	.088	.365	7.230	.000
2	(Constant)	6.603	.664		9.949	.000
	Political Discussion	.604	.088	.345	6.861	.000
	demo	1.994	.653	.221	3.055	.002
	repub	2.060	.654	.229	3.149	.002

a. Dependent Variable: Political Knowledge

Figure 15.1 SPSS output from a hierarchical regression estimating political knowledge from political discussion and then both discussion and political party identification.

output or equation 13.14). So it appears that group differences in political discussion do not completely account for the relationship between political party identification and political knowledge. Even after you account for the relationship between political knowledge and political discussion, and the fact that people who identify with different political groups differ in their frequency of political discussion, the group differences in political knowledge remain.

15.1.2   Partitioning Variability in Y in ANCOVA

It is worth again going through an exercise much like in the beginning of Chapter 14, where variability in Y was broken down into its components in analysis of variance. I will introduce some new notation here to clarify the discussion. First, recall from Chapter 13 that $SS_{regression}$ quantifies variation around $\overline{Y}$ attributable to all the variables in the regression model. If there is more than one predictor variable in the regression, then $SS_{regression}$ can be broken down into several components, each representing the contribution of each predictor variable to this explained variation. For instance, suppose the regression model contains two predictors, X and W. Define $SS_{effect(X)}$ as that part of the variation in Y that is attributable *uniquely* to X. It is the part of $SS_{regression}$ attributable uniquely to the relationship between X and Y. Similarly, $SS_{effect(W)}$ is the variation in Y attributable uniquely to W. $SS_{effect(X)}$ must be distinguished from a different quantity, $SS_{regression(X)}$, which is the regression sum of squares in a regression estimating Y from only the X variable. And define $SS_{regression(W)}$ as the regression sum of squares in a regression estimating Y from only W. To make very explicit just which variables are in a regression model in my discussion that follows, define $SS_{regression(W+X)}$ as the variability in Y attributable to W *and* X. And as we did in the previous chapters, define $SS_{residual}$ as everything left over—variation in Y not attributable to any of the variables in the regression model, and SS_{total} as total variability in Y. This notation is general, in that it can be used even if X and W are sets of variables rather than single variables. In what follows I am treating X as the set of dummy variables coding group membership and W as a single covariate, but W could be many covariates being controlled simultaneously.

Assume we have run a linear regression estimating Y from X and W. With the notation just defined,

$$SS_{effect(X)} = SS_{regression(X+W)} - SS_{regression(W)}$$

(15.1)

Because X and W are the only variables in the regression model, $SS_{regression(X+W)}$ is the total variability in Y explained by the model. Of that total explained variation, the part attributable uniquely to X must be the total explained variation minus the variation explained by W. So $SS_{effect(X)}$ represents how much explained variation in Y increases when X is added to the regression model containing W.

If Y is political knowledge, W is political discussion, and X is the two dummy variables coding political party affiliation, then from Figure 15.1,

$$SS_{regression(X+W)} = 1088.814$$

and

$$SS_{regression(W)} = 901.173$$

Therefore, from equation 15.1,

$$SS_{effect(X)} = 1088.814 - 901.173 = 187.641$$

Using this same logic, we can derive $SS_{effect(W)}$ as $SS_{regression(X+W)} - SS_{regression(X)}$. We know $SS_{regression(X+W)}$ from Figure 15.1, but $SS_{regression(X)}$ is not there. Remember from our previous definitions that $SS_{regression(X)}$ is the regression sum of squares in a regression estimating Y from just X. To get this, we can do two things. We can either run a regression estimating political knowledge from the two dummy variables coding political party identification, or we can conduct a oneway ANOVA comparing the mean political discussion of the three groups. In an ANOVA summary table, $SS_{regression(X)} = SS_{between}$. Either way you do it, you would find that $SS_{regression(X)} = 298.698$. Therefore,

$$SS_{effect(W)} = 1088.814 - 298.698 = 790.116$$

Wouldn't it be nice if $SS_{regression(X+W)} = SS_{effect(X)} + SS_{effect(W)}$, meaning that the sum of each variable's unique contribution to explaining variation in Y was equal to the sum of their combined explanatory power? But notice that this is not so: $187.641 + 790.116 \neq 1088.814$. The regression sum of squares left over ($1088.814 - 187.641 - 790.116 = 111.057$) is variability in Y attributable to either X or W but that cannot be attributed to either one of them *uniquely*. Let's call this $SS_{redundant}$, to symbolize that this is the variability in Y redundantly explained by X and W. Putting all this together, equation 15.2 is true:

$$SS_{regression(X+W)} = SS_{effect(X)} + SS_{effect(W)} + SS_{redundant}$$

(15.2)

$SS_{redundant}$ cannot be less than zero and will be zero only in the case where X and W are unrelated. In that special case where X and W are totally unrelated, then $SS_{redundant} = 0$ and so $SS_{regression} = SS_{effect(X)} + SS_{effect(W)}$. Because $SS_{redundant}$ can never be less than zero, we can say

$$SS_{regression(X+W)} \geq SS_{effect(X)} + SS_{effect(W)}$$

(15.3)

So we now have three components of the variability in Y: Variability in Y attributable uniquely to group membership (X), variability uniquely attributable to the covariate (W), and variability in Y attributable to both redundantly. There is one component left. Recall from Chapter 13 that $SS_{total} = SS_{regression} + SS_{residual}$. So as always, the total variability in Y not explained by the variables in the model is $SS_{residual} = SS_{total} - SS_{regression(X+W)}$. In this example (from Figure 15.1), $SS_{residual} = 5690.346$.[2] This completes our derivation of the four components of total variability in Y in ANCOVA:

$$SS_{total} = SS_{effect(X)} + SS_{effect(W)} + SS_{redundant} + SS_{residual}$$

(15.4)

In words, the total variance in Y, quantified as SS_{total}, is equal to the variance uniquely attributable to group membership, $SS_{effect(X)}$, plus the variance uniquely attributable to the covariate, $SS_{effect(W)}$, plus the variance redundantly explained by both group membership and the covariate, $SS_{redundant}$, plus variance not attributable to either, $SS_{residual}$.

These components of variability are more easily understood by examining a Venn diagram. Using Figure 15.2, the total variance in Y, SS_{total}, is represented as the area of the Y circle, or A + B + C + D. The component of the total variance in Y that is uniquely attributable to X is area A, quantified as $SS_{effect(X)}$. The component of the total variance in Y uniquely attributable to the covariate is area C, quantified as $SS_{effect(W)}$. B is $SS_{redundant}$—the component of the total variance in Y attributable to either the covariate or group membership but that can't be uniquely attributed to either. Everything left over—area D in Figure 15.2—is $SS_{residual}$.

I introduced ANCOVA as a form of multiple regression. However, ANCOVA is not traditionally conceptualized in these terms in social science statistics books, and the ANCOVA output from most statistical programs generate ANCOVA-relevant statistics in the form of an ANCOVA summary table rather than as multiple regression output. Figure 15.3 presents an ANCOVA output from SPSS's *general linear model* procedure. Most of the components derived above can be found in this table, and the one component not displayed, $SS_{redundant}$, can be derived from what is displayed. Also displayed are each component's degrees of freedom, mean square (defined as SS/df), F ratio

---

[2]Notice that there are actually two values of $SS_{residual}$ in Figure 15.1. Because we are interested in variability in Y unexplained in the analysis, the $SS_{residual}$ of interest is the one from the final model in the hierarchy.

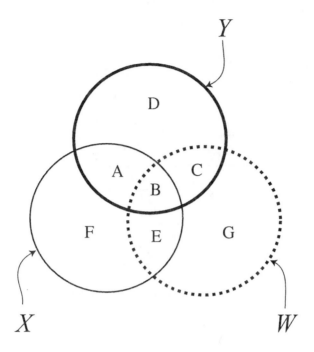

Figure 15.2 A Venn diagram illustrating the relationship between X, Y, and W.

(defined as in ANOVA as each effect's mean square divided by MS_{error}), and p-value. As can be seen, the effect of political identification, called PARTY in the output, is statistically significant, $F(2, 339) = 5.589, p = .004$. Notice that this F ratio and its corresponding p-value is identical to the F ratio for the change in R^2 for model 2 from the regression output in Figure 15.1.

The ANCOVA summary table also provides a test of the significance of political discussion, controlling for political group: $F(1, 339) = 47.071, p < .0005$. So independent of which group a person self-identifies, those who discuss politics more frequently have relatively more political knowledge. This test can also be found in the multiple regression output in the "Political Discussion" row in the model 2 regression output. Observe that the partial regression weight for political discussion is $b = 0.604, t(339) = 6.861, p < .0005$. So the partial regression weight for political discussion is different from zero. These two tests are mathematically equivalent, by the relationship $t^2 = F$ (observe that $6.861^2 = 47.073$, which agrees with Figure 15.1 within rounding error produced by our hand computations). And $SS_{residual}$ is listed in the ANCOVA summary table as SS_{error}. The only thing missing from this output is $SS_{redundant}$. But we can derive this from an algebraic manipulation of equation 15.4:

$$\boxed{SS_{redundant} = SS_{total} - SS_{effect(X)} - SS_{effect(W)} - SS_{residual}}$$

$$(15.5)$$

Plugging in the numbers from Figure 15.3 into equation 15.5,

$$SS_{redundant} = 6779.160 - 187.641 - 790.116 - 5690.346 = 111.057$$

just as we derived earlier.

Dependent Variable: Political Knowledge

Source	Type III Sum of Squares	df	Mean Square	F	Sig.
Discuss	790.116	1	790.116	47.071	.000
Party	187.641	2	93.821	5.589	.004
Error	5690.346	339	16.786		
Total	6779.160	342			

Estimated Marginal Means

Dependent Variable: Political Knowledge

Political Party Affiliation	Mean	Std. Error	95% Confidence Interval Lower Bound	95% Confidence Interval Upper Bound
democrat	11.513[a]	.345	10.834	12.193
republican	11.579[a]	.340	10.911	12.247
other	9.519[a]	.555	8.427	10.611

a. Covariates appearing in the model are evaluated at the following values: Political Discussion = 4.8309.

Figure 15.3 ANCOVA summary table and adjusted means from SPSS.

15.1.3   Measures of Effect Size

In Chapter 14, three measures of effect size were introduced. All three of these measures, η^2, ϵ^2, and ω^2, quantify the proportion of the variance in the outcome variable attributable to group membership. When one or more variables are being statistically controlled when comparing groups, there is considerable debate about how to quantify effect size (c.f., Cohen, 1973; Levine & Hullett, 2002; Maxwell, Camp, & Arvey, 1981). The controversy stems over the baseline against which "variance explained" is measured. Should it be based on *total* variance in Y, or should it be based on the proportion of variance in Y *remaining* after the covariate or covariates have been partialed out of Y? If the former, the choice is η^2, defined as

$$\eta^2 = \frac{SS_{effect(X)}}{SS_{total}}$$

(15.6)

In ANCOVA, η^2 is akin to the setwise squared semipartial correlation in multiple regression terms, in that it quantifies the proportion of the *total* variance in Y that can be uniquely attributed to group membership. Therefore, η^2 is equal to ΔR^2 at the final step of the hierarchical regression described in section 15.1.1.

An alternative is *partial* η^2, which quantifies effect size as the proportion of variance in Y remaining after controlling for the covariate(s) that can be uniquely attributed to group membership. Partial η^2 is defined as

$$\text{partial } \eta^2 = \frac{SS_{effect(X)}}{SS_{effect(X)} + SS_{error}}$$

(15.7)

In regression terms, partial η^2 is mathematically the same as the setwise squared *partial* correlation between group and the outcome controlling for the covariate(s).

If there is no relationship between the covariate(s) and the outcome variable, then partial η^2 and partial η^2 will be the same. Otherwise, η^2 is generally smaller than partial

η^2. For example, from Figure 15.3, the effect size for political party identification is either

$$\eta^2 = \frac{187.641}{6779.160} = 0.028$$

or

$$\text{partial } \eta^2 = \frac{187.641}{187.641 + 5690.346} = 0.032$$

Partial η^2 shares the same minor flaw as η^2, in that it is a slightly biased measure of variance explained in the population. But the bias is small with large sample sizes and, for all intents and purposes, trivial. Recall from Chapter 14 that an alternative measure of effect size, ϵ^2 overcomes much of this bias. There is also a version of ϵ^2 that is comparable to partial η^2. Partial ϵ^2 is defined as

$$\boxed{\text{partial } \epsilon^2 = \frac{SS_{effect(X)} - df_{effect(X)}MS_{error}}{SS_{effect(X)} + [n - df_{effect(X)}]MS_{error}}}$$

(15.8)

(Maxwell, Camp, & Arvey, 1981) where MS_{error} is the mean squared error from the analysis of covariance (or the $MS_{residual}$ in regression terms). Using the information in Figure 15.3, partial ϵ^2 for party identification is

$$\text{partial } \epsilon^2 = \frac{187.641 - 2(16.786)}{187.641 + (343 - 2)16.786} = \frac{154.069}{5911.667} = 0.026$$

In practice, if you are going use partial η^2 or partial ϵ^2 as your measure of effect size, it makes little difference which you choose.

The major problem with partial η^2 and partial ϵ^2 as measures of effect size is that they can be made nearly as large as desired merely by adding covariates to the analysis that are correlated with the outcome but that the groups do not differ on. This is most easily understood by considering equation 15.7. SS_{error} quantifies variability in Y not attributable to any of the variables in the analysis. The more covariates in the analysis that are correlated with Y the smaller SS_{error} will become. If those covariates are unrelated to the outcome variable, $SS_{effect}(X)$ will be largely unaffected by the inclusion of these additional covariates. So partial η^2 will increase (as will partial ϵ^2) inversely a function of the size of SS_{error}. By contrast, η^2 does not possess this limitation because the variance explained by group membership is benchmarked against total variance in the outcome (which does not change as a function of the predictors) rather than the variance left after partialing out the covariates from the outcome. Regardless of how strong the relationship is between the covariate(s) and the outcome, adding covariates to the analysis will not appreciably change η^2 if the groups do not differ on those covariates.

However, all of these measures are affected by the relationship between the covariate(s) and group membership. Adding covariates that the groups differ on will tend to lower all the measures of effect size discussed here. This also means that two investigators who have conducted otherwise identical studies but who control for different variables will end up with different estimates of effect size. Thus, effect sizes from analyses that differ with respect to the variables being statistically controlled are very hard to compare sensibly.

15.1.4 Adjusted Means

One of the more common mistakes when interpreting an analysis of covariance is to base the interpretation of group differences on the observed group means on Y just as would be done in a regular ANOVA. But this isn't correct, because analysis of covariance is testing a slightly different null hypothesis. The null hypothesis tested with analysis of covariance is not that the observed means are equal but that the *adjusted means* are equal. The adjusted means are the group means adjusted for group differences on the covariate(s). There is no single set of adjusted means, but many depending on the value of the covariate(s) used to define the adjustment. In the case of a *single* covariate W, the adjusted means are typically defined as

$$\overline{Y}'_j = \overline{Y}_j - b_w(\overline{W}_j - \overline{W})$$

(15.9)

where $\overline{Y}'_j$ is the adjusted outcome variable mean for group j, $\overline{Y}_j$ is the mean of the outcome variable for group j, $\overline{W}_j$ is group j's mean on the covariate, $\overline{W}$ is the mean of the covariate, and b_W is the partial regression weight estimating the outcome variable from the covariate, controlling for group membership. Defining Democrats, Republicans, and those who affiliate with neither party as groups 1, 2, and 3, respectively, from Chapter 14, $\overline{Y}_1 = 11.418$, $\overline{Y}_2 = 10.816$, $\overline{Y}_3 = 9.127$. Defining W as political discussion, $\overline{W} = 4.831$, $\overline{W}_1 = 4.674$, $\overline{W}_2 = 5.225$, $\overline{W}_3 = 4.182$. And from Figure 15.1, $b_W = 0.604$. Plugging these numbers into equation 15.9 yields

$$\overline{Y}'_1 = 11.418 - 0.604(4.674 - 4.831) = 11.513$$
$$\overline{Y}'_2 = 11.816 - 0.604(5.225 - 4.831) = 11.578$$
$$\overline{Y}'_3 = 9.127 - 0.604(4.182 - 4.831) = 9.518$$

These adjusted means can be interpreted as the expected group means in a group of people differing in their political affiliation but who report discussing politics 4.831 days a week.

A good look at equation 15.9 reveals that difference between a group's adjusted mean ($\overline{Y}'_j$) and observed mean ($\overline{Y}_j$) will vary as a function of the distance between a group's mean on the covariate and the overall covariate mean as well as the magnitude of the partial association between the covariate and the outcome. The closer a group's mean is to the overall covariate mean, the smaller the discrepancy between the group's adjusted and unadjusted mean. And the larger the regression weight, the larger the discrepancy between the adjusted and the unadjusted means.

The adjusted means can also be derived from the regression model, setting the covariate to its mean. From the model 2 output in Figure 15.1, the best fitting regression model is $\hat{Y} = 6.603 + 0.604(Discussion) + 1.994(Demo) + 2.060(Repub)$. Using the mean of political discussion as the adjustment point,

$$\overline{Y}'_1 = 6.603 + 0.604(4.831) + 1.994(1) + 2.060(0) = 11.515$$
$$\overline{Y}'_2 = 6.603 + 0.604(4.831) + 1.994(0) + 2.060(1) = 11.581$$
$$\overline{Y}'_3 = 6.603 + 0.604(4.831) + 1.994(0) + 2.060(0) = 9.521$$

The slight differences in the adjusted means that the two methods yield are attributable to rounding error produced through hand computations. Although equation 15.9 is appropriate whenever there is only one variable being statistically controlled in the ANCOVA, the use of the regression model is a more general approach, in that it can be used regardless of the number of covariates, as discussed in section 15.1.7.

Most good statistical programs that can conduct ANCOVA will display the adjusted means, sometimes called the *estimated means* or *least square means*, if you request them. An example from SPSS can be found in Figure 15.3.

15.1.5 Focused Contrasts Between Adjusted Means

Rejection of the null hypothesis of equality of adjusted means provides no information about which adjusted means differ from which. In Chapter 14, I described various procedures for conducting pairwise comparisons and contrasts between observed means, and the same logic and rational for comparing means applies to adjusted means. I only discuss focused contrasts here because any pairwise comparison can be represented using contrast coefficients in accordance with the rules described in section 14.3.2. To conduct these contrasts, a weighted combination of the means, δ, is constructed that quantifies the contrast of interest using contrast coefficients, but replacing the unadjusted means in equation 14.17 with the adjusted means from the ANCOVA. For example, to compare the political knowledge of people who self identify as either Democrat or Republican to those who identify with neither, the contrast coefficients of $1/2$, $1/2$, and -1 respectively would produce

$$\delta = \sum \lambda_j \overline{Y}'_j = (1/2)(11.513) + (1/2)(11.579) + (-1)(9.519) = 2.027$$

But the addition of a covariate changes the formula for the estimation of the standard error. Instead, of equation 14.18, the standard error is estimated as

$$s_\delta = \sqrt{MS_{error}\left(1 + \frac{MS'_{between}}{SS'_{error}}\right)\sum \frac{\lambda_j^2}{n_j}}$$

(15.10)

where the MS_{error} is the mean squared error from the ANCOVA or, identically, $MS_{residual}$ from the final model of the hierarchical regression, $MS'_{between}$ is the between-groups mean square from an ANOVA comparing the groups on the *covariate*, and SS'_{error} is the error sum of squares from this same ANOVA. From an ANOVA comparing the means of the three groups in their political discussion frequency, $MS'_{between} = 24.713$, $SS'_{error} = 2168.767$, and from Figure 15.3, $MS_{error} = 16.786$. Thus, the standard error of δ is estimated as

$$s_\delta = \sqrt{16.786\left(1 + \frac{24.713}{2167.767}\right)\left(\frac{(1/2)^2}{141} + \frac{(1/2)^2}{147} + \frac{(-1)^2}{55}\right)} = 0.606$$

and so the t ratio is $2.027/0.606 = 3.345$, which is larger than the critical t for $df_{error} = 339$, $\alpha = 0.05$, where df_{error} is from the ANCOVA. So the null hypothesis is rejected. Even after controlling for group differences in frequency of political discussion, affiliates of one of the two major political parties possess greater political knowledge than those who self-identify as neither. Remember that although these computations seem complicated and tedious, most good statistical packages will be able to do these computations for you.

Certain pairwise comparisons are printed in the regression output in Figure 15.1. For example, the coefficient for *Demo* in model 2 quantifies the difference between the adjusted mean for Democrats and the adjusted mean for those who identify as neither Republican nor Democrat controlling for frequency of political discussion (indeed, notice that $11.513 - 9.519 = 1.994 = b_{Demo}$). Similarly, the coefficient for *Repub* is the difference between the adjusted mean for Republicans and the adjusted mean for those who identify as neither Republican nor Democrat, again controlling for political discussion ($11.579 - 9.519 = 2.060 = b_{Repub}$). The t statistics and p-values for these coefficients can be used to test the null hypotheses that the difference between these pairs of adjusted means is equal to zero in the population from which the sample was derived. The missing pairwise comparison could be conducted by recoding the groups using a different group as the reference category and then reestimating the regression model.

The contrast coefficient approach to comparing adjusted means suffers from the same problem as when it is used to compare the unadjusted means. The contrast coefficients weight each group equally in the construction of the contrast, and this can give more weight than deserved to smaller groups in the computation of δ . When there are large differences in the sizes of the groups, I suggest that you instead recode the groups in the data into the two contrast groupings of interest and then conduct an analysis of covariance using this new grouping variable to conduct the contrast. Alternatively, you could use weighted contrast coding (see section 14.3.2).

15.1.6   Statistical Assumptions

ANCOVA has all the same assumptions as ANOVA and multiple regression, but it also has one additional assumption called *homogeneity of regression*. This assumption means that the regression weight estimating Y from the covariate must be the same in all groups. ANCOVA is based on statistical equating, by asking what the difference between the means would be if all groups had the same covariate mean. If the relationship between the covariate(s) and Y is different in the k groups, then the relative difference between the adjusted means as well as the test of significance between them will vary depending on the value of the covariate(s), and this would make the interpretation of the ANCOVA ambiguous and ultimately meaningless. Whether or not the homogeneity of regression assumption is warranted can be tested statistically by testing for an *interaction* between the covariate(s) and group membership in estimating the outcome variable. How to do so is discussed in Chapter 16.

15.1.7   Multiple Covariates

My example of ANCOVA has been based on a single covariate being statistically controlled. However, the only constraint on the number of covariates in ANCOVA is the number of cases in the data set. We can easily include a number of additional covariates without changing the basic method. For example, the analysis above indicates that group differences in political discussion do not account for differences in political knowledge between people who identify with different political parties. But political discussion is only one form of political communication. Perhaps if we statistically controlled for differences between the groups (even if not statistically significant) on television news exposure, newspaper use, and political talk radio use, the political knowledge differences would disappear. But we don't have to stop there, we can also control for demographics such as age, income, education, and sex, all in one fell swoop.

You already now how to do this. Define covariate set W as the set of 5 communication variables introduced in Chapter 13 (newspaper use, local TV news exposure, national network TV news exposure, political discussion, and political talk radio exposure) as well as age, income, education, and sex. And define variable set X as two dummy variables coding which political party a person self-identifies with. If the group differences in political knowledge remain after statistically controlling for these variables, we'd be hard pressed to explain these differences as the result of group differences in exposure to interpersonal and mass communication about politics or differences in their demographic makeup.

The statistical test is accomplished by first generating the best-fitting linear regression model estimating political knowledge (Y) from the nine covariates. As can be seen in Figure 15.4, $R^2_{YW} = 0.415$. So political communication and demographics explain about 41% of the variance in political knowledge. Does adding the two dummy variables coding political party self-identification increase the variance explained to a statistically significant degree. As can be seen, when these two variables are added to the model, $R^2_{YWX} = 0.429$, so $\Delta R^2 = SR^2_{YX.W} = 0.014$. That is, political party self-identification uniquely explains an an additional 1.4% of the variance in political knowledge, $F(2, 331) = 3.963, p = 0.020$. So groups differences in any or all of these 9 covariates cannot be entirely responsible for the observed differences Democrats, Republicans, and those who self-identify as neither in their average political knowledge.

Adjusted Means, Contrasts, and Effect Size. The adjusted means can be derived from the regression model by generating $\hat{Y}$ for each group using the dummy variables for *Demo* and *Repub* and the covariate means as the values of the covariates in the regression model. Doing so leads to adjusted means of $Y' = 11.624$ for Democrats, $Y' = 11.264$ for Republicans, and $Y' = 10.077$ for everyone else. A linear contrast comparing the means of those who identify as either Republican or Democrat to everyone else can be formed as

$$\delta = (1/2)(11.624) + (1/2)(11.264) + (-1)(10.077) = 1.367$$

With more than one covariate, equation 15.10 cannot be used to calculate the standard error. The formula for s_δ is quite complicated for multiple covariates. A good statistical package will know how to calculate it. SPSS tells me the standard error of δ is 0.514, yielding a t statistic of $1.367/0.514 = 2.659, p < .05$. Two pairwise comparisons are provided in the regression output, one comparing Democrats to Others (b_{Demo}), and one comparing Republicans to Others (b_{Repub}). Both of these comparisons are statistically significant.

The addition of several covariates related to political knowledge and the grouping variable shows how effect size can be affected by adding covariates. $SS_{effect(X)}$ can be derived as $SS_{regression(X+W)} - SS_{regression(W)}$. Using the information in Figure 15.4,

$$SS_{effect(X)} = 2904.993 - 2812.229 = 92.764$$

SS_{error} is $SS_{residual}$ from the second regression model. Using equations 15.6 and 15.7,

$$\eta^2 = \frac{92.764}{6779.160} = 0.014$$

and

$$\text{partial } \eta^2 = \frac{92.764}{92.764 + 3874.167} = 0.024$$

Model Summary

Model	R	R Square	Adjusted R Square	Std. Error of the Estimate	Change Statistics				
					R Square Change	F Change	df1	df2	Sig. F Change
1	.644[a]	.415	.399	3.45148	.415	26.230	9	333	.000
2	.655[b]	.429	.410	3.42117	.014	3.963	2	331	.020

ANOVA

Model		Sum of Squares	df	Mean Square	F	Sig.
1	Regression	2812.229	9	312.470	26.230	
	Residual	3966.932	333	11.913		
	Total	6779.160	342			
2	Regression	2904.993	11	264.090	22.563	
	Residual	3874.167	331	11.704		
	Total	6779.160	342			

Dependent Variable: Political Knowlege

Coefficients[a]

Model		Unstandardized Coefficients		Standardized Coefficients	t	Sig.
		B	Std. Error	Beta		
1	(Constant)	-2.950	1.545		-1.909	.057
	Age	.019	.014	.061	1.283	.200
	Years of Education	.590	.101	.278	5.846	.000
	Sex (Male = 1, Female = 0)	1.711	.385	.192	4.441	.000
	Household income (in $1000s)	.013	.005	.114	2.436	.015
	Political Discussion	.347	.079	.198	4.374	.000
	National Network News Exposure	.137	.084	.082	1.636	.103
	Newspaper Use	.234	.075	.148	3.124	.002
	Local News Exposure	-.253	.099	-.125	-2.566	.011
	Political Talk Radio Exposure	.525	.152	.152	3.446	.001
2	(Constant)	-3.937	1.572		-2.504	.013
	Age	.019	.014	.062	1.321	.187
	Years of Education	.586	.100	.276	5.854	.000
	Sex (Male = 1, Female = 0)	1.713	.382	.193	4.484	.000
	Household income (in $1000s)	.012	.005	.105	2.236	.026
	Political Discussion	.335	.079	.192	4.248	.000
	National Network News Exposure	.137	.083	.082	1.650	.100
	Newspaper Use	.218	.075	.138	2.919	.004
	Local News Exposure	-.247	.098	-.122	-2.519	.012
	Political Talk Radio Exposure	.547	.153	.158	3.579	.000
	Demo	1.546	.550	.171	2.811	.005
	Repub	1.187	.558	.132	2.125	.034

a. Dependent Variable: Political Knowledge

Figure 15.4 SPSS output from a hierarchical regression estimating political knowledge from communication and demographics and then adding political party identification.

Notice that $\eta^2 = \Delta R^2 = SR^2_{YX.W}$ and so can be interpreted as the proportion of total variance in political knowledge uniquely attributable to political party identification. By contrast, partial η^2 is $PR^2_{YX.W}$ and is interpreted as the proportion of variance in political knowledge remaining after partialing out the 9 covariates that can be uniquely attributed to political party identification. So when variance explained is benchmarked relative to variance in Y unexplained by the covariate rather than total variance in Y, the effect size of party self-identification nearly doubles in this example.

15.2 Analysis of Covariance in Experimental Designs

The previous discussion focused on the comparison of means after controlling for a variable or variables that the groups may also differ on. This is important because it allows the investigator to determine whether group differences on the outcome variable are simply an epiphenomenon of other differences between the groups that the outcome variable happens to correlate with. The ability to rule out this possibility allows the investigator to conclude that the difference between the groups is independent of other measured variables on which the groups might also differ on average.

In experiments, we are usually less concerned about the interpretational ambiguities caused by preexisting group differences on variables other than the dependent variable because such differences are minimized or eliminated entirely by the random assignment process. Groups of people constructed by randomly placing people into groups will, on average, be equal or nearly so on every conceivable variable measured prior to the manipulation of the independent variable. They will also be equal or nearly so, prior to the manipulation, on all *unmeasured* variables. But ANCOVA can still be useful in experiments because it can increase the power of the F test, leading to a greater probability of rejecting the null hypothesis of equality of the means if the manipulation does have an effect on the dependent variable. This is accomplished by statistically controlling for individual differences related to the *dependent variable* but that could not possibly be related to or affected by the manipulation. ANCOVA can also be useful as a means of assessing whether the effect of the manipulated independent variable on the dependent variable is *mediated* by some other variable that the independent variable affects. This is accomplished by measuring an additional variable or variables that are presumed to be causally between the manipulation and the outcome variable and then statistically controlling for them to see if this partialing process eliminates the relationship between the independent and dependent variable. So the distinction between these two uses of ANCOVA in experiments is based on whether the covariate is measured prior to or after the experimental manipulation or, more precisely, whether the covariate or covariates can be said to be *causally between* the manipulation and the outcome variable. We'll take each of these uses of ANCOVA in the analysis of experimental data in turn.

15.2.1 Controlling for Variables Unaffected by the Manipulation

At the beginning of the chapter, I noted that there are probably many things about a person that can predict how much they learn browsing online news sites, such as differences in experience on the Internet or general interest in public affairs. In the multimedia study described in Chapter 14 by Sundar (2000), participants were randomly assigned to one of the five experimental groups. By employing random assignment, we can be pretty sure that the groups don't differ on average on such variables as

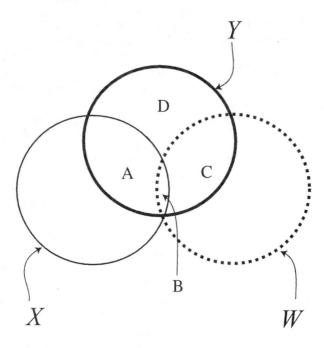

Figure 15.5 A Venn diagram illustrating the relationship between X, Y, and W.

experience with the Web. But that doesn't mean the potential influence of such an individual difference on learning during the experimental procedure somehow disappears. For example, people with less experience surfing the Web might be expected to learn less, and those with more experience perhaps would tend to learn more, regardless of which experimental condition they are assigned to.

When such variables are measured as part of the research procedure, it is possible to remove their influence from the analysis mathematically and increase the power of the test of the difference between the group means. To illustrate how this is so, consider the Venn diagram in Figure 15.5. This picture represents a situation where W, the covariate, is correlated with Y but only weakly with X (the independent variable being manipulated). I represent the relationship between the covariate and the independent variable as weak rather than zero to reflect the fact that even with random assignment of participants to groups, random assignment variation will still produce a small but likely nonsignificant and trivial difference between the groups on the covariate. If W is not in the analysis and a single-factor ANOVA conducted, the F ratio will be a function of the size of A + B ($SS_{between}$ or $SS_{regression}$) relative to the size of the sum of C + D (this sum being SS_{error}). But by including W in the analysis, variability in Y attributable to W is removed from Y, and SS_{error} is now just D. The result is that the ratio of A, ($SS_{effect(X)}$), to D (SS_{error}) will be larger than the ratio of A + B to C + D. After dividing these quantities by their respective degrees of freedom, this translates into a larger F ratio and smaller p-value for the effect of the independent variable on Y. A will be slightly smaller than A + B, but the difference will typically be much smaller than the difference between D and C + D. The effect that including W will have on the reduction of SS_{error} depends on the strength of the relationship between Y and W as well as the error degrees of freedom (Cox & McCullagh, 1982).

Dependent Variable: learn

A

Source	Type III Sum of Squares	df	Mean Square	F	Sig.
Condition	63.567	4	15.892	4.383	.004
Error	199.417	55	3.626		
Total	262.983	59			

Dependent Variable: learn

B

Source	Type III Sum of Squares	df	Mean Square	F	Sig.
WebExp	67.529	1	67.529	27.649	.000
Condition	63.114	4	15.779	6.460	.000
Error	131.888	54	2.442		
Total	262.983	59			

Dependent Variable: learn

C

Source	Type III Sum of Squares	df	Mean Square	F	Sig.
Time	68.179	1	68.179	28.053	.000
Condition	14.740	4	3.685	1.516	.210
Error	131.238	54	2.430		
Total	262.983	59			

Figure 15.6 The result of controlling for a covariate correlated with the outcome but unaffected by (B) or affected by (C) an experimental manipulation.

To illustrate, consider an analysis of covariance comparing learning in the 5 web conditions constructed by Sundar (2000), controlling for experience with the Web. (Sundar did not include this measure in his study, and I made the data up for the purpose of illustration). I include a hypothetical variable in the data set (see Appendix E8 on the CD) reflecting participants' response to the question: "About how how many hours did you spend browsing the World Wide Web last week?" (*Webexp*). Imagine the participants were asked this question before the experiment began, and so there is no way that what happened during the experiment could have possibly affected their responses to this question. The relationship between browsing experience and learning is positive, $r = 0.51$, but as would be expected through the random assignment process, mean web browsing experience does not vary across groups, $F(4, 55) = 0.125, p = 0.973$. Now compare the ANCOVA table from an analysis of covariance comparing mean learning across the groups controlling for web experience (Figure 15.6, panel B) to the ANOVA table where web experience is not statistically controlled (Figure 15.6, panel A). Notice that the F ratio for the experimental condition is larger in the ANCOVA than in the ANOVA. This reflects the reduction in the MS_{error} resulting from controlling for web experience (from 3.626 in the ANOVA to 2.442 in the ANCOVA). Because the covariate is largely unrelated to groups, the change in the sum of squares for the group effect has changed little (63.567 vs. 63.114), and thus neither has the mean square reflecting group variation in learning. The net result is a smaller F ratio for the effect of the experimental manipulation.

This example also illustrates how the inclusion of covariates can result in different effect size estimates depending on which approach to quantifying effect size you use. In the ANOVA, η^2 for the manipulation of information format on learning is $(63.567/262.983) = 0.242$. From the ANCOVA, $\eta^2 = (63.114/262.983) = 0.240$. So the inclusion of a covariate unrelated to the manipulated variable has not changed

η^2; experimental condition still explains about 24% of the total variance in learning. But partial $\eta^2 = 63.114/(63.114 + 131.888) = 0.324$. Which is the correct measure of effect size is an open question. Partial η^2 cannot be interpreted as the proportion of total variance in learning uniquely attributable to the manipulation of media format. Instead, it reflects the proportion of variance in learning *remaining after partialing out web browsing experience* that can be uniquely attributed to media format. As discussed in section 15.1.3, partial η^2 can be made as large as desired simply by adding covariates related to the outcome variable but unrelated to which group a person was randomly assigned to. Furthermore, two investigators who conducted the same study identically but who controlled for different variables would likely end up with different effect size estimates for the manipulated variable when using partial η^2 as the index of effect size. For this reason, I suggest you not use partial η^2 as a measure of effect size.

15.2.2 Controlling for Variables Affected by the Manipulation

By partialing out variables that are unaffected by an experimental manipulation but related to the outcome, the power of the F test comparing group means can be increased by sucking out predictable variation in the outcome that otherwise would end up in the denominator of the F ratio. This increase in power comes not only from the reduction in SS_{error} and MS_{error} but also by a corresponding lack of change in SS_{effect} and MS_{effect} quantifying the effect of the manipulation. So it is a good idea to partial out the relationship between the outcome and anything related to the outcome but not to the manipulation.

But the same cannot be said for variables that might be affected by the manipulation, especially if an argument can be made that such variables are *causally between* the independent variable and the outcome variable. Consider a twist on this study, where the researcher quantifies attention to the content by measuring how long each person spends viewing each web page during the experimental procedure. An argument could be made that the manipulation of format would affect how much attention participants devote to each web page. A photograph, for example, requires additional attention and processing time so the presence of pictures might increase how much time people spend on each page relative to the condition where no pictures are available. Or conversely, people may spend less time on a web page with audio or video because they may be less inclined to read the text as thoughtfully or thoroughly as someone not given an audio or video version of the same information. Or the amount of time that a person spends on each web page may reflect how interested the person is in the content of the page, with that interest being affected by the format in which the information is presented. Insofar as attention (or things attention is correlated with such as interest) affects how much a person learns, partialing out attention from the relationship between the experimental condition and learning may, in effect, partial out the very effect that researcher is interested in studying. Partialing out variables affected by the manipulation when assessing the relationship between the outcome and the experimental is sometimes called *over control*, and it is generally not a good thing to do.

To illustrate the effects of partialing out a variable affected by the manipulation, consider an analysis of covariance controlling for how many minutes the person spent viewing the web pages they were asked to view. Each case's score on this variable (*time*) can be found in the data described in Appendix E8 on the CD (again, these data are fabricated for the purpose of illustration). The correlation between time spent browsing the web pages and learning is positive, $r = 0.667, p < .001$. However, the addition of photographs or other forms of presentation also affected how much time the person spent browsing the web pages they were asked to view, $F(4, 55) = 3.286, p = .017$. Looking at the means, people appeared to spend less time browsing in the conditions that included an audio or video version of the content compared to those that contained just text or pictures. As we know from the ANOVA, the format of the web page did affect learning, but after controlling for time spent with the content, the effect becomes nonsignificant, $F(4, 54) = 1.516, p = 0.210$ (see Figure 15.6, panel C). But to say that the format of the information did not affect learning would be incorrect. The problem is produced by over control—partialing out a variable that is most likely causally between the independent and dependent variables. If greater learning is the result of greater attention (operationalized as time spent with the content), it shouldn't be surprising that after statistically equating the groups on how much attention was devoted to the content, there are no detectable differences between the groups in their learning. This would be equivalent to saying that unmarried men don't differ from unmarried women in how much taxes they pay after you partial out their annual income. If single men make more than single women, they probably pay more taxes *because* they make more money. Statistically removing the relationship between income and taxes paid would be statistically removing the mechanism that produces the differences in how much taxes are paid in the first place.

15.2.3 Mediation

In spite of the interpretational problems associated with partialing out a covariate affected by the independent variable, there is one good reason to conduct just such an analysis. If multimedia format affects learning as a result of how multimedia formats differentially affect attention paid to content, then we say that attention *mediates* the relationship between multimedia form and learning. A mediator variable is a variable that is *causally between* two variables and that *accounts for* the relationship between those two variables. So if W mediates the relationship between X and Y, this means that X and Y are related because of X's effect on W which in turn affects Y. The process of mediation is depicted graphically in Figure 15.7. The arrows in the figure depict a causal path between the variables, such that X is represented here to causally affect W while W causally affects Y. So X affects Y through the mediating variable W.

As with anything in science, there is no way of proving in no uncertain terms that a variable mediates a relationship between two variables. But it is possible to put together a statistical argument that is consistent with mediation. There are several strategies for testing a mediation hypothesis, but they all reduce down in some way to a set of criteria that must be met. A strategy is a four-step procedure popularized by Baron and Kenny (1986). To establish that W *completely mediates* the relationship between X and Y using this procedure, four criteria must be met: (a) the independent variable X must affect the proposed mediator variable W, (b) the proposed mediator variable W must affect the outcome variable Y, (c) the relationship between the proposed mediator and the outcome variable must persist even after controlling for the independent variable, and (d) the relationship between the independent and dependent variable must be eliminated after controlling for the proposed mediator variable. There are two other criteria that are implied but not explicitly stated by Baron and Kenny: (a) there must be a relationship between the independent and outcome variable—if there is no

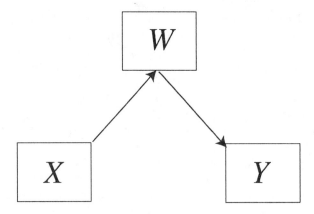

Figure 15.7 A graphical depiction of mediation.

relationship to be mediated, then there is no basis for arguing that anything mediates that relationship, and (b) all the effects must be in the direction consistent with the mediation process.

The first criterion is met in this example by the fact that the manipulation of the independent variable affected attention to the web pages, as evidenced by the statistically significant difference between the mean viewing times combined with the random assignment of people into conditions. The second criterion is met, at least statistically, because there is a significant relationship between how much time a person spent browsing the web pages and how much they learned, and the direction is consistent with the argument that greater attention leads to greater learning. Of course this is just a correlation, but a strong case can be made that the direction of cause, if any, must be from attention to learning. It would be hard to argue that greater learning leads to greater attention; a much more parsimonious explanation is that the causal path moves from attention to learning. Whether the third and fourth criteria are met can be established by examining the results of an analysis of covariance, comparing the means of the groups on the outcome variable controlling for the proposed mediator. The third criterion is that the mediator must be related to the outcome variable after controlling for the independent variable. As can be seen in Figure 15.6, panel C, even after controlling for which experimental condition a person was assigned to, there is a statistically significant relationship between time browsing and learning. It isn't apparent from this output, but a multiple regression estimating knowledge from time browsing and four dummy variables coding group would reveal that this partial relationship is positive, $b_{time} = 0.293$. So controlling for experimental condition, people who spent relatively more time browsing the site learned relatively more. The fourth criterion is met on the grounds that the statistically significant relationship between experimental condition and learning has disappeared after controlling for time (Figure 15.6, panel C). Together, these findings suggest that the relationship between multimedia format and learning from the web is completely mediated by attention.

When thinking about mediation as a concept, it is important to keep in mind that mediation describes a *causal* process. The criteria described above can be used to support a claim about mediation, but statistics cannot establish whether the process is a causal one. Assessing causality is a research design issue more than a statistical one. Causal processes are best tested with experimental designs such as this one. It is much more difficult to make a convincing case that a relationship between two variables is mediated by some third variable or set of variables when the data are correlational rather than experimental in origin, even if the criteria above are met.

Furthermore, the Baron and Kenny approach discussed above is only one way of thinking about mediation statistically. It has been criticized, and there are alternatives available. Assessing whether a pattern of relationships is consistent with a mediational argument is a complicated and controversial topic in statistics. For a good start familiarizing yourself with some of the arguments and controversies, see Holbert and Stephenson (2003), MacKinnon, Lockwood, Hoffman, West, and Sheets (2002), Preacher and Hayes (2004), and Shrout and Bolger (2002).

15.3 Summary

Groups can differ from each other on the variables measured in a research study for a number of different reasons. It is difficult to understand the mechanism producing differences between groups on some variable when those groups are naturally existing groups rather than groups created artificially by the researcher through random assignment to experimental conditions. The problem is that any other variable along which groups differ may produce differences in the outcome variable, so the difference observed between a set of group means may reflect nothing about the characteristics that define group membership. Analysis of covariance gives us a means of assessing group differences on some outcome variable after controlling for other variables that distinguish the groups from each other. It is easier to make the case that the characteristics that define the groups are driving the difference on the outcome variable if group differences exist even after controlling for those extraneous "nuisance" differences between the groups.

Even if the groups are created artificially in an experimental context, analysis of covariance can be used effectively to increase the power of tests of significance between group means. Power is increased when statistically controlling for variables that are unaffected by the experimental manipulation but related to the outcome variable because those variables reduce unexplained variation that is otherwise treated as unpredictable variation on the outcome variable. But it is dangerous to statistically control for variables that may have been affected by the experimental manipulation and that are causally related to the outcome variable, because partialing those covariates out of the relationship between X and Y partials out the very effect the you are trying to detect. The exception is when you are interested in testing a hypothesis about mediation. In that case, mediation can be tested statistically by examining if a relationship between two variables disappears after controlling for variables that are affected by the independent variable and that also affect the outcome. There are various strategies for testing a mediation hypothesis, but none of these strategies automatically yield causal conclusions, because causality is determined more by good research design rather than statistical methodology. Causal claims are justified only if the method of data collection and the quality of the study justifies such causal claims.

CHAPTER SIXTEEN

Interaction

Up to this point, we have discussed how to quantify and test for association between variables, determining whether a relationship exists between two variables after accounting for their shared relationship with another variable or set of variables, and how to determine whether "chance" is the most parsimonious explanation for differences between groups or a relationship that we observe between two variables. But there are questions that need to be answered before we can say we really have gained some understanding of communication processes and theory from our research: "Why?" "When?" and "How?" A scientist can make a career of demonstrating that two variables are related, but the more memorable studies, the more impressive studies, and ultimately the more influential studies in the field go further by discovering or explaining why such relationships exist, under what circumstances, or for whom the relationship exists strongly as opposed to weakly or not at all. We truly understand some phenomenon if we are able to determine when the phenomenon will occur, why or how it occurs, and for whom it occurs or will occur. As you become increasingly knowledgeable about the discipline of communication and increasingly expert in your specialty area, you will discover that the most sensible answer to almost every question you will confront as a scientist is "it depends." Such an answer is not a cop-out. What we study is often sufficiently complicated that it would be incorrect to say without condition or exception that X causes Y or that one group differs from another group on some outcome variable in all circumstances. Usually effects vary as a function of something else. For example, perhaps for some people exposure to televised violence causes aggressive behavior, but for others such exposure has no effect. Or perhaps the effect of such exposure differs depending on the consequences or form of the violence. Media violence that is perceived to be rewarded may lead people to engage in that behavior, whereas violence that is perceived to be punished may discourage such behavior. Or perhaps a message about the negative consequences of unsafe sexual practices could increase safe sexual practices among people of a certain background or age but decrease it or have no effect among people of a different background or age.

If a relationship between X and Y varies depending on the value of some other variable W, then it is said that W is a *moderator* of the relationship between X and Y, or that the relationship between X and Y is *moderated by* W. In other words, W moderates the relationship between X and Y if the value of W predicts the size or direction of the relationship between X and Y. Another term often used to describe moderation is *interaction*. We say that two variables X and W interact if the combination of X and W explain variation in Y independent of their additive effects. Thus, interaction is akin to the concept of synergy—when two things are combined they have a different effect than the sum of their parts. I will use the terms *interaction* and *moderation* interchangeably throughout this chapter.

The concept of interaction is perhaps more easily understood with a picture. Figure 16.1 illustrates three forms of interaction, as well as 3 examples of the absence of interaction. In the top row on the left, the relationship between X and Y, expressed as a regression line, varies depending on the value of W, where W can have only two values (e.g., $W = 0$ for males and $W = 1$ for females). But a lack of interaction between X and W is displayed in the top right panel. It is clear in that graph that the relationship between X and Y does not vary across the two groups defined by W, reflected in the fact that the slope of the regression line estimating Y from X is the same for both values of W. But W need not be dichotomous, as the middle two panels indicates. The graph in the left panel, middle row, depicts a relationship between Y and X that varies as a function of the values of W, whereas the relationship does not differ as a function of W in the right middle panel. The bottom row left panel illustrates how the relationship between X and Y might differ as a function of whether participants are assigned to an experimental or a control condition in an experiment. So the relationship between X and Y depends on the level of the experimental manipulation a participant was assigned to. A corresponding lack of interaction is displayed in the right panel of the bottom row. It should be apparent from these examples that interaction or moderation evidences itself graphically in the form of nonparallel regression lines. In all these examples on the left, the effect of X on Y (represented with the regression line) depends on some value W. A lack of interaction shows up graphically as parallel regression lines, reflecting the fact that the relationship between X on Y remains constant across all values of some third variable W.

In this chapter, I introduce some statistical approaches to testing for interaction between two predictor variables. This may be the most complicated of all chapters in the book, but it is arguably one of the more important chapters, because moderation is such a commonly tested hypothesis in communication science. It is also one of the more incomplete chapters in the book. We only begin to scratch the surface of statistical approaches to testing for interaction and the various forms that interaction can take. Whole books have been written on this topic (e.g., Aiken & West, 1991; Aquinis, 2002; Jaccard, Turrisi, & Wan, 1990), and there are literally dozens upon dozens of articles in the methodology literature about statistical interaction. But before focusing on the nuts and bolts of testing for interaction, let's first look at some examples in communication theory and research.

16.1 Interaction in Communication Research and Theory

Many of the hypotheses communication researchers test focus on interaction or moderation, and many of the theories that explain communication phenomena involve interaction between components of the theory. For example, Walther, Slovacek, and Tidwell (2001) were interested in how nonverbal information such as information contained in a person's face might affect the relational outcomes of a computer-mediated communication (CMC) task, and whether such an effect depends on whether the CMC

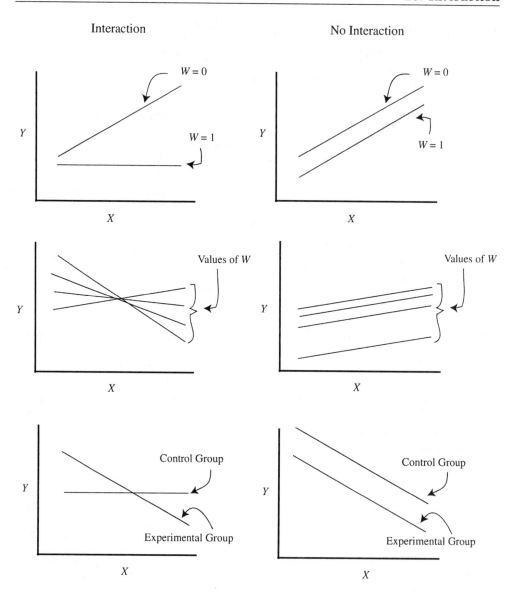

Figure 16.1 Graphical representation of interaction and lack of interaction.

partners had known each other for a long or relatively short period of time. In this study, Walther et al. (2001) manipulated whether the participants were given a photo of their interaction partners in a CMC context. They were also able to categorize the participants into two groups: whether the partners had interacted with each other in a CMC context only briefly during the procedure or had been interacting with each other more extensively over a long period of time. They found that the effect of the photograph on later judgments of feelings of intimacy and attraction toward the partners differed systematically as a function of the length of the CMC relationship. More specifically, they reported that in short term CMC relationships, a visual image of the interaction partners enhanced feelings of intimacy and attraction toward those partners, but in long-term CMC relationships, the presence of the photograph reduced such feelings. So we can say that the effect of the photograph on feelings of intimacy was moderated by the length of the CMC relationship or that the presence or absence of the facial information interacted with the length of the relationship in explaining variation in perceived intimacy.

Another example comes from research and theory on the knowledge gap (Tichenor, Donohue, & Olien, 1970). The knowledge gap refers to the differences in knowledge possessed by the "haves" and "have-nots" in society and the differential effect of information on such groups. More specifically, people who are relatively low in socioeconomic status tend to have less knowledge about a number of things, such as politics or world affairs, than people higher in socioeconomic status. There are a number of explanations for this phenomenon. One explanation is that people who are lower in education tend to have fewer of the cognitive skills and less of the background knowledge to make sense of information presented through the mass media. Thus, increased exposure to mass-mediated information is less likely to facilitate learning among the relatively less educated. But greater exposure should enhance learning among the more educated because they have the skills and aptitudes and prior knowledge that would help them to better understand and therefore learn from the mass media. Indeed, in a study to test this possibility, this is exactly what Eveland and Scheufele (2000) found. Using data from the 1996 National Election Study, they found that individual differences in media use were more predictive of individual differences in political knowledge among the more educated than among the less educated. Thus, education moderated the relationship between news exposure and political knowledge. That is, education and news exposure interacted in explaining person-to-person variation in political knowledge.

Yet another example is found in cultivation theory and the notion of *mainstreaming*. Cultivation theory attempts to explain the effects of television on the beliefs and attitudes of the public. According to cultivation theory, greater exposure to television leads to a greater internalization of the "television view" of the world. Thus, the more television a person watches, the more likely his or her perceptions of the world and the attitudes he or she holds will come to mirror the stories, world views, and attitudes that predominate the televised world. The notion of mainstreaming refers to the homogenizing effect that exposure to television produces among heavy viewers. People of different ethnicities, levels of education, or political orientations often have very different attitudes about social issues and different beliefs about the world, such as how dangerous it is or how trustworthy people are. The mainstreaming hypothesis predicts that individual differences such as ethnicity or education should be less related to attitudes or perceptions of the world among heavy viewers of television compared to light viewers, because heavy doses of the televised world leads to a convergence of the beliefs, attitudes, and perceptions of otherwise disparate groups of people toward the televised view of the world. Among light viewers, those who are less likely to have experienced the cultivating effect of television, such individual differences as education, ethnicity, and political orientation are more predictive of beliefs, attitudes, and perceptions because light viewers' world views are less likely to have been shaped by the images of television. Thus, cultivation theory and the mainstreaming hypothesis argue for a moderating effect of television viewing on the relationship between demographic variables such as education, ethnicity, and political orientation and beliefs, attitudes, and/or world views. In other words, frequency of television and such demographics are proposed to interact in the explanation of individual differences in beliefs, attitudes, or perceptions of the world. Although cultivation theory remains controversial, there is at least some evidence in the communication literature supporting cultivation theory and the mainstreaming hypothesis, summarized in such places as Gerbner, Gross, Morgan, and Signorielli (1986), and Shanahan and Morgan (1999).

Finally, the elaboration likelihood model of persuasion (Petty & Cacioppo, 1986) predicts an interaction between characteristics of a message or its source and a person's motivation or ability to process that message in determining how persuaded a person will be by that message. According to the elaboration likelihood model, people who are more motivated or more able to engage in thoughtful processing of message content are likely to be influenced by such features of a message as the strength of the arguments contained within it. People with relatively little motivation or ability, in contrast, are more influenced by the presence of "peripheral cues" of a message such as whether the source is likeable or attractive or the sheer number of arguments presented rather than their quality. Decades of research (summarized in Petty & Cacioppo, 1986) illustrates such interactions. For example, the effect of argument quality on persuasion depends on whether the content of the message is relevant to a person's life. Such "personal involvement" in an issue leads to deeper processing of message content, such that messages with predominantly strong arguments induce greater attitude change and greater memory for the content of the message than do messages with predominantly weak arguments. But when personal involvement is low, people are less likely to evaluate a message in terms of the quality of the arguments because they are less likely to engage in the kind of thoughtful message processing that would be required to determine whether a set of arguments is strong or weak. So attitude change and memory for arguments is largely unrelated to whether the arguments in the message are strong versus weak.

These examples all illustrate that much communication research and theory is based on the notion of interaction. Variables do not have consistent effects in the communication literature, or communication theory predicts that a variable's affect on some outcome will vary as a function of some other variable. For one reason or another, a variable may have one type of effect in some circumstances or among some people, but have a different effect in some other circumstance or among some other group. The ability to test hypotheses that focus on differences in effect and to discover such differences if they exist is an important skill that the communication researcher must possess.

There are two primary contexts in which questions about moderation are usually addressed statistically, with those contexts being defined in terms of whether all or only some of the predictor variables proposed to be interacting are categorical. When the predictor variables are all categorical, interaction is usually tested with *factorial analysis of variance*. For example, variables X and W may be experimental manipulations and the researcher is interested in knowing if the manipulation of variable X has the same effect across the levels of the manipulation of W. Or W may be a naturally occurring categorical variable like gender, ethnic group, or any other conceivable nominal variable. In that case, the question focuses on whether the experimental manipulation has the same effect in all groups defined by variable W. But if one or both of the predictor variables are quantitative dimensions, *moderated multiple regression* is more appropriate. In moderated multiple regression, the question focuses on whether the regression weight estimating Y from X varies as a function of some second variable W. Variable W can be either nominal with two or more possible categories, or quantitative with many possible values.

If W is categorical but X is quantitative, it is all too common to categorize cases in the data file based on their scores on X and then apply factorial analysis of variance rather than use the more efficient method of moderated multiple regression. I strongly discourage this strategy for reasons discussed toward the end of this chapter. This practice is common perhaps because factorial analysis of variance is a bit easier to grasp and therefore is probably more widely taught, understood, and therefore used. For this reason, I focus first on factorial analysis of variance. But as you will see, factorial analysis of variance is just a special form of multiple regression.

16.2 Factorial Analysis of Variance

Berger (2000) was interested in how media reports of increasing crime in a community contribute to people's perceptions of their risk of being a victim of crime. The media often reports frequency information about crime in a community over time and uses upward trends as evidence that crime is increasing. For example, a daily newspaper might report that in 2000 there were 200 crimes in Anytown whereas in 2005, there were 250 crimes. Understandably, knowledge that crime in your community has increased could make you feel uneasy and vulnerable. But such an increase in the frequency of crime would not be at all surprising if the population of Anytown also increased between 2000 and 2005. The more people there are in a region, the more crimes there are going to be, because there are more people, houses, business, etc. Berger (2000) argued that if the media included in their stories such information about population growth trends along with information about the trends in the frequency of crime, then the effect of information about upward trends in crime over time on people's feelings of vulnerability would be reduced. But he argued that such population trend information would not affect everyone the same. Specifically, he hypothesized that the reduction in perceived risk of being a victim of crime associated with the additional information about the size of the population over time would be smaller for women. This prediction was based on previous research that women seem to feel more vulnerable to crime than men and that this elevated feeling of vulnerability would interfere with a woman's ability to connect the information about the increase in population to the increase in the total number of crimes.

To test this hypothesis, a group of men and a group of women read a short news article describing how there had been an increase in the number of burglaries in the community in which they lived over a 5 year period. Half of the participants randomly assigned to the *Information Present* condition also read a second news article that described how the size of the population during the period had increased during this same 5-year period. The other half of the participants, randomly assigned to the *Information Absent* condition, did not get this story. After reading the story (or stories), the participants were asked a series of questions, including one that asked them to rate the likelihood that they would be a victim of a burglary on a 0 (certainly not) to 100 (certainly) scale. This was the dependent variable in their analysis that we will call *risk* or *perceived vulnerability*.

Berger (2000) was hypothesizing an *interaction* between gender and whether or not the participant received the population trend information on the participants' perceived risk judgments. That is, he proposed that the difference in perceived risk between men who received the population trend information and those who did not should be smaller than the corresponding difference in women. Rephrased, the size of the effect of population trend information on risk judgments should depend on whether the reader was a male or a female. If we call μ mean risk judgment, then the null and alternative hypothesis are

$$H_0 : (\mu_{MA} - \mu_{MP}) = (\mu_{FA} - \mu_{FP})$$
$$H_a : (\mu_{MA} - \mu_{MP}) \neq (\mu_{FA} - \mu_{FP})$$

where the first subscript refers to sex (**M**ale or **F**emale) and the second subscript refers to the population trend information (**P**resent or **A**bsent). The first difference in parentheses, $\mu_{MA} - \mu_{MP}$, is the effect of population trend information on the risk judgments of men, whereas the second difference, $\mu_{FA} - \mu_{FP}$ is the effect of population trend information on women. So the null hypothesis states that there is no difference between men and women in the effect of population trend information, whereas the alternative states that the effect of population trend information differs between men and women. But notice that as the research hypothesis is phrased, a one-tailed test is justified. That is, the research hypothesis could be framed statistically as

$$H_a : (\mu_{MA} - \mu_{MP}) < (\mu_{FA} - \mu_{FP})$$

but we will stick with two-tailed tests here because in more complicated ANOVA designs, it often isn't possible to test a directional alternative because of the way that ANOVA works mathematically. Furthermore, it is sensible to remain open to the possibility that the result could be the opposite of what was predicted.

Before continuing, a comment about the use of Greek symbols in the null and alternative hypothesis is warranted. As you know by now, is conventional in statistics to use Greek letters to refer to characteristics of a population and Roman letters to refer to characteristics of a sample from that population. The Greek letter μ is typically used to denote a population mean and a Roman character such as $\overline{Y}$ to refer to the mean computed of a sample from some population. In experimental contexts, the notion of a population is a bit different than in nonexperimental studies. In nonexperimental studies, the population refers to the universe of units (e.g., people) from which the sample was derived. In experiments, we often use the term "population" to refer to something more hypothetical. Consider μ_{MA}. This notation refers to a hypothetical population of males and what their average risk judgment would be expected to be in the information absent condition of the study. Of course we don't know μ_{MA}. At best, we can estimate this by obtaining some men and putting them in this condition and seeing what their judgments are. The population is strictly hypothetical because the experimental context is a world that we are creating. It doesn't exist in reality. There is no population of men who read stories about crime without corresponding information about population change over time. But imagine if we had unlimited resources and could conduct this study with a very large number men. If we could do this, then the sample mean, $\overline{Y}_{MA}$ would probably be a pretty good descriptor of how men, when placed in the *Information Absent* condition, would be expected to respond when asked how vulnerable they feel to burglary. Similarly, $\overline{Y}_{MP}$ would be a pretty good descriptor of how men, when placed in the *Information Present* condition, would be expected to respond. If the population trend information information has no effect on risk judgments in men, we are in making the claim that $\mu_{MA} = \mu_{MP}$ or, equivalently, $\mu_{MA} - \mu_{MP} = 0$. The same logic applies to the population means for women.

To test the hypothesis of interaction, the standard statistical method used is *factorial analysis of variance*. In analysis of variance, the independent variable or variables are often called *factors*, and the values of each factor are referred to as *levels*. In this study, there are two independent variables or factors, defined as gender and population trend information, each with two levels (male vs. female and population trend information present vs. absent). Thus, the analysis strategy described here is a "2 × 2" (pronounced "two by two") *between-groups factorial analysis of variance*, with the "2" referring to the number of levels of the factors. The "factorial" label comes from the fact that these two factors are perfectly crossed with each other, such that each each level of one factor occurs in the design at each level of the second factor. The factors in a factorial ANOVA can have any number of levels, but we will only discuss the 2 × 2 case in this chapter. The "between-groups" part of this description refers to the fact that each participant contributes data to one and only one of the 4 *cells* in this design. Each cell is defined by the combination of levels of the factors. So the four cells in the design are (a) males, information present, (b) males, information absent, (d) females, information present, and (d) females, information absent. Other types of factorial ANOVA commonly conducted in communication research include the completely repeated measures or "within-groups" factorial ANOVA, where each participant contributes data to each cell in the design, or a "mixed design" factorial ANOVA, where one factor is between groups while the other factor is "within-groups." We focus entirely on the between groups analysis of variance in this chapter. Entire books have been written about the analysis of data resulting from between, within, and mixed designs, and the many complicated issues that the analysis of complicated designs introduce. I refer you to one or more of the classic books on the topic, such as Keppel (1991), Keppel & Zedeck (1989), and the massive Winer, Brown, & Michels (1991) for detail on the analysis of more complicated designs.

16.2.1   Partitioning Variance in Y in a Balanced Factorial Design

Before showing how the hypothesis of interaction is tested in analysis of variance, it is worth going the process we went through in Chapter 14 of partitioning the variance of the dependent variable Y (risk judgment) into its components. The data for this exercise are presented in Table 16.1. For the purpose of illustration, I have made these data up, but they are consistent with the results reported in Berger (2000). In this hypothetical data set, 16 participants (8 men and 8 women) were randomly assigned in equal numbers to either the *Information Present* or *Information Absent* condition. The data show, for example, that the 4 men randomly assigned to the information present condition reported risk judgments of 30, 40, 20 and 30. This gives a mean for this cell of the design of $\overline{Y}_{MP} = 30$. This table also provides the *marginal means* for each factor, representing the average of the cases in that row or column of the table. So, for example, the mean risk judgment of the 8 males in the study was $\overline{Y}_M = 37.50$ and the mean risk judgment for the 8 participants who received no population trend information was $\overline{Y}_A = 50$. Finally, the table also shows that the mean risk judgment for all 16 people in the study was $\overline{Y} = 48.75$. The mean of all n units in the data is typically called the *grand mean* in the lingo of analysis of variance.

Observe in Table 16.1 that there is considerable variation in people's risk judgments around the grand mean. Some people perceived themselves to be more vulnerable than the grand mean, whereas others perceived themselves to be less vulnerable than the grand mean. Of course this isn't surprising because people will differ in how vulnerable they perceive themselves to be to crime in a community for any number of reasons. According to the logic and mathematics of between-groups factorial analysis of variance, such individual differences can be broken into several components. Much like in single-factor ANOVA, one component is how people in the different groups differ from grand mean. But here we have two ways of categorizing people into groups because we have two factors. Consider a man assigned to the population information absent condition. One of these men, call him John, had a perceived risk judgment of 40. His 40 can be attributed in part to how men differ from the grand mean $(\overline{Y}_M - \overline{Y})$ and also to how people who received no population trend information differ from the grand mean on average $(\overline{Y}_A - \overline{Y})$. But there is another source of variation that is attributable to being *both* a man *and* being assigned to the population trend information absent condition. On average, such people also differ from the grand mean in such a way that cannot be attributed merely to the additive effects of the two factors. Intuitively, we might want to symbolize this as $\overline{Y}_{MA} - \overline{Y}$, but doing so would be problematic because the size of $\overline{Y}_{MA}$ depends in part on both $(\overline{Y}_M - \overline{Y})$ and $(\overline{Y}_A - \overline{Y})$. The joint effect of being a man *and* being assigned to the information absent condition can be quantified as $\overline{Y}_{MA} - \overline{Y}_M - \overline{Y}_A + \overline{Y}$. Everything left over is individual differences between people in the same cell in the design (i.e., how John's Y differs from the other men in his condition in the study: $Y - \overline{Y}_{MA}$).

Before showing how John's score of 40 can be partitioned into these 4 components, I need to make the important distinction between a *balanced* and an *unbalanced* factorial design. In a balanced factorial design, the number of cases in each cell of the design is the same. The design in Table 16.1 is balanced because each cell contains 4 cases. In contrast, in an unbalanced design, the number of cases differs across the cells. The following discussion on apportioning variation in Y applies only to balanced designs. For unbalanced designs, the mathematics I am about to describe do not work, as I illustrate later.

Table 16.1
Hypothetical Data from Berger (2000), Balanced Design

Gender	Population Information				Marginal Means
	Present		Absent		
Male	30	40	40	50	
	20	30	50	40	$\overline{Y}_M = 37.5$
	$\overline{Y}_{MP} = 30$		$\overline{Y}_{MA} = 45$		
Female	60	60	50	60	
	80	60	60	50	$\overline{Y}_F = 60$
	$\overline{Y}_{FP} = 65$		$\overline{Y}_{FA} = 55$		
Marginal Means	$\overline{Y}_P = 47.5$		$\overline{Y}_A = 50$		$\overline{Y} = 48.75$

In a balanced design each case's Y score, expressed as deviation from the grand mean $(Y - \overline{Y})$, can be expressed as a sum of the 4 components just described. For example, for men (M) in the absent (A) condition, the following equation holds:

$$(Y - \overline{Y}) = (\overline{Y}_M - \overline{Y}) + (\overline{Y}_A - \overline{Y}) + (\overline{Y}_{MA} - \overline{Y}_M - \overline{Y}_A + \overline{Y}) + (Y - \overline{Y}_{MA})$$

So for John,

$$
\begin{aligned}
(40 - 48.75) &= (37.50 - 48.75) + (50 - 48.75) + (45 - 37.50 - 50 + 48.75) + (40 - 45) \\
-8.75 &= \quad\text{-11.25} \quad + \quad 1.25 \quad + \quad\quad\quad 6.25 \quad\quad\quad + \quad -5.00 \\
-8.75 &= \quad\quad\quad -8.75
\end{aligned}
$$

It works. In a balanced design, this is true for every case in the data.

Because we are ultimately interested in partitioning variability across the entire data set rather than for each person, we need to quantify these sources of variation across the entire data set. This is accomplished by computing each component for each case in the data set, squaring each component, and adding each squared component across all cases, just as we did in Chapter 14 for the single-factor ANOVA. The result is a sum of squares for each component. In a balanced design with two factors A and B, the following equation holds:

$$\sum(\overline{Y}_{ijk} - \overline{Y})^2 = \sum(\overline{Y}_{A_i} - \overline{Y})^2 + \sum(\overline{Y}_{B_j} - \overline{Y})^2 + \sum(\overline{Y}_{A_iB_j} - \overline{Y}_{A_i} - \overline{Y}_{B_j} + \overline{Y})^2 + \sum(Y_{ijk} - \overline{Y}_{A_iB_j})^2$$

(16.1)

where Y_{ijk} corresponds to case k's Y measurement, with case k belonging to level i of Factor A and level j of Factor B in the analysis. The summation is over all all cases in the data file. Equation 16.1 can be rewritten symbolically as

$$SS_{total} = SS_A + SS_B + SS_{A\times B} + SS_{error}$$

(16.2)

where SS_A and SS_B are the sum of squares for the effect of factor A and factor B on Y, and $SS_{A\times B}$ is the sum of squares for the *interaction* between A and B. SS_{error} is sometimes called the *within-group sum of squares* and denoted SS_{within}. I use SS_{within} and SS_{error} interchangeably. They mean the same thing.

Figure 16.2 contains an SPSS ANOVA summary table from a factorial analysis of variance showing all these sums of squares. Observe that indeed equation 16.2 works: $3375 = 2025 + 25 + 625 + 700$. This is true because the design is balanced. It is easy to show that in a balanced design, the sources of variation described above are *independent*, in that they carry unique information about variability in Y around $\overline{Y}$. Thus, their effects can be added up as above to produce the total variation in Y, quantified as SS_{total}. But in an unbalanced design, these components are partially redundant. They carry overlapping information, and the sources of variation cannot be added up to produce total variation in Y. An example of this will be provided in section 16.2.4.

Each sum of squares also has associated with it a *Mean Square* (MS), which is computed by dividing the sum of squares by its correspondent degrees of freedom. In a factorial design, df_A is the number of levels of the A factor minus 1, df_B is the number of levels of the B factor minus 1, $df_{A\times B} = df_A \times df_B$, and $df_{error} = n - df_A - df_B - df_{A\times B} - 1$, where n is the total sample size. An ANOVA summary table such as in Figure 16.2 will also contain the degrees of freedom and MS for each source of variation.

Dependent Variable: RISK

Source	Sum of Squares	df	Mean Square	F	Sig.
SEX	2025.000	1	2025.000	34.714	.000
INFO	25.000	1	25.000	.429	.525
SEX X INFO	625.000	1	625.000	10.714	.007
Error	700.000	12	58.333		
Total	3375.000	15			

Figure 16.2 SPSS ANOVA summary table from a 2×2 ANOVA of the data in Table 16.1.

16.2.2   Main and Interaction Effects

Notice in Figure 16.2 that unlike in a single factor ANOVA, in factorial ANOVA, there are several F ratios, one for each of the three main components described above (the fourth component is the error component, but it has no F ratio). These F statistics are all computed by dividing the mean square for the component by MS_{error}. Each of these F ratios can be used to test different null hypotheses by computing the p-value for F.

Main Effects. In a two-factor ANOVA, there are two *main effects*. A main effect refers to the effect of one of the factors, ignoring the existence of the other factor. These main effects correspond to differences in the marginal means on the outcome variable for each factor. In this study, the two main effects are the sex main effect (males vs. females) and the population trend information main effect (present vs. absent). The sex main effect refers to the difference between the mean risk judgments of men compared to women, corresponding in these data to the difference between $\overline{Y}_M = 37.50$ (the mean risk judgment for men) and $\overline{Y}_F = 60$ (the mean risk judgment for women). The F ratio for this main effect in these data is

$$F_{Sex} = \frac{MS_{Sex}}{MS_{error}} = \frac{2025.000}{58.333} = 34.714$$

This F ratio can be used to test the null hypothesis, $H_0 : \mu_M = \mu_F$ against the alternative: $H_a : \mu_M \neq \mu_F$. The degrees of freedom for this F ratio are $df_{numerator} = df_{sex}$ and $df_{denominator} = df_{error}$, and the p-value derived from a table of critical values of F or with a computer. In these data, $F_{Sex}(1, 12) = 34.712, p < .0005$. So we can reject this null hypothesis. The obtained difference between the risk judgments of men and women is too large to attribute it to chance. It seems that women perceive themselves as more vulnerable to burglary than do men.[1]

The second main effect corresponds to the effect of population trend information on risk judgments. In these data, this main effect corresponds to the difference between $\overline{Y}_P = 47.5$ (mean risk judgment for the 8 participants who received population

---

[1] Of course, we really have no basis for making a statistical statement about men and women from this design, given that the participants in Berger's study were conveniently available and not obtained through any kind of random sampling plan. But with a significant F-ratio, we can discount the null hypothesis of a random process pairing respondents of different sexes to particular risk judgments, as discussed in Chapter 10.

trend information) and $\overline{Y}_A = 50$ (mean risk judgment for the eight who received no population trend information). The F ratio is

$$F_{Info} = \frac{MS_{Info}}{MS_{error}} = \frac{25.000}{58.333} = 0.429$$

and is used to test the null hypothesis $H_0 : \mu_{Absent} = \mu_{Present}$ against the alternative $H_a : \mu_{Absent} \neq \mu_{Present}$. In these data, $F(1, 12) = 0.429, p = 0.525$, so the null hypothesis cannot be rejected. It seems that giving population trend information had no effect on the participant's risk judgments. The obtained difference can most parsimoniously be attributed to "chance."

As you will see, these main effects can be misleading, depending on whether the two factors interact. Because a sensible substantive interpretation of a main effect depends on whether or not there is an interaction between the two factors, the best strategy is to first focus on the *interaction* rather than the main effects.

Interaction. If two factors A and B interact, then the effect of factor A differs across levels of factor B, and the effect of B differs across levels of factor A. In this example, if the effect of population trend information depends on whether the reader is male or female, then we would say that sex and population information interact in explaining variation in risk judgments.

Interaction is most easily understood by considering the notion of a *simple effect*. A simple effect is the effect of one factor conditioned on the level of a second factor. For example, in this study there are 2 simple effects for population trend information. One is the simple effect of population information in men. The other is the simple effect of population information in women. In these data, the simple effect of population trend information in men is $(\overline{Y}_{MA} - \overline{Y}_{MP}) = 45 - 30 = 15$. Descriptively at least, men who had the population trend information perceived themselves less vulnerable to burglary than did men who were not given this information. The simple effect of population trend information in women is $(\overline{Y}_{FA} - \overline{Y}_{FP}) = 55 - 65 = -10$. On the surface, it would seem that giving females population trend information did not lower their perceived vulnerability. If anything, it increased it.

If 2 variables interact, then by definition of interaction, the simple effects are different. Here, we see that the simple effects descriptively are different (15 vs. -10). But we want to know whether they are *statistically* different. In other words, do we have reason to reject "chance" as the best explanation for the obtained difference between the simple effects? That is, can we reject the null hypothesis that $H_0 : (\mu_{MA} - \mu_{MP}) = (\mu_{FA} - \mu_{FP})$ in favor of the alternative $H_a : (\mu_{MA} - \mu_{MP}) \neq (\mu_{FA} - \mu_{FP})$? The F ratio gives us the key. If there is no interaction between population trend information, then we expect F to be about 1. Using information from the ANOVA summary table in Figure 16.2

$$F_{Sex \times Info} = \frac{MS_{Sex \times Info}}{MS_{error}} = \frac{625.000}{58.333} = 10.714$$

with a p-value of .007. We can reject the null hypothesis because the p-value is smaller than 0.05, $F(1, 12) = 10.714, p = .007$. It seems that population trend information and gender interact—the size of the effect of population information depends on whether the person is a male or female.

There is another way of interpreting this interaction because there are two more simple effects that we could compare. We could ask whether the differences in risk judgments between men and women differ depending on whether or not the person received population trend information. The simple effect of sex when no population

Model	R	R Square	Adjusted R Square	Std. Error of the Estimate
1	.890[a]	.793	.741	7.63763

a. Predictors: (Constant), Sex X Info, Info, Sex

	Unstandardized Coefficients		Standardized Coefficients		
	B	Std. Error	Beta	t	Sig.
(Constant)	48.750	1.909		25.531	.000
Sex	22.500	3.819	.775	5.892	.000
Info	2.500	3.819	.086	.655	.525
Sex X Info	-25.000	7.638	-.430	-3.273	.007

Figure 16.3 Regression output corresponding to a 2×2 ANOVA of the data in Table 16.1.

trend information is provided is $(\overline{Y}_{FA} - \overline{Y}_{MA} = 55 - 45 = 10)$. The simple effect of gender when population information is provided is $(\overline{Y}_{FP} - \overline{Y}_{MP}) = 65 - 30 = 35$. We can ask whether 35 is larger than 10 to a statistically significant degree, but we don't need to conduct another test because the F ratio for the interaction can also be used to test the null hypothesis that the simple effects are actually the same and differ from each other in the data available by just a chance mechanism. We can reject this null hypothesis and claim that females perceive themselves to be more vulnerable than men after reading the story, but more so when population trend information is provided compared to when it is absent.

When two factors interact, the main effects may not have a substantively useful interpretation, because the main effect of a factor is defined mathematically as the average simple effect of that factor. For example, notice the main effect of population trend information, $\overline{Y}_A - \overline{Y}_P = 2.50$, which is equal to the average of the two simple effects of population trend information: $(\overline{Y}_{FA} - \overline{Y}_{FP}) = 55 - 65 = -10$ and $(\overline{Y}_{MA} - \overline{Y}_{MP}) = 45 - 30 = 15$, so $(-10 + 15)/2 = 2.50$. If the simple effects are different from each other (which is what interaction is by definition), then the main effect of a factor will probably be a poor summary of the simple effects of that factor. So in the presence of a statistically significant interaction, it makes more sense to focus your interpretation on the interaction than on the main effects.

16.2.3 The Regression Equivalent of a 2×2 Factorial ANOVA

In the last two chapters, I made the point that ANOVA and ANCOVA are just special forms of multiple regression. The same is true for factorial analysis of variance. To illustrate, I provide the regression output from a multiple regression predicting perceived risk from population trend information, sex, and their interaction in Figure 16.3. Prior to running this analysis, I used a form of group coding called *effect coding*. For this coding scheme, the levels of the sex factor (*Sex*) were coded such that males $= -0.5$ and females $= 0.5$. Similarly, the population trend information factor (*Info*) was coded such that those assigned to the information present were assigned a score of -0.5

and those assigned to the information absent condition were given a score of 0.5. The following regression model was then calculated estimating risk judgment (Y):

$$\hat{Y} = a + b_1(Sex) + b_2(Info) + b_3(Sex \times Info)$$

where $Sex \times Info$ is a new variable defined as the product of Sex and $Info$ from the effect coding scheme described above.[2] In this model, b_1 quantifies the main effect of sex, b_2 quantifies the main effect of population trend information, and b_3 quantifies the interaction between sex and population trend information. In Figure 16.3 you will find the regression coefficients and tests of significance from this regression model. The best fitting regression model is

$$\hat{Y} = 48.750 + 22.500(Sex) + 2.500(Info) - 25.000(Sex \times Info)$$

Observe that the coefficient for $Info$ (b_2) of 2.50 is equal to the difference between the population information marginal means: $(\overline{Y}_A = 50.00) - (\overline{Y}_P = 47.50) = 2.50$. Furthermore, the p-value is the same as the p-value from the F ratio for the information main effect in the ANOVA (see Figure 16.2). This is because the tests are mathematically identical. Notice that the square of t for $Info$ from the regression analysis is equal to F for the information main effect in the ANOVA summary table (i.e., $-0.655^2 = 0.429$). Similarly, the coefficient for Sex (b_1) of 22.5 is exactly equal to the difference between the sex marginal means: $(\overline{Y}_F = 60.00) - (\overline{Y}_M = 37.50) = 22.50$, and the p-value for is the same as the p-value from the F ratio from the ANOVA, and the square of the t statistic is equal to F for the sex main effect from the ANOVA (i.e., $5.892^2 = 34.714$). Finally, it should come as no surprise now that the coefficient for the product of Sex and $Info$ (b_3) is equal to the difference between the simple effect of information for males and the simple effect of information for females: $(\overline{Y}_{FA} - \overline{Y}_{FP}) - (\overline{Y}_{MA} - \overline{Y}_{MP}) = (55 - 65) - (45 - 30) = -10 - (15) = -25$. Again, the the p-value for the regression coefficient for this product is the same as the p-value for the interaction in the ANOVA table, and $t^2 = F$.

16.2.4   Factorial ANOVA and Unbalanced Designs

In a perfect empirical world, our designs will be balanced. The effects we estimate will provide unique information about systematic variation in Y, and the four components of variance derived in section 16.2.1 will completely add up to the total variance in Y. But a factorial design often is not balanced. In experimental contexts, sometimes we have to throw out some of the data for whatever reason, producing certain cells that have a smaller number of participants. In nonexperimental contexts, factorial designs are almost certainly going to be unbalanced. For example, if we were to crossclassify respondents to a telephone poll into a 2×2 table (such as male vs. female and kids vs. no kids) and analyze how much TV people in these categories watch on average with a factorial ANOVA, it is highly unlikely that the four cells will contain the same number of people. When the design is unbalanced, we can still do factorial ANOVA and test for interaction, but there are few twists on the interpretation that need to be considered. Most computer programs can handle unbalanced designs as easily as balanced designs,

---

[2]Effect coding is typically described as a coding scheme using 1 and -1 to code various levels of the factors. However, effect codes can be multiplied by any constant without changing the results. But modification of the effect codes in this way changes the regression coefficients. By using 0.5 and -0.5 rather than 1 and -1, the regression coefficients exactly equal the differences between the marginal means.

Table 16.2
Hypothetical Data from Berger (2000), Unbalanced Design

Gender	Population Information		Marginal Means	
	Present	Absent	Unweighted	Weighted
Male	30 20 20 40 30 40 $\overline{Y}_{MP} = 30.00$	40 50 50 40 $\overline{Y}_{MA} = 45.00$	$\overline{Y}_M = 37.50$	$\overline{Y}_M = 36.00$
Female	60 60 80 60 $\overline{Y}_{FP} = 65.00$	50 60 40 50 60 50 60 70 $\overline{Y}_{FA} = 55.00$	$\overline{Y}_F = 60.00$	$\overline{Y}_F = 58.33$
Unweighted Marginal Means	$\overline{Y}_P = 47.50$	$\overline{Y}_A = 50.00$	$\overline{Y} = 48.75$	
Weighted Marginal Means	$\overline{Y}_P = 44.00$	$\overline{Y}_A = 51.67$		$\overline{Y} = 48.18$

so the real effort for you as the data analyst is to make sure you understand what the computer is telling you.

The data in Table 16.2 is largely a replication of Table 16.1, but I've added a few cases to some of the cells to produce an unbalanced design. Although the design is unbalanced, notice that the cell means are identical to the cell means in the balanced design, so I haven't done anything to the differences between the cell means. I've also added some new rows and columns that will be important in the forthcoming discussion. In Figure 16.4, panel A, I have provided the ANOVA summary table from a factorial ANOVA on these data, and in panel B you will find the output from a multiple regression equivalent using the coding scheme described in the previous section.

Partioning Variation in Y in an Unbalanced Design. Equation 16.2 says that the total variance in Y (quantified as SS_{total}) is equal to the sum of the sums of squares for the four components in this two-factor factorial ANOVA. But this applies only to balanced designs. Notice in 16.4, panel A, that the four sum of squares do not add up to the total sum of squares: $2557.895 + 31.579 + 789.474 + 1400.000 = 4778.948 \neq 4927.273$. This is typical when a design is unbalanced and results from the fact that in an unbalanced design, the factors and their interaction are intercorrelated variables. In this example, sex and population trend information factors carry redundant information as to the estimates of their effects. For example, the sex effect contains a part of the population information effect, because females are more likely than males to be in the population trend information absent condition in this unbalanced design.

In an unbalanced design, the sources of variation in Y cannot be derived using the logic and method described in section 16.2.1. Instead, the sums of squares can be derived much like they were derived in analysis of covariance by considering the analysis of variance as a linear regression using effect coding of the factors as was done in section 16.2.3. The sum of squares for a factor is assessed by quantifying how much the regression sum of squares decreases when a factor is excluded from the regression. Imagine running a regression estimating risk judgments Y from *Sex*, *Info*, and their product using coding scheme discussed in section 16.2.3. The regression sum of squares from this regression is listed in Figure 16.4 panel B.

To calculate the sum of squares for a specific effect, derive the difference between sum of squares for the model that includes the main effects and the interaction and the sum of squares from a regression model that excludes just that effect. Table 16.3 contains the regression sum of squares from the regressions necessary to derive the sums of squares for each effect. For example, to calculate the sum of squares for the sex main effect, SS_{Sex}, subtract the sum of squares for the model that excludes the

Table 16.3
Regression Sums of Squares for Different Models

Factors in Model	$SS_{regression}$
Sex, Info, Sex × Info	3527.273
Sex, Info	2737.799
Sex, Sex × Info	3495.694
Info, Sex × Info	969.378

main effect for Sex (969.378 in Table 16.3) from the full model including all main effects and the interaction (3527.273). The difference is $3527.273 - 969.378 = 2557.895$, which is exactly what the output in Figure 16.4, panel A says. The method yields the following sums of squares for each effect:

$$SS_{Sex} = SS_{Sex,Info,Sex \times Info} - SS_{Info,Sex \times Info} = 3527.273 - 969.378 = 2557.895$$
$$SS_{Info} = SS_{Sex,Info,Sex \times Info} - SS_{Sex,Sex \times Info} = 3527.273 - 3495.694 = 31.579$$
$$SS_{Sex \times Info} = SS_{Sex,Info,Sex \times Info} - SS_{Sex,Info} = 3527.273 - 2737.799 = 789.474$$

A

Dependent Variable: RISK

Source	Sum of Squares	df	Mean Square	F	Sig.
SEX	2557.895	1	2557.895	32.887	.000
INFO	31.579	1	31.579	.406	.532
SEX X INFO	789.474	1	789.474	10.150	.005
Error	1400.000	18	77.778		
Total	4927.273	21			

B

Model	R	R Square	Adjusted R Square	Std. Error of the Estimate
1	.846[a]	.716	.669	8.81917

a. Predictors: (Constant), Sex X Info, Info, Sex

ANOVA[b]

Model		Sum of Squares	df	Mean Square	F	Sig.
1	Regression	3527.273	3	1175.758	15.117	.000[a]
	Residual	1400.000	18	77.778		
	Total	4927.273	21			

a. Predictors: (Constant), Sex X Info, Info, Sex

b. Dependent Variable: RISK

Coefficients[a]

Model		Unstandardized Coefficients		Standardized Coefficients		
		B	Std. Error	Beta	t	Sig.
1	(Constant)	48.750	1.962		24.851	.000
	Sex	22.500	3.923	.749	5.735	.000
	Info	2.500	3.923	.083	.637	.532
	Sex X Info	-25.000	7.847	-.402	-3.186	.005

a. Dependent Variable: RISK

Figure 16.4 ANOVA summary table (A) and 2×2 ANOVA as a regression analysis (B) using the data in Table 16.2.

The remaining sum of squares, SS_{error}, is calculated as SS_{total} minus the sum of squares for the regression that includes all the main effects and the interaction. In these data, $SS_{error} = 4927.273 - 3527.273 = 1400.000$. Verify using Figure 16.4 that these sums of squares are all correct.

In an unbalanced factorial design with two factors A and B, the following equation holds:

$$SS_{total} = SS_A + SS_B + SS_{A \times B} + SS_{error} + SS_{redundant}$$

(16.3)

where $SS_{redundant}$ is variance in Y that cannot be uniquely attributed to any of the factors or their interaction because of the intercorrelation between the factors. A little algebraic manipulation tells us that

$$SS_{redundant} = SS_{total} - (SS_A + SS_B + SS_{A \times B} + SS_{error})$$

(16.4)

which in this example works out to

$$SS_{redundant} = 4927.273 - (2557.895 + 31.579 + 789.474 + 1400.000) = 148.325$$

Because $SS_{redundant}$ will be greater than 0 in an unbalanced design, it follows that in an unbalanced design, $SS_{Total} > (SS_A + SS_B + SS_{A \times B} + SS_{error})$.

The correlation between the factors that is produced by an unbalanced design does not produce a major mathematical problem (although it used to before computers were around to help out) because it is fairly easy to compute each variable's unique effect, defined as its effect after controlling for the effects of the other variables it is correlated with. Once each variable's unique sum of squares is derived as above, then the procedures for generating the mean squares, F ratios, and p-values described in section 16.2.2 can be used. But much like in multiple regression, if the factors are highly correlated, then even though one or both may have strong effects taken separately, they may have very small unique effects after the effects of the other factor and the interaction are considered and partialed out. So a small effect for one factor in an unbalanced design doesn't necessarily mean that the factor has a small effect when considered in isolation. It may simply have a small *unique* effect. In hypothesis testing contexts, what this means is that a main effect may be nonsignificant even if the variable has a large effect on the outcome measure because part of its effect is thrown out. Shared variation in explaining variation in Y is given to no factor or the interaction and instead is captured mathematically as $SS_{redundant}$.

Weighted versus Unweighted Marginal Means. To understand another important difference between balanced and unbalanced designs, you need to be understand the distinction between *unweighted* and *weighted* marginal means. Consider the mean risk judgment for males. There are 10 males in the data in Table 16.2. If you add up the 10 risk judgments provided by the males in the study, you will get 360. Divide 360 by 10 and you will get 36. This is the *weighted* mean risk judgment for males. It is a weighted because it is equivalent to the mean of the 2 male means in the table (males present and males absent) with each mean weighted by its sample size. That is, $36 = [6(30) + 4(45)]/10$. Similarly, the *weighted* mean risk judgment for females is the sum of the 12 female risk judgments divided by 12, which is $700/12 = 58.33$, which is the same as $[4(65) + 8(55)]/12$. In contrast, the *unweighted* marginal means (sometimes called *estimated means*, *e-means*, or *least squares means*), are derived by simple averaging of the means in that row or column in the table. So the unweighted mean male risk judgment is $(30 + 45)/2 = 37.50$, and the unweighted mean female risk judgment is $(65 + 55)/2 = 60$. So the difference between the marginal means depends on whether you define those means as weighted or unweighted. The difference between the weighted marginal means is 22.33, whereas the difference between the unweighted marginal means is 22.50.

This distinction between weighted and unweighted means was not made in section 16.2.2 because in a balanced design the weighted and unweighted means are the same. But when the design is unbalanced, the weighted and unweighted means are typically different and can be substantially different. In factorial ANOVA, the main effects are defined as the difference between the unweighted marginal means *not* the weighted means. So when interpreting the results of an unbalanced factorial ANOVA, you should base your interpretation on the unweighted marginal means, not the weighted means. A failure to recognize this can produce some seemingly bizarre situations that will be difficult to make sense of otherwise. For example, it is possible to get a statistically significant main effect for a variable even if the weighted marginal means are exactly the same. This can happen when there are large differences in the samples sizes across cells in the table.

As an informal proof that the main effects are tests of the difference between the unweighted marginal means and not the weighted marginal means, compare the p-values for the main effects in the ANOVA table (Figure 16.4, panel A) and the p-values for the regression weights in the regression output (Figure 16.4, panel B). Observe that they are the same, and that the F statistics in the ANOVA table are indeed the square of the t statistics from the regression output, as described earlier. Thus, these two tables show the results of mathematically identical hypothesis tests. But notice that the regression weight for sex is the difference between the unweighted marginal means, not the weighted marginal means. Similarly, the coefficient for population trend information is the difference between the unweighted marginal means, not the weighted marginal means.

The important message here is that when interpreting the results of ANOVA, it is easy (and common) to misinterpret these main effects as if they are comparisons of the means for different levels of one variable computed as if the second variable did not exist. If you compute the marginal means pretending as if the second variable did not exist in your design, you are computing the weighted means. The significance test for the main effect is not testing the difference between those weighted means. Instead, it is a test of the difference between the unweighted means. So remember, interpretations of the main effects in an unbalanced should be based on the unweighted means, not the weighted means.

16.2.5 Probing an Interaction in a Factorial ANOVA

So it seems that information about changes in the size of the population over time has a different effect on men's perceptions of vulnerability to burglary compared to women's following the reading a story about increasing crime in the community. But does that support Berger's hypothesis? Read it carefully before deciding:

> H4: Men exposed to a story showing increasing population frequencies before receiving a story depicting increasing threat during the same time period will show lower levels of victimization risk than will men receiving only a message depicting increasing threat. By contrast, among women, expo-

sure to population increase data will not lower victimization risk levels. (Berger, 2000, p. 31–32)

Rejecting the null hypothesis of no interaction does not mean that the pattern of differences is as predicted. To assess whether the patterns of means is as predicted, it is necessary to probe this interaction. Just how this is best accomplished is a bit controversial, and there are several ways of going about it. For the sake of illustration let's focus on the balanced design in Table 16.1. The simplest approach is to analyze the simple effects separately to see if the pattern of means is consistent with the predictions. For example, a simple t test comparing perceived risk judgments in men as a function of whether or not population trend information was provided reveals that risk judgments were in fact lower on average when population trend information was provided, Welch $t(5) = 3.000, p < .05$. In women, however, population trend information seemed to have no effect on average perceived risk, Welch $t(5) = -1.732, p = .146$. Thus, just as Berger predicted, providing population trend information lowered men's perceived vulnerability to crime but not women's. This strategy of simple t tests on the simple effects uses only information provided by participants in the study that contribute to the simple effect.

There is a more powerful but somewhat more complicated strategy that you could employ. This alternative approach is to construct a focused contrast corresponding to these t tests. Using the same method as described in Chapter 14, the following contrast would quantify the difference between population trend information and no population trend information among men (from equation 14.17):

$$\delta = 1(\overline{Y}_{MA}) - 1(\overline{Y}_{MP}) + 0(\overline{Y}_{FA}) + 0(\overline{Y}_{FP}) = 15$$

with standard error estimated as (from equation 14.18):

$$s_\delta = \sqrt{58.333\left(\frac{(1)^2}{4} + \frac{(-1)^2}{4} + \frac{(0)^2}{4} + \frac{(0)^2}{4}\right)} = 5.400$$

if you assume equality of variance in risk judgments over the four cells. With this assumption, $t(12) = 15/5.400 = 2.778, p < .05$. Using the same logic for the contrast for women produces $t(12) = -10/5.400 = -1.852, p = .09$. This contrast method will tend to be somewhat higher in power than the individual t test method when the assumption of equality of variance is met. If you don't want to make this assumption, then a t test on the simple effects of interest using the Welch-Satterthwaite approach should be used.

One can sensibly ask why the test for interaction is even necessary. Berger predicted that the population trend information should reduce perceived vulnerability among men but not among women. Why not just compare the two simple effects with a series of t tests? What information is gained by testing the interaction first? A case can be made that the interaction need not be tested at all if a set of comparisons such as these do in fact turn out as expected. But you need to recognize that what is left out from this strategy is an explicit test of whether the difference between these differences is statistically different. The interaction tests the significance of the difference between the differences. Whether or not that interaction must be statistically significant in order to make the desired claim is controversial and a matter of personal opinion. In my experience, potential critics of your research will want to see a test of the interaction, even if you personally don't feel that this test is informative or necessary.

The argument is that you need to provide some formal evidence that the differences are actually different before you can claim that the simple effects actually differ. It helps a lot to think about how the hypothesis is explicitly stated. As Berger's hypothesis 4 is stated, the hypothesis does not *explicitly* predict interaction but predicts instead that the simple effect of population trend information should be zero in women but not zero in men. Interaction is *implicitly* stated in the way the hypothesis is framed. This hypothesis can be legitimately tested with two simple effects tests without testing the interaction. But most readers would expect a test that the difference in the simple effects is statistically different, and Berger indeed reported a test of that interaction, finding it to be statistically significant.

It would be unfortunate if the the pattern of simple effects is consistent with predictions when there is no evidence of interaction. This would be unfortunate because it presents a logical paradox. How can a manipulation affect one group but not the other while, at the same time, there be no evidence that the effect differs between the groups? Unfortunately, such paradoxes arise in statistics all the time. For example, it is possible for a multiple correlation to not be statistically different from zero even if some of the partial regression weights are different from zero or for the omnibus null hypothesis to be rejected in ANOVA but to find that no means differ from each other to a statistically significant degree when all possible pairwise comparisons are conducted. The test you should focus on when interpreting an analysis is the test that is most directly relevant to the question you are trying to answer. If a hypothesis explicitly predicts an interaction, it should be tested and found to be statistically significant before you cam claim the prediction is supported in the data. But if the hypothesis doesn't explicitly state an interaction and instead proposes a pattern of simple effects, then whether or not the interaction needs to be statistically significant is controversial and a matter of personal opinion.

I have focused exclusively on the relatively simple 2×2 between-groups design. More complicated designs are possible. For example, one or more of the factors might have more than 2 levels. Although the conceptualization of interaction as inconsistent simple effects doesn't change, probing a significant interaction can become quite a bit more complicated. Consider for example two factors, each with 3 levels. A significant interaction can still be interpreted as simple effects that are statistically different. But each simple effect is based on 3 levels of the second factor, and there are three of these simple effects. It becomes necessary not only to probe which simple effects differ from which but also which means within a simple effect are statistically different from each other. The number of possible tests required to probe the interaction can become quite large very quickly.

Another complication involves the addition of a third or even fourth factor. When there are more than 2 factors, then it becomes possible to assess 3-way, 4-way, or even 5-way interaction. If there is a 3-way interaction between X, Z, and W, this means that the interaction between, for example, X and Z differs across levels of W. In other words, a 3-way interaction implies that two or more differences between differences are themselves different. Interpreting three-way interactions can become quite complicated, and interactions higher than the third order become nearly impossible to interpret. Nevertheless, some theories and hypotheses tested by communication researchers involve questions about three way interactions, necessitating such analyses in order to test the theory or hypothesis. I do not discuss the analysis of such designs in this book, and I refer to you more advanced books on analysis of variance such as Keppel (1991).

16.2.6   Quantifying Effect Size

In Chapters 14 and 15, several effect sizes in single factor ANOVA were introduced. When there is more than one factor, how to measure effect size becomes a bit ambiguous because there are several ways of talking about effect size, just as was the case in ANCOVA. One may ask what proportion of the *total* variance in the dependent variable Y is uniquely attributable to a specific independent variable of interest. Another conceptualization of effect size quantifies the size of the effect as the proportion of variance in the outcome remaining after partialing out the other effects on Y that is uniquely attributable to the effect of interest. You may recognize these as the distinction between the squared semipartial correlation and the squared partial correlation in Chapter 13, or η^2 and partial η^2 from Chapter 15. Focusing on η^2 and partial η^2:

$$\eta^2 = \frac{SS_{effect}}{SS_{total}}$$

(16.5)

$$\text{partial } \eta^2 = \frac{SS_{effect}}{SS_{effect} + SS_{error}}$$

(16.6)

where SS_{effect} is the sum of squares for the variable for which the effect size measure is desired. Plugging the numbers in from the the unbalanced design (Figure 16.4, panel A),

$$\text{SEX}: \quad \eta^2 = \frac{2557.895}{4927.273} = 0.519; \quad \text{partial } \eta^2 = \frac{2557.895}{2557.895 + 1400.000} = 0.646$$

$$\text{INFO}: \quad \eta^2 = \frac{31.579}{4927.273} = 0.006; \quad \text{partial } \eta^2 = \frac{31.579}{31.579 + 1400.000} = 0.022$$

$$\text{SEX} \times \text{INFO}: \quad \eta^2 = \frac{789.474}{4927.273} = 0.160; \quad \text{partial } \eta^2 = \frac{789.474}{789.474 + 1400.000} = 0.361$$

Choosing between these is sometimes difficult, and which is the correct measure of a factor's effect on Y is controversial. Contrary to popular belief, both η^2 and partial η^2 can be affected by the size of the effect of the other factors on Y, as well as how large the interaction is. Partial η^2 will tend to be more affected by the size of the other effects and will generally be larger than η^2. So if you want a measure of effect size for a factor in a factorial ANOVA that is less affected by the size of the other effects in the analysis, use η^2 rather than partial η^2. But both measures of effect size are affected by the intercorrelation between effects that occurs when a design is unbalanced.

In my judgment, partial η^2 is not a good measure of effect size and should not be used. The primary problem with partial η^2 is that an investigator can make it nearly as large as desired by increasing the complexity of the research design. By increasing the number of factors in an analysis of variance that have *some* effect on Y, partial η^2 for every variable will tend to increase because it gauges the unique effect of a variable relative to variance in Y left unexplained by the other factors. By contrast, η^2 indexes a variable's unique effect relative to *total* variance in Y. As a result, η^2 is not nearly so influenced by the number of factors in the design. To be sure, η^2 can be affected by the inclusion of additional variables if they are intercorrelated with the effect of interest, but this will *lower* η^2, not increase it. In addition, η^2 is conceptually equivalent to the change in R^2 in hierarchical regression—a measure of a variable's effect that is widely used in communication. That is, η^2 can be thought of as the incremental proportion of variance in Y that is explained by including that factor in the analysis relative to when it is excluded. Partial η^2 does not have this nice interpretation.

Because both of these measures of effect size depend in part on the other variables in the analysis, how intercorrelated the variables are, and the effect of those other variables on Y, it is hard to compare effect sizes across studies that differ in design. For example, suppose investigators A and B are both interested in the effect of online versus traditional print news on public affairs knowledge and conduct similar studies at the same time. They use the same measure of public affairs knowledge (a 20–item multiple choice test of knowledge of recent world events, Y) and a measure of form of news exposure (online versus print, X), and each study is based on 100 participants. Investigator A's study is the simplest, including only the single independent variable X manipulated in an experimental design, where participants are randomly assigned to be exposed to either a print or online version of a newspaper for 30 minutes, after which they are given a test of information contained in the news. Investigator B manipulates X in exactly the same way as A but has a second independent variable W crossed with X in a factorial design. Suppose W is a number of exposures manipulation, operationalized as the number of sessions of exposure the participant receives (30 minutes over one day or 30 minutes over 3 days, 10 minutes each). In short, both studies are identical with the exception of an additional manipulation in Investigator B's study and, of course, different participants. Each investigator reports a common measure of the effect of X on Y.

Regardless of whether A and B consistently report η^2 or partial η^2, their effect sizes are not necessarily comparable. Suppose for example that both report $\eta^2 = 0.20$. Without more information, we cannot necessarily say that X has the same effect on Y in these studies even though X appears to be explaining the same proportion of variance in Y. Because investigator B manipulated a second variable W, that manipulation as well as the interaction between X and W may increase variability in Y, with the amount of that increase being a function of how large those effects are. For example, distributing the same learning time over more sessions could increase the number of relatively high learning scores in B's study compared to what A observed because some (but not necessarily all) of the participants might be less fatigued over three short learning periods. So the total variance of Y (quantified as SS_{total}) may be quite a bit higher in B's study even though they have the same sample sizes. So an η^2 of 0.20 corresponds to more variability in learning explained by X in investigator B's study, even though X explains the same amount of relative variability (i.e., $SS_{effect(X)}/SS_{total}$). Without knowing more about between study differences in the variance of Y, the effect sizes cannot be meaningfully compared. Changing to partial η^2 does not solve the problem. Indeed, partial η^2 is even less comparable across these studies because partial η^2 quantifies the proportion of the variance in Y remaining after partialing out the other variables that X uniquely explains. Because investigator A included no other variables in the analysis, $\eta^2 =$ partial η^2. Just by including an additional independent variable in the design that has some effect on Y, the effect of X on Y increases in B's study using this measure of effect size. Partial η^2 is determined in part by the number of additional variables in the analysis and so isn't comparable across studies that differ in the number or nature of the additional variables. Had A included additional variables (manipulated or just measured) related to Y, partial η^2 likely would have been larger.

But even if W and $X \times W$ had absolutely no effect on Y in B's study (meaning they did not affect either the means or the total variability in Y relative to variability observed in A's study), the meaning of η^2 might be different in the two studies. Imagine that in B's study, the sample size in the print-multiple exposure condition was smaller than in the other three cells, perhaps because participants in this condition found the study less interesting and were less likely to return for the second or third exposure period. In that case, the independent variables (and their interaction) are intercorrelated. Most discussions of effect size in the communication and other literatures have assumed that the total sum of squares in an experiment can be partitioned perfectly into nonoverlapping components, as reflected in Levine and Hullet's (2002) examples and claim that "η^2 has the property that the effects for all components of variation (including error) will sum to 1.00" (p. 619). But life in science is not always so clean and perfect. Even in true experiments where the investigator has some control over the intercorrelation between variables through random assignment and control of cell sizes, things happen that induce correlation between the independent variables, such as procedural errors, discarding of participants due to suspicion about a deception, equipment malfunctions, and so forth. Unless there is some attempt to reequalize cell sizes (which introduces new design and analysis problems and can't generally be recommended), it becomes impossible to perfectly partition total variance into the effects of interest plus error. In this case, η^2 will be reduced in study B in proportion to how predictable X is from W and $X \times W$. Keep in mind that η^2 quantifies the proportion of *total* variance in Y uniquely attributable to X. When independent variables are correlated, some of the variance in Y that X might explain had X been the only factor in the analysis is not attributed to X statistically (or any other variable for that matter) because variability in Y attributable to more than one independent variable is eliminated from η^2 (and partial η^2 as well). Because A's study has only a single independent variable, this does not affect the interpretation of η^2 in that study. The fact that η^2 is the same in B's study in spite of the intercorrelation between W and X suggests that X may have a larger effect on Y in B's study, but it is impossible to know just how much larger. Using partial η^2 does not eliminate this ambiguity in the comparison of effect sizes, as it too is affected by the intercorrelation between independent variables.

16.3 Moderated Multiple Regression

In Berger's study, both of the independent variables were categorical. But sometimes a research design includes two groups (e.g., men and women, or participants in experimental or control group) both measured on a second *quantitative* variable, such as a personality variable or some other quantitative dimension. The researcher may be interested in whether the quantitative variable is related to the outcome variable differently in the two groups or whether the average difference between the groups on the outcome variable depends on the values of the quantitative variable. Or the researcher might have two quantitative variables and is interested in knowing if the relationship between one of those variables and the outcome varies systematically as a function of the values of the second variable.

Communication researchers sometimes approach the analysis of data from a design of this sort by categorizing one or both of the quantitative independent variables in some fashion and then subjecting the dependent variable to a factorial analysis of variance. For example, the researcher might place each case into a "high" or a "low" group based on whether the case's score is above or below the sample mean or median on one or both of the quantitative independent variables. But it is not necessary to categorize in this fashion, and doing so is an inefficient way to use the data available that I strongly discourage for reasons discussed in Section 16.5 (also see Bissonnette, Ickes, Berstein, & Knowles, 1990; Irwin & McClelland, 2001; Irwin & McClelland, 2003; MacCallum, Zhang, Preacher, & Rucker, 2002; Streiner, 2002; Veiel, 1988). A much more efficient approach is *moderated multiple regression*. In a moderated multiple regression, the goal is to assess whether the regression coefficient for a predictor variable in a model varies as a function of the values of a second predictor variable. It is worthwhile to compartmentalize this discussion as a function of the levels of measurement of the variables presumed to be interacting (i.e., all quantitative or one categorical and the other quantitative), although as you will see many of the same interpretational principles apply regardless.

16.3.1   Interaction Between a Dichotomous and a Quantitative Variable

Consider a simple hypothetical study similar conceptually to Monahan and Lannuitti (2000). The data from this hypothetical study will be used throughout this section, and the details about the data file used to generate the analyses here can be found in Appendix E9 on the CD. The question motivating this study is whether alcohol use moderates the relationship between a man's self-esteem and his willingness to engage in self-disclosure. An individual difference such as self-esteem may be less related to self-disclosure after drinking because alcohol serves as a "social lubricant," easing social anxiety during conversations and thereby reducing the effect of an individual difference such as self-esteem on social interaction. To conduct this study, the researcher recruited 40 men individually to a laboratory. Upon arrival at the laboratory, each man was given a self-report measure of self-esteem, with possible scores ranging between 1 and 5 (variable SE). Each participant was then placed by himself in a room for 60 minutes containing a keg of beer, a two-liter bottle of soda, a couch, a newspaper and several magazines, and a television. The participants randomly assigned to the *alcohol condition* ($C = 1$ in the data) were told that the investigator was interested in how people respond to new social encounters and how alcohol may affect those responses. During the 60 minute period, the participants were told they could watch television, relax or read, and that they were free to drink as much beer as desired from the keg. Participants randomly assigned to the *control condition* ($C = 0$ in the data) were treated identically, except they were told that the keg of beer was for a staff party later that day and not to drink anything from the keg. After the 60 minute period, the participants were escorted to another room that contained a female confederate of the experimenter. The experimenter gave them a task that they were to accomplish together (putting together a 50-piece jigsaw puzzle), and the female was instructed to flirt with the male during this task. These interactions were videotaped. Two coders then coded how much the man self-disclosed to the female, with self-disclosure scores (Y) ranging from 0 to 9.

The data for this example were constructed using a formula that produced a different relationship between self-esteem and self-disclosure in the two conditions. If high and low self-esteem groups are created using a median split and the data then subjected to a 2×2 ANOVA using the procedures described in section 16.2, only a main effect of alcohol use and a main effect of self-esteem is found. The interaction is not significant, $F(1, 36) = 2.046, p = .16$. This analysis would lead to the conclusion that the effect of self-esteem on self-disclosure does not vary depending on a person's alcohol use. Alternatively, this same lack of interaction means that alcohol use has the same effect on self-disclosure regardless of a person's self-esteem. But I strongly discourage this approach to analyzing the data from this study, for reasons discussed in section 16.5.

An analysis of the same data using moderated multiple regression, the procedure described in this section, yields a different but correct the conclusion. Figure 16.5 provides a scatterplot and the least squares regression lines for the control ($C = 0$) and alcohol groups ($C = 1$). As can be seen, there is a relationship between self-esteem and self-disclosure among students that did not drink alcohol. The regression weight for self-esteem in the control group, which I will symbolize as $b_{SE|C=0}$, is $0.663, t(19) = 2.919, p = .009$. But for students who were allowed to drink, the relationship appears different. Indeed, a formal hypothesis test reveals no statistically significant relationship between self-esteem and self-disclosure in the alcohol group. The regression weight for self-esteem in this group, $b_{SE|C=1}$, is $-0.087, t(19) = -0.350, p = .731$. Descriptively at least, the relationship between self-esteem and self-disclosure depends on whether a person has been drinking. But a formal test of interaction would allow us to rule out the possibility that the obtained difference in the regression coefficients is just "chance." In moderated multiple regression, this is easily accomplished by estimating the coefficients for the regression model below:

$$\hat{Y} = a + b_C(C) + b_{SE}(SE) + b_{C \times SE}(C \times SE)$$

where $\hat{Y}$ is a case's estimated self-disclosure and $C \times SE$ is a new variable defined as the product of a participant's self-esteem (SE) and the condition he was assigned to in the study (C). The latter term in the above equation, $b_{C \times SE}$, is sometimes called the *interaction term*. The variables that constitute the interaction, in this case C and SE, are sometimes called the *lower-order* variables in the model and the coefficients the *lower-order* effects.

The results of this regression analysis are displayed in Figure 16.6. The model is:

$$\hat{Y} = 3.094 + 2.922(C) + 0.663(SE) - 0.750(C \times SE)$$

For the question as to whether alcohol moderates the effect of social self-esteem on self-disclosure, the relevant section of the output is the size of and significance test for $b_{C \times SE}$, which here is -0.750 with a p-value of .034. This regression coefficient is statistically different from zero, so we conclude that alcohol use and social self-esteem interact in explaining variation in self-disclosure. Or we can say that self-esteem moderates the effect of alcohol on self-disclosure, or that alcohol moderates the effect of self-esteem on self-disclosure.

To illustrate just why $b_{C \times SE}$ quantifies the interaction, it is helpful to break down this model and assess the meaning of each regression coefficient. Let's start with b_{SE}. Remember that in a multiple regression *without* an interaction term, the partial regression weight for predictor variable i quantifies the estimated difference in Y between two people who differ by one measurement unit on variable i but who are equal on all the other predictor variables in the model. But when an interaction term is in a regression model, this changes the interpretation of the coefficients for the lower order variables. Consider the case where $C = 1$ and $SE = 3$, and thus $C \times SE = 3$. The regression equation yields

$$\hat{Y} = 3.094 + 2.922(1) + 0.663(3) - 0.750(3) = 5.755$$

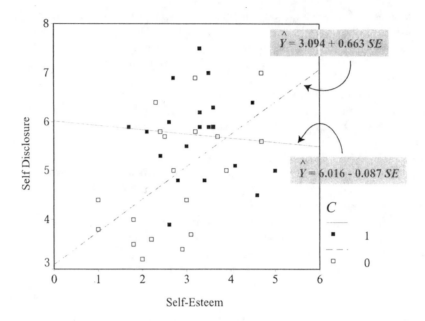

Figure 16.5 Scatterplot of the relationship between self-esteem and self-disclosure.

Keeping C constant but increasing SE to 4, the model gives

$$\hat{Y} = 3.094 + 2.922(1) + 0.663(4) - 0.750(4) = 5.668$$

Clearly, keeping C constant but increasing SE by one unit has not resulted in an increase of 0.663 in estimated self-disclosure. Instead, the estimated difference is $5.668 - 5.755 = -0.087$. Now repeat these computations, except this time using $C = 0$. In this case, when $SE = 3$, the model yields

$$\hat{Y} = 3.094 + 2.922(0) + 0.663(3) - 0.750(0) = 5.083$$

and when $SE = 4$, the model gives

$$\hat{Y} = 3.094 + 2.922(0) + 0.663(4) - 0.750(0) = 5.746$$

This time, the difference is $5.746 - 5.083 = 0.663$, which is b_{SE}. Regardless of which values of SE we choose, it would be the case that the predicted difference in self-disclosure associated with a one unit difference in SE is 0.663 when $C = 0$. So b_{SE} is the regression weight for self-esteem estimating self-disclosure when $C = 0$. In other words, it is the regression weight for SE for the control group in this study and exactly what we found when we analyzed the control group separately.

Recall that when $C = 1$, a one unit difference in SE was associated with a difference of -0.087 in estimated self-disclosure. It is no coincidence that this is exactly equal to the regression weight for the alcohol group, $b_{SE|C=1}$, from the earlier analysis. Notice as well that this difference of -0.087 is equal to $b_{SE} + b_{C \times SE}$. So the regression weight for SE when $C = 1$ is equal to $b_{SE} + b_{C \times SE}$. If $b_{SE} = b_{SE|C=0}$ and $b_{SE} + b_{C \times SE} = b_{SE|C=1}$, then simple algebra tells us that

$$b_{C \times SE} = b_{SE|C=1} - b_{SE|C=0}$$

Model Summary

Model	R	R Square	Adjusted R Square	Std. Error of the Estimate
1	.558[a]	.311	.254	.9692

a. Predictors: (Constant), C_X_SE, Self-Esteem (SE), Alcohol (C)

ANOVA[b]

Model		Sum of Squares	df	Mean Square	F	Sig.
1	Regression	15.272	3	5.091	5.419	.004[a]
	Residual	33.819	36	.939		
	Total	49.091	39			

a. Predictors: (Constant), C_X_SE, Self-Esteem (SE), Alcohol (C)

b. Dependent Variable: Self-Disclosure

Coefficients[a]

Model		Unstandardized Coefficients		Standardized Coefficients	t	Sig.
		B	Std. Error	Beta		
1	(Constant)	3.094	.637		4.859	.000
	Alcohol (C)	2.922	1.098	1.319	2.660	.012
	Self-Esteem (SE)	.663	.215	.569	3.083	.004
	C_X_SE	-.750	.341	-1.177	-2.199	.034

a. Dependent Variable: Self-Disclosure

Figure 16.6 SPSS output from a moderated multiple regression estimating self-disclosure from alcohol condition, self-esteem, and their interaction.

In other words, $b_{C \times SE}$ is the difference between the regression weight for self-esteem in the control group and the regression weight for self-esteem in the alcohol group. Rephrased, it can be interpreted as how the regression coefficient for self esteem changes with a one unit change in C. Indeed, observe that as C increases by one unit, the coefficient for SE changes by -0.750 (from 0.663 to -0.087). The significance test for $b_{C \times SE}$ tests the null hypothesis that this difference is attributable to "chance." Rejection of this null hypothesis means that the relationship between self-esteem and self-disclosure is statistically different in the two groups.

But what about b_C? Earlier I stated that b_{SE} is the regression weight for self-esteem estimating self-disclosure when $C = 0$. Using a similar logic, b_C is the regression weight estimating self-disclosure from alcohol use when $SE = 0$. So a one unit difference in C is associated with a 2.922 difference in estimated self-disclosure when $SE = 0$. The positive sign tells us that estimated self-disclosure is higher for people assigned to the alcohol group ($C = 1$) than the control group ($C = 0$). A visual examination of Figure 16.5 shows that when $SE = 0$, the two regression lines are indeed separated by just about 3 units. Finally, a, the regression constant, represents the estimated self-disclosure when both SE and C are equal to zero.

This example illustrates some general principles. In any regression model of the form

$$\hat{Y} = a + b_X(X) + b_W(W) + b_{XW}(XW)$$

where XW is the product of X and W, b_X represents the estimated effect of a one unit difference in X on Y when variable $W = 0$, b_W represents the estimated effect of a one unit difference in W on Y when $X = 0$, and b_{XW} represents how much b_X changes with a one unit increase in W or, conversely, how much b_W changes with a one unit increase in X. So in a regression model that includes X, W, and $X \times W$, the regression coefficients for X and W are *conditional regression weights, conditional effects,* or *local terms* (Darlington, 1990) and cannot be interpreted like main effects are interpreted in an analysis of variance, nor can they be interpreted as a partial regression weight would in a model without an interaction term. Instead, these regression coefficients quantify the effect of one predictor variable on the outcome variable conditioned on the other predictor variable being zero. This is important to keep in mind because it is possible that one or more of the lower order regression coefficients will have no sensible substantive interpretation whatsoever in a study if 0 is not a possible measurement on one of the predictor variables. In this example, self-esteem was measured on a scale from 1 to 5. Zero was not a possible score, so b_C and its test of significance has no meaningful interpretation here. And because SE cannot equal zero, the regression constant and its test of significance also has no substantive interpretation.

It is important to point out that the interpretational principles described here apply only to *unstandardized* regression coefficients. It is common for researchers to report standardized regression coefficients when reporting a moderated multiple regression model, but standardized regression coefficients in moderated multiple regression do not have the properties described here. Standardized regression coefficients are hard to interpret in this context, and I like to be able to apply the principles discussed above when I interpret other researchers' models, something that can't be done when standardized coefficients are reported. To ease interpretation by others, I suggest that if you feel you must report standardized regression coefficients (something I generally don't encourage), provide the unstandardized coefficients as well.

Probing a Significant Interaction. When testing for interaction with a factorial ANOVA, a significant interaction is typically followed by a simple effects analysis, where the investigator examines the effect of one independent variable at each level of the other independent variable. For example, had these data been analyzed after dichotomizing self-esteem at the median and a significant interaction found, the standard practice would be to do a simple effects analysis by either (a) examining the effect of the alcohol manipulation among people who are either "high" or "low" in self-esteem or (b) examining differences in self-disclosure as a function of self-esteem in each condition. But how would such an analysis be accomplished in moderated multiple regression given that self-esteem is not a categorical variable?

Before probing the interaction statistically, it is worth graphically representing the regression model by generating estimated values from the model using various values of the predictors. Moderated multiple regression is very holistic in its approach to assessing interactions, and much of the beauty of the method can be hidden by the mathematics. A picture can say a lot about what is happening in the data, so I strongly encourage you to first generate a set of $\hat{Y}$ values from the model and then plot them in the form of a scatterplot. In this example, this would be accomplished by first setting C to 0 and then plugging in several different values of SE into the regression formula. Repeat this process for the same values of SE but setting $C = 1$. Then generate a scatterplot, placing $\hat{Y}$ on the Y axis, SE on the X axis, and using different symbols in the plot for different values of C (see Figure 16.7).

There are two approaches to statistically probing this interaction. First, you could look at the regression weights separately in the two groups defined by the dichotomous variable. Recall that b_{SE} was interpreted as the conditional effect of self-esteem for those in the control group. So the regression output already provides information about the relationship between self-esteem and self-disclosure in the control group. We know from the output in Figure 16.6 that in the control condition, there is a positive

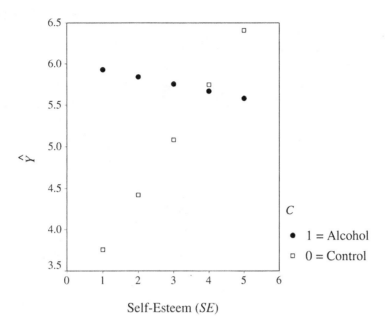

Figure 16.7 A visual representation of the interaction between self-esteem and alcohol consumption on self-disclosure.

and statistically significant relationship between self-esteem and self-disclosure, $b = 0.663, t(36) = 3.083, p = 0.004$. By rerunning the analysis, reversing the coding of C in the original data (so that $C = 0$ for the alcohol group and $C = 1$ for the control group) before computing $C \times SE$, we could get the conditional effect of self-esteem for those in the alcohol group. If you did this, you'd find $b = -0.087, t(36) = -0.350, p = .731$. So self-esteem is related to self-disclosure in the control condition but not in the alcohol condition.

But how do you assess the other kind of conditional effect—the effect of alcohol on self-disclosure at different self-esteem values? This can be accomplished using the interpretational principles outlined above. First, pick two or more "representative values" of SE at which to examine the alcohol effect and then transform the original data so that the regression output provides a test of the conditional effect of alcohol use at those values of SE. There are no hard and fast rules for selecting representative values. Aiken and West (1991) suggest using one standard deviation above the mean, the mean, and one standard deviation below the mean on one of the predictors. Or you could choose values that make some conceptual sense, or that have some kind of practical meaning. In these data, $\overline{SE} = 3.033, SD = 0.963$. One standard deviation below the mean is $3.033 - 0.963 = 2.070$ and one standard deviation above the mean is $3.033 + 0.963 = 3.996$. To test the effect of alcohol when $SE = 2.070$ (one standard deviation below the mean), create a new variable, SE', defined as $SE' = SE - 2.070$ as well as a new interaction term, $C \times SE'$, and then reestimate the regression model. The resulting regression model (see Table 16.4) is

$$\hat{Y} = 4.666 + 1.369(C) + 0.663(SE') - 0.750(C \times SE')$$

Table 16.4

Probing an Interaction in Moderated Multiple Regression

		Coeff.	s.e.	t	p
$SE' = SE - 2.070$					
	Constant	4.466	0.266	16.809	$< .001$
	Alcohol (C)	1.369	0.469	2.919	0.006
	SE'	0.663	0.215	3.083	0.004
	$C \times SE'$	-0.750	0.341	-2.199	0.034
$SE' = SE - 3.033$					
	Constant	5.104	0.223	22.870	$< .001$
	Alcohol (C)	0.647	0.318	2.036	0.049
	SE'	0.663	0.215	3.083	0.004
	$C \times SE'$	-0.750	0.341	-2.199	0.034
$SE' = SE - 3.996$					
	Constant	5.743	0.339	16.953	$< .001$
	Alcohol (C)	-0.075	0.445	-0.169	0.867
	SE'	0.663	0.215	3.083	0.004
	$C \times SE'$	-0.750	0.341	-2.199	0.034

Notice that $b_{SE'}$ and $b_{C \times SE'}$ are the same as b_{SE} and $b_{C \times SE}$, but b_C and a are different. Prior to this transformation of SE, b_C quantified the estimated difference between the control and alcohol groups when $SE = 0$. That interpretation still applies, but with this transformation, $SE' = 0$ when $SE = 2.070$, or one standard deviation below the sample mean SE in the data. So b_C can be interpreted as the effect of alcohol use for people one standard deviation below the sample mean SE. In this model, b_C is 1.369, $t(36) = 2.919, p = .006$. So when $SE = 2.070$, a one unit difference in C is associated with a statistically significant difference of 1.369 in self-disclosure, with the alcohol group having the higher expected self-disclosure score at this value of self-esteem (because the coefficient is positive).

Repeating the procedure setting $SE' = SE - 3.033$, yields (see Table 16.4)

$$\hat{Y} = 5.104 + 0.647(C) + 0.663(SE') - 0.750(C \times SE')$$

In this model, b_C quantifies the effect of alcohol when $SE' = 0$, but $SE' = 0$ when $SE = 3.033$, so the effect of alcohol at the mean SE is $b_C = 0.647, t(36) = 2.036, p = .049$. So alcohol results in greater self-disclosure at the sample mean SE. Finally, defining SE' as $SE - 3.996$, the regression model is (from Table 16.4 panel C):

$$\hat{Y} = 5.743 - 0.075(C) + 0.663(SE') - 0.750(C \times SE')$$

At one standard deviation above the sample mean SE, the effect of alcohol use is not statistically different from zero, $b_C = -0.075, t(36) = -0.169, p = .867$ (Table 16.4).

16.3.2   Interaction Between Two Quantitative Variables

In the previous section, I described the application of moderated multiple regression to testing and probing an interaction between a dichotomous and a quantitative predictor variable. In this section, the logic of moderated multiple regression is applied to the testing of interaction between two quantitative variables. As you will see, the general rules described previously apply to this situation.

Consider a slight modification to this study. In this variation, there was no experimental manipulation. Instead, all participants were simply placed in the room and told that they could drink as much beer as desired during the 60–minute period. Otherwise, the procedure was identical except that at the end of the 60–minute period, each participant's blood alcohol content was measured (variable BAC in the data set; see Appendix E9 on the CD) with a breathalyzer. Interest in this variation of the study still focuses on whether alcohol consumption moderates the relationship between self-esteem and self-disclosure, but alcohol consumption is not experimentally manipulated here. Instead, it is operationalized as the percent of a participant's blood content that is alcohol at the end of the 60-minute period.

To test this question, the following model is estimated:

$$Y = a + b_{BAC}(BAC) + b_{SE}(SE) + b_{SE \times BAC}(SE \times BAC)$$

where $SE \times BAC$ is the product of blood alcohol content and self-esteem. The results of this regression are presented in Figure 16.8. The regression model is:

$$\hat{Y} = 1.018 + 0.769(BAC) + 1.404(SE) - 0.239(SE \times BAC)$$

As can be seen from the computer output, the interaction term is significantly different from zero, meaning that self-esteem and alcohol consumption interact in explaining self-disclosure. The coefficient for the interaction ($b_{SE \times BAC}$) tells us that the regression weight estimating self-disclosure from self-esteem decreases by 0.239 as blood alcohol

Model Summary

Model	R	R Square	Adjusted R Square	Std. Error of the Estimate
1	.487[a]	.237	.174	1.0199

a. Predictors: (Constant), SE X BAC, Self-Esteem (SE), Blood Alcohol Content (BAC)

ANOVA[b]

Model		Sum of Squares	df	Mean Square	F	Sig.
1	Regression	11.645	3	3.882	3.732	.020[a]
	Residual	37.446	36	1.040		
	Total	49.091	39			

a. Predictors: (Constant), SE X BAC, Self-Esteem (SE), Blood Alcohol Content (BAC)

b. Dependent Variable: Self-Disclosure

Coefficients[a]

Model		Unstandardized Coefficients		Standardized Coefficients	t	Sig.
		B	Std. Error	Beta		
1	(Constant)	1.018	1.547		.659	.514
	Self-Esteem (SE)	1.404	.503	1.205	2.789	.008
	Blood Alcohol Content (BAC)	.769	.385	1.082	2.001	.053
	SE X BAC	-.239	.117	-1.571	-2.048	.048

a. Dependent Variable: Self-Disclosure

Figure 16.8 SPSS output from a moderated multiple regression estimating self-disclosure from blood alcohol content, self-esteem, and their interaction.

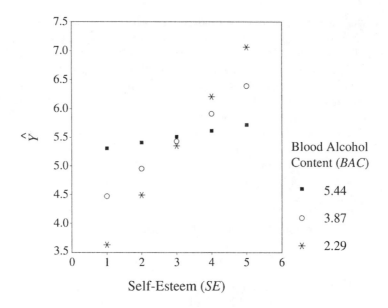

Figure 16.9 A Graphical Representation of the Interaction Between Blood Alcohol Content and Self-Esteem in Estimating Self-Disclosure

increases by one unit (because the coefficient is negative). Conversely, this interaction can be interpreted as the change in the regression weight for blood alcohol content with a one unit increase in self-esteem.

Interpretation of this interaction is made easier with a picture. Using the procedure described in the previous section, we generate estimated self-disclosure from the regression model for various values of BAC and SE. For reasons that will be clear soon, I used values of BAC equal to the mean (3.865), one standard deviation above the sample mean (5.443), and one standard deviation below the sample mean (2.287) and SE values 1 through 5 in increments of one. The estimated self-disclosure scores are then plotted in a scatterplot using different symbols for values of either SE or BAC (see Figure 16.9).[3]

The other coefficients in the regression model are interpreted just as in the previous example. The coefficient for self-esteem, b_{SE}, is the regression weight for self-esteem when $BAC = 0$. This is the relationship between self-esteem and self-disclosure if no alcohol is consumed (in which case BAC would be zero). This coefficient tells us that among a group of abstainers, two people who differ by one unit in self-esteem are expected to differ by 1.404 units in their self-disclosure, $t(36) = 2.789, p = .008$. For the same reasons as described previously, b_{BAC} has no sensible interpretation here because it is the conditional effect of blood alcohol content when $SE = 0$, but 0 is out of the range of possible values of self-esteem as measured in this study.

Probing the Interaction. We can probe this interaction using the procedure described in the previous section by estimating the conditional effect of one variable at various representative values of the other variable. To illustrate this, let's assess the relationship between self-esteem and self-disclosure at various values of blood alcohol content, using the sample mean, one standard deviation above the mean, and one

---

[3]The CD that comes with this book contains a couple of documents describing in detail how to generate such a plot in SPSS.

Table 16.5

Probing an Interaction in Moderated Multiple Regression

	Coeff.	s.e.	t	p
$BAC' = BAC - 2.287$				
Constant	2.778	0.796	3.492	0.001
Self-Esteem (SE)	0.857	0.271	3.162	0.003
BAC'	0.769	0.385	2.001	0.053
$SE \times BAC'$	-0.239	0.117	-2.048	0.048
$BAC' = BAC - 3.865$				
Constant	3.992	0.567	7.045	< .001
Self-Esteem (SE)	0.481	0.180	2.666	0.011
BAC'	0.769	0.385	2.001	0.053
$SE \times BAC'$	-0.239	0.117	-2.048	0.048
$BAC' = BAC - 5.443$				
Constant	5.206	0.864	6.028	< .001
Self-Esteem (SE)	0.104	0.243	0.426	0.672
BAC'	0.769	0.385	2.001	0.053
$SE \times BAC'$	-0.239	0.117	-2.048	0.048

standard deviation below the mean BAC as representative values. In the data, $\overline{BAC} = 3.865, SD = 1.578$, so one standard deviation below the mean is $3.865 - 1.578 = 2.287$ and one standard deviation above the mean is $3.865 + 1.578 = 5.443$. The results of the regressions after the necessary transformations can be found in Table 16.5. As can be seen, at one standard deviation below the mean BAC ($BAC = 2.287$) as well as at the mean ($BAC = 3.865$) the relationship between self-esteem and self-disclosure is positive and statistically significant. But at one standard deviation above the mean BAC ($BAC = 5.443$), the relationship is not significant.

16.3.3 Interaction Between a Quantitative and a Multicategorical Variable

Researchers often are interested in comparing the relationship between two variables in several naturally occurring groups or artificially created experimental conditions. For example, is the relationship between X and Y the same across all k levels of an experimental manipulation, or all k ethnic groups, $k > 2$? Or does the effect of an experimental manipulation with several different levels vary depending on the values of a second, quantitative predictor variable? When there is a multicategorical predictor variable, the same basic procedures described thus far can be applied, although there are some variations on the methodology required.

As discussed in Chapter 14, a categorical variable with more than two groups cannot be represented with a single variable in a regression model. To code group membership when there are several categories, $k - 1$ variables must be created coding group membership, where k is the number of categories. The same can be said about the required number of product terms to assess interaction between a multicategorical variable and a quantitative variable. Just as it requires $k - 1$ variables to code membership in one of k groups, it takes $k - 1$ product variables to test for interaction between a categorical variable with k categories and a quantitative variable. But because it requires more than one variable to quantify and test the interaction, it is not possible to test the hypothesis of interaction with a single regression coefficient, as was possible in the analyses described previously. Instead, one must resort to hierarchical regression analysis and determine how much R^2 changes when the $k - 1$ product terms coding the interaction are entered into a model without them.

To illustrate this procedure, we ask whether the relationship between exposure to political talk radio and political knowledge (Y) varies across party identification using the NES data set. First, we run a regression estimating political knowledge from political talk radio exposure and two dummy variables coding party identification. The model is:

$$\hat{Y} = 7.341 + 0.922(Talk) + 2.442(D) + 2.408(R)$$

where $Talk$ is exposure to talk radio (first discussed in Chapter 13), and D and R are two dummy variables coding whether a person self-identifies as a Democrat or Republican (see section 14.4 for details). Those who identify with neither party are treated in this analysis as the reference group.

The partial regression coefficient for $Talk$ is 0.922 and statistically different from zero, $t(339) = 5.125, p < 0.0005$, and the multiple correlation coefficient for this regression model is $R^2 = 0.113$. So controlling for party identification, two people who differ by one measurement unit in their exposure to political talk radio differ by 0.922 units in their political knowledge, with the person with greater exposure to political talk radio expected to have a higher political knowledge score. Combined, these three variables explain 11.3% of the variance in political knowledge. But this doesn't answer the question of interest. We want to know whether the relationship between political talk radio exposure and political knowledge depends on whether a person identifies as a Democrat, Republican, or neither of these groups. To answer this question, we ask whether a regression model that includes two additional variables that represent the interaction between political party identification and political talk radio exposure fits better than the model that excludes these interaction variables. The two variables added to the model are (a) the product of $Talk$ and the dummy variable coding Democrats (D), and (b) the product of $Talk$ and the dummy variable coding Republicans (R). We then estimate a regression model with the same predictors as model 1 but also including these two additional product variables. The resulting model is:

$$\hat{Y} = 7.173 + 1.009(Talk) + 3.854(D) + 1.514(R) - 0.789(Talk \times D) + 0.378(Talk \times R)$$

from the SPSS output in Figure 16.10). This model is presented graphically in Figure 16.11. The multiple correlation is $R^2 = 0.135$, so the incremental increase in variability in political knowledge explained by the addition of the two interaction terms is $\Delta R^2 = 0.135 - 0.113 = 0.022$. That is, these two variables explain an additional 2.2% of the total variance in political knowledge.

To test the null hypothesis that this increase in R^2 is attributable to a chance mechanism, we can use equation 13.14,

$$F = \frac{df_{residual} SR^2_{YX.W}}{m(1 - R^2_{YXW})}$$

To use this equation, think of variable set X as the two interaction terms $Talk \times D$ and $Talk \times R$ and variable set W as D, R, and $Talk$. In that case, ΔR^2 is the squared

Model Summary

Model	R	R Square	Adjusted R Square	Std. Error of the Estimate	Change Statistics				
					R Square Change	F Change	df1	df2	Sig. F Change
1	.336a	.113	.105	4.21207	.113	14.369	3	339	.000
2	.368b	.135	.122	4.17100	.022	4.354	2	337	.014

a. Predictors: (Constant), Political Talk Radio Exposure, D, R
b. Predictors: (Constant), Political Talk Radio Exposure, D, R, D_talk, R_talk

ANOVA^c

Model		Sum of Squares	df	Mean Square	F	Sig.
1	Regression	764.778	3	254.926	14.369	.000a
	Residual	6014.382	339	17.742		
	Total	6779.160	342			
2	Regression	916.290	5	183.258	10.534	.000b
	Residual	5862.870	337	17.397		
	Total	6779.160	342			

a. Predictors: (Constant), Political Talk Radio Exposure, D, R
b. Predictors: (Constant), Political Talk Radio Exposure, D, R, D_talk, R_talk
c. Dependent Variable: Political Knowledge

Coefficients^a

Model		Unstandardized Coefficients		Standardized Coefficients	t	Sig.	Correlations		
		B	Std. Error	Beta			Zero-order	Partial	Part
1	(Constant)	7.341	.666		11.018	.000			
	D	2.442	.670	.270	3.643	.000	.037	.194	.186
	R	2.408	.668	.268	3.604	.000	.116	.192	.184
	Political Talk Radio Exposure	.922	.180	.266	5.125	.000	.270	.268	.262
2	(Constant)	7.173	.982		7.301	.000			
	D	3.854	1.175	.427	3.281	.001	.037	.176	.166
	R	1.514	1.192	.169	1.270	.205	.116	.069	.064
	Political Talk Radio Exposure	1.009	.416	.291	2.426	.016	.270	.131	.123
	D_talk	-.789	.515	-.203	-1.530	.127	.052	-.083	-.078
	R_talk	.387	.490	.123	.790	.430	.260	.043	.040

a. Dependent Variable: Political Knowledge

Figure 16.10 SPSS output from a hierarchical multiple regression to estimate the interaction between political talk radio exposure and political party identification.

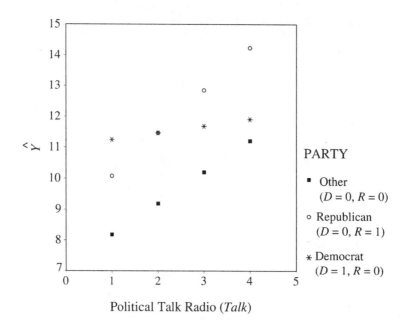

Figure 16.11 A graphical representation of the interaction between political talk radio exposure and political party self-identification in estimating political knowledge.

setwise semipartial correlation between X and Y controlling for W ($SR^2_{YX.W}$). The residual degrees of freedom for the model with the interaction terms is $df_{residual} = 337$, and $m = 2$ (the number of variables entered in the second regression model), so

$$F = \frac{337(0.022)}{2(1 - 0.135)} = 4.286$$

which is evaluated in reference to the F distribution with $df_{num} = 2$ and $df_{den} = 337$. The null hypothesis is that the relationship between political talk radio exposure and political knowledge does not vary across political identification groups. The obtained F of 4.286 exceeds the critical F for $\alpha = 0.05$ of 3.206 from Appendix D1. Using the SPSS output, we can see that the p-value for this increase is 0.014. We reject the null hypothesis and claim that the relationship between political talk radio exposure and political knowledge depends on whether a person self-identifies as a Democrat, a Republican, or some other political group.[4]

What do the Coefficients Mean? It may not be at all apparent to you how these two product variables and their corresponding regression coefficients quantify interaction. To illustrate how this is so, consider the simple regression models estimating political knowledge from political talk radio in each of the political party groups:

$$\text{Democrats:} \quad \hat{Y} = 11.028 + 0.220(Talk)$$
$$\text{Republicans:} \quad \hat{Y} = 8.687 + 1.396(Talk)$$
$$\text{``Others'':} \quad \hat{Y} = 7.173 + 1.009(Talk)$$

---

[4]The difference between the 4.286 computed here and from the SPSS output is simply rounding error in hand computations.

The regression coefficient for $Talk \times D$ is equal to the difference between the simple regression weight for $Talk$ in the Democrats and in the reference group. Indeed, notice that $0.220 - 1.009 = -0.789$. Similarly, the regression coefficient for $Talk \times R$ is equal to the difference between the regression weight for $Talk$ computed in the Republicans compared to the reference group: $1.396 - 1.009 = 0.387$. So these two regression coefficients do indeed quantify the differences in the regression weights. By testing the null hypothesis that both of these regression coefficients are zero, differing from each other in the sample by just chance, we are testing the null hypothesis that the relationship between political knowledge and political talk radio exposure does not vary across groups.

When an interaction term is in the model, the same rules for the interpretation of the coefficients apply. I've already discussed the interpretation of the regression coefficients for the two product terms. In the second model (model 2 in Figure 16.10), the coefficient for $Talk$ is the regression coefficient estimating political knowledge from talk radio exposure when all other variables are equal to zero. That occurs only when both D and R are equal to 0, which implies that this is the regression coefficient estimating political knowledge from talk radio exposure in the reference group. Indeed, that regression weight is 1.009, as above. The coefficient for D is the difference in estimated political knowledge between Democrats who don't listen to political talk radio (i.e., $Talk = 0$) and those who identify with neither party that don't listen to political talk radio. The coefficient for R is interpreted similarly, as the difference in estimated political knowledge between Republicans who don't listen to political talk radio and those who identify with neither party who don't listen to political talk radio.

In Chapter 15, I introduced analysis of covariance and noted in that ANCOVA assumes homogeneity of regression, meaning that the relationship between the covariate and the outcome variable is the same in all groups. You should recognize this as the assumption of no interaction between group membership and the covariate in estimating political knowledge, and now you know how to test this assumption. To do so, you follow the procedure just described.

16.3.4   Mean Centering of Predictors

It has been argued that the proper implementation of moderated multiple regression requires that the researcher first *mean center* the predictor variables prior to computing the product term representing the interaction. A variable is mean centered by subtracting the mean of the variable from each case. One argument advanced for mean centering in moderated multiple regression is that it reduces multicollinearity between the product and the constituent terms of the interaction (e.g., Aiken & West, 1991; Eveland, 1997). As discussed in Chapter 13, multicollinearity can reduce the power of significance tests in multiple regression because the variables tend to cancel each other out mathematically.

Indeed, the product of two variables X and W will tend to be highly correlated with both X and W. For instance, the correlation between self-esteem and the product of self-esteem and blood alcohol content in the example from section 16.3.2 is 0.745. And the correlation between blood alcohol content and this product is 0.846. As a result, the tolerances for the the predictors (BAC, SE, and $SE \times BAC$) are quite low—as small as 0.036 for ($SE \times BAC$). But when blood alcohol content and self-esteem are mean centered prior to computing the products, the intercorrelations are reduced substantially ($r = 0.159$ between self-esteem and $SE \times BAC$ and $r = 0.178$

Table 16.6

The Effects of Mean Centering on a Moderated Multiple Regression

		Coeff.	s.e.	t	p
Uncentered					
	Constant	1.018	1.547	0.659	0.514
	SE	1.404	0.503	2.789	0.008
	BAC	0.769	0.385	2.001	0.053
	$SE \times BAC$	−0.239	0.117	−2.048	0.048
Mean Centered					
	Constant	5.450	0.171	31.934	0.000
	SE	0.481	0.180	2.666	0.011
	BAC	0.045	0.110	0.408	0.686
	$SE \times BAC$	−0.239	0.117	−2.048	0.048
Standardized					
	Constant	5.450	0.171	31.933	0.000
	SE	0.463	0.174	2.666	0.011
	BAC	0.071	0.174	0.408	0.686
	$SE \times BAC$	−0.363	0.177	−2.048	0.048

between blood alcohol content and $SE \times BAC$), and the tolerances increase to greater than 0.85. Intuition would suggest that such mean centering would be beneficial in moderated multiple regression because it would lower the correlation between the variable representing the interaction and the two variables that define it, and this would increase the power of hypothesis tests for the regression weights.

But this is not true. Mean centering has absolutely no effect on the hypothesis test for the interaction term, as the regression weight, t statistic, and p-value will be the same regardless of whether the two predictor variables are mean centered prior to computing their product (Cohen, 1978; Cronbach, 1987; Dunlap & Kemery, 1987; Kromrey & Foster-Johnson, 1998). To illustrate, two regression models estimating self-disclosure from blood alcohol content, self-esteem, and their interaction are displayed in Table 16.6 one before mean centering and after mean centering. As you can see, the coefficient for $SE \times BAC$ is the same, as is the t statistic and p-value. Mean centering does not affect the coefficient or hypothesis test for the interaction one iota. To be sure, the regression coefficients, t statistics, and p-values for the lower order terms change as a result of mean centering, but the change is not the result of reduced multicollinearity. They change because their meaning is changed by centering, and the t statistics and p-values test a different null hypothesis.

As discussed in section 16.3.1, in a regression model of the form

$$\hat{Y} = a + b_X(X) + b_W(W) + b_{XW}(XW)$$

b_X represents the regression weight for X when $W = 0$, and b_W represents the regression weight for W when $X = 0$. But when X and W are mean centered, $X = 0$ corresponds to the mean of X and $W = 0$ corresponds to the mean of W. So b_X quantifies the regression weight for X at the mean of W, and b_W quantifies the regression weight for W at the mean of X. For example, in the regression with centered predictors in Table 16.6, b_{BAC} is the relationship between blood alcohol content and self-disclosure at the sample mean self-esteem. So two people who differ by one unit in blood alcohol content but who have a self-esteem score at the sample mean are estimated to differ by 0.045 in their self-disclosure. This difference is not statistically different from zero, $t(36) = 0.408, p = 0.686$. Similarly, b_{SE} is the relationship between self-esteem and self-disclosure at the mean blood alcohol content. Two people who differ by one unit in self-esteem but who are at the sample mean blood alcohol content are estimated to differ by 0.481 units in self-disclosure. This difference is statistically different from zero, $t(36) = 2.666, p = 0.011$.

Some argue that variables should be *standardized* prior to computing the product and estimating the moderated multiple regression model, again on the grounds that this reduces multicollinearity. True, multicollinearity is reduced when variables are standardized prior to computing the product, but as can be seen in Table 16.6, the hypothesis test for the interaction is unaffected by standardization. And although the coefficients are affected by standardization, the t statistics and p-values are not compared to when the variables are mean centered. The change in the regression coefficients has nothing to do with reduced multicollinearity. Instead, the change is the result of a difference in the unit of measurement. In regression with uncentered or centered measurements, the one-unit difference used to quantify the effect of a predictor on an outcome is a single unit in the original scale of measurement. But with standardization, one unit is *one standard deviation*. The difference between the lower-order coefficients in the regression with standardized variables compared to uncentered variables is due to the different meaning of "zero" on the measurement scales. With standardized scores, a measurement of zero is the mean, whereas with uncentered measurements, a measure of zero is just that—zero.[5]

So why all the recommendations to center or standardized predictors in moderated multiple regression? There is one reason why mean centering can be a good thing to do. In complicated models involving lots of predictors and several interactions, the tolerances can become so small that the mathematics of multiple regression explode, so to speak. Technically, the computation of a regression model requires something called *matrix inversion* in mathematics. If one predictor is very, very highly correlated with a linear combination of the other predictors, this can introduce rounding error into the computations of aspects of the regression model, yielding inaccuracies in the estimates and standard errors. That is the only sensible justification for mean centering, in my opinion. In most circumstances, it won't matter at all whether or not you mean center prior to computing the product and estimating a moderated multiple regression model. But if you choose to do so, remember that this changes the interpretation of the lower-order coefficients in the model.

---

[5]It is important to note that the coefficients in the moderated multiple regression model with standardized predictors are not the same as the coefficients in the *standardized regression equation* printed by most regression programs. In the latter, the product is created first, and then all the variables including the product and the outcome are standardized. In the former, only the lower order variables are standardized, after which the the product is created. The interpretation of the coefficient for the interaction in the standardized regression equation is very different than the interpretation of the interaction coefficient in the three models in Table 16.6.

16.3.5 Differences In Regression Coefficients vs. Differences in Correlations

A moderation hypothesis can also be framed as differences in correlations across groups. In the previous section, we found that the regression weight estimating political knowledge from political talk radio exposure differs between self-identifying Democrats, Republicans, and those who identify with some other political group. But perhaps the relationship between political knowledge and political talk radio exposure is stronger in one group rather than another. That is, perhaps the estimation of political knowledge from political talk radio exposure produces more accurate estimations in one group than in another. The regression weight is not a measure of strength of association in the way that a correlation coefficient is. It only quantifies how Y is estimated to change as X changes by one unit. There is a statistical test of the equality of a set of k Pearson correlation coefficients. The null hypothesis tested is that the population correlations are the same in the k groups. The alternative hypothesis is that at least two of the correlations are different.

Let's test the null hypothesis that the correlation between political talk radio and political knowledge is the same across these three groups. In the NES data, the sample correlations are $r = 0.059$, $r = 0.439$, and $r = 0.291$ in the 141 Democrats, 147 Republicans, and 55 respondents who identify as neither, respectively. To conduct this test, the difference between the sample correlations is converted to a chi-squared statistic with equation 16.7:

$$\chi^2 = \sum (n_j - 3)(Z_{r_j} - \overline{Z}_r)^2$$

$$(16.7)$$

where Z_{r_j} is the correlation between X and Y after Fisher's r-to-Z transformation (equation 12.19), n_j is the sample size in group j, and $\overline{Z}_r$ is the weighted mean of the k Fisher-transformed correlations, defined as

$$\overline{Z}_r = \frac{\sum (n_j - 3) Z_{r_j}}{n - 3k}$$

$$(16.8)$$

where n is the total sample size.

The conversion of r to Fisher's Z using equation 12.19 yields Z_r values of 0.059, 0.471, and 0.300 for Democrats, Republicans, and those who identify as neither, respectively. From equation 16.8,

$$\overline{Z}_r = \frac{(138)0.059 + (144)0.471 + (52)0.300}{343 - 9} = 0.274$$

Applying equation 16.7 yields

$$\chi^2 = (138)(0.059 - 0.274)^2 + (144)(0.471 - 0.274)^2 + (52)(0.300 - 0.274)^2 = 12.002$$

The p-value for $\chi^2 = 12.002$ assuming the null hypothesis is true can be derived from the χ^2 distribution with $(k-1)$ degrees of freedom. From Appendix C, the critical χ^2 for $df = 2$ and $\alpha = .05$ is 5.991. The obtained χ^2 statistic does exceed this critical value, so the null hypothesis is rejected, $p < 05$. Indeed, the obtained χ^2 exceeds the critical value for $\alpha = 0.01$, so the p-value is less than 0.01. So there is evidence that the correlation between political knowledge and exposure to political talk radio differs as a function of political party identification.

Although this test will tend to produce the same substantive conclusion about interaction as will moderated multiple regression, they can conflict. Which you use depends on the question of interest. The approach of comparing correlations asks whether the relationship between two variables is equally strong across the k groups, whereas the moderated multiple regression approach determines whether a one unit increase in a predictor is associated with the same expected difference in Y across all k groups. Although there are occasions where you might be interested in comparing the correlations, the problem with this approach is that the correlation between two variables can vary across groups if the range or variances of either the predictor or outcome varies substantially across groups.

This procedure should be used only if the correlations being compared are statistically independent. A necessary but not sufficient condition for correlations to be independent is that each unit must provide data to the computation of only one of the correlations involved in the comparison. This criterion is met in this example because the each person provides data to only the correlation between political discussion and knowledge in that person's group. This procedure could not be used to compare, for example, the correlation between political knowledge and political discussion and between political knowledge and newspaper exposure. In that case, each unit would be providing data to both of the correlations being compared. So they cannot be considered statistically independent. Correlations can also be nonindependent if units in the data are paired in some fashion, such as husband and wife couples. In this example, there is no pairing between units in the sample, so we are safe in using this procedure. Statistical procedures for comparing nonindependent correlations are described by Griffin and Gonzales (1995), Meng, Rosenthal, and Rubin (1992), Raghunathan, Rosenthal, and Rubin (1996), and Steiger (1980).

16.3.6   Statistical Control of Covariates

In moderated multiple regression, one or more covariates can be statistically controlled simply by including them in the regression model. The regression coefficient for the interaction in a moderated multiple regression model then quantifies the interaction controlling for the covariates. For example, in the analysis reported in section 16.3.2 we may have wanted to control for a participant's weight when assessing the interaction between blood alcohol content and self-esteem. Had weight been measured, it could have simply been included in the regression model, and all interpretations would be based on the statistical control of individual differences in body weight.

16.3.7   Required Terms in a Moderated Multiple Regression Model

In a regression model with an interaction between variables X and W, is it necessary to always include both X and W in the model, or can they be deleted if not statistically significant? The answers to these questions, respectively, are "yes" and "no." In order for the various terms in a moderated regression model to be estimated correctly and interpreted as described here, it is necessary that lower order variables that define the interaction be included in the regression model, regardless of whether or not their regression coefficients are statistically significant. A failure to do so will produce largely meaningless results that cannot be interpreted as described here. For this reason, you should *never* use stepwise variable entry (see section 13.6.4) to build a model that contains interactions because the variable entry algorithms used by stepwise procedures will not recognize this important constraint.

Although one should always include the lower order variables contributing to an interaction whenever the product of those variables is in a model, the same cannot be said about retaining a nonsignificant interaction term. Because the presence of an interaction term in a moderated multiple regression model changes the interpretation of the lower order coefficients from partial regression weights to conditional regression weights, it is a good idea to include product terms in a final model only if the interaction is statistically significant. If the interaction term is not significant, estimate a new regression model without it.

As I have illustrated throughout this section, the presence of an interaction term in a regression model changes the interpretation and tests of significance of the regression coefficients for the lower order variables that define the interaction. For this reason, hierarchical entry should be used if one is interested in first assessing the partial relationships between the predictor and outcome variables prior to assessing interaction. In the first stage of a hierarchical model, the predictor variables of interest are used to predict the outcome. At a second stage, the interaction is then added. If the interaction is nonsignificant, then all discussion of the results should be based on the first stage of the regression. If the interaction is significant, the coefficients for the lower order terms in the second stage model should be interpreted as conditional regression weights (which may or may not be meaningful), and the researcher can then probe the interaction using the methods described in this chapter.

16.3.8 The Pitfalls of Subgroup Analyses to Test Moderation

One strategy you will see in the communication literature for testing moderation hypotheses is to estimate a regression model several times, once for each of two or more subgroups in a sample, and then descriptively compare either the standardized or unstandardized regression coefficients for each variable across the groups. According to this approach, if one of the regression coefficients representing the partial relationship between a predictor and an outcome appears to differ across groups, then the grouping variable is considered a moderator of the relationship between that predictor and the outcome. For example, if predictor variable i is statistically significant in one group but not in another group, the grouping variable is deemed a moderator of the relationship between predictor i and the outcome.

There are two major problems with this strategy. First, a descriptive difference between regression coefficients (either standardized or unstandardized) for variable i across regression models does not imply that the relationship (simple or partial) between predictor i and the outcome variable differs across groups. Indeed, you'd expect regression coefficients from models estimated in different groups to differ from each other as a result of sampling error. Two coefficients may differ descriptively but not differ statistically (i.e., by more than "chance"). And evidence that the relationship between variable i and the outcome (again, simple or partial) is statistically significant in one group but not the other cannot be used as evidence of moderation when the groups differ in sample size, because the size of the standard error is determined in part by the size of the sample. And given that the standard error of a partial regression weight is determined in part by intercorrelations between predictors (see section 13.6.3), differences across groups in the predictor variable intercorrelations can also affect whether a variable is statistically significant in one group or the other. So sample size, predictor variable intercorrelations, and statistical significance are confounded.

Second, in spite of recommendations that standardized regression coefficients be routinely reported and used when comparing models across groups or studies (e.g., Hunter & Hamilton, 2002), standardized regression coefficients estimated in different subgroups are often not comparable. If the variance of either the predictor or the outcome variable differs across groups, standardized regression coefficients are expected to differ from each other even if predictor i has the same effect on Y across groups. Even minor differences in these variances across groups can produce differences in standardized coefficients. But such variations in variance across groups will have little to no effect on unstandardized coefficients (see, e.g., Blalock, 1967; Linn & Werts, 1969).

It is generally accepted in the field of statistics (even if not widely practiced in communication) that comparisons of regression coefficients for variable i between subgroups in a sample should be based on *unstandardized* coefficients, and a formal test of the significance of the difference using moderated multiple regression (or an equivalent strategy) should be conducted and the null hypothesis rejected before one can claim that a predictor variable's effect on an outcome variable differs across groups. Subgroup regression analyses, especially when based on standardized regression coefficients, are not informative about whether a variable's effect on an outcome differs across subgroups of the sample. For a good and very readable discussion on the problems of subgroup analysis to assess moderation hypotheses, see Newsom, Prigerson, Schultz, and Reynolds (2003).

16.4 Simplifying the Hunt for Interactions

In a moderated multiple regression with k predictors, there are "k choose 2" possible interactions between two predictors. For example, with 4 predictor variables, there are $4(3)/2 = 6$ possible 2-way interactions, with 5 predictors that are $5(4)/2 = 10$ possible 2-way interactions, and with 10 predictors there are $10(9)/2 = 45$ possible interactions between two predictors. Given the large number of possible interactions between two variables in even relatively simple multiple regression models, is it necessary to test for all of them? Some of them? If only some of them, which ones? In this section, I discuss some strategies for thinking about how to manage tests for interactions in linear models such as regression and analysis of variance.

The first question to address is whether one needs to bother with testing for interactions in the first place. It is clear from the communication literature that one common strategy is to assume that interactions don't exist. On the surface this might seem silly, but in fact there is some justification for ignoring the possibility that predictors may interact. There is no obligation that you test for interaction between predictors just because it is possible to do so. A failure to include interactions that should be in a regression model will of course lead to a regression model that is at best an oversimplification or, at worst, just plain wrong. But all regression models are wrong in some sense. For example, you might argue from the results of a regression analysis that because the relationship between X and Y persists even after controlling for W and Q that the relationship is not spurious. But there is an infinite number of other predictors that you could have included in the regression model but simply did not, either because you didn't measure the variables or you simply didn't think of including them in the model. If you had included them, the relationship between

X and Y may have disappeared. A regression model that fails to include potentially important predictors is called an *underspecified model*. The communication literature is filled with underspecified regression models, because we can never know for certain which potentially important variables have not been included in the model. Whether a model is underspecified or not is part a statistical judgment but also a theoretical judgment. A critic of your research may argue that you failed to control for something important. Such a criticism is usually a principled argument, in that the critic believes that there is a specific variable that you should have controlled for and that, had you done so, you would have ended up with a dramatically different result. By the same reasoning, a critic could make the case that a failure to include an interaction may lead to a misleading result, but such a criticism is usually principled, in that the critic typically would have particular reason for believing that there is an interaction that you should have included in your regression model.

My point is you should test for interaction if there is a principled argument leading you to expect there to be an interaction between two specific variables in the regression model. The primary principled argument for testing for an interaction is that your hypothesis or the theory you are testing postulates that an interaction between two of the variables should exist. If you are testing a theory or hypothesis that predicts an interaction, you darn well better test for it. If you don't test for it, you aren't testing the theoretical proposition correctly (c.f., Eveland, 1997). But if there is no reason to expect an interaction, and you can conceive of no principled arguments that a critic might make for why any of the variables should interact, then you have no obligation to test for interaction.

Nevertheless, the possibility of missing an interaction should loom large in your thinking. There is little harm in testing for interaction even if you don't have an a priori reason to believe such an interaction might exist. It is exciting to discover something unexpected, and unexpected discoveries can often lead to new research questions, new ways of thinking about old questions, or can even revolutionize and move theory in directions it otherwise wouldn't have gone. So I encourage you to explore your data in search of interactions for no reason other than the possibility that the unexpected may appear in your data. But how do you manage so many possible statistical tests given the number of possible interactions in even relatively small regression models?

One strategy is to test for interactions as a set. For example, in a regression model with 4 predictors, you might add all six possible interactions at a second step and see if R^2 increases significantly. If so, this suggests that there is at least one interaction between two of the predictors, and hopefully the coefficients for the interaction and tests of significance for each will tell you which interactions are significant in the set. Or you might define sensible subsets of possible interactions that are worth testing as a set. For example, if X is an experimental manipulation and the primary variable of interest in your study and W, Z, and Q are three covariates, you could see if adding $X \times W$, $X \times Z$, and $X \times Q$ as a set increases R^2 significantly. If not, this suggests no interaction between the experimental manipulation and any of the covariates. Having determined that X doesn't interact with W, Z, or Q, you could then test whether there are any interactions between W, Z, and Q by seeing if adding $W \times Z$, $W \times Q$, and $Z \times Q$ significantly increases R^2 compared to the model that includes only X, W, Z, and Q by themselves. If not, then stop searching and conclude that there are no interactions. If the increase in R^2 is statistically significant, look at the individual coefficients and their tests of significance. Another possibility is to test each interaction separately. So if there are 4 predictors, you run 6 additional regressions including one of the possible interactions in each regression model.

Of course, by fishing around in your data for statistically significant relationships, you are bound to find a small p-value now and then that reflects nothing other than sampling error or "chance." Some kind of multiple test correction (such as a Bonferroni correction) is justified when hunting in your data for something statistically significant worth reporting. Alternatively, repeat the study with a new set of participants to see if the interaction you found when mining the first data set replicates in the new data.

In factorial research designs, the default approach is to include both the main effects and the interactions in the ANOVA. This habit no doubt stems from where communication scientists have learned about the analysis of experiments. But the same logic I discussed above applies to factorial ANOVA. There is no obligation to test for interaction just because it is possible to do so. You should test for interaction if you have a reason to do so (such as your hypothesis predicts an interaction) or if you are just curious. If an interaction in a factorial ANOVA is not statistically significant, a strong argument can be made for eliminating it from the analyses (most good statistics programs have options for excluding interactions from an analysis of variance). If an interaction is not statistically significant, then the more parsimonious and better fitting model of the data is one that excludes the interaction term. And in unbalanced designs, the interaction is likely to be correlated with the main effects, so including the interaction when nonsignificant can lower the power of the F tests for the factors by reducing the sum of squares for the effect of interest and therefore the mean square for that effect. Conversely, including a nonsignificant interaction term can artificially lower MS_{error}, increasing the probability of a Type I error in tests for the factors.

16.5   Why Not to Categorize Prior to Testing for Interaction

In section 16.3, I introduced moderated multiple regression as a means of assessing whether the relationship between two variables X and Y varies as a function of a potential moderating variable W. Although moderated multiple regression is the preferred method for testing for interactions involving a quantitative predictor variable, unfortunately this procedure is not often used when it should be. A common strategy that you will see in the communication literature is for the researcher to take one of more of the quantitative predictor variables and place people into categories based on their scores on the quantitative predictor prior to testing for interaction using a factorial ANOVA. Such categorization of quantitative variables can take many forms, the most common being dichotomization through a median or mean split, where the investigator creates "low" and "high" groups prior to data analysis based on whether participants score below or above the sample median or mean on some quantitative measure. Other forms of categorization include trichotomization (the creation of three groups), bivariate group construction, where an investigator creates a special category of participants that exceed some criterion on more than one variable (e.g., classifying people into a group based on whether the person is above the median on 2 different measures), or arbitrary categorization, where the groups are defined based on whether a participant scores higher or lower than some arbitrary value other than the median or mean. For example, a researcher may classify participants as knowledgeable or unknowledgeable about a political candidate based on whether he or she can correctly answer 50% or more of the questions in a set about the candidate.

Many arguments have been presented against categorization of quantitative variables, although these arguments tend to focus on relatively simple analyses, such as testing for association or comparing two groups (Cohen, 1983; MacCallum, Zhang, Preacher, & Rucker, 2002). My interest in this chapter is tests of interaction, and in this section I try to make the case as to why such categorization should be avoided. But some of the arguments in the literature focused on simpler analyses are relevant, so I use them when necessary.

16.5.1 Classification Errors

One way of thinking about the damage to analyses caused by categorization is to ask how frequently participants are likely to be classified into the wrong group using a categorization procedure. Remember from Chapter 6 that the observed scores resulting from measurement are used as proxies for the true scores. Unless your measurement procedure is perfectly reliable, the observed scores on the variable being used to produce the categories are not going to be equal to the true scores of what is being measured. Our measurement procedures are not perfect. Measurements will almost always contain some random error, meaning that the match between each case's observed score and their true score is not going to be exact. So, for example, somebody whose observed score is below the sample median on some kind of individual difference variable such as communication apprehension may actually be above the median if his or her true score could be known exactly. Of course, the true scores are usually unknown, and so the observed scores are used to derive category membership. Random measurement error means that some participants that really are above (or below) the median on the true score may be misclassified as low (or high) on the variable being measured, with the frequency of misclassification depending on how reliably the construct is measured.

Table 16.7 illustrates the effect of measurement error on classification accuracy using either a median split or a trichotomization procedure (based on dividing the participants into "low," "middle," and "high" groups as a function of whether their observed scores are in the lower, middle, or upper third of the distribution). The numbers in this table were generated through a simulation and assume that the true scores and errors in measurement are normally distributed. For example, using a measurement

Table 16.7
Estimated Percent of Cases Misclassified As a Result of Categorization

Reliability of Measurement	Median Split	Tricho- tomization	2×2 Cross Class- Classification
1.00	0	0	0
0.90	10	18	19
0.80	15	26	27
0.70	18	32	33
0.60	22	37	39
0.50	25	41	44

procedure with minimally acceptable reliability to generate groups (generally, 0.70 is used by communication researchers), roughly 18% of participants are likely to be misclassified using a median split on the observed scores or 32% using a trichotomization procedure. Of course, the problem is less severe when the original measurements are more reliable, but even then the problem is not trivial. Using a second quantitative variable also measured with some error to produce a 2×2 classification of participants (as either above/below the median on one variable and above/below the median on the other) exacerbates the problem further. The last column in Table 16.7 provides expected misclassification assuming both variables are measured with the same reliability. For example, if both measures have reliability of 0.70, roughly 34% of participants will be misclassified in a 2×2 table based on a median split of each variable.

To put these numbers into a meaningful context, consider an investigator studying how men and women differ in communication apprehension. The misclassification estimates in Table 16.7 can be thought of as equivalent to the effect of misidentifying a person's sex in the data set. It would be potentially disastrous if a researcher of sex differences mistakenly misidentified the sex of 20% or more of his or her participants. Indeed, a researcher who later discovered such an error after publishing the results would likely feel an obligation to publish a correction of some sort. Yet categorization of quantitative variables produces such miscodings routinely and with certainty whenever a variable is measured with error.

16.5.2 Smaller Effect Sizes and Reduced Statistical Power

Categorization of a quantitative predictor prior to assessing interaction involving that variable tends to lower statistical power of tests of interaction as well as reduce the size of interaction effects. Remember that power is the ability of a hypothesis test to reject a false null hypothesis. Higher power is better.

To illustrate the effects of categorization on power and effect size, I present results of a small simulation in Table 16.8. To conduct this simulation, I generated samples of various sizes from two hypothetical populations with different relationships between an outcome variable and a quantitative predictor. In one population, the relationship between X_1 and Y was defined as $Y = \beta_1(X_1) + e$, where X_1 and e were random standard normal variables. This procedure was repeated but sampling from a different population, using not β_1 but β_2, where β_2 was set to a value different from β_1. In half of the simulations, X_1 was then dichotomized using a median split based on the sample median computed after combining both samples, creating "high" and "low" groups on X_1. X_1 was then recoded $X_1 = 0$ for the low group, and $X_1 = 1$ for the high group. The presence of interaction was then tested using a 2 (population sampled) $\times$ 2 (high vs. low on X_1) ANOVA. The proportion of the total variance in Y attributable uniquely to the interaction was computed, as was a test of significance for the interaction, using $\alpha = .05$ for rejection of the null hypothesis. In the other half of the simulations, these same statistics were computed testing for interaction using moderated multiple regression. This procedure was repeated 10,000 times for various combinations of β_1, β_2 and n (sample size in each group).

As can be seen in Table 16.8, both the proportion of variance in Y uniquely attributable to the interaction (η^2) and the power of the hypothesis test for interaction were lower for the ANOVA strategy compared to moderated multiple regression (although as you would expect, increasing the sample size reduced the differences in power because power converges to 1 for both tests with increasing sample size). Thus, the

Table 16.8
Comparing Factorial ANOVA to Moderated Multiple Regression

β_1	β_2	n per group	Mean Interaction η^2		Power	
			ANOVA	MMR	ANOVA	MMR
0	0.7	20	0.082	0.109	0.361	0.530
		50	0.070	0.102	0.748	0.913
		100	0.067	0.100	0.966	0.997
		250	0.064	0.099	1.000	1.000
0.3	0.5	20	0.029	0.030	0.080	0.090
		50	0.015	0.017	0.119	0.165
		100	0.010	0.012	0.192	0.282
		250	0.007	0.010	0.406	0.603
0.3	−0.3	20	0.071	0.096	0.285	0.411
		50	0.059	0.088	0.624	0.819
		100	0.056	0.085	0.908	0.984
		250	0.054	0.083	1.000	1.000
0.3	0.7	20	0.042	0.048	0.157	0.218
		50	0.029	0.038	0.330	0.493
		100	0.024	0.034	0.574	0.792
		250	0.021	0.032	0.924	0.993
0.7	−0.7	20	0.212	0.314	0.857	0.973
		50	0.210	0.321	0.999	1.000
		100	0.209	0.325	1.000	1.000
		250	0.210	0.327	1.000	1.000

categorization-followed-by-ANOVA strategy tended to produce smaller effect size estimates and was less likely to reject the false null hypothesis of no interaction when interaction was present than did moderated multiple regression.[6]

These results illustrate the lower statistical power and effect size estimates that result from categorization of quantitative variables prior to assessing interaction. Categorization of quantitative variables followed by factorial ANOVA reduces an investigator's ability to detect interactions when they are present compared to moderated multiple regression (e.g., Aiken & West, 1991, pg. 167–168; Bissonnette, Ickes, Berstein, & Knowles, 1990).

---

[6]The overall decline in the interaction η^2 as a function of sample size seen in Table 16.8 is attributable to the fact that η^2 is an upwardly biased estimate of effect size, but the bias decreases as sample size increases.

16.5.3   Spurious Statistical Significance

The skeptical reader may have another argument in favor of categorization followed by ANOVA. The power of a statistical test is irrelevant if one has successfully rejected a null hypothesis, so what harm is there in categorizing and testing for interaction using ANOVA if one has indeed found a number of interpretable effects after doing so? My argument thus far is that categorization of quantitative variables increases the probability of Type II errors (failing to reject a false null hypothesis). So why worry about failure to reject a null hypothesis if you have already done so successfully in spite of the problems with categorization?

In some circumstances, categorization of a quantitative variable can actual increase the likelihood of falsely rejecting a true null hypothesis and claiming support for a hypothesis or theory that is in fact false. That is, categorization of quantitative variables prior to analysis can yield spuriously significant effects. The statistical evidence is highly technical and summarized in a variety of sources. The most well known argument applies to non-experimental designs, where two quantitative variables are both dichotomized and interaction is tested with a 2×2 ANOVA. Maxwell and Delaney (1993) show that when two correlated variables are both dichotomized prior to analysis with a factorial ANOVA, the probability of a significant main effect can be much higher than the level of significance chosen for the test. In other words, the p-value for one of the main effects can be substantially underestimated, increasing the likelihood of a Type I error. If one of the dichotomous variables is an experimental manipulation and participants are randomly assigned to conditions, this is less likely to happen in a simple 2×2 design because random assignment would result in a zero or near zero correlation between the quantitative independent variable (in either the original or dichotomized form) and the levels of the experimental manipulation. But in more complicated analyses (e.g., a $2 \times 2 \times 2$ design), the presence in the analysis of any interaction involving the two dichotomized variables can produce spuriously significant effects. Dichotomization of variables and conducting an ANOVA can also yield a spuriously significant interaction if the true relationship between one of the IVs and the DV is curvilinear (Maxwell & Delaney, 1993). If an predictor variable is dichotomized prior to analysis, it is impossible to assess whether a curvilinear relationship exist between that variable and dependent variable, and any curvilinearity that does exist (i.e., prior to dichotomization) can show up as interaction.

16.5.4   Artifactual Failures to Replicate Findings

Anyone familiar with the communication literature knows that research findings are anything but consistent. In seemingly similar studies, one investigator may report one finding, and a different investigator might report something completely different. There are many different reasons an investigator may fail to replicate previous findings, among them being different populations studied, important between-study variations in the stimuli, differences in sample size, or simply time passing or society changing in an important way relevant to the phenomenon being studied. It is also true that two investigators who categorize quantitative variables prior to analysis may get very different results even though the same basic relationship between the variables exists in the data (c.f., Hirsch, 1980; Hunter & Schmidt, 1990; Sedney, 1981; Viele, 1988). Figure 16.12 graphically represents the relationship between a quantitative measure X (perhaps an individual difference like extroversion or a behavioral measure such as the number of hours spent watching television on a typical day) and some dependent

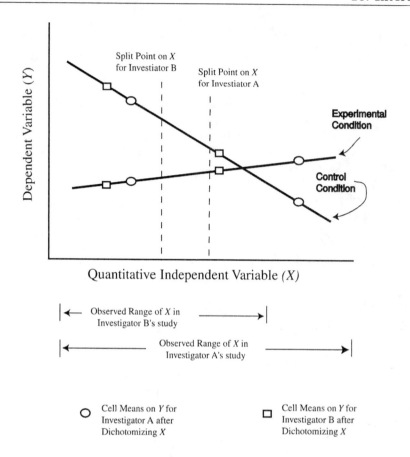

Figure 16.12 The effects of different median split points on study outcomes.

variable Y in a hypothetical experimental study. As can be seen, for participants in
a control group, the relationship between X and Y is negative. But the relationship
between X and Y is close to zero or perhaps positive in the experimental condition.
Investigator A has a sample of participants representing a wide range of values on X.
Investigator B, by contrast, has a sample that is restricted in the range of X, with
the bulk of the participants being in the low to middle range. Both investigators are
interested in the interaction between X and experimental treatment vs. control and
examine this by dichotomizing the participants at the median on X and analyzing the
study with a 2×2 ANOVA. As represented in Figure 16.12, investigator A's sample
median is much higher than investigator B's sample median. Notice that investigator
B's "high" group is not high at all relative to investigator A's sample. Indeed, what
investigator B calls "high" on X investigator A would consider "moderate" or about
average. In Figure 16.12, the circles and squares represent the cell means in this 2×2
design for investigator A and B, respectively. Investigator A would likely report an
interaction between experimental condition vs. control and X and perhaps a small
main effect of X. A simple effects analysis might show that among those low on
X, the control condition had a higher mean on the dependent variable compared to
the experimental condition. But among those high on X, exactly the opposite effect
occurred, with a larger mean in the experimental condition. In contrast, Investigator

B would likely report a main effect of experimental condition as well as an interaction between experimental condition and X. An analysis of simple effects might yield the finding that differences between the experimental and control group are much larger in the low group than in the high group (and thus the interaction), but the direction of the difference is the same.

So the apparent conflict in research findings between two studies can be an artifact of where on the quantitative variable two investigators split the sample. In this example, this problem might have been detected by one of the investigators if he or she knew prior to interpretation that samples in the two studies differed widely in their representation of the range of scores on X. But rarely do researchers have such intimate familiarity with the data of other researchers, so in most circumstances neither investigator would detect this problem (nor would journal reviewers or editors) and the result would be a conflicting and unnecessarily confusing literature. This might motivate some new investigator C to seek out some important difference between the methodologies of the two studies in attempt to design a study to explain the discrepancy in the hopes of advancing theory. Clearly, such attempts would be in vain, as there is no real discrepancy in the pattern of relationships between the individual difference and the dependent variable across the studies.

16.5.5 Is Categorization Ever Sensible?

Is there any reason why it might be sensible to categorize prior to analysis? There are two. First, categorizing is sensible when true categories exist and observed individual differences other than those attributable to category membership can be construed as measurement error. Second, it is sensible to categorize if there is a qualitative difference that results in a shift from one measurement to the next. For instance, if you asked people how many cigarettes they smoke each day, it might be sensible to categorize people into nonsmoking (zero cigarettes) and smoking (one or more cigarettes) groups if you were studying the effect of *any* smoking (rather than *how much*) on some outcome variable or as a moderator. But this wouldn't be sensible if you were interested in how small variations between people in the number of cigarettes smoked related to an outcome. Otherwise, in general, one should not categorize unless a convincing argument (as opposed to just an assumption) can be presented that categorization produces more meaningful measurement as it relates to the purpose of the research than does the use of the original measurements (c.f., Cohen, 1983; MacCallum et al., 2002).

16.6 Summary

Although the concept of interaction is relative simple conceptually, it can be tricky to test statistically. There are many forms that interaction can take, and may different statistical approaches to testing for interaction. We have only scratched the surface of the topic, and I encourage you to consult more advanced books referenced in this chapter for guidance on other forms of interaction and how to test for such forms of interaction in your data.

When the predictors are all categorical, the standard approach to testing for interaction is factorial analysis of variance. Although all good statistical programs can conduct a factorial ANOVA it is important to understand the interpretational differences that result when a design is unbalanced compared to when it is balanced. Most importantly, main effects are tests of differences between unweighted marginal means, not weighted marginal means, and so you can't just pretend that a variable in a factorial design doesn't exist when generating the means for your interpretation. If your statistics program doesn't automatically generate the unweighted marginal means, you need to calculate each of the cell means and then derive the unweighted means yourself before interpreting the main effects.

When one of the predictors presumed to interact with another predictor is quantitative, moderated multiple regression is the strategy of choice. Moderated multiple regression is used to test whether a regression coefficient (or a partial regression coefficient if there are covariates in the model) varies systematically as a function of variations in a second predictor variable. The inclusion of interaction terms in a regression model drastically alters the interpretation of the regression coefficients for variables that constitute the interaction. Rather than measures of partial association, those coefficients become measures of conditional association.

Although this may be the most difficult chapter in the book to read and master, your effort was well worth the effort. Understanding how interaction is conceptualized theoretically and tested statistically will take you a long way in life as a reader and producer of communication science.

APPENDICES

Appendix A: Table of Right-Tail Normal Probabilities

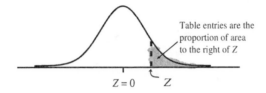

Table entries provide the proportion of area under the normal distribution to the right of the Z-score defined by the row and column. For example, looking in the 1.3 row, 4 column tells us that the proportion of area to the right of 1.34 is .0901. Area to the left of a negative Z-score is equal to the area to the right of the corresponding positive Z-score. Table generated with the SPSS IDF.NORMAL function. Proportions for $Z \geq 3.1$ are less than .001.

	Z									
	0	1	2	3	4	5	6	7	8	9
0.0	.5000	.4960	.4920	.4880	.4840	.4801	.4761	.4721	.4681	.4641
0.1	.4602	.4562	.4522	.4483	.4443	.4404	.4364	.4325	.4286	.4247
0.2	.4207	.4168	.4129	.4090	.4052	.4013	.3974	.3936	.3897	.3859
0.3	.3821	.3783	.3745	.3707	.3669	.3632	.3594	.3557	.3520	.3483
0.4	.3446	.3409	.3372	.3336	.3300	.3264	.3228	.3192	.3156	.3121
0.5	.3085	.3050	.3015	.2981	.2946	.2912	.2877	.2843	.2810	.2776
0.6	.2743	.2709	.2676	.2643	.2611	.2578	.2546	.2514	.2483	.2451
0.7	.2420	.2389	.2358	.2327	.2296	.2266	.2236	.2206	.2177	.2148
0.8	.2119	.2090	.2061	.2033	.2005	.1977	.1949	.1922	.1894	.1867
0.9	.1841	.1814	.1788	.1762	.1736	.1711	.1685	.1660	.1635	.1611
1.0	.1587	.1562	.1539	.1515	.1492	.1469	.1446	.1423	.1401	.1379
1.1	.1357	.1335	.1314	.1292	.1271	.1251	.1230	.1210	.1190	.1170
1.2	.1151	.1131	.1112	.1093	.1075	.1056	.1038	.1020	.1003	.0985
1.3	.0968	.0951	.0934	.0918	.0901	.0885	.0869	.0853	.0838	.0823
1.4	.0808	.0793	.0778	.0764	.0749	.0735	.0721	.0708	.0694	.0681
1.5	.0668	.0655	.0643	.0630	.0618	.0606	.0594	.0582	.0571	.0559
1.6	.0548	.0537	.0526	.0516	.0505	.0495	.0485	.0475	.0465	.0455
1.7	.0446	.0436	.0427	.0418	.0409	.0401	.0392	.0384	.0375	.0367
1.8	.0359	.0351	.0344	.0336	.0329	.0322	.0314	.0307	.0301	.0294
1.9	.0287	.0281	.0274	.0268	.0262	.0256	.0250	.0244	.0239	.0233
2.0	.0228	.0222	.0217	.0212	.0207	.0202	.0197	.0192	.0188	.0183
2.1	.0179	.0174	.0170	.0166	.0162	.0158	.0154	.0150	.0146	.0143
2.2	.0139	.0136	.0132	.0129	.0125	.0122	.0119	.0116	.0113	.0110
2.3	.0107	.0104	.0102	.0099	.0096	.0094	.0091	.0089	.0087	.0084
2.4	.0082	.0080	.0078	.0075	.0073	.0071	.0069	.0068	.0066	.0064
2.5	.0062	.0060	.0059	.0057	.0055	.0054	.0052	.0051	.0049	.0048
2.6	.0047	.0045	.0044	.0043	.0041	.0040	.0039	.0038	.0037	.0036
2.7	.0035	.0034	.0033	.0032	.0031	.0030	.0029	.0028	.0027	.0026
2.8	.0026	.0025	.0024	.0023	.0023	.0022	.0021	.0021	.0020	.0019
2.9	.0019	.0018	.0018	.0017	.0016	.0016	.0015	.0015	.0014	.0014
3.0	.0013	.0013	.0013	.0012	.0012	.0011	.0011	.0011	.0010	.0010

Appendix B: Table of Right-Tail Critical t Values

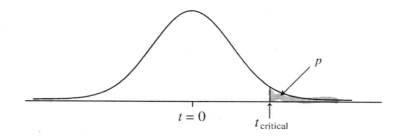

Table entries provide the values of t that cut off the upper p proportion of the t distribution from the test of the t distribution. For example, the $df = 13$ row, 0.050 shows that the proportion of area to the right of $t = 1.771$ is 0.050 when $df = 13$. In other words, 5% of the area under the $t(13)$ distribution is to the right of $t = 1.771$. Table generated with the SPSS IDF.T function.

df	p 0.250	0.100	0.050	0.025	0.010	0.005	0.0005
4	0.741	1.533	2.132	2.776	3.747	4.604	8.610
5	0.727	1.476	2.015	2.571	3.365	4.032	6.869
6	0.718	1.440	1.943	2.447	3.143	3.707	5.959
7	0.711	1.415	1.895	2.365	2.998	3.499	5.408
8	0.706	1.397	1.860	2.306	2.896	3.355	5.041
9	0.703	1.383	1.833	2.262	2.821	3.250	4.781
10	0.700	1.372	1.812	2.228	2.764	3.169	4.587
11	0.697	1.363	1.796	2.201	2.718	3.106	4.437
12	0.695	1.356	1.782	2.179	2.681	3.055	4.318
13	0.694	1.350	1.771	2.160	2.650	3.012	4.221
14	0.692	1.345	1.761	2.145	2.624	2.977	4.140
15	0.691	1.341	1.753	2.131	2.602	2.947	4.073
16	0.690	1.337	1.746	2.120	2.583	2.921	4.015
17	0.689	1.333	1.740	2.110	2.567	2.898	3.965
18	0.688	1.330	1.734	2.101	2.552	2.878	3.922
19	0.688	1.328	1.729	2.093	2.539	2.861	3.883
20	0.687	1.325	1.725	2.086	2.528	2.845	3.850
21	0.686	1.323	1.721	2.080	2.518	2.831	3.819
22	0.686	1.321	1.717	2.074	2.508	2.819	3.792
23	0.685	1.319	1.714	2.069	2.500	2.807	3.768
24	0.685	1.318	1.711	2.064	2.492	2.797	3.745
25	0.684	1.316	1.708	2.060	2.485	2.787	3.725

Table continues on the next page

Appendix B (continued)

df	0.250	0.100	0.050	0.025	0.010	0.005	0.0005
				p			
26	0.684	1.315	1.706	2.056	2.479	2.779	3.707
27	0.684	1.314	1.703	2.052	2.473	2.771	3.690
28	0.683	1.313	1.701	2.048	2.467	2.763	3.674
29	0.683	1.311	1.699	2.045	2.462	2.756	3.659
30	0.683	1.310	1.697	2.042	2.457	2.750	3.646
31	0.682	1.309	1.696	2.040	2.453	2.744	3.633
32	0.682	1.309	1.694	2.037	2.449	2.738	3.622
33	0.682	1.308	1.692	2.035	2.445	2.733	3.611
34	0.682	1.307	1.691	2.032	2.441	2.728	3.601
35	0.682	1.306	1.690	2.030	2.438	2.724	3.591
36	0.681	1.306	1.688	2.028	2.434	2.719	3.582
37	0.681	1.305	1.687	2.026	2.431	2.715	3.574
38	0.681	1.304	1.686	2.024	2.429	2.712	3.566
39	0.681	1.304	1.685	2.023	2.426	2.708	3.558
40	0.681	1.303	1.684	2.021	2.423	2.704	3.551
50	0.679	1.299	1.676	2.009	2.403	2.678	3.496
60	0.679	1.296	1.671	2.000	2.390	2.660	3.460
70	0.678	1.294	1.667	1.994	2.381	2.648	3.435
80	0.678	1.292	1.664	1.990	2.374	2.639	3.416
90	0.677	1.291	1.662	1.987	2.368	2.632	3.402
100	0.677	1.290	1.660	1.984	2.364	2.626	3.390
110	0.677	1.289	1.659	1.982	2.361	2.621	3.381
120	0.677	1.289	1.658	1.980	2.358	2.617	3.373
130	0.676	1.288	1.657	1.978	2.355	2.614	3.367
140	0.676	1.288	1.656	1.977	2.353	2.611	3.361
150	0.676	1.287	1.655	1.976	2.351	2.609	3.357
200	0.676	1.286	1.653	1.972	2.345	2.601	3.340
250	0.675	1.285	1.651	1.969	2.341	2.596	3.330
300	0.675	1.284	1.650	1.968	2.339	2.592	3.323
400	0.675	1.284	1.649	1.966	2.336	2.588	3.315
500	0.675	1.283	1.648	1.965	2.334	2.586	3.310
1000	0.675	1.282	1.646	1.962	2.330	2.581	3.300
∞	0.674	1.282	1.645	1.960	2.326	2.576	3.291

Appendix C: Table of Right-Tail Critical χ^2 Values

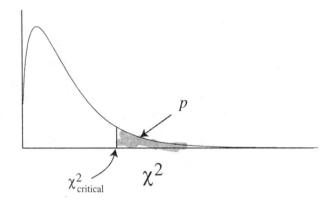

Table values are the values of χ^2 that cut off the upper p proportion of the χ^2 distribution from the rest of the distribution. For example, for the χ^2 distribution with $df = 3$, the proportion of area to the right of $\chi^2 = 7.815$ is 0.050. Table generated with the SPSS IDF.CHISQ function.

				p			
df	0.500	0.250	0.100	0.050	0.025	0.010	0.001
1	0.455	1.323	2.706	3.841	5.024	6.635	10.828
2	1.386	2.773	4.605	5.991	7.378	9.210	13.816
3	2.366	4.108	6.251	7.815	9.348	11.345	16.266
4	3.357	5.385	7.779	9.488	11.143	13.277	18.467
5	4.351	6.626	9.236	11.070	12.833	15.086	20.515
6	5.348	7.841	10.645	12.592	14.449	16.812	22.458
7	6.346	9.037	12.017	14.067	16.013	18.475	24.322
8	7.344	10.219	13.362	15.507	17.535	20.090	26.124
9	8.343	11.389	14.684	16.919	19.023	21.666	27.877
10	9.342	12.549	15.987	18.307	20.483	23.209	29.588
11	10.341	13.701	17.275	19.675	21.920	24.725	31.264
12	11.340	14.845	18.549	21.026	23.337	26.217	32.909
13	12.340	15.984	19.812	22.362	24.736	27.688	34.528
14	13.339	17.117	21.064	23.685	26.119	29.141	36.123
15	14.339	18.245	22.307	24.996	27.488	30.578	37.697
16	15.338	19.369	23.542	26.296	28.845	32.000	39.252
17	16.338	20.489	24.769	27.587	30.191	33.409	40.790
18	17.338	21.605	25.989	28.869	31.526	34.805	42.312

Appendix D1: Table of Critical F Ratios for $p \leq .05$

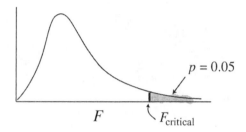

$p = 0.05$

F $F_{critical}$

Table values are the values of F that cut off the upper p proportion of the $F(df_{num}, df_{den})$ distribution from the rest of the distribution. For example, for the F distribution with $df_{num} = 3, df_{den} = 24$, the proportion of area to the right of $F = 3.009$ is 0.05. Table generated with the SPSS IDF.F function.

df_{den}	df_{num}							
	1	2	3	4	5	6	7	8
4	7.709	6.944	6.591	6.388	6.256	6.163	6.094	6.041
5	6.608	5.786	5.409	5.192	5.050	4.950	4.876	4.818
6	5.987	5.143	4.757	4.534	4.387	4.284	4.207	4.147
7	5.591	4.737	4.347	4.120	3.972	3.866	3.787	3.726
8	5.318	4.459	4.066	3.838	3.687	3.581	3.500	3.438
9	5.117	4.256	3.863	3.633	3.482	3.374	3.293	3.230
10	4.965	4.103	3.708	3.478	3.326	3.217	3.135	3.072
11	4.844	3.982	3.587	3.357	3.204	3.095	3.012	2.948
12	4.747	3.885	3.490	3.259	3.106	2.996	2.913	2.849
13	4.667	3.806	3.411	3.179	3.025	2.915	2.832	2.767
14	4.600	3.739	3.344	3.112	2.958	2.848	2.764	2.699
15	4.543	3.682	3.287	3.056	2.901	2.790	2.707	2.641
16	4.494	3.634	3.239	3.007	2.852	2.741	2.657	2.591
17	4.451	3.592	3.197	2.965	2.810	2.699	2.614	2.548
18	4.414	3.555	3.160	2.928	2.773	2.661	2.577	2.510
19	4.381	3.522	3.127	2.895	2.740	2.628	2.544	2.477
20	4.351	3.493	3.098	2.866	2.711	2.599	2.514	2.447
21	4.325	3.467	3.072	2.840	2.685	2.573	2.488	2.420
22	4.301	3.443	3.049	2.817	2.661	2.549	2.464	2.397
23	4.279	3.422	3.028	2.796	2.640	2.528	2.442	2.375
24	4.260	3.403	3.009	2.776	2.621	2.508	2.423	2.355
25	4.242	3.385	2.991	2.759	2.603	2.490	2.405	2.337

Table continues on the next page

Appendix D1 (continued)

df_{den}	df_{num}							
	1	2	3	4	5	6	7	8
26	4.225	3.369	2.975	2.743	2.587	2.474	2.388	2.321
27	4.210	3.354	2.960	2.728	2.572	2.459	2.373	2.305
28	4.196	3.340	2.947	2.714	2.558	2.445	2.359	2.291
29	4.183	3.328	2.934	2.701	2.545	2.432	2.346	2.278
30	4.171	3.316	2.922	2.690	2.534	2.421	2.334	2.266
31	4.160	3.305	2.911	2.679	2.523	2.409	2.323	2.255
32	4.149	3.295	2.901	2.668	2.512	2.399	2.313	2.244
33	4.139	3.285	2.892	2.659	2.503	2.389	2.303	2.235
34	4.130	3.276	2.883	2.650	2.494	2.380	2.294	2.225
35	4.121	3.267	2.874	2.641	2.485	2.372	2.285	2.217
36	4.113	3.259	2.866	2.634	2.477	2.364	2.277	2.209
37	4.105	3.252	2.859	2.626	2.470	2.356	2.270	2.201
38	4.098	3.245	2.852	2.619	2.463	2.349	2.262	2.194
39	4.091	3.238	2.845	2.612	2.456	2.342	2.255	2.187
40	4.085	3.232	2.839	2.606	2.449	2.336	2.249	2.180
50	4.034	3.183	2.790	2.557	2.400	2.286	2.199	2.130
60	4.001	3.150	2.758	2.525	2.368	2.254	2.167	2.097
70	3.978	3.128	2.736	2.503	2.346	2.231	2.143	2.074
80	3.960	3.111	2.719	2.486	2.329	2.214	2.126	2.056
90	3.947	3.098	2.706	2.473	2.316	2.201	2.113	2.043
100	3.936	3.087	2.696	2.463	2.305	2.191	2.103	2.032
110	3.927	3.079	2.687	2.454	2.297	2.182	2.094	2.024
120	3.920	3.072	2.680	2.447	2.290	2.175	2.087	2.016
130	3.914	3.066	2.674	2.441	2.284	2.169	2.081	2.010
140	3.909	3.061	2.669	2.436	2.279	2.164	2.076	2.005
150	3.904	3.056	2.665	2.432	2.274	2.160	2.071	2.001
200	3.888	3.041	2.650	2.417	2.259	2.144	2.056	1.985
250	3.879	3.032	2.641	2.408	2.250	2.135	2.046	1.976
300	3.873	3.026	2.635	2.402	2.244	2.129	2.040	1.969
400	3.865	3.018	2.627	2.394	2.237	2.121	2.032	1.962
500	3.860	3.014	2.623	2.390	2.232	2.117	2.028	1.957
1000	3.851	3.005	2.614	2.381	2.223	2.108	2.019	1.948
∞	3.841	2.996	2.605	2.372	2.214	2.099	2.010	1.938

Appendix D2: Table of Critical F Ratios for $p \leq .01$

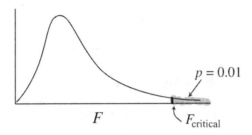

Table values are the values of F that cut off the upper p proportion of the $F(df_{num}, df_{den})$ distribution from the rest of the distribution. For example, for the F distribution with $df_{num} = 3, df_{den} = 24$, the proportion of area to the right of $F = 4.718$ is 0.01. Table generated with the SPSS IDF.F function.

df_{den}	1	2	3	4	5	6	7	8
4	21.198	18.000	16.694	15.977	15.522	15.207	14.976	14.799
5	16.258	13.274	12.060	11.392	10.967	10.672	10.456	10.289
6	13.745	10.925	9.780	9.148	8.746	8.466	8.260	8.102
7	12.246	9.547	8.451	7.847	7.460	7.191	6.993	6.840
8	11.259	8.649	7.591	7.006	6.632	6.371	6.178	6.029
9	10.561	8.022	6.992	6.422	6.057	5.802	5.613	5.467
10	10.044	7.559	6.552	5.994	5.636	5.386	5.200	5.057
11	9.646	7.206	6.217	5.668	5.316	5.069	4.886	4.744
12	9.330	6.927	5.953	5.412	5.064	4.821	4.640	4.499
13	9.074	6.701	5.739	5.205	4.862	4.620	4.441	4.302
14	8.862	6.515	5.564	5.035	4.695	4.456	4.278	4.140
15	8.683	6.359	5.417	4.893	4.556	4.318	4.142	4.004
16	8.531	6.226	5.292	4.773	4.437	4.202	4.026	3.890
17	8.400	6.112	5.185	4.669	4.336	4.102	3.927	3.791
18	8.285	6.013	5.092	4.579	4.248	4.015	3.841	3.705
19	8.185	5.926	5.010	4.500	4.171	3.939	3.765	3.631
20	8.096	5.849	4.938	4.431	4.103	3.871	3.699	3.564
21	8.017	5.780	4.874	4.369	4.042	3.812	3.640	3.506
22	7.945	5.719	4.817	4.313	3.988	3.758	3.587	3.453
23	7.881	5.664	4.765	4.264	3.939	3.710	3.539	3.406
24	7.823	5.614	4.718	4.218	3.895	3.667	3.496	3.363
25	7.770	5.568	4.675	4.177	3.855	3.627	3.457	3.324

Table continues on the next page

Appendix D2 (continued)

df_{den}	df_{num}							
	1	2	3	4	5	6	7	8
26	7.721	5.526	4.637	4.140	3.818	3.591	3.421	3.288
27	7.677	5.488	4.601	4.106	3.785	3.558	3.388	3.256
28	7.636	5.453	4.568	4.074	3.754	3.528	3.358	3.226
29	7.598	5.420	4.538	4.045	3.725	3.499	3.330	3.198
30	7.562	5.390	4.510	4.018	3.699	3.473	3.304	3.173
31	7.530	5.362	4.484	3.993	3.675	3.449	3.281	3.149
32	7.499	5.336	4.459	3.969	3.652	3.427	3.258	3.127
33	7.471	5.312	4.437	3.948	3.630	3.406	3.238	3.106
34	7.444	5.289	4.416	3.927	3.611	3.386	3.218	3.087
35	7.419	5.268	4.396	3.908	3.592	3.368	3.200	3.069
36	7.396	5.248	4.377	3.890	3.574	3.351	3.183	3.052
37	7.373	5.229	4.360	3.873	3.558	3.334	3.167	3.036
38	7.353	5.211	4.343	3.858	3.542	3.319	3.152	3.021
39	7.333	5.194	4.327	3.843	3.528	3.305	3.137	3.006
40	7.314	5.179	4.313	3.828	3.514	3.291	3.124	2.993
50	7.171	5.057	4.199	3.720	3.408	3.186	3.020	2.890
60	7.077	4.977	4.126	3.649	3.339	3.119	2.953	2.823
70	7.011	4.922	4.074	3.600	3.291	3.071	2.906	2.777
80	6.963	4.881	4.036	3.563	3.255	3.036	2.871	2.742
90	6.925	4.849	4.007	3.535	3.228	3.009	2.845	2.715
100	6.895	4.824	3.984	3.513	3.206	2.988	2.823	2.694
110	6.871	4.803	3.965	3.495	3.188	2.970	2.806	2.677
120	6.851	4.787	3.949	3.480	3.174	2.956	2.792	2.663
130	6.834	4.772	3.936	3.467	3.161	2.944	2.780	2.651
140	6.819	4.760	3.925	3.456	3.151	2.933	2.769	2.641
150	6.807	4.749	3.915	3.447	3.142	2.924	2.761	2.632
200	6.763	4.713	3.881	3.414	3.110	2.893	2.730	2.601
250	6.737	4.691	3.861	3.395	3.091	2.875	2.711	2.583
300	6.720	4.677	3.848	3.382	3.079	2.862	2.699	2.571
400	6.699	4.659	3.831	3.366	3.063	2.847	2.684	2.556
500	6.686	4.648	3.821	3.357	3.054	2.838	2.675	2.547
1000	6.660	4.626	3.801	3.338	3.036	2.820	2.657	2.529
∞	6.635	4.605	3.782	3.319	3.017	2.802	2.639	2.511

REFERENCES

Abeles, N., Iscoe, I., & Brown, W. F. (1954-1955). Some factors influencing the random sampling of college students. *Public Opinion Quarterly, 18*, 419–423.

Abelson, R. P. (1995). *Statistics as principled argument.* Mahwah, NJ: Erlbaum.

Abelson, R. P. (1997). On the surprising longevity of flogged horses: Why there is a case for the significance test. *Psychological Science, 8*, 12–15.

Agresti, A. (1990). *Categorical data analysis.* New York: Wiley.

Agresti, A., & Finlay, B. (1997). *Statistical methods for the social sciences* (3rd Ed.). Upper Saddle River, NJ: Prentice-Hall.

Aiken, L. S., & West, S. G. (1991). *Multiple regression: testing and interpreting interactions.* Newbury Park, CA: Sage.

Albarracin, D., & Kumkale, G. T. (2003). Affect as information in persuasion: A model of affect identification and discounting. *Journal of Personality and Social Psychology, 84*, 453–469.

Allison, P. D. (2002). *Missing data.* Thousand Oaks, CA: Sage.

Amir, Y., & Sharon, I. (1991). Replication research: A "must" for the scientific advancement of psychology. In J. W. Neuliep (Ed.), *Replication research in the social sciences* (pp. 51–70). Newbury Park, CA: Sage.

Anderson, C. A., Berkowitz, L., Donnerstein, E., Huesmann, L. R., Johnson, J. D., Linz, D., Malamuth, N. M., & Wartella, E. (2003). The influence of media violence on youth. *Psychological Science, Supp S*, 81–110.

Anderson, C. A., & Bushman, B. J. (2002). The effects of media violence on society. *Science, 295*, 2377–2379.

Aquinis, H. (2002). *Regression analysis for categorical moderators.* New York: Guilford Press.

Armstrong, G. B., & Chung, L. (2000). Background television and reading memory in context. *Communication Research, 27*, 327–352.

Aronson, E. (1977). Research in social psychology as a leap of faith. *Personality and Social Psychology Bulletin, 3*, 190–195.

Azen, R., & Budescu, D. V. (2003). The dominance analysis approach for comparing predictors in multiple regression. *Psychological Methods, 8*, 129–148.

Bakan, D. (1966). The test of significance in psychological research. *Psychological Bulletin, 66*, 423–437.

Baker, B. O., Hardyck, C. D., & Petrinovich, L. F. (1966). Weak measurements vs. strong statistics: An empirical critique of S. S. Stevens' proscriptions on statistics. *Educational and Psychological Measurement, 26*, 291–309.

Baker, F. B., & Collier, R. O. (1996). Some empirical results on variance ratios under permutation in the completely randomized design. *Journal of the American Statistical Association, 61*, 813–820.

Baldassare, M., & Katz, C. (1989). Who will talk to reporters? Bias in survey reinterviews. *Journalism Quarterly, 66*, 907–912.

Barnes, J. A., & Hayes, A. F. (1995). Integration of the language arts and teacher training: An examination of speech communication instruction in California high schools. *Communication Education, 44*, 307–320.

Baron, R. M., & Kenny, D. A. (1986). The moderator-mediator variable distinction in social psychological research: Conceptual, strategic, and statistical considerations. *Journal of Personality and Social Psychology, 51*, 1173–1182.

Baxter, L. A., & Babbie, E. (2004). *The basics of communication research*. Belmont, CA: Wadsworth.

Beatty, M. J. (2002). Do we know a vector from a scalar? Why measures of association (not their squares) are appropriate indices of effect. *Human Communication Research, 28*, 605–611.

Benoit, W. L., McKinney, M. S., & Stephenson, M. T. (2002). Effects of watching primary debates in the 2000 U.S. Presidential campaign. *Journal of Communication, 52*, 316–331.

Bearden, W. (1998). *Handbook of marketing scales*. Thousand Oaks, CA: Sage.

Beck, N. (2001). Time series-cross-section data: What have we learned in the past few years? *Annual Review of Political Science, 4*, 271–293.

Berger, C. R. (2000). Quantitative depictions of threating phenomena in new reports: The scary world of frequency data. *Human Communication Research, 26*, 27–52.

Bissonnette, V., Ickes, W., Berstein, I., & Knowles, E. (1990). Personality moderating variables: A warning about statistical artifact and a comparison of analytic techniques. *Journal of Personality, 58*, 567–587.

Blalock, H. M. (1967). Causal inferences, closed populations, and measures of association. *American Political Science Review, 61*, 130–136.

Boneau, C. A. (1960). The effects of violations of assumptions underlying the *t* test. *Psychological Bulletin, 57*, 49–64.

Borooah, K. V. (2002). *Logit and probit: Ordered and multinomial models.* Thousand Oaks, CA: Sage.

Bradley, J. V. (1977). A common situation conducive to bizarre distribution shapes. *American Statistician, 31*, 147–150.

Brennan, R. L., & Prediger, D. J. (1981). Coefficient kappa: Some uses, misuses, and alternatives. *Educational and Psychological Measurement, 41*, 687–699.

Breusch, T. S., & Pagan, A. R. (1979). A simple test for heteroscedasticity and random coefficient variation. *Econometrica, 47*, 1287–1294.

Brown, M. B., & Forsythe, A. B. (1974). Robust tests for the equality of variances. *Journal of the American Statistical Association, 69*, 364–367.

Bruschke, J., & Loges, W. E. (1999). Relationship between pretrial publicity and trial outcomes. *Journal of Communication, 49*, 104–120.

Budescu, D. V. (1993). Dominance analysis: A new approach to the problem of relative importance of predictors in multiple regression. *Psychological Bulletin, 114*, 542–551.

Byrne, D. (1971). *The attraction paradigm.* New York: Academic Press.

Campbell, D. T., & Stanley, J. C. (1963). *Experimental and quasi-experimental designs for research.* Boston, MA: Houghton-Mifflin.

Carmer, S. G., & Swanson, M. R. (1973). An evaluation of ten pairwise multiple comparison procedures by Monte Carlo methods. *Journal of the American Statistical Association, 68*, 66–74.

Carroll, R. J., & Ruppert, D. (1988). *Transformation and weighting in regression.* New York: Chapman and Hall.

Cegala, D. J. (1981). Interaction involvement: A cognitive dimension of communicative competence. *Communication Education, 30*, 109–121.

Chaffee, S. H., & Berger, C. R. (1987). What communication scientists do. In C. Berger & S. H. Chaffee (Eds.), *Handbook of communication science.* Newbury Park, CA: Sage.

Cheek, J. M., & Buss, A. H. (1981). Shyness and sociability. *Journal of Personality and Social Psychology, 41*, 330–339.

Ching, P., Willett, W. C., Rimm, E. B., Colditz, G. A., Gortmaker, S. L., & Stampfer, M. J. (1996). Activity level and risk of overweight in male health professionals. *American Journal of Public Health, 86*, 25–30.

Cohen, J. (1960). A coefficient of agreement for nominal scales. *Educational and Psychological Measurement, 20*, 37–46.

Cohen, J. (1968). Multiple regression as a general data-analytic system. *Psychological Bulletin, 70*, 426–443.

Cohen, J. (1973). Eta-squared and partial eta-squared in fixed factor ANOVA designs. *Educational and Psychological Measurement, 33*, 107–112.

Cohen, J. (1978). Partialed products are interactions; partialed products are curve components. *Psychological Bulletin, 85*, 858–866.

Cohen, J. (1983). The cost of dichtomization. *Applied Psychological Measurement, 7*, 249–253.

Cohen, J. (1990). *Statistical power analysis for the behavioral sciences*. Mahwah, NJ: Lawrenece Erlbaum Associates.

Cohen, J. (1994). The earth is round: ($p < .05$). *American Psychologist, 49*, 997–1003.

Cohen, J., Cohen, P., West, S. G., & Aiken, S. L. (2003). *Applied multiple regression/correlation for the behavioral sciences* (3rd ed.). Mahwah, NJ: Lawrence Erlbaum Associated.

Comstock, J., Rowell, E., & Bowers, J. W. (1995). Food for thought: Teacher nonverbal immediacy, student learning, and curvilinearity. *Communication Education, 44*, 251–266.

Conover, W. J., Johnson, M. E., & Johnson, M. E. (1981). A comparative study of tests for homogeneity of variances, with applications to the outer continental shelf bidding data. *Technometrics, 23*, 351–361.

Cox, D. R., & McCullagh, P. (1982). Some aspects of analysis of covariance. *Biometrics, 38*, 541-554.

Cronbach, L. J. (1951). Coefficient alpha and the internal structure of tests. *Psychometrika, 16*, 297–334.

Cronbach, L. J. (1987). Statistical tests for moderator variables: Flaws in analyses recently proposed. *Psychological Bulletin, 102*, 414–417.

Cronbach, L. J., & Meehl, P. E. (1955). Construct validity in psychological tests. *Psychological Bulletin, 52*, 281–302.

Darlington, R. B. (1968). Multiple regression in psychological research and practice. *Psychological Bulletin, 69*, 161–182.

Darlington, R. B. (1970). Is kurtosis really "peakedness?" *The American Statistician, 24(2)*, 19–22.

Darlington, R. B. (1990). *Regression and linear models*. New York: McGraw-Hill.

Davis, J. A. (1985). *The logic of causal order*. Newbury Park, CA: Sage.

Delli Carpini, M. X., & Keeter, S. (1993). Measuring political knowledge: Putting first things first. *American Journal of Political Science, 37*, 1179–1206.

Delli Carpini, M. X., & Keeter, S. (1996). *What Americans know about politics and why it matters*. New Haven, CT: Yale.

Denham, B. E. (2002). Advanced categorical statistics: Issues and applications in communication research. *Journal of Communication, 52*, 162–176.

Dixon, T. L., & Linz, D. (2000). Race and the mispresentation of victimization on local television news. *Communication Research, 27,* 547–573.

Dunlap, W. P., & Kemery, E. R. (1987). Failure to detect moderating effects: Is multicollinearity the problem? *Psychological Bulletin, 102,* 418–420.

Edgell, S. E., & Noon, S. M. (1984). Effects of violation of normality on the *t* test of the correlation coefficient. *Psychological Bulletin, 95,* 576–583.

Edgington, E. E. (1995). *Randomization tests.* New York: Dekker.

Edison Media Research & Mitofsky International (2005). *Evaluation of Edison/Mitofsky election system 2004.* Downloaded on January 22, 2005 from http://www.exit-poll.net (direct URL: http://www.exit-poll.net/election-night/EvaluationJan192005.pdf)

Efron, B., & Tibshirani, R. J. (1998). *An introduction to the bootstrap.* Boca Raton, FL: Chapman-Hall.

Embretson, S. E. (1996). The new rules of measurement. *Psychological Assessment, 8,* 341–349.

Embretson, S. E., & Reise, S. P. (2000). *Item response theory for psychologists.* Mahwah, NJ: Lawrence Erlbaum Associates.

Eveland, W. P. (1997). Interactions and nonlinearity in mass communication: Connecting theory and methodology. *Journalism and Mass Communication Quarterly, 74,* 400–416.

Eveland, W. P., & Scheufele, D. A. (2000). Connecting news media use with gaps in knowledge and participation. *Political Communication, 17,* 215–237.

Everitt, B. S. (1977). *The analysis of contingency tables.* London: Chapman & Hall.

Fisher, R. A. (1935). *The design of experiments.* London: Oliver & Boyd.

Fisher, R. A. (1966). *The design of experiments.* New York: Hafner.

Ford, L. A., & Ellis, B. H. (1998). A preliminary analysis of memorable support and nonsupport messages received by nurses in acute care settings. *Health Communication, 10,* 37-68.

Fowler, F. J. (2001). *Survey research methods* (3rd Ed.). Thousand Oaks, CA: Sage.

Fox, J. (1991). *Regression diagnostics.* Newbury Park, CA: Sage.

Frey, L. R., Kreps, G. L., & Botan, C. H. (1999). *Investigating communication: An introduction to research methods* (2nd ed). Boston: Allyn-Bacon.

Frick, R. W. (1998). Interpreting statistical testing: Process and propensity, not population and random sampling. *Behavior Research Methods, Instruments, and Computers, 30,* 527–535.

Games, P. A., & Howell, J. F. (1976). Pairwise multiple comparison procedures with unequal *N*'s and/or unequal variances: A Monte Carlo study. *Journal of Educational Statistics, 1,* 113–125.

Games, P. A., Keselman, H. J., & Rogan, J. C. (1981). Simultaneous pairwise multiple comparison procedures for means when sample sizes are unequal. *Psychological Bulletin, 90*, 594–598.

Gans, D. J. (1981). Use of a preliminary test in comparing two sample means. *Communications in statistics—Simulation and computation, 10*, 163–174.

Gant, C., & Dimmick, J. (2000). Making local news: A holistic analysis of sources, selection criteria, and topics. *Journalism and Mass Communication Quarterly, 77*, 628–638.

Gardner, W., Mulvey, E. P., & Shaw, E. C. (1995). Regression analyses of counts and rates: Poisson, overdispersed Poisson, and negative binomial models. *Psychological Bulletin, 118*, 392–404.

Gerbner, G., Gross, L., Morgan, M., & Signorielli, N. (1986). Living with television: The dynamics of the cultivation process. In J. Bryant & D. Zillman (Eds.), *Perspectives on media effects*. Hillsdale, NJ: Lawrence Erlbaum Associates.

Giles, H., Mulac, A., Bradac, J. J., & Johnson, P. (1987). Speech accommodation theory: The first decade and beyond. In M. L. Laughlin (Ed.), *Communication Yearbook, 10* (pp. 13–48). Newbury Park: Sage.

Gilovich, T. D. (1991). *How we know what isn't so: The fallibility of human reason in everyday life*. New York: Free Press.

Green, S. B. (1991). How many subjects does it take to do a regression analysis? *Multivariate Behavioral Research, 3*, 499–510.

Griffin, D., Gonzales, R. (1995). Correlational analysis of dyad-level data in the exchangeable case. *Psychological Bulletin, 118*, 430–439.

Goodman, L. A., & Kruskal, W. H. (1979). *Measures of association for cross classifications*. New York: Springer-Verlag.

Goertzel, T. (2002). Myths of murder and multiple regression. *The Skeptical Inquirer, 26*, 19–23.

Guttman, L. (1945). A basis for analyzing test-retest reliability. *Psychometrika, 10*, 255–282.

Hagan, R. L. (1997). In praise of the null hypothesis statistical test. *American Psychologist, 52*, 15-24.

Hamilton, D. (1987). Sometimes $R^2 > r^2_{yx_1} + r^2_{yx_2}$: Correlated variables are not always redundant. *The American Statistician, 41*, 129–131.

Hayes, A. F. (1996). The permutation test is not distribution-free: Testing $H_0 : \rho = 0$. *Psychological Methods, 1*, 184–196.

Hayes, A. F. (1998). SPSS procedures for approximate randomization tests. *Behavior Research Methods, Instruments, and Computers, 30*, 536–543.

Hayes, A. F., & Cai, L. (in press). Further evaluating the conditional decision rule for comparing two group means. *British Journal of Mathematical and Statistical Psychology*.

Hayes, A. F., Glynn, C. J., & Shahanan, J. (in press a). Willingness to self-censor: A construct and measurement tool for public opinion research. *International Journal of Public Opinion Research.*

Hayes, A. F., Glynn, C. J., & Shahanan, J. (in press b). Validating the willingness to self-censor scale: Individual differences in the effect of the climate of opinion expression. *International Journal of Public Opinion Research.*

Hendrick, C. (1991). Replications, strict replications, and conceptual replications: Are they important? In J. W. Neuliep (Ed.), *Replication research in the social sciences* (pp. 41–50). Newbury Park, CA: Sage.

Hertel, B. R. (1976). Minimizing error variance introduced by missing data routines in survey analysis. *Sociological Methods and Research, 4,* 459–474.

Hirsch, P. (1980). The "scary world" of the nonviewer and other anomalies: A reanalysis of Gerbner et al.'s findings on cultivation analysis. *Communication Research, 7,* 403–456.

Hoeffding, W. (1952). The large-sample power of tests based on permutations of observations. *Annals of Mathematical Statistics, 23,* 169–192.

Hoffner, C., Buchanan, M., Anderson, J. D., Hubbs, L. A., Kamigaki, S. K., Kowalcyzk, L., Pastorek, A., Plotkin, R. S., & Silberg, K. J. (1999). Support for censorship of television violence: The role of the third-person effect and news exposure. *Communication Research, 26,* 726–742.

Holbert, R. L., & Stephenson, M. T. (2003). The importance of indirect effects in media effects research: Testing for mediation in structural equation modeling. *Journal of Broadcasting and Electronic Media, 47,* 556–572.

Holm, S. (1979). A simple sequentially rejective multiple test procedure. *Scandanavian Journal of Statistics, 6,* 65–70.

Holsti, O. R. (1969). *Content analysis for the social sciences and humanities.* Reading MA: Addison-Wesley.

Hosmer, D. W., & Lemeshow, S. (2000). *Applied logistic regression* (2nd ed). New York: Wiley

Howell, D. C. (1997). *Statistical methods for psychology* (4th ed). New York: Duxbury.

Hunter, J. E. (1997). Needed: A ban of the significance test. *Psychological Science, 8,* 3–7.

Hunter, J. E., & Hamilton, M. A. (2002). The advantages of using standardized scores in causal analysis. *Human Communication Research, 28,* 552–561.

Hunter, J. E., & Schmidt, F. L. (1990). Dichtomization of continuous variables: The implications for meta-analysis. *Journal of Applied Psychology, 75,* 334–349.

Infante, D. A., & Rancer, A. S. (1992). A conceptualization and measure of argumentativeness. *Journal of Personality Assessment, 46,* 72–80

Irwin, J. R., & McClelland, G. H. (2001). Misleading heuristics and moderated multiple regression models. *Journal of Marketing Research, 38*, 100–109.

Irwin, J. R., & McClelland, G. H. (2003). Negative consequences of dichotomizing continuous predictor variables. *Journal of Marketing Research, 40*, 366–371.

Jaccard, J., Becker, M. A., & Wood, G. (1984). Pairwise multiple comparison procedures: A review. *Psychological Bulletin, 96*, 589–596.

Jaccard, J., Turrisi, R., & Wan, C. K. (1990). *Interaction effects in multiple regression*. Newbury Park, CA: Sage.

Jackson, J. M., Procidano, M. E., & Cohen, C. J. (1989). Subject pool sign-up procedures: A threat to external validity? *Social Behavior and Personality, 17*, 29–43.

Johnson, A., & Kaid, L. L. (2002). Image ads and issue ads in U.S. Presidential advertising: Using videostyle to explore stylistic differences in televised political ads from 1952 to 2000. *Journal of Communication, 52*, 281–300.

Kennedy, P. E. (1995). Randomization tests in econometrics. *Journal of Business and Economic Statistics, 13*, 85–94.

Kenny, D. A., & Judd, C. M. (1986). Consequences of violating the independence assumption in analysis of variance. *Psychological Bulletin, 99*, 422–431.

Kenny, D. A., Mannietti, L., Pierro, A., Livi, S., & Kashy, D. A. (2002). The statistical analysis of data from small groups. *Journal of Personality and Social Psychology, 83*, 126–137.

Keppel, G. (1991). *Design and analysis: A researcher's handbook* (3rd ed.). Englewood Cliffs, NJ: Prentice Hall.

Keppel, G., & Zedeck, S. (1989). *Data analysis for research designs: Analysis of variance and multiple regression/correlation approaches*. New York: Freeman.

Kim, J. O., & Ferree, G. D. (1981). Standardization in causal analysis. *Sociological Methods and Research, 10*, 187–210.

Kim, J. O., Mueller, C. W. (1976). Standardized and unstandardized coefficients in causal analysis: An expository note. *Sociological Methods and Research, 4*, 428–438.

Kincaid, D. L. (2000). Mass media, ideation, and behavior: A longitudinal analysis of contraceptive change in the Philippines. *Communication Research, 27*, 723–763.

Klockars, A. J., & Sax, G. (1986). *Multiple comparisons*. Thousand Oaks, CA: Sage.

Koehler, K. J., & Larntz, K. (1980). An empirical investigation of goodness-of-fit statistics for sparse multinomials. *Journal of the American Statistical Association, 75*, 336–344.

Kowalski, C. J. (1972). On the effects of nonnormality on the distribution of the sample product-moment correlation coefficient. *Applied Statistics, 21*, 1–12.

Krippendorff, K. (2003). *Content analysis: An introduction to its methodology*. Thousand Oaks, CA: Sage.

Krippendorff, K. (2004). Reliability in content analysis: Some common misconceptions and recommendations. *Human Communication Research, 30*, 411–433.

Kromrey, J. D., & Foster-Johnson, L. (1998). Mean centering in moderated multiple regression: Much ado about nothing. *Educational and Psychological Measurement, 58*, 42–67.

Kuder, G. F., & Richardson, M. W. (1937). The theory of the estimation of test reliability. *Psychometrika, 2*, 151–160.

Kwak, N. (1999). Revisiting the knowledge gap hypothesis: Education, motivation, and media use. *Communication Research, 26*, 385–413.

Lang, A. (1996). The logic of using inferential statistics with experimental data from nonprobability samples. *Journal of Broadcasting and Electronic Media, 40*, 422–430.

Lehmann, E. L. (1975). *Nonparametrics: Statistical methods based on ranks.* San Francisco, CA: Holden-Day

Levene, H. (1960). Robust tests for the equality of variance. In L. Olkin (Ed.), *Contributions to probability and statistics.* Palo Alto, CA: Stanford University Press.

Leventhal, L., & Huynh, C. (1996). Directional decisions for two-tailed tests: Power, error rates, and sample size. *Psychological Methods, 1*, 278–292.

Levine, T. R., & Hullet, C. R. (2002). Eta-squared, partial eta-squared, and misreporting of effect size in communication research. *Human Communication Research, 28*, 612–625.

Liao, T. F. (1994). *Interpreting probability models: Logit, probit, and other generalized linear models.* Thousand Oaks, CA: Sage.

Liebert, R. M., & Liebert, L. L. (1995). *Science and behavior: An introduction to psychological research methods* (4th ed.). Englewood Cliffs, NJ: Prentice-Hall.

Liebertrau, A. M. (1983). *Measures of association.* Beverly Hills, CA: Sage.

Linn, R. L., & Werts, C. E. (1969). Assumptions in making causal inferences from part correlations, partial correlations, and partial regression coefficients. *Psychological Bulletin, 72*, 307–310.

Littlejohn, S. W. (2001). *Theories of human communication* (7th ed.). Belmont, CA: Wadsworth.

Lombard, M., Snyder-Duch, J., Bracken, C. C. (2002). Content analysis in mass communication: Assessing and reporting intercoder reliability. *Human Communication Research, 28*, 507–604.

Long, J. S. (1997). *Regression models for categorical and limited dependent variables.* Thousand Oaks, CA: Sage.

Long, J. S., & Erwin, L. H. (2000). Using heteroscedasticity-consistent standard errors in the linear regression model. *The American Statistician, 54*, 217–224.

Lord, F. M. & Novick, M. R. (1968). *Statistical theories of mental test scores.* Reading MA: Addison-Welsley.

Luke, D. A. (2004). *Multilevel modeling.* Thousand Oaks, CA: Sage.

Lunneborg, C. E. (2000). *Data analysis by resampling: Concepts and applications.* Pacific Grove, CA: Duxbury.

MacCallum, R. C. (2003). Working with imperfect models. *Multivariate Behavioral Research, 38,* 113–139.

MacCallum, R. C., Zhang, S., Preacher, K. J., & Rucker, D. D. (2002). On the practice of dichtomization of quantitative variables. *Psychological Methods, 7,* 19–40.

MacKinnon, D. P., Lockwood, C. M., Hoffman, J. M., West, S. G., & Sheets, V. (2002). A comparison of methods to test mediation and other intervening variable effects. *Psychological Methods, 7,* 83–104.

Manusov, V. L. (2005). *Sourcebook of nonverbal measures.* Mahwah, NJ: Erlbaum.

Maxwell, S. E., Camp, C. J., & Arvey, R. D. (1981). Measures of strength of association: A comparative examination. *Journal of Applied Psychology, 66,* 525–534.

Maxwell, S. E., & Delaney, H. D. (1993). Bivarate median splits and spurious statistical significance. *Psychological Bulletin, 113,* 181–190.

McLeod, D. M., & Perse, E. M. (1994). Direct and indirect effects of socioeconomic status on public affairs knowledge. *Journalism Quarterly, 71,* 433–442.

McFleur, M. L., & Ball-Rokeach, S. (1989). *Theories of mass communication* (5th Ed.). New York: Longman.

Menard, S. (2001). *Applied logistic regression analysis* (2nd ed.). Thousand Oaks, CA: Sage.

Meng, X., Rosenthal, R., & Rubin, D. B. (1992). Comparing correlated correlations. *Psychological Bulletin, 111,* 172–175.

Merton, R. K., Reader, G. G., & Kendall, P. L. (1957). *The student physician: Introductory studies in the sociology of medical education.* Cambridge, MA: Harvard University.

Micceri, T. (1989). The unicorn, the normal curve, and other improbable creatures. *Psychological Bulletin, 105,* 156–166.

Mielke, P. W., & Berry, K. J. (1994). Permutation tests for common locations among samples with unequal variances. *Journal of Educational and Behavioral Statistics, 19,* 217–236.

Monahan, J. L., & Lannutti, P. J. (2000). Alcohol as a social lubricant: Alcohol myopia theory, social self-esteem, and social interaction. *Human Communication Research, 26,* 175–202.

Mondak, J. J. (1999). Reconsidering the measurement of political knowledge. *Political Analysis, 8,* 57–82.

Mook, D. G. (1983). In defense of external invalidity. *American Psychologist, 38*, 379–387.

Mooney, C. Z., & Duvall, R. D. (1993). *Bootstrapping: A nonparametric approach to statistical inference.* Thousand Oaks, CA: Sage.

Moors, J. J. A. (1986). The meaning of kurtosis revisited: Darlington reexamined. *The American Statistician, 40*, 283–284.

Morrison, D. E., & Henkel, R. E. (1969). Significance tests reconsidered. *American Sociologist, 4*, 131–140.

Moser, B. K., & Stevens, G. R. (1992). Homogeneity of variance in the two-sample means test. *American Statistician, 46*, 19–21.

Moser, B. K., Stevens, G. R., & Watts, C. L. (1989). The two-sample t test versus Satterthwaite's approximate F test. *Communications in Statistics—Theory and Methods, 18*, 3963–3975.

Murphy, B. P. (1976). Comparison of some two sample means tests by simulation. *Communication in Statistics-Simulation and Computation, B5*, 23–32.

National Institutes for Health (1998). *Clinical guidelines on the identification, evaluation, and treatment of overweight and obesity in adults.* NIH Publication 98–4083

Neuendorf, K. (2001). *The content analysis guidebook.* Thousand Oaks, CA: Sage.

Newsom, J. T., Prigerson, H. G., Schultz, R., & Reynolds, C. F. (2003). Investigating moderator hypotheses in aging research: Statistical, methodological, and conceptual difficulties with comparing separate regressions. *International Journal of Aging and Human Development, 57*, 119–150.

Noelle-Neumann, E. (1993). *The spiral of silence: Public opinion—Our social skin* (2nd ed.). Chicago, IL: University of Chicago Press.

Nunnally, J. C. (1978). *Psychometric theory.* New York: McGraw-Hill.

O'Connor, B. P. (2004). SPSS and SAS programs for addressing interdependence and basic levels-of-analysis issues in psychological data. *Behavior Research Methods, Instruments, and Computers, 36*, 17–28.

Pampel, F. C. (2000). *Logistic regression: A primer.* Thousand Oaks, CA: Sage.

Perreault, W. D., & Leigh, L. E. (1989). Reliability of nominal data based on qualitative judgments. *Journal of Marketing Research, 26*, 135–148.

Petty, R. E., & Cacioppo, J. T. (1986). The elaboration likelihood model of persuasion. In L. Berkowitz (Ed.), *Advances in experimental social psychology, 19*, 123–199.

Pfanzagl, J. (1974). On the Behrens-Fisher problem. *Biometrika, 61*, 39–47.

Picard, R. G. (1998). A note on the relations between circulation size and newspaper advertising rates. *Journal of Media Economics, 11*, 47–55.

Potter, W. J., Cooper, R., & Dupagne, M. (1993). The three paradigms of mass media research in mainstream communication journals. *Communication Theory, 3*, 317–335.

Potter, W. J., & Levine-Donnerstein, D. (1999). Rethinking validity and reliability in content analysis. *Journal of Applied Communication Research, 27*, 258–284.

Preacher, K. J., & Hayes, A. F. (2004). SPSS and SAS procedures for estimating indirect effects in simple mediation models. *Behavior Research Methods, Instruments, and Computers, 36*, 717–731.

Press, S. J., & Wilson, S. (1978). Choosing between logistic regression and discriminant analysis. *Journal of the American Statistical Association, 73*, 699–705.

Raghunathan, T. E., Rosenthal, R., & Rubin, D. B. (1996). Comparing correlated but nonoverlapping correlations. *Psychological Methods, 1*, 178–183.

Rasmussen, J. L. (1989). Computer-intensive correlation analysis: Bootstrap and approximate randomization techniques. *British Journal of Mathematical and Statistical Psychology, 42*, 103–111.

Ratcliff, R. (1993). Methods for dealing with reaction time outliers. *Psychological Bulletin, 114*, 510–532.

Reichardt, C. S., & Gollub, H. F. (1999). Justifying the use and increasing the power of a *t* test for a randomized experiment with a convenience sample. *Psychological Methods, 4*, 117–128.

Richardson, J. T. E. (1996). Measures of effect size. *Behavior Research Methods, Instruments, and Computers, 28*, 12–22.

Rimal, R. N. (2001). Perceived risk and self-efficacy as motivators: Understanding individuals' long-term use of health information. *Journal of Communication, 51*, 633–655.

Robinson, J. P., Shaver, P. R., & Wrightsman, L. S. (1990). *Measures of personality and social psychological attitudes.* San Diego, CA: Academic Press.

Robinson, J. P., Shaver, P. R., & Wrightsman, L. S. (1998). *Measures of political attitudes.* San Diego, CA: Academic Press.

Romer, D., Kenski, K., Waldman, P., Adasiewicz, C., & Jamieson, K. H. (2004). *Capturing campaign dynamics: The national Annenberg election survey.* New York: Oxford University Press.

Rosenthal, R., & Rosnow, R. L. (1975). *The volunteer subject.* New York: Wiley.

Rosenthal, R., Rosnow, R. L., & Rubin, D. B. (2000). *Contrasts and effect sizes in behavioral research.* Cambridge, UK: Cambridge University Press.

Rosenthal, R., & Rubin, D. B. (1984). Multiple contrasts and ordered Bonferroni procedures. *Journal of Educational Psychology, 76*. 1028–1034.

Ross, S. (1988). *A first course in probability* (3rd ed). New York: MacMillan.

Rossiter, C. M. (1976). The validity of communication experiments using human subjects: A review. *Human Communication Research, 2,* 197–206.

Roth, P. L. (1994). Missing data: A conceptual review for applied psychologists. *Personnel Psychology, 47,* 537–560.

Rubin, R. B., Palmgreen, P., & Sypher, H. E. (2004). *Communication research measures: A sourcebook.* Mahwah, NJ: Erlbaum.

Ryan, T. A. (1959). Multiple comparisons in psychological research. *Psychological Bulletin, 56,* 26–47.

Ryan, T. A. (1960). Significance tests for multiple comparison of proportions, variances, and other statistics. *Psychological Bulletin, 57,* 318–328.

Ryan, T. A. (1980). Comment on "Protecting the overall rate of Type I errors for pairwise comparisons with an omnibus test statistic." *Psychological Bulletin, 88,* 354–355.

Satterthwaite, F. E. (1946). An approximate distribution of estimates of variance components. *Biometrics Bulletin, 2,* 110–114.

Scheffe, H. (1943). On solutions to the Behrens-Fisher problem based on the *t* distribution. *The Annals of Mathematical Statistics, 14,* 35–44.

Scheffe, H. (1953). A method for judging all contrasts in the analysis of variance. *Biometrika, 40,* 87-104.

Scheffe, H. (1959). *The analysis of variance.* New York: Wiley.

Scott, S. C., Goldberg, M. S., & Mayo, N. E. (1997). Statistical assessment of ordinal outcomes in comparative studies. *Journal of Clinical Epidemiology, 50,* 45–55.

Scott, W. A. (1955). Reliability of content analysis: The case of nominal scale coding. *Public Opinion Quarterly, 19,* 321-325.

Sears, D. O. (1986). College sophomores in the laboratory: Influences of a narrow data base on social psychology's view of human nature. *Journal of Personality and Social Psychology, 51,* 515–530.

Sedney, M. A. (1981). Comments on median split procedures for scoring androgyny measures. *Sex Roles, 7,* 217–222.

Selvin, H. C. (1957). A critique of tests of significance in survey research. *American Sociological Review, 22,* 519–527

Severin, W. J., & Tankard, J. W. (2001). *Communication theories: Origins, methods, and uses in the mass media* (5th ed.). Boston: Allyn-Bacon

Shadish, W. R., Cook, T. D., & Campbell, D. T. (2002). *Experimental and quasi-experimental designs for generalized causal inference.* Boston, MA: Houghton-Mifflin.

Shahanan, J., & Morgan, M. (1999). *Television and its viewers: Cultivation theory and research.* Cambridge University Press.

Shrout, P. E., & Bolger, N. (2002). Mediation in experimental and nonexperimental studies: New procedures and recommendations. *Psychological Methods, 7*, 422–445.

Siegel, S. (1956). *Nonparametric statistics for the behavioral sciences.* New York: McGraw-Hill.

Slater, M. D. (2003). Alienation, aggression, and sensation seeking as predictors of adolescent use of violent film, computer, and website content. *Journal of Communication, 53*, 105–121.

Slater, M. D., Henry, K. L., Swaim, R. C., & Anderson, L. L. (2003). Violent media content and aggressiveness in adolescents: A downward spiral model. *Communication Research, 30*, 713–736.

Solomon, D. H., & Williams, M. L. M. (1997). Perceptions of social-sexual communication at work: The effects of message, situation, and observer characteristics on judgments of sexual harassment. *Journal of Applied Communication Research, 25*, 196–216.

Sparks, G. G. (1995). Comments concerning the claim that mass media research is "prescientific": A response to Potter, Cooper, and Dupagne. *Communication Theory, 5.* 273–280.

Sparks, G. G. (2002). *Media effects research: A basic overview.* Belmont, CA: Wadsworth.

Spearman, C. (1907). Demonstration of formulae for true measurement of correlation. *American Journal of Psychology, 15*, 201-292.

Spearman, C. (1913). Correlation of sums and differences. *British Journal of Psychology, 5*, 417–426.

Spector, P. E. (1992). *Summating rating scale construction.* Thousand Oaks, CA: Sage.

Squire, P. (1988). Why the 1936 *Literary Digest* poll failed. *Public Opinion Quarterly, 52*, 125–133.

Steiger, J. H. (1980). Tests for comparing elements in a correlation matrix. *Psychological Bulletin, 87*, 245–251.

Stevens, S. S. (1958). Problems and methods of psychophysics. *Psychological Bulletin, 55*, 177–196.

Stewart, T. D. (2001). *Principles of research in communication.* Boston: Allyn-Bacon.

Stonehouse, J. M., & Forrester, G. J. (1998). Robustness of the t and U tests under combined assumption violations. *Journal of Applied Statistics, 25*, 63–74.

Streiner, D. L. (2002). Breaking up is hard to do: The heartbreak of dichotomizing continuous data. *Canadian Journal of Psychiatry, 47*, 262–266.

Stuart, A. (1984). *The ideas of sampling.* New York: MacMillan.

Sundar, S. S. (2000). Multimedia effects on processing and perceptions of online news: A study of picture, audio, and video downloads. *Journalism and Mass Communication Quarterly, 77*, 480–499.

Tewksbury, D., & Althous, S. L. (2000). Differences in knowledge acquisition among readers of the paper and online versions of a national newspaper. *Journalism and Mass Communication Quarterly, 77*, 457–479.

Thompson, B. (2003a). Understanding reliability and coefficient alpha, really. In B. Thompson (Ed.), *Score reliability: Contemporary thinking on reliability issues.* Thousand Oaks, CA: Sage.

Thompson, B. (2003b). A brief introduction to generalizability theory. In B. Thompson (Ed.), *Score reliability: Contemporary thinking on reliability issues.* Thousand Oaks, CA: Sage.

Tichenor, P., Donohue, G., & Olien, C. (1970). Mass media flow and differential flow in knowledge. *Public Opinion Quarterly, 34*, 159–170.

Tremblay, M. S., & Willms, J. D. (2003). Is the Canadian childhood obesity epidemic related to physical inactivity? *International Journal of Obesity, 27*, 1100–1005.

Tucker, L. A., & Bagwell, M. (1991). Television viewing and obesity in adult females. *American Journal of Public Health, 81*, 908–911.

Ulrich, R., & Miller, J. (1994). Effects of truncation on reaction time analysis. *Journal of Experimental Psychology: General, 123*, 34–80.

Van Eijck, K., & Van Rees, K. (2000). Media orientation and media use: Television viewing of specific reader types from 1975 to 1995. *Communication Research, 27*, 574–616.

Veiel, H. O. F. (1988). Base-rates, cut-points, and interaction effects: The problem with dichotomized continuous variables. *Psychological Medicine, 18*, 703–710.

Verba, S., Schlozman, K. L., & Brady, H. E. (1995). *Voice and equality: Civic volunteerism in American politics.* Cambridge, MA: Harvard University.

Viswanath, K., & Finnegan, J. R. (1996). The knowledge gap hypothesis: Twenty-five years later. *Communication Yearbook, 19*, 187–227.

Walther, J. B., Slovacek, C. L., & Tidwell, L. (2001). Is a picture worth a thousand words? Photographic images in long-term and short-term computer-mediated communication. *Communication Research, 28*, 105–134.

Wang, A. Y., & Jentsch, F. G. (1998). Point-of-time effects across the semester: Is there a sampling bias? *Journal of Psychology, 132*, 211–219.

Welch, B. L. (1937). The significance of the difference between two means when the population variances are unequal. *Biometrika, 29*, 350–362.

Welch, B. L. (1951). On the comparison of several means: An alternative approach. *Biometrika, 38*, 330–336.

Wilcox, R. R. (1987). New designs in analysis of variance. *Annual Review of Psychology*, *38*, 29–60.

Wilcox, R. R. (2002). Comparing the variances of two independent groups. *British Journal of Mathematical and Statistical Psychology*, *55*, 169–175.

Wilcox, R. R., & Keselman, H. J. (2003). Modern robust data analysis methods: Measures of central tendency. *Psychological Methods*, *8*, 254–274.

Williams, F., & Monge, P. (2001). *Reasoning with statistics: How to read quantitative research* (5th ed.). Fort Worth, TX: Harcourt.

Winer, B. J., Brown, D. R., & Michels, K. M. (1991). *Statistical principles in experimental design* (3rd Ed.). Boston: McGraw-Hill.

Wright, R. E. (1995). Logistic regression. In L. G. Grimm & P. L. Yarnold (Eds.), *Reading and understanding multivariate statistics*. Washington, D.C.: American Psychological Association.

Zhao, X., & Gantz, W. (2003). Disruptive and cooperative interruptions in prime-time television fiction: The role of gender, status, and topic. *Journal of Communication*, *53*, 347–362.

Zimmerman, D. W. (2002). A warning about statistical significance tests performed on large samples of nonindependent observations. *Perceptual and Motor Skills*, *94*, 259–263.

Zimmerman, D. W. (2004). A note on preliminary tests of variance equality. *British Journal of Mathematical and Statistical Psychology*, *57*, 173–181.

Zimmerman, D. W., Williams, R. H., & Zumbo, B. D. (1993). Effect of nonindependence of sample observations on some parametric and nonparametric statistical tests. *Communications in Statistics—Simulation and Computation*, *22*, 779–789.

INDEX